ANNUALS
for Every Purpose

ANNUALS
for Every Purpose

Choose the Right Plants for Your Conditions, Your Garden, and Your Taste

Larry Hodgson

RODALE

WE INSPIRE AND ENABLE PEOPLE TO IMPROVE THEIR LIVES AND THE WORLD AROUND THEM

Printed in the United States of America on acid-free ∞, recycled ♻ paper

On the cover: Tiny water-filled cells in a Livingstone daisy (*Dorotheanthus bellidiformus*) reflect light, causing the blooms to blaze like a beacon in the garden.

We're always happy to hear from you. For questions or comments concerning the editorial content of this book, please write to:

Rodale Book Readers' Service
33 East Minor Street
Emmaus, PA 18098

Look for other Rodale books wherever books are sold. Or call us at (800) 848-4735.

For more information about Rodale Organic Living magazines and books, visit us at:

www.organicgardening.com

Editor: **Karen Bolesta**

Contributing Editor: **Nancy Ondra**

Cover and Interior Book Designer: **Nancy Smola Biltcliff**

Interior Illustrator: **Allison Mia Starcher**

Garden Designers: **Stephanie Cohen, Sarah Wolfgang Heffner, Nancy Ondra, and Pamela Ruch**

Cover Photographer: **Andrew Lawson**

Photography Editor: **Lyn Horst**

Photography Assistant: **Jackie L. Ney**

Layout Designer: **Keith Biery**

Digital Imaging Specialist: **Dale Mack**

Researchers: **Diana Erney, Sarah Wolfgang Heffner, and Pamela Ruch**

Copy Editors: **Candace B. Levy and Linda Brunner**

Production Specialist: **Jodi Schaffer**

Indexer: **Lina Burton**

Editorial Assistance: **Susan L. Nickol, Kerrie A. Cadden, and Megan O'Connell**

RODALE ORGANIC LIVING BOOKS

Editorial Director: **Christopher Hirsheimer**

Executive Creative Director: **Christin Gangi**

Executive Editor: **Kathleen DeVanna Fish**

Art Director: **Patricia Field**

Content Assembly Manager: **Robert V. Anderson Jr.**

Studio Manager: **Leslie M. Keefe**

Copy Manager: **Nancy N. Bailey**

Projects Coordinator: **Kerrie A. Cadden**

Library of Congress Cataloging-in-Publication Data

Hodgson, Larry.
    Annuals for every purpose : choose the right plants for your conditions, your garden, and your taste / Larry Hodgson.
        p.   cm.
    Includes bibliographical references (p.   ) and index.
    ISBN 0–87596–824–4   (hardcover : alk. paper)
    1. Annuals (Plants)   I. Title.
SB422 .H64   2001
635.9'312—dc21   2001004078

Distributed in the book trade by St. Martin's Press

2 4 6 8 10 9 7 5 3 1 hardcover

RODALE
ORGANIC GARDENING STARTS HERE!

Here at Rodale, we've been gardening organically for more than 60 years—ever since my grandfather J. I. Rodale learned about composting and decided that healthy living starts with healthy soil. In 1940 J. I. started the Rodale Organic Farm to test his theories, and today the nonprofit Rodale Institute Experimental Farm is still at the forefront of organic gardening and farming research. In 1942 J. I. founded *Organic Gardening* magazine to share his discoveries with gardeners everywhere. His son, my father, Robert Rodale, headed *Organic Gardening* until 1990, and today a third generation of Rodales is growing up with the new *OG* magazine. Over the years we've shown millions of readers how to grow bountiful crops and beautiful flowers using nature's own techniques.

In this book, you'll find the latest organic methods and the best gardening advice. We know—because all our authors and editors are passionate about gardening! We feel strongly that our gardens should be safe for our children, pets, and the birds and butterflies that add beauty and delight to our lives and landscapes. Our gardens should provide us with fresh, flavorful vegetables, delightful herbs, and gorgeous flowers. And they should be a pleasure to work in as well as to view.

Sharing the secrets of safe, successful gardening is why we publish books. So come visit us at www.organicgardening.com where you can tour the world of organic gardening all day, every day. And use this book to create your best garden ever.

Happy gardening!

Maria Rodale

Maria Rodale
Rodale Organic Gardening Books

CONTENTS

Part 2: Choosing the Best Annuals
page 36

A Letter from Larry

It's so nice to see annuals back in style again
after the dark days of the 1960s through 1990s,
when, if it wasn't a perennial, it just wasn't cool.

Dear Reader,

I don't remember when I first started growing annuals: Probably I was still in diapers! I do recall that each of us kids had his or her own little square in the family vegetable plot where we could grow what we liked, and what we liked were usually tall, impressive plants like sunflowers and kiss-me-over-the-garden-gate. By the age of 7 or so, I was already borrowing my father's seed catalogs. My dad, a self-taught gardener, would direct my attention to the easy plants he felt I could handle. By age 10, I had my own garden, equal in size to the entire family vegetable plot, where I could experiment as I wished . . . and my father was now letting me make my own mistakes. I loved then (and still do) annuals that self-sowed: poppies, calendula, and cosmos. I just couldn't wait until spring to see where they popped up next! I also began to try making my own crosses (although my insipid purplish pink petunias looked more like a step back, not an advancement). And I devoured my father's *Organic Gardening* magazines: They were pretty much the family Bible!

By then I was already a confirmed plantaholic. While my brother and sisters used their allowances to buy candy and comic books, I'd save up all my cash to buy seeds.

Then in high school, I discovered that the greenhouse off the biology room was scarcely being used, so I commandeered that as well. That's where I learned to make cuttings (I started a great collection of fancy-leaf geraniums) and how to overwinter "annuals" that were in fact tender perennials. While the other teens reveled in long weekends, I came to hate them: I couldn't get into the greenhouse to water my plants!

High school also taught me that a reputation for having a green thumb got you no points with women, so by university I had learned to bury my horticultural inclinations and spent 4 years pretending I knew nothing about plants and wanted to know even less. As soon as I had settled into marriage, though, it all came gushing out again. The balcony of our first apartment was so covered in flowers and vegetables that there was literally no room for people. And I begged, borrowed, and stole vacant spaces throughout the neighborhood so I could also garden in the ground.

By my early 30s, I had become such a passionate gardener I gave up my day job to work full time as a garden writer. The earnings were meager, especially at first, but I was just thrilled when anything I wrote was published. Who needs food when you have fame? Now I actually make a decent living at it, although I do wish writing would leave me more time for gardening!

Making Things Easier

One of my goals in writing this book was not only to present you with hundreds of great annuals, many of which you have probably never seen, but also to help make growing them easier. After all, there's nothing at all difficult about it. You drop a seed into the ground, water it a few times, and it *will* grow. On the other hand, I tried to take a "warts and all" approach, making no effort to hide the downsides of certain annuals, as I find many garden writers tend to make all plants seem just perfect. Let's admit it: Many annuals *do* self-sow too abundantly and others need constant deadheading, some can't stand hot summers, and others can't stand cool ones. I've tried to tell you all the pros and cons and then let you judge whether the plant is suited to you and your gardening style.

And I don't believe in complicating things with difficult, time-consuming procedures, not if there's an easy way out. If you mulch, use soaker hoses, and learn to cover up weeds under a newspaper barrier rather than spread them by turning soil over. Caring for your garden is easier than you'd have ever imagined.

An Encyclopedia with a Purpose

You'll notice this book is not organized the way most gardening books are, with annual after annual presented in alphabetical order.

I get a kick out of my home garden: It's not big but it's jammed full of fun plants. Self-sowing is not only allowed, but also encouraged.

There's nothing wrong with that, but most of the time, you'll be looking for annuals to meet a particular need, not ones that start with "C" or "D." Instead, I've grouped the plants together based on special features, such as growing ease, use, and location. For example, if you're looking for annuals to grow in poor, dry soil, go straight to my selection of "Drought-Resistant Annuals," starting on page 96. This organization makes it simpler for you to choose plants according to *your* needs.

In each plant entry, I've summarized the main attributes of the plant right at the start for quick reference, then followed that with a more complete description and a few juicy details on growing it successfully. You'll even notice warning icons: Self-sowing (🌱), if the plant tends to spread via seed, and Think Twice (✋), if it has a flaw so major you might want to consider not growing it.

Whether you sit down and read it page by page or just pull it out for reference every now and again, I hope you'll enjoy this book and learn from it and, even more important, that it will help you enjoy gardening as much as I do.

Larry Hodgson

PART 1

ANNUAL GARDENING MADE EASY

Why make gardening complicated? Planting and sowing annuals is easy! It's so easy, in fact, that you might feel you can skip this introductory section on how to garden with annuals and jump right into the heart of this book—the plant descriptions. If you have lots of gardening experience, feel free to get right to the good stuff! I have included quite a few tips and tricks that you may not know, so come back and read through this section on one of those rainy days when you just can't get into the garden.

If you're still a beginner, though, this section will probably be the most important part of the book for you. It shows you how to start off on the right track—and how to stay there. I don't believe in making gardening complicated, so I've tried to avoid including the unnecessary little steps that many gardeners traditionally take but that really don't give results. Follow the information in this section, and you'll be sipping lemonade on the porch while you watch your plants do all the work. Give it a read and see: Annual gardening has never been so easy!

GETTING YOUR
Garden Started

I have good news for you: Annuals are "no-brainers." They're such fast-growing, high-performance plants that they do almost all the work. Of course, you *do* have to do a bit of site preparation, but if you already have a flowerbed, it will be minimal. And if you don't, well, I have an easy way around that, too!

Getting off on the right foot: That's what this chapter is all about. So roll up your shirt sleeves; it's time to get to work.

◄ Perk up a dark spot with splashes of color. Deep purples and pinks will sparkle like jewels as you pass through the garden.

Annuals and Their Place in the Garden

Each type of plant has its particular use: Trees give shade, slow down strong winds, and cool your yard; perennials add seasonal accents that change as they come in and go out of bloom. As for annuals, the most temporary of plants since they live only one season, their whole purpose is to add color, color, color, from spring right through to frost.

You could either try for carpet bedding—varying colors of annuals all about the same height, giving the effect of a massive carpet of color—or go for a more three-dimensional annual garden, with short-edging annuals along the border, medium-size ones in the center, and tall annuals at the back. Gardeners tend to get tired of replanting entire flowerbeds year after year, though, so beds composed only of annuals are not as common as they once were. Mass plantings of annuals, however, remain an excellent way of filling in a new bed until you get around to planting more permanent plants.

More often these days, annuals play a complementary role to other plants. Use them to fill in spaces left by spring bulbs and early perennials, like Oriental poppy (*Papaver orientale*), that go dormant after blooming. They are also ideal choices for planting around slow-to-establish shrubs and perennials that will one day need lots of space. Annuals are perfect for adding splotches of summer-long color to perennial beds, rock gardens, and shrub borders, too. In fact, I don't even believe in "perennial borders"; instead, I think *all* borders should include at least a few spaces where clusters of annuals can add season-long color.

Preparing the Site

Just about any site will do, although for greatest color, try for full or nearly full sun with well-drained soil and little root competition from established trees and shrubs.

For a fast and easy flowerbed with no weeds, just put down a newspaper barrier and cover it with weed-free soil.

Old-timers will tell you the way to start a new garden is to cut out the old sod, then to dig out any weed roots and turn the soil deeply while mixing in plenty of compost, manure, or peat moss. You can do it that way, of course, but it's a lot of work. You end up with a lot of weeds, too, because this process brings long-dormant weed seeds to the surface, and there will also be lots of weed roots left in the soil.

Years ago I learned a faster, no-stress method that gave me a weed-free garden from the start. Wherever you want a new garden, mow the lawn or cut any brush to the ground, leaving all the clippings where they fall. *Don't* remove the sod unless you need it elsewhere. Now cover the entire area with a layer of newspaper at least five to ten pages thick, making sure the newspaper overlaps at all edges. If the day is windy, soak the newspaper in a bucket of water before laying it to keep it from blowing away. Finish by covering the whole area with a generous layer of top-quality, weed-free soil or a mix of weed-free soil and good-quality compost. A full 1 foot (30 cm) is best, but if there are nearby trees or shrubs you want to preserve, I suggest using only 8 inches (20 cm) so you don't smother their roots. The newspaper acts as a temporary weed barrier, keeping grass and weed roots and seeds deep in the ground and away from your plantings. It will decompose within a year or so. In the meantime, you'll be gardening in fresh, rich, weed-free soil!

You can use the same layering method to convert former vegetable gardens, decomposed brush piles, or tired, weedy flowerbeds into fresh gardening space. Remember: You remove nothing, not even the worst weeds; just cover them up!

Starting from Seed

Not all annuals are available as young plants ready to set out in your garden. And even if plants *are* available, they can get quite pricey if you need lots of them. Fortunately, it's not as difficult as you might think to raise your own annuals from seed. And if you're on a limited budget, growing from seed can supply you with a yardful of annuals for less than $20! This is also the best way to get the latest introductions or unusual cultivars that your local nursery or garden center doesn't yet carry.

My main reason for starting annuals from seed, though, is that it's fun! I have a basement room nearly full of plant lights, and from about mid-February on, I can't wait to get up in the morning to see what has germinated and how the seedlings are doing. In fact, I enjoy growing from seed so much that the only annuals I buy as plants are those that are particularly slow or delicate from seed, like begonias and impatiens.

The plant descriptions in Part 2, starting on page 36, will help you decide which plants to grow from seed and whether you should start them indoors or out in your climate. Let's take a look at both methods here.

Sowing Outdoors

Sowing outdoors is the most natural way of growing annuals because you simply copy what Mother Nature does. It's the ideal approach for annuals that don't like to be transplanted, as well as those that grow very quickly from seed. It's also perfect for establishing annuals around bulbs and summer-dormant perennials. However, it does mean your annuals will likely flower later in the season than if you set out young plants, so direct sowing is most often used in climates with very long growing seasons.

When you sow depends on your climate. Usually, you'll be sowing in early spring, often before the last frost date; the seeds will germinate when the weather is right. In mild climates (Zones 6 and south) and colder areas where you can depend on a good snow cover over winter, you can also sow many annuals in late fall for germination in spring. In *very* mild climates (Zones 9 to 11), you'll also be sowing some annuals in early fall for winter bloom.

Start with a freshly cleared section of garden. This could be a newly prepared flowerbed full of fresh, rich soil or an older bed where you've removed dead leaves, last year's debris, and any mulch. In the latter case, add a 2-inch (5-cm) layer of finished compost and a handful or two of organic fertilizer, and rake lightly to mix these amendments. *Do not* turn over the whole bed; if you do, you'll bring up unwanted weed seeds and disturb the delicate framework of microbial life in the soil.

Once the site is ready, scatter the seeds evenly over the area where you want them to grow. Rake the spot lightly if the seeds need to be covered with soil; if they don't, place a board over the sown area, press lightly to settle the seeds, remove the board, and then water. If you're sowing annual seeds for a simple edging, the technique is slightly different. Trace a furrow of the proper depth, sprinkle the seeds into it, cover them lightly, and water: It's that simple!

Seed Needs

Most seeds have very simple sowing needs—just plant them at a depth equal to three times their diameter—but some do have special needs. It's a good idea to read the plant description or seed pack before you sow to check; you may see some of the following recommendations:

- *Don't cover.* Some seeds are so tiny they would be smothered by even a thin layer of seed-starting mix or soil. Simply press them lightly into the mix or the ground with a piece of board.

- *Needs light to germinate.* As above, press them lightly into the mix or soil with a piece of board.

- *Needs darkness to germinate.* Outdoors, simply covering these seeds with soil usually provides enough darkness; for extra cover, you could place an inverted tray over the planting spot. Indoors, place the sown seeds in darkness or cover them with a sheet of dark plastic, such as a dark green garbage bag. Check covered seeds daily and expose them to light as soon as you see growth.

- *Sow into peat pots.* Pots made of pressed peat let roots grow right through them when planted into the ground. They're great for starting annuals that won't tolerate root disturbance.

- *Soak seeds.* This softens up really hard seeds and speeds their germination. Let them sit in an old thermos of hot, but not boiling, water overnight, or as long as recommended.

- *Scarify seeds.* This means to nick the seed coat with a sharp knife or to file it so you expose the inner part of the seed covering. Scarifying can be difficult and time-consuming, so it's usually easier to soak the seeds, which gives the same result.

- *Refrigerate for 2 (or 3 or 4) weeks.* Some seeds won't germinate without having been exposed to cold and moist conditions. Sow these seeds outdoors early, while there is still danger of frost, or sow them indoors, seal the pot or tray in a plastic bag, and place them in the refrigerator or a cold room for the recommended time.

When seeds have sprouted, remove their mini-greenhouse to improve air circulation.

starting). Or make your own by mixing equal parts of peat moss, perlite, and vermiculite, or two parts of screened compost to equal parts of perlite and vermiculite (compost can help prevent disease problems in seedlings), plus 1 teaspoon (5 ml) of dolomitic limestone per gallon (4 l) of mix. (Wear a mask so you don't inhale any irritating dust.) If you're starting seeds that need particularly good drainage, blend your chosen mix with an equal amount of clean sand. Premoisten the mix (add enough water so it feels like a damp sponge), then scoop it into pots or trays that have drainage holes. Add the mix to within ½ inch (1.25 cm) of the rim, then even out the surface with your fingers.

Scatter seeds evenly over the surface or sow one by one in rows. Cover the seeds to the suggested depth with fresh mix, then spray lightly with warm water. Or, if the recommendation is to *not* cover them, simply press lightly with a piece of board to settle them into the mix, then remove the board and spray lightly. Either way, cover with a plastic bag or sheet of plastic to create a mini-greenhouse that maintains high humidity.

Give the seedlings the recommended conditions for germination. Most seeds prefer lots of light, so place them under fluorescent lights that are left on 12 to 18 hours a day, or give them a windowsill with an ample amount of bright but indirect light. (Avoid full sun, or they could cook inside their mini-greenhouses.) After germination, remove the plastic to increase air circulation and prevent damping-off, and start giving the brightest light possible. Give trays on windowsills a quarter turn every few days to keep them from bending toward the sun. If possible, lower temperatures to about 65°F (18°C) during the day and 55°F (13°C) at night; this produces sturdier plants.

Water as needed by placing the containers or pots in a tray of warm water when they approach dryness. When the potting mix becomes moist on the surface, remove the containers or pots and let them drain. Thin out the seedlings

Growing from seed inevitably results in *too many* plants, so once your seedlings are up and growing, thin them out to the recommended spacing by cutting off the surplus plants at the base with scissors.

No matter whether you sow indoors or out, always prepare a label in indelible ink and insert it at sowing time. You'd be surprised how easy it is to forget just what you've sown!

Sowing Indoors

Indoor sowing isn't at all difficult if you have a window that gets a lot of light or a spot under fluorescent lights: I start probably 90 percent of my annuals this way.

You can buy pasteurized growing mixes already prepared (look for one recommended for seed (either pinch or cut them off at soil level) when their leaves begin to touch, or if you want to keep all of them, carefully repot them into a larger container. After transplanting, tamp the mix lightly around the seedlings, let the new pot soak in a tray of warm water until the mix is fully moist, then let drain.

Once the seedlings have four true leaves (the leaves that form after the very first pair of leaves), begin spraying them with foliar fertilizer, following the recommendations on the product label. (Liquid seaweed is perfect for this purpose.)

When temperatures outdoors start to warm up, begin acclimating the seedlings to outdoor conditions—a process called hardening off. Start by setting them outside only a few hours per day in moderate shade, then increase the length of time and intensity of light until they are receiving the kind of conditions (full sun, partial shade, or full shade) they will grow in as adults.

Multiplying by Cuttings

True annuals grow only from seeds: They die at the end of the year and simply will not root from cuttings. Many annuals, though, are actually tender shrubs or perennials (see "What Is an Annual" on page 11), and these are usually easy to

Never hold fragile seedlings by their stems: You could accidentally crush them. Instead, hold a leaf with one hand and use a Popsicle stick, pen, or other small tool to dig the seedling up and lift it to its new home.

Growing under Lights

You can grow healthy seedlings in natural light, but you need *lots* of it: A window with full southern exposure, with the trays placed right up against the window frame, is not too much light for most annuals. If you lack light, though, you can switch to growing under lights. All you need is a shop-type, fluorescent lamp fixture suspended over a table. Look for a lamp that takes two 40-watt, 4-foot (1.2-m) tubes; this is the standard length and so both the lamps and the tubes are relatively cheap. Inexpensive "cool white" tubes are the best for seedlings. Set the lights only 2 to 6 inches (5 to 15 cm) above the plants, then adjust their height upward as the seedlings grow. Unless the seeds have a special day-length need, such as tuberous begonias, leave the lights on 14 to 18 hours per day. (You can buy inexpensive timers to turn your lights on and off for you.) With this simple setup, you can produce professional-quality plants right in your own home!

multiply by stem cuttings. You'll generally take cuttings either in late summer, to overwinter them, or in the early spring, using stems from overwintered plants to start a whole bunch of new plants for the summer garden.

With a sharp knife, cut off a 4- to 6-inch (10- to 15-cm) stem tip. Remove the lower leaves, baring 2 to 3 inches (5 to 8 cm) of the base of the stem. Fill a small pot with moistened growing mix and poke a hole in the center with a pencil. Insert the bottom 2 to 3 inches of the cutting into the hole and firm the mix so the cutting remains upright. Cover with a clear plastic bag and set in a warm spot (bottom heat can be helpful) with bright light (but not full sun). When new growth appears (this can take from a few days to more than a month), remove the plastic covering and move the plant to a brighter, cooler spot. From this point on, begin watering, fertilizing, pinching, and pruning it as if it were an adult plant.

Planting Annuals in the Garden

Transplanting nursery-bought and homegrown annuals into the garden is a snap. First, spread a 2-inch (5-cm) layer of compost and a few handfuls of organic fertilizer over the planting area. Don't bother digging this in; you'll mix much of it automatically as you plant.

A handheld trowel is the only tool you need for creating planting holes. Space the holes according to the suggested spacing for the plants you are growing. Unless you're using annuals as an edging—in which case planting them in a straight line is fine—set them out in a triangular pattern, with each plant equidistant from its neighbors. The planting will look thin at first, but don't be tempted to overplant; most annuals fill in rapidly and look best when they have room to spread.

Create a rich tapestry of color and texture when you combine cherry pie (*Heliotropium arborescens*), ivy geranium (*Pelargonium peltatum* 'Burgundy Mesh'), and golden creeping Jenny (*Lysimachia nummularia* 'Aurea').

Once the planting holes are ready, remove the plants from their containers. On individually potted plants, slip one hand, palm down, over the potting mix with the stems between your fingers; carefully invert the pot over that hand. With your other hand, tap the pot to loosen it, then lift it off. If the plants are growing in flexible cell packs, simply push up on the bottom of each cell to pop them out. And if multiple plants are growing together in one tray, cut between the plants with a sharp knife to give each its fair share of roots.

Seedlings growing in peat pots are particularly easy; just set them out—pot and all—in a hole that's deep enough to hold the entire pot. Make sure all of the pot rim is covered when you backfill around the pot with soil. For other transplants, make sure their rootball is buried to its original level. Or, if the plants are weak and wobbly at the base, dig the hole a bit deeper and plant them to the depth of their lowest leaves. Once you've set out all the plants, finish by watering well with tepid water.

The Container Option

Annuals have always been the top choice for containers. Just plant them in early spring, either indoors a few weeks before the last frost date or outdoors when the air has warmed up. All containers should have drainage holes to let excess water drain out; but to prevent the growing mix from trickling out, place a bit of screening or a pot shard over the hole before planting. There is no need for a drainage layer of gravel at the container's base—it only wastes valuable root space and doesn't help drainage one bit!

You'll find more information on growing in containers in the chapters "Flowering Annuals for Containers & Hanging Baskets," starting on page 304, and "Foliage Plants for Containers & Hanging Baskets," starting on page 332.

SITE PROBLEMS

Fortunately, most annuals will get by—and even do well—with less-than-ideal conditions. Since most of us have a range of conditions in our gardens, here are some suggestions for getting the best from your annuals even in less-than-perfect sites.

CONDITIONS	SOLUTIONS
Shady conditions	Choose shade-tolerant plants. (See "Annuals That Bloom in the Shade," starting on page 150, and "Annuals with Decorative Fruits or Foliage," starting on page 278.) Grow sun-lovers in containers and move them into shade for up to 2 weeks while they're blooming well, then set them back in the sun until they bloom again. Open up wooded areas by removing some lower tree branches.
Root competition	Water more often or add an irrigation system. Or, instead of planting among tree and shrub roots, set pots of container-grown annuals throughout the area.
Fast-draining soil (including sandy and dry soils)	Choose drought-resistant plants. (See "Drought-Resistant Annuals," starting on page 96.) Add plenty of organic material to the soil. Mulch abundantly. Make raised beds with good topsoil and compost mixture. Install an irrigation system.
Heavy clay soil	Grow your annuals in raised beds. You can instead use the old-fashioned method of digging the soil deeply and working in plenty of organic material, but you'll need to repeat it every year; it helps for only a few months.
Nutrient-poor soil	Test soil to identify problem. Choose plants adapted to poor soil. (See "Soil Preference" under the individual plant descriptions in Part 2.) Grow your plants in raised beds filled with good topsoil. Add plenty of organic material and long-lasting organic fertilizers annually. Apply foliar sprays in midseason to perk up yellowing plants.
Wet soil	Create a bog garden or water garden to take advantage of your site conditions. Choose plants adapted to damp or wet soil. (See "Soil Preference" under the individual plant descriptions in Part 2.) Grow plants in raised beds filled with well-drained soil. Install a drainage system.
Saline soil	Choose drought-resistant plants or those recommended as salt tolerant. Water more abundantly. Leach soil in early spring. Use raised beds or replace soil if problem is severe.
"Rain shadow" effects	Choose drought-resistant plants. (See "Drought-Resistant Annuals," starting on page 96.) Add plenty of organic matter and mulch heavily to combat the drought-causing effects of roof overhangs and nearby walls. Install an irrigation system.
Poor air circulation	Choose disease-resistant plants. Allow more space between plants than usual. Consider removing lower branches of overhanging trees.
Windy conditions	Water more frequently. Mulch heavily. Stake taller annuals. Install a living windbreak of shrubs, evergreens, or perennial grasses, or add trellising or fencing and grow climbing annuals over them.
Slopes and hillsides	Use erosion-control mats (made of burlap, wool mat, or paper), and cover them with mulch. Perennial groundcovers are actually better than annuals in such conditions because they'll hold the soil all year long.

PICKING THE PERFECT
Annuals

I have the secret to end all secrets when it comes to growing annuals: Discover which annuals are considered easy to grow under your growing conditions—then plant lots of them! There's little use trying to grow cool-weather annuals in a Florida summer, or moisture-loving annuals where summers are always dry. But if you pick the right plants for your conditions, they'll practically grow themselves!

With hundreds of new annuals released yearly, it is hard to know which to choose, but I always go for those that have won the prestigious All-America Selections award. Many of these stand the test of time to become classic garden plants!

◄ Small specialty nurseries are the answer if you're on the make for plants that add visual interest to your gardens and borders.

What Is an Annual?

As the very name "annual" suggests, true annuals are plants that go through their entire life cycle—from seed to bloom to seed production to death—within one calendar year.

Actually, though, only a few of the plants we know as annuals really do go through their full cycle in just one year (on their own, at least). The other "annuals" are actually biennials, perennials, or shrubs that we can trick into blooming the first year by extending their growing season artificially. In other words, we start them indoors to encourage early bloom. We then treat them as annuals because they give the results we expect of an annual; that is, they come into bloom quickly and remain in bloom over the whole summer. When they die in the fall, it's not because they *couldn't* have lived longer, but because they can't take the cold or damp winters common in much of North America.

From Hardy to Tender

Since they have different origins, the plants we group together as annuals have somewhat different needs. It's easy to tell these needs at a glance if you just understand three terms: hardy, half-hardy, and tender.

- Hardy annuals are extremely fast-growing plants that you can sow directly outside in all climates. They are tough enough to sow outdoors in very early spring, *before* the last frost date, although you can also start them indoors a few weeks before the last frost date for even earlier bloom. Many are so tough you can sow them the previous fall for germination the following spring.
- Half-hardy annuals can be started indoors in short-season climates, 6 to 8 weeks before the last frost date. Where summers last 4 months or more, they grow fast enough that you can sow them directly outdoors. Set out transplants or direct-sow around the last frost date.

Annuals are perfect "filler materials," hiding gaps in older beds and quickly filling newer ones.

■ Tender annuals are usually tender biennials, perennials, or shrubs. Unless you live in a frost-free climate, you'll sow these indoors, usually 10 or more weeks before the last frost. These plants don't like cold temperatures, so keep them indoors until 2 or 3 weeks *after* the last frost date.

10 Things to Look For in an Annual

Most gardeners probably first choose a particular annual for its color or flower shape—but that can be a mistake. Even the most beautiful flowers can be fleeting if you try to grow a plant in conditions it doesn't like. To get the best results, first pick out annuals that adapt well to your conditions, *then* look at the flower colors and forms of the plants in that group. I suggest choosing your annuals according to the following 10 criteria:

1. The plant should be adapted to a wide range of general conditions (sun and shade, rain and drought, and so on).

2. It should also be well adapted to any particularities in *your* climate (hot summers or humid air, for example).

3. It should bloom all summer.

4. It should grow from seed to full bloom in no more than 3 months.

5. It should be resistant to insects and diseases.

6. It should grow more strongly than most weeds, yet not strongly enough to *become* a weed.

7. It should need little in the way of fussy maintenance (such as pruning, staking, or deadheading).

8. It should be widely available.

9. It should come true from seed.

10. It should transplant readily at all stages of growth.

Of course, no annual meets all 10 of my criteria (wouldn't that be wonderful, though?). The best most can usually manage is 7 out of the 10, which are *very* good plants. And 5 out of 10 is really not that bad. However, if the plant rates less than 4, you're better off looking for something else.

A Note of Caution

In Part 2 of this book, you'll see two logos that appear often. Here's what they mean and why they are important.

🖊 Self-Sowing

Annuals That Self-Sow
The Self-Sowing logo indicates that the plant's seeds tend to sprout all on their own the following year. This can be a good thing or a bad thing. It's great if they sprout where you want them to, but it's not so great if they sprout in the wrong spots. Whether you like self-sowing plants or not will depend partly on the style of your garden. In cottage-style gardens, for example, self-sowing is considered a major plus. In carpet bedding or other more formal styles, where each plant has a specific space, interlopers are *not* appreciated. Of course, you can always pull out or move self-sown annuals, but they can still be an annoyance.

If you don't want your annuals to self-sow, regularly remove their dead flowers before they set seed. Adding a fresh layer of mulch to the garden each spring will also help a lot because it will cover up last year's seeds and discourage them from sprouting. To *encourage* self-sowing, don't deadhead, and do leave a few mulch-free spots in your garden.

🖊 Think Twice

"Think Twice" Annuals
Annuals that rate the Think Twice logo have a serious problem of some sort: one that may mean they are not a good choice for you. Some annuals, for instance, self-sow to the point of weediness; they can even escape from gardens entirely and cause damage to the local environment. Other annuals are particularly subject to insects or disease in certain situations. Whether

New and Improved

You'll note that I rarely recommend specific cultivar names for annuals (like 'Plum Carpet' petunia, for just one example), in the individual plant descriptions in Part 2, even though there are thousands of them on the market, that's because so many annual cultivars are introduced each year. Cultivars popular today may be supplanted by newer introductions in just a few years. Rather than waste space writing about cultivars that will already be out-of-date before this book is even in your hands, I suggest you check out seed catalogs each year to see what's hot.

or not you should hesitate before selecting a Think Twice annual depends on your conditions. For example, many of the most weedy annuals, such as lantana (*Lantana camara*), are problems only in tropical climates; there's absolutely no danger in growing them elsewhere. And if you *always* deadhead, weediness is simply not a concern.

Buying Annuals

There was a time when you had only two choices when purchasing annuals: Either you bought wooden boxes of ready-to-plant annuals, or you bought seed packs. Well, those wooden boxes (and the fiber ones that followed) have pretty much gone the way of the dinosaur having been replaced by plastic containers. Seed packs still exist, of course, and in many ways, they've scarcely changed from a century ago. Let's take a quick look at the options:

Seed Packs
You'll find these for sale both in local stores and in seed catalogs, but the latter have by far the widest choice. Seed packs are relatively inexpensive, so they're a great choice if you are on a

limited budget. In most cases, each annual you grow from seed costs you only a few cents! The downside of seed packs is that they *do* mean extra work.

Boxes, Flats, and Cell Packs

The standard containers for nursery-grown annuals include boxes, flats, and cell packs. Single pots—usually 4 inches (10 cm) in diameter for annual plants—are the most costly, and cell packs (4 to 6 plants) and six packs are the most commonly sold. In the United States, flats usually contain 8 to 12 cell packs and are the cheapest, most surefire route to a lush, full garden. Outside the states, annual containers hold anywhere from 4 to 36 plants.

The plants grown in these containers are generally raised from seed; in fact, it's the same seed you could have bought from a seed rack or a catalog, but someone else has done all the work. Container-grown seedlings can be a big plus if you're really busy; just pop the plants into the ground and water. In return, you pay a bit more, but most annuals come in at less than 50 cents a plant, so that's not exorbitant.

Plugs

For years, nurseries have been buying the more-delicate annuals prestarted in trays with tiny little compartments. Normally, they pot them up into larger containers, then jack up the price. Some nurseries, however, are now selling these "plugs" (as the tiny seedlings are called) directly at greatly reduced prices. I buy all my "difficult" annuals (such as begonias and impatiens) this way. Of course, you'll have to pot up the plugs yourself, but the savings are considerable: less than one-quarter the cost of buying the same plant in a cell pack. Buy plugs early and pot them into 2½-inch (6.5-cm) pots or sectioned trays, then grow them indoors until planting-out time.

You can also buy larger plugs (in this case, starter plants) of the usually expensive annuals grown from rooted cuttings—such as Australian fan flower (*Scaevola aemula*)—once again with the idea of potting them up yourself.

Annuals come in a variety of different containers. Just pop out plants from containers or peat pots, and cut through roots to separate plants if they are growing in an undivided flat.

Individual Pots

Rooted cuttings of container annuals are usually sold in individual pots at quite a cost: $2 or more per pot. And the larger the pot, the more you pay! If you only need a few plants for a container, though, the cost won't seem so bad. Since all these plants can be propagated by cuttings, I suggest you buy just one plant and multiply it by rooting the cuttings yourself. That will bring the price down!

Preplanted Pots and Baskets

These "finished" container plantings are the most expensive option of all. Plus, they limit your creativity since you're stuck with choosing from the available color combinations and plant choices. Personally, I prefer to plan my own mixed containers. But hey, if you find a preplanted container that you like and it's at a reasonable price, go for it!

Buying Smart

You can tell true gardeners by the annuals they purchase. Everyone around them is picking up plants in full, gorgeous bloom, yet the true gardeners select plants with nary a blossom. Why?

They know that blooming plants kept in cramped quarters all their lives are overmature. When you put these plants in the ground, they are slow to produce new roots and tend to grow poorly or even die back. Slightly younger plants—perhaps in bud, but not yet in bloom—react differently; put them in the garden and they immediately send out new roots in all directions, then new branches and new leaves. Soon, they are far larger, healthier, and more floriferous than the planted-when-blooming annuals will ever be.

Unfortunately, already-flowering plants sell quickest, so nurseries have no reason to set out younger, not-yet-blooming plants. If you must buy container-grown seedlings al-

You can buy preplanted containers, but preparing your own is cheaper and more fun!

ready in bloom, you can still get good results if you pinch out all the flowers and all the buds at planting time. This extra step encourages the plant to sprout new roots and shoots galore, giving you blooming plants of top quality in no time.

Going for Quality

Besides choosing annuals that are not yet in full bloom, watch out for any that have been mistreated. Yellowed leaves, leaf spots, straggly growth, wilting stems, and visible insects are *not* good signs. Instead, look for plants with dense, lush, dark green foliage.

Designing WITH ANNUALS

Boy, are you in luck! There is no plant group easier to design with than annuals. For one thing, most bloom throughout the growing season. That means you don't need to account for "downtime," as you would in a perennial garden, or to plan on a color scheme that changes constantly. And annuals let you *experiment!* You wouldn't dare try a bold design or color combination with permanent plants like perennials or shrubs unless you're sure it will work. With annuals, though, anything goes! You don't like it? Just try something different the following year!

If there's any set rule for designing with annuals, it's to be yourself. Other people's plans are fine for starters, but as soon as you feel at ease with already-planned designs, learn to add your own favorite colors and plants, combining them in ways that suit your eye. After all, it's your garden!

◄Place cool colors, like the deep violet of these heliotropes, in the foreground with warm shades, like those of celosia and summer poinsettia, in the background.

Design Basics

I don't consider myself an expert on design. Like most gardeners, I just follow a few basic rules and change things when I don't like them. And I confess to breaking the rules every now and then: sometimes with great results, sometimes not. Oh well, that's what I use annuals for—to experiment! Three of the basic keys to a beautiful garden are color, texture, and form. Get them to mesh and you'll be doing just fine.

Color

Of the three, color is probably the most influential factor when you choose the annuals you grow. Cool colors, like green and blue, make the garden seem calmer and more peaceful, and they can make a small garden look larger.

Warm colors, like yellow and red, stimulate the eye. They make a garden seem vibrant and alive and can make a large garden seem more intimate.

How you use warm and cool colors is up to you. You can use only one or mix the two groups. If you do choose to mix them, use about half again as many cool-colored annuals as warm-colored ones; if you use equal numbers, the warm colors will dominate. And in general, put cool colors in front of warm colors; otherwise, they'll hardly be visible.

Color Combinations

There is nothing wrong with mixing colors at random, especially if you enjoy an all-mixed-up, everything-goes appearance. If so, you'll find white flowers (and silver and gray foliage) make great moderators. You can use them to separate and soften excessively strong impacts and dilute overbearing colors.

Red

Orange

Violet

Blue

Yellow

Green

Combining colors is easier if you use a color wheel. Neighboring colors always work well together, or try a "complementary color": one from the direct opposite side of the wheel.

Texture and Form

While flower color is undeniably important when planning a garden, you'll want to consider texture and form as well.

Texture can refer to either flowers or foliage. Just think fine, medium, and coarse, and you'll have a handle on it. Fine foliage creates a soft, intimate look, whereas a few spots of bold, coarse foliage can wake up a humdrum border.

Form refers to a plant's general outline; it may be vertical, rounded, open, spreading, or prostrate (practically flat). The most successful gardens usually include some of each form, with spreading or prostrate plants in the foreground, rounded plants to the middle, and vertical ones at the back or standing tall here and there as "vertical accents."

Beyond "Borders"

Most modern flower gardens feature a broad bed backed by a tall background element, such as a hedge or fence, and are laid out with plants of graduating height (shortest in the front to tallest

in the back). Or if the border is to be seen from both sides, the tallest plants are in the middle with shorter plants to either side. But with annuals offering so many possibilities, why not try going beyond the border?

Carpet Bedding

This type of formal bedding is back in style. You've probably seen it in parks or in front of corporate offices: neatly trimmed, low-growing plants set out in precise geometrical patterns or even in company or municipal logos. You can adapt simpler carpet-bedding styles to the home garden. Just choose low-growing plants of contrasting colors, and set them out in relatively geometric patterns. Often a tall, upright centerpiece plant, like castor bean (*Ricinus communis*), will give carpet beds more impact.

Flower Meadows

The ultimate in informality! Best suited for vast spaces you don't have the time (or the money!) to cover with individual bedding plants, a flower meadow involves simply sowing seeds of mixed, fast-growing annuals. In fall or early spring, simply till or plow under whatever was there before. (*Don't* bother worrying about weeds; the nice thing about a flower meadow is that weeds fit right in!) Then sow annual wildflower seed by hand or with a spreader. Don't think flower meadows are self-maintaining, though. You'll have to till the meadow under and resow it annually; otherwise, weeds and grasses *will* dominate and flowers will be few.

Cut-Flower Gardens

If you're fond of gathering flowers and foliage for fresh and dried arrangements, consider growing an area of annuals just for that purpose. You'll find details on this type of garden in "Annuals for Cut & Dried Arrangements," starting on page 242.

The 10 Commandments of Annual Design

Over the years, I've learned a lot both from my successes and my failures. Here are the best tips I know about gardening with annuals.

1. Mix 'em up! Gone are the days when annuals had to be in a bed of their own. You can—and should—plant them among shrubs and perennials.

2. Don't plant too densely. A newly planted garden always looks barren at first, but annuals fill out in only a few weeks. So respect the spacing indicated in the descriptions in Part 2 and be patient. Crowded plants rarely give good results.

3. Plan before you plant. It's always wise to take a few minutes to make a rapid sketch of a garden plan and then pencil in a few plant names you've chosen from Part 2 of this book. Next, trace the plan on the garden surface with flour or powdered lime before planting. If you make a mistake, you just have to rake the lines out and redraw. It's much easier than having to dig plants up and replant them!

4. Use annuals abundantly for new gardens. Even if you plan to have a garden mostly based on shrubs or perennials, use annuals until the permanent plants fill in.

5. Avoid straight lines whenever possible. Lines are too hard to maintain and rarely look their best; it takes only one dead plant to destroy the whole effect. Instead, go for curves and undulations when planning edges and for spots of color inside the garden. Save planting in lines for very formal styles, such as carpet bedding.

6. Repeat spots of color. You can mix any colors you like with total impunity, as long as you repeat them. One spot each of a dozen different plants will seem discordant, but if you repeat the spots (each at least twice and preferably more), the whole garden will "pull together" visually. And while you're at it, write down your successful combinations so you'll remember the following year.

7. Stake discreetly or not at all. A few twiggy branches, a bit shorter than the plants themselves, will look much nicer than a forest of upright stakes. And if possible, grow plants that don't require staking.

8. Watch out for self-sowing annuals. They have many good qualities, but that doesn't mean you should let them grow anywhere they want! Pull or dig out any annuals that appear where you don't want them.

9. Don't be afraid to experiment. One of the great advantages to annuals is that they are temporary, so you can easily replace plants that don't work with others when you replant next year.

10. Don't always follow the rules. All rules are meant to be broken, especially in design. Break or bend a few—and watch your garden come alive!

Garden Designs with a Purpose

Still not sure you're ready to design a garden on your own? Try borrowing or adapting the ideas in the following section! I've included four annual garden designs created by professionals especially for home gardeners like you.

Look over the design layouts on the next several pages to see how the designers combine color and texture, use repetition, and choose plants that have different habits. You may find a plan that's just perfect for your yard or one that inspires you to take the plunge to design a garden of your own. Good luck and have fun!

GRANDMOTHER'S BACKDOOR GARDEN

Heirloom flowers are enjoying a resurgence of popularity—and with good reason. The annuals our grandmothers and great-grandmothers knew and grew are colorful, sturdy, easy-to-grow plants. Many of these old-time favorites are also wonderful in cut-flower arrangements. Designed by heirloom-flower aficionado Sarah Wolfgang Heffner, this backdoor garden in shades of pink, blue, and lavender starts its show in late spring with larkspur and cornflowers, then keeps the color coming with cleome, ageratum, and zinnias for an abundance of bloom from midsummer through early fall (the midsummer view is shown here). This low-maintenance planting will do well in direct sun and fertile, well-drained soil.

Sowing and planting: Start ageratum seeds indoors 6 to 8 weeks before the last frost date. Sow cleome, cornflower, and larkspur seeds outdoors in early spring. Sow zinnia seeds outdoors around the last frost date, and set out dusty miller plants around the same time.

Plant List

1 Cleome
(*Cleome hassleriana*)
(8 plants)

2 Larkspur
(*Consolida ajacis*)
(6 plants)

3 Bachelor's buttons
(*Centaurea cyanus*)
(12 plants)

4 'Blue Bouquet' ageratum
(*Ageratum houstonianum*
'Blue Bouquet')
(6 plants)

5 Zinnia
(*Zinnia elegans*)
(8 plants)

6 Dusty miller
(*Senecio cineraria*)
(5 plants)

SCALE OF PLAN
¼" = 1'

AN ELEGANT ENTRANCE BORDER

There's nothing like a flower-filled garden to welcome visitors to your home. Designed by Pam Ruch, this inviting planting (shown in midsummer) combines a touch of formality loosened up by an exuberant mix of colors and heights on either side of the walk. The drought-resistant zinnias add a blast of bright color for months on end, while the Brazilian vervain adds a lively second layer of purple haze. The cool green 'Envy' zinnias provide a pleasant break for the eye. (If your 'Envy' zinnias start looking forlorn by mid- to late summer, Pam suggests pulling them out and letting the remaining plants fill the space—which they'll happily do!) The flowering tobacco offers an extra bonus of evening fragrance. Give this garden a full-sun site with average, well-drained soil.

Sowing and planting: Sow Brazilian vervain seeds outdoors in early spring. Start zinnia seeds indoors 4 to 6 weeks before the last frost date or sow outdoors around the last frost date. Sow flowering tobacco seed outdoors in late spring or indoors at the same time as the zinnias for earlier bloom. Set out mealy-cup sage plants after the last frost date.

Plant List

1 Flowering tobacco (*Nicotiana sylvestris*) (8 plants)

2 'Victoria' mealy-cup sage (*Salvia farinacea* 'Victoria') (72 plants)

3 'Profusion Orange' hybrid zinnia (*Zinnia elegans* × *angustifolia* 'Profusion Orange') (about 70 plants)

4 'Envy' zinnia (*Z. elegans* 'Envy') (12 plants)

5 'Star White' narrow-leaved zinnia (*Z. angustifolia* 'Star White') (about 70 plants)

+ Brazilian vervain (*Verbena bonariensis*) (about 30 plants)

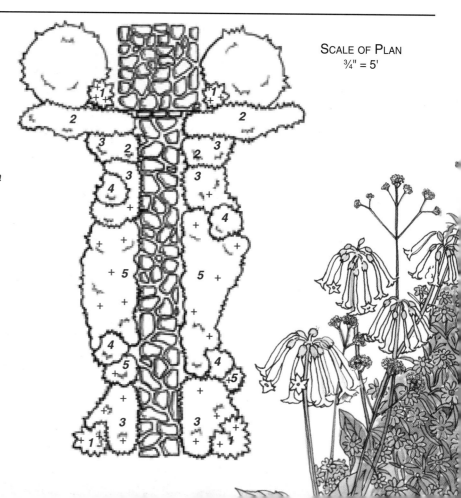

SCALE OF PLAN
¾" = 5'

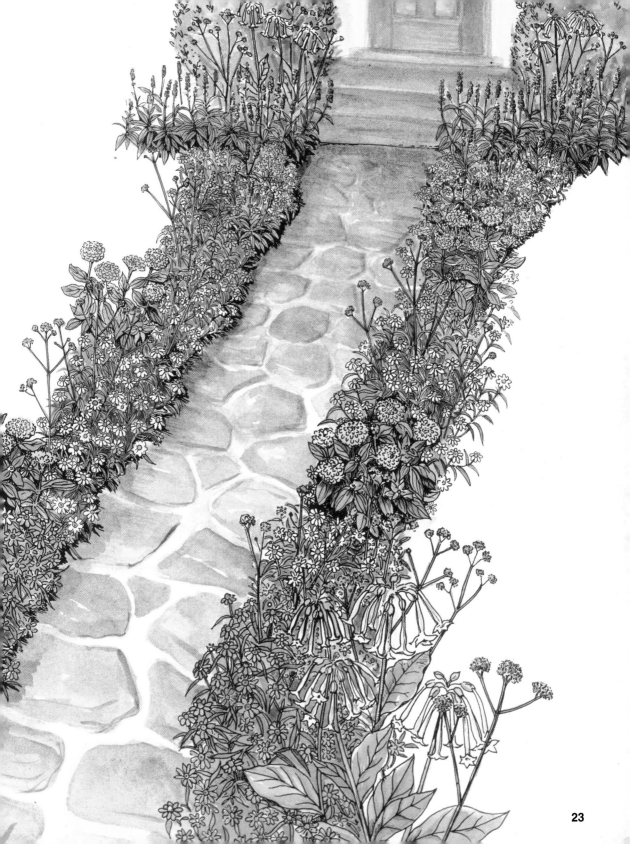

A Regal Red Garden

This dramatic collection of rich red flowers and foliage is sure to attract plenty of attention in midsummer (shown here), whether you tuck it into an otherwise boring corner or give it a prominent spot near a sidewalk or patio. 'Lady in Red' Texas sage is even a great draw for hummingbirds. To set off the red flowers, this garden includes a variety of other complementary companions, including the chartreuse flowers of 'Lime Green' flowering tobacco, the bright green, red-veined leaves of 'Rhubarb' chard, and the dark purple foliage of 'Purple Ruffles' basil and purple fountain grass. For a more vivid effect, you might replace the purple basil with ferny, bright green parsley. Designed by Nancy Ondra, this garden works well in evenly moist but well-drained soil in either full sun or light shade.

Sowing and planting: Start snapdragon plants indoors 8 to 10 weeks before the last frost date and flowering tobacco seed indoors 6 to 8 weeks before the last frost date. Sow chard seed outdoors in early spring or indoors 6 to 8 weeks before the last frost date. Set out basil, fountain grass, impatiens, and Texas sage plants after all danger of frost has passed.

Plant List

1 'Accent Red' impatiens (*Impatiens walleriana* 'Accent Red') (12 plants)

2 'Purple Ruffles' basil (*Ocimum basilicum* 'Purple Ruffles') (12 plants)

3 'Rhubarb' Swiss chard (*Beta vulgaris cicla* 'Rhubarb') (2 plants)

4 'Black Prince' snapdragon (*Antirrhinum majus* 'Black Prince') (12 plants)

5 'Lime Green' flowering tobacco (*Nicotiana* 'Lime Green') (6 plants)

6 'Lady in Red' Texas sage (*Salvia coccinea* 'Lady in Red') (6 plants)

7 Purple fountain grass (*Pennisetum setaceum* 'Purpureum') (1 plant)

SCALE OF PLAN
$\frac{3}{8}$" = 1'

8'

2'

A GARDEN WITH CLASSICAL APPEAL

Designer Stephanie Cohen created a layout that rivals any formal perennial garden for elegance, yet it's composed entirely of easy-care annuals. Shown in midsummer, the mixture of strong spikes, billowing mounds, and cheerful climbers blooms from early summer to midfall. Full sun and average, well-drained soil are ideal for this garden.

Sowing and planting: Start snapdragon plants indoors 8 to 10 weeks before the last frost date. Sow sweet alyssum seeds outdoors in early to mid-spring. Start ageratum and hyacinth bean seeds indoors 6 to 8 weeks before the last frost date. Start zinnia seeds indoors 4 to 6 weeks before the last frost date or sow outdoors around the last frost date. Set out fountain grass, mealy-cup sage, and marguerite daisy plants, and sow morning glory seeds outdoors after the last frost date.

Plant List

1 'Pearly Gates' morning glory (*Ipomoea tricolor* 'Pearly Gates') (1 plant)

2 Hyacinth bean (*Lablab purpurea*) (1 plant)

3 'Rocket White' snapdragon (*Antirrhinum majus* 'Rocket White') (6 plants)

4 'Splendor Pink' zinnia (*Zinnia* 'Splendor Pink') (6 plants)

5 'Victoria' mealy-cup sage (*Salvia farinacea* 'Victoria') (16 plants)

6 Purple fountain grass (*Pennisetum setaceum* 'Purpureum') (4 plants)

7 'Comet Pink' and 'Comet White' marguerites (*Argyranthemum* hybrids 'Comet Pink' and 'Comet White') (10 plants)

8 'Blue Horizon' ageratum (*Ageratum houstonianum* 'Blue Horizon') (7 plants)

9 'Carpet of Snow' sweet alyssum (*Lobularia maritima* 'Carpet of Snow') (20 plants)

SCALE OF PLAN
⅝" = 1'

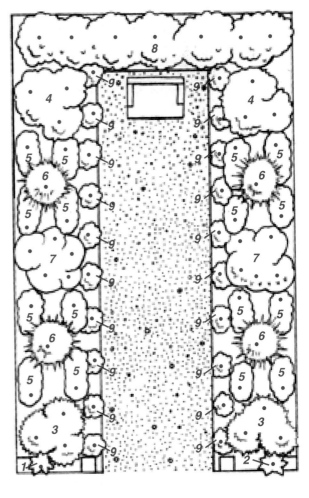

27

KEEPING ANNUALS
Alive & Kicking

When it comes to annual maintenance, I'm on the minimalist side of the garden gate. I don't believe in spending all of my waking hours caring for a garden. I prefer to *enjoy* my gardens, and I think you should do the same. Therefore, in this chapter, don't look for persnickety little details on coaching a plant to its maximum bloom. Instead, you'll find "easy ways out": how to get the most of your annuals with the least possible effort.

The degree of effort required in maintaining a garden is directly related to its degree of formality. Formal beds and carpet bedding, when every dead flower sticks out, need the most care. Mixed borders need only moderate care. Cottage gardens and flower meadows, on the other hand, need so little upkeep that they practically take care of themselves!

◄ An abundant assortment of upright and trailing plants give you a garden's worth of beauty in a small container.

Back to Basics

So, you've just finished planting or sowing your annuals, and you've watered thoroughly. What next?

Mulching as a Way of Life

My next step is always mulching. I can't say enough about this important practice! Mulching simply means covering the soil with a layer of organic material. Chopped leaves, lawn clippings (mix them with chopped leaves), pine needles, small pieces of bark, cocoa hulls, and similar materials are widely available and sometimes even free. A 2-inch (5-cm) layer is perfect for accomplishing what mulches are supposed to accomplish, which includes minimizing weed problems, keeping the soil evenly moist, enriching the soil as they decompose, and providing a haven for beneficial insects. Since I began mulching about 20 years ago, I've put away my hoe entirely and almost never water, plus I keep fertilizing to a minimum. Try it and see!

There are, however, a few things to keep in mind when using mulches. Plants that prefer dry soil, for example, may find conditions too moist under an organic mulch. For these plants, I instead use decorative stones, which help keep the base of the plants dry. Also remember that organic mulches decompose readily, so you'll need to replace them regularly. Even in my cool summer climate, my chopped leaf mulch is all but gone by fall; in hot, humid climates, you'll have to apply such mulches twice a year. And certain mulches will, in the long run, change the soil's characteristics. Pine and other conifer needles, as well as sawdust, for example, acidify the soil, so you should use them only on plants that prefer an acidic environment.

To my mind, the major flaw with mulches is that they prevent annuals from self-sowing. Of course, that's not always a bad thing; they also prevent weed seeds from germinating in the same way. But if you

Deadheading is a persnickety practice I try to avoid, but it is useful for some annuals, especially those in the foreground of a garden bed.

enjoy the casual, easy-care nature of self-sowing annuals, you'll need to leave a few mulch-free spots in your garden for them . . . or wait until self-sown annuals have sprouted (in late May or June) before you apply mulch.

You can apply organic mulches either before or after planting. If the garden is already mulched, just dig right through the mulch as you plant, adding a bit more to fill in at the end. Don't worry if some organic mulch gets mixed in with the soil; it will simply decompose that much faster. If the bed is not already mulched, just apply fresh mulch around the plants when you finish. Since you can't sow seeds through a mulch, rake it off the area where you want to sow, then push it back into place once the seedlings are up and growing strongly.

Keeping Weeds at a Minimum

If you begin with weed-free soil and mulch abundantly, weeds simply won't be a major problem. Remove the few you *do* see by hand,

then fill the gap that's left with mulch to prevent new weeds from seeding themselves in. Hoeing and cultivating are largely a waste of time: They simply bring fresh weed seeds to the surface!

The ABCs of Grooming

Annuals grow quickly and will usually fill in all on their own if you pinched them back when they were seedlings. Don't hesitate to pinch back any straggly looking plants at other times as well. Full-scale pruning with pruning shears, as you might do on shrubs, is not necessary with annuals, although gardeners in the South may have to prune back, often to ground level, those "annuals" that grow as shrubs or perennials in their climate—lantanas, for example.

A more important step for many annuals is deadheading. This simply means removing faded flowers. You can cut off individual flowers by snipping them off. When flowers grow in clusters, it is often easier to wait until the entire cluster has nearly finished blooming, and then to cut off the whole stem at the base.

Deadheading is useful for several reasons. For one, it cleans up a potentially messy appearance, because some annuals, like marigolds, hold onto a dense mass of browning petals after the blooms have long gone. More important, though, it "tricks" the plant into prolonging its blooming season. You see, once they begin producing seed, many plants stop flowering. But if you remove flowers before they set seed, they just keep on blooming.

Deadheading is *not* necessary on all annuals. Many, like impatiens, seem perfectly able to bloom and produce seeds at the same time and are self-cleaning (their faded petals drop off on their own). Others produce attractive seed capsules that you wouldn't want to remove. And if you want to collect seed or allow self-sowing, you should, of course, allow at least some flowers to produce seed capsules.

Clean-Up Time

Most annuals, however, are simply allowed to die their natural death with the arrival of cold fall weather. You can clean up their stems, leaves, and faded flowers after they die back in fall, or in early spring. *Don't* pull out dead annuals! This leaves the bed open to erosion and provides a gaping hole for weeds to seed into. Instead, cut them off at ground level and leave the roots alone where they will rot and add organic matter to the soil. Put cut material in your compost pile. *Don't* compost disease-infested stems and foliage, though, because the temperature in your compost pile might not be high enough to kill disease spores; burn such parts or put them out with the garbage.

Harvesting Seed for Next Year's Bloom

There's not much use in harvesting seed of hybrid plants; the resulting seedlings won't look like their parents. Other annuals, though, *will* come true—at least if you plant them where they can't be cross-pollinated by others of a different size or color. For example, a patch of pink cosmos (*Cosmos bipinnatus*) in the same bed as a patch of white cosmos may well yield seed giving mixed colors. Where there is no chance of crossing, though, simply harvest the seed when it is ripe (usually when the seed capsule turns brown). Just cut the capsule off at its base and let it drop into a paper envelope.

Store envelopes or packets of seed over the winter in a cool, dry spot indoors. I seal mine in a wide-mouth bottle and store it in the refrigerator, inserting a small envelope of powdered milk to absorb excess humidity. Replace the powdered milk annually. Most annual seeds will last 2 to 5 years when stored this way.

Water Wisely

Mulching, as mentioned previously, can reduce watering needs to almost zero in many climates. And drought-resistant annuals won't need much water, either. But when you do water, do it wisely: Water is too precious a resource to waste. That's why I rarely water with a sprinkler or watering can any more; most of the water applied that way evaporates rather than going to the plants. Also, watering plants from above can spread disease. If you must water from above, try to do it in the morning, so the leaves have time to dry off before nightfall.

I now use a soaker hose for almost all watering needs in the garden and drip irrigation to water plants in pots. Both keep the leaves dry and the soil moist. And that *should* be your goal, at least for most annuals: keeping the soil evenly moist at all times. Don't wait until they wilt; sink a finger through the mulch and feel. If the soil is dry to the touch, it is time to water.

A soaker hose is simply my favorite garden tool. I just run it through my beds and turn it on as needed.

Fertilizing for Good Growth

Start with good soil and add organic matter annually, and you'll find you won't need to fertilize very much. Just using organic mulch that gradually works its way into the soil as it decays is sufficient to keep most annuals perfectly happy. You may still want to add some slow-acting organic fertilizer at planting time, such as bonemeal, if your soil is naturally poor or if you're gardening in containers.

Sometimes certain plants falter in midseason, becoming yellowed or failing to bloom properly. Since this rarely affects the whole bed, why fertilize all the plants? This is a case for foliar fertilizer; spray the leaves of the weak plants only. I use liquid seaweed or fish emulsion according to the directions on the label, and the plants green up overnight!

Overwintering Annuals

You can bring many annuals indoors at the end of the growing season, either as cuttings or as plants dug up from the garden. Besides giving you winter color for your home or greenhouse, it's a great way to keep expensive or difficult-to-replace annuals from year to year. Not all annuals can be maintained this way, though; check the individual descriptions in Part 2 to see which ones do adapt.

Indoors, supply the brightest light possible. The full sun of a south window is ideal. Or grow your annuals under fluorescent lights, much as you would seedlings. Pinch the plants regularly through the winter to keep them bushy. If you can keep temperatures cool indoors—less than 60°F (15°C) at night—their water needs will be minimal. Under warm conditions, though, most plants will need watering regularly, up to once a week. Don't fertilize overwintered plants (unless you're growing plants under lights, where it is always "summer"), until day lengths increase in late February; then work some organic fertilizer into their mix. This is also the time to take cuttings to have lots of plants for the summer garden.

Plants overwintered indoors need help getting used to outdoor conditions again. Start by setting them outside only a few hours per day in moderate shade, then increase the length of time and intensity of light until they are receiving the kind of conditions they will grow in as adults.

Know Thine Enemies

Annuals tend to be far less susceptible to pests and diseases than other plants, mostly because they don't live long. If you grow different annuals in each spot each year, the pests and diseases won't be able to build up to problem level. Ornamental annuals tend to have plentiful natural defenses against pests. That doesn't mean you will never have any problems, but the chances are reduced. For more details, refer to "Annual Diseases" on the opposite page and "Annual Pests" on page 34.

ANNUAL DISEASES

Annuals generally don't live long enough to pick up most diseases, but if they do, the damage normally isn't evident until near the end of the season. Diseases are usually highly specific (one race of powdery mildew attacks only begonias, for example, while another affects only verbenas), so if a disease returns again and again, try growing something else! In general, good drainage and good ventilation will go a long way toward preventing diseases on annuals.

DISEASE NAME AND SYMPTOMS	CONTROLS	LARRY'S HELPFUL HINTS
Downy mildew Fuzzy, cottony, gray or tan "mold" appears under leaves, which then turn yellow and die back.	Space plants well and thin out to encourage air circulation. Avoid water-logged soil. Remove and destroy infected leaves.	Downy mildew is especially prevalent during humid, rainy weather when days are hot and nights are cool.
Gray mold (botrytis blight) Leaves, stems, or flowers become covered with grayish, powdery growth. Shoots may wilt and fall over, and stem bases can blacken and rot.	Cut off infected parts and destroy severely infected plants. Don't add infected material to the compost. Ensure good drainage to prevent a recurrence.	Gray mold usually attacks only weak or dying foliage at first, but it can spread to healthy growth, so keep it under control.
Leaf spots A variety of bacterial diseases with the same symptoms: brown or purple leaf spots. Severely infected leaves yellow and drop.	Maintain good ventilation, keep foliage dry, and destroy infected leaves. Allow 4 years before planting the same annual again in that spot.	If you keep having problems with leaf spot, try growing something else!
Powdery mildew Leaves appear grayish because they are covered with white, powdery masses. As the disease advances, leaves blacken and die. The disease strikes when the air is moist, and the soil is dry.	Choose mildew-resistant strains of plants known to be susceptible, like verbena or zinnias. Provide good air circulation. Remove damaged lower leaves in early stages to prevent spreading.	Powdery mildew is a common disease that's usually only a problem at the end of the season when most of the flowering is done anyway, so you can simply pull out infected plants.
Rots and wilts Plants wilt even when soil is moist. Wilt usually shows few other symptoms; in rot, the plant's roots or crown will also be soft, soggy, or brown.	To prevent, grow cultivars that are disease resistant, and provide good air circulation. You may be able to take cuttings from unaffected parts. Little can be done to save seriously infected plants; pull out and destroy.	Rots and wilts tend to develop due to poor drainage or lack of ventilation. Try raised beds and use wider spacings if the problem occurs the following year.
Rust Yellow or pale spots are visible on the upper leaf surface. Powdery orange spores are visible underneath.	Grow disease-resistant cultivars. Mulching and watering with a soaker hose will help prevent spores from reaching leaves.	Mostly a problem in cool, humid climates or during especially rainy summers. Rust damage usually occurs so late in the season that it rarely affects bloom.

ANNUAL PESTS

If you can see the pest itself, glance through the description column to identify it. If you instead see mostly the results of the pest's raids, look through the damage column until you find a match. Once you've found the cause, read on to see how to control that particular pest.

PEST NAME AND DESCRIPTION	DAMAGE	CONTROLS	LARRY'S HELPFUL HINTS
Aphids Little pear-shaped insects ranging from green to black to orange. Most are wingless.	They damage plants by pumping out the sap, causing the plant to yellow and distort, and often by transmitting viruses as they feed.	A strong spray of water will knock them off. Insecticidal soap and light horticultural oil can also be effective.	Hummingbirds and lady beetles are voracious eaters of aphids.
Caterpillars These creepy crawlers have wormlike, smooth to fuzzy bodies.	They eat holes in leaves, stems, or flowers. Some roll themselves in leaves, then eat their way out.	Hand-pick or spray with insecticidal soap. *Bacillus thuringiensis* (BT), reapplied after every rain, also works.	Remember that caterpillars are young butterflies and moths. If you want to attract fluttery visitors to your garden, you'll have to accept some damage. Especially learn to identify the larvae of those species of butterflies you want to encourage.
Japanese beetles Rounded beetles with metallic green bodies and coppery brown wing covers.	They eat leaves and flowers, leaving small, round holes at first, then often skeletonize the leaves.	Hand-pick if they are not numerous, then crush underfoot or drop into soapy water. Spot-spray with insecticidal soap.	The larvae of Japanese beetles are lawn grubs, so join with your neighbors to treat the area's lawns with milky spore disease (*Bacillus popillus*).
Leafminers You'll probably never see either the tiny, winged adults or the scarcely visible green larvae.	The larvae burrow inside leaves, leaving pale, twisting tunnels just under the leaf surface.	Cut off and destroy infected leaves.	Plant dill or another carrot-family member to attract beneficial wasps that will, in turn, control the miners.
Mammals Deer, gophers, groundhogs, rabbits, and so on.	As they feed, these critters can tear large chunks out of leaves or eat whole plants to the ground.	Blood meal can help keep them away. Spray predator urine.	Sometimes the only solution is a good fence, partly buried in the ground.
Mealy bugs Slow-moving pink or gray insects that seem covered in tufts of cotton.	Cottony masses form at leaf axils and under leaves; plants weaken and yellow. Black sooty mold forms on lower leaves.	Touch each insect with a cotton swab dipped in rubbing alcohol. Spray with insecticidal soap.	They are usually only a major problem indoors over the winter. Putting plants outdoors for the summer often allows natural predators to control them.

PEST NAME AND DESCRIPTION	DAMAGE	CONTROLS	LARRY'S HELPFUL HINTS
Slugs and snails Slimy mollusks with tentacles on their heads. Snails have shells; slugs don't.	Lower leaves show irregular holes. Small plants are totally eaten. A glistening trail is left behind.	Hand-pick at night (use a flashlight) and crush the ones you see. Leave out bowls of beer; they'll drop in and drown.	A barrier of diatomaceous earth (DE) or a strip of copper around each plant can repel these pests. Ducks love to eat slugs and snails, so if you live in the country, get a duck!
Spider mites You'll see spiderweb-like strands over leaves. The dustlike particles that move over them are the spider mites.	They pierce tiny holes in the leaves and drink the sap that leaks out. Leaves may turn yellow and curl under.	Hose down regularly with water or spray with insecticidal soap or light horticultural oil.	Spider mites are mostly a problem indoors and in dry climates. In humid climates, they are washed away by rains.
Whiteflies Tiny white flies, looking like dandruff particles, flutter about when you touch the foliage, then quickly return to their host or its neighbors.	Both the adults and the tiny, dome-shaped larvae suck up sap and cause yellowing and stunted, droopy growth. Sooty mold may form on lower leaves.	Spray with insecticidal soap or light horticultural oil. If possible, treat at night because the adults fly away in daylight.	Wash both sides of leaves of all plants you bring inside in the fall because whiteflies can multiply quickly and cause serious damage indoors.

Aphids quickly form huge colonies, but you can knock them off with a sharp spray of water.

Snails (shown here) and slugs are a menace in humid conditions: I just usually handpick and crush.

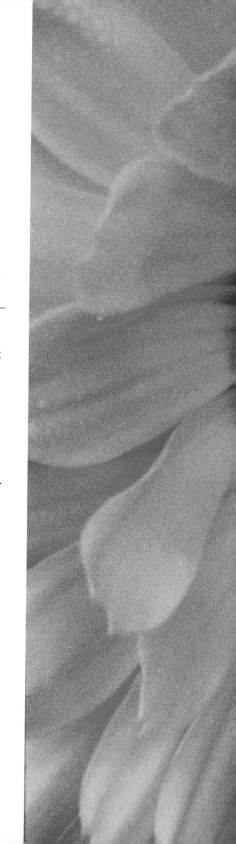

PART 2

Choosing the Best Annuals

With so many wonderful annuals to choose from, where do you start? I suggest picking your annuals not simply by color, but by how you intend to use them. And that's why this section is divided as it is, so you can pick annuals that suit your exact purpose. Just decide what you need and turn to the chapter in question; it couldn't be easier!

Are you looking for bedding plants or easy-to-direct-sow annuals to fill empty spots in your garden? Turn to "Multipurpose Annuals," starting on page 38, and "Annuals to Sow Directly Outdoors," starting on page 70. Need something tall to give height to your garden or dress up your walls and fences? Try "Giants for the Back of the Garden," starting on page 192, or "Climbing Annuals," starting on page 214.

Are you into container gardening? If so, you'll find two chapters for your perusal, "Flowering Annuals for Containers & Hanging Baskets," starting on page 304, and "Foliage Plants for Containers & Hanging Baskets," starting on page 332. Whatever your needs, you'll find an answer in this section. Now just flip through to the right chapters and prepare to be amazed!

Multipurpose ANNUALS

They're tall or short; they're upright, rounded, or creeping; they're great in borders or in containers; they grow under a wide range of conditions; and they come in an incredible range of flower forms and colors. They're multipurpose annuals: plants that offer a bit of everything to every garden-planting scheme. You could easily design a complete annual garden around just these 13 versatile plants! Oh, but did I mention they also mingle well with bulbs, perennials, and shrubs? You simply can't go wrong when you use multipurpose annuals throughout your landscape.

◄Celosias, both the plumed type and the cockscomb type, are among the most brilliant of all annuals. Adding a patch or two will bring even the dullest bed to life!

Traditional Yet Ever-Changing

If you're looking for something totally new, a plant of a genus never before seen on the shelves of your local nursery, look elsewhere in this book! The multipurpose group is made up strictly of plants that have been popular for generations. Snapdragon, pansy, geranium, petunia, marigold: They're all names you've heard before, even if you've never lifted a hoe in your life. That's not to say that multipurpose annuals don't occasionally yield new characteristics: new flower forms or colors or never-before-seen growth habits. It's their tried-and-true performance, however, that you'll learn to love; just stick them in the ground and watch 'em grow. They'll bloom and bloom and bloom, making your garden look good right through the summer.

Tailor-Made to Suit Our Tastes

There are many annuals whose entire range consists of one or two cultivars. When you head to the garden center or market to buy one of these, you have little choice: just pink or white perhaps, or maybe tall or taller. Compare this sort of meager selection to nursery displays of any of the plants featured in this chapter. Even corner stores offer dozens of varieties of each in an equally wide range of colors and forms. And if you *really* want choice, go beyond local stores and delve into one of the larger seed catalogs: There are literally pages and pages of petunias, pansies, marigolds, and China asters, for example.

No matter what your tastes in plants are, each of the multipurpose annuals probably offers at least a few varieties that you'll just love. Of course, this wide range of plants wasn't always available. When these multipurpose annuals were first introduced a few centuries back, there

Plain and ordinary? Never! Petunias take center stage in many annual gardens and are just as lively as many newfangled introductions.

was usually only *one* species . . . and it wasn't always that impressive. For example, would you believe that the original petunia, now available in such a wide range of cultivars, was a scrawny, creeping plant with tiny white flowers? None of the multipurpose annuals we grow today was any different: The original plants offered little variety and certainly didn't seem to offer much potential.

And then the hybridizers got a hold of them! Under their guiding hands, the wild species morphed into the varied plants we know and love today. Tall, ungainly plants were brought down to size, climbers and creepers became dense and compact mounders, and simple little flowers became large blooms with extra petals that bloomed in a vastly wider range of colors. The end result with each multipurpose annual has been a profusion of cultivars of each plant.

Small Is Beautiful . . .

One of the most remarkable and obvious changes in multipurpose annuals is that they have come down in size over the years. Most of the dense, low-growing annuals we're so used to today were once tall, rangy plants suitable only for the back of the border or scraggly spreaders that needed to be mingled with others to create a worthwhile effect. Hybridization has lead to plants with shorter and shorter internodes (the spaces between the stem leaves), resulting in dense, compact plants suitable for edging and bedding.

In fact, the entire concept of a bedding plant (and all multipurpose annuals make superb bedding plants) implies dense, short growth with abundant bloom that creates a carpet of blossoms. The shortening of annual plants over time is so universal that most gardeners would scarcely recognize the gangly ancestors of their common garden annuals. And the trend still continues, with each year bringing ever-shorter cultivars. If it never ends, I can only surmise that future generations of annuals will bloom underground!

. . . But Only in Plant Size

If short plants are generally seen as desirable, small flowers most certainly are not. So another major trend has been toward the development of larger and larger flowers, or at least denser clusters of flowers. Here, too, there seems to be no limit. Many modern annuals have blooms so large that they are beaten to a pulp by the slightest rain (Grandiflora petunias, for example), but gardeners will forgive even that—as long as the plant quickly replaces its damaged blooms with new blooms.

Other trends are easy to see just by looking at what the average nursery offers. Double flowers, for example, are clearly highly prized (although that trend does seem to be abating these days). And increases in color range are a must. Is it any wonder dahlias and pansies are so popular? They are now offered in about every color of the artist's palette—and then some!

Although the trend is toward dense, short-growing annuals, don't totally rule out the more old-fashioned, taller strains of yore. Tall snapdragons, for example, can add great impact to the mid or back border—and make great cut flowers. And the old-fashioned, climbing nasturtiums look just as great on a trellis as their dwarf brethren do at the front of the border.

Annuals for Everyone

And there you have a portrait of the average multipurpose annual: dense and compact, with large, often double, flowers in a wide range of colors and forms. These versatile annuals are the wallpaper of the flower garden. There is so much choice, you can't help but find exactly what you want!

Creating New Cultivars

Originally, new selections of annuals came about by chance. A gardener or nurseryman would notice that one plant out of the hundreds he or she grew was different. Perhaps it had larger flowers or a shorter stem. Left on their own, such mutations inevitably submerged back into the gene pool. But if the mutation was attractive, wise growers collected seed from the oddballs and sowed them again the following year. Over time, pure strains carrying the desirable trait were developed, and new cultivars were born.

Early on, this kind of selection happened without any real knowledge of genetics. By the early nineteenth century, however, simple selection was replaced by true hybridization: a technique that speeds up the process considerably. Pollen from a plant with one desirable trait, say a unique flower color, is manually transferred to the flower of a plant with another interesting characteristic, like a more compact habit; the pollinated flower is then isolated so no insect can bring in foreign pollen. Because annuals grow from seed to bloom in one single year, new lines of annuals are often developed and are ready for the market in as few as 3 years.

15 More Multipurpose Annuals

As hybridizers work their magic, developing a wider and wider range of sizes, colors, and forms, more and more plants join the list of multipurpose annuals. The following are just a few others you should consider:

Antirrhinum

Snapdragon

Snapdragons are instantly recognizable by their terminal spikes of unique flowers. The tubular blooms with a pouting lower lip seem closed to all traffic until you lightly pinch the sides; then they quickly open to reveal a gaping maw, as if they were dragons ready to snap off your finger! Of course, the flowers are perfectly harmless, but they have fascinated generations of young and young-at-heart gardeners for decades.

Plant Profile

ANTIRRHINUM
an-tir-RYE-num

- **Bloom Color:** Pink, purple, red, orange, yellow, white; bicolor

- **Bloom Time:** Summer; fall through spring in mild climates

- **Height:** 6 to 36 inches (15 to 90 cm)

- **Spread:** 6 to 12 inches (15 to 30 cm)

- **Garden Uses:** Container planting, cut-flower garden, edging, mass planting, mixed border, rock garden

- **Attracts:** Bees, hummingbirds

- **Light Preference:** Full sun or partial shade

- **Soil Preference:** Humus-rich, moist but well-drained, neutral to very acid soil

- **Best Way to Propagate:** Sow seed indoors in late winter or outdoors in early spring

- **Hardiness:** Tender perennial grown as a half-hardy annual

Growing Tips

Snapdragons are easy-to-grow annuals with a long blooming season, particularly in cool summer areas. On the down side, they tend to peter out quickly in hot summer climates. If you live where summer temperatures soar, get your snapdragons into the ground early to take full advantage of their spring bloom; and plant them in partial shade, where it is naturally cooler.

You *could* sow snapdragons outdoors in early spring, as soon as the ground is workable, but then you'll miss half their blooming season. Instead, start them indoors 8 to 10 weeks before your last frost date. Sprinkle seed over the surface of the growing mix—don't cover it; mist lightly and expose the tray to light to stimulate germination. Look for the first seedlings in 10 to 21 days. Snapdragons germinate readily under cool conditions, down to 50°F (10°C), but they do fine under lights at warm temperatures as well. When the seedlings have four to six leaves, pinch the stem tips lightly to encourage bushy growth. Water carefully, preferably from below; young seedlings are subject to rot if overwatered. Plant outdoors 2 to 3 weeks before your last frost date; snapdragons can take even relatively heavy frosts without complaint.

Snapdragons' excellent cold resistance makes them a great choice for winter bloom in mild-winter areas. Just sow them outdoors in August or September in an out-of-the way spot, then transfer them to your flowerbed when nights start to turn cool.

If you're buying plants, look for healthy, dense, leafy growth. Snapdragons that are planted when already in bloom tend to fade out after their first flowering, so for the best long-term results, remove all of the flower spikes at planting time. In the garden, deadhead regularly, cutting out flower spikes when the last few flowers are opening in order to stimulate rebloom.

Although they are offered as annuals, snapdragons are actually tender perennials and occasionally survive winter even in my cold climate. When they do, though, they tend to start blooming late in the season only to suffer in summer's heat. You're best off planting new ones each spring and then yanking them out when their flowering season ends.

Good Neighbors

Snapdragons are valuable as a vertical accent in the mixed plantings of annuals and perennials. In groupings of three to six, taller cultivars can offset postbloom mounds of lady's-mantle (*Alchemilla mollis*) or perennial geraniums (*Geranium* spp.), bringing color to an otherwise green season. The range of available colors gives you all kinds of combination options, but I think the most useful of all is the cream shade, which looks great with any other color. Picking up a couple of dozen to use as filler is never a mistake.

Problems and Solutions

Rust can be a problem, especially in rainy climates. Look for resistant cultivars and avoid overhead watering. When rust has been a problem in the past, avoid planting snapdragons in the same spot 2 years in a row. Taller cultivars may need discreet staking. (See "Annual Diseases" on page 33.)

Top Performer

Antirrhinum majus (common snapdragon): Originally tallish plants bearing spikes of flowers over a bushy cluster of stems, most snapdragons are now low-growing, compact plants with short, dense spikes. The original dragon's-head–like flower form is still common, but there are now many open-flowered snapdragons with trumpet-shaped blooms as well as double-flowered forms. There are dozens of cultivars, ranging in height from tall to knee-high to dwarf; and all make good garden plants, so choose according to your tastes.

Common snapdragon
(*Antirrhinum majus*)

Container Choices

In recent years, the common snapdragon has been crossed with other *Antirrhinum* species, resulting in various forms of creeping or trailing plants in an increasingly wide range of colors. Some of these bear the typical (if short) flower spikes at the stem tips, but others bloom from leaf axils all along the creeping stems. All look great in containers! Some strains of creeping snapdragons are available from seed, but most are sold as rooted cuttings; look for them at better nurseries and garden centers.

Callistephus

China aster

The huge blooms of the China aster are a flower arranger's dream, and they don't look half bad in the garden either! The range of flower forms is remarkable, from single, daisylike blooms to double pompoms to those shaggy spider types that seem to be having a continuously bad-hair day. The color range is just as amazing: They've long been available in every possible shade of white, pink, red, and purple, and now there are even shades of yellow and peach. All have dark green, somewhat triangular, coarsely toothed leaves.

Plant Profile

CALLISTEPHUS
ka-LISS-tee-fuss or
ka-liss-TEE-fuss

- **Bloom Color:** Near blue, lavender, pink, purple, violet, peach, red, rose, yellow, white

- **Bloom Time:** Midsummer into fall; early summer for day-neutral cultivars

- **Height:** 6 to 36 inches (15 to 90 cm)

- **Spread:** 12 to 18 inches (30 to 45 cm)

- **Garden Uses:** Container planting, cut-flower garden, edging, mass planting, mixed border, rock garden

- **Light Preference:** Full sun to partial shade

- **Soil Preference:** Average, well-drained, slightly acid to alkaline soil

- **Best Way to Propagate:** Sow seed indoors in late winter or outdoors after all danger of frost has passed

- **Hardiness:** Half-hardy annual

Growing Tips

Although pretty as a picture, China asters have picked up a bad rap over the years as being difficult to grow. While that reputation isn't fully merited, I still wouldn't necessarily recommend the China aster for your first attempt at growing annuals from seed. For your first try, I suggest either buying plants or sowing the seed outdoors when all danger of frost has passed for bloom into late summer and fall.

If you're feeling adventurous, you *can* grow China asters from seed indoors—*if* you start them under lights. The problem with growing China asters indoors is that they grow poorly during short days, and because you should start them indoors 6 to 8 weeks before the last frost, the days are *always* short at sowing time. Giving them 12-hour days from the start, however, produces beautiful, dense, healthy plants. Just barely cover the seed; it germinates readily at room temperature in 10 to 20 days. Water lightly; soggy mix can cause seedlings to rot. Their roots are fragile, so transplant carefully, or sow in peat pots to avoid transplant shock. And prick the seedlings out with the crown at the same depth as before.

In the garden, China asters prefer full sun or only very light shade. Keep their soil moderately moist, and mulch to keep the roots cool. Cut-flower types may need staking, or you can surround them with sturdier plants to keep them upright. Individual plants bloom for only 3 to 4 weeks, so try successive sowings to prolong flowering until fall; or sow early, midseason, and late cultivars. Don't bother deadheading; China asters won't rebloom—just pull out the plants when they finish blooming.

Good Neighbors

China asters and grasses share an affinity for soil of neutral pH, which makes the two good companions. Try direct-sowing them around medium-height grasses, such as blue oat grass (*Helictotrichon sempervirens*) or northern sea oats (*Chasmanthium latifolium*). Sowing tall China aster cultivars around stiffer plants, such as *Artemisia* 'Powis Castle' or *Sedum* 'Autumn Joy', may help you avoid staking.

Problems and Solutions

Aster wilt, which causes the plants to blacken at the base and keel over, was formerly very common; but most modern China asters are now very resistant to the disease. The same can't be said for aster yellows, an incurable virus carried by insects. As the name suggests, the infected plants turn yellow, and then they die. Although leafhoppers and aphids are the main culprits, don't panic when you see them—your plants will likely have time to bloom before the disease affects them. But do destroy obviously diseased plants on sight. The real secret to controlling both aster yellows and aster wilt is to choose a different planting site for your China asters each year and to avoid replanting in the same spots for at least 4 years.

Top Performer

Callistephus chinensis (China aster): It's the only species available, but it makes up for the lack of choice by offering literally hundreds of cultivars. One important development in China asters has been the introduction of "day-neutral" plants. In the past, it was difficult to get asters to bloom early (other than under lights) because they needed the long days of summer to initiate buds, meaning they weren't in full bloom until mid-July at the earliest. Day-neutrals, on the other hand, will start to flower once they reach their adult size, regardless of day length. You won't always find the words "day neutral" noted on the seed pack, though: Look for "early blooming," "blooms within 90 days," or some other phrase that suggests the pack's contents are especially rapid from seed.

China aster
(*Callistephus chinensis*)

Larry's Garden Notes

Despite its common name, China aster is *not* a true aster but an entirely different plant. The error came about when the plant was first introduced to Britain around 1730 as *Aster sinensis*. It quickly became apparent the new flower wasn't a true aster, but the damage was done and the plant has forever since gone under the wrong name in England and America. In France, however, the mess was fixed quickly, and our China aster goes under the regal name of *reine marguerite* (queen of the daisies).

Celosia

Celosia, cockscomb

Celosia is a plant of tropical origin, and it looks every bit the part! The shiny, deep maroon or light green leaves are topped by tiny flowers clustered into plumy feather dusters or twisted brain- or coral-like masses, generally in fiery shades of red, yellow, orange, or shocking pink. Some puritanical gardeners disdain celosia's brilliant coloration and complain it stands out too much from the crowd. If it offends *your* tastes, try something else—but if you want to add a bit of zing to an otherwise drab landscape, this brazen beauty may be just what the doctor ordered.

Plant Profile

CELOSIA
sell-OH-zee-uh

- **Bloom Color:** Pink, red, orange, yellow, cream

- **Bloom Time:** Late spring through early fall; fall through winter in mild climates

- **Height:** 8 to 36 inches (20 to 90 cm)

- **Spread:** 6 to 16 inches (15 to 40 cm)

- **Garden Uses:** Container planting, cut-flower garden, edging, mass planting, mixed border

- **Light Preference:** Full sun to partial shade

- **Soil Preference:** Humus-rich, evenly moist but well-drained soil

- **Best Way to Propagate:** Sow seed indoors in spring or outdoors in early summer

- **Hardiness:** Frost-sensitive perennial grown as a tender annual

Growing Tips

Although you can sow celosia seed outdoors, you should wait until the ground has warmed up thoroughly, 1 or 2 weeks after the last frost date. You'll probably find, however, that you get better results by sowing the seed indoors, just barely covering it, 4 to 8 weeks before the last frost date. The seed sprouts in 5 to 14 days at 70° to 80°F (21° to 27°C). Celosias resent root disturbance, so for best results, start the seed in peat pots. Wait 1 or 2 weeks after your last frost date, until the night temperatures have warmed up a bit, before setting out the seedlings. When you plant them out, keep the rootball at the same depth as it was in the pot.

Slow and steady is the key to success with celosia. Abrupt changes in conditions, drought, and even just cold water from the hose can stunt its growth. Even buying plants already in bloom is risky; they often stop growing and fail to fill out. When buying celosias, look for sturdy plants not yet in flower. Failing that, remove all existing flower clusters at planting time. Six packs or cell packs are a better choice than flats because there's less root disturbance at planting time.

Good Neighbors

When planted in masses, celosia can be too much of a good thing; used judiciously, however, it can add a rich accent to a perennial bed. The dark foliage of 'New Look', a plumed cultivar with deep red flowers, makes a great foil for postbloom candytuft (*Iberis sempervirens*) or perennial geraniums (*Geranium* spp.). Try yellow plumes around purple globe amaranth (*Gomphrena globosa*) for an interesting low border. An edging of a tightly crested cultivar can provide a fascinating contrast in front of feathery Oriental fountain grass (*Pennisetum orientale*). Wheat celosia (*Celosia spicata*) has a unique look that can be quite interesting in a natural-istic garden among grasses and meadow plants.

Problems and Solutions

The most common problem is stunted growth due to planting shock or abrupt changes in conditions, so careful planting when temperatures have warmed up is essential. Root rot is possible in soggy soil.

Top Performer

Celosia argentea plumosa (plumed celosia, feathered amaranth): This plant comes in dwarf, knee-high, and tall cultivars with green or red leaves and remarkable feathery clusters of flowers. Taller cultivars form a solid, summer-long mass of flowers at the tip of the bushy plant with smaller plumes toward its base. Dwarf cultivars produce nu-merous shorter clusters, all reaching much the same height. Dwarf cultivars make excellent bedding plants; taller selections are spectac-ular cut flowers. Height: 8 to 36 inches (20 to 90 cm). Spread: 6 to 16 inches (15 to 40 cm).

More Recommended Celosia

Celosia argentea cristata (cockscomb): Resulting from a curious muta-tion that comes true from seed, the flowers of the normally spiky celosia become crested like a rooster's comb. Cockscomb celosias occasionally produce normal plumed flowers; just prune these out on sight. Height: 8 to 36 inches (20 to 90 cm). Spread: 6 to 16 inches (15 to 40 cm).

    C. spicata (wheat celosia): These plants are thinner, more open, and less flamboyant in both form and color than their showier cousins—and they are easier to fit into mixed plantings. The spiky flower clusters, in pale pink to deep pink, do look rather like wheat, and they take on a bicolor appearance as the lower flowers on the spike turn paler over time. Height: 28 inches (70 cm). Spread: 6 inches (15 cm).

Plumed celosia
(*Celosia argentea plumosa*)

Larry's Garden Notes

Celosias look great in the garden, but they're also fun indoors. They make excellent fresh-cut flowers and dry well, keeping plenty of color, although they do lose a bit of their tropical brilliancy in the process. Hang them upside down in a hot, dry spot, such as over a stove; they tend to become moldy if they dry out too slowly. Celosias also make attractive houseplants for a sunny, humid spot. Container-grown specimens handle the move indoors more readily than garden-grown plants.

Dahlia

Dahlia

There's no lack of choice when it comes to dahlias! There are some 20,000 different cultivars in just about every color but true blue, and they range from 1-foot (30 cm) bedding dahlias to 10-foot (3-m) border giants that fill nearly a whole flowerbed by themselves. There are so many flower forms that the American Dahlia Society has designated 16 different classes: everything from spiky cactus dahlias to fully rounded ball dahlias, formal-looking decorative dahlias, and old-fashioned single-flowered dahlias. Even the foliage ranges from dark green to deep purple!

Plant Profile

DAHLIA
DAH-lee-uh

- **Bloom Color:** Near black, lavender, pink, purple, violet, red, orange, yellow, white

- **Bloom Time:** Summer through early fall for bedding dahlias; mid-summer to early fall for border dahlias

- **Height:** 1 to 10 feet (30 to 300 cm)

- **Spread:** 12 to 18 inches (30 to 45 cm) for bedding dahlias; 18 to 48 inches (45 to 120 cm) for border dahlias

- **Garden Uses:** Container planting, cut-flower garden, edging, annual hedge, mass planting, mixed border

- **Attracts:** Butterflies

- **Light Preference:** Full sun to partial shade

- **Soil Preference:** Average, evenly moist but well-drained soil

- **Best Way to Propagate:** Sow seed indoors in late winter; divide tuberous roots

- **Hardiness:** Frost-sensitive tuberous root grown as a tender annual

Growing Tips

You can start dahlias either from seed or from tuberous roots; nurseries and mail-order sources offer both in early spring. You'd think that those grown from tubers would be faster growing, but oddly enough, seed-grown dahlias usually beat the tubers to the punch. Start the fine seed indoors 6 to 10 weeks before the last frost, barely covering it, and keep it at 65° to 85°F (18° to 30°C) until seedlings emerge in 5 to 21 days. Pinch when the seedlings are about 3 inches (8 cm) tall to promote bushier growth and more abundant bloom. Wait until all danger of frost has passed and the ground has warmed up before setting them out. You can also start the seed directly outdoors, but the seedlings won't bloom until mid- to late summer.

Maintenance is simple: Water when the soil is nearly dry, mulch to keep the weeds in check, and deadhead to encourage rebloom.

I have a basic rule about whether or not to overwinter dahlias: I carefully dig up and store for the winter my favorite tuber-grown cultivars, but I let the seed-grown types freeze. It sounds cruel, but it is actually faster to grow border dahlias from seed each spring than from tubers . . . and just as easy. If you do want to keep your tubers, dig them up after frost has destroyed their foliage; cut off the dead leaves; and store the tubers in peat moss, vermiculite, or perlite in a cool, frost-free spot.

FUN FACTS

Watch out for confusing terminology with dahlias. Miniature dahlias have small flowers but often on tall plants. If you want low-growing dahlias, look for border or dwarf cultivars. And note that even dwarf dahlias can have fairly large flowers!

Check them monthly during the winter and spray them with tepid water if they seem to be shriveling. In spring, plant them directly in the garden when all danger of frost has passed, or start them indoors in pots 4 weeks before the last frost.

Good Neighbors

Shorter cultivars mound nicely and present a formal face, making them useful as edging plants, and they look great in containers, too. Combine the taller cultivars, which are excellent for cutting but not the most generous of bloomers, with Brazilian vervain (*Verbena bonariensis*) to add continuous color for those times when the dahlias aren't in flower. The dark foliage of red-leaved selections, such as the seed-grown 'Diablo' strain, makes a handsome accent in perennial borders.

Problems and Solutions

When earwig populations are large, they do considerable damage, entirely emptying out buds before they open. Leave out boards they can hide under, then crush them underfoot. Staking is almost essential with tall dahlias. Otherwise, they are pretty much trouble-free plants.

Top Performer

Dahlia cultivars (dahlia): Almost all dahlias currently grown are complex hybrids and listed either without a species name or as *Dahlia* × *hortensis*. This category includes everything from the tiniest border types to the huge dinner-plate-flowered, back-of-the-border cultivars. Only a handful of these come true enough from seed to be sold in seed packs. Most of the latter are border-type dahlias: short, dense plants with an early-blooming, nonstop-flowering characteristic that makes them outperform even the best of the tuberous cultivars. Seed-grown dahlias *do* produce small tuberous roots, but they grow so quickly from seed that it is rarely worthwhile trying to maintain them over the winter.

Dahlia
(*Dahlia* x *hortensis*)

Looking Back

The dahlia was first sent to Spain around 1789 as a potential substitute for the potato, a new vegetable causing quite a stir in Europe at that time. Unfortunately, people found dahlia tubers unpalatable, so the dahlia was kept as a simple botanical curiosity. The first species grown, *Dahlia imperialis*, reached 20 feet (6 m) tall. By the early 1800s, however, hybrid dahlias were catching on as ornamentals, and within 20 years, more than 1,000 cultivars were already available.

Dianthus

China pink, sweet William

China pinks get top ratings for their incredibly long season of bloom. They're frost hardy, so you can plant them out *before* the last frost date for extra-early blossoms; under the right conditions, they'll still be in full bloom late the following fall! Their flat-faced, toothed or smooth-edged, 1- to 2-inch (2.5- to 5-cm) blooms are usually bicolored, with contrasting eyes or halos, and are held over mounds of grasslike, gray-green foliage. Some offer a very light clove scent.

Plant Profile

DIANTHUS
dye-AN-thus

- ■ **Bloom Color:** Pink, wine purple, red, white; bicolor
- ■ **Bloom Time:** Early spring through late fall; fall through winter in mild climates
- ■ **Height:** 6 to 30 inches (15 to 75 cm)
- ■ **Spread:** 8 to 14 inches (20 to 36 cm)
- ■ **Garden Uses:** Container planting, cut-flower garden, edging, groundcover, mass planting, mixed border, rock garden
- ■ **Attracts:** Butterflies
- ■ **Light Preference:** Full sun to partial shade
- ■ **Soil Preference:** Average, well-drained, neutral to alkaline soil
- ■ **Best Way to Propagate:** Sow seed indoors in late winter or outdoors in early spring
- ■ **Hardiness:** Hardy perennial grown as a hardy annual

Growing Tips

China pinks are easy to grow, whether you start them from seed or buy them in six packs or cell packs. They have only two flaws: They hate hot weather (protection from afternoon sun is best where summers are hot) and they like soil on the alkaline side. Although the slightly acid soil of most gardens is acceptable, they prefer a pH of 7.0 or more; so I suggest sprinkling a bit of powdered limestone or wood ashes into the soil at planting time.

Start China pinks indoors 8 to 10 weeks before the last frost or buy plants already in bud. You can also sow them directly in the garden 3 weeks before the last frost for somewhat later bloom; in mild climates, sow in fall for bloom the following spring. Indoors, sow at room temperature, just covering the seed. After germination, in 5 to 21 days, bring the temperatures down to 50° to 60°F (10° to 15°C). Set out these cold-tolerant plants 2 to 3 weeks before the last frost date. During summer, keep them well watered and deadheaded regularly to help maintain constant flowering.

Good Neighbors

Planted in masses, pinks create a low river of intense color that looks super edging a bed or snaking through low-growing shrubs or late-flowering mums. They can also be useful as an underplanting for roses of a complementary color range or as a filler to color the niches of a rock garden.

FUN FACTS

Pinks got their name not from their flower color (although they do include pink in their repertoire) but for their toothed petals, which look like they've been trimmed with pinking shears.

Problems and Solutions

When grown as annuals, pinks rarely suffer from insects or diseases, although slugs are sometimes a problem (see page 35 for control suggestions). Rust or wilt sometimes affects established plants; destroy diseased plants and set out new pinks in a different site.

Top Performer

Dianthus barbatus × *chinensis* (hybrid China pink): Almost all modern strains of so-called *D. chinensis* actually belong here. Crossing China pinks with sweet William (*D. barbatus*) has added greater frost resistance, clustered instead of solitary flowers, more fringing (true China pinks tend to have smooth-edged blossoms), and occasionally some perfume. Most modern China pinks are compact plants, which are ideal for edging and containers, although the long-stemmed cultivars seem to be coming back in style. Growing 18 to 30 inches (45 to 75 cm) tall, these taller cultivars make great cut flowers but may require staking. Height: 6 to 30 inches (15 to 75 cm). Spread: 8 to 14 inches (20 to 35 cm).

More Recommended Dianthus

Dianthus barbatus (sweet William): These plants are very similar to China pinks, but they produce clusters of more deeply fringed flowers in pink, red, white, purple, and bicolors—each stem makes a complete bouquet! Sweet Williams were originally highly scented flowers, but modern strains have lost much of their perfume. Originally biennials or short-lived perennials, sweet Williams—through careful selection—now bloom the first year from early-sown seed. Sow annual strains as recommended above; sow the biennial strains outdoors in early summer for bloom the following year. Height: 6 to 24 inches (15 to 60 cm). Spread: 4 to 12 inches (10 to 30 cm).

D. *chinensis* (China pink): Pure China pinks are now quite rare. Plants sold under the name *D. chinensis* are inevitably hybrids between *D. chinensis* and *D. barbatus*. Height: 6 to 30 inches (15 to 75 cm). Spread: 8 to 14 inches (20 to 35 cm).

'Melody Pink' China pink
(*Dianthus chinensis* 'Melody Pink')

Larry's Garden Notes

When you buy annual pinks, you get more than you pay for! China pinks and sweet Williams are actually short-lived perennials, but they're commonly sold in six packs at the same price as annuals. In the perennials section of the same nursery, you'll likely find these plants sold one per pot—at about the same price as a whole six pack of annuals! So buy them as annuals, but don't pull them out in the fall; leave them in place and enjoy them as they rebloom the following year.

Nicotiana

Nicotiana, flowering tobacco

Yep, this delicate summer beauty really *is* a close relative of the tobacco plant (*Nicotiana tabacum*). Don't try smoking any of the ornamental kinds, though; they're considered toxic! Instead, grow them for their summer-long bloom and often-exquisite perfume. Most nicotianas form a dense cluster of apple green leaves topped with spikes of tubular, five-petaled flowers. Be forewarned, though, that their blooms often close during the day, opening fully only in the evening, at night, and on cloudy days. If you want daytime bloom, look for cultivars labeled "open all day long."

Plant Profile

NICOTIANA
ni-koh-shee-AH-nuh

- **Bloom Color:** Green, pink, salmon, red, white
- **Bloom Time:** Late spring through early fall
- **Height:** Varies by species; see individual listings
- **Spread:** Varies by species; see individual listings
- **Garden Uses:** Container planting, cut-flower garden, edging, annual hedge, mass planting, meadow garden, mixed border
- **Attracts:** Sphinx moths, hummingbirds
- **Light Preference:** Full sun to partial shade
- **Soil Preference:** Evenly moist, well-drained soil
- **Best Way to Propagate:** Sow seed indoors in late winter, outdoors in late spring
- **Hardiness:** Frost-sensitive perennial grown as a half-hardy annual

Growing Tips

Nicotianas are adaptable, easy-to-care-for annuals that thrive in most climates and under most conditions, even alkaline soil and partial shade. They're pretty much problem-free plants with lots of visual impact in the garden.

Whether you grow them from seed or buy plants is mostly a question of how much time you have on your hands: Even raw novices will find them a snap to grow from seed. Although *Nicotiana sylvestris* is fast enough to grow from direct-sown seed (in fact, it will often self-sow), it's best to start most other types indoors 6 to 8 weeks before the last frost, at least if you want to have early bloom. Don't cover the fine seed, though: It needs light to germinate. They sprout at 65° to 85°F (18° to 30°C) in 10 to 20 days. For maximum bloom, keep the plants moist throughout the entire growing season (mulch can be a big help).

Good Neighbors

Planted in groups of six or more, the more-compact nicotianas add color and elegance to a perennial garden or a shrub border. Lime green *Nicotiana langsdorffii* looks terrific with any other color but makes an especially handsome contrast with dark foliage; try it with deep purple basil or one of the tall, dark-leafed coleus cultivars that

FUN FACTS

Nicotianas got their name from Frenchman Jean Nicot, who first introduced the tobacco plant to Europe in the sixteenth century as a "good-for-whatever-ails-ya" medicinal plant. I think we can now safely say that tobacco has killed more people than it has ever healed!

can take a bit of sun. Tuck a plant or two of *N. sylvestris* into the back of a border for wonderful evening scent.

Problems and Solutions

Nicotianas are not particularly subject to pests, but aphids can occasionally be a problem. Knock them off with sprays of water. Reduce the chance of mildew, damping-off, stem rot, and other diseases associated with wet stems and leaves by mulching and watering from below. To help prevent tobacco mosaic virus, keep nicotianas away from other members of the Solanaceae family, which includes tomatoes, potatoes, and the like.

Top Performer

Nicotiana × *sanderae* (common nicotiana, flowering tobacco): Although often sold as *N. alata* or *N. affinis,* the common nicotiana generally belongs in the hybrid genus *N.* × *sanderae.* True *N. alata* is a tall plant, up to 5 feet (150 cm), with highly scented, yellowish green flowers that open only at night. Crossing with other *Nicotiana* species has resulted in shorter plants in a much wider range of colors. The flowers of most modern hybrids stay open all day long, but many have entirely lost the scent that was half the charm of the species! Height: 8 to 24 inches (20 to 60 cm). Spread: 8 to 10 inches (20 to 25 cm).

More Recommended Nicotiana

Nicotiana langsdorffii (flowering tobacco): This curious plant, with small, bottle-shaped, lime green flowers dangling from upright, branching stems, is actually much more attractive than the description suggests and should be more widely grown. Its flowers remain open all day but are scentless. Height: 3 to 5 feet (90 to 100 cm). Spread: 12 to 14 inches (30 to 35 cm).

   N. sylvestris (flowering tobacco): This is perhaps the most highly perfumed of the flowering tobaccos, with tall, candelabra-like stems of white flowers with extremely long tubes that half close on sunny days. Scent is faint or absent during the day but remarkable at night. Height: 3 to 6 feet (90 to 180 cm). Spread: 2 feet (60 cm).

'Domino Salmon Pink' flowering tobacco (*Nicotiana* × *sanderae* 'Domino Salmon Pink')

Larry's Garden Notes

Nicotianas used to be so fragrant they were called jasmine tobaccos, yet most modern hybrids have little or no scent. What happened? Hybridizers managed to "improve" nicotianas by selecting flowers that remain open all day long and display a wider range of colors. However, the genes for day-opening flowers and brighter colors seem to cover up those offering scent. If you're looking for perfume in a modern nicotiana, look for cultivar descriptions that emphasize fragrance over beautiful colors.

Pelargonium × hortorum

Zonal geranium, bedding geranium

Zonal geraniums are so ubiquitous on winter windowsills and in summer containers and gardens that one could argue they need no introduction. For the benefit of true novices, though, these are the geraniums with thick, somewhat fuzzy stems and rounded, oddly scented leaves, either all green or marked with a dark, horseshoe-shaped band (the "zone" in zonal). Their main claim to fame, though, comes from their stalks of large, rounded clusters of single or double flowers, often in brilliant, eye-catching colors.

Plant Profile

PELARGONIUM × HORTORUM
pe-lar-GO-nee-um hor-TO-rum

- **Bloom Color:** Pink, purple, salmon, red, orange; bicolor

- **Bloom Time:** Late spring through early fall; all year indoors and in frost-free climates

- **Height:** 10 to 36 inches (25 to 90 cm)

- **Spread:** 8 to 14 inches (20 to 35 cm)

- **Garden Uses:** Container planting, edging, mass planting, mixed border, rock garden, specimen plant

- **Light Preference:** Full sun to partial shade; partial shade in hot summer climates

- **Soil Preference:** Humus-rich, well-drained soil; tolerates alkaline soil

- **Best Way to Propagate:** Sow seed indoors in winter; take stem cuttings at any season

- **Hardiness:** Frost-sensitive sub-shrub grown as a tender annual

Growing Tips

These easy-care annuals have few special needs: Simply give them full sun or just a bit of shade (partial shade is a must in hot summer climates), water moderately, and you should have no problems. It's when you multiply them that geraniums become more difficult. Beginners would be wise to buy geraniums already started, skipping the seed stage entirely.

If you're adventurous, however, you can start seed indoors in early winter, 14 to 16 weeks before the last frost to get plants that will bloom by summer. That means you'll be starting seed in the dark days of winter and will probably need artificial lights. You may, therefore, prefer to start yours 10 to 12 weeks before the last frost, when days are longer, even if that means your plants won't bloom quite as early in the season.

Seed germinates in 3 to 21 days at 70° to 85°F (21° to 30°C). Barely cover them with mix. Move the seedlings to a cooler spot—60° to 70°F (15° to 21°C)—and pinch them once when they are about 4 inches (10 cm) high to promote bushy growth.

To reproduce favorite plants by cuttings, snip off a few stem sections about 6 inches (15 cm) long and remove the lower leaves. Apply rooting hormone and insert the cut end into damp perlite or sand. Traditionally, gardeners let freshly cut stems "heal over" by

FUN FACTS

Although members of the Geranium family, zonal geraniums are not true geraniums (*Geranium*), a genus of mostly hardy perennials. They belong to the genus *Pelargonium* and should properly be called zonal pelargoniums, but even I have trouble remembering that one!

setting them in a sunny spot for a week or so before inserting them into the growing mixture, but this actually does more harm than good. This is also one of the rare cases when you shouldn't cover cuttings in clear plastic because geranium cuttings tend to rot without good air circulation.

Good Neighbors

Traditionally used in garish bedding displays and in "you-can-see-it-a-mile-away" pots, geraniums have been somewhat maligned recently by garden connoisseurs who find them too brilliant for more understated modern beds. However, zonal geraniums do come in a number of subdued colors, making them suitable for softer planting schemes. Even the bright reds can be great garden accents: Tuck small numbers of them around dark-leaved neighbors, such as purple-leaved amaranths (*Amaranthus* spp.), or dot them throughout a planting of rambling nasturtiums. In containers, try combining a zonal geranium with blue lobelia and the chartreuse-gray leaves of licorice plant (*Helichrysum petiolare* 'Limelight').

Zonal geranium
(*Pelargonium* x *hortorum*)

Problems and Solutions

Stem rot (black leg) is common in cuttings. Increased air circulation can reduce the chance of infection. Edema, seen as raised brown patches on the undersides of leaves, is not a disease but a physiological problem resulting from excess watering. For control of aphids and whiteflies, both occasional pests, see page 34.

Top Performer

Pelargonium × *hortorum* (zonal geranium): Modern hybrids tend to be dense plants that branch with little pinching: quite a contrast to Grandma's stringy geraniums! They come in a wide range of shades, including bicolors, with single or double blooms. There are dozens of categories, such as rosebuds, cactus-flowered, miniatures, and beautiful fancy-leaved geraniums with colorful foliage that's variegated with white, pink, yellow, or red. Blooms of double geraniums tend to be particularly durable, but you need to pinch them off when they do fade or they become moldy. Single-blossom types are usually self-cleaning.

Larry's Garden Notes

Is it worthwhile overwintering zonal geraniums? It depends. Seed-grown types will be available at a fair price the following spring and are probably not worth saving. Cutting-grown types are more expensive and harder to find, so it can be worth overwintering them. It is easiest to sink them, pot and all, into the ground or a container in spring, then dig up and rinse off the pots in fall. Otherwise, you'll need to dig the plants in August, prune them back, and pot them up, or you'll need to take stem cuttings.

Petunia

Petunia

Modern petunias are branching, semi-upright to creeping plants with sticky, hairy, spoon-shaped leaves and medium to large, trumpet-shaped, five-lobed blossoms in a wide range of colors and forms. Double, ruffled, striped, netted, picoted: There's practically no limit to their variety, and even flower colors long considered impossible, like yellow, are now common. They all bloom right through summer in most climates; although in hot, humid climates they are best considered for fall planting and winter through spring bloom.

Plant Profile

PETUNIA
peh-TOON-yuh

- **Bloom Color:** Pink, violet-blue, red, yellow, white
- **Bloom Time:** Late spring through early fall; fall through winter in mild climates
- **Height:** 6 to 24 inches (15 to 60 cm)
- **Spread:** Varies by species; see individual listings
- **Garden Uses:** Container planting, cut-flower garden, edging, groundcover, mass planting, mixed border, rock garden; on slopes, in wet areas
- **Attracts:** Hummingbirds, moths
- **Light Preference:** Full sun to partial shade
- **Soil Preference:** Light, evenly moist, well-drained soil
- **Best Way to Propagate:** Sow seed indoors in late winter or spring; take stem cuttings in late summer
- **Hardiness:** Frost-sensitive perennial grown as a half-hardy annual

Growing Tips

Petunias are among the easiest of all annuals to grow, if you buy them already started. Pinch them before you plant them, and spray occasionally during the summer with organic foliar fertilizer to stimulate continuous growth. Deadheading helps encourage more bloom and keeps the plants tidy. If your petunias get scraggly, prune them back by half, and they'll soon grow back.

Given the wide variety of petunias offered in most nurseries, it is usually not worthwhile to start them yourself from seed, unless you want a cultivar not available locally. Start them indoors 8 to 10 weeks before the last frost (12 to 14 weeks for the slower-growing doubles). Don't cover the seed; it needs light to germinate. Look for seedlings in 7 to 21 days at 70° to 80°F (21° to 27°C). After germination, drop the temperature to about 60°F (15°C). When thinning seedlings, don't methodically eliminate the smaller, weaker-looking ones; they're often the ones with the best color or most interesting forms. Plant out when all danger of frost has passed, giving the seedlings a pinch to stimulate better branching. You can also sow single-flowered petunias directly outdoors, when the soil warms up, for late-season bloom.

Petunias can be highly perfumed, especially at night, so don't hesitate to use them at nose level in flower boxes, on walls, or in hanging baskets.

Good Neighbors

Petunias are extravagant bloomers, which makes them very useful in containers. Combine them with foliage plants, such as lotus vine (*Lotus berthelotii*) or sweet potato vine (*Ipomoea batatas*), for sure success. They can also be useful in the garden as a groundcover beneath the airy clumps of gaura (*Gaura lindheimeri*) or *Artemisia* 'Powis Castle' or surrounding the blades of irises.

Problems and Solutions

Usually petunias are quite pest free, but aphids are occasional problems. Knock them off with a spray of water. Look for weather-resistant cultivars in climates with frequent heavy rains; these cultivars also tend to be less susceptible to gray mold and soft rot, which can otherwise affect both foliage and flowers in humid climates.

Top Performer

Petunia × *hybrida* (petunia): Almost all the petunias sold today are complex hybrids, which are divided into various classes. Grandifloras, with single or double flowers 4 to 5 inches (10 to 12 cm) across, come in both semi-upright and cascading cultivars; the latter are mostly used in containers. Multifloras have smaller flowers—about 2 inches (5 cm) across—but they tend to grow faster, bloom more freely, and have more weather-resistant petals. Space both types about 1 foot (30 cm) apart so they can grow together and form a carpet. Millifloras are newcomers with tiny 1- to 1½-inch (2.5- to 4-cm) flowers over mounded plants. Space them about 6 inches (15 cm) apart. Groundcover petunias, of which the 'Wave' and 'Surfinia' series are the best known, are low-growing spreaders highly popular for hanging baskets, since they can trail 3 feet (90 cm) or more. Although they are very floriferous, they need constant fertilizing to perform well. Height: 1 to 2 feet (30 to 60 cm). Spread: 6 to 36 inches (15 to 90 cm).

More Recommended Petunias

Petunia integrifolia (violet-flowered petunia): One of the rare species of petunias offered, violet-flowered petunia is a low-growing spreader that looks and behaves exactly like a groundcover petunia, of which it is a parent. It bears numerous small violet flowers throughout the growing season. Height: 1 to 2 feet (30 to 60 cm). Spread: 2 to 3 feet (60 to 90 cm).

Petunia
(*Petunia* x *hybrida*)

Looking Forward

A few short years ago, all petunias were grown from seed, but now an increasing number are available only from cuttings. Obviously, vegetative petunias take more work to produce, so they are more expensive. This price may be justified for petunias whose traits can't be passed on by seed (such as variegated leaves). Seed strains of most other types *could* be developed, but since gardeners willingly pay more for cutting-grown petunias, growers have little incentive to bring prices down by introducing seed-grown strains!

Tagetes

Marigold

There's no denying that marigolds have sometimes been overused, but think of it this way: Their enormous popularity is a sure sign they are easy to grow. Whether you grow them from seed or buy six packs of plants, you simply can't go wrong! The way I see it, there is always room for such a workhorse, even in the gardens of the most sophisticated plant collectors! There's hardly a need to describe this common annual; the deeply cut, aromatic leaves and yellow to orange flowers are a dead giveaway.

Plant Profile

TAGETES
TAH-jeh-teez

- **Bloom Color:** Varies by species; see individual listings
- **Bloom Time:** Summer through early fall
- **Height:** Varies by species; see individual listings
- **Spread:** Varies by species; see individual listings
- **Garden Uses:** Container planting, cut-flower garden, edging, mass planting, mixed border, rock garden
- **Light Preference:** Full sun to partial shade
- **Soil Preference:** Not excessively rich, well-drained soil
- **Best Way to Propagate:** Sow seed indoors in mid-spring or outdoors in late spring
- **Hardiness:** Half-hardy annual

Growing Tips

Marigolds are a snap from seed, started either indoors 4 to 6 weeks before the last frost date, at 65° to 85°F (18° to 30°C), or directly in the garden, after all danger of frost has passed. Sown ¼ inch (6 mm) deep, they germinate quickly, usually in 4 to 14 days, and are often in bloom in less than 2 months. Of course, they are also widely available in six packs and transplant very well, even when already in bloom. Wash your hands when you've finished planting, though: When handled, marigolds give off a scented oil to which some people are allergic.

Naturally quite drought tolerant, marigolds actually do better in soil that is on the poor side. Pinch young African marigolds at least once or they may produce only one large bloom. Deadheading can help maintain continuous bloom.

Good Neighbors

Enjoy the smaller marigolds as fillers around bold plants, such as yuccas, dark-leaved cannas, or cardoon (*Cynara cardunculus*). The imposing pompoms of African marigold (*Tagetes erecta*) look super as a mass of color around evergreen shrubs. The ferny foliage of signet marigold (*T. tenuifolia*) makes a satisfying companion for more-vibrant flowers, such as zinnias.

FUN FACTS

Things aren't always what they seem, and with flower names, that's usually the case. Both French and African marigolds actually come from Mexico. The French marigold got its misleading name when it was introduced into Britain via France; the African marigold had escaped culture in Northern Africa and was originally mistaken for a native.

Problems and Solutions

Leaf spot, gray mold, powdery mildew, and other leaf diseases can be problematic, especially in humid climates: Look for weather- and disease-resistant strains. Taller African marigold hybrids tend to snap off under the weight of their huge flowers; plant them more deeply than in their original cell packs so the lower part of the stem can root, providing extra support.

Top Performer

Tagetes patula (French marigold): These relatively small, bushy plants bear numerous 1-inch flowers in yellow or orange, often mixed with mahogany red. Blooms can be single, double, or crested and are often bicolored. The foliage has a vaguely unpleasant "greenery" odor. Height: 6 to 18 inches (15 to 45 cm). Spread: 8 to 12 inches (20 to 30 cm).

More Recommended Tagetes

Tagetes erecta (African marigold): This species offers huge yellow, orange, or creamy white flowers from 3 to 5 inches (8 to 13 cm) in diameter. This species is perhaps the stinkiest of all marigolds, but fortunately the odor is emitted only if you touch the leaves or stick your nose into the bloom. Height: 10 inches to over 4 feet (25 to 120 cm). Spread: 12 to 18 inches (30 to 45 cm).

T. erecta × patula (triploid marigold): This sterile plant is an F_1 hybrid, a handmade cross between African and French marigolds. It is a perfect mixture of the two and usually displays pompomlike flowers 2 to 3 inches (5 to 8 cm) across. Since they produce no seed, triploids bloom up a storm and need no deadheading. Unfortunately, their germination rate is low and seed is very expensive. Height: 10 to 18 inches (25 to 45 cm). Spread: 12 to 16 inches (30 to 40 cm).

T. tenuifolia (signet marigold): A delightful but lesser-known plant with extremely fine, lacy foliage that has a pleasant lemon scent. The numerous tiny single yellow or orange flowers don't overwhelm the plant but mingle delicately with the foliage, and they attract beneficial, pest-eating insects. Height: 1 to 2 feet (30 to 60 cm). Spread: 12 to 16 inches (30 to 40 cm).

French marigold
(*Tagetes patula*)

Larry's Garden Notes

Companion planting enthusiasts often plant marigolds throughout their vegetable gardens because their scent is said to confuse harmful insects and keep them from finding their host plants. (It hasn't worked for me, but maybe you'll be luckier.) Marigold roots also emit a toxic substance that kills harmful nematodes (eelworms). Plant a bed entirely in marigolds for one summer and you'll have 2 to 3 years without any nematode damage, no matter what you plant there.

Tropaeolum

Nasturtium, Canary creeper

Nasturtiums offer both intriguing leaves and complex and colorful flowers, so they look good practically from the time they germinate. I could easily have put these fun-to-grow plants in the chapter "Climbing Annuals" since the original species are very much climbers. Hybridizers have worked long and hard to cut the nasturtium down to size, however; and most modern nasturtiums are "dwarf" or trailing types.

Plant Profile

TROPAEOLUM
tro-PEE-o-lum

- **Bloom Color:** Varies by species; see individual listings

- **Bloom Time:** Early summer through early fall; fall through spring in mild climates

- **Height:** Varies by species; see individual listings

- **Spread:** Varies by species; see individual listings

- **Garden Uses:** Container planting, cut-flower garden, edging, hanging basket, mass planting, mixed border, vegetable garden; on slopes or covering trellises, fences, and pergolas

- **Attracts:** Hummingbirds

- **Light Preference:** Full sun to partial shade

- **Soil Preference:** Average to poor, well-drained soil

- **Best Way to Propagate:** Sow seed indoors in peat pots in mid-spring or outdoors in late spring

- **Hardiness:** Tender annual or frost-sensitive perennial

Growing Tips

Nasturtiums are fast-growing annuals that seem to thrive on neglect. Sow the large seed directly outside once the ground warms up, covering it with ¼ inch (6 mm) of soil. Or get a head start on the season by starting it indoors in peat pots, in darkness, 2 to 4 weeks before planting out. It usually germinates in 7 to 12 days at 60° to 65°F (15° to 18°C). If you prefer to buy plants in the spring, cell packs are the best choice because there is less risk of transplanting shock.

The secret to great nasturtiums is benign neglect. Plant them in soils that are average to low in fertility, and don't fertilize or over-water them because rich soils can stimulate lush, rapid foliage growth with few flowers. Full sun is usually best, but partial shade is recommended in hot summer areas.

Except in mild climates (Zones 9 to 11), nasturtiums are best treated as annuals. You can, however, overwinter a particularly nice nasturtium by taking stem cuttings in late summer and growing them indoors in a sunny spot.

Good Neighbors

Always a cheerful presence in the garden, nasturtiums can be an easy answer to the problem of unsightly bulb foliage. Even the dwarfs remain distinctly rambling plants, so they are ideal for containers, hanging baskets, borders, and filling in gaps in the landscape. Attractive neighbors include sturdy plants with finely cut foliage, such as artemisias, or plants with stiff upright foliage, such as irises and blackberry lilies (*Belamcanda* spp.). Planted near a large shrub or hedge, canary creeper (*Tropaeolum peregrinum*) will wander happily among the branches.

Problems and Solutions

Aphids are a major problem. Blast them off with a strong spray of water. Caterpillars, whiteflies, flea beetles, and slugs are occasional problems; see page 34 for suggestions for controlling pests.

Top Performer

Tropaeolum majus (nasturtium, common nasturtium): This is the plant most people think of when the word *nasturtium* is mentioned, although, in fact, the botanical name *Nasturtium* belongs to an entirely different plant—watercress (*N. officinale*). Our nasturtium bears unique, round, shieldlike leaves in deep to light green. Some cultivars, like 'Alaska' (dwarf) and 'Jewel of Africa' (climbing) are heavily marbled with cream. The 2- to 2½- inch (5- to 6.5-cm) flowers form wide-open trumpets and usually have a long spur at the back. The blooms come in a wide range of colors—yellow, orange, cream, red, mahogany, and cherry pink, often splotched with a contrasting color—and are commonly delightfully scented. Double types are generally sterile and must be propagated by cuttings; semidoubles are available from seed. Height: 8 to 15 inches (10 to 38 cm) for dwarfs and trailers; 10 feet (3 m) for climbers. Spread: 12 to 18 inches (30 to 45 cm).

More Recommended Tropaeolum

Tropaeolum peregrinum (Canary creeper, Canary vine): This is a very different plant with different needs. The small, gray-green leaves are divided into fingerlike lobes. The curious flowers, with two large, highly fringed petals over a smaller cluster of three petals, may be canary yellow, but they actually get their name because of the plant's place of discovery. Botanists first saw this Mexican native growing on the Canary Islands. Canary creeper needs a richer, moister soil than its cousin does. Plants started indoors can bloom faster, but they also tend to peter out before the end of summer. Seed started directly in the garden blooms until fall. This superb climbing plant needs a thin support that the leaf stems can wrap themselves around. Height: 8 to 12 feet (2.5 to 4 m). Spread: 18 inches (45 cm). **Self-sowing** 🌱

Nasturtium
(*Tropaeolum majus*)

Larry's Garden Notes

All parts of the common nasturtium are edible, so this annual is actually considered a vegetable in some parts of the world. The peppery flavor spices up the taste of otherwise bland foods, such as green salads. Classy restaurants often use the flowers as garnishes, and the blooms add lots of color to salads. Flower buds and green seed capsules can be pickled in vinegar and used as a substitute for capers. If you plan to eat your nasturtiums, though, be sure you do not treat them with toxic pesticides!

Verbena

Verbena

Gardeners have more than 250 species of verbenas to choose from, and a good number of those make great garden plants. The genus includes annuals, perennials, and shrubs; and the different plants vary considerably in appearance and in care. In general, though, they are bushy to creeping plants with four-sided stems and tubular flowers with five well-spaced lobes, often notched at their tip. Although the individual flowers are small, they're held in dense clusters that will knock your socks off, both in the garden and in containers.

Plant Profile

VERBENA
ver-BEAN-uh

- **Bloom Color:** Lavender, pink, purple, salmon, red, white

- **Bloom Time:** Late spring through early fall; much of the year in mild climates

- **Height:** Varies by species; see individual listings

- **Spread:** Varies by species; see individual listings

- **Garden Uses:** Container planting, cut-flower garden, edging, hanging baskets, groundcover, mass planting, mixed border, rock garden; on slopes

- **Attracts:** Butterflies, hummingbirds

- **Light Preference:** Full sun to partial shade

- **Soil Preference:** Average, well-drained soil

- **Best Way to Propagate:** Sow seed indoors in late winter; take stem cuttings in late summer

- **Hardiness:** Frost-sensitive perennial grown as a half-hardy annual

Growing Tips

Unless you have a home greenhouse or grow under lights, you're better off buying six packs or cell packs of young verbena plants than trying to start your own from seed. If you like a challenge, though, you can save a considerable amount of money by sowing them yourself. Just don't expect high germination: With verbenas, especially the popular hybrid types, 50 percent germination is considered good; 70 percent is excellent!

Start the seed indoors, 8 to 10 weeks before the last frost. Barely cover the seed; then place in the dark until seedlings appear, usually in 14 to 28 days at 50° to 75°C (10° to 24°C). After germination, try to keep the temperatures toward the lower end of that range. Water very carefully, preferably from below to avoid damping-off, and make sure there is good ventilation.

There are fast-growing verbenas, like Brazilian vervain (*Verbena bonariensis*), that you can sow directly outdoors in early spring for late-season bloom. Even these are best started indoors, though. For good germination, place the six packs or cell packs in the fridge for 2 weeks before exposing them to warmth.

Verbenas may be delicate as seedlings, but once in the garden, they are no-brainers. They prefer full sun (some shade in the afternoon is best in hot summer areas) and do well in ordinary garden soil. They are quite drought resistant, although watering in very dry weather is always wise. Avoid wetting the leaves, if possible, to reduce the spread of the fungal disease powdery mildew. If bloom becomes sparse in midsummer, shear the plants back harshly and spray them with organic foliar fertilizer; they'll soon be in full flower again.

To keep favorite plants from year to year, start cuttings in late summer and grow them indoors in bright light all winter or dig up and bring in a few plants.

Good Neighbors

Because of their cascading nature, low-growing verbenas are ideal choices for pots, but they're useful as groundcovers as well. The lacy foliage and purple flowers of 'Imagination' mingle beautifully with bold kales, yuccas, or Siberian irises (*Iris sibirica*). Combine garden verbena (*Verbena* × *hybrida*), lantana (*Lantana camara*), and tall Brazilian vervain (*V. bonariensis*) in a large pot and you will have a long season of layered, flowering interest.

'Peaches and Cream' garden verbena (*Verbena* × *hybrida* 'Peaches and Crea[m]'

Problems and Solutions

Powdery mildew and other leaf diseases are a major problem in humid climates: Grow only disease-resistant strains, like the 'Quartz' series. Control whiteflies, spider mites, and scale insects by spraying with insecticidal soap.

Top Performer

Verbena × *hybrida* (garden verbena): This is definitely a mixed bag of plants! Some types are bushy and upright, while others are spreading, mat forming, or even trailing. The green to gray-green leaves can be simple, toothed, or deeply cut; and the fragrant or odorless flowers come in a wide range of bright and pastel colors. Many modern hybrids, like the 'Temari' and 'Tapien' series (both of which come in an astounding range of colors), are available only as vegetatively produced (cutting-grown) plants. The seed-grown strains—most either bushy or only slightly spreading—are particularly popular for garden use; the more expensive cutting-grown types—most either trailers or semi-trailers—are widely used in containers. Take your pick; they're all great plants! Height: 10 to 20 inches (25 to 50 cm). Spread: 12 to 20 inches (30 to 50 cm).

More Recommended Verbena

There are many great verbenas to recommend. For examples of this popular plant, see "Larry's Last Look: Verbena" on page 68.

Kissing Cousins

Aloysia triphylla (lemon verbena): You'll grow this herb not for its less-than-impressive pale lavender or white flowers but for its narrow, pointed leaves that give off a delicious lemon scent when touched. Enjoy the fresh or dried foliage in cooking, in sachets, and wherever else you want a lemon scent. Lemon verbena is sometimes hardy to Zone 8, with a good mulch; but it's best as a container plant in most climates. Give it full sun and excellent drainage, water moderately, and watch out for whiteflies!

Viola

Pansy, horned violet, Johnny-jump-up

The rounded, flat-faced flowers of most pansies look just like a chubby-faced baby: How could you *not* love them? Garden favorites for generations, they are widely available just about everywhere and are often the first annuals to bloom. They likewise make cute little bouquets and are a standard offering in posies. If only they were a bit more heat resistant, they would be just about the perfect annual. Instead, you have to plan carefully to get the most out of them before the dog days of summer knock them flat on their faces!

Plant Profile

VIOLA
vy-OH-luh

- **Bloom Color:** Blue, lavender, purple, red, orange, bronze, yellow, white

- **Bloom Time:** Early spring through summer; fall through winter in mild climates

- **Height:** Varies by species; see individual listings

- **Spread:** Varies by species; see individual listings

- **Garden Uses:** Container planting, cut-flower garden, edging, groundcover, mass planting, mixed border, rock garden, woodland garden; along paths

- **Light Preference:** Full sun to moderate shade

- **Soil Preference:** Humus-rich, evenly moist but well-drained soil

- **Best Way to Propagate:** Sow seed outdoors in fall or indoors in winter

- **Hardiness:** Hardy perennial or biennial grown as a hardy annual

Growing Tips

The secret to happy pansies is to remember they like things cool. In temperate climates, you'll get best results from young transplants set out in fall (for the earliest spring bloom) or in early spring, as soon as the ground can be worked. Where summers are generally cool—not over 90°F (32°C)—they bloom best in full sun and keep on going until fall. In hotter climates, look for heat-resistant cultivars and plant them in moderate shade. Where winters are mild, plant pansies in fall for bloom right through winter; then pull them up when the heat gets to them.

The easiest way to grow pansies from seed is to treat them like biennials. Sow them outdoors in midsummer, then plant them in their final home in fall, mulching well in cold winter areas. It *is* possible to sow pansies indoors, although it is a bit of a challenge. Sow the seed indoors 14 to 16 weeks before the last frost date, barely covering it. Place the containers in your refrigerator for 2 weeks, and then expose the seed to room temperatures; it should sprout in about 10 days. After germination, keep the temperature as low as you can; 50° to 65°F (10° to 18°C) is ideal, but room temperature is acceptable. Plant out hardened-off seedlings as soon as the soil is workable.

Outdoors, water pansies as needed and deadhead them to help maintain blooming. Cut straggly plants back severely to stimulate renewed growth.

Good Neighbors

One of the few annuals that can be planted in fall for early-spring bloom, pansies play a unique role in the garden. Let them take the spring shift in an impatiens bed or front-door planter or fill in the ground level around tall daffodils. Tuck them around plants that thrive in part shade, such as ferns or purple-leaved heucheras (*Heuchera* hybrids), and they'll bloom well into summer.

Problems and Solutions

Pansies are somewhat susceptible to leaf diseases: Choose disease-resistant strains, and rotate plantings if you notice repeated damage. Hand-pick slugs and snails if they become a problem.

Top Performer

Viola × *wittrockiana* (pansy): These large-flowered plants with overlapping petals are offered in an almost infinite range of colors, including a violet so deep it appears black. Most are bicolored with facelike markings, but some are all one color. Pansies are usually borderline hardy in Zone 4. Height: 6 to 9 inches (15 to 23 cm). Spread: 9 to 12 inches (23 to 30 cm).

More Recommended Viola

Viola cornuta (horned violet, viola): Horned violet is one of the parents of the pansy and is very similar to it, but with smaller flowers. The species is a long-lived plant with violet to lavender flowers, but most plants now sold under this name have been crossed with the garden pansy. They come in a similar range of colors and tend to act as short-lived perennials or annuals. Height: 8 inches (20 cm). Spread: 6 to 12 inches (15 to 30 cm). **Self-sowing**

Think Twice: *V. tricolor* (Johnny-jump-up, heartsease): An even smaller viola than horned violet, it has 1-inch (2.5-cm) flowers that have bright yellow faces, dark purple Mickey Mouse ears, and cute little mustaches. The many hybrids come in a color range similar to that of pansies. They come somewhat true from seed but return to the purple-and-yellow theme over time. Usually annual or biennial, the fast-growing plants self-sow abundantly but rarely dominate other plants, so I just let them be. Pickier gardeners, though, consider this species little more than a weed. Height: 3 to 5 inches (8 to 13 cm). Spread: 4 to 6 inches (10 to 15 cm). **Self-sowing**

'Melody Purple and White' pansy (*Viola* x *wittrockiana* 'Melody Purple and White')

Larry's Garden Notes

Where botanists see just one large genus, *Viola*, gardeners see a host of different plants. Violets are the small-flowered ones with backward-curving petals, usually blooming in spring; they tend to be long-lived perennials. Pansies have large, flat-faced flowers, often with facelike markings. They are short-lived perennials or even annuals, rarely lasting more than a year or so. Violas are intermediate, with flat-faced, pansylike flowers but of a much smaller size. They too tend to be short-lived perennials.

Zinnia

Zinnia

Bright, long-lasting, daisylike flowers are the trademark of the zinnia, a New World native that has taken the plant world by storm. Modern zinnias come in a wide range of sizes and shapes, from upright, cut-flower types to multistemmed, multiflowered border zinnias. The flowers can be single or double, big or small, and the color range is just about complete: Only true blue is lacking. If that weren't enough, they are particularly easy to grow!

Plant Profile

ZINNIA
ZIN-ee-uh

- **Bloom Color:** Varies by species; see individual listings

- **Bloom Time:** Summer through early fall

- **Height:** 4 to 48 inches (10 to 120 cm)

- **Spread:** 10 to 24 inches (25 to 60 cm)

- **Garden Uses:** Container planting, cut-flower garden, edging, mass planting, meadow garden, mixed border

- **Attracts:** Butterflies

- **Light Preference:** Full sun

- **Soil Preference:** Humus-rich, well-drained soil

- **Best Way to Propagate:** Sow seed outdoors in late spring or indoors in mid-spring

- **Hardiness:** Half-hardy annual

Growing Tips

No doubt about it, the easiest way to grow zinnias is to sow them directly outside as soon as the ground warms up. They grow quickly, reaching blooming size in just 6 weeks. Just loosen up the soil, toss in the seed, cover lightly, and water; it'll do the rest. Nurseries often offer cell packs, but zinnias generally don't transplant well once they've reached flowering size. If you do buy plants, try pruning them back by one-third at planting time to help them make a successful transition.

You can also start zinnias indoors at 60° to 85°F (15° to 27°C). They're up like a shot (in only 4 to 7 days) and need only a 4- to 6-week head start on the season. Sow them in peat pots or cell packs to reduce transplant shock.

Full sun is a must, and good air circulation is important for preventing powdery mildew. For bushy plants with lots of bloom, pinch young zinnias when they have developed their third set of leaves. Don't put zinnias outside too early because cool air stunts their growth; wait until all danger of frost has passed and the weather warms up. Keep deadheading through summer to stimulate continuous bloom.

Good Neighbors

Combine mixed-color zinnias with tall ageratum (*Ageratum houstonianum*) for an exuberant display. Chartreuse green 'Envy' looks great with just about any other color: Tuck it among perennials in a mixed border. For an eye-catching planting that will bloom freely even through summer drought, pair mildew-resistant, narrow-leaved zinnias (*Zinnia angustifolia*) or the hybrid 'Profusion' series with mealycup sage (*Salvia farinacea* 'Victoria').

Problems and Solutions

Powdery mildew is a major problem in humid climates. Mildew-resistant cultivars are really the only viable option under those conditions. Excessively moist soil can lead to root or stem rot. Where Japanese beetles are a problem, hand-pick and drop them into a container of soapy water.

Top Performer

Zinnia elegans (common zinnia): The most widely grown zinnia, this species has an upright habit, with opposite, bright green, broadly lance-shaped leaves and a wide range of flower colors, sizes, and forms. It is also the species the most susceptible to powdery mildew, so it's best in dry climates and well-ventilated spots in the garden. Height: 4 to 48 inches (10 to 120 cm). Spread: 10 to 24 inches (25 to 60 cm).

More Recommended Zinnias

Zinnia angustifolia, formerly *Z. linearis* (narrow-leaved zinnia): This species is a more modest plant, with smaller, simple flowers in orange to white with a yellow heart and narrower, pointed leaves. Its main claim to fame is that it seems entirely mildew resistant. The easy-to-grow 'Star' and 'Crystal' series belong here. Height: 8 to 24 inches (20 to 60 cm). Spread: 8 to 12 inches (20 to 30 cm).

Z. angustifoia × elegans (hybrid zinnia): This cross between the common and narrow-leaved zinnia produces plants much like the latter (and just as disease resistant) but in a wider color range, including orange, pink, red, and white. The highly popular 'Profusion' series falls here. Height: 8 to 24 inches (20 to 60 cm). Spread: 8 to 12 inches (20 to 30 cm).

Z. haageana, formerly *Z. mexicana* (Mexican zinnia): The species name is in doubt, but it's a handy place to place two old-fashioned but still popular narrow-leaved doubles, 'Old Mexico', 16 inches (40 cm) tall, and 'Persian Carpet', 12 inches (30 cm) tall. Both have multicolored blooms: orange or red flowers that are tipped in either white or yellow. Height: 12 to 18 inches (30 to 45 cm). Spread: 8 to 12 inches (20 to 30 cm).

Common zinnia
(*Zinnia elegans*)

Larry's Garden Notes

When I was a kid, zinnias were right up there with petunias and marigolds as the stars of the annual border, but that was when most people still grew their annuals themselves. Zinnias took a nosedive when buying plants in full bloom came into style because they just don't transplant well, particularly when in flower. Now that gardeners are growing their own plants again and using some of the high-performance, mildew-resistant strains, zinnias are working their way back to the top of the heap again.

LARRY'S LAST LOOK: VERBENA

There were just too many verbenas to cover in just a couple of pages, so here is a quick presentation of some of the other possibilities. All of the following are tender to half-hardy perennials grown as annuals—and all will amaze you with their beauty!

COMMON AND BOTANICAL NAMES	LIGHT AND SOIL PREFERENCES	DESCRIPTION
Brazilian vervain *Verbena bonariensis*, formerly *V. patagonica*	Full sun or partial shade Average to poor, well-drained soil	Forms a low clump of narrow dense leaves overshadowed by upright stems of clustered purple flowers. This tall, thin plant looks ungainly on its own but shines when interplanted with other plants or grown in masses. Pinch it back hard when young to stimulate branching. This plant can easily reach 6 feet in height in southern climates but will top out at 4 feet in colder areas. Warning: It produces copious amounts of seed and can become highly invasive if you don't deadhead. Hardy to Zone 7 with protection. Height: 4–6 feet (120–180 cm) Spread: 1–3 feet (30–90 cm)
Rose verbena *V. canadensis*	Full sun or partial shade Fertile, well-drained soil	A creeping plant with deeply lobed green leaves and domed clusters of often scented flowers in purple, red, pink, or white. There are lots of selections, with mildew-resistant 'Homestead Purple' leading the pack. It often self-sows, sometimes to the point of weediness, especially in hot, humid climates. Once established, rose verbena can tolerate dry weather but does best when watered regularly. One of the hardiest of the "annual" verbenas, it can be perennial into Zone 6. Height: 6–18 inches (15–45 cm) Spread: 18–36 inches (45–90 cm)

Brazilian vervain
(*Verbena bonariensis*)

'Homestead Purple' rose verbena
(*Verbena canadensis* 'Homestead Purple')

COMMON AND BOTANICAL NAMES	LIGHT AND SOIL PREFERENCES	DESCRIPTION
Peruvian verbena *V. peruviana*, formerly *V. chamaedrifolia*	Full sun or partial shade Average, well-drained to dry soil	A lesser-known verbena that merits more attention, especially for use in containers since it hangs beautifully from baskets and flower boxes. And what a great groundcover: The plants are densely clothed in small leaves that produce a nearly flat carpet. The blooms form a flattened dome in red, pink, or white, depending on the hybrid. The species has red flowers with a white eye. Less hardy than most others (only to Zone 9), it is not as likely to become a weed, but you'll still want to deadhead it regularly to prevent unwanted seedlings. Height: 3–6 inches (8–15 cm) Spread: 1–3 feet (30–90 cm)
Vervain *V. rigida*, formerly *V. venosa*	Full sun or partial shade Average, well-drained soil	The same rigid flowerstalks, long, toothed leaves, and well-spaced clusters of tiny flowers as Brazilian vervain (*V. bonariensis*) but on a much smaller plant. The original species is almost the same purple as well, although crosses with other species now give this plant a color range nearly equal to garden vervain (*V. × hybrida*). It can be clump-forming or spreading, and most lines are delightfully scented. Deadhead regularly to ensure constant bloom and to keep it from self-sowing too abundantly. Hardy to Zone 8. Height: 6–24 inches (15–60 cm) Spread: 12–18 inches (30–45 cm)
Moss verbena *V. tenuisecta*	Full sun or partial shade Average, well-drained soil	A naturally spreading or even trailing plant, ideal for containers. It gets its name from its deeply cut, almost feathery leaves. The color range includes blue, purple, lilac, mauve, and white. Purple-flowered 'Imagination', a popular seed-grown selection, is an example of a hybrid type. This species does not self-sow too aggressively. It is relatively hardy—to Zone 8—but best grown as an annual. Height: 8–20 inches (20–50 cm) Spread: 12–18 inches (30–45 cm)

Vervain
(*Verbena rigida*)

Moss verbena
(*Verbena tenuisecta*)

ANNUALS TO
Sow Directly OUTDOORS

In the good ol' days, when gardening was considered as natural as breathing, there was only one way to sow annuals: You took a hoe from the tool shed, scratched up the ground a bit, tossed in some seed saved from the year before, and watered like crazy. In a couple of days, the seed sprouted; a few weeks later, the flowers were in bloom. So why have things gotten so complicated? Peat pots, heating mats, cold treatments, artificial lights, transplanting: There's almost no limit to what we'll do to get our precious modern annuals started! Why not take a step back and sow some annuals directly in the garden, the way nature always intended it?

◀ Self-sowing annuals, like this calendula, can be among the easiest of all annuals to grow— as long as you are open to their easy-going, "pop-up-where-it-pleases-me" nature!

How Easy Can It Get?

With our modern techniques and our need for instant gratification, we've made producing annual flowers so complex that we forget how easy it used to be. Real annuals don't need babying or special care of any sort: You just sow them where you want them to grow, and they're in full bloom within 8 to 10 weeks, or sooner. It's that simple.

The odd thing is that even many experienced gardeners don't realize you can grow annuals this way. They see annuals as something you buy in six packs, cell packs, or flats in spring, or maybe start indoors. Sowing them directly outdoors sounds as strange as growing flowers on the moon, and just as unlikely. I've even heard a so-called expert, a graduate of a well-known horticultural school, insist that it couldn't be done. When I protested, he countered, "Well, we didn't learn anything about it when *I* was in school!" That explains a lot about how schools teach horticulture—and perhaps why direct sowing seems to be a lost art.

Of course, you *do* need a bit of patience. You can't expect to sow annuals directly in the garden and have flowers as quickly as if you bought trays of blooming beauties and stuck them in the ground. But all the plants described here grow fast—really fast. If you've never tried them before, you'll be surprised at how quickly they come into bloom. And you'll be pleased as punch when you find out that growing annuals from seed is so much fun!

Take a walk on the wild side. Let poppies self-sow with abandon to create a field of blazing color.

Why Sow at All?

Why would you want to wait even 5 or 6 weeks for plants to bloom, when you can get instant results? There are actually lots of reasons, but perhaps the most obvious is the fact that you can save money! Most of the plants described here cost a fraction of a cent per seed. Compare that to annuals sold in six packs, cell packs, or flats. You'd be hard pressed to find any at less than 25 cents a plant. With sow-and-grow annuals, you can fill in an entire border with a wide variety of flowers for only a few dollars.

Sow-and-grow annuals are also great fillers. Those first years after you put it in, a mixed border can look pretty barren; permanent plants like shrubs, perennials, and bulbs take years to fill in entirely. It's tempting to set them close together at planting time, but then you'll have to divide or move them within a few years. Instead, toss seed of fast-growing annuals into the open spaces, and your garden will soon be brimming with color.

In established gardens, sow-and-grows are perfect companions to spring bulbs and early-blooming perennials that die back in summer, such as Oriental poppy (*Papaver orientale*) and common bleeding-heart (*Dicentra spectabilis*). In spring, as the early bloomers are just sprouting, scatter seed of the annuals around them. As the perennials bloom, the sow-and-grows are starting to sprout; by the time the early bloomers' foliage starts to yellow, the annuals will be in flower, quickly covering up the fading foliage.

I also keep a few packs of seed on hand for a fast fix. If something dies back unexpectedly in midsummer, it's easy to toss in a few seeds of sow-and-grow annuals. Even in my short-season climate, I can sow flaxes and calendulas in August and still get my money's worth—not that I spent much on them in the first place!

Self-Sowing Guaranteed

⊎ **Think Twice:** Unless you deadhead them rigorously (and self-sowing annuals bloom so abundantly, you'd have to be a true maniac to get to *all* of their flowers), sow-and-grow annuals *will* self-sow. It is in their nature to sprout quickly and easily from seed, and all have seed that will survive the rigors of winter. As discussed on page 13, this is either an advantage or a disadvantage, depending on your point of view. I confess to being fascinated by self-sowing plants: I just love to see where they'll turn up next. And since I tend to plan my flowerbeds a bit formally, the volunteers add a touch of whimsy to what could otherwise be a rather "by the book" garden display.

Of course, you'll find sow-and-grow annuals self-sowing abundantly only when there is a lot of space in which they can grow. They all need sun and therefore bare soil in order to sprout. In established gardens, where open space is rare, they'll be present—but in minute quantities. Mulching also greatly reduces the number of self-sown seedlings you'll see—the only down side to this important part of good garden maintenance. Now I deliberately leave bare patches in my garden for the self-sowers. All I have to do is watch those spaces carefully and pull out the few weeds that appear, allowing the self-sowers to flourish.

The Lost Art of Direct Sowing

How to sow annuals directly outdoors is explained in detail in the section "Starting from Seed" on page 4. It's so easy that even a child can do it! In fact, having your children and grandchildren sow their own flowers, plus a few vegetables while they're at it, is a great initiation to gardening and to the appreciation of life on this planet. And if a 3-year-old can do it—well, I suggest that you try direct sowing to see for yourself!

Fast Flowers for New Beds

I use sow-and-grow annuals most abundantly when I've just finished preparing a brand new bed. By the time I've finished, I no longer have the energy to get down on my hands and knees and plant individual flowers, and much of my summer's budget has been blown on bringing in top-quality soil. So I buy a few seed packs of sow-and-grow annuals and simply broadcast sow, tossing the seed in the air and letting it fall where it may. All that remains is to rake lightly and water. Of course, there is some logic to my sowing—the seed of taller plants gets tossed toward the back of the bed, that of shorter ones to the front—but I still let the plants mingle together as they wish. This gives me great swaths of color the first year for almost nothing and with minimal effort. In following years, I begin adding shrubs and perennials, plus cell packs of annuals, but I still let the sow-and-grow annuals self-sow in any empty spaces.

18 More Sow-and-Grow Annuals

There are many other annuals you can sow directly in your garden for bloom the same summer. Here are just a few of the more popular ones.

Asperula (Annual woodruff) . . .154	*Iberis* (Candytuft) . . .378
Beta (Swiss chard) . .282	*Lablab* (Hyacinth bean) 234
Clarkia (Clarkia) 130	*Lathyrus* (Sweet pea) 236
Consolida (Larkspur) 132	*Lupinus* (Lupine) 140
Cynoglossum (Chinese forget-me-not) 134	*Malope* (Malope) 204
Eschscholzia (California poppy) . .112	*Nemophila* (Baby-blue-eyes) . . .168
Euphorbia (Snow-on-the-mountain) . . .290	*Nigella* (Love-in-a-mist) 268
Helianthus (Sunflower) 200	*Phaseolus* (Scarlet runner bean) 238
Humulus (Japanese hops) . . .224	*Reseda* (Mignonette) 388

Calendula

Calendula, pot marigold

With its bright sunny flowers over spoon-shaped leaves, this easy annual helps brighten up any garden. The British simply call this plant marigold—a word we North Americans reserve for *Tagetes* spp. (see page 58)—but the term "calendula" is understood on both sides of the pond. The name calendula, by the way, dates back to the time of the Romans and is derived from the same word as is "calendar," because the plant was said to bloom in every month of the year. Indeed, gardeners in mild areas *can* sow seed in late winter for spring into summer bloom and in early fall for bloom through fall and winter.

Plant Profile

CALENDULA
ka-LEND-yew-luh

- ■ **Bloom Color:** Apricot, orange, yellow, cream
- ■ **Bloom Time:** Summer through early fall; fall through winter in mild climates
- ■ **Height:** 12 to 30 inches (30 to 75 cm)
- ■ **Spread:** 12 to 18 inches (30 to 45 cm)
- ■ **Garden Uses:** Container planting, cut-flower garden, edging, groundcover, mass planting, herb garden, meadow garden, mixed border, rock garden
- ■ **Light Preference:** Full sun to partial shade
- ■ **Soil Preference:** Fertile, well-drained soil
- ■ **Best Way to Propagate:** Sow seed outdoors in early spring or fall
- ■ **Hardiness:** Hardy annual

Growing Tips

I well recall sowing the curious scimitar-shaped seed of calendulas when I was a kid; they were included in every pack of "children's garden seeds" I ever tried. Calendulas are still a great kid's plant: The seed is easy to handle, and the plants will grow in just about any situation (short of deep shade or truly soggy soil).

For earliest bloom, sow calendulas early in spring, as soon as the frost is out of the ground, at a depth of about ¼ inch (6 mm). You can even sow in late fall for bloom the following spring; the seed comes through the coldest winters unscathed. In mild winter climates, treat calendulas as cool-season annuals and start in fall for winter bloom. If you are really impatient, you can sow the seed inside about 6 weeks before the last frost. Plants sold in six packs or cell packs tend to be already past their prime and rarely make it through an entire season: I prefer homegrown calendulas!

Full sun is ideal, although partial shade is a better choice in hot summer climates. The older cultivars tend to weaken in hot weather, but modern selections bloom on and on, especially if you deadhead regularly. Thin plants to about 8 inches (20 cm) apart. For best results, water before the soil is completely dry.

I like to leave the final flowers of the season in place so they can go to seed, which allows the

FUN FACTS

Calendulas have only recently gained fame as ornamentals. They were originally grown for their edible leaves and flowers; in fact, the name "pot marigold" refers its use as a pot herb (stewing vegetable). Modern gardeners still enjoy tossing the petals in salads or adding them to rice for a lovely orange tint.

plant to self-sow. This saves me the effort of having to resow the following year. You can also harvest the seeds and store them in a dry spot over winter. Most cultivars seem perfectly stable, coming true from seed year after year.

Good Neighbors

As the season progresses, calendulas tend to become ungainly at ground level, so it's a good idea to front them with shorter plants. They look especially good with dark foliage, such as a sun-tolerant coleus or 'Blackie' sweet potato vine (*Ipomoea batatas* 'Blackie'). Red fountain grass (*Pennisetum setaceum* 'Purpureum') also makes an attractive backdrop.

Problems and Solutions

Aphids are the most common problem. They get down inside the flowers and around the base of the leaves and are hard to eliminate, although a dousing of insecticidal soap can help. You can also use insecticidal soap to treat whiteflies, occasional pests. Calendulas are subject to several leaf diseases, notably mildew; water from below to avoid wetting the leaves.

Top Performer

Think Twice: *Calendula officinalis* (calendula, pot marigold): The old, single-flowered, golden calendulas are still around, but we now have several others to choose from. You can find doubles and semidoubles, with wide to narrow to quilled petals (actually ray florets), variously colored centers, and a range of flower colors that is inching beyond the usual yellows and oranges toward cream and pink, sometimes even with a touch of red. Modern cultivars tend to be dense and low growing. One old-fashioned cultivar still worth trying is the curious and beautiful hens-and-chicks calendula (*C. officinalis* 'Prolifera'), with single, golden yellow flowers surrounded by a circle of smaller flowers. Do remember that all calendulas self-sow, if given a chance, but I don't consider them to be dangerously invasive. **Self-sowing** 🖊

Calendula
(*Calendula officinalis*)

Kissing Cousins

One of my favorite annuals is the criss-cross plant (*Cladanthus arabicus*, also called *Anthemis arabica*). It's a feathery plant with aromatic, grayish green leaves and bright golden yellow flowers, just like single calendula blooms. It's called "criss-cross" because of its growth habit: Four or five side branches form just below each flower head, then each forms its own four or five branches, and so on. It's just as easy and fast to grow as calendulas and takes the same care. Height: 16 to 24 inches (40 to 60 cm). Spread: 16 inches (40 cm). **Self-sowing** 🖊

Centaurea

Bachelor's buttons, cornflower

Beloved by generations of cottage gardeners, cornflowers have nearly disappeared from modern gardens because they don't adapt well to nursery culture. But once you get them started, they'll return year after year with minimal fuss from you. And it doesn't take much knowledge of ancient Greek to figure out that *Centaurea* gets its name from the centaur: half man, half horse. It's said the leaves of a cornflower were used to heal the wound of Chiron the centaur, who had been struck by a poison arrow. Cornflowers are rarely used medicinally anymore; today, they're mostly ornamental plants.

Plant Profile

CENTAUREA
sen-TOR-ee-uh

- **Bloom Color:** Varies by species; see individual listings

- **Bloom Time:** Early summer through early fall; fall through winter in mild climates

- **Height:** Varies by species; see individual listings

- **Spread:** Varies by species; see individual listings

- **Garden Uses:** Cut-flower garden, edging, mass planting, wildflower meadow, mixed border

- **Attracts:** Beneficial insects, butterflies, seed-eating birds

- **Light Preference:** Full sun

- **Soil Preference:** Average to poor, well-drained soil

- **Best Way to Propagate:** Sow seed outdoors in late spring or fall

- **Hardiness:** Hardy annual

Growing Tips

There are literally hundreds of *Centaurea* species, most of them perennials, such as the popular mountain bluet (*C. montana*). The annual ones may not be as well known, but they are particularly easy to grow. All they need is a bit of open ground and some bright sun, and they're up and growing!

For summer bloom, sow cornflowers in early spring, when the ground is still cool, or (in all but the coldest climates) in late fall, about ¼ inch (6 mm) deep. The seed and young plants are quite frost hardy. For prolonged bloom, sow a second time in early summer, although modern cornflowers tend to be much longer blooming than the rather fleeting wild types, especially if they are deadheaded regularly. In mild winter areas, treat them as winter bloomers: They'll bloom until spring from a midfall sowing.

If you can't wait a few weeks for annual cornflowers to come into bloom in the garden, you can instead sow them indoors, but use peat pots so the roots won't be disturbed at planting. Start them about 6 weeks before the last frost. For faster germination, slip the containers into the fridge for a 5-day cold treatment before exposing them to room temperatures. The seed germinates in 8 to 10 days. After germination, grow the seedlings at cooler temperatures—60° to 65°F (15° to 18°C)—before hardening them off to outdoor conditions.

Their poor response to transplanting means you'll rarely find cornflowers in six packs or cell packs. If you do see them, cut off all the flowers and buds and transplant with care; you may then have some luck in establishing them in your garden.

Cornflowers are about to take center stage in organic gardens, as scientists have discovered they have unique extrafloral nectaries that release a solution that is 75 percent sugar. This sugar attracts all kinds of beneficial (pest-eating) insects, including lady beetles, lacewings, and flower flies.

Good Neighbors

Old-fashioned bachelor's buttons (*Centaurea cyanus*) are a good choice for an informal cottage garden or meadow planting. Taller cultivars benefit from the support of sturdier annuals, such as Mexican sunflower (*Tithonia rotundifolia*). A casual combination of bachelor buttons and corn poppies (*Papaver rhoeas*) is an effective and time-tested pairing. The newer cultivars are much smaller and denser and are appropriate for edging.

Problems and Solutions

Cornflowers are usually trouble free, although leaf diseases, like powdery mildew, can be a problem when summers are dry. To prevent this, try to keep their soil evenly moist in hot weather, watering carefully from below so as not to wet the leaves.

Top Performer

❚ **Think Twice:** *Centaurea cyanus* (bachelor's buttons, cornflower, blue bonnets, bluebottle): The fastest-growing cornflower, this species often blooms within 5 to 6 weeks of sowing. Its original form was indeed very buttonlike: a medium blue inflorescence somewhat like a frizzy daisy with a compressed blue center. Modern cultivars are often so double as to be ball shaped. The narrow, grayish green leaves are sparse on the taller types but form masses at the base of the modern, self-branching hybrids. Watch out: This plant sometimes self-sows eagerly! Height: 8 to 32 inches (20 to 80 cm). Spread: 6 to 8 inches (15 to 20 cm). **Self-sowing**

More Recommended Centaurea

Centaurea americana (basket flower): This tall-growing cornflower has huge flowers—up to 6 inches (15 cm) across in some cultivars. The heavily webbed buds are intriguing, and the rose pink or white flowers are spectacular and make great cut and dried flowers. A little known annual that deserves *much* greater recognition! Height: 4 to 5 feet (120 to 150 cm). Spread: 30 inches (75 cm). **Self-sowing**

'Florence Violet' bachelor's buttons (*Centaurea cyanus* 'Florence Violet')

Kissing Cousin

Once considered part of the genus *Centaurea*, sweet sultan (often still labeled *C. moschata*, but now called *Amberboa moschata*) still looks like a cornflower—but it sure doesn't smell like one! Unlike the odorless common cornflower, sweet sultan is highly perfumed, with an exotic musky scent. The 2-inch (5-cm), white, pink, purple, or yellow flowers are delicately fringed with a thistlelike center. Grow it as you would *C. cyanus*, although you'll find it is much more heat tolerant. Height: 18 to 36 inches (45 to 90 cm). Spread: 9 inches (23 cm).

Chrysanthemum

Annual chrysanthemum

Chrysanthemums are so associated with the fall season that we forget there are dozens of other species. One group that is often overlooked is the annual chrysanthemums, all summer bloomers of extremely easy culture yet often spectacular bloom. Few annuals are as attractive and floriferous, yet just try to find them! Few nurseries carry the plants, even though they transplant very well, and they're often absent from seed racks as well. Fortunately, most seed catalogs *do* carry these beautiful plants with deeply cut leaves and daisylike blooms.

Plant Profile

CHRYSANTHEMUM
kris-ANN-theh-mum

- Bloom Color: Varies by species; see individual listings

- Bloom Time: Early summer through early fall; fall through winter in mild climates

- Height: Varies by species; see individual listings

- Spread: Varies by species; see individual listings

- Garden Uses: Container planting, cut-flower garden, edging, mass planting, mixed border

- Attracts: Butterflies

- Light Preference: Full sun to partial shade

- Soil Preference: Average, well-drained soil

- Best Way to Propagate: Sow seed indoors in early spring, outdoors in late spring

- Hardiness: Hardy annual

Growing Tips

Annual mums give you lots of sowing options. You can sow directly outdoors in spring, as soon as the soil can be worked or as late as the last frost date for summer bloom; in mild winter areas, sow in fall for winter bloom. Indoors, sow 6 to 8 weeks before planting time. Indoors or out, sow the seed about ⅛ inch (3 mm) deep. It germinates in 10 to 13 days indoors—a little more slowly outdoors if the weather is cool. Give the young plants a pinch when they have six to eight leaves. The fast-growing plants start to bloom about 6 weeks after pinching.

Annual chrysanthemums do best in full sun, except in hot summer climates where some midday shade is preferable. In really hot climates, you may want to sow twice: Plant in early spring for bloom to midsummer, then pull out the fading plants and sow again for fall bloom. In cool climates, they bloom all summer long without special care. Deadheading is not really essential unless you're a neatness freak; they continue to bloom heavily whether you deadhead them or not. Some self-sow to a certain degree, but don't depend on them; it's best to sow fresh seed each year.

All annual chrysanthemums fill out nicely, making excellent container plants either on their own or in mixed plantings. And all make great, long-lasting cut flowers.

Good Neighbors

Pick up one of the colors of painted daisy (*Chrysanthemum carinatum*) with a neighboring snapdragon (*Antirrhinum majus*) or celosia, or simply echo the form with other daisy-type flowers. An informal pairing with bells-of-Ireland (*Moluccella laevis*) is another good option.

Buttercup yellow crown daisy (*Chrysanthemum coronarium*) is an easy mixer, bringing out the best in mahogany reds or deep purples; try it with a deep red snapdragon such as 'Black Prince'.

Problems and Solutions
Not particularly subject to problems with insects or diseases.

Top Performer
Chrysanthemum carinatum (painted daisy, tricolor chrysanthemum): Gaudy, you say? I prefer delightfully colorful! The tricolor or even quadricolor blooms, 3 to 4 inches (8 to 10 cm) in diameter, have to be seen to be believed: pinks, reds, yellows, oranges, salmons, and purples form concentric circles around a darker center. Most types have single blooms, but there are also double-flowered forms. The deeply cut, rich green, almost succulent foliage is charming in and of itself. You'll most often find it in mixed colors, but there are now several single-color strains, including 'German Flag' (scarlet ray flowers with a yellow halo). Height: 2 to 3 feet (60 to 90 cm). Spread: 1 foot (30 cm).

Painted daisy
(*Chrysanthemum carinatum*)

More Recommended Chrysanthemums
⚑ **Think Twice:** *Chrysanthemum coronarium* (crown daisy, chop-suey greens, shungiku): This chrysanthemum has single, semidouble, or double, yellow daisylike flowers. The light green, deeply cut, fernlike leaves are attractive in their own right. Crown daisy has a long tradition of use as a vegetable in Asia. The Chinese enjoy the cooked leaves as a basic ingredient of chop suey, and the Japanese prefer to lightly sauté the flowers. This species sometimes escapes from culture to become a pest, so keep it deadheaded. Height: 24 to 32 inches (60 to 80 cm). Spread: 12 to 16 inches (30 to 40 cm).

C. *segetum* (corn marigold): This is a particularly fast-growing species with coarsely toothed, gray-green foliage and bright yellow 2½-inch (6.5-cm) daisies that have yellow to dark brown centers. It is popular in wildflower mixes. Height: 8 to 32 inches (20 to 80 cm). Spread: 1 foot (30 cm).

Kissing Cousins

Formerly classified as a chrysanthemum and still sold uniquely under that name, butter daisy (*Coleostephus myconis* or *Chrysanthemum multicaule*) has yellow flowers that resemble those of its relatives but in a smaller size: only 1½ inches (4 cm) across. It is a low, mounding plant, excellent as an edger and in containers. Another similar annual is baby marguerite (usually sold as C. *paludosum*, but considered by some botanists to be *Hymenostemma paludosum* or *Leucanthemum paludosum*); it has white ray flowers and a yellow center. Height: 8 to 12 inches (20 to 30 cm). Spread: 1 foot (30 cm).

Coreopsis

Calliopsis

This North American native is amazingly variable, in height and color as well as in habit. There are plants only 1 foot (30 cm) tall, others twice as high, and yet others twice as tall again. And while the daisylike blooms typically bear yellow ray flowers with a tiny trace of mahogany red at their base, many are entirely yellow, others are all mahogany except for a yellow tip, and others still are all reddish brown. Calliopsis is a very airy, open plant, even it its densest forms: The branching stems bear very narrow leaves and most of them are at the base of the plant.

Plant Profile

COREOPSIS
ko-ree-OP-sis

■ **Bloom Color:** Purple, mahogany, yellow; may be bicolor

■ **Bloom Time:** Early summer through early fall; fall through winter in mild climates

■ **Height:** Varies by species; see individual listings

■ **Spread:** Varies by species; see individual listings

■ **Garden Uses:** Container planting, cut-flower garden, mass planting, meadow garden, mixed border

■ **Attracts:** Bees and other pollinators, butterflies, seed-eating birds

■ **Light Preference:** Full sun to partial shade

■ **Soil Preference:** Average to rich, well-drained soil

■ **Best Way to Propagate:** Sow seed outdoors in late spring

■ **Hardiness:** Hardy annual

Growing Tips

There is nothing difficult about growing calliopsis: Just toss the seed into the air, rake it in a bit, water, and then thin lightly if too many seedlings come up. The plants will do the rest!

You can sow seed any time from snow melt to early summer, although an early sowing will give earlier blooms. In all but the very coldest climates, you can also sow in fall. In mild winter areas, you can sow twice a year: once in late winter for spring to summer bloom, once in fall for fall to winter bloom. The plant flowers with remarkable speed, often only 40 days after sowing.

If you prefer, you can also start the seed indoors, about 6 weeks before the last frost date in your area. It's best to use peat pots to avoid disturbing the roots at planting time. Just cover the seed and water, placing the tray in full sun after germination. This will give you only a 1- or 2-week head start on the flowering season, though.

Calliopsis naturally blooms over a very long season but will eventually wear itself out. To extend the show, either deadhead regularly or cut the whole plant back by half when flowering decreases. However, always let a few flowers mature at the end of the season, so they can supply replacement plants. Either collect the seed and store it in a dry place over winter or let the plant self-sow.

Low-growing calliopsis strains—those less than 2 feet (60 cm) high—rarely need support. Taller ones, though, need something to lean on. Stick a few branches into the ground in spring for them to cuddle up against, or plant them densely—about 6 inches (15 cm) apart—so they use each other for support.

All calliopsis make great cut flowers and they're ideal in meadow gardens and mixed borders, as well as being a staple for country-look cottage gardens. The dwarf varieties also make nice container plants, particularly when potted with foliage plants.

Good Neighbors

Calliopsis (*Coreopsis tinctoria*) is a standard ingredient in meadow mixes, and it makes a great mid-border filler in perennial and shrub borders. It is also an ideal companion to marigolds, being similar in color range but airier in habit.

Problems and Solutions

Slugs and snails feed on leaves, notably in rainy weather. Hand-picking is one solution. Leaf diseases, such as powdery mildew, are sometimes a problem. To help prevent them, water from below so as not to moisten the leaves. If the problem comes back, try rotating your plantings to spots where coreopsises have not been grown for several years.

Calliopsis
(*Coreopsis tinctoria*)

Top Performer

Coreopsis tinctoria (calliopsis, annual coreopsis): Although there are other species of annual coreopsis, this is the only one popularly grown. See "Growing Tips" for a complete description. Height: 1 to 4 feet (30 to 120 cm). Spread: 12 to 18 inches (30 to 45 cm). **Self-sowing**

More Recommended Coreopsis

Coreopsis grandiflora (large-flowered coreopsis) and *C. lanceolata* (lance-leaved coreopsis): These two plants are actually perennials, hardy to Zone 3, but they grow so quickly from seed that many seed companies offer them as annuals. The two species are almost indistinguishable; in fact, most plants sold under one name or the other are hybrids of the two. The flowers are generally entirely yellow or only slightly marked with mahogany at the base and can be single, semidouble, or double. To use them as annuals, start seed indoors 6 to 8 weeks before the last frost. Unlike calliopsis, they generally transplant well. Height: 18 to 36 inches (45 to 90 cm). Spread: 1 to 3 feet (30 to 90 cm). **Self-sowing**

Larry's Garden Notes

Many years ago, I broadcast a wildflower mix over a new flowerbed, just to fill in for the first year until I could afford to plant something more permanent. Among the many plants that germinated were several colors of calliopsis in all different heights, including a tall one with beautiful mahogany red blooms. It's come back every year since through self-sown seed, and I look forward to seeing just where this beautiful annual will pop up each year. So much pleasure for so little effort!

Cosmos

Cosmos

The bright flowers of cosmos are such a staple of the annual garden that they scarcely need any introduction. Both common species are fast-growing annuals, often reaching considerable heights in nature, although careful selection has led to hybrids of more restrained growth. They seem to thrive on neglect: The less you fuss with them, the better they do. And they even self-sow! You really can't ask for much more in a no-nonsense, low-care annual: I can't imagine a garden without them.

Plant Profile

COSMOS
KOS-mus

- **Bloom Color:** Varies by species; see individual listings

- **Bloom Time:** Early summer through early fall; fall through winter in mild climates

- **Height:** Varies by species; see individual listings

- **Spread:** 12 to 18 inches (30 to 45 cm)

- **Garden Uses:** Container planting, cut-flower garden, annual hedge, mass planting, meadow garden, mixed border, screening

- **Attracts:** Beneficial insects, butterflies, seed-eating birds

- **Light Preference:** Full sun

- **Soil Preference:** Average to poor, well-drained soil

- **Best Way to Propagate:** Sow seed outdoors in late spring, indoors in mid-spring

- **Hardiness:** Half-hardy annual

Growing Tips

Cosmos are a snap to grow if you provide their basic needs: full sun and soil that is not overly rich. In fertile soil, they tend to grow tall and then flop over, or simply produce lots of leaves but few if any flowers.

The easiest way to grow cosmos is to broadcast seed lightly over tilled soil toward the last frost date, work it in slightly, then water well. You can also start seed indoors 6 to 8 weeks before the last frost, covering the seed with ⅛ inch (3 mm) of mix. Either way, germination is rapid: 3 to 10 days. Thin seedlings or set transplants to stand 12 to 18 inches apart (30 to 45 cm). They reach flowering size in 10 to 12 weeks.

Even without deadheading, cosmos tend to bloom right through summer in cooler areas. Where summers are hot, though, cosmos sometimes bloom themselves to death. Either deadhead them regularly so they won't use all their energy producing seed, or cut them back by half when they start to flower less energetically. Do let at least a few flowers mature in fall, though, so the plants can self-sow (or so you can collect seed). The seedheads also attract hordes of seed-eating birds.

Dwarf and medium-height cosmos rarely need staking, although taller cultivars may need a solid support, especially in humid climates.

All cosmos make great cut flowers. Tall selections are excellent for backgrounds and living screens, while dwarf cosmos make good container plants.

Good Neighbors

The finely cut foliage of *Cosmos bipinnatus* can form an interesting cloud around shrubs or dark-leaved cannas, and these sturdy companions provide welcome support. Soft pink and purple cosmos look great paired with purple coneflowers (*Echinacea* spp.). In the border, give

C. sulphureus a rear seat or a low companion to conceal its leggy stems. It's marvelous rising up from a mound of 'Homestead Purple' verbena (*Verbena canadensis* 'Homestead Purple') or bouncing around a clump of variegated 'Pretoria' canna.

Problems and Solutions

Insects and diseases are few and far between, rarely requiring any intervention on your part.

Top Performer

Think Twice: *Cosmos bipinnatus* (cosmos): This species is the star of the genus, with saucer-shaped, 4-inch (10-cm), yellow-centered blooms that look like a broad-petaled daisy. They come in white, pink, or crimson, sometimes with a halo of a darker color around the center, and can be single, semidouble, or double. There are even yellow-flowered varieties, although they tend to be so late blooming they won't have time to bloom in short-season areas. The branching stems are cloaked in deeply cut, ferny, mid-green leaves. Cosmos range widely in height, but the most popular strains are semidwarf to mid-height, measuring between 30 and 48 inches (75 and 120 cm). 'Seashells' (available in a mix and separate colors) stands out from the crowd, with florets rolled into wide open tubes, rather like an old-fashioned hearing aid. All forms can self-sow a bit excessively. Height: 15 inches to 8 feet (45 to 240 cm). Spread: 12 to 18 inches (30 to 45 cm). **Self-sowing**

More Recommended Cosmos

Think Twice: *Cosmos sulphureus* (yellow cosmos): The common name isn't too accurate any more; the original species was indeed bright yellow, but most modern cultivars come in shades of orange. The ones sold as scarlet red need hot, dry conditions; otherwise, they, too, tend toward orange. This species used to be a true giant, but most modern cultivars are in the dwarf category: from 10 to 30 inches (25 to 75 cm) tall. Their flowers are much smaller than those of *C. bipinnatus* but also more numérous. Sometimes they're a bit too enthusiastic about self-sowing. Height: 10 inches to 7 feet (25 to 210 cm). Spread: 12 to 18 inches (30 to 45 cm). **Self-sowing**

Cosmos
(*Cosmos bipinnatus*)

Larry's Garden Notes

Think Twice: Chocolate cosmos (*Cosmos atrosanguineus*) is not a true annual, but it's often grown as one. It gets its name not from the velvety textured, reddish chocolate flowers but from its scent: No flower smells quite as much like rich Belgian chocolate! Nice-smelling blooms aside, this is one persnickety plant, prone to blooming poorly and dying for unknown reasons. Perfect drainage seems to be the secret to getting it through summer. Although theoretically hardy in Zones 7 to 10, it often rots away in winter.

Gilia

Gilia, Queen Anne's thimble, thimble flower, bird's eyes

How Queen Anne's thimble and bird's eyes could be in the same genus is beyond me, yet, botanically, they're both *Gilia*. They do share feathery leaves and a rather informal appearance, and they need much the same care, but unless you look very closely, the flowers couldn't be more different. Queen Anne's thimble (*G. capitata*) produces dense, globular clusters of lilac-blue, tubular flowers with protruding stamens, while bird's eyes (*G. tricolor*) produces much larger, cup-shaped, tricolored flowers, either singly or in small clusters.

Plant Profile

GILIA
JILL-ee-uh or GILL-ee-uh

- ■ **Bloom Color:** Lilac-blue
- ■ **Bloom Time:** Late spring through early fall; early spring in mild climates
- ■ **Height:** Varies by species; see individual listings
- ■ **Spread:** 8 to 9 inches (20 to 23 cm)
- ■ **Garden Uses:** Container planting, cut-flower garden, meadow garden, mixed border
- ■ **Attracts:** Butterflies, hummingbirds
- ■ **Light Preference:** Full sun to partial shade
- ■ **Soil Preference:** Average, light, well-drained soil; tolerates sandy soil
- ■ **Best Way to Propagate:** Sow outdoors in early spring
- ■ **Hardiness:** Hardy annual

Growing Tips

No use looking for six packs or cell packs of gilia in your local garden center: It will just never happen. The plants are too weak stemmed to tolerate being moved around without ending up flopping all over: hardly conducive to good sales. Nor is there any pressing reason to start them indoors from seed. You *can* do it, about 6 to 8 weeks before the last frost, but the resulting plants are just never as attractive as those sown directly in the garden.

Sow these cold-tolerant annuals outdoors as soon as you can work the ground in spring, or even in fall. The seed needs only a light cover—no more than ⅛ inch (3 mm) deep—so it's easiest to simply loosen up the soil beforehand, scatter the seed over the surface you want to cover, then lightly rake it in. Both species make great filler plants around perennials and bulbs, so you might want to direct-sow them into open spaces in the perennial border. Or mix their seed in with other wildflowers when you prepare your own meadow garden.

Gilias are perfect sow-and-grow annuals: They sprout readily (within about 1 week) and come into bloom about 6 weeks later. They bloom all summer long in cool summer climates as long as you deadhead (or if you keep harvesting them as cut flowers, as my wife always does). In hot, humid summer areas, though, expect the plants to fade out over time—all the more reason to plant early so you get a maximum of bloom in spring and early summer, before the heat of summer beats them down. In Zones 10 and 11, you can even sow them in late fall or early winter for bloom in February or March.

Being naturally weak stemmed, these plants may need some help standing up to the elements. A few twiggy branches placed here and there can help, but I like to let them grow closely together in drifts, thinning to no more than 6 inches (15 cm) apart so they can hold each other up. In a mixed border, they'll lean a bit on their neighbors for support.

Good Neighbors

Both species make interesting filler plants in the cooler part of the growing season. Sow them directly around more upright plants that thrive in well-drained conditions: Oriental poppy (*Papaver orientale*) and mulleins (*Verbascum* spp.) are just two good choices.

Problems and Solutions

Powdery mildew and rust can be occasional problems for gilia, especially in humid climates. Avoid planting them in spots where rust was a problem in the past, and improve air circulation to help prevent both diseases. (See "Annual Diseases" on page 33.)

Top Performer

Gilia capitata (Queen Anne's thimble, thimble flower): Rough-textured stems bear deeply cut, ferny foliage and rounded, dense, 1-inch (2.5-cm) clusters of tiny tubular flowers with extended stamens, held well above the foliage. They are usually lilac-blue, although white individuals occasionally appear. Height: 14 to 24 inches (35 to 60 cm). Spread: 8 to 9 inches (20 to 23 cm). **Self-sowing**

More Recommended Gilia

Gilia tricolor (bird's eyes): The foliage of this plant is similar to that of *G. capitata* although even lacier—much like the foliage of fern asparagus. The flowers seem to float directly over the leaves and are borne singly or in open clusters of two to five. The cup-shaped blossoms measure about ½ inch (1.25 cm) in diameter and are pale lilac, fading to white with a deep violet ring around the yellow center. Height: 12 to 18 inches (30 to 45 cm). Spread: 8 to 9 inches (20 to 23 cm). **Self-sowing**

Queen Anne's thimble
(*Gilia capitata*)

Kissing Cousins

The two main species of *Gilia* don't look like they belong together, yet the similar looking mountain phlox (*Linanthus grandiflorus*), which has blooms almost like *G. tricolor,* is in a totally different genus. Of course, the leaves *are* different: *Gilia* species have pinnately lobed (featherlike) leaves, whereas those of mountain phlox are palmately lobed (hand shaped). The 1¼-inch (3-cm), cupped flowers come in shades of purplish pink, lavender, or white, with a yellow center. Culture as per *Gilia.* Height: 12 to 20 inches (30 to 50 cm). Spread: 8 to 9 inches (20 to 23 cm). **Self-sowing**

Hibiscus

Annual hibiscus

This diverse genus has a lot to offer: shrubby forms, perennial types, and even houseplants. But even some experienced gardeners don't realize that these showy plants can be annuals, too, which just goes to show how much we all have to learn. There *are* annual hibiscus that are just as attractive as the shrubs, perennials, and tropicals we already know, with exotic-looking flowers that will make your neighbors jealous. Best of all, they're particularly easy to grow: Just toss the seed on the ground and let 'em rip!

Plant Profile

HIBISCUS
hi-BIS-cus

- **Bloom Color:** Yellow, cream
- **Bloom Time:** Midsummer through early fall to late fall
- **Height:** Varies by species; see individual listings
- **Spread:** Varies by species; see individual listings
- **Garden Uses:** Container planting, mass planting, meadow garden, mixed border
- **Attracts:** Hummingbirds
- **Light Preference:** Full sun
- **Soil Preference:** Humus-rich, evenly moist but well-drained soil
- **Best Way to Propagate:** Sow seed outdoors in late spring
- **Hardiness:** Half-hardy annual

Growing Tips

Direct-sowing outdoors is the traditional way to start annual hibiscus, although this does delay their blooming season. Soaking the hard seed in hot water for 1 hour can speed up germination considerably, from the usual 30 days or more to 10 or less. Sow the seed on the soil surface; don't cover it.

You can also sow annual hibiscus indoors—a definite plus in areas where summer is short or cool or rainy (or cool *and* rainy!). Sow them into peat pots (seedlings don't transplant well) 8 to 10 weeks before the last frost.

Once they're up and growing, annual hibiscus need little attention; just keep them well-watered, adding a bit of diluted organic fertilizer as you go. Even without deadheading, they bloom on until frost or cool nights nip them back. Deadhead only if you're afraid of them self-seeding too abundantly.

Good Neighbors

Bushy and free-flowering, *Hibiscus trionum* makes an excellent addition to a shrub border, especially where the soil is moist. In the mixed border, it's a super successor to moisture-loving Virginia bluebells (*Mertensia viriginica*), which will vanish as the season progresses.

Problems and Solutions

Annual hibiscus usually don't have the disease problems often associated with their perennial brethren. Insects can be an annoyance, especially whiteflies, aphids, and Japanese beetles: See "Annual Pests" on page 34 for control suggestions.

Top Performer

Think Twice: *Hibiscus trionum* (flower-of-an-hour): In the "everything old is new again" category, here's a plant gardeners haven't heard from in a long, long time. A true Victorian, it went out of style when buying bedding plants in six packs or cell packs came into vogue because it simply does not transplant well. **Self-sowing**

Flower-of-an-hour is a shrubby plant with spreading branches. The dark green leaves are almost heart-shaped at the base of the plant but three to five lobed at the top. The 2- to 3-inch (5- to 8-cm), bowl-shaped flowers are yellow to cream in color with a dark brown center, followed by inflated seed capsules. The original form had flowers that often closed before noon, giving the plant its common name: flower-of-an-hour. The blooms of modern strains, such as 'Simply Love', stay open until early evening. As with most hibiscus, each flower lasts only 1 day.

In Zones 10 and 11, flower-of-an-hour survives winter for a second season of bloom, but it acts as a self-sowing annual elsewhere. It can be invasive, so deadhead where that could be a problem. Height: 30 inches (75 cm). Spread: 2 feet (60 cm).

Flower-of-an-hour
(*Hibiscus trionum*)

More Recommended Annual Hibiscus

Hibiscus rosa-sinensis (tropical hibiscus, Chinese hibiscus, rose-of-China): Not a true annual by any means, this popular houseplant is often grown outdoors for summer. Its 4- to 8-inch (10- to 20-cm) flowers come in a wide range of colors. Bring it indoors in fall or let it freeze: It is not hardy north of Zone 10. Height: 15 inches to 15 feet (38 cm to 4.5 m). Spread: 1 to 4 feet (30 to 120 cm).

H. sabdariffa (roselle, Jamaican sorrel): Although best known in tropical climates, this short-lived tropical perennial grows well anywhere where summers are at least moderately warm. It looks like a taller *H. trionum* with pure yellow flowers. It is actually grown more as a fruit than as a flower: The swollen base of the flower, usually red, has a delicious sweet-and-sour taste and is used in jellies, drinks, and sauces. The fruit doesn't mature, however, in areas with cool or short summers. Grow it as you would *H. trionum*. Height: 4 to 5 feet (1.2 to 1.5 m). Spread: 3 feet (90 cm).

Larry's Garden Notes

It is rare for a tropical plant to do well as a sow-and-grow annual. Most plants of tropical origin take a few months to sprout, a few more to grow, and even more to reach flowering size. That's why there are so few tropical sow-and-grow annuals; these plants simply feel no rush to fit their life cycle into one growing season. Flower-of-an-hour is a major exception: It's up and blooming within 3 months and keeps going until frost kills it back. If only all tropical plants were that easy!

Linum

Flax

It's a mystery to me why annual flax species aren't more widely planted! They're incredibly easy to grow, and their silky-textured flowers have no equal elsewhere in the garden. I figure the problem is a commercial one: They don't like to be transplanted, and since *the* way to sell annuals these days is in flats and cell packs, they simply don't fit modern marketing strategies. From the point of view of someone who *wants* to sow annuals directly in the garden, though, they really should be at the top of the list of "best garden annuals," not at the bottom.

Plant Profile

LINUM
LIE-num

- **Bloom Color:** Varies by species; see individual listings

- **Bloom Time:** Summer to early autumn

- **Height:** Varies by species; see individual listings

- **Spread:** 4 to 6 inches (10 to 15 cm)

- **Garden Uses:** Container planting, cut-flower garden, mass planting, meadow garden, mixed border

- **Light Preference:** Full sun

- **Soil Preference:** Average, not overly humus-rich, well-drained soil

- **Best Way to Propagate:** Sow seed outdoors in late spring

- **Hardiness:** Hardy annual

Growing Tips

Growing annual flax takes amazingly minimal effort: Simply till the soil, broadcast the seed, and lightly rake it in. The ideal sowing season is in early spring, when the soil is still cool. Don't worry about frost; young flax plants are hardy. In fact, except in the very coldest areas, you can also sow flax in fall and the seed will overwinter perfectly. Can you start flax indoors? Sure, in peat pots, about 6 to 8 weeks before the last frost. The recommended sowing depth is ⅛ inch (3 mm).

Don't worry if nothing happens at first when you sow flax: the seed takes about 3 weeks to germinate. After that, though, they go straight into overdrive, and the plants will probably be in bloom within 6 weeks.

Flax doesn't require a lot of space and, in fact, looks better when its relatively thin stems mingle with those of its neighbors: thin to about 4 inches (10 cm) apart. Insert a few short branches here and here for support, especially in windy spots.

To keep flax blooming, either deadhead regularly or prune the plants back by one-half when blooming starts to falter. Deadheading and pruning aren't as effective where summers are hot: The plants tend to go rapidly downhill after their first flush of bloom. For continuous bloom in hot summer areas, make a second sowing about 3 weeks after the first, and yet another 3 weeks later. That should get you through summer and well into fall.

Be careful when you weed the flax patch; flax resents root disturbance. Hand-weed around young plants, then let them shade out any interlopers.

As long as you leave some open space in your garden, flax will self-seed quite abundantly, coming back from year to year. Just pull out any wayward plants.

Good Neighbors

Think about sowing this weak-stemmed plant with slightly sturdier companions, such as strawflowers (*Bractentha bracteata*). Flax is also at home in a meadow garden amid bachelor's buttons (*Centaurea cyanus*), California poppies (*Eschscholzia californica*), and calliopsis (*Coreopsis tinctoria*).

Problems and Solutions

Damping-off can be a problem if you sow seed indoors. Otherwise, diseases are rarely a problem for flax. Knock off any aphids with a strong spray of water. As for slugs and snails, rather than fight them, sow densely and let them eat a few plants: You won't notice the loss.

Flowering flax
(*Linum grandiflorum*)

Top Performer

Linum grandiflorum (flowering flax, scarlet flax): This is probably the only flax you'll find offered as an annual. It's a slightly fuzzy plant with narrow, gray-green leaves at its base and numerous thin, upright flowerstalks, each bearing several buds. The five-petaled flowers have a striking velvety sheen to them that helps compensate for their relatively small diameter: 1½ to 2 inches (4 to 5 cm). The color range includes scarlet red, white, pink, and lilac-blue, usually with a darker eye, plus a striking white form with a red center called 'Bright Eyes'. Look quickly—the flowers fade fast. Height: 16 to 30 inches (40 to 75 cm). Spread: 4 to 6 inches (10 to 15 cm). **Self-sowing** 🌱

More Recommended Linum

Linum usitatissimum (common flax): The flax used in making linen, this species offers superb blue flowers with darker veins. It forms a broom-shaped plant that dries to a nice flaxen (pale golden brown) color. Common flax will not rebloom, so let it dry on the spot, then harvest it as filler material for dried arrangements in fall. Look for the seed in drugstores and health-food stores, under the name linseed. Height: 2 to 3 feet (60 to 90 cm). Spread: 4 to 6 inches (10 to 15 cm). **Self-sowing** 🌱

Larry's Garden Notes

Many people don't know that common flax was once used as a fiber (and, in fact, still is, on a limited scale). Making linen was very labor intensive, however, so cotton largely replaced it even before the development of synthetic fibers. Flax is still grown for other purposes, though. The dried seed (called linseed) is used for medical purposes and the crushed seed gives linseed oil, used in making paints and inks. The residues of the oil-making process are compressed into linseed cake, valued as animal fodder.

Papaver

Poppy

The silky, crumpled petals of annual poppies seem so delicate, yet they are tough plants that can take whatever Mother Nature dishes out. The buds first hang upside down, then right themselves to crack open into bowl-shaped blooms. Afterward, they leave curious rounded seedpods with a flattened top and tiny little openings that, when it's windy, act like a salt shaker, releasing the fine seed all around them.

Plant Profile

PAPAVER
pa-PAH-ver

- **Bloom Color:** Varies by species; see individual listings
- **Bloom Time:** Late spring through early fall; fall through winter in mild climates
- **Height:** Varies by species; see individual listings
- **Spread:** Varies by species; see individual listings
- **Garden Uses:** Container planting, cut-flower garden, mass planting, meadow garden, mixed border; along paths
- **Attracts:** Beneficial insects, butterflies
- **Light Preference:** Full sun
- **Soil Preference:** Average to poor, well-drained soil
- **Best Way to Propagate:** Sow seed outdoors in early spring or late fall
- **Hardiness:** Hardy annual

Growing Tips

Outdoor sowing is definitely the way to go with annual poppies. They hate being moved. Sow them in early spring where you want them to bloom, or in late fall. You can even broadcast the seed over snow! In mild winter areas, sow in early fall for fall and winter bloom. The seed is so small and light that there's no need to cover it; the seed easily slips between the particles of freshly tilled soil, thus getting the darkness they need in order to germinate.

If you *insist* on starting poppies indoors, sow in peat pots about 6 to 8 weeks before the last frost date. But be aware that transplants just don't perform as well in the garden as plants produced by direct-sown seed.

The main secret to happy poppies is to thin them out. It's easy to sow the fine seed too thickly, but crowded plants will be weak and flower poorly. Give them space and you'll get sturdier plants with much more bloom.

All annual poppies self-sow abundantly, as long as there's a sunny, open spot for them in the garden. This can make them weedy (and explains the "Think Twice" warnings), but it's easy to find the seedpods and cut them off if you want to minimize self-sowing.

Most annual poppies have a short blooming season, so make sure you've provided some back-up bloom to cover when they die back.

FUN FACTS

Annual poppies make super cut flowers, but they need special treatment or they quickly wilt. Harvest when the bud is just beginning to unfurl, and sear the cut end (it will be oozing milky sap) with a match or in boiling water. Properly treated, cut flowers last as long as they do in the garden!

Good Neighbors

Scarlet corn poppy (*Papaver rhoeas*) is lovely floating in a cloud of baby's breaths (*Gypsophila* spp.) or surrounding silver artemisias (*Artemisia* spp.). It's also nice with blues, such as larkspur (*Consolida ajacis*) or bachelor's buttons (*Centaurea cyanus*). Sprinkle mixed poppy seed liberally in mixed borders for a bright accent.

Problems and Solutions

Poppies have few insect pests and are only rarely bothered by diseases.

Top Performer

Think Twice: *Papaver rhoeas* (corn poppy, Shirley poppy, Flander's field poppy): Modern mixes now include white, pink, orange, red, salmon, and bicolors! My favorite blend is 'Mother of Pearl' (also called 'Fairy Wings'), which contains the softest shades of pink, lilac-blue, and an exquisite, subtle dove gray. The single, semidouble, or double blooms are 2 to 3 inches (5 to 8 cm) across, held on slender hairy stems with fuzzy, gray-green, irregularly cut leaves. Let a few pods mature so they'll self-sow. Height: 1 to 3 feet (30 to 90 cm). Spread: 6 to 12 inches (15 to 30 cm). **Self-sowing**

Corn poppy
(*Papaver rhoeas*)

More Recommended Papaver

Think Twice: *Papaver commutatum* (field poppy): The blooms look exactly like a wild corn poppy (*P. rhoeas*), except the base of the petals is heavily blotched in black. Luminous red 'Lady Bird' is the usual cultivar. Height: 18 inches (45 cm). Spread: 6 inches (15 cm). **Self-sowing**

Think Twice: *P. somniferum* (opium poppy): This species offers blue-green, deeply lobed leaves on sturdy stems that bear 4-inch (10-cm), bowl-shaped flowers in a range of reds, pinks, whites, and even near black, plus some striking bicolors, with or without dark blotching. Modern cultivars are usually fully double and may be erroneously sold as *P. paeoniflorum* (peony-flowered poppy)*, while those with frilly petals are sold as *P. laciniatum*. After flowering (they will not rebloom), yank out the plants, leaving just a few for self-seeding. Height: 3 to 4 feet (90 to 120 cm). Spread: 1 foot (30 cm).

Larry's Garden Notes

Yes, *Papaver somniferum* is the plant from which opium, and secondarily heroin, is produced, but no, you don't have to worry about your teens getting into the poppy patch. The process of producing opium is complicated and takes many fields of poppies. It just can't be done in a North American context. Hundreds of thousands of people grow opium poppies and the seed is widely available through the most respectable of seed companies, so don't worry about the police paying a visit!

Rudbeckia hirta

Black-eyed Susan, gloriosa daisy

The summer-long bloom of this North American native is obvious as you drive through the countryside. Only something as bold as this plant's brilliant golden yellow blooms could catch the eye when you're rolling along at 65 miles (100 km) an hour! Happily, domesticated forms are now enjoying a place in our gardens. The species described here has the same type of blooms as its longer-lived cousins: a central cone of fertile, seed-producing flowers surrounded by a circle of long yellow florets that serve as a lure and landing platform for the butterflies that love it so.

Plant Profile

RUDBECKIA HIRTA
rood-BECK-ee-uh HER-ta

- **Bloom Color:** Mahogany, orange, russet, yellow

- **Bloom Time:** Summer through fall

- **Height:** 10 to 48 inches (25 to 120 cm)

- **Spread:** 12 to 18 inches (30 to 45 cm)

- **Garden Uses:** Container planting, cut-flower garden, edging, mass planting, meadow garden, mixed border

- **Attracts:** Butterflies, seed-eating birds

- **Light Preference:** Full sun to partial shade

- **Soil Preference:** Rich and relatively moist soil; tolerates any well-drained soil

- **Best Way to Propagate:** Sow seed outdoors in late spring, indoors in late winter

- **Hardiness:** Biennial or short-lived perennial grown as a hardy annual

Growing Tips

Black-eyed Susan grows just about everywhere, except in deep shade or constantly wet soil. It even adapts to poor soil and, once established, is very drought resistant. For best results, though, give it full sun and rich, evenly moist soil.

Outdoors, sow the seed in early spring, a few weeks before the last frost date, just pressing it into place because it needs light to germinate. Indoors, a 6- to 8-week head start is sufficient. It sprouts quickly, in only 5 to 10 days, and the seedlings grow quickly, reaching blooming size in as little as 8 weeks (in some faster-growing cultivars). You can also buy six packs or cell packs in just about any garden center.

Generally speaking, the smaller-flowered types are the quickest to come into bloom but the shortest-lived; they're often true annuals. Some of the larger-flowered kinds don't bloom much the first year, but they make up for that by living for 4 or 5 years. They tend to be tetraploid strains: plants with a double set of chromosomes, which also seems to confer extra longevity. The term *gloriosa daisy* was originally coined to represent this longer-lived group but has since become generalized to mean any *Rudbeckia hirta* cultivar. Since catalogs rarely hint at which types are more perennial, take a guess and test drive a few under your conditions; you'll soon find out.

When the mother plant has decided it has had enough—after 1, 2, or 3 years or so—it simply dies. But you probably won't notice that. It self-sows so readily that new plants quickly fill in the gaps. If you don't want too much self-seeding going on, take cut flowers. The blooms are incredibly long lasting (sometimes up to 4 weeks!), and the dried cones are nice in dried arrangements.

Most rudbeckias are quite sturdy, but the taller kinds may need staking.

Good Neighbors

Black-eyed Susans are most at home in a casual garden setting. Use them to pick up the color tones of French marigold (*Tagetes patula*), signet marigold (*T. tenuifolia*), or calliopsis (*Coreopsis tinctori*). For contrast, add spikes of deep blue mealy-cup sage (*Salvia farinacea*) or tall wands of Brazilian vervain (*Verbena bonariensis*). A combination of black-eyed Susan and 'Homestead Purple' verbena (*Verbena canadensis* 'Homestead Purple') creates a lively picture for much of summer.

Problems and Solutions

Powdery mildew is the number one problem. In very dry summers, the whole plant turns white, then black. Keeping the soil evenly moist will minimize mildew. Aphids can be pesky; knock them off with a spray of water. Hand-pick slugs and snails.

Top Performer

Think Twice: *Rudbeckia hirta* (black-eyed Susan, gloriosa daisy): This species is the only rudbeckia commonly grown as an annual. The wild plant, bright yellow with a black cone and about 3 feet (90 cm) tall, is a classic addition to meadow garden seed mixes. Cultivated selections in the same yellow-and-black color scheme range from 10-inch (25-cm) dwarfs, ideal for borders or containers, to 4-foot (1.2-m) giants with flowers 9 inches (23 cm) across. 'Irish Eyes' differs from other yellow cultivars by its bright green cones. There are many other strains of all heights and bloom sizes, with flowers that are orange or russet or marked with mahogany, not to mention double and semidouble types. All these form a basal clump of mid-green leaves with smaller, narrower leaves on the stems. Both leaves and stems are covered in short bristles, somewhat akin to a 5-day beard, which actually gave the plant its botanical name: *Hirta* means "hairy." **Self-sowing**

Black-eyed Susan
(*Rudbeckia hirta*)

Larry's Garden Notes

My wife keeps complaining there's too much yellow in our backyard, but what she means is that there are too many rudbeckias. I've yet to meet a rudbeckia I didn't absolutely adore. I love the way they bloom for months at a time and add bright color to borders, even when everything else is in that midsummer slump. Too much yellow? Well, when hybridizers break the color barrier (yellow *does* predominate with rudbeckias) and start producing them in everything from baby blue to fire-engine red, I'll grow them, too!

LARRY'S LAST LOOK: SOW-AND-GROW ANNUALS

Of all the annuals, my favorites are the ones I can grow myself from seed, so here are a few more. All are beautiful and easy to grow, but do be aware that most of these plants *will* self-sow—often more than you'd like.

COMMON AND BOTANICAL NAMES	LIGHT AND SOIL PREFERENCES	DESCRIPTION
Pheasant's eye *Adonis aestivalis*	Full sun to partial shade Average, well-drained soil	The deeply cut, almost threadlike leaflets are attractive in their own right, but the buttercup-shaped, deep bloodred flowers with a black center are stupendous. Easy and prolific mid-summer bloomer. Height: 16–18 inches (40–45 cm) Spread: 6–12 inches (15–30 cm)
Burning bush, summer cypress *Bassia scoparia trichophylla* (also called *Kochia scoparia trichophylla*)	Full sun Average to humus-rich, well-drained soil	This annual has a dense, shrubby habit, forming a beautiful bright green, fine-leaved, barrel-shaped plant that turns bright red in the fall. It's an excellent annual hedge that you can even prune to shape, and it looks great as the focal point in an island bed. Watch it, though: It spreads readily by self-sowing in dry climates! Green flowers are insignificant. Height: 1–5 feet (30–150 cm) Spread: 12–18 inches (30–45 cm)
Rock purslane *Calandrinia grandiflora* (*Cisanthe grandiflora* is similar, if not identical)	Full sun Average, very well-drained soil	This succulent annual has thick, leathery, shiny green leaves and tall stems of cup-shaped, silky-textured flowers. It can be perennial in dry, frost-free climates and also makes a good houseplant. Height: 2 feet (60 cm) Spread: 18 inches (45 cm)
Viper's bugloss *Echium vulgare* (dwarf hybrids)	Full sun Average to poor, well-drained to dry soil	This compact annual or biennial has soft, nonirritating bristles on its leaves and an abundance of violet-blue, purple, pink, or white flowers. Ideal for sunny, dry sites where little else will grow. If soil is too rich, this plant may fail to bloom. The ultimate bee plant! Height: 1 foot (30 cm) Spread: 12–15 inches (30–38 cm)
Blazing star *Mentzelia lindleyi* (also called *Bartonia aurea*)	Full sun Average, well-drained soil	Beautifully cut leaves and golden yellow, cup-shaped flowers centered on a fuzzy pincushion of long stamens. The flowers open at night and are highly scented; by morning most of the scent is gone, but the flowers remain open until noon. Cut back after first bloom to enjoy a second show of blossoms. Height: 6–30 inches (15–75 cm) Spread: 6–9 inches (15–23 cm)

COMMON AND BOTANICAL NAMES	LIGHT AND SOIL PREFERENCES	DESCRIPTION
Desert evening primrose *Oenothera deltoides*	Full sun Poor to average, well-drained to dry soil	This is a fast-growing, erect, branching plant with large, cup-shaped, white or pale yellow flowers fading to pink. Despite its common name, it is a day bloomer. It can be perennial in Zones 9–11; elsewhere, grow it as an annual. Height: 1 foot (30 cm) Spread: 8 inches (20 cm)
Venus's navelwort *Omphalodes linifolia*	Full sun to partial shade Humus-rich, light, well-drained soil	Fast-growing, early-blooming, cool-season annual with silvery gray leaves and one-sided, branching, open stems of blue or white, scented flowers to ½ inch (1.25 cm) across. Height: 12–18 inches (30–45 cm) Spread: 6 inches (15 cm)
Cream cups *Platystemon californicus*	Full sun Average, loose, well-drained soil	Very attractive annual with fuzzy, gray-green, narrow leaves, a spreading to sprawling habit, and numerous, 1-inch (5 cm), cup-shaped, creamy yellow, poppylike flowers with multiple stamens. May die back in hot weather but resprouts in fall. Often included in seed mixes, but hard to find solo. Height: 4–12 inches (10–30 cm) Spread: 6–9 inches (15–23 cm)
Night phlox *Zaluzianskya capensis*	Full sun Average, moist but well-drained soil	Night-opening, honey-scented flowers have five deeply notched petals that are pure white above and deep maroon below. Plant in groups to intensify the aroma. Height: 18–24 inches (45–60 cm) Spread: 6 inches (15 cm)

'Howellii' desert evening primrose
(*Oenothera deltoides* 'Howellii')

Venus's navelwort
(*Omphalodes linifolia*)

Drought-Resistant
ANNUALS

There are lots of ways to fight an occasional drought: hauling watering cans, setting out sprinklers and soaker hoses, and applying mulches, to name just a few. But if you live in a climate that's dry much of the year, if your garden is subject to prolonged droughts every growing season, or if you just have a spot that dries out faster than other parts of your garden, it's smart to consider growing plants that are naturally adapted to dry conditions. This sort of garden won't have the lush exuberance of a moist-soil planting, but it can still be beautiful and flower filled—especially with a generous dose of drought-tolerant annuals!

Top Picks

◀ Not all annuals need rich, moist soils: The ones described in this chapter, like bush morning glory, will grow all summer from just a few sprinklings after sowing.

Annuals in Dry Gardens

To be honest, annuals generally aren't the first plants that come to mind when you think of low-water landscaping. By their very nature, annuals are fast-growing plants, and quick growth usually requires abundant water. More-permanent plants (such as trees, shrubs, and perennials) are naturally much more adapted to dry spells, due to their abundant and far-reaching roots. Yes, you need to water them well for the first year or two, until their root system has had enough time to develop, but from then on, they're quite drought tolerant.

Not so for annuals! Their entire life cycle is designed around blooming quickly and producing seed at record speed, and not around producing long roots or storing up water for a dry spell. Of all the plants in the garden, only aquatic plants and vegetables need more rain (or when it is lacking, watering) than annuals. An annual bed that lacks water is a sorry thing indeed: leaves ranging from yellow to brown and few if any flowers. Most annuals do all right in climates that get regular rainfall, but for maximum performance, they appreciate a helping hand from you when the weather fails to provide rain on a regular basis.

So much for *most* annuals—because there *are* drought-resistant annuals! As you read through this chapter, you'll discover a dozen varieties that really don't need supplementary watering, except in the very driest climates. Just water once, at planting or sowing time (even drought-resistant annuals need *some* water to get started), and watch 'em grow.

For a meadow of California poppies (*Eschscholzia californica*), just sow seeds directly into the garden in very early spring, then lightly rake them in. If blooms are only minimal by midsummer, encourage a new round of blooms by cutting back the plants by one-third.

Coping with Drought

Dry-climate annuals have developed a number of ways to cope with their environment. Some have the accoutrements of drought resistance you find in succulents:

- Thick leaves or stems that store water for future use
- Silvery, bluish, waxy, or reflective leaves that don't let water vapor escape easily
- Prickly or bitter leaves so they don't get chomped on by predators and thus lose precious liquid
- A low-growing, ground-hugging habit so the plant is less exposed to drying winds

Other plants protect themselves from drought in less visible ways, notably with thickened underground roots that you'd never notice unless you dug them out. And several of the drought-resistant plants we grow as annuals aren't really annuals at all but rather long-lived tender perennials that save water simply by growing more slowly. We treat them as annuals only because they don't survive cold winters.

Then there are the speed demons, which are mostly annuals native to truly arid regions. Their trick is simple: They sprout during periods of heavy rain, then they race through their entire life cycle before dry conditions return. Their seed is inevitably very hard coated and long lived, surviving for decades, if necessary, until enough rain falls. When it does, they sprout rapidly, absorb as much water as they can through their fast-growing roots, and then quickly bloom, produce seed, and die. They're among the fastest of all annuals, often blooming within 6 weeks or less. These super-fast annuals usually work best when sown directly in the garden and watered just once. They'll do the rest.

The More the Merrier?

Many annuals for dry climates are abundant self-sowers. It's in the very nature of typical dry-climate annuals to produce copious quantities of seed that germinate readily whenever the soil is moist. Whether you find this a good thing or not depends on what kind of gardener you are: whether you prefer to keep your plants under control or are happy with whatever comes up, *wherever* it comes up! It's a blessing in a cottage-style garden but appalling if yours is a carefully planned, formal planting.

Fortunately for the control freaks among us, almost all the self-sowing, dry-climate annuals need full sun to germinate. They won't sprout well in a garden jam-packed with other plants, each shading out its neighbor. Nor will they self-sow much if you use a mulch because it, too, will shade the soil below to help prevent germination. But it's still smart to watch where you plant these eager-to-seed annuals!

Adaptable to Many Areas

Drought-resistant annuals are a blessing for those who garden in truly arid conditions. Many of the plants in this chapter can simply be broadcast over beds or into rock gardens or paths where they'll come up when the time is right with no fuss or bother. In the mild winter, arid climates of the Southwest, where rain tends to come in late fall, they often sprout in the short days of winter to bloom to perfection with the first days of spring, then fade away with the coming of the hot days of summer. In colder climates, they'll sprout in spring, blooming all summer if you deadhead.

Drought-resistant annuals are useful in rainier climates, too. They're ideal for those drier spots you'd otherwise have to water constantly, such as the upper parts of an exposed slope or at the base of a wall with an overhanging roof. They'll often surprise you with their durability: Other plants around them may be stunted or wilting, while they'll still be growing strong. They also make ideal choices for window boxes and containers, especially those that are beyond the reach of your watering can. Containers planted with moisture-loving annuals often fizzle out when hot summer days repeatedly dry out their soil. But if you use drought-resistant selections, your planters will still be full of color long after your neighbors have emptied theirs in frustration.

And don't worry that the plants described here will rot if they get a bit of rain. They're drought *tolerant,* not drought *dependent.* All will do perfectly well planted with other annuals and perennials in areas with regular rainfall or in irrigated sections of the garden. In fact, they'll do better if they get regular rainfall or waterings than if they dry out entirely. Any well-drained site will do—just avoid truly soggy soils.

Being a Responsible Citizen

To water or not to water? If you live where rainfall is abundant, of course, you can water whenever you want and not feel guilty about it. But where water is in short supply—and it *can* be scarce in almost all climates at some point in time—we need to think seriously about using such a precious commodity to maintain plants that serve simply as decorations. I suggest gardening responsibly, using as little water as possible in any climate, and none at all where it is rare. And drought-resistant annuals, which won't need watering at all if planted or sown during a naturally rainy period, are among the most guilt-free plants you can imagine for a dry-climate garden.

14 More Drought-Resistant Annuals

Although the annuals described in this chapter are among those best known for their drought resistance, there are others—in fact, many others! The following are just a few additional plants you might want to try if drought is a concern where you live.

Argemone

Prickly poppy, Mexican poppy

This fascinating annual seems to me the very epitome of the desert, even when it's growing in a climate way too cold for traditional desert plants, such as cacti. The spiny, gray-green, silver-veined leaves are charming in their own right, and even the prickly seedpods attract the eye—but what flowers! It's amazing that such a prickly, unapproachable plant could have such soft, silky petals. The large, bowl-shaped flowers have the same crinkly texture as the much softer-leaved poppies (*Papaver* spp.) we know and grow. Prickly poppies are a knockout for any dry spot your garden may provide!

Plant Profile

ARGEMONE
ar-GEH-mow-nee

- **Bloom Color:** Varies by species; see individual listings
- **Bloom Time:** Summer through early fall
- **Height:** Varies by species; see individual listings
- **Spread:** 12 to 16 inches (30 to 40 cm)
- **Garden Uses:** Container planting, mass planting, meadow garden, mixed border, rock garden, specimen plant; on slopes
- **Light Preference:** Full sun
- **Soil Preference:** Average to poor, even stony, very well-drained, neutral to alkaline soil
- **Best Way to Propagate:** Sow outdoors in late spring
- **Hardiness:** Frost-sensitive perennial or half-hardy annual

Growing Tips

This plant was *made* for poor growing conditions—no matter how stony your soil, how lacking in humus, or how alkaline, it will thrive. In fact, the poorer the soil, the better it blooms. And few annuals are more heat resistant: When your backyard feels like an oven and everything else is limp, prickly poppies will still be going strong.

Although prickly poppies are sometimes biennial or perennial in mild climates, most gardeners use them as annuals. It's best to start them by direct sowing in late spring, 1 or 2 weeks before your last frost date, while the soil is still a bit cool. Just scratch the seed into the soil with a rake; they need only a very light covering. You can try starting them indoors 4 to 6 weeks before the last frost, but germination is often irregular under indoor conditions. Sow the seed about ⅛ inch (3 mm) deep in peat pots; they produce thick tap roots and don't appreciate root disturbance. They germinate best at cooler temperatures, 55° to 60°F (13° to 15°C). Keep the seedlings just slightly moist while indoors. Plant out when all danger of frost has passed.

Don't expect strong, straight stems when growing prickly poppies; the first ones inevitably flop over. But staking won't be necessary: The plant then produces more stems that will lean on the earlier ones and soon make a nice clump. Plants bloom all summer with no need for deadheading.

Think Twice: For most gardeners in moister climates, prickly poppy is simply another annual that will self-sow modestly, never becoming truly weedy. If you're surrounded by arid land, though, you should definitely think twice about prickly poppy and even consider not growing it. Under such conditions, it can become a noxious weed, all the more unwanted in that its prickly foliage is irritating to livestock, and its seed and sticky yellow sap are somewhat poisonous. Of course, if the plant is already native or well established in your area (as it is in many of the drier parts of the southern United States), that's not a concern. But elsewhere, be very, very careful! **Self-sowing**

Good Neighbors

Grasses such as blue fescue (*Festuca glauca*), blue oat grass (*Helictotrichon sempervirens*), and fountain grass (*Pennisetum orientale*), which thrive in similar conditions and would not compete with the decorative foliage of prickly poppy, are appropriate companions.

Problems and Solutions

This plant is mostly free from disease and insect problems.

Top Performer

Argemone mexicana (prickly poppy, Mexican poppy, devil's fig): Of the nearly 30 species of prickly poppy, this is perhaps the most commonly offered. A true annual, it has bright yellow, lightly perfumed flowers that contrast well with the blue-green leaves. There are also orange and white cultivars. Height: 18 to 36 inches (45 to 90 cm). Spread: 12 to 16 inches (30 to 40 cm).

More Recommended Argemone

Argemone grandiflora (prickly poppy): This taller species of poppy can be a short-lived perennial in drier areas of Zones 8 to 11. Its 4-inch (10-cm) flowers are usually white, but there are also pale yellow cultivars. Some seed companies offer a similar plant under the name *A. polyanthemus*. Height: 3 to 5 feet (90 to 150 cm). Spread: 12 to 16 inches (30 to 40 cm).

 A. platyceras (prickly poppy): This species also has white flowers, but they're even larger than *A. grandiflora*. It is the least spiny of the three prickly poppies described here. Height: 18 to 36 inches (45 to 90 cm). Spread: 12 to 16 inches (30 to 40 cm).

Prickly poppy
(*Argemone mexicana*)

Kissing Cousins

Horned poppy (*Glaucium flavum*) is a short-lived perennial (Zones 6 to 11) that flowers the first year from direct-sown seed. It forms an incredible rosette of glaucous, spineless, blue-green, undulating leaves topped by poppylike, 2-inch (5-cm), golden yellow flowers and interesting seedpods. Grow it as you would prickly poppies, although horned poppy is more cold tolerant; sow it as soon as the frost leaves the ground. Height: 1 to 3 feet (30 to 90 cm). Spread: 12 to 18 inches (30 to 45 cm). **Self-sowing**

Argyranthemum

Marguerite, Paris daisy, Boston daisy

After a long history of popularity as a cut flower, this charming plant practically disappeared from culture between the two World Wars when higher fuel prices closed down many greenhouses. Fortunately it was "rediscovered" back in the mid-1990s and is again very much in style. The marguerite is not a true annual at all but actually a tender evergreen shrub; it bears single, semidouble, or double daisylike flowers in white, pink, or yellow over finely cut foliage ranging from dark green to almost silver gray.

Plant Profile

ARGYRANTHEMUM
ar-geh-RAN-the-mum

- **Bloom Color:** Pink, yellow, white

- **Bloom Time:** Early summer through early autumn

- **Height:** 18 to 48 inches (45 to 120 cm)

- **Spread:** 18 to 36 inches (45 to 90 cm)

- **Garden Uses:** Container planting, cut-flower garden, annual hedge, mixed border, rock garden, specimen plant, screening

- **Attracts:** Butterflies

- **Light Preference:** Full sun to partial shade

- **Soil Preference:** Average, well-drained soil

- **Best Way to Propagate:** Take stem cuttings at any time of the year

- **Hardiness:** Frost-sensitive shrub grown as a tender annual

Growing Tips

Marguerite seed is often hard to find, although you can sometimes get *Argyranthemum frutescens,* usually under its old name of *Chrysanthemum frutescens.* If you do find it, the seed is easy to grow: Start it indoors 6 to 8 weeks before the last frost date, without covering it. Seed germinates in about 2 weeks at room temperatures. Plant out when all danger of frost has passed.

Most marguerites commonly sold today are hybrids that don't come true from seed and are reproduced only by cuttings. They're usually sold in pots at fairly high prices, all the more reason to try to save them from fall frosts. Bring in plants in fall, cutting them back fairly hard, although not to old wood (they don't resprout well from truly woody stems). Or take cuttings from nonflowering shoots in any season. Grow the plants in a greenhouse or on a sunny windowsill over the winter.

Pinch young plants regularly until they reach whatever height you desire. Pinching not only controls height but also gives a fuller, bushier plant and far more abundant bloom.

Although marguerites are reliably hardy only under nearly tropical conditions (Zones 10 to 11), gardeners in warmer parts of Zone 9 can risk leaving the plant outdoors in winter. If well mulched, it will often come back from the roots even if the upper part is killed back by frost. It is still wise, though, to keep a few rooted cuttings indoors, just in case.

Good Neighbors

In containers, combine marguerites with edging lobelia (*Lobelia erinus*), or group them around plants with blade-shaped leaves such as New Zealand flaxes (*Phormium* spp.). In the garden, use them with restful green plants—perhaps ornamental grasses or *Nicotiana* 'Lime Green'—or around a bold, structural plant such as a dark-leafed canna.

Problems and Solutions

Marguerites normally have few insect or disease pests. If leaf miners cause leaf discoloration, pick them off and destroy infested foliage.

Top Performer

Argyranthemum hybrids (marguerite, Paris daisy, Boston daisy): Most plants sold under the name *A. frutescens* (see below) or even as *Chrysanthemum frutescens* or *Anthemis frutescens*, two former names, actually belong here. Few of the wild species of marguerite are still grown, but there are dozens of hybrids. Most produce flowers with a bright yellow center with white, pink, apricot, or yellow ray florets forming a daisylike bloom that is 1 to 2 inches (2.5 to 5 cm) in diameter. The semidouble and double forms, however, don't have the yellow eye of the singles. Those called anemone-flowered marguerites form a rounded central dome surrounded by ray florets of the same color. The fully double ones form perfect balls of florets all in the same shade. The deeply cut foliage can range in texture from quite coarse (like carrot leaves) to extremely fine, even almost feathery. Most modern hybrids have mid-green leaves, but some of the older ones have leaves that are a lovely silver gray. Height: 18 to 48 inches (45 to 120 cm). Spread: 18 to 36 inches (45 to 90 cm).

More Recommended Argyranthemum

Argyranthemum frutescens (marguerite): There are over 20 species of *Argyranthemum*, but this is one of the few offered for sale. Most plants sold under the name *A. frutescens* will turn out to be one of the hybrid forms. The true species has bright green leaves and small white flowers with yellow centers, about ¾ inch (2 cm) in diameter. Height: 24 to 28 inches (60 to 70 cm). Spread: 24 to 28 inches (60 to 70 cm).

'Summer Eyes' marguerite (*Argyranthemum* 'Summer Eyes')

Kissing Cousins

Euryops pectinatus is often confused with the marguerite, although the 1½- to 2-inch (4- to 5-cm) flowers are a much brighter yellow than the yellowest marguerite. If not pinched regularly, it can also be a much larger plant, easily reaching 6 feet (1.8 m). The species has deeply cut, silvery gray leaves; 'Viridis' has deep green ones. In most respects, it needs the same culture as *Argyranthemum*; the seed, however, needs cool temperatures of 50° to 55°F (10° to 13°C) to germinate. Height: 3 to 6 feet (90 to 180 cm). Spread: 3 feet (90 cm).

Catharanthus

Madagascar periwinkle, rose periwinkle

If your garden is hot, hot, hot, you'll probably adore Madagascar periwinkle! This heat-tolerant annual is just as resistant to high humidity as to dry air, so you can grow it equally well in Florida and in California. Even northern gardeners can grow it, although they're wise to wait until the air warms up before putting it outside. As the common name suggests, it is related to the popular dwarf periwinkle (*Vinca minor*), a hardy perennial, and you may still find it sold as *Vinca rosea*.

Plant Profile

CATHARANTHUS
cath-ah-RAN-thus

- **Bloom Color:** Lavender, pink, red, rose, white
- **Bloom Time:** Early summer through late fall
- **Height:** 4 to 24 inches (10 to 60 cm)
- **Spread:** 1 to 2 feet (30 to 60 cm)
- **Garden Uses:** Container planting, edging, hanging baskets, groundcover, mass planting, mixed border, rock garden
- **Light Preference:** Full sun to partial shade
- **Soil Preference:** Average to humus-rich, well-drained soil
- **Best Way to Propagate:** Sow seed indoors in late winter; take stem cuttings in spring or summer
- **Hardiness:** Frost-sensitive perennial grown as a tender annual

Growing Tips

Although seed of Madagascar periwinkle is widely available, it's one of the more difficult annuals to start at home. Since it's easy to find in six packs or cell packs in any flower market or nursery, I suggest skipping the starting-from-seed process entirely and just buying the plants. Of course, that means you'll be limited to what is available locally; so if you really do want to grow a particular color from scratch, sow indoors about 12 to 16 weeks before the last frost. Cover the seed with ¼ inch (6 mm) of growing mix; then place the tray in complete darkness at about 70° to 80°F (21° to 27°C). Germination takes from 15 to 20 days.

When the tiny seedlings are visible, move the tray to a bright spot and remove any covering to increase air circulation. Wait until the mix is nearly dry before watering again; then stand the tray in warm, shallow water for no more than 10 to 15 minutes, just enough to moisten the mix from below, leaving the surface dry. Keep them in a state closer to dry than to wet until the young plants (and they are very slow growing at first) start producing larger, thicker leaves. Pinch them once when they have 6 to 8 true leaves to encourage them to branch out.

Don't even think of putting Madagascar periwinkle outdoors until both the ground and the air have warmed up because temperatures below 60°F (15°C) can stunt its growth. (As you can imagine, it is *not* a good choice for cool summer climates.) Full sun is best, except in areas with very hot summers, where the plants appreciate some midday shade. Once in the garden, the plants are very easy to maintain, taking rainy periods and prolonged droughts with equal aplomb. They don't even need deadheading.

Madagascar periwinkles are not true annuals but rather tender perennials, so you can overwinter them indoors. Take cuttings or bring in whole plants while nights are still warm. They'll need full sun indoors. In Zones 10 and 11 and in warmer parts of Zone 9, Madagascar periwinkles will often overwinter and act like true perennials; they'll likewise self-sow to a certain degree. **Self-sowing** 🌱

Good Neighbors

A very useful plant for foregrounds, Madagascar periwinkle is most effective when planted in masses. Although it often comes in mixed colors, using plants that are all the same shade makes for a more attractive display. Match the flower color with that of a nearby neighbor, such as a large-flowered hibiscus or a grouping of tall snapdragons (*Antirrhinum majus*). Or try pairing a pale lavender-flowered form with deep purple heliotrope (*Heliotropum arborescens*). For a low-care display, use Madagascar periwinkle around a drought-resistant, architectural plant, such as yucca.

Problems and Solutions

Diseases are an occasional problem, especially in hot, humid conditions. Aster yellows, in which the whole plant turns yellow, is a serious problem; destroy infected plants. Pests (notably spider mites and whiteflies) tend to be a problem only while the plant is overwintering indoors: Control with insecticidal soap. (See page 35 for more information on these pests.)

Top Performer

Catharanthus roseus (Madagascar periwinkle, rose periwinkle): Although there are about half a dozen species in the genus *Catharanthus,* this is the only species currently grown. Spreading, shrubby plants have glossy, pale-veined leaves and broad, flat-faced flowers, usually with a darker eye. **Self-sowing** 🌱

Madagascar periwinkle
(*Catharanthus roseus*)

Container Choices

With its love of heat and its drought resistance, Madagascar periwinkle is a natural choice for pots of any kind. The original species was distinctly upright, but many modern selections, like the 'Carpet' series, are low growing and well branched, making better container choices. And now there's a series of trailing Madagascar periwinkles: the 'Mediterranean' series. These plants creep over the surface of the potting mix, then drip down over the pot's edges, making a perfect carpet of bloom.

Convolvulus

Dwarf morning glory, bush morning glory

If you're looking for the morning glories that are climbing plants with trumpet-shaped flowers, turn to *Ipomoea* on page 232. The genus *Convolvulus* also has its share of climbers—notably the nearly inextricable field bindweed (*C. arvensis*)—but those grown as annuals are low-growing, bushy plants, not climbers. And the name "morning glory" really doesn't suit them either because their flowers remain open all day. The plants described here are tender shrubs or short-lived perennials, but they grow fast enough to act like annuals. These easy-care plants make great choices for edging and containers.

Plant Profile

CONVOLVULUS
con-VOL-view-lus

- **Bloom Color:** Varies by species; see individual listings

- **Bloom Time:** Early spring through early fall

- **Height:** Varies by species; see individual listings

- **Spread:** Varies by species; see individual listings

- **Garden Uses:** Container planting, edging, hanging baskets, groundcover, mass planting, rock garden, woodland garden

- **Attracts:** Hummingbirds

- **Light Preference:** Full sun to partial shade

- **Soil Preference:** Average to poor, well-drained soil

- **Best Way to Propagate:** Sow seed indoors in spring

- **Hardiness:** Frost-sensitive perennial or shrub grown as a half-hardy annual

Growing Tips

Dwarf morning glories tend to transplant poorly, so you'll rarely find them for sale in six packs or cell packs. If you want to try them, you'll have to grow your own from seed. Fortunately, that's not too difficult a thing to do.

In areas with a long summer, you can sow dwarf morning glory seed directly outdoors 1 week or so before the last frost. (Where winters are mild, you can even sow in late fall.) Elsewhere, though, you can give them a head start by sowing them indoors from 5 to 6 weeks before the last frost. The seed is very hard and germinates best if soaked for 24 hours in tepid water before being sown. Sow them about ⅛ inch (3 mm) deep in peat pots to minimize any disturbance at transplanting time, and place the trays in a warm spot—70° to 80°F (21° to 27°C). The seed germinates quite rapidly, often starting to sprout in less than 1 week. Plant out when the soil has warmed up and there is no further danger of cold nights.

A site with full sun is best, but some protection from the afternoon sun will help prolong the flowering period in hot summer areas. Just about any soil will do, although soils that are too rich tend to result in abundant leaves and few flowers. Once established, dwarf morning glories are very heat and drought tolerant and need little care in the garden. Even deadheading seems unnecessary.

The shrubbier species (see "More Recommended Convolvulus" on the opposite page) are generally reproduced by stem cuttings. Where they aren't hardy, the shrubby morning glories can overwinter indoors in full sun.

Good Neighbors

Combining one of the blue cultivars with other blues, such as trailing lobelia (*Lobelia erinus*), will make their yellow throats shine like stars. White alyssum (*Lobularia maritima*) brings out the white that rims each yellow throat, making it a perfect partner for any shade of *Convolvulus tricolor*.

Problems and Solutions

Dwarf morning glories aren't particularly subject to pests and diseases when grown outdoors but may suffer from aphids or spider mites while overwintering indoors. Repeated treatments with insecticidal soap should help.

Top Performer

Convolvulus tricolor (dwarf morning glory, bush morning glory): By far the most popular of the nonclimbing morning glories, this is a fast-growing annual (or sometimes a short-lived subtropical perennial) that's easy to grow from seed. It produces dark green, lance-shaped leaves on reddish stems that are at first bushy and upright, then spreading or even trailing. The showy, trumpet-shaped, 2-inch (5-cm) flowers are inevitably multicolored: a ring of red, purple, blue, pink, or white surrounding a throat feathered white with a yellow center. Height: 6 to 16 inches (15 to 40 cm). Spread: 9 to 15 inches (23 to 38 cm).

More Recommended Convolvulus

Convolvulus cneorum (silverbush): This is a shrubby species usually multiplied by cuttings. It produces a dense mound of delightfully silvery narrow leaves and numerous 1¼-inch (4-cm) white flowers springing from pink buds. It is hardy in Zones 8 to 11 but most often used as a container annual in all zones. Height: 2 feet (60 cm). Spread: 3 feet (90 cm).

   C. sabatius (Mauritius bush morning glory): Most often sold under its former name, *C. mauritanicus,* this creeping tender perennial has medium green leaves and hordes of tiny, funnel-shaped, lavender to purple flowers. It's hardy in Zones 8 to 11 but is more often grown as an annual. Multiply by taking cuttings. Height: 6 inches (15 cm). Spread: 20 inches (50 cm).

'Blue Ensign' dwarf morning glory (*Convolvulus tricolor* 'Blue Ensign')

Kissing Cousins

Not many plants have true blue flowers, so the few that do exist tend to attract a lot of attention. Such is the case of *Evolvulus pilosus* (also called *E. glomeratus* or *E. nuttallianus*), a relatively new introduction that is becoming very popular as a container plant, an edging plant, or (in Zones 8 and above) a perennial ground-cover. Its trailing stems bear small, silver-gray leaves and numerous flowers that look exactly like miniature blue morning glories! Height: 20 inches (50 cm). Spread: 20 inches (50 cm).

Dimorphotheca

African daisy, Cape marigold

The arid regions of South Africa are home to an incredible range of fast-growing annuals that sprout from nowhere when heavy rains fall, then bloom, produce seed, and disappear in short order. One such group includes the various species and genera of the Compositae (or daisy) family, which are collectively known as African daisies or Cape marigolds. It's a varied group of plants, all with large daisylike flowers that close at night and in poor weather. Trying to find your way through this maze of plants is not easy; let's take a look together!

Plant Profile

DIMORPHOTHECA
dye-more-foe-THEE-kuh

- **Bloom Color:** Varies by species; see individual listings

- **Bloom Time:** Early summer through early fall; fall through winter in mild climates

- **Height:** Varies by species; see individual listings

- **Spread:** Varies by species; see individual listings

- **Garden Uses:** Container planting, cut-flower garden, edging, mass planting, meadow garden, mixed border, rock garden

- **Attracts:** Butterflies

- **Light Preference:** Full sun

- **Soil Preference:** Average to poor, even stony or sandy, very well-drained soil

- **Best Way to Propagate:** Sow seed indoors or outdoors in spring

- **Hardiness:** Half-hardy annual or tender perennial

Growing Tips

All African daisies grow well from seed sown directly outdoors a week or so before the last frost. (In nearly frost-free climates, you can also sow in fall for winter bloom.) To get flowers earlier in summer, sow indoors 6 to 8 weeks before the last frost, barely covering the seed. Germination takes about 2 weeks at 60° to 70°F (15° to 21°C). Or buy plants in six packs or cell packs: Just about every nursery or garden center carries at least one African daisy. After planting, they need little care—just regular deadheading.

Think Twice: Generally speaking, African daisies do best in full sun and are very heat tolerant, as long as the air isn't humid. In hot, humid climates they tend to be short lived; but in relatively cool conditions (they make great seashore plants, for example), they are more tolerant of humid air. In cold winter climates, they self-sow only moderately. They can, however, be extremely invasive in drier areas; in these climates, do not plant them near open areas where they can escape into the wild. **Self-sowing**

Some African daisies are true annuals, but most are tender perennials. They may overwinter in arid areas of Zones 9 through 11.

Good Neighbors

Their mounding habit makes African daisies ideal for use in the front of beds and borders. Pair them with other compact, drought-tolerant plants, such as low-growing sedums, thymes, and sea thrifts (*Armeria* spp.). Or group them around a taller plant of a noncompetitive color, such as an ornamental grass.

Problems and Solutions

African daisies have few problems in most climates, but hot, humid conditions may lead to various leaf spots and diseases. Try setting them outdoors early so that their main flowering will take place before the heat waves occur.

Top Performer

Dimorphotheca sinuata (star of the veldt): Of the many African daisies, this one rates top performer status simply because of its greater resistance to the double whammy of heat and humidity. It forms a clump of narrow, aromatic, toothed leaves and white, yellow, orange, or pink ray florets, often bluish underneath, with a maroon central disk. It is also called *D. aurantiaca.* Height: 1 foot (30 cm). Spread: 1 foot (30 cm).

Star of the veldt
(*Dimorphotheca sinuata*)

More Recommended African Daisies

Arctotis fastuosa (monarch of the veldt): *Arctotis* is closely related to *Dimorphotheca* and requires the same care. This species, formerly sold as *Venidium fastuosum*, is the most easily identified of the African daisies: Its flowers always have two levels of ray florets instead of the usual one. It forms a rosette of deeply lobed, dandelion-like leaves covered in silver-white felt. The flowers are orange, yellow, or white, often with a ring of purple surrounding a dark purple disk. Height: 1 to 2 feet (30 to 60 cm). Spread: 1 foot (30 cm).

Arctotis 'Harlequin' hybrids (hybrid African daisy): Sold under the name *Arctotis* × *hybrida* or × *venidioarctotis,* this hybrid offers a wide range of colors (golden yellow, orange, pink, white, or red) around a dark center. Some of the most beautiful African daisies belong to this category. Height: 18 to 20 inches (45 to 50 cm). Spread: 1 foot (30 cm).

Dimorphotheca pluvialis (rain daisy, weather prophet): Taller and hairier than *D. sinuata,* with more deeply cut leaves. The white flowers are purplish underneath and have a purple halo on top surrounding a maroon center. The common names come from the fact that the flowers won't open, even if it is brilliantly sunny at the time, if rain is due. Height: 12 to 16 inches (30 to 40 cm). Spread: 6 to 12 inches (15 to 30 cm).

Kissing Cousins

In the vast array of African daisies, *Ursinia anethoides* (fern-leaf African daisy) stands out due to its deeply cut, fernlike foliage. Not only do the medium green leaves look like those of dill (*anethoides* means "resembling dill"), they also smell vaguely like it if you take a few seconds to run your fingers through the foliage. The feathery leaves perfectly set off the daisy-like, dark-centered, yellow-orange flowers. Height: 12 to 18 inches (30 to 45 cm). Spread: 8 to 12 inches (20 to 30 cm).

Dorotheanthus

Livingstone daisy, ice plant

Diamonds in the garden: That's what you get with ice plants! The leaves are covered with tiny crystalline protuberances that sparkle in the sun. And if that weren't enough, the flowers have a satiny sheen and seem to glitter as well. They look like the common daisy-type blooms we're all familiar with, but while a true daisy is made up of many individual flowers, each ice plant blossom is a single flower. These plants are actually much more closely related to the famous "living stones" (mostly *Lithops* spp.), also of South Africa, than to daisies of any kind.

Plant Profile

DOROTHEANTHUS
door-oh-thee-ANN-thus

- **Bloom Color:** Varies by species; see individual listings
- **Bloom Time:** Late spring through early fall
- **Height:** Varies by species; see individual listings
- **Spread:** Varies by species; see individual listings
- **Garden Uses:** Container planting, edging, groundcover, mass planting, mixed border, rock garden
- **Attracts:** Bees
- **Light Preference:** Full sun
- **Soil Preference:** Poor, sandy, even stony, very well-drained soil
- **Best Way to Propagate:** Sow seed indoors or outdoors in spring; take cuttings at any time (perennial types)
- **Hardiness:** Half-hardy annual or tender perennial

Growing Tips

Ice plants bloom profusely even in the poorest soils and hottest sites. For early color in the summer garden, start your first batch of seedlings indoors, 8 to 10 weeks before the last spring frost date. Don't cover the fine seed; just press it into the soil surface. Germination is better if you place the tray in darkness. After all danger of frost has passed, plant out the seedlings, then lightly broadcast more seed in the same spot to start a second group. A third sowing in the same area about 6 weeks later will guarantee bloom right through the season, even in areas where summers are particularly long.

Think Twice: In areas where other annuals can't compete (notably, in sites with poor, dry soil or those covered with stone mulches), Livingstone daisy will self-sow. In arid climates with mild winters, it sometimes escapes from culture and establishes itself in the wild. There's greater competition for growing space in moist, fertile sites, so it generally doesn't get out of hand in those conditions.

Self-sowing

Other than possibly deadheading, the plants need little care.

Good Neighbors

Ice plants are ideal for rock walls, edging, containers, and wherever else you'll appreciate their compact habit and drought tolerance. They can help soften the bold forms of yuccas and cactus and add a bit of pizzazz to barren

FUN FACTS

There are plenty of succulent perennials, but true annuals that are also succulents are extremely rare. Livingstone daisy is one of the exceptions! A true succulent, it stores water in the gelatinous interior of its leaves, releasing it as needed to keep the plant going through the driest weather.

stone mulches. The low-growing nature of the Livingstone daisy (*Dorotheanthus bellidiformis*) and its extreme drought tolerance make it an ideal choice for dry slopes and rock gardens.

Problems and Solutions

Rot and slug and snail damage are possible in moist sites. In the dry, sunny conditions they prefer, ice plants are usually problem free.

Top Performer

Dorotheanthus bellidiformis (Livingstone daisy, ice plant): The leaf form of these variable plants ranges from cylindrical to spoon shaped, but the foliage is always fleshy and is covered with the crystalline structures that give it its brilliance. The 1½-inch (4-cm) flowers are borne singly on fleshy stems. They are made up of a dark center surrounded by numerous, shiny, narrow petals in cream, orange, pink, purple, red, or white, often with a contrasting white halo. The flowers close at night and open only in full sun. Formerly known as *Mesembryanthemum criniflorum*. Height: 4 to 6 inches (10 to 15 cm). Spread: 1 foot (30 cm).

More Recommended Ice Plants

Lampranthus hybrids (ice plant, highway daisy): There are almost 200 *Lampranthus* species, but those most commonly enjoyed for summer planting are usually of hybrid origin. They're often grown as permanent groundcovers in waste sites and road sides in subtropical, arid climates. (They are so ubiquitous along roadways in southern California that they're often simply lumped together under the name "highway daisies"!) Most have cylindrical or three-sided, green to blue-green, succulent leaves and trailing stems with numerous small, glistening, daisylike flowers in orange, pink, purple, red, or yellow. Although commonly referred to as ice plants, they get that name more from association with their cousin *Dorotheanthus* than from real merit; their leaves lack the crystalline protuberances that make the latter's leaves sparkle in the sun. Their flowers, though, do have the same satiny glimmer as those of *Dorotheanthus*. They're widely available in southern California, but often difficult to find elsewhere. *Malephora* is similar, although no more widely available. Height: 6 to 18 inches (15 to 45 cm). Spread: Indefinite.

Livingstone daisy
(*Dorotheanthus bellidiformis*)

Larry's Garden Notes

The perennial ice plants (*Lampranthus* spp.) need somewhat different care than the annual Livingstone daisy (*Dorotheanthus bellidiformis*). You *can* grow them from seed started indoors, as explained here, but it's easier to multiply them by cuttings. In nearly frost-free climates (Zones 9 to 11), they survive the winter outdoors. In colder areas, however, they make great summer annuals, often covering quite vast surfaces during their summer outside. Overwinter cuttings of your favorite plants on a bright, sunny windowsill.

Eschscholzia

California poppy

Has there ever been a wildflower seed mixture for sun that didn't include California poppies? It's easy to see why: They bloom so quickly and so spectacularly under such a wide range of conditions that they are practically guaranteed to perform! California poppies aren't true poppies (*Papaver* spp.), but they are nonetheless close relatives. The branching plants produce blue-green stems and equally blue-green, deeply cut, lacy foliage. They form a billowing mound that is attractive in its own right but even more so when dotted with a profusion of golden flowers.

Plant Profile

ESCHSCHOLZIA
esh-HOLT-zee-uh

- **Bloom Color:** Pink, red, orange, yellow, cream, white

- **Bloom Time:** Late spring through early fall; fall through winter in mild climates

- **Height:** 6 to 12 inches (15 to 30 cm)

- **Spread:** 6 to 12 inches (15 to 30 cm)

- **Garden Uses:** Container planting, cut-flower garden, edging, mass planting, meadow garden, mixed border, rock garden; along paths, on slopes

- **Attracts:** Beneficial insects, seed-eating birds

- **Light Preference:** Full sun

- **Soil Preference:** Average to poor, well-drained soil

- **Best Way to Propagate:** Sow seed outdoors in late spring

- **Hardiness:** Frost-sensitive perennial grown as a hardy annual

Growing Tips

You'll occasionally see California poppies for sale in six packs or cell packs, but they react poorly to transplanting, so it is much better to sow them yourself. If you *have* to buy transplants, try cell packs: It is far easier to extract the plants with their rootballs intact.

If you're desperate for color early in the season, you can sow California poppies indoors, in peat pots, 2 to 3 weeks before the last frost. But they're so quick from seed that you'll see results almost as soon by sowing them directly outdoors when the soil has warmed up a bit (or even, where winters aren't too harsh, in late fall). In areas with frost-free winters, you can also sow them in early fall for winter bloom. In all cases, barely cover the seed and water lightly. Look for seedlings in 10 to 14 days.

California poppy seed is so fine you'll almost inevitably sow it too thickly, so thin the plants to about 6 inches (15 cm) apart. Well-spaced plants flower much more abundantly than crowded ones and are less likely to go into decline after their first blooming.

California poppies perform best in poor, even sandy, soil. Good drainage is a must! The plants are extremely heat and drought tolerant, although you can expect to have better bloom if you water them occasionally.

In many climates, and especially hot, humid ones, California poppies tend to die out after their first wave of blooms. To keep them going strong, deadhead them regularly and water during very dry periods. In their native environment, they are short-lived perennials, but only rarely will you see them survive winter anywhere else. That's not a big loss, though: they bloom most profusely their first year anyway.

Good Neighbors

California poppy looks lovely among rocks and will self-sow in the cracks and crevices of a wall or rock garden, or even in a gravel walk or driveway. Any drought-tolerant neighbor will do, but the dissected foliage will add a nice softness to iris foliage, to myrtle euphorbia (*Euphorbia myrsinites*), or to yucca plants.

Problems and Solutions

Root rot and leaf diseases occur occasionally, but you can usually prevent them by avoiding overly moist conditions and increasing air circualtion.

Top Performer

Think Twice: *Eschscholzia californica* (California poppy): The floral emblem of California, this is by far the most common species. It was originally orange or yellow, but the color range has expanded to include cream, white, pink, and red, as well as some lovely salmon and apricot shades. The 2- to 3-inch (5- to 8-cm) flowers can be single, semidouble, or double, and some strains have beautifully fluted petals. All types self-sow, although the hybrid cultivars tend to revert back to golden yellow or orange after a few years. Be forewarned that this plant has escaped from culture many times in arid regions around the world. Where it's not native, don't plant it near wilderness areas where it might escape. Height: 6 to 12 inches (15 to 30 cm). Spread: 6 to 12 inches (15 to 30 cm). **Self-sowing**

More Recommended Eschscholzia

Eschscholzia caespitosa (tufted California poppy): Occasionally you'll see other species of California poppy offered in catalogs; they all require much the same care as *E. californica*. This particular species is about half the size of regular California poppy, and it produces very fine, hairlike leaves. The scented flowers are golden yellow to lemon yellow, depending on the cultivar. Height: 6 inches (15 cm). Spread: 6 inches (15 cm). **Self-sowing**

California poppy
(*Eschscholzia californica*)

Kissing Cousins

The Mexican tulip poppy (*Hunnemannia fumariifolia*) is one of my favorite annuals. Think of it as a California poppy for the middle of the flowerbed and you'd be pretty close. It produces a taller stem and a slightly larger, more cup-shaped flower in golden yellow to yellow. Mexican tulip poppy is a tender perennial (Zone 11), but it blooms the first year, so you can grow it as an annual in colder climates. It self-sows moderately. Height: 2 feet (60 cm). Spread: 8 inches (20 cm). **Self-sowing**

Gazania

Gazania, treasure flower

Gazanias's ground-hugging rosettes aren't especially exciting, but you'll hardly notice them when their glorious daisylike flowers are on display! The base of the ray florets are often marked by a deep black spot with what appears to be a brilliant diamond, sapphire, emerald, or other crystalline jewel in the center. No wonder one of its common names is treasure flower! Take a closer look the next time you're near a gazania and you'll see: It's almost like a sparkling eye staring back at you.

Plant Profile

GAZANIA
gah-ZAY-nee-uh

- ■ **Bloom Color:** Pink, red, orange, bronze, yellow, white

- ■ **Bloom Time:** Late spring through early fall; fall through winter in mild climates

- ■ **Height:** Varies by species; see individual listings

- ■ **Spread:** Varies by species; see individual listings

- ■ **Garden Uses:** Container planting, edging, ground-cover, meadow garden, mixed border, rock garden

- ■ **Attracts:** Butterflies

- ■ **Light Preference:** Full sun

- ■ **Soil Preference:** Light, sandy, well-drained soil

- ■ **Best Way to Propagate:** Sow seed indoors in spring

- ■ **Hardiness:** Frost-sensitive perennial grown as a half-hardy annual

Growing Tips

Gazanias are widely sold in six packs or cell packs and transplant very well, so go ahead and buy plants if you want instant results. Pinch off all flowers and buds before you plant to help the young plants settle in quickly.

If you prefer to sow your own, that's easy, too! Sow indoors 6 to 8 weeks before the last frost date or directly outside when there is no longer any danger of frost. Sow the seed about ⅛ inch (3 mm) deep. Indoors, place the tray with the sown seed in complete darkness at 60° to 65°F (15° to 18°C) for about 7 days, then bring it back to a bright spot. Water the seedlings lightly; they don't like to be wet. Gazanias also don't appreciate cool temperatures, so wait until the soil is thoroughly warmed up (usually about 2 weeks after the last frost date) before setting them outside.

Plant gazanias in your hottest, windiest, most-exposed spot; they'll love it! Any well-drained soil will do fine. Gazanias are highly drought tolerant once established, although they will bloom more abundantly if you water them occasionally. Deadhead if you want to have continuous bloom.

Gazanias are actually perennials and will overwinter in many climates, especially in the drier parts of Zones 8 to 11. In fact, in nearly frost-free climates, they'll bloom heavily in spring and early summer, and then sporadically throughout the rest of the year. In cold winter climates, you can dig up your favorite plants and grow them on a sunny windowsill for winter. If you want to multiply a particular plant, take basal cuttings of nonflowering stems at any season.

Good Neighbors

Try a carpet of gazania as a unique groundcover for a sunny bank. In containers, combine it with a trailing plant such as creeping Jenny (*Lysimachia nummularia*) or edging lobelia (*Lobelia erinus*). Its compact size and drought tolerance make it an ideal choice for a window box.

Problems and Solutions

Crown rot and leaf spots are common in poorly drained soil. Powdery mildew can also be a problem when the air is humid but the soil is dry; a bit of extra watering in late summer will help prevent the disease.

Top Performer

Gazania hybrids (gazania, treasure flower): Almost all gazanias on the market these days are complex hybrids. The array of colors is quite stupendous—yellows, oranges, pinks, bronzes, reds, and whites—often with black and jewel-like markings at the base and stripes of a contrasting color running down the center of each ray floret. The central disk can be yellow to orange to dark brown or purple. The flowers range in size from about 3 inches (8 cm) in diameter for the dwarf, multiflowering types to over 5 inches (13 cm) in some of the full-size hybrids. Normally gazania flowers close in cloudy or rainy weather, but some newer strains stay open all day. The foliage too is quite variable: Some have nearly lance-shaped leaves, while others are lobed along the sides (rather like dandelion leaves). All types have rich silver matting under the leaves, but there are also several strains whose leaves are bright silver both above and below. Height: 6 to 10 inches (15 to 25 cm). Spread: 8 to 10 inches (20 to 25 cm).

More Recommended Gazania

Gazania linearis (hardy gazania): A small species with narrow, linear leaves and orange to yellow, star-shaped flowers. It's proven surprisingly hardy, with some selections coming through Zone 4 winters unscathed. Expect a range of hardy perennial gazanias in a much wider color range if breeders can work that characteristic into the gene pool of the current hybrid lines! Height: 6 inches (15 cm). Spread: 6 inches (15 cm).

Gazania
(*Gazania* hybrid)

Larry's Garden Notes

Black is not a common color in flowers—mainly because it's not a color that attracts pollinating insects—yet the markings on gazania flowers appear to be a true jet black. The secret, though, is that they really aren't black, but ultraviolet. Our eyes can't see ultraviolet and so see black (the absence of color). But insect eyes *do* see ultraviolet, and to them, it is a particularly vibrant color. Those little "black" spots are, therefore, like neon lights to insect eyes, directing pollinators toward the nectar in the center of the flower.

Pennisetum

Fountain grass

The genus *Pennisetum* is best known for cold-hardy grasses, such as hardy fountain grass (*P. alopecuroides*), but it also includes a few frost-tender plants generally grown as annuals. The most obvious characteristics of these grasses are the narrow, arching leaves that sway in the slightest breeze and the foxtail-like flower spikes that arch up well above the foliage, then hang lazily downward. Even more exciting than the green types are the purple-leaved cultivars, by far the most deeply colored of any ornamental grass.

Plant Profile

PENNISETUM
penn-ih-SEE-tum

■ **Bloom Color:** Varies by species; see individual listings

■ **Bloom Time:** Late summer and fall

■ **Height:** Varies by species; see individual listings

■ **Spread:** Varies by species; see individual listings

■ **Garden Uses:** Container planting, cut-flower garden, annual hedge, mass planting, meadow garden, mixed border, specimen plant, screening

■ **Attracts:** Lady beetles, ground beetles, and other beneficial insects

■ **Light Preference:** Full sun

■ **Soil Preference:** Average to fertile, well-drained soil

■ **Best Way to Propagate:** Sow seed indoors in spring, divide in early spring

■ **Hardiness:** Frost-sensitive perennial grown as a half-hardy annual

Growing Tips

Grow all-green forms of fountain grass from seed sown directly outdoors around the last frost date or indoors 6 to 8 weeks earlier. Just barely cover the seed with soil, then water well.

The purple-leaved forms do *not* come true from seed. If you want purple fountain grasses, buy a plant in spring. After that, you can obtain more by division; even young plants quickly form dense clumps. You can also take stem cuttings with at least one node (leaf joint) and root it in moist growing mix.

Fountain grasses like any well-drained soil and full sun. They are slow growing in spring but pick up speed when temperatures warm up. They're extremely drought tolerant but they put on a better show if kept evenly moist.

The two fountain grasses described here are hardy only in Zones 9 through 11. In Zone 8, you can try overwintering them in the ground by mulching abundantly with weed-free straw or some other dry mulch. Elsewhere, dig up a clump, cut it back severely to stimulate new growth, and bring it indoors over winter to a frost-free spot, watering it moderately. Don't expect much in the way of color while the plant is indoors (short days and weaker light will turn even the purple ones green), but it will pick up again once it's back in the garden the following summer.

Think Twice: All tender fountain grasses are extremely invasive in mild winter areas (Zones 9 to 11). They've escaped from cultivation in many areas and are crowding out native vegetation. (In Hawaii, in fact, it is *illegal* to import them.) If you grow them where there is any chance they could escape, be sure to remove the flower spikes as they begin to turn brown. This will prevent any escape because they are clump-forming grasses and spread only through seed.

Good Neighbors
In a mixed border, repeat the dark red of purple-leaved fountain grass with dark-leaved selections of other plants, such as heucheras or coleus. Or plant it in a mass with a large-flowering hibiscus (*Hibiscus moscheutos*), or with drifts of rudbeckia. In a large pot, pair it with sweet potato vines (*Ipomoea batatas*), a couple plants of chartreuse 'Margarita,' and a single 'Blackie' (to echo the dark color); this combination looks super all season long!

Problems and Solutions
Powdery mildew and other foliar diseases can develop if the soil is too moist or if air circulation is lacking in the garden. (See "Annual Diseases" on page 33.) Slugs and snails can also cause problems in poorly drained spots. In conditions more to their liking, fountain grasses are usually trouble free.

Top Performer
Pennisetum setaceum (fountain grass): This tender perennial grass produces narrow, arching leaves and, in late summer, feathery, pendulous, foxtail-like flower spikes about 1 foot (30 cm) long. They are pinkish in color on green-leaved forms and purplish on the purple-leaved types. 'Purpureum' is the classic, 3-foot (90-cm), reddish purple cultivar; plants sold as 'Atropurpureum', 'Rubrum', and 'Cupreum' are apparently the same thing. 'Burgundy Giant' is a taller selection—up to 5 feet (1.5 m)—with even deeper purple leaves. Height: 3 to 5 feet (90 to 150 cm). Spread: 18 to 24 inches (45 to 60 cm).

More Recommended Pennisetum
Pennisetum villosum (feathertop): This smaller grass is especially popular in dried and fresh arrangements, but it's lovely in borders and containers as well. It produces narrow, medium green, arching leaves and cylindrical, feathery, 4- to 5-inch (10- to 13-cm), greenish to white spikes that turn purple as they mature. Height: 2 feet (60 cm). Spread: 2 feet (60 cm).

'Rubrum' fountain grass (*Pennisetum setaceum* 'Rubrum')

Kissing Cousins
Another deep purple grass you might want to try is purple-leaved sugar cane (*Saccharum officinarum* 'Pele's Smoke'). This tall, thick-stalked grass has glossy purple leaves and stems and makes quite a statement in containers. Try it as a vertical accent to the bright blooms of 'Profusion Orange' zinnias—very showy! You'll need to overwinter it indoors in all but the mildest climates. It rarely produces flower spikes outside of tropical climates. Height: 6 feet (180 cm). Spread: 3 feet (90 cm).

Phacelia

California bluebells

I first discovered this North American native in England, at the world-famous Sissinghurst Garden, where it is considered an essential element of the equally famous blue garden. It had such strong azure-blue flowers, I thought it was a gentian or something equally complicated to grow. It wasn't until I got home and did some research that I realized it was an annual. An *annual*—one you can sow directly outdoors. You learn something new every day!

Plant Profile

PHACELIA
fah-SEE-lee-uh

- **Bloom Color:** Blue
- **Bloom Time:** Spring in hot climates, summer elsewhere
- **Height:** Varies by species; see individual listings
- **Spread:** Varies by species; see individual listings
- **Garden Uses:** Container planting, cut-flower garden, edging, meadow garden, mixed border, rock garden
- **Attracts:** Pollinating bees, other beneficial insects
- **Light Preference:** Full sun to partial shade
- **Soil Preference:** Average to poor, well-drained soil
- **Best Way to Propagate:** Sow seed outdoors in early spring or late fall
- **Hardiness:** Half-hardy annual

Growing Tips

Spectacular as it is in bloom, California bluebell will probably never be highly popular. For one thing, it transplants poorly, so you'll never see plants sold, only seed. Its appeal is also limited by its specific needs. If you can't offer it hot days and cool nights, plus very well-drained soil, its blooming period will be reduced to just a few weeks in late spring or early summer. But if you *can* grow it, you won't want to be without it!

In mild winter areas, especially those with hot, humid summers, grow California bluebells as a spring flower. Sow outdoors in late fall and it will sprout with the first warming rays of spring. It's extremely fast growing (from seed to bloom in about 7 weeks) and will provide a carpet of deep blue for about a month and a half. You can then pull it out and plant something else for summer and fall color

In colder climates, sow seed outdoors 2 or 3 weeks before the last frost date, then sow again every 4 weeks for bloom right through the summer. You can also start the seed indoors, in peat pots, 6 to 8 weeks before the last frost. But remember, this plant likes things cool: If you can't provide 50° to 55°F (10° to 13°C) during germination, you're better off sowing it directly outdoors.

California bluebell needs darkness to germinate. Outdoors, make sure you rake lightly so the seed is at least lightly covered; indoors, place it in darkness until sprouts appear (in about 10 days).

FUN FACTS

In its native Southwestern United States, as well as in Mexico, you'll sometimes see fields of cultivated California bluebells grown as a honey plant. (Do stop and take a picture!) If you miss the all-too-brief show, you can at least pick up "bluebell honey," a more durable souvenir.

Thin seedlings to about 2 inches (5 cm) apart; it likes to wind its way through neighboring vegetation, using it as a support.

While the plant is in bloom, you can pretty much ignore it. When the flowering slows down, cut the plant back harshly and water it a bit more. It will often send out new shoots and then bloom again in fall.

Good Neighbors
California bluebells look great weaving their way through sweet alyssum (*Lobularia maritima*) or California poppy (*Eschscholzia californica*). They also make handsome companions for taller drought-tolerant plants, such as sea hollies (*Eryngium* spp.) or medium to large sedums.

Problems and Solutions
Downy and powdery mildew are sometimes a problem. To prevent these diseases, keep the ground a bit moister when dews are heavy. In moister climates, a slug barrier is practically a necessity: Slugs and snails *adore* this plant! (See "Annual Pests" on page 35.)

Top Performer
Phacelia campanularia (California bluebells): This compact, branching, upright to semitrailing annual has sticky, hairy, toothed, dark green leaves. The flowers are to die for: clusters of deep rich blue, bell-shaped, 1-inch (2.5-cm) blooms with pale yellow stamens. The leaves emit a somewhat sweet aroma when crushed, but I don't recommend testing this out: Some people are allergic to the sticky bristles that cover the leaves. Height: 6 to 12 inches (15 to 30 cm). Spread: 4 to 6 inches (10 to 15 cm).

More Recommended Phacelia
Phacelia tanacetifolia (fiddleneck): This is a taller, more upright plant with bristly, narrow-lobed leaves. The branching flowerstalks rise well above the foliage and curl under at the tips, with cup-shaped, ½-inch (1.25-cm), lavender-blue flowers. This species is much easier to grow than *P. campanularia*, and it blooms throughout much of the summer. Height: 18 to 48 inches (45 to 120 cm). Spread: 12 to 18 inches (30 to 45 cm).

California bluebells
(*Phacelia campanularia*)

Larry's Garden Notes

Reading over the stringent requirements of California bluebell, you might imagine you could never grow it. But it's always been my opinion that you can grow anything if you really want to! Experiment with it in different parts of your garden, and you just might find the perfect spot. With my cool, generally rainy summers, I didn't think I'd have a chance, but it turns out it positively thrives in my garden at the top of a slope, in what is practically pure sand. And if *I* can grow it, I'll bet you can too!

Portulaca

Portulaca, moss rose, sun plant

Ask a gardener to name a drought-tolerant annual, and portulaca is likely one of the first plants he or she will think of. The ornamental species are all low-growing, spreading, tender perennials grown as annuals, with thick, succulent leaves and comparatively large, cup-shaped, satiny flowers in a wide range of particularly vibrant colors. True sun-worshipers, portulacas all love hot, dry conditions, but they adapt to average growing conditions as well. Anything but truly soggy soil will do—but do give them sun or their flowers won't even open!

Plant Profile

PORTULACA
por-chew-LACK-uh

- **Bloom Color:** Pink, purple, magenta, salmon, red, orange, yellow, white

- **Bloom Time:** Late spring until frost; year-round in frost-free climates

- **Height:** 4 to 8 inches (10 to 20 cm)

- **Spread:** 6 to 18 inches (15 to 45 cm)

- **Garden Uses:** Container planting, edging, hanging baskets, groundcover, mass planting, rock garden, wall planting; along paths

- **Light Preference:** Full sun

- **Soil Preference:** Average to poor, even sandy, well-drained soil

- **Best Way to Propagate:** Sow seed indoors in spring, outdoors in late spring

- **Hardiness:** Frost-sensitive perennial grown as a half-hardy annual

Growing Tips

Portulacas are widely available in six packs or cell packs, but they often suffer shock at transplanting time. Cutting them back harshly at planting will help them settle in more quickly.

They're also easy to start from seed. In long-season areas, just rake the soil surface lightly and sow the seed outdoors, without covering it, around the last frost date. For faster results in short-season areas, start seed indoors in peat pots 6 to 8 weeks earlier, just pressing the seed into the mix. It germinates readily at room temperature.

Portulacas self-sow reliably, although not to the point of becoming a nuisance. You'll appreciate the way they sow themselves into the same tiny cracks and crevices that true weeds like to work their way into, thus stealing the space from the bad guys. Be aware, though, that hybrid cultivars don't come true, so expect smaller flowers in fewer colors in subsequent years. **Self-sowing** 🖊

Summer care is almost nonexistent. Water at planting time; that's about it. There's no need to deadhead. If the plants get straggly, you can shear them back. And don't fertilize too heavily; that will give you lots of thick, healthy foliage, but few flowers.

It's easy to propagate portulacas by cuttings. They'll bloom all winter long indoors as long as they are in full sun, so you might want to carry any really nice plants over winter as houseplants.

Good Neighbors

Portulacas look great livening up rock crevices or the edges of gravel paths. Scatter the seed around a planting of prickly pear cactus (*Opuntia humifusa*) to complement the cacti's beautiful but extremely short blooming season. Or try it as a living mulch to cover the soil between roses or other shrubs. Low care and low in stature, all portulacas work well in window boxes. For contrast, combine them with equally low-care trailing types of plectranthus (*Plectranthus* spp.).

Problems and Solutions
Damping-off and crown rot can be problems in moist conditions; avoid these diseases by planting in well-drained soil.

Top Performer
Portulaca grandiflora (portulaca, moss rose, sun plant): Popular since the late-nineteenth century, this species produces thick, creeping stems covered with succulent, medium green, cylindrical, pointed leaves—I always think they look like obese pine needles. The satiny, ruffled flowers are about 1 inch (2.5 cm) in diameter and can be single, semidouble, or double. They come in a wide range of strong colors, including magenta, cerise, neon pink, red, yellow, and orange. More recent introductions also include some pastel shades: apricot, soft pink, cream, and white. The flowers of some are even mottled or streaked in other colors. Originally, the flowers closed up around noon, but the blooms of most modern strains stay open right through the afternoon. All species, however, still need sun to start the floral display: They won't open up on cloudy days. Height: 4 to 8 inches (10 to 20 cm). Spread: 6 to 18 inches (15 to 45 cm).

More Recommended Portulaca
Portulaca umbraticola (broad-leaved portulaca): Since the mid-1990s, a mysterious new type of portulaca has been making its way onto the market. This species produces paddle-shaped, plump leaves and brilliant, single, 1- to 1½-inch (2.5- to 4-cm) flowers in magenta, red, pink, lavender, yellow, orange, and bicolors. It's widely available as an annual grown from cuttings, often in hanging baskets, under the name 'Yubi' hybrids. You may see these plants labeled as either *P. grandiflora* or *P. oleracea,* but these names don't match the plant being sold. European growers are, however, offering it as *P. umbraticola:* Could that be it's correct name? Height: 4 to 8 inches (10 to 20 cm). Spread: 1 to 2 feet (30 to 60 cm).

Portulaca
(*Portulaca grandiflora*)

Larry's Garden Notes

Think Twice: Another portulaca, purslane (*Portulaca oleracea*), is sometimes offered for sale in seed catalogs as a summer vegetable. Avoid it at all costs! Purslane is a noxious weed, and it has little ornamental value. Each plant can produce more than *one million* seeds per season, and they can remain viable for more than 20 years, sprouting each time you hoe. If you really want to taste purslane, buy it in a farmer's market or harvest the wild plants. Or try eating some trimmings from your ornamental portulacas: They're just as edible as purslane!

Salvia

Salvia, sage

There are so many salvias that you could easily do an entire garden using nothing else! Here are three of the most popular species, all tender perennials generally grown as annuals. Traits they all share include erect spikes of tubular, two-lipped flowers, leaves that are scalloped or toothed and often scented, and stems that are square in cross-section. You'll find more salvias in "Larry's Last Look: Salvia" on page 124 and yet more in the chapter "Annuals for Cut & Dried Arrangements," on page 242.

Plant Profile

SALVIA
SAL-vee-uh

- **Bloom Color:** Varies by species; see individual listings
- **Bloom Time:** Late spring through fall
- **Height:** Varies by species; see individual listings
- **Spread:** Varies by species; see individual listings
- **Garden Uses:** Container planting, cut-flower garden, edging, mass planting, meadow garden, mixed border
- **Attracts:** Butterflies, hummingbirds
- **Light Preference:** Full sun to partial shade
- **Soil Preference:** Average to humus-rich, well-drained soil
- **Best Way to Propagate:** Sow seed indoors in late winter or spring
- **Hardiness:** Frost-sensitive perennial grown as a half-hardy annual

Growing Tips

Salvia seedlings can be tricky to grow, so consider buying started plants in six packs or cell packs. Wait for the soil to warm up before planting them out; most salvias are very frost sensitive.

If you want to try growing them from seed, start with fresh seed and soak it overnight. Sow indoors 6 to 8 weeks before the last frost date (10 to 12 weeks for mealy-cup sage). Most red-flowered sages need light to germinate, so don't cover their seed; just press it into the growing mix. The other sages are indifferent about light, but the seed is so tiny it's best not to cover them anyway. Water carefully, keeping the mix just slightly moist. In Zones 9 to 11, you can sow salvias outdoors in early spring.

During summer, salvias need little care. Sun or partial shade is fine, as is any well-drained soil.

Of the three common sages, only mealy-cup sage is easy to keep from year to year. It will even overwinter outdoors in Zones 8 to 11. Elsewhere, bring it inside (dig up a plant or take cuttings) and grow it on a bright windowsill.

Good Neighbors

Create a simple but stunning combination of border flowers with a dwarf blue mealy-cup sage (such as *Salvia farinacea* 'Victoria') and 'Profusion Orange' zinnias. Or, if you need more height, try a taller mealy-cup sage (perhaps 'Blue Bedder') with lemon yellow sunflowers or red-orange Mexican sunflower (*Tithonia rotundifolia*). Modest groupings of red-flowered sages spotted among ornamental grasses or silver-leaved plants can make a memorable visual display.

Problems and Solutions

Seedlings are subject to damping-off; keep them barely moist. Good air circulation will help prevent mildew. Slugs are a problem early in the season; mature plants seem to be more resistant. If aphids or whiteflies appear, control them with insecticidal soap.

Top Performer

Salvia farinacea (mealy-cup sage): A bit slower off the mark than the others, this species catches up by midsummer and is often the star of the garden right through into fall. The common name refers to the mealy powder that covers the stems and calyces. The plants form thick clumps of small, narrow leaves and slender, upright stalks of colorful calyces and blossoms: Blue and violet-blue are the main colors, but white is also available. Usually the calyx is the same color as the bloom, but 'Strata' has white calyces and blue flowers. Mealy-cup sage may self-sow somewhat in Zones 8 to 11. Height: 14 to 30 inches (35 to 75 cm). Spread: 1 foot (30 cm). **Self-sowing**

'Victoria' mealy-cup sage
(*Salvia farinacea* 'Victoria')

More Recommended Salvia

Salvia coccinea (Texas sage): The original species had scarlet blooms, but modern hybrids also come in pinks and whites as well as bicolors. The plants have very open spikes, so they create a nice effect when you want just a touch of bright color. This species will self-sow in mild climates. Height: 18 to 36 inches (45 to 90 cm). Spread: 1 foot (30 cm). **Self-sowing**

   S. splendens (scarlet sage, salvia): This once-tall plant has been brought down to size; most modern hybrids measure in at just 1 foot (30 cm) or so. It forms dense clumps of dark green leaves that are topped with thick flower spikes. Originally brilliant red, the flowers now also come in white and shades of pink, orange, lavender, and purple. Pinching them at planting time and regular deadheading will help prolong bloom. This species does better with moist soil and a bit of shade. Height: 10 to 48 inches (25 to 120 cm). Spread: 9 to 14 inches (23 to 35 cm).

Larry's Garden Notes

Salvias make up a varied group, so their culture needs also vary. Mealy-cup sage (*Salvia farinacea*) and Texas sage (*S. coccinea*), for example, are drought resistant and prefer average to poor soil, whereas scarlet sage (*S. splendens*) needs regular watering and does best in rich soil. Scarlet sage and Texas sage tend to die out if not deadheaded; mealy-cup sage keeps on blooming with no care. Even cold tolerance varies; scarlet sage and Texas sage need warm weather, but mealy-cup sage can even come through light frosts unscathed!

LARRY'S LAST LOOK: SALVIA

I warned you there were too many salvias to describe in just a couple of pages, so here is a quick presentation of some of the others. Most are tender perennials grown as annuals, but some can overwinter outdoors in mild winter areas.

COMMON AND BOTANICAL NAMES	LIGHT AND SOIL PREFERENCES	DESCRIPTION
Pineapple sage *Salvia elegans*	Full sun to partial shade Average to rich, well-drained soil	Soft, smooth, pineapple-scented leaves used in cold drinks and fruit salads. Shrubby growth habit. Late-summer and fall bloom in cold climates, winter bloom in mild ones. Loose spikes of bright scarlet, 1-inch (2.5-cm) flowers. Hardy in Zones 8–10. Height: 6 feet (1.8 m) Spread: 3 feet (90 cm)
Autumn sage *S. greggii*	Full sun to partial shade Average to poor, well-drained soil	A short, shrubby species with leathery, crinkled leaves on branching, nearly woody stems. Spikes bear pairs of ¾-inch (2-cm) flowers, each with an extended lip. Blooms from late summer until frost. Needs perfect drainage; tolerates drought. Prefers light shade in hot climates. Prune back occasionally for more compact growth. Hardy in Zones 7–10. Height: 1–2 feet (30–60 cm) Spread: 12–20 inches (30–50 cm)
Blue anise sage *S. guaranitica*	Light shade Average to rich, evenly moist but well-drained soil	Shrublike plant with wrinkled, fuzzy, medium green leaves. Blooms in late summer and fall. Striking 2-inch (5-cm) long flowers in blue, purple, or white, usually with darker purple calyces. Prefers light shade and evenly moist soil. Produces tuberous roots that you can store indoors over winter like a dahlia. Formerly *S. concolor*. Hardy in Zones 7–10. Height: 4–6 feet (1.2–1.8 m) Spread: 4–5 feet (1.2–1.5 m)
'Indigo Spires' sage *S. 'Indigo Spires'*	Full sun Average to rich, well-drained soil	Bushy plant with medium green basal leaves. Produces long, often arching, flower spikes in summer. Blue bracts and deep purple, ½-inch (1.25-cm) long flowers. Hybrid between *S. farinacea* and *S. longispicata*. Hardy in Zones 7–10. Height: 3 feet (90 cm) Spread: 1 foot (30 cm)
Rosyleaf sage *S. involucrata*	Partial to dense shade Average to rich, well-drained soil	Tall, shrubby, little-branched plant with large velvety leaves. Produces dense, 1-foot (30-cm) spikes of purplish pink flowers with rose-pink bracts in late summer and fall. For large gardens and containers. Hardy in Zones 9–10. Height: 5 feet (1.5 m) Spread: 3 feet (90 cm)

COMMON AND BOTANICAL NAMES	LIGHT AND SOIL PREFERENCES	DESCRIPTION
Mexican bush sage *S. leucantha*	Full sun to partial shade Average to rich, well-drained soil	Shrubby plant with hairy, white, arching stems and narrow, gray-green leaves. Dense spikes bear short purple or white flowers nearly hidden by showy purple calyces. Blooms in late summer and fall but attractive all summer. Drought-tolerant. Easy to propagate by cuttings. Hardy in Zones 10–11. Height: 24–40 inches (60–100 cm) Spread: 16–36 inches (40–90 cm
Gentian sage *S. patens*	Full sun to partial shade Average to rich, well-drained soil	Compact plant with long, hairy, medium green leaves. Open, 16-inch (40-cm) spikes of deep blue flowers held in pairs. Blooms from midsummer to fall. 'Cambridge Blue', paler than the species, is a common cultivar. Good drainage is critical. Blooms best in a warm, protected spot. Tubers can be over-wintered indoors. Hardy in Zones 8–10. Height: 18–36 inches (45–90 cm) Spread: 18 inches (45 cm)
Bog sage *S. uliginosa*	Full sun Average to rich, evenly moist to wet soil	One of the rare sages that prefers moist and even soggy soil, but adapts well to the well-drained soil of most gardens. Clumping habit, spreading by rhizomes where hardy. Deeply toothed, narrow, medium green leaves, larger at the base of the plant than the top. Spikes of clear blue flowers in late summer and fall. Hardy in Zones 8–10. Height: 4–6 feet (1.2–1.8 m) Spread: 3 feet (90 cm)

Mexican bush sage
(*Salvia leucantha*)

Gentian sage
(*Salvia patens*)

ANNUALS FOR
Cool Conditions

Some like it hot; others like it cold. You can't please every plant, so if you live in an area where cool temperatures reign, why even try growing annuals like castor bean (*Ricinus communis*) or Madagascar periwinkle (*Catharanthus roseus*)? These heat seekers take forever to get going in cool weather, and they may not mature fast enough to bloom before frost. If you're more likely to be wearing a sweater than a bikini in July, get a jump on gardening success with annuals that thrive in cool conditions—like the plants described here. If you're a warm-climate gardener, don't just skip this chapter: Most of the annuals in this chapter will thrive in the winter months in frost-free climates, so they are great for winter color!

◄Why fight Mother Nature? If you live in a climate where summers are cool, simply choose annuals that enjoy cool conditions, like the clarkias seen here. In hotter climates, these annuals make great choices for winter or early spring bloom.

Cool Comfort

Not everyone has to turn on the air conditioner from May through October. There are plenty of regions in North America where summer days are barely warm and nights can be downright chilly, even in July. The most obvious of these areas are at high altitudes and in the North where, to makes things worse, cool summers often combine with a short growing season. So not only are your summers cool, but they're over practically before they have even begun. Fast-growing, cold-tolerant annuals are an absolute must in this kind of climate. Many coastal regions also have cool summers: Fresh air blowing in off the sea keeps things almost nippy most of the time. San Francisco is a good example of a maritime climate with cool summers; in fact, its summers are usually colder than its winters.

Growing the more typical heat-loving annuals in cool summer areas can be very discouraging. You usually have to start them indoors if you want to get any results at all, then they often just sit there, showing little growth for a few weeks before starting to bloom halfheartedly. And then summer is over. It's enough to make you think annuals just aren't for you!

But that won't be the case if you grow annuals that really like cool conditions. The plants described here all originate from climates with cool growing seasons. Some are summer bloomers in alpine, coastal, or northern regions. Others are from Mediterranean climates like southern Europe, California, Chile, or Australia, where it's too hot and dry in summer for most plants

Cool-loving annuals, like larkspur, shown here with scabiosa, will really enjoy a cooling mulch.

plant can't take heat during part of its life cycle. In hot climates, cool-season annuals typically do well enough early in the season but then tend to die back when things really start to heat up. If that worries you, plant them next to more heat-tolerant annuals that have a somewhat spreading habit, such as begonias, ageratum, and verbenas. They'll happily fill in the gaps when the cool-season plants start to fade.

There are also some other things that warm-climate gardeners can do to give their cool-season annuals the best possible chance. Plant them in partial shade, for instance, rather than in full, direct sun. They are particularly good in spots that get plenty of morning sun but are in the shade when the hot afternoon sun starts to beat down.

Soil temperatures are more critical than air temperatures when it comes to these plants' well-being, so anything you can do to keep the soil cooler will help them to grow and flower better. Just making sure the soil stays slightly moist at all times, for example, brings the temperature down a few degrees because water uses heat to evaporate, and moist soil is thus usually much cooler than dry soil.

Also use an organic mulch to shade the soil and keep the sun off, or else plant densely, so less sun actually reaches the surface of the soil. Heat *and* stagnant air are often a deadly combination, so planting cool-weather annuals in spots that profit from at least some air movement, such as containers, can help, too.

The Whole Gamut of Conditions

Just because certain annuals love things on the chilly side doesn't mean that they all need the same growing conditions. You'll find that some of the annuals described here are best when started indoors, others outside;

to grow; so annuals there switch over and grow during the cooler, moister winter months. In all cases, though, these annuals make great plants for climates where daytime temperatures rarely reach much above 72°F (22°C).

Keeping Them Cool

You can, of course, grow the cool-season annuals described here in warm summer areas, and even in out-and-out hot places. Being cold tolerant does not necessarily mean the that some need deadheading to bloom all season long, whereas others just bloom on and on without any help from you at all. Their degree of frost resistance is also variable. Just because a plant likes things cool doesn't necessarily mean it will tolerate below-freezing temperatures. On the other hand, many plants in this chapter *do* tolerate a bit of frost, and so they can make great annuals for those climates where unseasonable frosts are not unknown.

Of course, their love of cool conditions *does* mean you can get all of the plants in this chapter into the garden early in the season, often a few weeks before the last frost date (unless spring in your area has been abnormally cold). In fact, they *prefer* being planted early: Waiting until the ground is warm will only delay or shorten their flowering season.

Inverting the Seasons
In frost-free (or nearly frost-free) climates, such as those of the Gulf States and southern California, you can replace your fading warm-weather annuals with cool-season plants in late summer or early fall. They'll keep blooming for you right through the fall and winter. When they weaken in their turn as warmer conditions begin to return in the spring, just replace them with more heat-tolerant annuals. Two flowering seasons in just one year? It almost makes me wish I, too, lived in the South!

A Cool Start
Many of the annuals described here prefer cooler germination temperatures than most seeds. Sow as usual, then seal the trays in the refrigerator for a week or so. Sometimes they'll sprout in the fridge, but most often they'll wait until you move them into light before germinating.

Frost Prevention, Summer-Style

In some climates, notably in the North and at higher altitudes, there really is no season where frost can't be a threat. The sad thing is that summer frosts are inevitably very temporary—one or two nights, then things warm up again—but the damage they do to unprotected plants can be permanent. Fortunately, there are a number of tricks you can use to keep your garden from getting blasted by summer frosts.

First, start with cold-tolerant flowers. Several of the annuals described in this chapter and listed below are very frost tolerant. They'll breeze through a frost without losing a bloom.

If frost is announced, there are two things you can do. One is to cover your plants for the night with an old sheet, blanket, tarp, or newspaper held in place with stakes. Or turn on the sprinkler: Plants won't freeze if there is water flowing over their leaves. Frost inevitably hits just before dawn, so set a timer for 4 A.M. Turn off the sprinklers or remove your coverings when the frost has left the air.

17 More Cool-Season Annuals

Besides the plants described in this chapter, there are many other annuals that prefer cool growing conditions. Many of the following do quite well in the heat—but just wait until you have one of those cool "it-can't-be-fall, we-haven't-even-had-a-summer" years and watch them really strut their stuff!

Clarkia

Clarkia, farewell-to-spring

We can thank the Lewis and Clark Expedition for this pretty annual, which they brought back (with hundreds of other species) from the Pacific Coast of North America in the early 1800s. In fact, the genus was named *Clarkia* in honor of William Clark. The genus remained little known outside botanical circles until David Douglas, another plant explorer, reintroduced it in 1823; but that time, it quickly became a staple in cottage and cutting gardens. The genus contains dozens of species of very pretty, long-blooming annuals, but only the few mentioned here are regularly available.

Plant Profile

CLARKIA
KLARK-ee-uh

- **Bloom Color:** Lavender, pink, purple, violet, salmon, red, orange, creamy yellow, white

- **Bloom Time:** Early summer through early fall; fall through winter in mild climates

- **Height:** Varies by species; see individual listings

- **Spread:** 8 to 12 inches (20 to 30 cm)

- **Garden Uses:** Container planting, cut-flower garden, mass planting, meadow garden, mixed border, woodland garden

- **Attracts:** Hummingbirds

- **Light Preference:** Full sun to partial shade

- **Soil Preference:** Average, not overly humus-rich, very well-drained soil

- **Best Way to Propagate:** Sow seed outdoors in fall or late spring

- **Hardiness:** Hardy annual

Growing Tips

It's a shame that clarkias aren't better known: They're a snap to grow, they flower abundantly, and few flowers are more impressive. On the other hand, they don't adapt well to commercial production because they transplant poorly and their stems tend to snap off if mishandled, so they're best for gardeners who start their own annuals from seed. I first tried clarkias as a kid and wouldn't be without them now.

Fast-growing and cold-tolerant, clarkias grow best if you sow them directly in the garden, either in fall or in cold winter areas in early spring. You can also start them indoors, preferably in peat pots, 4 to 6 weeks before the last frost date. Don't cover the seed, though; it needs light to germinate. Look for seedlings to appear in 7 to 14 days at 55° to 70°F (13° to 21°C). After they sprout, try to grow them on the cool side: about 50°F (10°C). Young plants need abundant watering, but they are quite drought tolerant when they reach flowering size. Once they're up and growing, clarkias need no care at all.

Most clarkias have an upright growth habit, but their stems are weak. Therefore, they look best when grown close together so one plant can lean on its neighbor; just sow densely and then thin to 4 to 6 inches apart. Or stick a few twiggy branches into the ground when they are young to use as support later.

Avoid hot, humid conditions if possible; they result in straggly plants and a shortened blooming period. (Planting in partial shade and mulching well can help clarkias cope with the heat.) They're fairly frost tolerant once established, although a really hard frost can cut them back considerably.

Good Neighbors

Clarkia's willowy, upright habit works well among broad-leaved perennials or low-growing shrubs. Sow seed directly among later-flowering perennials, such as purple coneflower (*Echinacea purpurea*). In bloom, clarkias mingle well with low-growing campanulas and dark-leaved heucheras.

Problems and Solutions

Leaf diseases such as downy mildew and leaf spot are occasionally a problem in hot climates. Keeping the roots cool and moist will help prevent any problems.

Top Performer

Clarkia unguiculata (clarkia, farewell-to-spring, garland flower): Also known as *C. elegans*. Frilly, crepelike flowers are the main characteristic of this beautiful annual. It comes in both single and double forms, but the doubles are far more popular. The upright, reddish to pink stems bear lance-shaped to elliptic leaves. The flowers appear at leaf axils from the top to the bottom of the wiry stems. Height: 1 to 3 feet (30 to 90 cm). Spread: 8 to 12 inches (20 to 30 cm). **Self-sowing**

Clarkia
(*Clarkia unguiculata*)

More Recommended Clarkia

Clarkia concinna (red ribbons): Also called *Eucharidium concinnum*. This very pretty, although much less common, clarkia has much thinner petals than *C. unguiculata* that split into three lobes at the tip, giving the petals a ribbonlike appearance. It comes in shades of red, pink, and white and is one of the few clarkias that really does well in hot, dry conditions. Seed sold under this name sometimes turns out to be *C. pulchella*. Pink ribbons (*C. brewerii*) is very similar but with rose pink flowers. Height: 1 foot (30 cm). Spread: 1 foot (30 cm). **Self-sowing**

   C. pulchella (pretty clarkia): This attractive clarkia has petals that are narrow at the base, like *C. concinna,* and spread out at the tip into a ruffled wing, like *C. unguiculata*. Most cultivars sold are semidoubles and come in shades of red, pink, and white. Height: 12 to 16 inches (30 to 40 cm). Spread: 8 to 12 inches (20 to 30 cm). **Self-sowing**

Kissing Cousins

Godetia, or satin flower, is now a clarkia (*Clarkia amoena*), but it was known so long under the name *Godetia amoena* or *G. grandiflora* that I think of it as a separate plant. Besides, the flat, open, only slightly fluted flowers are very different from the ruffled flowers of the other clarkias. The 2- to 4-inch (5- to 10-cm), pink, red, or white flowers are often outlined in a contrasting color and have a silky texture. Height: 9 to 30 inches (23 to 75 cm). Spread: 6 to 12 inches (15 to 30 cm). Self-sowing

Consolida

Larkspur, annual delphinium

If you think delphiniums are charming to look at but a pain to grow, you should take a look at this annual! Larkspur is so closely related to the delphinium that it was once classified in the same genus (*Delphinium*). Both plants produce upright flower spikes in just about the same range of shades; larkspur, however, is pretty much resistant to diseases and insects and requires only minimal staking, if any. And better yet, if deadheaded, it will bloom throughout the summer. A classic of old-fashioned gardens, larkspurs are well worth a try in today's gardens, too.

Plant Profile

CONSOLIDA
con-SAH-lih-duh

- **Bloom Color:** Blue, pink, purple, violet, red, white
- **Bloom Time:** Late spring to late summer; fall through winter in mild climates
- **Height:** 1 to 4 feet (30 to 120 cm)
- **Spread:** 9 to 12 inches (23 to 30 cm)
- **Garden Uses:** Cut-flower garden, mass planting, meadow garden, mixed border, screening
- **Attracts:** Butterflies, hummingbirds
- **Light Preference:** Full sun to partial shade
- **Soil Preference:** Fertile, light, well-drained soil
- **Best Way to Propagate:** Sow seed outdoors in fall or late spring
- **Hardiness:** Hardy annual

Growing Tips

Larkspurs are among the easiest annuals to grow. Sow the seed directly outdoors, in fall or very early spring for spring bloom or in early fall for winter bloom (in climates where frost is rare). Just rake the seed in lightly and add water; it'll sprout even if the ground is still cold. And as long as you let a few plants produce seed, larkspurs will self-sow readily. In future years, you'll simply have to remove any surplus plants!

If you insist, you can try starting larkspurs indoors. Sow them in peat pots (they *hate* transplanting) about 8 weeks before the last frost, barely covering the seed; then place the container in the refrigerator for 2 weeks. Next, cover the container (the seed needs darkness to germinate) and supply it with cold conditions: 50° to 55°F (10° to 13°C). After germination, in 2 to 3 weeks, continue to grow the plants under the coolest conditions possible. I think you'll agree that sowing directly outdoors is by far the easiest way to go!

There are two ways of growing larkspurs. For cut-flower use or mass plantings, thin the plants from 6 to 9 inches (15 to 23 cm) apart. This will give you shorter plants but more flower-stalks and thicker foliage. For tall, delphinium-like spires, choose naturally taller cultivars and plant them 12 to 18 inches (30 to 45 cm) apart so they will have enough room to grow.

FUN FACTS

Larkspur seeds are highly toxic but, like many poisonous plants, have had medical uses in the past. The name *Consolida* ("to consolidate or thicken") is said to be derived from the plant's use in favoring healing and stopping bleeding. Modern herbalists, though, have banished this pretty but dangerous remedy from their shelves.

Dwarf and multistemmed larkspurs are usually self-supporting, but the taller ones may need some staking. Simply insert twiggy branches in the seedling larkspur patch.

Larkspurs have the reputation of dying out in midsummer under hot conditions. In a cool summer climate, though, you can keep them in bloom right through the summer. Just deadhead regularly, cutting off each spike as it nears the end of its blooming season, and the plant will obligingly produce more. Frost is not a problem with larkspurs: They sail right through even moderate frosts without losing a petal.

Good Neighbors

The cool blues and purples of larkspur can form nice associations with other tall annuals, such as pale yellow *Chrysanthemum coronarium*. In warm climates, planting it with cosmos, flowering tobacco (*Nicotiana sylvestris*), and other longer-lasting flowers will prevent the holes that can occur when the larkspur succumbs to summer's heat.

Problems and Solutions

Larkspurs are rarely seriously troubled by insects or diseases, although a light dusting of powdery mildew is possible toward the end of the season. Slugs and snails may cause some damage early in the season, but the plants usually recover.

Top Performer

Consolida ajacis (common larkspur): This is the best-known larkspur to gardeners and comes in the full range of colors, from blues and purples to pinks and white. The leaves are extremely deeply cut, giving them a very feathery appearance. There are lots of different strains, ranging from dwarf types only 1 to 2 feet (30 to 60 cm) in height to the traditional background larkspurs that can reach 3 to 4 feet (90 to 120 cm) tall. They come in either branching or upright forms, with dense or open spikes of single to double-spurred flowers that are 1½ inches (4 cm) in diameter. In catalogs and internet sources, you may find larkspur seed sold under a wide range of botanical names other than *C. ajacis,* including *C. ambigua, Delphinium ajacis,* and *D. consolida.* **Self-sowing**

Common larkspur
(*Consolida ajacis*)

Kissing Cousins

Most people think of delphiniums as perennials, but some species of these larkspur relatives can (and probably should) be grown as annuals. The Chinese or bouquet delphinium (*Delphinium grandiflorum*) is one such plant: a bushy, short-lived perennial with blue or white flowers that tends to die out after its first season of bloom. The scarlet-flowered red delphinium (*D. nudicaule*) is similar in dimensions (and in its short-lived nature) to the Chinese delphinium. Height: 8 to 20 inches (20 to 50 cm). Spread: 9 to 12 inches (23 to 30 cm).

Cynoglossum
Chinese forget-me-not, hound's tongue

If you like forget-me-nots (*Myosotis* spp.) but wish they'd bloom longer, you'll probably be thrilled by their Chinese cousin. It produces a rounded mound of a plant that's covered with blue flowers right through summer and well into fall. The flowers are tiny but numerous and, unlike the paler-centered true forget-me-nots, are blue through and through. The flowerstalks have a curious habit: They are rolled up like a scorpion's tail at first, then unravel as the buds mature until, at the end of summer, they have entirely straightened out.

Plant Profile

CYNOGLOSSUM
sigh-no-GLOSS-um

- **Bloom Color:** Blue, pink, white

- **Bloom Time:** Summer to frost; fall through winter in mild climates

- **Height:** 1 to 2 feet (30 to 60 cm)

- **Spread:** 1 foot (30 cm)

- **Garden Uses:** Container planting, cut-flower garden, edging, groundcover, mass planting, meadow garden, mixed border, rock garden, woodland garden

- **Light Preference:** Full sun to partial shade

- **Soil Preference:** Average to poor, evenly moist but well-drained soil

- **Best Way to Propagate:** Sow seed outdoors in fall or late spring

- **Hardiness:** Half-hardy biennial grown as a hardy annual

Growing Tips

The Chinese forget-me-not can't seem to decide if it is a biennial or an annual. If you sow it early enough in fall, it will germinate and start to grow, then overwinter (in Zone 5 and south) as a young plant to bloom the following spring. If you sow it later in fall, when the ground is already cold, or early in spring, it will act as an annual, sprouting quickly in spring to begin blooming by early summer. And, of course, in warm winter climates, it will bloom all winter from a fall sowing. Just make sure you cover the seed by scratching it in to a depth of about ¼ inch (6 mm), as it needs darkness to germinate. If you really want to, you can start Chinese forget-me-nots indoors, although you don't really gain much in terms of flowering. Just sow the seed indoors 6 to 8 weeks before the last frost. It germinates in 5 to 10 days at room temperature or cooler.

While it's easy to get this annual started, the plants need proper placement to thrive after that. They bloom best in poor soil, or at least soil that is not overly fertilized. Unlike some plants in this chapter, Chinese forget-me-not *will* grow in hot summer areas, although it does prefer cooler conditions. Just make sure to mulch it and keep its soil slightly moist at all times; planting in partial shade also helps. Where summers are cool,

FUN FACTS

The tongue-shaped, rough-textured, grayish green leaves of the Chinese forget-me-not are said to be the reason it was called *Cynoglossum*, which means "hound's tongue." Now, I beg to differ with the botanists who named it: I have both a dog and a cat, and I can assure you the scratchy leaves are *much* closer in texture to that of a cat than of a dog. Maybe we should change the name to *Felixoglossum*?

no such precautions are needed; it will do fine in full sun and is quite drought tolerant once established. It is likewise tolerant of light frosts and is killed back only when really hard fall frosts hit.

Chinese forget-me-not is very much a low-maintenance plant. It needs no pinching, no pruning, no fertilizing, and essentially no deadheading. As with many easy-to-grow annuals, it self-sows abundantly, but it's easy to remove the seedlings if they become too invasive. Its self-sowing habit makes it a great plant for cottage gardens, flower meadows, and semiwild areas; but it is likewise a great, although an often underused, border plant.

One of the great mysteries with this plant is why it is not offered for sale more often in six packs or cell packs: It transplants well and certainly requires little effort on the part of the nurseries. In most areas, though, you'll have a hard time finding it in anything other than seed packets.

'Blue Showers' Chinese forget-me-not (*Cynoglossum amabile* 'Blue Showers')

Good Neighbors

Chinese forget-me-not's combination of blue flowers with grayish green foliage blends well with multicolored flowers. For an early spring display in Zones 6 to 10, sow in early fall alongside pansies. Calendula (*Calendula officinalis*), nasturtium (*Tropaeolum majus*), and painted tongue (*Salpiglossis sinuata*) also make lovely companions.

Problems and Solutions

Chinese forget-me-not is rarely bothered by insects or disease, although downy and powdery mildew can occur late in the season, and root rot is possible in overly moist soil.

Top Performer

Cynoglossum amabile (Chinese forget-me-not): Although the genus *Cynoglossum* includes more than 50 different species of annuals, biennials, and short-lived annuals, only this one is currently cultivated. It is a dense, bushy plant with gray-green leaves that produces numerous flowerstalks. There are several cultivars, varying mostly in height and flower color: Blue is the usual color, but pink- and white-flowered cultivars also exist. **Self-sowing** 🥾

Kissing Cousins

🛈 Think Twice: *Anchusa capensis*, much better known as bugloss or summer forget-me-not, has sky blue flowers with a white throat, just like the spring-blooming, true forget-me-nots (*Myosotis* spp.). Pink- and white-flowered cultivars also exist. Start it as you would Chinese forget-me-not, but cut it back by half after the first flush of bloom to ensure repeat blooming. Be aware, though, that this plant can self-sow to the point of invasiveness. Height: 6 to 18 inches (15 to 45 cm). Spread: 6 to 9 inches (15 to 23 cm). Self-sowing 🥾

Diascia

Twinspur

Truly a new kid on the block, this South African plant has risen from horticultural oblivion to near stardom in only a few years, mainly due to its great performance in containers. A rather small plant with creeping leafy stems, it is topped off with upright to arching flowerstalks bearing trumpet-shaped flowers. They bear two downward-pointing spurs, as indicated by the name twinspur. And on closer inspection, the spurs are equipped with bright yellow, translucent "windows." Once you've taken a close look, this is one flower you'll never mistake for any other!

Plant Profile

DIASCIA
dye-AH-see-uh

■ **Bloom Color:** Pink, salmon, rose

■ **Bloom Time:** Late spring through early fall; fall through winter in mild climates

■ **Height:** 6 to 12 inches (15 to 30 cm)

■ **Spread:** 20 to 24 inches (50 to 60 cm)

■ **Garden Uses:** Container planting, cut-flower garden, edging, groundcover, hanging baskets, mass planting, mixed border, rock garden

■ **Attracts:** Butterflies, hummingbirds

■ **Light Preference:** Full sun to partial shade

■ **Soil Preference:** Fertile, moist but well-drained soil

■ **Best Way to Propagate:** Sow seed indoors in late winter or spring; take stem cuttings anytime

■ **Hardiness:** Frost-sensitive perennial grown as a half-hardy annual

Growing Tips

The twinspurs usually sold in nurseries are cutting-grown transplants. Because they are expensive compared to seed-grown annuals, it is worthwhile trying to maintain your plants from year to year or even to multiply them. You can bring whole plants indoors for winter, overwintering them in a bright sunny spot, or bring in cuttings (they root readily in moist growing mix).

Twinspur seed is expensive and hard to find. That's because the only insect that can pollinate twinspur is found nowhere in the world but South Africa. Plants grown elsewhere, therefore, simply don't produce seed unless carefully hand-pollinated. If you can obtain seed, though, it is easy enough to grow. Sow indoors 6 to 8 weeks before the last frost or directly outdoors in spring a few weeks before the last frost, just covering the seed. They germinate in 2 to 4 weeks. Pinch the plants when they are about 3 inches (8 cm) tall to help stimulate branching.

One of the least heat resistant of all the plants in this chapter, twinspur often blooms well in early spring, then stops blooming entirely until cooler temperatures arrive in fall. Thus, in hot summer areas, do your best to keep it cool: Give it afternoon shade, mulch well, and keep the soil evenly moist. Also, cutting it back

FUN FACTS

The long, downward-pointing spurs of the twinspur serve as a nectar source for a very strange bee. It has extra-long forearms so it can reach down into the spurs to get at the nectar. The spur even has a translucent window to show the bee where to look! In positioning itself to reach the nectar, the bee accidentally picks up the flower's pollen and transports it to other flowers, thus ensuring the plant's reproduction.

harshly after one flush of bloom may help stimulate another. Despite all these efforts, twinspurs often refuse to perform well in hot summer climates. In cool summer climates, though, it will bloom for months! When it does start to slow down, prune it back by one-third and it will bloom again.

Twinspur is actually a perennial in areas where winter cold isn't too severe: Zones 8 to 10. Occasionally, it will come through winter unscathed in much colder climates, but I'd recommend keeping at least a cutting going indoors, just in case. Remember, too, that container-grown plants are more sensitive to cold than those grown in the ground and less likely to come through winter, even in Zone 9.

Twinspur
(*Diascia barberae*)

Good Neighbors

Enjoy twinspur in front of the blue spikes of mealy-cup sage (*Salvia farinacea*) or as a color accent against a silver planting of artemisia or lamb's-ears (*Stachys byzantina*). It's an excellent choice for containers, too: licorice plant (*Helichrysum petiolare*) and marguerites (*Argyranthemum* spp.) are just two great partners.

Problems and Solutions

Slugs and snails can cause some damage to plants grown in the ground (see page 35 for control suggestions).

Top Performer

Diascia barberae (twinspur): These low, mat-forming plants have small, shiny, narrow, heart-shaped leaves. Loose, open spires of ½- to ¾-inch (1.25- to 2-cm), pink, rose, or salmon flowers rise well above the foliage from summer to fall. Height: 6 to 10 inches (15 to 25 cm). Spread: 20 to 24 inches (50 to 60 cm).

More Recommended Diascia

Diascia rigescens (rigid twinspur): This is a slightly taller species with similar but more deeply toothed leaves, a more erect habit, and a denser flowerstalk. The flowers are pink to deep pink and have curved spurs. It is probably the hardiest of the twinspurs. Height: 10 to 12 inches (25 to 30 cm). Spread: 20 to 24 inches (50 to 60 cm).

Kissing Cousins

Related to twinspur but from a South American branch of the family, *Angelonia angustifolia* has been catching on as an outdoor plant, especially for containers and baskets. It produces upright, hairless stems with lance-shaped leaves and spikes of two-lipped, cupped flowers in shades of purple, blue, white, and bicolors. Unlike its cousin, it prefers hot summers, but keep it moist at all times. This frost-sensitive perennial is not hardy outside Zones 9 to 11. Height: 1 to 2 feet (30 to 60 cm). Spread: 12 to 18 inches (30 to 45 cm).

Gerbera

Transvaal daisy, Barberton daisy

Probably the most spectacular of all the daisies, Transvaal daisy produces huge, brilliantly colored, daisylike flower heads from 3 to 6 inches (8 to 15 cm) in diameter with yellow or dark centers. The slender ray flowers surrounding the center come in a wide range of colors, and there are single, double, and "duplex" strains (the latter have an extra row of ray flowers). The flower heads are borne individually on sturdy stalks over a large, ground-hugging rosette of spreading, mid-green, deeply lobed leaves that are woolly underneath: They look vaguely like giant dandelion leaves.

Plant Profile

GERBERA
GER-ber-uh

- **Bloom Color:** Pink, red, orange, yellow, cream
- **Bloom Time:** Early to late summer; fall through winter in mild climates
- **Height:** 10 to 18 inches (25 to 45 cm)
- **Spread:** 1 to 2 feet (30 to 60 cm)
- **Garden Uses:** Container planting, cut-flower garden, mass planting, mixed border
- **Attracts:** Butterflies
- **Light Preference:** Full sun to partial shade to deep shade
- **Soil Preference:** Average to humus-rich, evenly moist but well-drained soil
- **Best Way to Propagate:** Sow seed indoors in late winter or divide in spring
- **Hardiness:** Frost-sensitive perennial grown as a tender annual

Growing Tips

The Transvaal daisy is rapidly building a triple career for itself: as a potted gift plant for indoors, as a commercial cut flower, and now as a bedding plant for outdoor use. It's perennial in warmer parts of the country (Zones 8 to 10); elsewhere, use it as an annual.

Transvaal daisies are occasionally available in six packs or cell packs but are found more often in individual pots. Due to the cost of buying plants individually, you might want to try to grow Transvaal daisy from seed. (Seed is expensive as well but still much less costly than the plants.) Remember that double-flowered strains don't come entirely true from seed, though: Expect about 40 percent to have single blooms. Sow fresh seed indoors 12 to 18 weeks ahead of the planting-out season. The Transvaal daisy dislikes root disturbance, so it's best to sow the seed in peat pots. Simply press the seed into the growing mix; it needs light to germinate. It will sprout in 15 to 30 days at 70° to 75°F (21° to 24°C).

Plant Transvaal daisy outdoors when the weather has warmed up and all danger of frost has passed. Full sun is ideal in cool summer areas, but provide protection from the afternoon sun in hot climates. Choose a site that has excellent drainage and set the plants with their crowns at least ½ inch (1.25 cm) above the soil surface. It is often best to sink a potted Transvaal daisy into the garden or into a larger

FUN FACTS

To use Transvaal daisies as cut flowers, wait until the flowers are fully open but the centers are still tight. After harvesting, cut a slit into the base of each stem before plunging them into tepid water: This will help the flowers absorb more water. Cut flowers will last for 1 week or more.

container without removing it from its pot; that makes it easy to bring indoors later. A mulch of pebbles will help keep the soil cool while ensuring perfect aeration around the plant's delicate crown.

During the growing season, keep the soil at least slightly moist at all times and fertilize regularly with a liquid organic fertilizer. Cut off faded leaves and flowers as needed. When fall comes, you can bring container-grown plants indoors; give them a cool spot—45° to 50°F (7° to 10°C)—in full sun and keep them just barely moist.

Where winters are mild, you can plant Transvaal daisies directly in the garden and grow them as perennials. They'll flower year-round (though most heavily in spring and fall) in hot summer areas, and right through the summer in cooler ones. In areas of marginal hardiness (the colder parts of Zone 8), mulch them well with pine needles, hay, or some other light, well-aerated material during the coldest part of winter.

Transvaal daisy
(*Gerbera jamesonii*)

Good Neighbors

Outstanding container plants, Transvaal daisies contrast well with delicate-looking partners such as twinspurs (*Diascia* spp.), sweet alyssum (*Lobularia maritima*), and lotus vine (*Lotus berthelotii*).

Problems and Solutions

In poorly drained soil, especially, diseases such as root or crown rot, gray mold, and powdery mildew can be problems. Providing a site with full sun and perfectly well-drained soil and keeping the soil slightly moist will help prevent diseases. Leafminers can chew winding tunnels in leaves; remove and destroy infested foliage.

Top Performer

Gerbera jamesonii (Transvaal daisy, Barberton daisy): There are some 40 different species of *Gerbera* but only this one, originally from South Africa, is at all commonly grown. It is available in a wide range of cultivars, from the dwarf, small-leaved strains designed for pot use to the large, upright kinds ideal for cut flowers, flowerbeds, and larger containers.

Larry's Garden Notes

Most people think of Africa as being either hot and dry or hot and humid and, therefore, assume that plants coming from that continent are going to like hot conditions. But not all of Africa is hot: Much of South Africa has distinct seasons, and its winter temperatures can drop close to the freezing point. Since the cold season corresponds to the rainiest season of the year and thus to the growing season, many South African plants—including Transvaal daisies and twinspurs (*Diascia* spp.)—actually bloom best when grown under cool conditions.

Lupinus

Lupine

The very existence of annual lupines has to be one of the best-kept secrets of modern horticulture. The perennial 'Russell' lupines get all the attention, even though the annual types are just as attractive and, in many ways, easier to grow. Even better, the annuals are seldom troubled by the aphids and leaf diseases that attack their perennial cousins. They come in a wide range of colors and appear in more and more seed catalogs each year. Let's hope they soon reach the level of popularity they deserve!

Plant Profile

LUPINUS
lu-PIE-nus

- **Bloom Color:** Varies by species; see individual listings

- **Bloom Time:** Summer

- **Height:** Varies by species; see individual listings

- **Spread:** Varies by species; see individual listings

- **Garden Uses:** Cut-flower garden, mass planting, meadow garden, mixed border

- **Attracts:** Hummingbirds

- **Light Preference:** Full sun

- **Soil Preference:** Average, well-drained soil

- **Best Way to Propagate:** Sow seed outdoors in spring

- **Hardiness:** Hardy annual

Growing Tips

Annual lupines are best adapted to cool, moist climates and simply will not grow well under hot, humid conditions. Where summer heat is a problem, sow them in fall or very early in spring, while the ground is still cool; they grow quickly and bloom well before torrid temperatures arrive. Or you can start them indoors 6 to 8 weeks earlier in peat pots (they resent root disturbance) to gain a good head start on the season. Of course, the arrival of hot weather will likely cut off their flowering, but they still bloom over a much longer period of time than the perennial lupines. In hot climates, simply cut annual lupines back when they start to falter.

In cool climates, most annual lupines start to bloom in summer and continue right through to fall. Sow them directly outdoors in fall or spring, nicking the hard seed beforehand or soaking it in tepid water for 24 hours before planting. There is little advantage to starting it indoors. Sow the seed about ⅛ inch (3 mm) deep. It starts to germinate in 2 to 3 weeks.

Lupines are legumes and as such live in symbiosis with bacteria that are capable of extracting nitrogen from the air and converting it into a form the plants can use. That means lupines will do wonderfully even in nitrogen-poor soil. In fact, the colonies of bacteria that lupines need for healthy growth will build up much more readily if you *don't* fertilize them. Ordinary garden soil is, therefore, perfectly suitable for lupines—and they'll actually improve the soil for future plants.

All annual lupines self-sow quite readily, but they rarely spread to the point of becoming invasive.

Good Neighbors

Lupines' upright spikes contrast handsomely with mound-forming companion plants, such as lady's-mantle (*Alchemilla mollis*) and bloody cranesbill (*Geranium sanguineum*). They also look great planted in clumps among shrubs.

Problems and Solutions

Pests and diseases are rarely serious, although rust and powdery mildew can appear toward the end of the flowering season if you plant annual lupines in the same spot year after year.

Top Performer

Lupinus hartwegii (Hartweg's lupine): This Mexican species is the most widely available of the annual lupines. It comes in a range of colors from the original blue to pinks and whites, all highlighted by secondary colors. It forms a branching plant with hairy, mid-green leaves and dense, upright, 8-inch (20-cm) flower spikes from summer through fall. Height: 18 to 36 inches (45 to 90 cm). Spread: 18 to 30 inches (45 to 75 cm). **Self-sowing**

'Giant King' Hartweg's lupine
(*Lupinus hartwegii* 'Giant King')

More Recommended Lupinus

Lupinus luteus (yellow lupine): This is a shorter species but otherwise quite similar in form and habit to Hartweg's lupine. It bears delightfully scented, golden yellow flowers on 10-inch (25-cm) spikes. Height: 18 to 24 inches (45 to 60 cm). Spread: 1 foot (30 cm). **Self-sowing**

   L. nanus (dwarf lupine): Despite its name, this plant is not all that much smaller than the others. It produces 8-inch (20-cm) spikes of blue, pink, lavender, white, or bicolored flowers in summer. Height: 20 inches (50 cm). Spread: 9 inches (23 cm). **Self-sowing**

   L. texensis (Texas bluebonnet): This lupine is a smaller plant with much more compact flower spikes—to about 3 inches (8 cm) long. The flowers come in a range of shades of blue to purple, usually with attractive white markings. Texas bluebonnet is a beautiful native plant, but it is one of the more difficult annual lupines to grow in the home garden, needing perfect drainage, cool weather, and full sun to thrive. Height: 10 to 12 inches (25 to 30 cm). Spread: 9 inches (23 cm). **Self-sowing**

Smart Substitutes

For a lupinelike flower in shadier conditions, consider Chinese houses (*Collinsia bicolor*, also called *C. heterophylla*). Although not related to true lupines, the whorled flower spikes and bicolored flowers have a lupinelike appearance, at least from a distance. The flowers have a two-lobed, white upper lip, while the three-lobed lower lip is usually rose-purple but sometimes pink, purple, or white. Sow directly outdoors in fall or early spring. Height: 2 feet (60 cm). Spread: 12 to 18 inches (30 to 45 cm).

Nemesia

Nemesia

This intriguing annual looks a bit like an edging lobelia (*Lobelia erinus*) but with larger flowers in a much wider range of colors. It forms a low, mounding plant of narrow green leaves that are usually hidden by masses of somewhat orchidlike flowers. They have a curious, tubular shape, with a hidden spur at the back and two lips of often contrasting color: a fan-shaped upper one with four lobes and a much larger lower one, often incised in the middle. The effect of nemesia in bloom is out-and-out spectacular, as long as you can provide it with the cooler temperatures it needs.

Plant Profile

NEMESIA
neh-MEE-see-uh

- ■ Bloom Color: Varies by species; see individual listings
- ■ Bloom Time: Late spring through early fall; fall through winter in mild climates
- ■ Height: Varies by species; see individual listings
- ■ Spread: Varies by species; see individual listings
- ■ Garden Uses: Container planting, edging, hanging baskets, groundcover, mass planting, mixed border, rock garden, woodland garden, wall planting
- ■ Light Preference: Full sun to partial shade
- ■ Soil Preference: Humus-rich, evenly moist but well-drained soil
- ■ Best Way to Propagate: Sow seed indoors in spring
- ■ Hardiness: Frost-sensitive perennial or tender annual

Growing Tips

"Cool" is the key word here because this South African plant really does need chilly nights to do well. Grow it for late spring and early summer bloom in hot climates, or for summer-long bloom in cool ones; either way, it's a winner!

In most climates, it's best to start nemesia indoors. It will need the biggest boost in hot summer climates: Start it indoors 8 to 10 weeks before the last frost date so you can get it blooming outdoors early, while the air is still cool. In cooler climates, there is less of a rush: A 4- to 6-week head start is just fine. Of course, in regions with very long, cool summers, you can also sow it outdoors. And it makes a great winter annual in climates where frost is absent.

You should have no trouble finding six packs or cell packs of plants at the appropriate planting time. Just try not to buy them at too advanced a stage because mature plants tend to recover poorly from transplanting. Ideally, they should have lots of buds but only a few open flowers. Otherwise, sow the seed in vermiculite, watering only from below to help prevent damping-off. It germinates in 5 to 21 days at 55° to 70°F (13° to 21°C). When the seedlings have four true leaves, prick out and repot into trays or flats. Pinch them when they are about 2 inches (5 cm) tall to stimulate a bushier habit; then just let them grow!

Full sun is ideal, but you'll have to compromise in warm climates if you want the show to go on for the longest possible time. Partial shade is a must there, as is mulching and careful watering to make sure the soil remains evenly moist. In cool summer areas, nemesias are much less fussy, but they still prefer evenly moist soil. When the plants start blooming less, chop them back by one-third, and (in cooler climates, at least) they will be back in bloom in no time. Nemesias have a tendancy to flop, so plant them densely, spacing them from 4 to 6 inches (10 to 15 cm) apart.

Good Neighbors

Planted at border's edge, nemesia can act as a placeholder for more heat-tolerant annuals such as sweet alyssum (*Lobularia maritima*) and moss rose (*Portulaca grandiflora*), which will take over when nemesia's short flowering season ends. In cool summer areas, of course, nemesia can hold its own as a border plant right though the summer months.

Problems and Solutions

Overly enthusiastic watering can result in root or stem rot. Try to keep the soil evenly moist but don't let it become soggy. Nemesia needs good drainage.

'Blue Gem' nemesia
(*Nemesia strumosa* 'Blue Gem')

Top Performer

Nemesia strumosa (nemesia): The most common species, it's a true annual and will self-sow somewhat in cooler climates. It produces flowers in an extremely wide range of colors—in fact, just about every shade but green. Many cultivars have starkly contrasting differences between the upper and lower lobes: the self-descriptive 'Mello Red & White' is one, while 'KLM', featuring the blue and white colors of that famous airline, is another. Recent years have seen flower size double from ½ inch (1.25 cm) to 1 inch (2.5 cm). Height: 7 to 12 inches (18 to 30 cm). Spread: 4 to 6 inches (10 to 15 cm).
Self-sowing 🖊

More Recommended Nemesia

Nemesia caerulea (nemesia): Also called *N. foetens* and *N. fruticans*. This is a perennial species (Zones 9 and 10) in its native South Africa, and you can easily keep it from year to year by taking cuttings. It bears small flowers, no more than ½ inch (1.25 cm) in diameter, in shades of purple, blue, pink, and white. Height: 1 to 2 feet (30 to 60 cm). Spread: 1 foot (30 cm).

Kissing Cousins

Nemesia's relatives, the slipper flowers (*Calceolaria* spp.)—also called pocketbook flowers—are renowned for their pouchlike flowers. *C.* 'Herbeohybrida Group', a hybrid plant, is often sold as a flowering houseplant, and *C. integrifolia* (syn. *C. rugosa*), is a tender perennial grown as an annual (and classified as *C.* 'Fruticohybrida Group' by some botanists). The 'Herbeohybrida Group' comes in yellow, orange, red, and bicolors; *C. integrifolia* has yellow flowers. Grow as for *Nemesia* but start indoors about 3 months before the last frost. Height: 12 to 18 inches (30 to 45 cm). Spread: 12 to 18 inches (30 to 45 cm).

Nierembergia

Cupflower

They say everything old is new again—and here's living proof! Cupflower was a favorite back in Victorian times, then gardeners practically ignored it for nearly 100 years. Then one cultivar, 'Mont Blanc', won an All-America Selection award, and suddenly the whole genus is very hot again. Cupflower forms a lovely compact spreading mound of finely cut foliage and is topped off by numerous cup-shaped flowers in violet or white. It's one of those "try it, you'll like it" plants that every home gardener should grow.

Plant Profile

NIEREMBERGIA
near-em-BER-gee-uh

■ **Bloom Color:** Violet, white

■ **Bloom Time:** Late spring through early fall; fall through winter in mild climates

■ **Height:** Varies by species; see individual listings

■ **Spread:** Varies by species; see individual listings

■ **Garden Uses:** Container planting, edging, hanging baskets, groundcover, mass planting, mixed border, rock garden, wall planting

■ **Light Preference:** Full sun to partial shade

■ **Soil Preference:** Rich, evenly moist but well-drained soil

■ **Best Way to Propagate:** Sow seed indoors in spring or outdoors in late spring

■ **Hardiness:** Frost-sensitive perennial grown as a half-hardy annual

Growing Tips

It's fairly easy to find cupflower in six packs or cell packs in spring (or in fall in mild winter areas). Look for young plants not yet in bloom: They recover much more quickly from transplanting.

Of course, you can also grow it easily from seed. If you have a full 4 or 5 months of growing season, sow seed directly outside, either in early fall or early spring. You can also sow cupflowers in early fall for winter bloom in frost-free areas. For earlier results, or if you live in a shorter-season climate, start it indoors 8 to 10 weeks before the last spring frost. Just barely cover the seed and expose it to room temperatures; it'll germinate in 2 to 4 weeks.

As with most annuals that prefer cool temperatures, cupflower has two quite different care regimes, depending on your local climate. In cool summer areas, it does best in full sun and is quite drought tolerant. In hotter climates, though, give it partial shade, keep the soil cool by using an organic mulch, and make sure it remains slightly moist at all times. To maintain flowering throughout the summer, simply cut the plant back by one-third after each heavy period of bloom.

Although sold as an annual, cupflowers may come through winter quite nicely, especially if the soil is well drained. It is often hardy into Zone 7, especially if well protected for winter with a loose, fluffy mulch. In colder areas, you can maintain it over winter by taking stem cuttings in fall and growing the young plants indoors. Or simply bring a container-grown plant indoors for winter. You can also grow cupflower as a houseplant for a cool room: You'll find it blooms best in late winter, when days are getting longer but temperatures are still cool.

Good Neighbors

Cupflowers' ground-hugging, cup-shaped flowers make it perfect for the sunny or partly shaded border edge, window box, or rock garden. It also looks terrific when paired with taller foliage plants. Sweet alyssum (*Lobularia maritima*) and silver-leaved dusty miller (*Senecio cineraria*) are just two of the many possible charming companion plants.

Problems and Solutions

Outdoors, cupflower has few enemies, although slugs and snails can be a nuisance in rainy weather. Hand-picking is one way to control them, or leave out bowls of beer—they'll fall in and drown.

Top Performer

Nierembergia caerulea (cupflower): Also called *N. hippomanica.* This is a branching, mounding plant with small, stiff, ferny leaves. The lavender-blue, yellow-throated flowers measure about ¾ inch (2 cm) across. 'Purple Robe' has rich violet-blue flowers; 'Mont Blanc' is pure white. These cultivars are less heat sensitive than others in the species and are better choices for hot summer climates. Height: 8 inches (20 cm). Spread: 8 inches (20 cm).

More Recommended Nierembergia

Think Twice: *Nierembergia repens* (white cup): Also called *N. rivularis.* This lesser-known species is a much lower-growing plant, forming a ground-hugging carpet of spoon-shaped foliage. The bell-shaped, upward-facing flowers are white in this species and measure from 1 to 2 inches (2.5 to 5 cm) in diameter. There are also purple-flowered cultivars. This species is less heat tolerant than *N. caerulea;* but where it is happy (cool summer areas in Zones 7 to 10), it often spreads aggressively via underground stolons and can become weedy. Try it in a restricted spot in a rock garden or between cracks between paving stones for a truly lovely effect! Height: 2 inches (5 cm). Spread: 2 feet (60 cm).

Cupflower
(*Nierembergia caerulea*)

Smart Substitutes

If you like cupflower, you'll probably love blue stars. (Most botanists agree it should be *Solenopsis axillaris*, but you're more likely to find it sold as *Laurentia axillaris*; another possible name is *Isotoma axillaries*.) This Australian species has star-shaped flowers, usually in shades of blue or white. Grow it like cupflower; it is more heat-tolerant but still prefers cool summer conditions. It is perennial in Zones 9 and 10 and annual elsewhere; it sometimes self-sows. Height: 1 foot (30 cm). Spread: 1 to 2 feet (30 to 60 cm).

Osteospermum

Osteospermum, Cape daisy

Osteospermums first began to hit the garden world in a big way in the early 1990s, mostly on the West Coast. Since then, they have gained considerable popularity, selling on sight practically everywhere they are available. They are clumping to shrublike plants with toothed, green to gray-green leaves and upright stems bearing 2- to 3-inch (5- to 8-cm) daisylike flowers, with yellow, violet-blue, or dark centers and violet blue on the undersides. The range of colors is already quite impressive and seems to improve every year as dozens of new hybrids are launched annually.

Plant Profile

OSTEOSPERMUM
oss-tee-oh-SPUR-mum

- **Bloom Color:** Pink, purple, yellow, white
- **Bloom Time:** Spring through early fall
- **Height:** 1 to 5 feet (30 to 150 cm)
- **Spread:** 1 to 4 feet (30 to 120 cm)
- **Garden Uses:** Container planting, cut-flower garden, mass planting, mixed border
- **Attracts:** Butterflies
- **Light Preference:** Full sun
- **Soil Preference:** Light, moderately fertile, well-drained soil
- **Best Way to Propagate:** Take stem cuttings in spring or fall
- **Hardiness:** Frost-sensitive perennial grown as a tender annual

Growing Tips

Osteospermums are yet another of those South African plants that simply can't stand the heat. They absolutely thrive in the cool coastal areas of the West Coast and wherever else summers are cool and sunny, but they rarely live up to their end of the bargain elsewhere. And, for once, you can't compensate for the heat by putting them in partial shade: They really do need full sun to bloom. In fact, the flowers won't even open in shade or in cloudy weather.

Interestingly, many osteospermums do seem to do all right in intense heat—if it is *dry* heat. When heat combines with humidity, though, they inevitably fail to bloom. One solution, of course, is to buy plants in full bloom early in spring, then to simply enjoy them while the flowers last—and last they will, often for several months—until temperatures start to rise.

Of course, if you live in a cool-summer area, none of the above applies. For you, osteospermums are simply spectacular, summer-long bloomers posing no particular problems. You'll usually find them as full-grown, blooming container plants, but if you want to save money, look into local or mail-order nurseries that specialize in producing rooted cuttings. You can find small plants for a fraction of the cost of a mature plant; and if you buy them in early spring, they'll have time to reach maturity by the blooming

FUN FACTS

The genus *Osteospermum* used to be included in *Dimorphotheca* (see page 108), which differs by the fact that the ray flowers (the "petals" surrounding the seed-producing central disk) produce seed. In *Osteospermum*, as in most other daisies, the ray flowers are sterile.

season. Or grow osteospermums from seed. 'Passion Mix' (see "Up and Coming," below right) is one strain that is readily available from seed and easy to grow. Start the seed indoors 6 to 8 weeks before the last frost, at 60° to 65°F (15° to 18°C), just barely covering it with soil. It germinates in about 2 weeks. Where summers are long, you can sow the seed directly outside in early spring. During the summer, the only maintenance needed is deadheading to promote rebloom.

Once you have osteospermums, you can easily multiply them by taking stem cuttings. Overwinter adult plants or rooted cuttings in a cool spot—about 50°F (10°C)—and keep the soil barely moist. In Zones 10 and 11, and in protected spots in Zone 9, they can be overwintered outdoors.

Osteospermum
(*Osteospermum ecklonis*)

Good Neighbors

Osteospermums add a cheerful presence to containers, beds, and borders. Pick up the slate blue disks of white 'Whirligig' with the richly colored blooms of edging lobelia (*Lobelia erinus*), or try a classy combination of pastel osteospermums with licorice plant (*Helichrysum petiolare*).

Problems and Solutions

Diseases are seldom a problem in sites with well-drained soil and good air circulation. If aphids cause sticky, distorted foliage, try knocking them off with a strong spray of water.

Top Performer

Osteospermum ecklonis hybrids (osteospermum): Most plants sold today as osteospermum are hybrids derived from *O. ecklonis* and other species, notably *O. jucundum*. Most hybrids have simple flowers, although doubles are not unknown. One interesting characteristic is the "whirligig" pattern, named after a white-flowered cultivar with ray flowers that are crimped in the middle, giving them a spoon-shaped pattern. This trait has been bred into many modern hybrids.

Up and Coming

Researchers around the world have targeted *Osteospermum* as a genus with tremendous potential but a serious flaw: its lack of heat resistance. As a result, thousands of crosses are being made annually to develop heat-resistant osteospermums. In 1999, an All-America Selections award was given to a new strain of osteospermums—'Passion Mix'—with a more compact habit than previous varieties and, most especially, better heat resistance. And it is very likely that more heat-resistant strains will be released over the next few years.

Salpiglossis

Salpiglossis, painted tongue, satin flower

If I had to give a prize for the flower with the most incredible texture, I'd award it to salpiglossis. I can think of no other flower that looks so much like velvet! The 2-inch (5-cm), funnel-shaped, five-lobed flowers have a soft, strokable appearance that is furthermore highlighted by deep veins and overlaid with a metallic sheen closer to true gold than just about any other color in the vegetable world. It is certainly a flower fit for a king; and, indeed, the overall effect is nothing less than regal!

Plant Profile

SALPIGLOSSIS
sal-pih-GLOSS-iss

- **Bloom Color:** Pink, purple, red, mahogany, orange, gold, yellow
- **Bloom Time:** Summer through early fall; fall through winter in mild climates
- **Height:** 18 to 36 inches (45 to 90 cm)
- **Spread:** 1 foot (30 cm)
- **Garden Uses:** Container planting, cut-flower garden, mass planting, meadow garden, mixed border
- **Light Preference:** Full sun or partial shade
- **Soil Preference:** Humus-rich, evenly moist but well-drained soil
- **Best Way to Propagate:** Sow seed indoors in spring
- **Hardiness:** Tender annual

Growing Tips

Salpiglossis dislikes hot, humid weather, but it is not as demanding as most of the other plants in this chapter. Temperatures up to 80°F (27°C), as long as they don't go on for weeks at a time, are quite acceptable. It's only in areas with truly torrid summers that it simply gives up the ghost entirely and dies. Even there, you can start the plants indoors and plant them outside early for color in late spring and early summer. For most gardeners, though, even in moderately hot climates, salpiglossis will bloom nonstop right through summer, especially when they are deadheaded.

Salpiglossis is sometimes available in six packs or cell packs in spring, but it's most often one of those annuals you have to grow yourself from seed. Since it doesn't appreciate root disturbance, it's best to sow the seed in peat pots. Start it indoors 8 to 10 weeks before the last frost date. Sprinkle two or three seeds into each pot and press them into the growing mix; then cover with dark plastic to keep out the light because they germinate best in total darkness. Germination takes 1 to 4 weeks at 70° to 75°F (21° to 24°C). Thin to one seedling per pot. Set the plants about 1 foot (30 cm) apart; closer spacing results in wispy plants.

If you have a long growing season (4 months or more), you can instead sow the seed directly outside. Just press the fine seed into the soil: Don't cover it. To keep out the sun until germination takes place (remember, the seed needs darkness to germinate), cover the planting site with an overturned pot or seed flat. After germination, remove the covering. Thin seedlings so they will stand about 1 foot (30 cm) apart.

When the plants have about six true leaves, pinch back the stems to stimulate better branching. In hotter climates, begin mulching the plants at this point to help keep them cooler. Full sun usually gives the best results, but in hot summer areas, afternoon shade is preferable.

During the growing season, let the plants dry out slightly before watering. Stick a few twiggy branches into the bed for extra support, especially for the taller-growing types because salpiglossis is rather weak-stemmed. Deadhead regularly to stimulate continuous bloom, and feed occasionally with a liquid organic fertilizer if your soil is on the poor side.

Salpiglossis
(*Salpiglossis sinuata*)

Good Neighbors

Try these intriguing annuals in a large pot with companions that will accentuate their rich dark throats, such as a dark-leaved canna or sweet potato vine (*Ipomoea batatas* 'Blackie'). In the garden, a dark-leaved heuchera (such as *Heuchera* 'Palace Purple') will perform the same function.

Problems and Solutions

Poor drainage can result in various leaf diseases, such as gray mold or even stem rot; in heavy, clay soil, raised beds may be a solution. Aphids love salpiglossis (as they do most plants in the petunia family), causing sticky, distorted foliage: Insecticidal soap sprays will help control them.

Top Performer

Salpiglossis sinuata (salpiglossis, painted tongue): There are only two species of *Salpiglossis* and only this one is currently grown. It has an upright, open habit with oval to lance-shaped leaves and branching stems (both of which are covered with sticky hairs) and terminal clusters of flowers. Although the tall cultivars are best for cutting, most modern hybrids are relatively compact plants, 18 to 24 inches (45 to 60 cm) tall, and these create the best impact in containers and in the garden.

Larry's Garden Notes

The flowers of salpiglossis are lovely, but its foliage and silhouette are not nearly so attractive. It's actually a rather ungainly plant, with an open habit. This isn't so obvious when the plant is well spaced in the garden and surrounded by others of its kind or by companion plants. Sold in crowded six packs or cell packs, however, the plants tend to stretch and look rather horrible. Take heart, though: If you prune them back by one-third at planting and take care not to disturb their roots, they will recover quite nicely.

ANNUALS THAT
Bloom in the Shade

And partial shade for that matter! Let's face it, fellow gardeners: Shade is *not* the best environment for annuals. They're quick to bloom and die, and an accelerated life cycle requires lots of energy. And for plants, the only natural source of energy is sunlight. That's why 98 percent of all annuals are sun lovers (or, at best, tolerate a bit of shade). The remaining 2 percent include plants that pack quite a punch. Nothing gives color to shady spots better than the nonstop bloom of annuals—and if there's one thing a shady garden needs, it's color!

Top Picks

◄Believe it or not, there actually are many good annuals that thrive in the shade. Use plants of this type, like baby-blue-eyes, when you garden in more shade than sun.

Shade Is as You Find It

There's nothing quite like trying to define what shade really is. All gardeners *know* what parts of their gardens are shady—or if they don't, they quickly learn—but it's almost impossible to nail down a definition on paper.

"Full shade" is easy enough: It describes places that receive no direct sun at all and where any light is filtered through deep foliage or reflected from nearby objects. To that definition, you can add spots that do get direct sun, but for only 1 or 2 hours a day. You'll find full-shade sites on the north side of a tall fence or wall or under a full, unbroken canopy of trees where no ray of light ever penetrates.

Partial shade is more difficult to define, but it's much easier to live with. It includes sites that get full sun for 2 to 4 hours each day followed by shade for the rest of the day. And make that 6 hours of sun a day if the only sun received comes early or late in the day when the sun is weaker, or in the North, where even direct sun is less intense than in the South. Sites that get no direct sun at all, but where rays of sunlight filter through overhanging leaves over much of the day, are also considered partial shade. In general, even shade-tolerant annuals will bloom better with partial shade than full shade. That is, by the way, why the term "shade tolerant" is better than "shade loving"; there are several shade-*tolerant* annuals, ones that perform well enough in full shade, but there really aren't any shade-*loving* plants. They'd all prefer more light than that.

Testing Shade Levels

Personally, I don't spend time trying to name the shade my gardens get; instead, I look and test. If I find a shady spot that looks relatively

Shade gardens can be alive with color. Choose light, brightly colored flowers such as white and pink varieties to pop out of the shadows rather than fade into the dim light.

shade. Petunia is a good example of a *somewhat* shade-tolerant plant; it prefers full sun but will tolerate partial shade. It *won't* do well, however, in full shade. Any spot where petunias don't grow well, I'll know in the future to use those few annuals that really do tolerate deep shade, such as impatiens. But if the petunias do fairly well, blooming all summer—although perhaps less than they do in full sun—I know I can use the much wider choice of annuals that tolerate partial shade.

Shade Plants in the Sun?

Just because an annual is listed as a shade plant doesn't mean it can't take full sun. Most of the annuals in this chapter do perfectly well in the sun, especially in cool climates and in the North, where the sun is less intense. In very hot climates, though, at least some protection from afternoon sun is recommended for all the plants in this chapter.

Reduced Care for Shade-Grown Plants

Plants grown in shade usually require less effort on your part than the same plant grown in full sun, the main difference being, of course, that they lose much less water to evaporation and, therefore, don't dry out as quickly. In many truly shady spots, especially in regions that receive regular summer rain, watering needs will be negligible. Where tree roots and annuals cohabit, though, any water saved by lessened evaporation will be eliminated by the drying effect of the tree roots. Applying an organic mulch will help, but you may still find yourself watering tree-shaded annual beds as much as any other.

bright, I put a few sun-loving annuals there and see how they perform. If they do well enough, I consider it to be full sun—for the purpose of growing flowers, anyway. If they don't thrive— well, the big advantage of annuals is that they only live one summer, so I can try other, more shade-tolerant plants there next year.

My two favorite test plants for shade levels are portulacas (page 120) and petunias (page 56)— partly because both are widely available and inexpensive, but mostly because I know what to expect from them. Portulaca is a perfect example of a full-sun plant. If it does well in what appears to be a partially shady spot, I know I can consider that spot to be full sun. If it doesn't, I have partial

Winning the Battle of the Roots

Shade often means root competition. That's because, in many cases, shade comes from overhanging trees, and they won't always willingly share their space with plants they consider competitors. Not all trees are culprits, though. Honey locusts (*Gleditsia* spp.), ashes (*Fraxinus* spp.), and oaks (*Quercus* spp.) are among those trees with deep roots; you can usually plant right up to the base of their trunks with no problem. Other trees, though, including maples (*Acer* spp.) and most conifers, are shallow rooted; just digging in the soil at their base is going to be an effort. Yet they create the very conditions for which color is most appreciated: shaded, dry soil where vegetation is sparse or even nonexistent.

Annuals are *not* the best plants for use under shallow-rooted trees. Digging in such spots is already difficult enough because you have to cut through tough roots, but with annuals, you'd have to repeat the process yearly as pruned roots grow back. It is usually easiest to grow shade-tolerant permanent plants, such as shrubs, perennials, and groundcovers, but annuals do make nice additions the first few years, while the permanent ones are filling in. To make planting easier, cover the area around the base of each tree with newspaper (it will act as a temporary barrier to hold its roots back while the other plants establish themselves), then cover with 4 inches (10 cm) of light soil mixed with compost; just plant in this new layer of soil. Don't worry that the tree will be harmed by this: As long as the soil isn't so deep it could smother the roots—certainly 1 foot (30 cm) would be too much—the tree will actually *improve* in health as its sends its new roots up through the new layer of soil.

There's actually an easier way of ensuring color where root competition is a problem: Simply place pots of annuals over the bare surface (or on top of the mulch) or, better yet, pile a couple inches of mulch against the pots. If you set the pots closely enough—about 2 inches (5 cm) less than the plants' spread at maturity—you can create a perfect carpet of flowers. Or you can use bigger containers of mixed annuals, placed here and there, to draw the eyes away from the bare ground.

Not Made for the Shade

Relatively few shade-tolerant plants are true annuals because annuals living on the meager sunlight available in shady spots generally just don't have enough energy to reach blooming size before frost. Instead, annuals for shady conditions tend to be flowering perennials of tropical origin. We've learned how to trick them into blooming early; then we profit from their ability to flower all summer. After all, they're used to an eternal summer in their native lands and lack the internal clock annuals from colder climates have to warn them it's all going to come to an end. Thus they bloom happily right through to fall, only to die a sudden death with the first frosts.

13 Other Shade-Tolerant Annuals

The list of annuals that truly prefer shady conditions is very short, but there are many annuals that will *tolerate* shade. The following plants are just a few of them. For others, see the chapter on "Foliage Plants for Containers & Hanging Baskets." Foliage plants in general tolerate more shade than do flowering plants. In the list below, the plants most tolerant of shade are identified with an asterisk.

Asperula

Annual woodruff, woodruff

Here's a shade-tolerant flower that certainly deserves more attention! Annual woodruff is a low-growing annual that readily forms a beautiful carpet of narrow, whorled leaves on thin, branching square stems. The fragrant blue flowers are tubular in outline and quite small, but they're produced in dense clusters. Sometimes you can scarcely see the foliage for the flowers! Even the somewhat fuzzy seed capsules are interesting, especially when they catch the morning dew. Annual woodruff blooms right through summer and well into fall, often surviving the first winter snows to flower some more.

Plant Profile

ASPERULA
as-PER-oo-luh

- ■ **Bloom Color:** Blue, white
- ■ **Bloom Time:** Summer through early fall; fall through winter in mild climates
- ■ **Height:** 8 to 12 inches (20 to 30 cm)
- ■ **Spread:** 3 to 4 inches (8 to 10 cm)
- ■ **Garden Uses:** Container planting, cut-flower garden, edging, groundcover, mass planting, meadow garden, mixed border, rock garden, woodland garden; along paths, in wet areas
- ■ **Light Preference:** Full sun to deep shade
- ■ **Soil Preference:** Humus-rich, damp but well-drained soil; tolerates alkaline soil
- ■ **Best Way to Propagate:** Sow seed outdoors in fall or late spring
- ■ **Hardiness:** Hardy annual

Growing Tips

Woodruff is a true annual that somehow manages to find enough light to sprout and grow to flowering size in only about 8 weeks, even in the shadiest spots. It does best, however, in light to medium shade: a spot where a little sunlight will filter through much of the day or where it can bask in morning sunshine, then be protected from the torrid afternoon heat. Annual woodruff loves cool temperatures and moist soil, so it's often at its best near a stream or a water garden, especially if you've planted it in sun. In hot, humid climates, give it as much shade as you can; otherwise, it has a nasty habit of dying out in midsummer. Elsewhere, you can count on it for nonstop bloom until hard frost.

Don't look for annual woodruff at your local garden center or nursery; it seems to be a home gardener's secret, totally ignored by professional nurseries. That means you'll have to start it yourself from seed. It grows quickly and seems to prefer cool temperatures for germination. It's easiest to sow directly outdoors, either in late fall or very early spring, when there is still some chance of frost (in frost-free areas, sow it in early fall for winter bloom). It sprouts readily, in 4 to 21 days, although if sown in warm soil, it may not germinate until fall. Since it looks best in drifts, simply broadcast the seed over

FUN FACTS

You'll probably have to plant annual woodruff only once because it self-sows where happy, although not to the point of becoming weedy. In my backyard, it has mingled with a patch of similar-looking sweet woodruff (*Galium odoratum*). Since the latter blooms in the spring in white and annual woodruff all summer in blue, it's as if the same plant suddenly changed color!

the soil surface and water it in; do not cover the fine seed. Don't worry much about thinning; in a dense planting, the weak stems can lean on each other and hold up their neighbors.

You can also sow annual woodruff indoors, although that requires a bit more effort. Start it 8 to 10 weeks before the last spring frost. Use peat pots, so you won't disturb the roots at transplanting. Sprinkle a few seeds over each pot, press lightly, and seal in a plastic bag. For best germination, place the pots in the refrigerator for 2 weeks because it germinates most readily after a cold treatment. It will germinate best at cool temperatures, 50° to 65°F (10° to 18°C), so a coldframe is usually a better place to start them than on a windowsill or under lights.

During the summer, mulch helps keep the roots cool and moist. Deadheading doesn't seem very useful; it blooms on and on whether you remove the faded flowers or not. In long-season climates, it fades out on its own by midfall; elsewhere, it only succumbs when the really severe frosts hit, although flowering does slow down somewhat with the arrival of cold weather.

Good Neighbors

Annual woodruff looks best in massed plantings or edging beds of perennial shade-lovers such as ferns and hostas. Shade- and moisture-loving astilbes, epimediums (*Epimedium* spp.), gingers (*Asarum* spp.), and violets (*Viola* spp.) also make lovely neighbors.

Problems and Solutions

Annual woodruff seldom has insect or disease problems.

Top Performer

Asperula orientalis (annual woodruff): Also called *A. azurea* and *A. azurea setosa*. Although there are some 200 species of *Asperula,* most are perennials or shrubs and none are frequently offered. Other than the closely related sweet woodruff (once *A. odorata* but now *Galium odoratum*), which is a perennial with clusters of white flowers over similarly whorled foliage, this annual species is the only woodruff you're likely to find. **Self-sowing** 🥚

Annual woodruff
(*Asperula orientalis*)

Smart Substitutes

❗ Think Twice: For blue flowers earlier in the spring, consider garden forget-me-not (*Myosotis sylvatica*). Sow seeds in summer for bloom the following spring, or start indoors 8 to 10 weeks before the last frost date for bloom in the first year. Grow forget-me-not as you would annual woodruff, although it needs darkness for germination and prefers sun or partial shade to full shade. Its prolific self-sowing makes it great for naturalizing, but it can be a problem in a formal flowerbed. Height: 5 to 12 inches (13 to 30 cm). Spread: 6 inches (15 cm). Self-sowing 🥚

Begonia Semperflorens

Wax begonia, fibrous begonia

This highly popular, easy-to-grow plant is a true workhorse, both in containers and directly in the garden. From early summer until the first fall frosts, it's never without abundant flowers. This popularity, however, belies a rather modest appearance: Its rounded shape and relatively small flowers have little impact on their own. In mass plantings, though, where the individual plants combine to form a carpet of bloom, it is quite simply spectacular. And the fact it can create such a display in the deep shade is nothing less than a miracle!

Plant Profile

BEGONIA SEMPERFLORENS
bih-GOAN-yuh sem-per-FLOR-enz

- **Bloom Color:** Pink, red, white, bicolor
- **Bloom Time:** Summer through early fall
- **Height:** 6 to 16 inches (15 to 40 cm)
- **Spread:** 6 to 12 inches (15 to 30 cm)
- **Garden Uses:** Container planting, edging, hanging baskets, groundcover, mass planting, mixed border, rock garden, woodland garden
- **Light Preference:** Full sun to partial shade to deep shade
- **Soil Preference:** Humus-rich, evenly moist soil
- **Best Way to Propagate:** Divide or take stem cuttings in fall or early spring
- **Hardiness:** Frost-sensitive perennial grown as tender annual

Growing Tips

Forget about growing this plant from seed: It's widely available in six packs or cell packs each spring, and at a good price; so why go through all the hassle of trying to get this plant through its very delicate first months as a seedling?

If you insist on trying, remember it needs a very long growing period before reaching blooming size (usually 15 to 20 weeks). Sow the dustlike seed (or pelleted seed, which is easier to handle) indoors, as thinly as possible, on the surface of a fine-textured, already-moist growing mix. Press the seed very lightly and cover the tray with clear plastic or a pane of glass. Place the tray at 65° to 75°F (18° to 24°C). Although light isn't necessary for germination, it will be immediately afterward, so it's usually easiest to place the trays under fluorescent lights or in bright sunlight (but not direct sun) from the start. Germination takes 15 to 21 days. The tiny seedlings are very susceptible to damping-off, so remove the covering to increase air circulation as soon as they appear and water only from below. When the seedlings are large enough to handle, carefully transplant them to trays or individual cells.

Wait until your soil is warm to the touch before moving the seedlings to the garden. Partial shade to fairly deep shade is best, although most modern hybrids

FUN FACTS

When you sow seed of mixed wax begonia hybrids, you'll notice that some seedlings look more vigorous than others; make sure you keep some of the weaker ones along with the strong. The strongest-growing seedlings tend to be white-flowering plants. By keeping some of the weaker, shorter seedlings, you'll also get pink- and red-flowering plants.

are quite sun tolerant if you keep the soil evenly moist. And in hot climates, they need afternoon shade at the very least. Plant them about 1 foot (30 cm) apart in the garden, half that in containers.

Summer care is minimal. They don't even need deadheading. Mulching helps keep the soil moist. If your soil isn't rich in humus, apply an organic foliar fertilizer every few weeks.

In fall, you can bring in cuttings or lift plants and grow them in a bright spot indoors for the winter. Since most wax begonias are widely available in spring, I bring in only rare, more expensive cultivars, such as those with double flowers or variegated foliage.

Wax begonia
(*Begonia* Semperflorens-Cultorum)

Good Neighbors

Enjoy wax begonias in masses for a carpet of bloom, or as ribbons of color for edging walkways or beds of green hostas and ferns. These carefree plants are also well suited for containers. Using a variegated coleus to pick up the color of dark-leaved types can create a pretty combination.

Problems and Solutions

Fungal diseases such as stem rot and gray mold are problems in poorly drained soil. Raised beds may give better results. Control slugs by handpicking or other methods (see page 35), especially early in the season.

Top Performer

Begonia Semperflorens-Cultorum hybrids (wax begonia): Succulent stems support irregularly shaped, waxy leaves in green or bronze (occasionally variegated). The ½- to 1-inch (1.3- to 2.5-cm) flowers are composed of two large petals and two smaller ones. Both single- and double-flowered cultivars are available. Height: 6 to 12 inches (15 to 30 cm). Spread: 6 to 12 inches (15 to 30 cm).

More Recommended Begonias

Begonia 'Dragon Wing' (angel-wing begonia): There are hundreds of other fibrous begonias that are suitable for garden use, but only a few are presently used that way. One such plant is 'Dragon Wing', with large, dark green leaves and dangling clusters of scarlet flowers. Height: 14 to 16 inches (35 to 40 cm). Spread: 1 foot (30 cm).

Larry's Garden Notes

Wax begonias are often referred to as "fibrous begonias." This in no way refers to a stringy appearance, but rather to their place in the vast begonia clan. You see, there are over 1,300 species of begonias, and they fall into three main groups. Some produce tubers, while others have creeping, thickened, horizontal stems called rhizomes. A third class has no special underground structure, just numerous thin roots that look like fibers. Wax begonia is just one of many hundred species of fibrous-rooted begonias.

Begonia Tuberhybrida

Tuberous begonia

These bold-flowered beauties offer large blooms in a wide range of colors—but that's just the beginning! They also have handsome foliage: large, angel-wing-shaped leaves in either green or bronze, produced on thick, succulent stems that grow from a potato-like tuber. There are many different categories, from the trailing Pendula types to the smaller bedding types called Multifloras to the huge-flowered "show" types. Only the trailing and bedding types are commonly offered as seed-grown plants suitable for growing as annuals.

Plant Profile

BEGONIA TUBERHYBRIDA
bih-GOAN-yuh
TEW-bur-HIGH-brid-uh

- ■ **Bloom Color:** Pink, peach, red, orange, yellow, white, bicolors

- ■ **Bloom Time:** Summer through early fall

- ■ **Height:** 8 to 24 inches (20 to 60 cm)

- ■ **Spread:** 10 to 12 inches (25 to 30 cm)

- ■ **Garden Uses:** Container planting, edging, hanging baskets, mass planting, mixed border, woodland garden, specimen plant

- ■ **Light Preference:** Partial shade

- ■ **Soil Preference:** Humus-rich, evenly moist but well-drained soil

- ■ **Best Way to Propagate:** Take stem cuttings in spring

- ■ **Hardiness:** Frost-sensitive perennial grown as a tender annual

Growing Tips

It just makes sense to let someone else grow your tuberous begonias from seed. If something isn't to the plants' liking—if it's too cold, or too dry, or the days are too long—they stop growing, produce tubers, and go dormant; if the plant is still tiny, however, the tuber will be too small to sprout.

Fortunately, most nurseries sell seed-grown tuberous begonias in six packs or cell packs in the spring at very reasonable prices. They've done all the work and taken all the risks, and you get to reap the rewards. Sounds fair to me!

Still insist on trying? Then grow tuberous begonias *exactly* as you would wax begonias, described on page 156. Surface sow, using pelleted seed if possible, and keep humid until it sprouts. Afterward, grow a bit on the cool side—no warmer than 70°F (21°C)—and keep barely moist, watering carefully from below. If you grow the seedlings under lights, keep the day length shorter than 15 hours because overly long days encourage dormancy.

Whether you buy six packs or cell packs or start your own tuberous begonias indoors, careful planting is important. Wait until the ground has warmed up and there is no danger of frost. Partial to fairly deep shade is best, although some modern strains of Multifloras will take sun in cooler climates. And cool temperatures are impor-

FUN FACTS

With tuberous begonias, male flowers are fully double, while the female blooms (easily recognized even before the buds open by the three-sided ovary at their base) are single with a yellow stigma in the center. Since they use up energy that would otherwise go to the prettier male flowers, pinch off the females as soon as you see them.

tant. As much as they hate the cold, tuberous begonias can't stand hot, humid weather either. A good mulch and a semishady location will help keep them cool enough in most climates. The thick stems of tuberous begonias are not as solid as they look, so keep your plants out of strong winds or they can snap off.

Now comes the big question: What do you do with the plants in fall? You can't keep them growing over winter; they need to go dormant. Traditionally, you harvest the tubers, dry them out, and store them in a frost-free place for winter. Many modern hybrids, however, have been so carefully developed to put their energy into blooming all summer that they barely make any tuberous growth. I suggest saving only those that do make tubers at least the size of a Ping-Pong ball. Restart those tubers indoors, in 4-inch (10-cm) pots, in February or March.

Besides growing tuberous begonias from seed, you can also take stem cuttings in the spring or cut old tubers in half, between two growth points, at planting time.

Good Neighbors

Tuberous begonias are showy enough to look good by themselves, but they also look handsome with attractive foliage plants, such as a trailing ivy (*Hedera helix*). For an eye-catching combination, try pairing a red-flowered tuberous begonia with the delicate purple-blue blooms of edging lobelia (*Lobelia erinus*), which will climb up and through the bold foliage.

Problems and Solutions

Providing good air circulation and keeping soil evenly moist will help avoid the leaf diseases and rots that affect tuberous begonias.

Top Performer

Begonia Tuberhybrida hybrids (tuberous begonia): This is an entirely manmade species, created by crossing different summer-blooming tuberous species from the Andes. Popular seed-grown lines of Pendula (hanging types) available in a wide range of colors include 'Illumination' and 'Show Angels,' whereas 'Non Stop', 'Clips', and 'Pin Up' are common bedding-type tuberous begonias (Multifloras).

'Pin Up' tuberous begonia (*Begonia* Tuberhybrida 'Pin Up')

Larry's Garden Notes

Some experts recommend mixing the dustlike seed of begonias with fine sand and sowing the resulting mix with a salt shaker. While this works with other small seed, I have yet to find sand fine enough for begonias! In my experience, the best way of sowing begonia seed is to spend more and buy pelleted seed, which you can easily manipulate with your fingers. Or pour the seed into the crease in a sheet of paper and then tap lightly as you point one end of the sheet down toward the growing mix while moving it slowly over the surface.

Browallia

Browallia, bush violet

At last: a tough, workhorse of a plant that can replace impatiens! With bushy, upright to somewhat sprawling branches tipped in 2-inch (5-cm) trumpets with broad, pointed, starlike lobes, it looks quite like perennial bellflowers (*Campanula* spp.). The real excitement with this plant is that it has about the same size and impact of the often-overused impatiens, yet it comes in a different range of colors and has a totally different texture. So whenever you find yourself looking at your shady borders or containers and wanting something a little different, remember this super but underused annual.

Plant Profile

BROWALLIA
bro-AL-ee-uh

- **Bloom Color:** Purple, violet-blue, white

- **Bloom Time:** Late spring through early fall

- **Height:** 10 to 24 inches (25 to 60 cm)

- **Spread:** Varies by species; see individual listings

- **Garden Uses:** Container planting, edging, hanging baskets, mass planting, mixed border, woodland garden, specimen plant

- **Light Preference:** Full sun to deep shade

- **Soil Preference:** Humus-rich, evenly moist but well-drained soil

- **Best Way to Propagate:** Sow seed indoors in late winter

- **Hardiness:** Frost-sensitive perennial grown as a tender annual

Growing Tips

Now that browallia is starting to become available in six packs or cell packs in the spring, it's bound to catch on in a bigger way. Of course, unlike some of the plants in this chapter, there is no particular challenge in growing it from seed, so if your local nursery doesn't yet carry started plants, don't let that stop you.

Except in the South, where the longer growing season means you can sow it directly outdoors after all danger of frost is over, browallia needs a bit of a head start on the season. Sow it indoors 8 to 10 weeks before the last frost. Just press the seeds into the surface of a premoistened mix without covering it; it needs light to germinate. Place the tray at 65° to 75°F (18° to 24°C). The seed germinates rapidly, in 6 to 15 days, and the sprouts grow quickly. Pinch them back by about one-third when they're 4 inches (10 cm) tall to promote bushier growth.

Browallia doesn't appreciate cold conditions, so wait until the soil has started to warm up to plant it outside. A spacing of about 1 foot (30 cm) will give plants the room they need to meld together and form a lovely carpet, either in the garden or in a container.

The ideal placement is a spot in bright shade and evenly moist soil, with a thick mulch to ensure the roots stay cool at all times. Hot temperatures and full sun are a deadly combination, although browallia will take full sun in cooler climates. In hot climates, especially, it blooms happily even in the deepest shade; in the North, a bit more light will give better bloom.

Avoid letting the plant dry out: It does recover when watered again, but it loses leaves and buds each time and soon becomes unattractive. Otherwise, summer care is minimal. Deadheading and pruning seem to be of little benefit, although cutting a nearly leafless, drought-stricken plant back harshly can encourage new growth.

In the South (Zones 9 to 11), browallia will often come through winter and may even self-sow to some degree, although without becoming weedy.

Good Neighbors

Low-growing *Browallia speciosa* hybrids have a loose, bushy habit that looks particularly fine cascading from a container. Try them with nemesia (*Nemesia strumosa*), polka dot plants (*Hypoestes* spp.), or white petunias or begonias. The more substantial but less easily available *Browallia americana* is an excellent long-flowering annual for the shade garden. Use it as a follow-up to Virginia bluebells (*Mertensia pulmonarioides*) or bleeding-hearts (*Dicentra spectabilis*).

Browallia
(*Browallia speciosa*)

Problems and Solutions

Aphids and whiteflies love browallia; control them by spraying with insecticidal soap. Keeping insects under control will also help prevent tomato spotted wilt virus, which results in spotted leaves and lack of bloom. Destroy any plants that do become infected.

Top Performer

Browallia speciosa (browallia, bush violet, sapphire flower): This is the most common species, with rather pale green leaves and a bushy habit. The flowers have sunken veins that give them a lovely textured look; they come in shades of violet to blue that always have a contrasting white center, and they also are available in pure white. White and the paler shades of blue are the most striking in deep shade. Height: 10 to 24 inches (25 to 60 cm). Spread: 1 foot (30 cm).

More Recommended Browallia

Browallia americana (browallia, bush violet): Similar to *B. speciosa* but with darker leaves and denser overall growth. The species has deep violet flowers with a white center, but there are now cultivars available in white and various shades of blue. Height: 2 feet (60 cm). Spread: 2 feet (60 cm).

Smart Substitutes

Most bellflowers (*Campanula* spp.) are hardy perennials grown in borders or rock gardens. There are, however, several subtropical species that make super basket plants for the summer garden. The most common of these is *C. isophylla*, called variously falling stars, Italian bellflower, and star of Bethlehem. Its pale blue to white flowers are remarkably like those of browallia. It has very fine seed that takes months to bloom, so it is easiest to buy plants. Height: 6 to 8 inches (15 to 20 cm). Spread: 1 foot (30 cm).

Impatiens

Impatiens

Easy to grow and constantly in flower, impatiens are now the number one bedding plant in North America, beating out even such longtime favorites as petunias and geraniums. Not only do they bloom up a storm all summer long, in even the darkest corners, but they come in an incredibly wide range of colors: orange, pink, scarlet, red, purple, lavender, and all manner of bicolors. In fact, were I to steal a line from a fruit promotion ad, I'd say they were "nature's most perfect flower."

Plant Profile

IMPATIENS
im-PAY-shens

- **Bloom Color:** Varies by species; see individual listings

- **Bloom Time:** Late spring through early fall; year-round in frost-free climates

- **Height:** Varies by species; see individual listings

- **Spread:** Varies by species; see individual listings

- **Garden Uses:** Container planting, edging, hanging baskets, groundcover, mass planting, mixed border, woodland garden, specimen plant

- **Attracts:** Hummingbirds

- **Light Preference:** Full sun to deep shade

- **Soil Preference:** Humus-rich, evenly moist but well-drained soil

- **Best Way to Propagate:** Sow seed indoors in late winter, take stem cuttings in fall or spring

- **Hardiness:** Frost-sensitive perennial grown as a tender annual

Growing Tips

Impatiens seed is expensive and difficult to germinate, so it's easiest to buy trays of plants in the spring.

If you do want to try growing it from seed, though, sow it indoors 8 to 10 weeks before the last frost. Press the seed into the soil without covering it. Impatiens seed needs warmth—70° to 75°F (21° to 24°C)—and high humidity to sprout; covering the tray with a sheet of clear plastic will help increase humidity while preventing cool air from getting in. Germination takes 2 to 3 weeks. When seedlings appear, take off the plastic and lower night temperatures to about 60°F (15°C).

Wait until the ground has warmed up (usually about 2 weeks after the last spring frost) before setting these warmth-loving plants outdoors. Plant them in rich soil in anything from deep to light shade. They tolerate full sun only in cool or cloudy climates.

Summer care is simple: Just keep them moist. Deadheading isn't necessary. If they get straggly after a few months, prune them back by a third and they'll soon be as good as new.

Some impatiens are annuals, but most species are tropical perennials, surviving the winter only in totally frost-free climates (Zones 10 and 11). Elsewhere, you can either pot up a few favorite plants in fall or take cuttings and bring them indoors. I only bother saving cultivars that don't come true from seed, such as those with variegated or golden foliage or with double flowers.

Good Neighbors

As effective as they are popular, garden impatiens (*Impatiens walleriana*) are truly workhorses in the garden, looking great any way you use them. For an interesting variation, try interplanting drifts of garden impatiens with large-leaved caladiums (*Caladium bicolor*). New Guinea impatiens make a beautiful groundcover in front of a shrub border. Or, in a large pot, combine them with a trailing plant such as sweet potato vine (*Ipomoea batatas* 'Blackie').

Problems and Solutions

Watch out for slugs in spring; hand-pick them for control. Mites are a problem in dry weather; spraying regularly with insecticidal soap will help keep their populations under control.

Top Performer

Impatiens walleriana (garden impatiens, busy Lizzie, patience plant): This garden favorite is a shrubby tropical perennial with succulent stems and green to bronze (sometimes variegated) leaves. The innumerable flat-faced flowers, each with a spur in the back, come in every shade but true blue: There are even yellow and double-flowered cultivars now! Height: 6 to 24 inches (15 to 60 cm). Spread: 6 to 24 inches (15 to 60 cm). **Self-sowing**

More Recommended Impatiens

Impatiens balsamina (garden balsam): This old-fashioned annual species is a more pyramidal plant than the others. The cup-shaped, hooded, single or double flowers are borne in the leaf axils, partly hidden by foliage. They come in shades of pink, red, purple, and white. Height: 12 to 30 inches (30 to 75 cm). Spread: 12 to 18 inches (30 to 45 cm). **Self-sowing**

Impatiens New Guinea Group: This is a hybrid group of tropical perennial impatiens, based on species found in New Guinea. They are sturdy plants with large flowers in shades of rose, red, salmon, lilac-pink, purple, and white, as well as bicolors. The bronze or green foliage is often variegated with cream, pink, or yellow. Most types are cutting propagated, but some strains can be grown from seed as above. They prefer brighter light than the garden impatiens but still need some protection from full sun in the South. Height: 8 to 24 inches (30 to 60 cm). Spread: 12 to 18 inches (30 to 45 cm).

Garden impatiens
(*Impatiens walleriana*)

Larry's Garden Notes

Having trouble with the irregular, sporadic germination of garden impatiens (*I. walleriana*) seed? Here's a trick I learned from a gardening friend, and it really works! Rather than placing the seed tray in light after sowing, as usually recommended, set it in a warm spot, but in total darkness. After 48 hours, set it under plant lights or on a bright windowsill (but out of direct sunlight) Not only will the plants germinate much more quickly (in 9 to 14 days) but they sprout all at the same time.

Lobelia

Edging lobelia

There are actually more than 350 species of lobelia from around the world, ranging from perennials and annuals to shrubs, treelike plants, and even aquatics. All share narrow leaves and two-lipped tubular flowers with a two-lobed upper lip and a much larger, three-lobed lower lip—but that's about all they have in common. In the annual category, the most widely grown species is edging lobelia (*Lobelia erinus*), with its bushy to trailing growth habit and unbelievable number of ½-inch (1.3-cm) flowers in some of the richest shades you'll see in the plant world.

Plant Profile

LOBELIA
low-BEE-lee-uh

- **Bloom Color:** Blue, lilac, purple, wine red, white
- **Bloom Time:** Late spring through early fall
- **Height:** 4 to 9 inches (10 to 23 cm)
- **Spread:** 4 to 6 inches (10 to 15 cm)
- **Garden Uses:** Container planting, edging, hanging baskets, mass planting, mixed border, rock garden, wall planting
- **Attracts:** Butterflies; also provides nectar for beneficial insects
- **Light Preference:** Full sun to deep shade
- **Soil Preference:** Humus-rich, evenly moist soil
- **Best Way to Propagate:** Sow seed indoors in late winter
- **Hardiness:** Frost-sensitive perennial grown as a tender annual

Growing Tips

Edging lobelia isn't a true annual but instead is a tender perennial. If you want good results, therefore, don't sow it outdoors; it would take too long to begin blooming. Instead, either buy transplants (they're readily available) or start it indoors from seed so it has a good jump on the season. Since it is widely available in six packs or cell packs and also a bit tricky to grow from seed, a trip to the nursery is the easiest way to go.

Notwithstanding, you *can* grow edging lobelia from seed; you just have to be aware of its special needs. Start seed indoors 8 to 10 weeks before the last frost, just pressing the fine seed into the mix, as it needs light to germinate. Sow relatively densely, which is easy enough to do since the seed is so fine and dustlike you'd never be able to sow it one by one anyway.

Germinate at 65° to 75°F (18° to 24°C). The seedlings will be up in 2 to 3 weeks. After germination, keep the soil slightly moist by watering from below to help prevent damping-off. When the seedlings are about 1 inch (2.5 cm) tall, prick them out in clumps of three to five, and move them to peat pots, cell packs, or individual pots.

Wait until nighttime temperatures are above 40°F (4°C) and there's no more danger of frost before daring to put your lobelias outside for the summer. They are at their best under cool condi-

FUN FACTS

You'll also find lobelia seed sold as "multipellets": pellets containing four to six seeds. This gives more easily handled seed you can sow directly into cell packs or individual pots. The plants will naturally come up in clusters of three or four plants, just the way you'd want them.

tions in evenly moist soil; that's one reason they do so well in partial shade. You can grow them in full sun in the North or in cooler coastal areas; but in the South, where things get really hot and humid, err on the side of more shade rather than less.

Edging lobelia is a knockout early in the season, but it has a nasty habit of drying up and dying in midsummer. There are two ways of coping with this. One is "planned obsolescence": Use edging lobelia as a filler in pots or borders that will later be jammed full of the slower-to-fill-out annuals, such as petunias; then just cut out its dead stems as the other plants take over. (This is the best choice in hot summer areas, where it won't be happy in the heat anyway.) The other approach is the "midsummer trim," which is better adapted to the cooler regions of the country: When the plant has been blooming for a while and is just beginning to look a bit thinner, hack it back by half. It will quickly sprout anew and bloom until frost.

'Sapphire' edging lobelia (*Lobelia erinus* 'Sapphire')

Good Neighbors

A traditional favorite in containers and window boxes, edging lobelia mixes beautifully with just about any other flower color, as well as with chartreuse, silver, blue-gray, and bright green foliage. In the garden, it adds sparkle to a planting of lady's-mantle (*Alchemilla mollis*), hostas, and other plants that thrive in moist, partially shaded conditions.

Problems and Solutions

Other than damping-off at the seedling stage and dying back in midsummer, edging lobelia is not particularly prone to health problems.

Top Performer

Lobelia erinus (edging lobelia): This frothy little "annual" may have either green or bronze-tinted foliage. The tiny flowers come in pure blues, purples, pinks, lilacs, wine reds, and whites; some cultivars also have contrasting eyes. Take your pick between the "border" types, which are more upright (but still look great in containers), and the "trailers," which dangle downward to a greater degree.

Kissing Cousins

Lobelia × speciosa cultivars (hybrid lobelia): These upright lobelias are clump-forming plants with comparatively broad leaves. Tall stalks bear distinctly tubular flowers—mostly in shades of intense red but also purple, pink, or mauve—that are beloved by hummingbirds. The shiny foliage is often flushed with red or deep purple-maroon. Red-leaved, scarlet-flowered 'Queen Victoria' is a popular strain. Although partly derived from the very hardy cardinal flower (*L. cardinalis*), treat these plants as annuals in Zone 7 and north—they rarely seem hardy beyond that. Height: 20 to 48 inches (50 to 120 cm). Spread: 9 to 12 inches (23 to 30 cm).

Mimulus

Monkey flower

I keep looking at the flower, but I *still* don't see the monkey face promised in the common name. Regardless, this is an attractive mounding annual with hairy stems and medium green, toothed leaves. The tubular flowers flare out into an open mouth and very broad, flashy lobes: two on the upper lip, three on the bottom one. Monkey flower looks equally striking in the garden and in containers and inevitably attracts a lot of attention. With blooms this striking, you can be sure it won't go unnoticed!

Plant Profile

MIMULUS
MIM-you-lus

- **Bloom Color:** Pink, burgundy-red, orange, yellow, cream

- **Bloom Time:** Late spring through early fall

- **Height:** 6 to 36 inches (15 to 90 cm)

- **Spread:** 6 to 36 inches (15 to 90 cm)

- **Garden Uses:** Container planting, edging, hanging baskets, groundcover, mass planting, mixed border, rock garden, woodland garden; in wet areas

- **Attracts:** Hummingbirds

- **Light Preference:** Full sun to partial shade

- **Soil Preference:** Rich, moist, slightly acid soil

- **Best Way to Propagate:** Sow seed indoors or out in spring

- **Hardiness:** Frost-sensitive to hardy perennial grown as a tender annual

Growing Tips

Unless you really love a challenge, it's best to buy transplants of monkey flower. Fortunately, they're becoming quite widely available in garden centers.

The challenge in growing monkey flower from seed is doing the right thing at the right time. Sow the seed indoors 14 to 15 weeks before the last frost, simply pressing the seed into the soil surface because it needs light to germinate. Now seal the tray inside a plastic bag and refrigerate for 3 weeks. Next, place the container in good light, but not direct sun, at 70° to 75°F (21° to 24°C). After their cold treatment, the seeds germinate quite readily, in 1 to 3 weeks. After germination, take off the covering and give them bright light and cool conditions. (If you're using lights, set the timer at 13 hours a day to get nicely compact plants). Keep them moist at all times: They will not tolerate drought.

Plant out your monkey flowers after all danger of frost has passed. The secret to their success is to place them somewhere they'll *always* have abundant soil moisture. You can even plant them on the border of a stream or water garden with their roots in soggy muck. Monkey flower is said to need shade and cool conditions, but the truth is that it will also grow in full, blazing sun as long as the soil is moist enough. If you wish to grow monkey flower in average garden soil, it's much easier to plant it in partial shade, using a mulch and watering it regularly.

FUN FACTS

Most monkey flowers are complex hybrids with equal amounts of hardy Alaskan stock and tender South American blood. Some are quite perennial, even to Zone 4; others you can't get through the winter in Zone 8!

During summer, deadhead regularly and cut wispy plants back harshly to encourage new growth and bloom.

Good Neighbors

In the moist, partly shaded border, good neighbors for monkey flowers include sweet flag (*Acorus calamus*), irises, rodgersias, and astilbes. In a container, monkey flowers can add personality to a shaded patio, either alone or combined with other moisture-lovers, such as creeping Jenny (*Lysimachia nummularia*).

Problems and Solutions

Leaf diseases are a problem where the ground is dry and the air humid. Keeping the soil moist, but without wetting the foliage, can help prevent them. Aphids, whiteflies, and mites can distort and discolor foliage; control them with insecticidal soap.

Top Performer

Mimulus × *hybridus* (hybrid monkey flower): The most common monkey flower, these hybrids come in both solid colors and spotted forms. There are many different seed strains. Height: 6 to 36 inches (15 to 90 cm). Spread: 1 to 3 feet (30 to 90 cm). **Self-sowing**

More Recommended Mimulus

Mimulus cardinalis (scarlet monkey flower): This species offers scarlet flowers, sometimes with yellow markings in the throat. Height: 18 to 36 inches (45 to 90 cm). Spread: 1 to 2 feet (30 to 60 cm).

M. cupreus (copper monkey flower): Yellow flowers turning coppery red. Height: 18 to 24 inches (45 to 60 cm). Spread: 1 foot (30 cm).

M. guttatus (common monkey flower): One of the parents of the hybrid monkey flower. Yellow, orange, or red flowers, usually spotted with burgundy. Quite hardy (Zone 4 with protection), spreading widely where happy. Height: 15 to 24 inches (38 to 60 cm). Spread: 1 to 2 feet (30 to 60 cm). **Self-sowing**

M. luteus (yellow monkey flower). Similar to the other species, with brown-spotted yellow flowers. Height: 18 to 36 inches (45 to 90 cm). Spread: 1 to 2 feet (30 to 60 cm). **Self-sowing**

'Mystic Orange' hybrid monkey flower (*Mimulus* × *hybridus* 'Mystic Orange')

Larry's Garden Notes

So you like the look of monkey flower but can't find a wet spot to grow it in? How about under that leaky outside faucet you never seem to find time to repair? Or that spot where water keeps dripping from the eaves even days after the rain has stopped? Beds at the base of a slope are also a good possibility; they tend to be moister than surrounding areas. Or grow monkey flower in a container set in a large saucer that you keep filled with water: This is one plant that is *not* going to complain if its soil is always soggy!

Nemophila

Nemophila, baby-blue-eyes, five spot

The very name of this annual indicates its preferred growing conditions: from the Greek *nemo* ("wooded place"—that is, shade) and *philo* ("to love")! The two common species are California natives, and like many plants native to Mediterranean climates, they have learned to bloom after the fall or winter rains, usually sprouting in winter to bloom in early spring. Both species produce slender stems and deeply cut, gray-green leaves, plus clouds of bell-shaped, upward-facing, five-petaled flowers in shades of blue and white. They are easy to grow and they bloom abundantly, but they remain relatively little known as garden annuals.

Plant Profile

NEMOPHILA
nem-oh-FILL-uh

- **Bloom Color:** Blue, white

- **Bloom Time:** Late spring through early fall; late winter to spring in mild climates

- **Height:** 6 to 12 inches (15 to 30 cm)

- **Spread:** 6 to 12 inches (15 to 30 cm)

- **Garden Uses:** Container planting, edging, hanging baskets, groundcover, meadow garden, mixed border, rock garden, woodland garden

- **Light Preference:** Full sun to partial shade

- **Soil Preference:** Fertile, evenly moist but well-drained soil

- **Best Way to Propagate:** Sow seed indoors or outdoors in spring; in fall in mild climates

- **Hardiness:** Hardy annual

Growing Tips

Nemophila should be easy to produce commercially in six packs or cell packs, but you'll almost never find plants for sale, so you'll have to start them yourself. The key to success is growing nemophila only when your climate can offer cool temperatures and moist soil.

In cool summer areas, such as the Pacific Northwest, the Atlantic coast, and the North, you can simply sow seed outdoors in early spring. It will sprout quickly and bloom right through summer. Notwithstanding its "shade-loving" name, nemophila will do wonderfully in full sun in such climates, although partial shade is better in borderline areas.

In mild winter climates (Zones 8 to 10), usually the only cool weather is in fall and winter. In these areas, sow directly outdoors in late summer and again in late fall. This will give you two periods of bloom: from midfall to winter, then from midwinter to spring.

And in areas with frosty winters and hot summers, enjoy nemophila as a spring-flowering annual by starting it indoors (to give it a head start on the season) and putting it outside while the air is still cool, even if there is still some danger of frost. It will bloom all spring, usually with the tulips and other spring-flowering bulbs, and then fade away when summer temperatures get toasty. If you plant it where it will get afternoon shade at least, and add a good mulch, that will help prolong the flowering period. Ideally, it should go in a spot that gets *no* direct sun but plenty of light, such as on the north side of a building. If you have a really long frost-free season, try sowing a second time in mid-August for blooms in October and November.

When sowing nemophila outdoors, simply broadcast the seed liberally over the soil surface, rake it in lightly, and water well. It usually sprouts in a little more than a week. Thin the resulting plants from 6 to 12 inches (15 to 30 cm) apart. Since nemophila transplants well, you can also start it indoors in flats, just barely covering the seed, and plant it out when the seedlings are developing well. If possible, give it cool temperatures when it is indoors: nights of around 55°F (13°C) or less.

In most of North America, nemophila will self-sow, finding its own niche and blooming according to most appropriate conditions for that region.

Good Neighbors

Enjoy dainty nemophilas as edging plants or in containers. Try them with white sweet alyssum (*Lobularia maritima*) for a delicate border in a partly shaded, moist location. *Nemophila menziesii* 'Pennie Black' makes an interesting companion to a dark coleus or to purple-leaved basil.

Problems and Solutions

Powdery and downy mildew can be problems when the plants are stressed. Prevent these diseases by keeping the soil slightly moist at all times. Eliminate aphids by spraying with insecticidal soap.

Top Performer

Nemophila menziesii (baby-blue-eyes): Also called *N. insignis*. This hairy-leaved, low-growing, spreading annual produces 1½-inch (4-cm), bright blue flowers with a lighter blue to white center. 'Pennie Black' has deep purple flowers set off by a silvery white edge. *N. menziesii* var. *atromaria* 'Snowstorm' has white flowers liberally speckled with tiny black dots. Height: 8 inches (30 cm). Spread: 1 foot (30 cm). **Self-sowing** 🌰

More Recommended Nemophila

Nemophila maculata (five spot): A similar plant but with less-fuzzy leaves and a somewhat more mounding habit. The flowers are absolutely charming: white, with petals tipped by a deep violet-blue spot and veins often faintly tinted with violet. Height: 6 to 12 inches (15 to 30 cm). Spread: 6 to 12 inches (15 to 30 cm). **Self-sowing** 🌰

Baby-blue-eyes
(*Nemophila menziesii*)

Smart Substitutes

If you like lavender-blue flowers but can't meet nemophila's need for cool temperatures, here's a plant to try: Persian violet (*Exacum affine*). This plant is quickly catching on as a heat-tolerant summer annual. It forms a compact, bushy plant with shiny, rounded leaves and slightly fragrant, five-petaled, ¾-inch (2-cm) flowers with prominent yellow stamens. Start this short-lived tender perennial indoors 10 to 12 weeks before the last frost or buy plants in spring. It does best in bright shade but can take full sun in cool summer areas.

Torenia

Wishbone flower, bluewings

Want something a little different for your shade garden? Look no further! Wishbone flower gets its name from the curious construction of its anthers. When the flower first opens, the two anthers rise from either side of the flower, then arch inward and join at the tip, creating a shape like a wishbone. When the first bee enters the flower, its movements trigger the anthers to break apart and crash down on its back, coating it in pollen. When it moves to another flower, the pollen brushes onto the new flower's stigma and then the bee gets another dusting. This way, both the bee and the flower get what they need!

Plant Profile

TORENIA
tor-REE-nee-uh

- **Bloom Color:** Varies by species; see individual listings

- **Bloom Time:** Summer through early fall; much of the year in frost-free climates

- **Height:** 6 to 12 inches (15 to 30 cm)

- **Spread:** Varies by species; see individual listings

- **Garden Uses:** Container planting, edging, hanging baskets, groundcover, mass planting, mixed border, rock garden, woodland garden, wall planting

- **Attracts:** Hummingbirds

- **Light Preference:** Partial shade to deep shade

- **Soil Preference:** Humus-rich, evenly moist but well-drained soil

- **Best Way to Propagate:** Sow seed indoors in spring

- **Hardiness:** Tender annual

Growing Tips

Wishbone flower is widely available in six packs or cell packs, at least in larger nurseries. Look for very young plants because mature torenias don't transplant very well.

It's also easy to grow wishbone flower from seed. Sow it 6 to 8 weeks before the last frost, in peat pots. Just press the fine seed into the surface of the mix without covering it because it needs light to germinate. Keep evenly moist and warm—70° to 75°F (21° to 24°C)—until it sprouts, 1 to 3 weeks later. Afterward, move the plants to a cooler spot if possible, with night temperatures around 55°F (13°C) because this yields much more compact plants. (If your seedlings do become a bit spindly, you just have to pinch them a few times and they'll fill in quite nicely.)

In climates with very long summers, you might prefer to sow the seeds outside, directly where they are to bloom, starting about 1 week before the last frost. Thin them to 6 to 8 inches (15 to 20 cm) apart for the bushy types and 12 to 18 inches (30 to 45 cm) for the trailing kinds.

Plant out homegrown or store-bought wishbone flowers a few weeks after the last spring frost, when the soil has warmed up. A spot in partial shade is best, with protection from afternoon sun. Wishbone flowers do very well in deep shade too, especially in hot summer climates. Only in truly cool summer areas should you even think of growing them in full sun.

Wishbone flowers dislike hot, humid weather. They'll do best where summers are naturally cool, or in hot climates, with a combination of a thick mulch, regular watering, and shade to keep them air-conditioned. If you apply foliar fertilizer, especially one that is rich in potassium, every few weeks throughout the summer, you'll get a maximum amount of bloom. Growing them in a soil with plenty of added compost gives great results too. There isn't much use in deadheading this plant: The seed capsules aren't unattractive and going to seed doesn't seem to slow their flowering one iota.

Good Neighbors

Small in stature and delicate in habit, wishbone flower makes a good edger for shady beds filled with ferns or hostas. In a container, pair *Torenia fournieri* with yellow pansies and blue edging lobelia (*Lobelia erinus*) to accentuate their yellow throats and varying shades of blue and purple.

'Clown Rose' wishbone flower (*Torenia fournieri* 'Clown Rose')

Problems and Solutions

Leaf and stem diseases are possible when the plant is stressed. To avoid these problems, plant in rich, moist, and well-drained soil. Keep wishbone flower cool and well watered but without moistening the leaves.

Top Performer

Torenia fournieri (wishbone flower, bluewings): This is a small, bushy, upright annual with pale green leaves. The 1½- to 2-inch (4- to 5-cm) long flowers come in lavender and white, violet and purple, and pink and rose, as well as pure white. Most have a paler throat and a bright yellow spot in the center of the lower "lip." Height: 4 to 12 inches (10 to 30 cm). Spread: 6 to 9 inches (15 to 23 cm).

More Recommended Torenia

Torenia flava (yellow wishbone flower): Also called *T. baillonii*. The 1-inch (2.5-cm) flowers are a rich golden yellow with a contrasting dark maroon throat, and the "wishbone" is nearly black: very striking! The plant is more spreading than *T. fournieri* and trails wonderfully when grown in a basket or container. Height: 8 to 12 inches (20 to 30 cm). Spread: 1 to 2 feet (30 to 60 cm).

Up and Coming

Most wishbone flowers have a bushy habit, but there are some new hybrids with a very interesting trailing habit. Plants in the 'Summer Wave' series, for instance, make a great groundcover for a shady spot or dangle gracefully from containers and hanging baskets. 'Summer Wave' has light blue flowers marked in deep blue; 'Summer Wave Violet' is violet and deep purple. Future years should bring the full color range of *Torenia fournieri* into this exciting new type of plant. Height: 8 to 12 inches (20 to 30 cm). Spread: 18 to 36 inches (45 to 90 cm).

LOW-GROWING ANNUALS FOR
Beautiful Borders

Of all the ways you can enjoy annuals, using them for edging flowerbeds is probably the most popular. The human eye adores lines, be they straight or squiggly. If you edge your flowerbeds with a low border of plants of a similar height and shape, you can do just about whatever you want with the rest of the bed, and it will look just great. You can even edge a scraggly, unmanaged forest in annuals and get neighbors commenting on your "beautiful garden"! And the choice is enormous: Just about all the plants in this book (expect perhaps those in the chapter "Giants for the Back of the Garden" on page 192) can eventually make good border plants, so take your pick! Many annuals of particular interest as edging plants, though, are highlighted in this chapter.

◀ Low-growing annuals are so popular as edging material for flowerbeds that the term "edging plant" has come to mean an annual flower. There is a wide range of "edgers," including ageratum.

Edging Matters

The ideal edging plant has dense, compact growth; melds readily into its neighbors to form a perfectly even miniature hedge; and either blooms up a storm all summer or has colorful foliage from spring to fall. It's easy to transplant or quick to bloom from seed and is abundantly available (you need lots of plants to make a good edging). Even with all these criteria, you have nearly unlimited options: *Most* annuals are either naturally low-growing or offer compact selections that would look great in a border situation.

Perfect Edges, Every Time

Of course, you could treat edging annuals as hedges and trim them neatly every few weeks to create a perfectly straight line or even the intricate patterns of knot gardens and Victorian carpet beds. Constant trimming is, however, a lot of work, and not everyone wants such a formal look to their borders. That's why most gardeners simply use annuals planted in a line to create an edge that is generally straight without being geometrically perfect, since it is formed of plants that are generally rounded. The result is at least as charming as the "cut-with-a-knife" look of formal carpet bedding but softer and friendlier: more suited to the less rigid garden styles of today and to the decided lack of manpower in the average garden. (After all, the Victorians given to perfectly trimmed carpet bedding usually had a full-time gardener at their service!)

Creating a narrow border is easy: Simply plant multiples of a single kind of annual either in a straight line or following the contours of the garden. Since you want the plants to merge with each

Formal carpet bedding is enjoying a surge in popularity once again. Botanical gardens and city parks are terrific places to look for ideas and plant combinations.

other, set them a bit closer together than usual. If the plant has a spread of 1 foot (30 cm), for example, set them 8 to 10 inches (20 to 25 cm) apart. For wider beds, a single line of plants can be a bit thin, though. Unless the edging annual is very bushy, consider instead planting two or three rows deep for more impact. Don't align the rows on a square pattern, though. Instead, plant them in a triangular pattern equidistant from one another to give the bed a fuller look. Don't panic at the thin look of a newly planted border; young annuals fill in quickly. Within weeks, you'll have the full effect you've been striving for.

Mix and Match

Traditionally, of course, edgings are done all in one type of annual in one single color. And why not? Such a border has a nice unifying effect and is certainly easy enough to plan!

You can, however, also mix different colors of the same plant or even two or more different species in the same border, especially if all are about the same height. A checkerboard pattern caused by following an overly precise pattern, such as one white sweet alyssum (*Lobularia*

maritima) followed by one purple one, ad infinitum, can be a bit tedious, though. Instead, group the plants together. You might have 2 or 3 feet (60 to 90 cm) of white alyssum, 4 or 5 feet (1.2 to 1.5 m) of purple, then 6 feet (1.8 m) of white, and so on. Mixing groups of different types of plants also works well, especially in informal garden styles. Combine white sweet alyssum with blue ageratum (*Ageratum houstonianum*) for a calming effect, or set fire to the border's edge by growing brilliant yellow marigolds with fiery red salvias (*Salvia splendens*) of the same height.

And, yes, you can also mix differently colored plants with impunity. Don't try for any type of pattern: Simply pluck one plant after the other from a tray of mixed colors and plant, without looking at what you're doing. After all, flower colors mix in nature, so why not in the garden?

Beyond Edging

Of course, the naturally dense, compact growth of edging annuals makes them wonderfully suited for all sorts of other uses. Instead of planting them in thin lines toward the edge of the garden, for example, just spread them back toward the middle and you can create an incredible mass planting. They really shine in containers, too. The taller ones make great fillers, and the very lowest ones look great along the outer edges. (Most have a naturally spreading habit and will at least reach out and over the edge of the container; many will trail at least slightly.) Their dense habit and capacity to mingle with their neighbors also makes them a great choice for planting alone in containers. Four or five plants of any "edging" annual sharing the same pot will create a marvelous effect.

Is There Carpet Bedding in Your Future?

Carpet bedding is a style of garden very closely related to the parterre or knot garden of France. It caught on in the 1800s and remained popular—especially in estate gardens and municipal parks—well into the twentieth century. Bedding plants, usually those with colorful foliage, were planted in very precise patterns, like a tapestry. At the extreme limit, carpet bedding was so precise that the plants were trimmed weekly, something modern gardeners would scarcely have the time to do. But simpler patterns requiring only mass plantings of plants in contrasting colors are not only possible, they're actually easy to carry out. And carpet bedding, after nearly a century of neglect, seems to be coming back in a big way in city parks. Will home gardeners be able to resist the sway? If you have a bit of a slope (carpet beds *are* best admired from an angle) and want something unusual and ornamental, give this style a try!

In carpet beds, low-growing foliage plants still reign supreme, but you can also use any low-growing flowering annual. If a rainy summer causes plants to grow more than they usually would, just go over the bed with a string trimmer when it threatens to get out of control, cutting plants back by half. Within 2 weeks, your carpet bed will look better than ever!

The Lower the Better?

Not all the annuals used in edging are naturally short and compact. Most, in fact, were originally much taller plants. Gardeners have a thing for dense growth, however, so hybridizers have long seen "compact yet floriferous" as the ultimate goal. The result is that annuals become shorter and shorter as time goes on. The original ageratum (*Ageratum houstonianum*), for example, was over 30 inches (75 cm) tall, but some modern lines scarcely reach 4 inches (10 cm). And there are even what can only be called "edging" sunflowers (*Helianthus annuus*) reaching just 16 inches (40 cm) tall—quite a change from a plant that originally grew to 15 feet (4.5 m). With many annuals coming down a good 2 inches (5 cm) every 5 or 6 years, we may be seeing more plants that bloom after barely breaking ground.

16 More Low-Growing Annuals

No problem here: If there's any annual that doesn't yet have a low-growing form, you can be pretty sure that hybridizers are working hard at trying to create one. Here are just a few of the most popular of the *hundreds* of annuals that make great edging plants.

Antirrhinum (Snapdragon)	.42	Petunia (Petunia)	.56
Begonia Semperflorens (Wax begonia)	.156	Portulaca (Portulaca)	.120
Calendula (Calendula)	.74	Salvia splendens (Scarlet sage)	.123
Dahlia (Dahlia)	.48	Senecio (Dusty miller)	.298
Eschscholzia (California poppy)	.112	Tagetes (Marigold)	.58
Impatiens (Impatiens)	.162	Torenia (Wishbone flower)	.170
Lobelia (Edging lobelia)	.164	Viola (Pansy)	.64
Pelargonium × hortorum (Zonal geranium)	.54	Zinnia (Zinnia)	.66

Ageratum

Ageratum, flossflower

Once a tallish annual for the mid-border, ageratum has morphed into the ideal edging plant. It forms a low mound of heart-shaped leaves often almost covered by dense clusters of fuzzy, ball-shaped flowers. The main color is lavender-blue: It's a hard color to capture in photos, so it ends up looking pinkish purple in some catalogs and nearly pure blue in others. It's a lovely and unusual color for the garden, and the flowers last and last. In fact, the name *Ageratum* means "long-lived"; it's derived from the Greek *a* ("not") and *geras* ("age").

Plant Profile

AGERATUM
ah-ger-AY-tum

- **Bloom Color:** Lavender-blue; other shades vary by species

- **Bloom Time:** Late spring through early fall; fall through winter in mild climates

- **Height:** Varies by species; see individual listings

- **Spread:** Varies by species; see individual listings

- **Garden Uses:** Container planting, cut-flower garden, edging, groundcover, mass planting, mixed border, rock garden

- **Attracts:** Butterflies

- **Light Preference:** Full sun to partial shade

- **Soil Preference:** Humus-rich, evenly moist but well-drained soil; tolerates very acid soil

- **Best Way to Propagate:** Sow seed indoors in spring; late summer for winter bloom in mild climates

- **Hardiness:** Frost-sensitive perennial grown as half-hardy annual

Growing Tips

You can find ageratum plants for sale in any nursery or garden center. They transplant quite well, even when in full bloom.

Of course, if you're looking for one of the less common cultivars, you'll need to know how to grow ageratum from seed. You *could* sow it directly outside, but it needs warm conditions to sprout and grow, so unless you live in a mild climate with a very long frost-free season, it's better to give it a head start indoors. Sow the seed 6 to 8 weeks before the last frost date, just pressing it into the growing mix; it needs light to germinate. Seed sprouts quickly, in 5 to 14 days, at room temperature. After that, lower the air temperature to about 60°F (15°C) to get stockier plants. If that's not possible, pinch the plants back by a third before you plant them outside and you'll get the same results.

Wait to set out plants until all danger of frost is over and the soil has thoroughly warmed up. In climates with frost-free winters (Zones 10 and 11), ageratum makes a great winter-flowering annual.

Plant edging types about 6 inches (15 cm) apart for a full look; space taller cultivars 1 foot (30 cm) apart. Full sun to light shade is fine under most circumstances, but ageratum tends to burn out quickly in extreme heat. In areas where torrid summers are a problem, give it partial shade, or at least protection from the afternoon sun. Ageratum is very shallow-rooted and, therefore, suffers rapidly from drought. To keep it happy, mulch well and water before the soil dries out.

In short-season areas, many of the lavender-blue cultivars bloom right through summer with no need for deadheading, but the white-flowered cultivars and some of the pinks go downhill more quickly.

Keep cutting off the clusters when the first flowers turn brown to stimulate renewed bloom. Where summers are long, deadhead all the colors to maintain bloom. In warm climates, ageratum may self-sow.

Good Neighbors

Compact ageratums in front of slightly taller yellow marigolds is a classic combination. For something a little different, consider trying the taller, more open types, which can mix more casually with their companions. Signet marigolds (*Tagetes tenuifolia*), lantana (*Lantana camara*), and annual rudbeckias (*Rudbeckia hirta*) all make attractive companion plants.

Problems and Solutions

Whiteflies and aphids can distort and discolor foliage; control them with repeat sprays of insecticidal soap. Good air circulation and regular waterings (without wetting the foliage) will help prevent mildew. Or water in the morning so foliage has a chance to dry out.

Top Performer

Ageratum houstonianum (common ageratum, common flossflower): Also called *A. mexicanum.* Once a Central American wildflower, common ageratum is now a standard in flower gardens the world over. Besides the usual dwarf types, there are cut-flower types up to 30 inches (75 cm) tall that are just starting to be rediscovered. Another interesting development is the bicolor ageratum—the center of the flower is white, while the fuzzy outer part is blue. Height: 4 to 30 inches (10 to 75 cm). Spread: 6 to 12 inches (15 to 30 cm). **Self-sowing**

More Recommended Ageratum

Think Twice: *Ageratum conyzoides* (wild ageratum): This tropical species is catching on as a garden plant, and no wonder! It forms a tall, upright bush with flattened clusters of pale blue flowers. A real knockout, both in the garden and as a cut flower. Be forewarned, though: It can be a real weed in mild climates! Height: 3 feet (90 cm). Spread: 12 to 16 inches (30 to 40 cm). **Self-sowing**

'Blue Horizon' common ageratum (*Ageratum houstonianum* 'Blue Horizon')

Kissing Cousins

Lonas annua (golden ageratum, yellow ageratum): Also called *L. inodora.* Although only a very distant relative of the ageratum, this plant *does* share the same type of flower: dense clusters of fuzzy, ball-shaped blooms. However, the color—a bright, golden yellow—couldn't be more different. Start this one indoors in darkness, just barely covering the seed. In the garden, it tolerates drier conditions than ageratum and probably won't need mulch. Height: 12 to 18 inches (30 to 45 cm). Spread: 6 to 10 inches (15 to 25 cm). **Self-sowing**

Alternanthera

Garden alternanthera, Joseph's coat, calico plant

Garden alternanthera is a carpet-bedding plant *par excellence*. Pruned low to the ground, its variously colored foliage is super for tracing intricate knots and geometric forms of all kinds. If you decide to let it do its own thing, it will form a more open but still attractive mound of color that's perfect for edging or containers. The leaves come in a wide range of different shades, including burgundy, red, orange, yellow, and lime green—sometimes all in one leaf! Don't count on alternanthera for flowers, though; the button-shaped whitish flowers are scarcely noticeable.

Plant Profile

ALTERNANTHERA
all-ter-NAN-ther-uh

- ■ **Foliage Color:** Varies by species; see individual listings

- ■ **Foliage Time:** Late spring through early fall; year-round in mild climates

- ■ **Height:** Varies by species; see individual listings

- ■ **Spread:** Varies by species; see individual listings

- ■ **Garden Uses:** Container planting, edging, groundcover, mass planting, mixed border, rock garden

- ■ **Light Preference:** Full sun to partial shade

- ■ **Soil Preference:** Average, evenly moist but well-drained soil

- ■ **Best Way to Propagate:** Take stem cuttings in spring or fall

- ■ **Hardiness:** Frost-sensitive perennial grown as a tender annual

Growing Tips

Don't look for alternanthera seed in your local nursery; you won't find it. Nor is it often available from even the best mail-order seed specialists. That's because most strains of alternanthera don't come true from seed. With the renewed interest in carpet bedding, some of the more progressive nurseries are starting to offer individual pots or even trays of alternanthera, but most gardeners still get their first starter plant from exchanges with other gardeners (see "Larry's Garden Notes" on the opposite page).

If all you managed to find was a single cutting, use it the first year as a simple spot of color in a flowerbed or in a container. Before the first frost, take several cuttings from it. If you bring in four or five cuttings and keep them in bright light indoors for the winter, pinching them occasionally, you will have plenty of stems to use for further cuttings in late February.

Don't put alternanthera outdoors until about 2 weeks *after* the last frost date, when the air and soil have warmed up. This annual thrives in hot, humid summers; just don't let it dry out entirely. The foliage color is most intense in full sun, but alternanthera grows perfectly well in partial shade as well.

To use alternanthera as a formal edging, plant densely—about 2 inches (5 cm) apart for dwarf cultivars and 4 inches (10 cm) for others—and trim lightly as needed to keep it dense. Rather than bending over with pruning shears and clipping each stem individually, use a string trimmer to shear the whole planting in seconds. If you prefer a less formal look, space the plants out more—8 to 10 inches (20 to 25 cm) apart—and let them grow untrimmed to form nice spreading mounds.

Good Neighbors

Choose companions for Joseph's coat (*Alternanthera ficoidea*) based on their foliage colors. You might, for instance, pair a red-, yellow-, and green-leaved selection with bright red salvias, yellow melampodium (*Melampodium paludosum*), and green ornamental grasses. Maroon-leaved indoor clover (*A. dentata* 'Rubiginosa') makes a handsome background for delicately colored petunias.

Problems and Solutions

Choose a site with good air circulation to prevent the development of mildew. (See "Annual Diseases" on page 33.)

Top Performer

Alternanthera ficoidea (Joseph's coat, parrot leaf, calico plant): Also called *A. bettzichiana, A. amoena,* and *A. versicolor.* This small-leaved alternanthera bears its flowers hidden at the leaf axils. It offers the widest variety of foliage colors: red, orange, burgundy, yellow, and lime green, including bicolors and multicolors. It's also available in dwarf types—some are only 2 inches (5 cm) tall—and in broad-leaved and narrow-leaved forms. Be aware that the same plant may be sold under several different cultivar names. The situation with the botanical name is no clearer. Many experts consider *A. bettzichiana* a separate species from *A. ficoidea,* but I've lumped them together here because the average gardener won't be able to tell them apart anyway: I certainly can't! Height: 2 to 12 inches (5 to 30 cm). Spread: 4 to 24 inches (10 to 60 cm).

More Recommended Alternanthera

Alternanthera dentata 'Rubiginosa' (indoor clover): This is a taller, more open plant, with glossy, purple leaves up to 3 inches (8 cm) long. The common name comes from its clover-shaped, white inflorescences, which appear in winter. If it isn't deadheaded, this cultivar self-sows and usually comes true from seed. Height: 2 to 3 feet (60 to 90 cm). Spread: 12 to 18 inches (30 to 45 cm). **Self-sowing** 🖊

'Brilliantissima' Joseph's coat (*Alternanthera ficoidea* 'Brilliantissima')

Larry's Garden Notes

Until recently, there were only two ways of obtaining any alternanthera: through mail-order tropical plant catalogs and through exchanges with other gardeners. Alternanthera is what I call a "hand-me-down plant," along with other old favorites such as beefsteak plant (*Iresine herbstii*). These are plants that were popular generations ago but then forgotten by commercial nurseries. However, they have been maintained over all that time by gardeners passing them down within their family or exchanging cuttings with friends.

Brachyscome

Swan River daisy

Once used only as a flowering houseplant, this delightful Australian native is catching on in a big way as a summer annual. When well grown, it is nothing less than spectacular: airy mounds of soft, billowy foliage topped with innumerable, small, daisylike blooms, usually in shades of violet-blue, with yellow or black centers. Swan River daisy looks stupendous as an edging plant and even better cascading from a hanging basket or container. Gardeners living near the ocean will be pleased to know it is both wind and salt tolerant. If it were only more heat tolerant, it would be very nearly the perfect garden annual!

Plant Profile

BRACHYSCOME
brah-keys-KO-mee

- **Bloom Color:** Varies by species; see individual listings

- **Bloom Time:** Late spring through early fall; fall through winter in mild climates

- **Height:** 8 to 18 inches (20 to 45 cm)

- **Spread:** 12 to 18 inches (30 to 45 cm)

- **Garden Uses:** Container planting, cut-flower garden, edging, hanging baskets, groundcover, mass planting, meadow garden, mixed border, rock garden

- **Light Preference:** Full sun

- **Soil Preference:** Humus-rich, well-drained soil; tolerates dry conditions

- **Best Way to Propagate:** Sow seed indoors in spring or outdoors in late spring or fall

- **Hardiness:** Frost-sensitive perennial or half-hardy annual

Growing Tips

In the Australian outback, Swan River daisy is a winter or early-spring bloomer, sprouting and blooming rapidly after rains during the cooler months. In Zones 10 and 11 (and parts of Zone 9 where frost is rare), therefore, Swan River daisy performs best when sown or planted in fall for winter bloom.

In most climates, though, you can grow it as a summer-blooming annual. One possibility is to sow it outdoors after the last frost and then thin the plants to about 8 inches (20 cm) apart for border use or 4 inches (10 cm) apart for a dense edging. Many gardeners prefer starting Swan River daisy indoors 6 to 8 weeks before the last frost so it will bloom earlier in the season. In either case, just cover the seed and keep it slightly moist, at 65° to 75°F (18° to 24°C). Expect germination in 10 to 21 days. Since the seedlings are quite susceptible to damping-off when young, water from below and keep them a bit drier than other seedlings. Never plant out until all danger of frost has passed.

In the garden, full sun and perfect drainage give the best results. Avoid mulching because Swan River daisy prefers soil that dries a bit between waterings. The taller types may need a bit of support (a few twiggy branches stuck into the soil, for example). Cut the plants back by a third when about two-thirds of the blooms are spent; they'll rapidly rebloom.

FUN FACTS

Most books spell this plant's name *Brachycome*, but I've used the "correct" spelling here. Although the spelling without an "s" has been used for nearly 300 years, it was recently discovered that the originally published spelling was *Brachyscome*. And in botany, the original name always has precedence.

Good Neighbors

A combination of silvery dusty miller (*Senecio cineraria*), deep purple heliotrope (*Heliotropium arborescens*), and blue or purple Swan River daisy creates a nice foliage mix along with a pleasing color harmony. For an interesting textural contrast, pair Swan River daisy's ferny foliage with more upright plants, such as scented geraniums (*Pelargonium* spp.) or an ornamental pepper (*Capsicum annuum*).

Problems and Solutions

Swan River daisy rarely suffers from insects or diseases, but slugs or snails can be a problem in wet weather (hand-picking is one control).

Top Performer

Brachyscome iberidifolia (common Swan River daisy): This true annual is still the "usual" species, but it's being rapidly replaced by longer-lived, more heat-tolerant hybrids (see below). It produces lightly scented, 1- to 2-inch (1.25- to 2.5-cm) flowers in various shades of violet-blue, plus pink, mauve, and white. Height: 8 to 18 inches (20 to 45 cm). Spread: 12 to 18 inches (30 to 45 cm).

More Recommended Brachyscome

Brachyscome hybrids (hybrid Swan River daisy): The commonly available cutting-propagated cultivars, such as the 'Outback' series, are complex hybrids resulting from crosses with perennial species. They tend to keep blooming right through summer, in shades of violet-blue, pink, mauve, white, or lemon yellow. Height: 8 to 18 inches (20 to 45 cm). Spread: 12 to 18 inches (30 to 45 cm).

 B. multifida (rock daisy): This spreading species is more frost resistant than the others, so you can plant it out earlier. The leaves are even finer than those of *B. iberidifolia*. The flowers, only about ¾ inch (2 cm) in diameter, come in shades of blue, purple, pink, white, and pale yellow. Height: 10 to 15 inches (25 to 38 cm). Spread: 18 inches (30 to 45 cm).

Common Swan River daisy
(*Brachyscome iberidifolia*)

Smart Substitutes

Dahlberg daisy, also called golden fleece, requires similar growing conditions to those of Swan River daisy, but it's much more heat resistant. The threadlike leaves are highly aromatic; some people find them unpleasantly musky. The upward-facing, bright yellow, daisylike flowers are about ½ inch (1.25 cm) wide. You'll find this annual sold under two different botanical names: *Thymophylla tenuiloba* (currently considered to be correct) and *Dyssodia tenuiloba*. Height: 1 foot (30 cm). Spread: 1 foot (30 cm).
Self-sowing 🌱

Felicia

Blue daisy, blue marguerite

Blue is such a rare color in the garden that it's surprising this plant isn't more popular. And the flowers on the best cultivars really are a true blue, with none of the violet overtones common to so many "blue" flowers. There are mauve, pink, and white cultivars too, but I think it's a shame to substitute such everyday flower colors for the rich blue of the real thing. This African genus of some 80 species contains a wide variety of plants, from annuals to perennials to shrubs. The commonly available selections described here all have small, daisylike flowers with a contrasting yellow center.

Plant Profile

FELICIA
feh-LEE-see-uh

- **Bloom Color:** Blue, mauve, pink, or white

- **Bloom Time:** Late spring through early fall; fall through winter in mild climates

- **Height:** Varies by species; see individual listings

- **Spread:** Varies by species; see individual listings

- **Garden Uses:** Container planting, cut-flower garden, edging, hanging baskets, groundcover, mass planting, mixed border, rock garden

- **Attracts:** Butterflies

- **Light Preference:** Full sun

- **Soil Preference:** Very well-drained, even sandy, soil; tolerates poor soil

- **Best Way to Propagate:** Sow seed indoors in spring or late winter

- **Hardiness:** Tender annual or frost-sensitive subshrub grown as a tender annual

Growing Tips

Trays and cell packs of blue daisies are becoming more widely available in nurseries, so if you prefer, you can start with plants that are already blooming.

If you'd rather raise your own from seed, sow indoors 10 to 12 weeks before the last frost, just barely covering the seed. After sowing, seal the tray in a clear plastic bag and place it in the refrigerator for 3 weeks; then expose it to temperatures 60° to 70°F (15° to 21°C). Seeds will germinate in about 1 month. You can skip the precooling treatment and start the seeds only 6 to 8 weeks early, but germination will be more irregular. Pinch the seedlings as they grow to stimulate good basal branching. Plant out when all danger of frost or even cool nights has passed, in full sun and just about any kind of well-drained soil.

If desired, you can instead sow the seed directly outdoors at about the last frost date, while the soil is still cool. This technique works best in climates where summers are cool: Hot weather too soon after germination can kill the young seedlings. In Zones 10 and 11, you can sow blue daisy seed in fall for winter and spring bloom.

Space the smaller types about 6 inches (15 cm) apart, and the taller types up to 18 inches (45 cm) apart. During summer, water only enough to keep them from drying out. Deadhead regularly to stimulate continuous bloom.

The perennial species of blue daisies are hardy only in Zones 10 and 11. Elsewhere, either dig up the plants in fall in order to overwinter them indoors in full sun, or take stem cuttings in late summer for the next season.

Good Neighbors

Combining this blue daisy with yellow companions, such as yellow lantana (*Lantana camara*) will bring out the yellow centers of the flowers. In a container, pair blue daisy with a plant that has some foliage interest, such as the broad, silvery leaves of *Plectranthus argentatus*.

Problems and Solutions

Rot and botrytis (a fuzzy gray mold) can attack plants growing in poorly drained soil.

Top Performer

Felicia amelloides (blue daisy, blue marguerite): Also called *F. aethiopica*, *Aster amelloides*, *A. capensis*, and *A. coelestis*. By far the most commonly grown species, it is available from both seed and cuttings. It's actually a small shrub in the wild, but you can grow it that way outdoors only in the very mildest climates. Elsewhere, treat it as an annual or bring plants or cuttings in over the winter. There are lots of cultivars, mostly in shades of light to deep blue but also in white, pink, and mauve. Flower size ranges from ¾ to 2 inches (2 cm to 5 cm). Leaves range from linear to oval and are often quite succulent. Height: 10 to 24 inches (25 to 60 cm). Spread: 10 to 24 inches (25 to 60 cm).

More Recommended Felicia

Felicia amoena (blue daisy): Also called *Aster pappei*. A less common but equally attractive perennial species, with downy leaves and bright blue flowers. It is best known through its cream variegated cultivar, 'Variegata', probably the most common of several variegated blue daisies. Height: 12 to 20 inches (30 to 50 cm). Spread: 12 to 20 inches (30 to 50 cm).

F. bergeriana (kingfisher daisy): This charming annual species is much smaller than the others but is even more free flowering. It produces a low-growing mat of hairy foliage and copious, 1¼-inch (3-cm), light blue flowers borne well above the foliage. It is remarkably wind resistant and, therefore, popular in coastal and mountainous areas. Height: 8 to 10 inches (20 to 25 cm). Spread: 10 to 18 inches (25 to 45 cm).

Blue daisy
(*Felicia amelloides*)

Kissing Cousins

Looking for a blue daisy that's native to North America? Tahoka daisy (*Machaeranthera tanacetifolia*, also called *Aster tanacetifolius*) fills the bill quite nicely. It's a bushy, upright plant with deeply cut leaves and 2-inch (5-cm), violet-blue, yellow-centered daisies throughout summer. Treat it as *Felicia*, although you can also sow the seed in fall for bloom earlier the following summer. Can't find it in your usual seed catalog? Try looking in the wildflower section. Height: 15 to 24 inches (38 to 60 cm). Spread: 1 foot (30 cm). Self-sowing

Gypsophila

Baby's breath

Some plants "just don't get no respect," to quote a famous comedian. Such is the case with the annual baby's breath. The fine, lacy, open clumps of foliage are covered with numerous flowers, giving them a billowing, cloudlike appearance similar to the much better-known perennial baby's breath (*Gypsophila paniculata*) but on smaller plants. In spite of their beauty, though, you never seem to see them mentioned. I must admit I'm a serious fan of wall baby's breath (*G. muralis*), in particular; I consider it one of the very best of all the edging plants!

Plant Profile

GYPSOPHILA
jip-SOFF-ill-uh

■ Bloom Color: Pink, white

■ Bloom Time: Late spring through early fall; fall through winter in mild climates

■ Height: Varies by species; see individual listings

■ Spread: Varies by species; see individual listings

■ Garden Uses: Container planting, cut-flower garden, edging, hanging baskets, groundcover, meadow garden, mixed border, rock garden, wall planting

■ Light Preference: Full sun to partial shade

■ Soil Preference: Average, well-drained soil; tolerates poor, sandy, alkaline soil

■ Best Way to Propagate: Sow seed indoors or outdoors in spring

■ Hardiness: Hardy annual

Growing Tips

You may find wall baby's breath (*Gypsophila muralis*) sold in six packs or cell packs at better nurseries in spring, but common annual baby's breath (*G. elegans*) is rarely sold this way. Fortunately, both are extremely easy to grow from seed. Sow these hardy annuals outdoors a few weeks before the last frost, or even the previous fall, for summer bloom. (For earlier flowers on wall baby's breath, you can sow indoors 6 to 8 weeks before the last frost.) In mild winter areas, you can direct-sow either species in fall for winter bloom.

Just barely cover the seed with soil and water well. It's up in less than 2 weeks and will often start to bloom in 6 to 8 weeks. In the garden, baby's breaths need minimal care; just water them enough to keep them from drying out completely. They seem to grow fine in average garden soil, but add a bit of lime if you know your soil is highly acidic.

Wall baby's breath is a long-blooming plant that breezes through the summer. In really hot climates, give it a bit of afternoon shade and cut it back harshly in midseason to stimulate rebloom if it seems to be faltering. Common annual baby's breath, on the contrary, tends to bloom for only a short period, about 6 weeks. Sow it again every 2 to 3 weeks until July if you want nonstop bloom.

Plant wall baby's breath about 6 inches (15 cm) apart if you use it as an edging plant. If you want to accentuate its domelike appearance, give it more space: about 8 to 10 inches (20 to 25 cm).

Taller common annual baby's breath is very floppy, so plant it densely—about 4 inches (10 cm) apart—so it can lean on its neighbors; otherwise, mix it in with other plants that can hold it up. A few twiggy branches placed here and there will also help. Like perennial baby's breath, it makes a great cut flower (although it doesn't dry well) and is used as filler in summer bouquets.

Both annual baby's breaths self-sow, perhaps a bit too readily in the case of *G. elegans*.

Good Neighbors

If there was ever a plant that requires a companion, common annual baby's breath (*Gypsophila elegans*) is it: It's simply too wispy to stand alone. Heliotrope (*Heliotropium arborescens*), roses, and yuccas are a few excellent partners. Wall baby's breath (*G. muralis*) is a particularly choice edging plant, and its pastel shades complement most other colors.

Problems and Solutions

The annual species don't seem to have any major problems.

Top Performer

Gypsophila muralis (wall baby's breath): When the double, pale pink cultivar 'Gypsy' won an All-America Selection award in 1997, I figured this beautiful annual had finally hit the big time, but it remains poorly known in most garden centers and nurseries. Wall baby's breath is a very low-growing, dome-shaped plant with extremely thin stems and even thinner leaves. The tiny, ⅛- to ¼-inch (3- to 6-mm), white or pale pink flowers seem to float on air—an incredibly charming effect! They are borne in incredible numbers over a long season. Height: 6 to 12 inches (15 to 30 cm). Spread: 1 foot (30 cm). **Self-sowing** 🌱

More Recommended Gypsophila

❗**Think Twice:** *Gypsophila elegans* (common annual baby's breath): This is a branching, open, weakly upright plant with white, pink, or rose flowers about ½ inch (1.25 cm) across, sometimes with darker veins. It's much more at home in the middle of the garden than as an edging because it can depend on surrounding plants for support, although some of the lower-growing types—like the 20-inch (50-cm), white-flowered 'Snow Fountains'—could work as edging plants in a tall border. Height: 18 to 30 inches (45 to 75 cm). Spread: 1 foot (30 cm). **Self-sowing** 🌱

Wall baby's breath (*Gypsophila muralis*)

Smart Substitutes

❗**Think Twice:** From a distance, Mexican daisy (*Erigeron karvinskianus*, also called *E. mucronatus*) looks much like wall baby's breath (*Gypsophila muralis*); close up, though, it couldn't be more different. Mexican daisy's ¾-inch (2-cm) blooms are true daisies: yellow-centered, with white ray flowers that fade to pink. It's perennial in Zones 9 to 11. Where it's too hot for baby's breath, this may do the trick! Watch it, though: It can self-sow to the point of weediness. Height: 6 to 12 inches (15 to 30 cm). Spread: 20 inches (50 cm). **Self-sowing** 🌱

Linaria

Toadflax, spurred snapdragon

How could you not be charmed by toadflax? Its tiny blossoms in myriad colors look just like miniature snapdragons, with the same puffy lower lip and jaws that open when you press on them. The main difference is that, if you look below the flower, you'll see it has a nectar-filled spur that will make your yard's hummingbirds very happy. Plus the upper lip is very extended and divided into two parts, looking a bit like rabbit ears.

Plant Profile

LINARIA
lin-AIR-ee-uh

- **Bloom Color:** Pink, purple, red, orange, yellow, white
- **Bloom Time:** Late spring through early fall; fall through winter in mild climates
- **Height:** Varies by species; see individual listings
- **Spread:** Varies by species; see individual listings
- **Garden Uses:** Container planting, cut-flower garden, edging, hanging baskets, meadow garden, mixed border, rock garden, wall planting
- **Attracts:** Hummingbirds
- **Light Preference:** Full sun to partial shade
- **Soil Preference:** Average to humus-rich, well-drained soil; tolerates sandy soil
- **Best Way to Propagate:** Sow seed indoors in spring or outdoors in late spring; early fall in mild winter areas
- **Hardiness:** Hardy annual

Growing Tips

You'll often find six packs or cell packs of toadflax in nurseries in the spring, usually in full bloom. If you buy them this way, trim them back by about a third before planting. They'll sprout again from the base and bloom with renewed vigor in only a few weeks.

You can also grow toadflax from seed. For the earliest possible bloom from an outdoor sowing, sow in fall or as soon as you can work the soil in spring, barely covering the seed. For yet earlier bloom, sow indoors 10 to 12 weeks before the last frost, just pressing the seed into the planting mix; then seal the tray inside a plastic bag and place in the refrigerator for 3 to 4 weeks. Afterward, set the tray in a relatively cool spot, about 55° to 60°F (13° to 15°C).

For a somewhat later flowering, sow toadflax outdoors 2 or 3 weeks before the last frost. In mild winter areas, sow in early fall for winter bloom.

Set out transplants in small clumps 8 to 10 inches (20 to 25 cm) apart, or thin seedlings to stand 3 to 4 inches (8 to 10 cm) apart. A site with excellent drainage is important. Full sun is best, although afternoon shade in hot summer areas will help maintain blooming through the dog days.

Although toadflax is drought tolerant, you'll find that it blooms better with regular watering. After the first flush of bloom, cut plants back by a third and spray them with organic foliar fertilizer; they'll quickly come into bloom again.

Don't confuse these annual toadflaxes, which do self-sow but rarely become weedy, with common toadflax or butter-and-eggs (*Linaria vulgaris*), a yellow-flowered perennial species that spreads by runners and has become a common weed.

Good Neighbors

The compact forms of Morocco toad-flax (*Linaria maroccana*) blend well with the shorter cultivars of annual phlox (*Phlox drummondii*) and silver-leaved licorice plant (*Helichrysum petiolare*). Use the warm red, orange, and yellow colors of 'Crown Jewels' purple-net toadflax (*L. reticulata*) to set off the deep purple foliage of purple basil or *Heuchera* 'Palace Purple'.

Problems and Solutions

Fungal diseases can be a problem, notably where air circulation is limited; thin out the plants to improve air movement. Control aphids with insecticidal soap sprays.

Morocco toadflax
(*Linaria maroccana*)

Top Performer

Linaria maroccana (Morocco toadflax): Most modern strains are dwarf, with spreading stems of narrow leaves reaching no more than 9 to 12 inches (23 to 30 cm) in height, although there are also taller strains for use in the middle of the border. For years, you could find only mixed colors of this plant, but recently separate colors have become available. (Be aware that the resulting seedlings will not be identical, but rather shades of yellow, shades of red, and so on.) Height: 9 to 18 inches (23 to 45 cm). Spread: 6 inches (15 cm). **Self-sowing**

More Recommended Linaria

Linaria anticaria (dwarf yellow toadflax): This is a relatively new one—a natural dwarf with cream flowers highlighted by a bright lemon yellow spot. The narrow leaves are blue-green. Height: 6 to 8 inches (15 to 20 cm). Spread: 4 inches (10 cm). **Self-sowing**

L. reticulata (purple-net toadflax): Although originally a taller species, the most commonly available cultivars, such as 'Crown Jewels', are much more compact. Wild forms have purple flowers with yellow netting and a yellow mark on the lower lip; modern cultivars range into such shades as red, maroon-red, orange, or yellow, usually with contrasting veins and lip. Height: 9 to 48 inches (23 to 120 cm). Spread: 4 to 9 inches (10 to 23 cm). **Self-sowing**

Larry's Garden Notes

With a name like toadflax, *Linaria* has a definite PR problem. It makes the flower sound brown and warty, something you'd be more likely to add to a witch's brew than a flower garden. Yet there's nothing ugly about toad-flax; it's a charming and colorful plant that's well worth growing. It does, however, deserve its name for another reason. In Old English, adding the word "toad" to the name of any plant or animal meant that it was poisonous (in the case of toadflax, it's poisonous if you eat it). Come to think of it, maybe it *would* be perfect for a witch's brew!

Lobularia

Sweet alyssum, alyssum

Is there an easier (or more fragrant) annual to grow than sweet alyssum? Probably not. It's a snap from seed or from transplants; reaches blooming size at record speed; grows just about anywhere but in deep shade or soggy soil; and in general, outperforms just about every other garden plant. As a bonus, the flowers attract beneficial flower flies that help control aphids and other pests. Minute as the flowers may be, they are borne in such huge numbers that the plant is often almost hidden by flowers throughout the entire growing season. Is it any wonder that this simple little edging plant is one of the most popular annuals of all?

Plant Profile

LOBULARIA
lob-you-LAIR-ee-uh

- **Bloom Color:** Lavender, pink, purple, apricot, rose, lemon yellow, white

- **Bloom Time:** Late spring through early fall; year round in mild climates

- **Height:** 2 to 12 inches (5 to 30 cm)

- **Spread:** 8 to 12 inches (20 to 30 cm)

- **Garden Uses:** Container planting, cut-flower garden, edging, hanging baskets, groundcover, mass planting, meadow garden, mixed border, rock garden, wall planting

- **Light Preference:** Full sun to partial shade

- **Soil Preference:** Average to poor, well-drained soil; tolerates poor, sandy soil

- **Best Way to Propagate:** Sow seed outdoors in late spring

- **Hardiness:** Hardy annual

Growing Tips

Every garden center and nursery carries six packs or cell packs of sweet alyssum in spring, and these transplants certainly provide instant results. One downside is that transplants often don't settle into the garden very well. (If you go this route, look for smaller plants with more leaves than bloom, or trim heavily blooming plants back by half at planting time.) The other downside is that you inevitably pay far too much. Sweet alyssum is just about the easiest plant that nurseries can produce, so it should be much cheaper than plants like petunias or pansies that require months of culture plus special growing conditions. But usually nurseries sell all their annuals at the same price (except they may charge more for a few really tough-to-grow ones). Thus figure that you've paid twice or three times what the alyssum plants are really worth.

It's actually quite simple to start sweet alyssum yourself from seed. (It's so easy to do that sweet alyssum is considered a prime choice for first-time seed sowers!) Just sprinkle some seed over moist growing mix 5 to 6 weeks before the last spring frost; then press lightly. Place them in a bright spot (they do need light to germinate) at anywhere from 55°F (13°C) up to room temperature, and they'll germinate in as little as 5 days. After the last frost, plant them outdoors in sun or partial shade in any kind of well-drained soil, setting the plants 6 to 8 inches (15 to 20 cm) apart. Water once, then let them grow. Within 5 to 6 weeks, they'll already be blooming lightly.

Even easier yet, if that's possible, just sprinkle the seed on the ground right where you want the plants to grow. In cold winter climates, sow outdoors a few weeks before the last frost; in mild winter areas, sow once each season—spring, summer, fall, and winter—for bloom 6 weeks later. When the plants come up, thin them to 6 to 8 inches (15 to 20 cm) apart.

In cool summer areas, sweet alyssum blooms right through the summer with no effort on your part (except a bit of watering during periods of drought), and it survives the first fall frosts, blooming on until nearly winter. In hot summer climates, it will do best in partial shade, or at least with protection from afternoon sun. After the first flush of bloom, trim it back by half and it will soon be flowering again. It may quit blooming during the hottest weather in some climates, but then it will pick up where it left off when the air cools again. Or simply sow more, even as late as early August; that way, you'll be sure to have healthy young plants for fall bloom.

Sweet alyssum
(*Lobularia maritima*)

Good Neighbors

It's hard to go wrong if you just scatter sweet alyssum seed along paths or in front of flower borders. Seed sprinkled over maturing daffodil foliage will result in a soft sheet of color above the dormant bulbs. Deep purple heliotrope (*Heliotropium arborescens*) growing out of a sea of purple alyssum creates an elegant combination with a somewhat formal look.

Problems and Solutions

Watch out for damping-off if you start seeds indoors; water from below to avoid. Slugs and snails seem to love it, but sweet alyssum usually grows in faster than they can eat it.

Top Performer

Lobularia maritima (sweet alyssum, alyssum): Also called *Alyssum maritimum*. This tiny, spreading, mat-forming plant has simple, narrow leaves and domed clusters of tiny, four-petaled blooms. There are many cultivars, not only in the traditional colors—white, purple, pink, lavender, and rose—but also in newer shades, such as apricot and lemon yellow. They're all great! **Self-sowing** 🌱

Larry's Garden Notes

Where fragrance is concerned, not all colors are created equal. Whites are the most highly scented, whereas the deep purple ones often have no scent at all. To get the most pleasure out of the fragrant ones, plant at least a few of them at nose level: at the top of a stone wall, in a window box, in a patio planter, or in hanging baskets. And alyssum looks wonderful in all those situations, cascading from walls and containers like billowing, frothy foam. You can even try sowing some in pots indoors to enjoy the perfume in winter as well!

Phlox

Annual phlox, Drummond phlox, Texas pride

Most gardeners know the various perennial phloxes quite well, but surprisingly few realize that there's an annual phlox as well. Annual phlox has the same dense clusters of tubular flowers that spread at the tip into flat, five-lobed blossoms, and the lance-shaped foliage is similar, too. Although shorter, it was originally as sturdily upright as garden phlox (*Phlox paniculata*), but most modern hybrids are now instead low-growing spreaders. While annual phlox loses points because of its near lack of scent, it gains them all back by being nearly immune to mildew. All in all, it's a plant to discover!

Plant Profile

PHLOX
FLOCKS

■ **Bloom Color:** Lavender, pink, purple, salmon, red, yellow, white

■ **Bloom Time:** Late spring through midfall

■ **Height:** 4 to 18 inches (10 to 45 cm)

■ **Spread:** 6 to 10 inches (15 to 25 cm)

■ **Garden Uses:** Container planting, cut-flower garden, edging, hanging baskets, groundcover, mass planting, meadow garden, mixed border, rock garden

■ **Attracts:** Butterflies, hummingbirds

■ **Light Preference:** Full sun to partial shade

■ **Soil Preference:** Average to humus-rich, evenly moist but well-drained soil

■ **Best Way to Propagate:** Sow seed indoors or outdoors in spring

■ **Hardiness:** Hardy annual

Growing Tips

Annual phlox is available in six packs or cell packs, but it usually doesn't sell well that way because it has an undeserved reputation for being difficult to transplant. True, you shouldn't go out of your way to twist or squeeze the roots, or to knock the soil out of the rootball, but if you leave the roots reasonably intact, there is no major problem. Just to be safe, look for annual phlox sold in cell packs, so you can remove the rootball with a minimum of disturbance. Annual phlox is frost tolerant, so you can even plant it out a few weeks before the last frost date if the spring isn't particularly cool.

Of course, you can also grow phlox from seed. In long-season areas, simply sow outdoors a few weeks before the last frost date, while the soil is still cool. Barely cover the seed. When the plants come up, in 10 to 21 days, thin or transplant them to stand 4 to 6 inches (10 to 15 cm) apart for the more common dwarf types or 12 to 18 inches (30 to 45 cm) for the taller types.

Indoors, sow the seed directly into cell packs or peat pots. (Alternately, sow them into trays and then transplant them into cell packs or pots when they have four to six leaves.) Lightly sprinkle growing mix over the seed; then cover with black plastic until germination, which is quite irregular and takes 10 days to 3 weeks. Cool temperatures—55° to 65°F (13° to 18°C)—give the best results. After germination, expose seedlings to bright light and thin to one plant per pot. Pinch plants at least once, when they have four or eight leaves, to help stimulate branching.

Annual phlox grows best in full sun where summers are cool, but some protection from afternoon sun is best in hot summer areas. To keep the plants cool, mulch and make sure the soil remains evenly moist. Deadhead to remove faded flowers and stimulate continued bloom. If your plants seem to stall in the heat and look close to death, cut them back severely, to about 2 inches (5 cm) from the ground, or sow them again for fall bloom.

Good Neighbors

The mixed colors and various heights of annual phlox makes it very useful as a bedding plant, either in a formal scheme or a more natural-style garden. By picking up colors in a mix—for example, echoing the warm colors of 'Phlox of Sheep' with taller snapdragons—you can easily create a very colorful, long-blooming border. The taller types make an attractive underplanting for airier Brazilian vervain (*Verbena bonariensis*).

Problems and Solutions

Mildew rarely bothers annual phlox, usually showing up only when the plants are drought stressed. Keep them at least slightly moist at all times, and you should have no problems.

Top Performer

Phlox drummondii (annual phlox, Drummond phlox, Texas pride): These days, you'll most often see the dwarf, spreading, edging hybrids. They range between 6 and 8 inches (15 and 20 cm) tall. Most seed catalogs also offer at least one of the taller cut-flower types, 15 to 18 inches (38 to 45 cm) tall. Many annual phlox flowers are bicolor or even tricolor, typically with a darker eye. Single, semi-double, and double cultivars are available, as are small- and large-flowered strains. 'Sternenzauber' (also called 'Twinkle') has star-shaped flowers with fringed petals. My favorite, though, is 'Phlox of Sheep', with beautiful pastel shades, including apricot and lemon yellow. **Self-sowing**

Annual phlox
(*Phlox drummondii*)

Larry's Garden Notes

Annual phlox gets its botanical name (*Phlox drummondii*) from its discoverer, Englishman Thomas Drummond, who noticed the plant in eastern Texas in 1835. The wild plant had red flowers only; all the shades we know and love today showed up as mutations over the years and were improved by intensive breeding programs. The original phlox was upright but also tended to flop. Hybridizers corrected this by developing strains with extra-tough stems (the cut-flower types of today) as well as dwarf strains that spread sideways more than up.

GIANTS FOR THE
Back of the Garden

Most of the true "giant" plants we use in gardens are trees and shrubs: plants that take years to reach any size at all. So, how can a plant grow from a seed to giant status in just one summer? Well, somehow, some annuals do manage to do it. Of course, being tall is very practical—a plant that can grow from seed and reach up above its neighbors in only a few short weeks will be able to grab the lion's share of solar energy in that area; and to plants, light means life. Tall annuals may be the exceptions, but those that do find the strength to reach for the sky are often very successful in the wild, and they certainly add a dramatic touch to our gardens as well!

◄ Only a few years ago, tall-growing annuals seemed destined to go the way of the dinosaur: Everyone was into dwarf, edging annuals. But "big" is back in style again, so don't hesitate to try giant annuals, like kiss-me-over-the-garden-gate.

Bodacious Beauties

Big, bold, and bodacious: That's how I'd describe the plants in this chapter. All are either tall or massive; many are both. I didn't have any specific height in mind in choosing "giant annuals," as height is only one factor. Some, indeed, are only about 3 feet (90 cm) tall, just a bit bigger than many of the "regular" annuals. But the shorter giants (now *there's* an oxymoron!) make up for any lack in height by being massive plants: true "Mack trucks" of the plant world. Wide and dense, these full-figured plants fill space more like a shrub than a typical annual. They truly stand out from the crowd, so you often need only a few of them to create the impact you're looking for.

Putting Giants to Good Use

As this chapter's title suggests, the main use for giant annuals is at the back of the flower garden. The typical annual border rises from a low edge to a slightly taller middle, and then—in recent years at least—tends to stop with a few medium-height annuals. Now, that may be all right if you're trying not to hide an incredible view, but if there's just an endless fence or a rather boring view of the neighbor's yard behind your annual bed, a row or two of humungous annuals will concentrate the view on your garden instead of its surroundings. You don't necessarily need a solid wall of plants to create an interesting background: A few patches of tall plants here and there can also create a lovely effect.

In perennial and mixed borders, tall annuals are especially useful in the early years, to give height quickly while you're waiting for

Sunflowers are the epitome of giant annuals. Once considered old-fashioned, they're now among the most trendy of all annuals, especially those with bright colors or unusual forms, like 'Teddy Bear', which is fully double.

I Screen, You Screen

Have a view you don't want to see (your neighbor's collection of pink flamingos, for example) and don't want to wait 15 years until your shrub border fills in? Use giant annuals to block it from sight in the meantime. There's nothing stopping you from planting two parallel hedges: the permanent one and the annual one. You can stop planting the annual one when the other gets big enough. Or use just the annual hedge by itself: It's great when you want to hide a summer view but like looking out on a vaster panorama in winter. In my yard, for example, I don't particularly want to see what the neighbors are doing all summer but love the feel of a seemingly endless field of snow in winter, so I break up my property-line plantings of shrubs with patches of big, bold annuals that grow sky high. They give me privacy in summer while allowing a clear view in winter.

In cold climates, hedges of tall annuals are useful for summer screening along roads and other paved areas where snowplows and snow throwers deposit crystallized ice and snow in winter. Typical shrub and evergreen hedges can't withstand this kind of abuse, even if it only happens once, but the annuals are gone by that time of year and couldn't care less!

Where strong winds are a problem, giant annuals can likewise do a great job of protecting more tender plants to the lee side. Traditionally, plains gardeners have used sunflowers as a windbreak for their vegetable and flower gar-

shrubs and taller perennials to fill in. Even in mature gardens, it's still worth leaving a bit of room for a few favorite taller annuals. Since many of them self-sow, you can take advantage of their largesse by letting them make their own decisions as to where they'll look good. And, let's be honest, often Mother Nature knows best!

In flowerbeds of all types, tall annuals can help you avoid monotony. If you have nicely organized things so your plants slope gradually from short in the front to tall in the back, that can be very soothing to the eye, but also—how can I put this without insulting anyone?—more than a bit boring. Toss a taller annual into the middle or even the foreground every now and then, and you'll find your flowerbed just comes alive visually!

dens, leaving the stalks standing in winter and removing them only in spring. They not only nicely buffer the winds but also prevent wind erosion and even trap snow, which then melts and helps keep the garden moister in summer. And if you get tired of sunflowers, you'll find many other giant annuals that will do an equally good job.

Starring in a Container near You

Obviously, a 15-foot (4.5-m) sunflower might be a bit much for even the largest container garden, but most giant annuals have a few somewhat smaller-size cultivars, in the 3- to 4-foot (90- to 120-cm) range, which can be very striking in containers. Because of their size, they make super centerpieces in mixed plantings. When used this way, you'll only need one per pot, usually dead center; then fill in around it with bushy or creeping annuals. Tall annuals look great grown on their own, as well. Often, container growing will restrain their height somewhat, but these are still big plants and will automatically dominate the scene.

Keeping Your Giants Happy

Most of the giant annuals are fast-growing, easy plants that have no particularly difficult needs to meet. Many, in fact, self-sow readily, always a sure sign of an easy-to-grow plant. Obviously, if you want the biggest, tallest, bushiest annuals, you should supply them with deep, rich soil and keep them well watered. Most, however, will still reach an imposing size on very ordinary soil and with little special care. Tall annuals generally have strong, deep roots, especially if they were sown directly in the garden, and usually only need staking in very windy sites. Transplants can be weak rooted at first, though: In a windy spot, use a short stake to hold them in place for 2 or 3 weeks, until they have had time to settle in.

A Blast from the Past

You'll note that the plants in this chapter are all old-fashioned annuals, popular back in the Victorian era or even much earlier. Several of them are so old-fashioned they're going to seem new to many readers, but I assure you, your great-grandparents probably knew them on a first-name basis. Don't think, though, that because they're all oldies that they aren't interesting. On the contrary, in recent years, a few of these annuals—particularly angel's trumpets (*Datura* spp.) and sunflower (*Helianthus annuus*)—have been so thoroughly revived they're now among the hottest of all annuals. Some are still not well known, but I think we'll be seeing a lot of the giant annuals in the near future.

12 More Giant Annuals

Giant annuals are actually quite few and far between: Most of the spectacular ones are described in this chapter. There are, however, other annuals that can be tall growing, at least in some selections. While they may not all be giants, the plants below do offer some cultivars over 3 or 4 feet (90 to 120 cm) tall that are massive enough to make good background plants.

Amaranthus

Amaranth, love-lies-bleeding, tassel flower, prince's feather

These easy-to-grow, warm-weather annuals pack quite a punch in the landscape. There are some 60 species of amaranth, including some weeds, such as pigweed (*Amaranthus retroflexus*), and grain crops (*A. cruentus* and *A. hypochondriacus*). The ornamental types range from plants with flamboyantly colored foliage to those with fascinating tassel-like flowers, and yet others have both attractive foliage and plumy flowers. Use these giants with restraint, though, as they can be quite overbearing when planted in large numbers.

Plant Profile

AMARANTHUS
am-ah-RAN-thus

- **Bloom Color:** Varies by species; see individual listings

- **Bloom Time:** Early summer through early fall; year-round in mild climates

- **Height:** Varies by species; see individual listings

- **Spread:** Varies by species; see individual listings

- **Garden Uses:** Container planting, cut-flower garden, annual hedge, mass planting, mixed border, specimen plant, screening

- **Attracts:** Seed-eating birds

- **Light Preference:** Full sun to partial shade

- **Soil Preference:** Average, evenly moist but well-drained soil

- **Best Way to Propagate:** Sow seed indoors in spring

- **Hardiness:** Frost-sensitive, short-lived perennial grown as a half-hardy annual

Growing Tips

You can buy amaranths in six packs or cell packs, but the secret is to get them while they are still young. Plants already in bloom rarely thrive when they are transplanted, although pruning them back harshly at planting can help.

Amaranths are easy to grow from seed. In areas with a long growing season, you can sow outdoors, where you want the plants to bloom, after all danger of frost has passed and the soil has warmed up. Elsewhere, start the seeds indoors 4 to 6 weeks before the last frost date. You can sow it in trays as long as you transplant it outdoors while it is still small, as mature plants resent root disturbance, or avoid the risk and sow it into peat pots. Barely cover the seed. Germination is quite fast at 70° to 75°F (21° to 24°C), sometimes in only 3 to 4 days.

Plant outside in full sun, if possible; although it will grow in partial shade, amaranth is rarely as colorful or as full. Ordinary soils are fine. In fact, in overly rich soils, the selections with colorful foliage are not as brilliantly colored. About the only thing it *won't* stand is wet feet, so make sure drainage is good. Give the plants a good 3 feet (90 cm) to spread for specimen plants; half that if you want a mass display or annual hedge.

Direct-sown amaranths generally don't require staking, but transplants are less solid and may need support until they settle in. Deadheading isn't necessary. You can, however, harvest the flowers for both fresh and dried arrangements.

Think Twice: Most amaranths will self-sow but the resulting seedlings rarely reach full size in shorter-season areas. They are not invasive in most climates, but gardeners in parts of Zones 10 and 11 (where amaranths have been known to escape from culture) might want to grow something less risky.

Good Neighbors

Amaranths make outstanding vertical accents in the garden. Balance their strong appearance with large drifts of other tall-to-medium–height annuals, such as wheat celosia (*Celosia spicata*), green-flowering tobacco (*Nicotiana* 'Lime Green'), and clouds of cosmos (*Cosmos bipinnatus*).

Problems and Solutions

Spray occasional outbreaks of aphids or red spider mites with either water or an insecticidal soap. Well-drained soil will help prevent root rot.

Top Performer

Amaranthus caudatus (love-lies-bleeding, tassel flower, tassel amaranth): This plant is an absolute knockout! The upright, red, green, or purplish stems bear pale green to reddish ovate leaves and long, tassel-like clusters of red flowers right through summer into fall. 'Viridis', with apple green blossoms, is highly popular in cut-flower arrangements. Height: 3 to 5 feet (90 to 150 cm). Spread: 18 to 30 inches (45 to 75 cm). **Self-sowing**

More Recommended Amaranthus

Amaranthus hypochondriacus (prince's feather, grain amaranth): Also called *A. hybridus*. A variable plant with green to purple leaves and massive upright panicles of yellow, green, golden, red, or purple flowers. *A. cruentus* is very similar but usually taller, to 6 feet (1.8 m). Height: 18 to 48 inches (45 to 120 cm). Spread: 12 to 18 inches (30 to 45 cm). **Self-sowing**

A. tricolor (Joseph's coat, summer poinsettia, tampala): This tall annual bears only insignificant flowers, but what leaves! Green-leaved (or green with dark markings) when young, the whole plant changes color at flowering time, becoming brilliant gold, yellow, red, cerise, purple, or tricolor. There are lots of cultivars in different colors. Height: 4 feet (1.2 m). Spread: 12 to 30 inches (30 to 75 cm). **Self-sowing**

Love-lies-bleeding
(*Amaranthus caudatus*)

Larry's Garden Notes

All the "ornamental" amaranths are also grown as edible plants. The young leaves of Joseph's coat (*Amaranthus tricolor*) can be boiled and eaten like spinach. The other species are mostly grown for their protein-rich seeds. In fall, dry the flower spikes and thresh them inside a cloth bag to free the seed, then pour over a window screen to separate the seed from the chaff. You can eat the seed cooked, popped, or sprouted or grind it into flour, using it to replace up to one-quarter of the flour in any bread recipe for a protein-rich treat.

Datura

Angel's trumpet, datura, thornapple

If you enjoy exotic-looking flowers, you definitely need to try daturas! These shrubby plants have stout stems clad in large leaves that are foul smelling (but only when crushed). Their attraction, though, comes from the huge, trumpet-shaped flowers in shades of white to lilac or purple. They unravel from rolled-up, cigarlike buds in early evening, then exude a striking, intense perfume. The scent seems sweet and enticing at first but gradually becomes overpowering if you remain right next to a plant in bloom. The show is over early the next day, by noon at the latest, then starts all over again.

Plant Profile

DATURA
da-TOUR-uh

■ **Bloom Color:** Varies by species; see individual listings

■ **Bloom Time:** Summer through early fall; year-round in mild climates

■ **Height:** Varies by species; see individual listings

■ **Spread:** Varies by species; see individual listings

■ **Garden Uses:** Container planting, cut-flower garden, annual hedge, specimen plant, screening

■ **Attracts:** Sphinx moths

■ **Light Preference:** Full sun

■ **Soil Preference:** Humus-rich, evenly moist but well-drained soil

■ **Best Way to Propagate:** Sow seed indoors in late winter

■ **Hardiness:** Frost-sensitive perennial grown as a tender annual

Growing Tips

Some nurseries and garden centers sell daturas in spring as individually potted plants, ready to set out in the garden.

You can also start daturas from seed. In Zones 9 to 11, sow directly outdoors in early spring. Elsewhere, start the seed indoors 10 to 12 weeks before the last frost, just covering it with growing mix. The seed germinates in 2 to 3 weeks at 60° to 70°F (15° to 21°C), and growth is quite rapid.

Wait until all danger of frost has passed and both the air and the soil have warmed up before setting out transplants. Plant them 3 to 4 feet (90 to 120 cm) apart, and take care not to disturb their roots. If you intend to stake them, you can reduce that spacing by half because supported plants will grow upward rather than sprawl. If you're going to plant them in a container, give them the largest planter you can find; crowding their roots can stunt their growth.

Daturas have a curious growth habit: The first flower forms at the tip of the plant, which then produces two branches just below the bud. When these branches bloom in turn, the plant again doubles its branches. By midsummer, there can be a veritable forest of stems, with several flowers opening every night. All this without any pinching from you!

Daturas do best if they're allowed to grow without any impediments or shocks, so keep them evenly moist. Deadheading is not necessary, unless you want to prevent the plants from self-sowing. Daturas are essentially annuals, although they can be perennial in Zones 9 to 11, where they often die back to their roots in winter.

Warning: Angel's trumpet is a more appropriate name than you might think since these trumpetlike flowers are highly poisonous and can send you straight to the angels. Keep it and its seed out of reach of children and pets, and warn your adolescents as well: It is known as a mind-altering drug, yet causes horrible suffering or even death to those who dare take it. All species of *Datura* and *Brugmansia* are identified here with the "Think Twice" logo because of their poisonous nature.

Good Neighbors

At their best on a moonlit night, the trumpets of daturas always create a strong presence in the garden. For extra interest, combine them with a partner that has feathery, silvery foliage, such as 'Powis Castle' artemisia.

Angel's trumpet
(*Datura metel*)

Problems and Solutions

Whiteflies, mealy bugs, and spider mites can cause foliage to become distorted or discolored; treat with insecticidal soap.

Top Performer

 **Think Twice:** *Datura metel* (angel's trumpet, thornapple)—or maybe that's *D. wrightii, D. meteloides,* or *D. inoxia.* The nomenclature of the genus *Datura* is incredibly complicated, but the plants are similar enough so that distinguishing between them really has little importance to the gardener. Single or double, upright-facing trumpets in white, yellow, lilac, or purple measure up to 6 inches (15 cm) long. All seem to come true from seed, and there are several different cultivars. Height: 3 to 5 feet (90 to 150 cm). Spread: 18 to 48 inches (45 to 120 cm). **Self-sowing**

More Recommended Datura

Think Twice: *Datura stramonium* (jimsonweed, common thornapple, Jamestown weed): This plant has green to purple stems and lobed or toothed leaves. Its white or pale lavender flowers (more rarely purple) are 3 to 5 inches (8 to 13 cm) long; they open at dawn and close by midday. This is by far the easiest datura to grow but also the most invasive since it succeeds in maturing seed into Zone 4. Height: 2 to 4 feet (60 to 120 cm). Spread: 18 to 30 inches (45 to 75 cm). **Self-sowing**

Kissing Cousins

Think Twice: Also called angel's trumpets, brugmansias (*Brugmansia* spp.) are tall tropical shrubs with large apple green leaves and huge trumpet flowers. Unlike daturas, which have short-lived, semi-upright blooms, the flowers of brugmansias are always pendulous and last for several days. *B.* × *candida* blooms in shades of white, pink, yellow, or apricot. *B. versicolor*, sometimes mistakenly sold as *B. arborea*, a much rarer plant, has white flowers. Overwinter plants indoors. Height: 4 to 30 feet (1.2 to 9 m). Spread: 5 to 8 feet (1.5 to 2.5 m).

Helianthus

Sunflower, annual sunflower, common sunflower

Just about everyone knows the commercial-type sunflower: the really tall one with one broad yellow bloom filled with large seeds. And if you haven't seen one, you've tasted it! Its seeds, once divested of their white-and-black striped coats, can be eaten sprouted, roasted or raw, or ground into flour for cooking. Garden sunflowers, however, offer much more variety than that, coming in a wide range of heights and habits and ranging in color from the usual golden yellow to white, lemon yellow, orange, red, and mahogany. Few annuals are as trendy, or as easy to grow!

Plant Profile

HELIANTHUS
hee-lee-AN-thuss

- **Bloom Color:** Varies by species; see individual listings

- **Bloom Time:** Mid- to late summer through early fall

- **Height:** 10 inches to 15 feet (30 cm to 4.5 m)

- **Spread:** 1 to 3 feet (30 to 90 cm)

- **Garden Uses:** Container planting, cut-flower garden, annual hedge, mass planting, meadow garden, mixed border, specimen plant, screening

- **Attracts:** Beneficial insects, seed-eating birds

- **Light Preference:** Full sun

- **Soil Preference:** Average, evenly moist but well-drained soil

- **Best Way to Propagate:** Sow outdoors in late spring

- **Hardiness:** Half-hardy annual

Growing Tips

It is now possible to buy dwarf sunflowers in pots, already in bloom, but be prepared to pay handsomely for one single flower whose season will be over in about 3 weeks. Think of them as glorified cut flowers, good for instant color for the living room, but not really plants for the garden.

Seed is really the way to go for best results with sunflowers. You *can* start them indoors, but why bother: They grow so quickly that little is gained by a head start. If you insist, start them 1 to 3 weeks before your last frost date. Sow in peat pots so the roots won't be disturbed at planting time. Keep the pots at about 70° to 85°F (21° to 30°C); germination takes only 1 week or so.

Sowing outdoors is the way to go for 99.9 percent of us. Do so after the last frost at a depth of about ¼ inch (6 mm). They need little special care after sowing, although the occasional watering during periods of drought certainly won't hurt. Too much feeding can produce lush foliage but reduce or delay flowering. Very tall cultivars may need staking if they're growing in shallow soil or near a wall or other source of shade because the plant will bend toward the light, then take a tumble.

Deadheading is pointless with single-stem sunflowers: They won't rebloom anyway, and half the fun of growing them is watching them produce seed. Do deadhead multistemmed types, at least until late summer because this will stimulate more bloom. If you want to save the seed for yourself, cover fading flower heads with cheesecloth so birds won't eat them. Otherwise, leave them in the garden into winter as free-standing bird feeders. Birds inevitably toss enough seed to the ground to ensure replacement plants for the following year.

Sunflowers make excellent cut flowers, lasting up to 3 weeks. There are even pollen-free hybrids designed to last longer both in the garden and when cut.

Good Neighbors

To create a colorful and functional annual screen, combine several cultivars of different heights and colors. A few well-placed sunflowers can really liven up a planting of ornamental grasses. Underplanting sunflowers with climbing nasturtiums (*Tropaeolum majus*) can create a pleasing color echo as well as a cover-up for the lower leaves, which tend to become ragged by the end of summer.

Problems and Solutions

Leaf diseases can be a problem but usually only damage lower leaves (remove these if desired). Hand-pick beetles and other leaf pests; spray with insecticidal soap to control aphids. Inject *Bacillus thuringiensis* (BT) into stems to control borers.

Common sunflower
(*Helianthus annuus*)

Top Performer

Helianthus annuus (common sunflower, annual sunflower): This is by far the most popular of the annual sunflowers and includes single or double flowers in golden yellow, orange, red, mahogany, and bicolors. It has a thick, rough stem bearing heart-shaped leaves. The original species was single stemmed, but multistemmed cultivars are now common. Normally, sunflowers start to bloom only in August, but there are now day-neutral cultivars (meaning these cultivars don't need a set number of hours of daylight in order to bloom), such as deep mahogany 'Prado Red', which begins flowering within 60 days or so after sowing. Height: 10 inches to 15 feet (30 cm to 4.5 m). Spread: 1 to 3 feet (30 to 90 cm). **Self-sowing**

More Recommended Helianthus

Helianthus debilis (cucumber-leaved sunflower): Naturally multibranching, this species produces narrower leaves and small flower heads of bright to pale yellow flowers. 'Italian White', with creamy white flowers, is one common cultivar. Height: 3 to 6 feet (90 to 180 cm). Spread: 1 to 2 feet (30 to 60 cm). **Self-sowing**

Larry's Garden Notes

If you're looking for beauty in sunflowers, stick with the multi-stemmed ornamental types. But if you want to try for record-breaking height, try agricultural types instead: Those giant sunflowers produce only one massive flower-stalk ending in an equally massive inflorescence. Try 'Russian Giant', 'Mammoth', or whatever your seed supplier recommends as their biggest; heights to 15 feet (4.5 m) are common. Give your "prize winners" lots of space; full sun; relatively rich, well-drained soil; a solid stake; and regular watering.

Lavatera

Lavatera, annual rose mallow, tree mallow

This old-fashioned cottage garden annual has been rediscovered by modern gardeners and is now as popular as ever. The gorgeous, shrublike plants nearly bloom themselves to death with large, satiny, 3- to 4-inch (8- to 10-cm), saucer-shaped flowers that are the spitting image of a single hollyhock. Lavatera is no persnickety diva, but rather a real workhorse of a plant, thriving under ordinary conditions (as long as it gets full sun) and growing readily from seed. Best of all, it is self-cleaning and blooms for months: The botanical name *trimestris*, in fact, means "3 months."

Plant Profile

LAVATERA
la-va-TARE-uh

- **Bloom Color:** Pink, rose, white

- **Bloom Time:** Midsummer until frost

- **Height:** 1 to 5 feet (30 to 150 cm)

- **Spread:** 12 to 18 inches (30 to 45 cm)

- **Garden Uses:** Container planting, cut-flower garden, annual hedge, mass planting, meadow garden, mixed border, specimen plant, screening

- **Light Preference:** Full sun to partial shade

- **Soil Preference:** Average to poor, well-drained soil

- **Best Way to Propagate:** Sow seed outdoors in fall or early spring

- **Hardiness:** Hardy annual

Growing Tips

You'll often hear that lavateras transplant poorly, but in my experience, there's no problem if you're at all careful to keep root disturbance to a minimum. Thus, if you can find them in six packs or cell packs in the spring, don't hesitate to try them.

Most people simply grow their lavateras from seed, and that certainly isn't complicated. In short-season climates, start it indoors 6 to 8 weeks before the last frost. Sow in individual pots or peat pots so you can move the plants apart as they begin to spread, and barely cover the seed. Look for seedlings in 2 to 3 weeks. Elsewhere, sow outdoors early in the season, a few weeks before the last spring frost; the seed seems to germinate better when it has been exposed to cold. Or sow in fall for germination the following spring. Thin the seedlings or set the transplants 1 foot (30 cm) apart for a hedgelike appearance, double that if you want to see the full mounding form of individual plants.

Grow in average garden soil; overly rich conditions produce lush, attractive foliage but result in few flowers. Full sun is needed for really spectacular bloom, but since lavatera is basically a cool-season annual, partial shade—and especially protection from afternoon sun—is necessary in hot summer areas. (Mulching and keeping the soil evenly moist can also help the plants beat the heat.) There's no real need to deadhead if you start the seed outdoors because the plants will bloom until frost no matter how you treat them. Plants started indoors, however, will start to decline early; cutting them back by half in early August will keep them blooming until frost. Let some seed mature to collect for next year's garden, or allow the plants to self-sow, which they will do modestly.

Summer care consists mostly of watering during periods of drought. In very windy situations, staking may be necessary, especially if plants were started indoors.

Lavatera makes a spectacular cut flower. Each flower lasts only a day or two, but if you choose a stem with lots of buds and only a few open flowers, the show will go on for over a week.

Good Neighbors

This abundant bloomer is a good companion for early-flowering shrubs, particularly roses. Its pink hues also mix well with blues, purples, and silvers, such as mealy-cup sage (*Salvia farinacea*) and 'Powis Castle' artemisia.

Problems and Solutions

Lavateras are seldom bothered by any pest or diseases problems.

Annual lavatera
(*Lavatera trimestris*)

Top Performer

Lavatera trimestris (annual lavatera, annual rose mallow): This is the plant described in the introduction above. It comes in a wide array of cultivars, varying in form, height, and color (white, pink, or rose; solid shades or veined). Most of the modern hybrids are of medium height and form perfect mounds of foliage, but the taller, shrubbier, old-fashioned types are just as attractive. Height: 1 to 5 feet (30 to 150 cm). Spread: 12 to 18 inches (30 to 45 cm). **Self-sowing**

More Recommended Lavatera

Lavatera arborea 'Variegata' (variegated tree mallow): A huge, thick-stemmed plant with nearly rounded, 8-inch (20-cm) leaves that are beautifully variegated in cream, especially in cooler weather. Start it indoors; it grows slowly at first and needs a long growing season. It doesn't always succeed in blooming in short-season climates, even when started indoors, but if you grow it for its foliage, that's not a problem. Elsewhere, it produces 2-inch (5-cm), deep rose flowers in abundance in late summer or fall. This biennial may overwinter in Zones 8 to 10. Height: 4 to 10 feet (1.2 to 3 m). Spread: 5 feet (1.5 m).

Kissing Cousins

Although actually a biennial or short-lived perennial, high mallow (*Malva sylvestris*) is probably best grown as an annual, especially north of Zone 6 and in hot, humid areas, where it likewise rarely overwinters. It will produce shrublike, upright plants with 2½-inch (6.5-cm), saucer-shaped flowers in pink, white, or violet-blue, usually beautifully veined. Start it indoors as you would for lavatera. Height: 3 to 4 feet (90 to 120 cm). Spread: 1 to 2 feet (30 to 60 cm). **Self-sowing**

Malope

Malope, annual mallow

Everything old is new again, or so they say. If so, this cottage-garden favorite, which has all but disappeared from the gardening scene since its last wave of popularity back in the 1920s, is already overdue for fame and fortune. It's hard to explain why it hasn't already caught on: It's a beautiful, shrubby annual with hairy leaves and 2- to 3-inch (5- to 8-cm), trumpet-shaped flowers in beautiful shades of pink, rose, violet-blue, and white, often with beautifully contrasting veins. It's at least as lovely as its similarly showy cousins, lavateras (*Lavatera* spp.), and it's just as easy to grow.

Plant Profile

MALOPE
ma-LOW-pee

- **Bloom Color:** Pink, violet-blue, red, white

- **Bloom Time:** Midsummer through early fall

- **Height:** 2 to 4 feet (60 to 120 cm)

- **Spread:** 9 to 12 inches (23 to 30 cm)

- **Garden Uses:** Container planting, cut-flower garden, annual hedge, mass planting, meadow garden, mixed border, specimen plant

- **Light Preference:** Full sun to partial shade

- **Soil Preference:** Average to humus-rich, evenly moist but well-drained soil

- **Best Way to Propagate:** Sow seed indoors in late winter or outdoors in late spring or fall

- **Hardiness:** Hardy annual

Growing Tips

There is little use searching for six packs or cell packs of malope in nurseries and garden centers: They just don't seem to be available.

If you want to try malope, you'll have to grow it yourself. Its seed resists the coldest weather, so you can sow it outdoors in mid- to late fall, or in spring as soon as you can work the soil. Barely cover the seed. It'll germinate (although irregularly) as the ground warms up. Thin to about 1 foot (30 cm) apart for mass plantings, or at least 2 feet (60 cm) if you want the individual plants to stand out more. Pinch once when the plants are about 6 inches (15 cm) tall to help stimulate branching.

You can also sow malope indoors. Since the seed needs a cold treatment to germinate well, start early: about 12 weeks before the last frost. Sow the seed in peat pots (seedlings dislike root disturbance), then seal them inside a plastic bag and place in the freezer for 3 to 4 weeks. After that, place under warmer conditions: 65° to 75°F (18° to 24°C). Look for seedlings in 2 to 4 weeks. Pinch once and plant outside as per the spacing suggested above.

Full sun is ideal in cool summer climates where malope will have no trouble blooming right through summer until the last frost. Partial shade, or at least protection from the afternoon sun, plus a good mulching and

FUN FACTS

You may not have to go far to find malope: It has maintained itself over the years by self-sowing in old, abandoned gardens. In fact, sometimes cleaning up an old garden and thus letting more light reach the ground will result in malopes sprouting from buried seed where they haven't been seen in generations!

regular waterings will help keep it happier in hotter climates. Malope does fine in average, well-drained garden soil. Some experts suggest it will tend to produce more leaves than flowers in rich soil. But in my garden at least, the contrary has been true: The most free-flowering plants were in the richest soil.

Usually malope is quite sturdy, but it can be a bit "weak in the knees" if it is surrounded by competitors. In such cases, try staking the plants when they are still young to prevent damaging their roots later on.

Deadheading is wise, especially in hot summer areas, to stimulate continuous bloom. Do let some seed capsules mature, though, to ensure some seeds for next year's garden. Malope self-sows willingly but without becoming invasive.

Malope
(*Malope trifida*)

Good Neighbors
A planting of Brazilian vervain (*Verbena bonariensis*) will mingle appealingly with the pinks and purples of malope. Several plants of deep purple heliotrope (*Heliotropium arborescens*) or 'Homestead Purple' verbena make a flattering foreground addition.

Problems and Solutions
Control aphids with insecticidal soap. The same rust that attacks hollyhocks can also cause orange spots on malope foliage, although usually only at the end of the season. To prevent problems, avoid growing these plants together. If the disease does appear, don't grow malope in that spot for the next 3 years.

Top Performer
Malope trifida (malope, annual mallow): The flowers of this species resemble those of lavateras (except the petals don't quite join at the base), leaving a starlike pattern of five little windows through which you can see the green calyces. With backlighting, this can create a beautiful appearance, like a stained-glass cathedral window. There are several different cultivars. In the South, try the tetraploid cultivars, such as 'Vulcan' (deep magenta pink with dark purple veins); they seem more heat resistant. **Self-sowing**

Kissing Cousins

Musk mallow (*Abelmoschus moschatus*) produces hibiscus-like flowers 3 to 4 inches (8 to 10 cm) in diameter. The original species has yellow flowers with a purple center, but most cultivars are red, pink, or orange-red with a white eye. The species is quite tall, but the most common series, 'Pacific', reaches only 12 to 18 inches (30 to 45 cm) tall. Care for musk mallow is the same as for malope. Height: 1 to 5 feet (30 to 150 cm). Spread: 18 inches (45 cm). **Self-sowing**

Nicandra

Shoo-fly plant, apple of Peru

Shoo-fly plant offers two great features: beautiful blooms and interesting seed pods. A tall, branching, sturdy plant with broad, toothed, wavy-margined leaves, it produces bell-shaped, white-centered, pale violet-blue flowers from summer into early fall. The flowers open in the morning and fade the same day, but they're quickly replaced by others. Each bloom leaves behind an inflated, papery calyx hiding a green fruit. Don't even think of tasting the fruit, though: It is poisonous.

Plant Profile

NICANDRA
nye-CAN-druh

■ **Bloom Color:** Violet-blue

■ **Bloom Time:** Early summer through early fall

■ **Height:** 3 to 4 feet (90 to 120 cm)

■ **Spread:** 2 to 4 feet (60 to 120 cm)

■ **Garden Uses:** Container planting, cut-flower garden, annual hedge, mass planting, meadow garden, mixed border, specimen plant, screening

■ **Light Preference:** Full sun or partial shade

■ **Soil Preference:** Humus-rich, evenly moist but well-drained soil

■ **Best Way to Propagate:** Sow seed indoors in spring or outdoors in fall or early spring

■ **Hardiness:** Half-hardy annual

Growing Tips

Unless shoo-fly plant undergoes a sudden wave of popularity, you are not likely to find it sold in six packs or cell packs, except perhaps at specialist nurseries.

In most cases, you'll need to grow your own plants from seed. In areas with long summers, you can sow seed outdoors in early spring, several weeks before the last frost, or even in fall for germination the following spring. In Zones 6 and below, though, it's best to start the plants indoors. Sow the seed 6 to 8 weeks before the last frost, just barely covering it. Use peat pots or individual pots because the plants are very fast growing and quickly get too crowded in six packs or cell packs. Seeds germinate in 10 to 20 days at 60° to 75°F (15° to 24°C). Thin to one plant per pot.

You can set the plants outside 2 (or even 3) weeks before your last frost date, unless the spring is unseasonably cold. Don't worry if there is a light frost: Young plants don't seem bothered in the slightest by cold snaps. Give them lots of room to grow, spacing them at least 3 feet (90 cm) apart. Full sun is best, although they will tolerate some shade. Don't worry about shading them from afternoon sun: In fact, the hotter and more humid the summer, the better shoo-fly plants grow. They

FUN FACTS

If the papery calyces of shoo-fly plant make you think of lantern-shaped envelopes of the ground cherry, you'd be right on the mark. *Nicandra* is a close relative of the ground cherry (*Physalis peruviana*) and its cousin, Chinese lantern (*P. alkekengi*), and the most commonly grown species *Nicandra physaloides* makes reference to that fact with its name—*physaloides* means "like a physalis."

positively thrive in the unbearably humid Deep South. They'll do well in any type of well-drained soil as long as you can ensure relatively even moisture. If you want giant plants, give them rich soil; if you prefer them more restrained, try using unimproved soil.

Summer care consists mainly of keeping the soil evenly moist. Mulching can be a great help in areas where droughts are common. Deadheading doesn't seem to help stimulate further flowering, and since part of shoo-fly plant's charm is its curious inflated seed capsules, removing flowers would only limit its ornamental effect. And it doesn't usually seem to need any staking.

While shoo-fly plant hangs on right through summer, it certainly knows when to call it quits and begins to become brown and unattractive in September, even if there is still no frost on the horizon.

Shoo-fly plant
(*Nicandra physaloides*)

Good Neighbors

Planted among lower-growing annuals such as 'Star White' zinnias or nasturtiums (*Tropaeolum majus*), a single plant can create an interesting presence. Or combine three of the smaller cultivar 'Splash of Cream' in a large container, underplanted with Swan River daisies (*Brachyscome* spp.) or other cascaders.

Problems and Solutions

Shoo-fly plant rarely suffers from insects or plant diseases when it is grown outdoors.

Top Performer

Think Twice: *Nicandra physaloides* (shoo-fly plant, apple of Peru): The species, with pale violet flowers that are 2½ inches (6.5 cm) across, is what you're most likely to find in seed catalogs. 'Violacea' is deeper purple at the base of the flower, with purplish stems and calyces. 'Splash of Cream' is a slightly smaller plant—2 to 3 feet (60 to 90 cm) tall—with irregular yellow to cream variegation, which, I must confess, I find quite sickly looking. Both come true from seed. Shoo-fly plant self-sows somewhat in all climates but can actually become invasive in Zones 9 to 11. **Self-sowing**

Larry's Garden Notes

I first grew shoo-fly plant as a child because I wanted to see if it really did chase flies from the garden. Unfortunately, I really couldn't say whether it worked or not. Later, hearing it was supposed to be even more effective indoors on whiteflies, I tried growing it in the house. The first thing I learned is that it's a very big plant to be growing indoors. The other is that instead of being repelled, whiteflies settle on it in large colonies. My conclusion? I think it does shoo flies, at least whiteflies—but from other plants onto itself!

Persicaria

Kiss-me-over-the-garden-gate, knotweed

The genus *Persicaria* contains some 60 species, including many popular perennials and a few annuals. The common name, knotweed, makes perfect sense because the stems of all the species have prominent "knots" (that is, joints or nodes). Of the two commonly grown annual species, the one I'll concentrate on here is kiss-me-over-the-garden-gate (*P. orientale*). This has to be one of the longest common names for any plant, but it's also one of the most appropriate: The dangling spikes of flowers can indeed reach over the garden gate to kiss the plants on the other side.

Plant Profile

PERSICARIA
per-sih-CARE-ee-uh

- **Bloom Color:** Pink, red, white
- **Bloom Time:** Midsummer through early fall
- **Height:** 3 to 10 feet (90 to 300 cm)
- **Spread:** 2 to 4 feet (60 to 120 cm)
- **Garden Uses:** Cut-flower garden, annual hedge, meadow garden, mixed border, specimen plant, screening; in wet areas
- **Light Preference:** Full sun to partial shade
- **Soil Preference:** Any evenly moist to damp soil
- **Best Way to Propagate:** Sow seed indoors or outdoors in spring
- **Hardiness:** Hardy annual

Growing Tips

Few, if any, nurseries are growing this old-fashioned annual for sale, but that's no bother: It's a snap to grow from seed. In fact, it's a common ingredient in cottage-garden seed mixes, not only because it's perfectly suited to cottage gardens, but because it really does give guaranteed results when sown outdoors.

After your last frost date, scatter the seed where you want the plants to grow, and rake it into the ground. It will sprout as soon as the soil warms up. From there on, the plants grow at a rapid rate: They can reach 10 feet (3 m) in only 6 to 10 weeks!

If you want even faster results, you can also sow indoors 4 to 6 weeks before your last frost date. Barely cover the seed and expose it to warmth: 70° to 75°F (21° to 24°C). They sprout in 2 to 3 weeks. Plant them outside when all danger of frost is gone, in full sun (partial shade in hot, humid climates).

Steady soil moisture is the key to success with this annual. In drier gardens, mulching will go a long way toward keeping it happy. If you can't keep the soil moist but you like the look of the weeping flower spikes, you might instead try growing love-lies-bleeding (*Amaranthus caudatus*), which has vaguely similar although longer and thicker hanging spikes.

Summer care for kiss-me-over-the-garden-gate is largely limited to watering it as needed.

FUN FACTS

If the name *Persicaria* seems new to you, don't be surprised. The former genus *Polygonum* has been broken into several parts, so *Persicaria*, the genus into which most of the species have been shifted, is a new classification to most gardeners.

Deadheading seems of little importance because the plants will keep blooming into fall whether or not you cut off the faded blooms.

Be forewarned, though, that kiss-me-over-the-garden-gate will self-sow, although rarely to excess. The tall stems rise quickly above the surrounding vegetation, so it's quite easy to find them and yank out any unwanted seedlings.

Good Neighbors

Combine kiss-me-over-the-garden-gate with bold plants such as cannas and castor bean (*Ricinus communis*), or envelop it in a cloud of cosmos (*Cosmos bipinnatus*) and spider flower (*Cleome hassleriana*). Echo the gently arching habit of the flowers with an ornamental grass, such as red fountain grass (*Pennisetum setaceum* 'Rubrum') or with Oriental fountain grass (*P. orientale*).

Problems and Solutions

Aphids can cause distorted or discolored foliage; spray them with a strong stream of water or with insecticidal soap. Whichever control you use, make sure you hit the undersides of the leaves where aphids can hide. Hand-pick Japanese beetles or see page 34 for other pest-control suggestions.

Top Performer

Persicaria orientale (kiss-me-over-the-garden-gate, prince's feather, princess feather): Usually called *Polygonum orientale*. This Victorian annual seems to be making a modest comeback. It is a massive plant, with thick, branching stems that bear large, heart-shaped, olive green leaves. Its height varies according to conditions. Theoretically, it could be just 3 feet (90 cm) one year and then 10 feet (3 m) the next, but 5 to 7 feet (1.5 to 2 m) is about the average. When it has reached its full height for the season, it starts to produce arching, branching stems that end in 2- to 3-inch (5- to 8-cm), pendulous spikes of tiny, bell-shaped flowers. Pink or rose-red are the usual colors, but white is not unknown.

Self-sowing 🖊

Kiss-me-over-the-garden-gate (*Persicaria orientale*)

Kissing Cousins

❗ **Think Twice:** *Persicaria capitata* (magic carpet plant): Usually called *Polygonum capitatum*. This compact species produces purplish green leaves with a purple, V-shaped mark, then adds ball-shaped clusters of tiny pink blooms throughout the summer. It is hardy in Zones 8 through 10, where it spreads through rooting stems and by self-sowing, possibly becoming very weedy. Elsewhere, grow it as a half-hardy annual; it self-sows but not enough to become a pest. Height: 3 inches (8 cm). Spread: 20 inches (50 cm) or more.
Self-sowing 🖊

Ricinus

Castor bean

With castor bean, the tropics come right into your yard, no matter where you live! The huge plant produces thick, sturdy stems and giant, star-shaped leaves that can range from 6 inches to 3 feet (15 to 90 cm) in diameter. Foliage color ranges from dark green to deep purple; stem color from blue green to red. Until recently, the flowers could have been called insignificant, but the spiny, rounded, reddish brown seed capsules were always of some interest. However, there are now cultivars with red or pink flowers and seed capsules, meaning castor bean is spreading beyond its original "foliage plant" classification.

Plant Profile

RICINUS
RI-sin-us

- ■ **Bloom Color:** Pink, red, yellowish green
- ■ **Bloom Time:** Late summer; much of the year in mild climates
- ■ **Height:** 3 to 15 feet (90 cm to 4.5 m)
- ■ **Spread:** 2 to 4 feet (60 to 120 cm)
- ■ **Garden Uses:** Container planting, annual hedge, mixed border, specimen plant, screening
- ■ **Light Preference:** Full sun to partial shade
- ■ **Soil Preference:** Average to humus-rich, well-drained soil
- ■ **Best Way to Propagate:** Sow seed indoors or out in spring
- ■ **Hardiness:** Frost-sensitive shrub grown as a tender annual

Growing Tips

Many nurseries and garden centers sell individual castor bean plants in pots, at the end of springtime.

Growing your own plants from seed is also an option. In long-season areas, you can sow it outdoors after all danger of frost is gone and the soil has warmed up; elsewhere, it's best to sow indoors. Start 6 to 8 weeks before the last frost date. Soak the large, hard seed for 24 hours in tepid water (pour the water into an old thermos so it doesn't cool off) or file them to weaken their thick coating. Plant two seeds per peat pot or individual pot; the plants grow much too quickly to be worth growing in six packs or cell packs. Cover the seed with ¼ inch (6 mm) of potting mix and place in a warm spot: 70° to 75°F (21° to 24°C). The seed tends to germinate irregularly over a period of 2 to 4 weeks.

The secret to large, healthy castor bean plants is to protect the young plants from any condition that can stunt their growth. Indoors, keep the seedlings in warmth and full sun or very bright light. As they grow, pot them on regularly into larger and larger pots. (They'll stop growing if their roots are restricted.) When there is absolutely no further danger of frost, the soil has warmed up, and night temperatures remain above 50°F (10°C), you can plant them outdoors.

FUN FACTS

That horrible-tasting purgative hated by kids the world over, castor oil, is derived from the seeds of castor beans. Fortunately for all of us who still recall its terrible taste and swore we'd never put our children through that, it is rarely used as a purgative any more. The oil, however, is still widely employed in manufacturing cosmetics, soaps, industrial oils, and varnishes.

Plant castor beans in any kind of well-drained soil, although rich soil produces the largest, bushiest plants. And although they are very drought resistant, regular waterings will ensure the healthiest growth and largest leaves. Full sun is best, but partial shade is acceptable. Castor beans take the hot, humid summers of the Deep South with no trouble.

If you plan to grow castor beans in containers, give them plenty of room: A half whiskey barrel is a minimum for a full-size plant. In smaller containers, the plants tend to stop growing and start blooming once their roots fill the pot.

Castor beans are likely to self-sow only in Zones 10 and 11. (Actually, they can become a weed in those climates if you don't remove the seed capsules before they mature.) In these areas, the plants themselves can survive the winter and grow on as large shrubs or even 30-foot (9-m) trees.

Castor bean
(*Ricinus communis*)

Good Neighbors

This exotic attention-getter can be useful as an annual screen or as a back-of-the-border presence. Create a bold display by pairing the deep red foliage of 'Carmencita' with orange Mexican sunflower (*Tithonia rotundifolia*), then echo the dark foliage color with red fountain grass (*Pennisetum setaceum* 'Rubrum').

Problems and Solutions

Spider mites are a problem where the air is dry. Spray regularly with water or use insecticidal soap to control them. (See "Annual Pests" on page 35.)

Top Performer

Think Twice: *Ricinus communis* (castor bean): There is an increasing array of cultivars, ranging from "dwarf" strains only 4 feet (1.2 m) high to green-leaved 'Zanzibarensis', which can grow more than 15 feet (4.5 m) in just one season. Many cultivars have bronze or purple leaves. 'Carmencita', with red seed capsules, and 'Carmencita Pink', with pink seed capsules, are making castor beans just as interesting in seed as they are in foliage. **Self-sowing**

Larry's Garden Notes

Warning: The castor bean plant is extremely poisonous, especially the large, beautifully colored seeds that children could easily mistake for candy. Two seeds are enough to kill a child! Where summers are long and hot, it is probably best to cut off all seed capsules before they mature; otherwise, they can shoot their seeds as far as 20 feet (6 m) away, where they could easily fall into the wrong hands. Furthermore, some people are allergic to this plant's sap. If you tend to suffer from skin allergies, it is best to wear protective gloves.

Tithonia

Mexican sunflower, torch flower

This giant flowering plant seems at last to be catching on and certainly deserves its increased popularity. It's a fast-growing, easy-to-care-for annual that provides spectacular bloom over a long season. Plus, it thrives under conditions that would roast most other annuals, making it a great choice for people who find many of the other plants in this book difficult to grow. Mexican sunflower is a tall, abundantly branched plant with dark green leaves in a variety of shapes, from triangular to ovate, sometimes even lobed—in fact, just about every shape but round, yet oddly, its botanical epithet, *rotundifolia,* means "round-leaved"!

Plant Profile

TITHONIA
ti-THO-nee-uh

- **Bloom Color:** Orange, orange-red, or yellow

- **Bloom Time:** Summer through early fall

- **Height:** 28 to 96 inches (70 to 240 cm)

- **Spread:** 1 to 3 feet (30 to 90 cm)

- **Garden Uses:** Container planting, cut-flower garden, annual hedge, mass planting, meadow garden, mixed border, specimen plant, screening

- **Attracts:** Butterflies, hummingbirds

- **Light Preference:** Full sun

- **Soil Preference:** Poor to average, well-drained soil

- **Best Way to Propagate:** Sow seed outdoors in late spring

- **Hardiness:** Tender annual

Growing Tips

Mexican sunflower has started to come onto the market in six packs and cell packs, which is very good news—sort of. The problem is that limited root space can easily stress the fast-growing seedlings, stunting later growth. Try to buy young plants, and avoid those that have yellow lower leaves or no lower leaves at all (a sign they have been mistreated.)

It's also easy to start plants yourself. For early bloom, sow indoors 6 to 8 weeks before the last frost. Scatter the large seed over the growing mix and press it into the surface. Germination is rapid at room temperature: They start to sprout in about 5 days. As with many "giant" plants, the secret to success with Mexican sunflowers is to avoid any checks to their growth. Keep the seedlings warm, supply even moisture (adult plants are drought tolerant, but the youngsters aren't), and keep moving them up to larger pots before they get root-bound. Wait until there is no further danger of frost and night temperatures remain above 50°F (10°C) before setting out transplants. (In other words, when it is time to plant out your tomatoes, the conditions are right for Mexican sunflower as well!)

Where summers are longer, it is easier by far to sow Mexican sunflower right where it is to bloom when the soil has warmed

FUN FACTS

The botanical name of this plant derives from Tithonius, the handsome king of Troy. Aurora, the goddess of dawn, loved the king so much that she asked Zeus to grant him eternal life, which he did. Unfortunately, she forgot to ask for eternal youth as well, so Tithonius turned into a hideous, wrinkled old man while she stayed young.

up. This also makes the plants sturdier and less likely to need staking.

For best results, plant or thin Mexican sunflowers to at least 2 feet (60 cm) apart, even 3 feet (90 cm) for the tallest cultivars. This is one plant that actually does better in poor to average soils than in rich ones. In humus-rich or abundantly fertilized soil, plants tend to produce more foliage than flowers and also become weak stemmed, needing very sturdy staking. Gardeners in the Deep South will appreciate the fact that Mexican sunflower is not bothered by heat and humidity. A slight lack of rain won't faze this plant at all—at least, not once it is established—although it does appreciate some water during periods of extreme drought. (Cool, rainy weather is not at all to this plant's liking, however, so if your summers are composed of gray days and lots of drizzle, you should probably try something else.) Deadheading is important to keep Mexican sunflowers blooming right through the summer.

Mexican sunflower
(*Tithonia rotundifolia*)

Good Neighbors

The striped foliage and orange flower of 'Pretoria' canna makes a striking companion, echoing the bloom color of the Mexican sunflower. Try planting green-flowering tobacco (*Nicotiana* 'Lime Green') alongside of it for extra interest.

Problems and Solutions

Mexican sunflower is not terribly subject to diseases. Watch out for slug and snail damage (see page 35 for solutions) during rainy weather, and spray with insecticidal soap to control whiteflies.

Top Performer

Tithonia rotundifolia (Mexican sunflower, torch flower): There are about 10 species of *Tithonia,* but only this one is commonly grown. Recent years have seen a profusion of dwarf cultivars of this normally giant plant: Some reach no more than 28 inches (70 cm) tall—under the right conditions. All Mexican sunflowers will respond to overly rich soil with vigorous growth, so don't be surprised if your "dwarf" cultivar tops out at 5 feet (1.5 m) tall if you feed it too heavily!

Larry's Garden Notes

With its long stems and long-lasting blooms, Mexican sunflower makes a great cut flower, but it does have one problem: Its hollow stems need extra care at harvesting time, or they will quickly flop over. Sear the stem in boiling water or over a flame, then plunge the entire length of stem in a bucket of warm water for a few hours to condition it. After that, you can use it in arrangements however you wish. Properly prepared, the flowers can last for nearly 2 weeks.

Climbing ANNUALS

The sky's the limit when you grow climbing annuals! These amazing plants grow to incredible heights with equally incredible speed: often to 30 feet (9 m) or more in only a few weeks. Of course, climbers do have a dark secret: They quickly take advantage of any and all means to achieve their goal—that is, to grow as tall as possible. They'll clamber up and over trellises, fences, and pergolas, of course, but also up other plants, lawn furniture, and even rusting car carcasses. I suspect they'd even grow up your leg if you held still long enough! That said, I suggest you simply turn the tables on them and use their attributes to best advantage without letting them know your plans! Given their opportunistic nature, use climbing annuals for your own means: to hide ugly fences, embellish a bare wall, decorate a forlorn arbor, or disguise a compost pile.

◄Where speed is of the essence, annual climbers are simply *the* top choice for vast cover. Plants like black-eyed Susan vine can completely cover a trellis or pergola in only a few weeks.

Up, Up, and Away!

You've got to give them credit: Climbing annuals have certainly learned to turn their major flaw into their major advantage. Reaching the light, you see, is the key to success for plants. So most plants pile on the cellulose to produce strong, sturdy stems they can use to hold their leaves well above those of their neighbors. It's a slow process, though, and those plants richest in cellulose are also the slowest growing. Eventually, though, woody (that is, full of cellulose) plants like trees and shrubs do win the race for the sun and shade, out-competing annuals. Climbing plants, though, evolved from races of weak, floppy plants that could survive only by leaning on others for support. In the unforgiving race to survive, they should have been left in the dust.

But climbing plants have actually developed quite a successful survival strategy. Rather than producing energy-expensive but sturdy cellulose, they produce totally floppy stems with only a minimal amount of cellulose, then sneakily wrap themselves around fellow plants, using their "competitor's" sturdy stems as a personal staircase to the stars. In short order, they quickly reach the top of their host plant and deploy their leaves in full sun, soaking up energy while expending almost none themselves. Profiting from their place in the sun, they produce a profusion of flowers and hordes of fresh seeds—then use their great height to toss their seeds far and wide. Sneaky, isn't it? But there's no denying their ploy is enormously successful; just about every environment on this planet has its share of climbing plants.

Use an annual vine for those spots where you long for foliage and color without the commitment of keeping a perennial vine trained and pruned.

Something to Grow On

Left with nothing to climb up, most climbers will simply spread out in all directions. You can use them as temporary groundcovers, or let them cascade out of a pot or over a low wall. But since there are so many naturally creeping plants you can use for these purposes, why not let the climbers do what they do best: clamber upward. For that, however, they need a support.

Self-sown climbers, true to their opportunistic nature, will simply climb up nearby trees and shrubs. In doing so, though, they may harm their hosts by cutting off much of their light, and by adding extra weight the host plant can't always support. You *could* let an annual climber or two race up a solid tree or shrub, but in most cases, it's wisest to provide your vines with their own support system.

There is practically no limit to what structures climbers will grow on. Trellises, fences, pergolas, and arbors are the traditional means of supporting them, but that's just the beginning! You can also let them clamber up and over lampposts, a railing, a free-standing obelisk, a garden gate (yes, they'll tolerate the swinging back and forth!), a gazebo, or garden shed, or even simply strings you've run up a wall. If it's upright and they can wrap themselves around it, they'll gladly use it!

Think Thin

Unlike many perennial or shrubby climbers, few annual climbers will cling to a flat surface. With one exception—cup-and-saucer vine (*Cobaea scandens*)—they have no sticky aerial roots, stickers, or spines to allow them to grow up a wall. Instead, they climb by winding themselves through or around their support. Some have twining stems, others twisting leaf or flowerstalks, and still others have special corkscrew-shaped extensions called tendrils. All of these will "cling" only if their support is relatively thin, usually no more than 3 inches (8 cm) in diameter. Therefore, if you want your climbers to grow up a thick post or flat wall, you'll have to supply some thinner means of support.

For wall plantings, of course, the trellis immediately comes into mind. You'll find plenty of commercial models in wood, plastic, or a host of other materials and in a variety of shapes. And you can also build your own trellis to match the needs of your outdoor decor. However, climbing plants will grow just as readily up an inexpensive trellis net: a nearly transparent netting usually sold for use with climbing vegetables like peas and beans. You can easily hook, nail, or tack it over any flat surface, wrap it around posts, or use it to cover just about anything. Alternatively, you can simply attach string to nails hammered to the top and the bottom of the support of your choice to make an inexpensive and effective trellis.

Occasionally a young climber may seem like it doesn't know where to go, or it may start wrapping itself around another plant. In this case, take the wayward stem and "direct" it to its support: Just delicately grasp it and wrap it lightly around the stake or string. If it lets go, tie it lightly in place with a piece of nylon stocking. From then on, the stem should climb with no further aid.

Temp Service

Annual climbers are often at their most useful in the early days of a landscape. You may already have planned to include more permanent climbing plants, like clematis or Boston ivy (*Parthenocissus tricuspidata*), but they can take years to reach their full height. Annual vines, however, reach their maximum height—and that can be 30 feet (9 m) or more—in just one growing season. Talk about instant results! As the permanent climbers fill in, you can cut back gradually on the annuals or even eliminate them entirely.

From Shade to Sun

Most climbing annuals are sun lovers. The whole point of their rapid growth is to be able to bask in the glorious rays of unfiltered sunlight. But that doesn't mean you can't grow them in shady spots! You see, climbing annuals have a contingency plan. Most produce very large seeds chock full of carbohydrates they can burn for speedy growth during their first weeks of life. Plant them where their base is in the shade, but where sun is within reach, and they'll use that stored energy to grow toward the light as fast as possible. Since shady spots can also be cool, though, you might want to give shade-grown climbers a jump on the season by starting them indoors in the warmth and then transferring them outside once they're up and growing.

Round and Round They Go

Many annual vines like to twist around their supports, but have you ever wondered how they do that? Rather than growing straight up, as do most plants, twining annuals naturally grow in spirals, sometimes clockwise, sometimes counterclockwise, depending on the species. Their long stems actually spin, something like a lasso although far more slowly. If the slowly spinning stem touches an upright object, it reacts by coiling around it, often in only a few hours. Then the plant will continue to wrap itself around its host until it reaches the top, where it again starts spinning, looking for something even taller to hoist itself onto. This spinning trick even has a name: It's called circumnutation.

4 More Climbing Annuals

Truly climbing annuals are rather a select group, and there aren't too many you can choose from. Or, to look at it from another point of view, climbing annuals are so different from other annuals they really don't belong in any other chapter but this one. So the list of climbing annuals listed elsewhere in this book is very, very short.

Hedera helix (English ivy) 342	*Tropaeolum majus* (Nasturtium) 61
Ipomoea batatas (Sweet potato vine) . .346	*Tropaeolum peregrinum* (Canary creeper) 61

You will, however, find several *trailing* annuals: They don't really climb unless you attach them to a support, but their naturally long, floppy stems do offer material for climbing up small trellises if you want to try that. You'll find them described in the chapter "Flowering Annuals for Containers & Hanging Baskets," starting on page 305.

Asarina

Climbing snapdragon, chickabiddy

Popular with Victorian gardeners, this old-fashioned annual seemed to almost disappear from culture for more than 75 years. But now, it's suddenly being promoted as the latest thing in climbing plants! The trumpet-shaped flowers have five flaring lobes—three on the bottom, two at the top—and they hang downward and outward, creating an attractive cascading appearance. Although the climbing snapdragon is a rather fragile-looking plant, with thin, apparently weak twining stems, its seemingly delicate appearance belies the plant's tough-as-nails nature: It really is a snap to grow.

Plant Profile

ASARINA
a-SAH-ree-nuh

- **Bloom Color:** Varies by species; see individual listings

- **Bloom Time:** Late spring through fall; into winter in mild climates

- **Height:** 3 to 10 feet (90 to 300 cm)

- **Spacing:** 1 foot (30 cm)

- **Garden Uses:** Container planting, hanging baskets, groundcover, screening; on trellises, fences, and pergolas

- **Attracts:** Hummingbirds

- **Light Preference:** Full sun to partial shade

- **Soil Preference:** Well-drained, evenly moist, neutral soil

- **Best Way to Propagate:** Sow seed indoors in late winter or take stem cuttings at any time

- **Hardiness:** Frost-sensitive perennial grown as a half-hardy annual

Growing Tips

Larger nurseries are starting to sell pots of climbing snapdragon in spring. The price tends to be fairly steep, though; so if you need several plants, it makes sense to grow your own from seed.

Except in the warmest climates, where you can sow directly outdoors, start the seed inside 10 to 12 weeks before your last frost date. Climbing snapdragon is somewhat sensitive to root disturbance, so it's best to plant into peat pots, just pressing the small winged seed into the mix. Seed germinates in 10 to 21 days at 60° to 75°F (15° to 24°C). Growth is slow at first but picks up after a few weeks. Support young plants with a stake if they begin to climb before they are in the garden.

Since climbing snapdragon actually prefers cool temperatures, don't hesitate to plant it out early as long as there is little danger of frost. Although it prefers neutral or even alkaline soil, slightly acid soil is acceptable as well. Plant about 1 foot (30 cm) apart in full sun, but preferably with some shade during the heat of the day. In hot summer climates, mulch to keep the soil cooler and evenly moist.

Give climbing snapdragon only a thin support to climb up, not much more than 1 inch (2.5 cm) in diameter because it has trouble wrapping itself around thick stakes. Deadheading will help prolong bloom through summer.

If you're growing climbing snapdragon in a pot, either supply a support for it to climb on, or allow it to trail. It will cascade very gracefully, and many people actually prefer its look that way.

Although climbing snapdragon is actually a perennial, it will survive winter outdoors only in Zones 10 and 11 and protected parts of Zone 9. Elsewhere, you can bring plants in from the garden for winter (easiest to do if they are still in pots) or take cuttings. They grow well over winter, although more slowly than in summer, and they are not as floriferous.

Good Neighbors

An interesting up-close flower, climbing snapdragon can be a great addition to a small garden. In a container or in the ground, surround its feet with pink globe amaranth (*Gomphrena globosa*), dusty miller (*Senecio cineraria*), and other cool-hued annuals for extra color.

Problems and Solutions

Climbing snapdragons rarely have insect or disease problems.

Top Performer

Asarina scandens (climbing snapdragon, chickabiddy, creeping gloxinia): Also called *Maurandya scandens* and *Lophospermum scandens*. At the time of this writing, all of the so-called climbing snapdragons are being sold under the botanical name *Asarina*. They certainly *look* like members of the same genus, but there is a complicated set of name changes under way; look for them under any or all of the mentioned alternative names as time goes on. The 1½- to 2-inch (4- to 5-cm) long flowers of chickabiddy come in shades of violet-blue, lavender, pink, and white with a white to greenish throat, and the leaves are heart or arrow shaped. Most of the increasingly wide range of hybrids belong here or are crosses with *A. barclayana* (or *Maurandya barclayana*). Height: 3 to 10 feet (90 to 300 cm).

More Recommended Asarina

Asarina antirrhiniflora (violet climbing snapdragon): Also called *Maurandella antirrhiniflora*. Like *A. scandens* but with broader flowers whose throats remain nearly closed, making them look more like true snapdragons. The flowers are usually purple to violet but sometimes pink, and often spotted at the base. Height: 3 to 10 feet (90 to 300 cm).

  A. barclayana (Barclay's climbing snapdragon): Also called *Maurandya barclayana*. Often confused with *A. scandens,* but with larger, more tubular flowers in a similar range of colors. Height: 3 to 10 feet (90 to 300 cm).

  A. erubescens (blushing climbing snapdragon): Also called *Lophospermum erubescens*. This species is very similar to the others, but with fuzzier leaves and more pendant, rose-pink flowers. Height: 3 to 10 feet (90 to 300 cm).

'Mystic Pink' chickabiddy (*Asarina scandens* 'Mystic Pink')

Smart Substitutes

If you enjoy dainty annual vines like climbing snapdragon, chances are you'll also like purple bell vine (*Rhodochiton atrosanguineum*, also called *R. volubile*). The flowers start off with a bell-shaped, reddish purple calyx, which could easily pass for the flower itself. A dark purple tube emerges from the center of the calyx, opening into a hanging flower with pure white stamens. Grow as per climbing snapdragon, but use only fresh seed for sowing. Height: 6 to 8 feet (1.8 to 2.4 m).

Cobaea

Cup-and-saucer vine, cathedral bells, Mexican ivy, monastery vine

Cup-and-saucer vine's tenacious and tough nature makes it a good choice for a quick cover-up on a sturdy structure. But this vigorous annual is more than just practical: Its blooms are intriguing as well. The paler green calyces (which become the saucers) hide buds that slowly open into 2-inch (5-cm)-long, nodding flowers (the cups). The blooms are greenish at first, with an unpleasant scent, then slowly darken to deep violet with a honeylike fragrance. The calyces remain attractive after the flowers fade, and the foliage looks good even through the first frost.

Plant Profile

COBAEA
COE-bee-uh

- **Bloom Color:** Purple or white
- **Bloom Time:** Mid- to late summer through midfall
- **Height:** 20 to 70 feet (6 to 21 m)
- **Spacing:** 2 to 3 feet (60 to 90 cm)
- **Garden Uses:** Container planting, groundcover, specimen plant, screening; on trellises, fences, and pergolas
- **Light Preference:** Full sun
- **Soil Preference:** Well-drained, evenly moist soil
- **Best Way to Propagate:** Sow seed indoors in late winter; take stem cuttings in summer
- **Hardiness:** Frost-sensitive perennial grown as a tender annual

Growing Tips

You can sometimes buy individual plants in pots in spring, but the price can be surprisingly high, considering how quickly cup-and-saucers can grow. On the other hand, you will rarely need more than one or two plants of this vine, so buying started plants can be an easy route to go.

Start cup-and-saucer vine indoors, in large-size peat pots, at least 6 to 8 weeks before the last frost date. Beware of sowing much earlier than 10 weeks, though, because this is a massive plant that is hard to accommodate indoors. To speed up germination, nick the large, flat seed with a sharp knife before planting, or soak it overnight in an old thermos of warm water. Plant it long edge down, with the upper edge at the soil surface because seed placed flat tends to rot. Sow two or three seeds per peat pot. Germination is often quite irregular, taking 10 to 30 days (sometimes even longer) at 70° to 75°F (21° to 24°C). Cut out all but one plant per pot. As the seedlings grow, pinch each once or twice to encourage branching.

Plant out only when all danger of frost has passed and the soil has warmed up—preferably in a somewhat protected spot because young plants are sensitive to cold. Give them a site with well-drained soil in full sun (partial shade is acceptable in mild climates). Avoid fertilizing with a nitrogen-rich product because it can stimulate rapid growth but delay flowering: something you'll not want in cool summer areas, where the blooms already come late enough. Water as needed to keep the soil partially moist. The plants become considerably hardier as summer advances and will easily take light frost by summer's end, often surviving and blooming until nights get really frigid in October or November.

If you're trying to cover an eyesore fast, just let cup-and-saucer vine grow. Otherwise, pinch repeatedly when the stems reach eye level to concentrate the bloom on the lower parts. (There's not much use having flowers so high up you'd need binoculars to see them, especially since their colors are rather muted; they're most striking up close.)

You can also grow cup-and-saucer vine in containers, but you'll really need large ones—such as a half-barrel with a very solid trellis—if you want a great show.

This fast-growing climber is hardy outdoors only in Zones 9 through 11. Don't bother trying to dig it up to bring indoors: It hates transplanting. Bring in container-grown plants if you have the space; otherwise, simply start new plants each spring.

Good Neighbors

Cup-and-saucer vine is a vigorous climber that needs a large arbor, trellis, or pergola to show you what it is made of. Combine it with a shorter, bushier vine such as yellow flag-of-Spain (*Ipomoea lobata* 'Citronella') to add color closer to eye level.

Problems and Solutions

Cup-and-saucer vine seldom has pest or disease problems.

Top Performer

Cobaea scandens (cup-and-saucer vine, cathedral bells, Mexican ivy, monastery vine): This tropical climber can reach unheard-of heights in mild climates—up to 70 feet (21 m)! Don't expect quite so much of it elsewhere, though; 25 feet (7.5 m) is more common. While often quite late to bloom, especially where summers are cool, this vine produces lots of exotic foliage beforehand. The rich green pinnate leaves end in a cluster of long, twisting tendrils that wrap around nearby objects. The tendrils end in tiny hooks that can work their way into tiny cracks in rough surfaces such as wood or even concrete, making this the one annual vine that doesn't require something to twist around. Besides the usual purple-flowered form, there is also a "white" flowered form: 'Alba' (whose flowers are actually more green than white).

Cup-and-saucer vine
(*Cobaea scandens*)

Larry's Garden Notes

To my mind, there's something vaguely unsettling, or even sinister, about the flowers of cup-and-saucer vine. Their shades of green to violet, plus the odd odor they give off when they first open, would seem to make them suitable for funeral arrangements or perhaps Halloween decorations. Not that they are unattractive; it's just that they aren't bright, sunny flowers that bring a happy smile to the face. I still like to grow cup-and-saucer vine for the great cover-up job it does—and to have something curious to show visitors.

Cucurbita

Ornamental gourd, bottle gourd, squash, minipumpkin

Ornamental gourds really come into their own *after* their multicolored and often curiously formed fruit is harvested for use in crafts and seasonal displays. That's not to say that the plants themselves have no ornamental qualities, however! The large, deeply lobed, mid- to light green leaves are great for screening unsightly views, and the charming white or yellow flowers appear nonstop through summer. The gourds themselves are also of great garden interest, of course, especially as they ripen to their mature colors.

Plant Profile

CUCURBITA
cue-CUR-bih-tuh

- **Bloom Color:** Varies by species; see individual listings

- **Bloom Time:** Summer

- **Height:** 10 inches to 10 feet (25 cm to 3 m)

- **Spacing:** 10 to 12 inches (25 to 30 cm) if trellis-grown; 5 to 10 feet (1.5 to 3 m) if allowed to sprawl

- **Garden Uses:** Container planting, hanging baskets, groundcover, vegetable garden, screening; on trellises, fences, and pergolas

- **Light Preference:** Full sun

- **Soil Preference:** Humus-rich, evenly moist but well-drained soil

- **Best Way to Propagate:** Sow seed indoors or out in spring

- **Hardiness:** Tender annual

Growing Tips

Gourds grow quickly but transplant poorly, so there's no use looking for them to be sold as individual plants in a nursery. It's usually fairly easy to find the seed, though.

You can start the faster-maturing, yellow-flowered gourds directly outdoors when there is no danger of frost and the soil is at least 60°F (15°C). In most areas, however, it's best to start these heat-loving annuals—especially the white-flowered types—indoors in peat pots. There is no use starting them too early, though: They grow far too quickly and would become impossible to transplant. A mere 3 weeks before the last spring frost date is all the head start they need. Plant two or three seeds per peat pot, about ¼ inch (6 mm) deep. They germinate quickly at 70° to 75°F (21° to 24°C). Once they're up, eliminate all but one per pot. Don't even think of transplanting gourds outside until the soil temperature has reached 70°F (21°C). Let them scramble if you have lots of space, otherwise supply a strong support they can clamber up using their tendrils. Full sun and rich soil are ideal.

For drying purposes, harvest the fruits when the foliage begins to die back but before frost hits. Leave a bit of stem on each gourd and handle it carefully; bruises or nicks can lead to rot. Dry in a warm, well-ventilated room. Some people

FUN FACTS

Gourds produce separate male and female flowers on the same plant. You can tell which ones are females by the swollen ovary (the future gourd) at their base. If a female flower opens when there are no bees around (in cool or rainy weather), pollinate it yourself by plucking a male flower and touching the yellow pollen of the anther to the clublike pistil in the center of the female bloom.

like to wax or lacquer their gourds to ensure longer life, but even air-dried gourds can last a year or so if they're perfectly intact. You can also try opening and hollowing out gourds before drying them for use as ladles, bowls, bird houses, or whatever use their shape suggests. However, expect a certain percentage of loss due to rot: Whether an open squash rots or dries has always been pretty much a toss-up, even back when ancient peoples used the fruits as tools and utensils.

Good Neighbors

A high, sturdy arbor planted with ornamental gourds would make an interesting garden entrance, either as a yearly feature or as a temporary measure while perennial vines such as clematis are getting a foothold.

Problems and Solutions

Vine borers, squash bugs, and beetles are sometimes problems, damaging leaves or introducing bacteria that cause plants to wilt. Hand-picking is one solution for visible bugs and beetles. If you notice leaf wilt, look for holes in the main stem in that area, and inject *Bacillus thuringiensis* (BT) to control the squash borer.

Top Performer

Cucurbita pepo (ornamental gourd, squash, minipumpkin): Don't look for this or any other gourd under its botanical name. They are all sold simply as "ornamental gourds" (if offered as a mix) or according to the description of the fruit: crown-of-thorns, warted gourd, minipumpkin, Turk's turban, and so on. The range of colors and shapes is incredible—just take your pick! Height: 10 inches (25 cm) if allowed to sprawl; 5 to 10 feet (1.5 to 3 m) if trellis-grown.

More Recommended Ornamental Gourds

Lagenaria siceraria (white-flowered gourd, bottle gourd, calabash): These white-flowered gourds are sold either separately under such fun names as "caveman's club" or in mixtures with *Cucurbita pepo*. White-flowered gourds need a longer growing season than the yellow-flowered species, so be sure to start them indoors. Height: 10 inches (25 cm) if allowed to sprawl; 5 to 10 feet (1.5 to 3 m) if trellis-grown.

Ornamental gourd
(*Cucurbita pepo*)

Kissing Cousins

For a gourdlike plant that is a true ornamental, try balsam apple (*Momordica balsamina*) or balsam pear (*M. charantia*). This vining plant produces numerous thin stems clad in attractive, dark green, maplelike leaves. Bright yellow flowers produce strangely lumpy green fruits that mature to bright orange, then split open to reveal striking red flesh. Start balsam apples or pears indoors 6 to 8 weeks before your last frost date. Train to some kind of support to show off the fruits. Height: 5 to 10 feet (1.5 to 3 m) if trellis grown.

Humulus

Japanese hops

Want to hide something from sight—fast? Have I got the plant for you! It grows fast, tall, and wide, and it provides the densest cover you could imagine. Japanese hops is great as a twining climber on trellises, arbors, pergolas, and other structures, but it's equally effective when used as a groundcover to hide a pile of rubble, a stump, or whatever unsightly feature you might have in your landscape.

Plant Profile

HUMULUS
HEW-mew-lus

- **Bloom Color:** Green
- **Bloom Time:** Late summer and early fall
- **Height:** 10 to 20 feet (3 to 6 m)
- **Spacing:** 2 to 3 feet (60 to 90 cm)
- **Garden Uses:** Container planting, hanging baskets, groundcover, screening; on trellises, fences, and pergolas
- **Light Preference:** Full sun to partial shade
- **Soil Preference:** Humus-rich, fertile, evenly moist but well-drained soil
- **Best Way to Propagate:** Sow seed indoors or outdoors in late spring or fall
- **Hardiness:** Short-lived perennial grown as a hardy annual

Growing Tips

You're not likely to find pots of Japanese hops for sale at your local garden center. Even the seed is rarely available in stores; you usually have to order it by mail.

How you start the seed depends on how much of a hurry you're in for it to hide that eyesore or cover that pergola. You can't wait? Start it indoors, in individual peat pots, 6 to 8 weeks before the last frost; then plant it outdoors after all danger of frost has passed. You're in no hurry? Sow it outdoors, a few weeks before the last frost, or even in the fall for growth the following spring. Seed sown outdoors while the soil is still cool will germinate when the time is right. Indoors, nick the hard seeds or soak them in an old thermos of warm water overnight to stimulate faster germination. (Even with the help, germination can take a while: from 2 weeks to more than 1 month.) Indoors or out, sow the seeds about ¼ inch (6 mm) deep.

Japanese hops is one tough plant and can take just about any conditions you throw at it, including poor soil, drought, strong wind, and extreme heat and humidity. For truly luxuriant growth, though, give it full sun and moist but well-drained, humus-rich soil, and supply extra water (without wetting the leaves) during dry spells.

Unless you're using it as a groundcover, hops need a truly solid support. Even though it is

FUN FACTS

Unfortunately, this is *not* the kind of hops used in making beer. That honor goes to common hops (*Humulus lupulus*), a vigorous species that's perennial at least into Zone 3. The species has plain green leaves that aren't especially interesting, but 'Aureus' is a lovely golden-leaved cultivar of great ornamental value.

an annual, this is a big, heavy plant and it could easily tear right through lightweight trellis netting. It does make a great privacy screen, though.

Although frost tolerant to a considerable degree once it is established, Japanese hops will begin to die back at season's end. You can either cut it back and clean it up or leave the brown stems and leaves where they are: Sometimes they are more attractive than whatever they are hiding! Theoretically, Japanese hops is a perennial, but it rarely makes it through the winter even in moderate climates.

Think Twice: Once you've planted Japanese hops in your garden, you'll probably never need to sow it again: It will self-sow with a vengeance. It is, in fact, already well established as a weed species in most temperate regions of the world. To keep it from becoming a weed in *your* yard, mulch abundantly to keep the seed from getting started, and pull out unwanted plants as soon as you see them germinating in your garden bed. **Self-sowing**

'Variegatus' Japanese hops (*Humulus japonicus* 'Variegatus')

Good Neighbors

Japanese hops primarily provides foliage interest, so consider combining it with a flowering vine, such as sweet peas (*Lathyrus odoratus*) or morning glories (*Ipomoea* spp.), for extra color.

Problems and Solutions

Plants stressed by very wet or very dry soil are prone to leaf diseases, such as downy and powdery mildew. There's not much you can do once you notice the discolored foliage; instead, correct the growing conditions the following year.

Top Performer

Humulus japonicus (Japanese hops): Twining stems bear dark green, maplelike leaves that are 6 to 8 inches (15 to 20 cm) across. Both the leaves and stems are very rough textured. The male blooms are scarcely noticeable, but the female ones, covered with pale green, pendulous bracts that turn beige in the fall, look a bit like pinecones and do add a bit of interest. 'Variegatus' has dark green leaves irregularly marbled with gray and white and is less invasive than the species.

Smart Substitutes

If you're worried about the invasive nature of Japanese hops but still want abundant cover without very flashy flowers, try balloon vine (*Cardiospermum halicacabum*). This daintier climber has tiny, greenish white flowers that are followed by inflated, green seed pods that bob in the wind. Turning brown as they age, the mature pods contain dark seeds, each marked with the white heart that gives the plant its other common names: heartseed and love-in-a-puff. Start indoors as per Japanese hops. Height: 10 to 12 feet (3 to 3.6 m). Spacing: 1 to 2 feet (30 to 60 cm).

Ipomoea alba

Moonflower

What a wonderful name for a delightful flower! The huge blooms really do open with the moon, early in the evening, and then remain open all night. They seem to glisten in the moonlight, reflecting the slightest bit of light from the heavens above. With the first rays of dawn, they slowly start to close, and, by noon (a little later on cloudy days), the show is over. Fortunately, it starts all over again in the evening, until either the shortening days of fall or the first frost closes down the display.

Plant Profile

IPOMOEA ALBA
ih-poe-MEE-uh AL-buh

- **Bloom Color:** White
- **Bloom Time:** Early summer through fall
- **Height:** 6 to 15 feet (2 to 5 m)
- **Spacing:** 1 foot (30 cm)
- **Garden Uses:** Container planting, cut-flower garden, hanging baskets, ground-cover, specimen plant, screening; on trellises, fences, and pergolas
- **Attracts:** Sphinx moths
- **Light Preference:** Full sun to partial shade
- **Soil Preference:** Average, evenly moist well-drained soil
- **Best Way to Propagate:** Sow seed indoors in spring
- **Hardiness:** Frost-sensitive perennial grown as a tender annual

Growing Tips

Don't count on finding moonflower plants for sale at your local garden center. In most cases, you'll have to grow your own plants from seed.

Except in the mildest climates, where you could sow it outdoors, you'll probably want to start moonflower indoors. Otherwise, it is so slow getting started that the summer will be nearly over before it begins to bloom.

Indoors, sow the seed about 8 weeks before the last frost. Before planting, nick it with a sharp knife or soak it in an old thermos of warm water for 24 to 48 hours. Moonflower doesn't like having its roots disturbed, so sow it into a peat pot, two or three seeds per pot. Barely cover the seed, then place the pots in a warm spot: 70° to 75°F (21° to 24°C). Germination takes about 2 weeks. Cut out all but the strongest plant in each pot. When the young plants have several leaves, pinch out the shoot tip to force them to fill out more.

Don't be in a rush to put moonflowers outdoors; they are true tropical plants and will expect nothing less than warmth. If needed, move them up to bigger peat pots to keep them growing indoors. When the weather finally does warm up, gradually acclimate them to outdoor conditions, and then plant them out in well-drained, evenly moist soil—ideally in full sun. In cooler climates, look for a spot protected from strong winds, perhaps against a wall that radiates some heat at night.

FUN FACTS

Moonflower makes a short-lived but spectacular cut flower. Just cut it in the early evening and let it float in a clear bowl. The intoxicatingly sweet perfume seems even more remarkable indoors than out.

Once in the ground, moonflowers grow rapidly and will need a sturdy support to twist around. In tropical areas, they often climb right to the top of surrounding trees, up to 70 feet (21 m), but expect about 10 to 15 feet (3 to 4.5 m) in cooler climates. Deadheading doesn't seem to make a difference in bloom production. The appearance of rounded seedpods, each with a minaret-like point at their tip, does not mean you'll have seeds to harvest, however. The seeds are only ripe when they turn brown on their own, and they won't have time to mature in many areas. (Turning brown due to frost does *not* count!)

Warning: The seeds of moonflower are poisonous, so keep them out of reach of children and pets.

If you grow your moonflowers in a container, you could theoretically bring them indoors for the winter. They need lots of room, though! Cut them back harshly when you bring them in and keep pruning them through the winter if they threaten to take over your home or greenhouse.

Moonflower
(*Ipomoea alba*)

Good Neighbors

Moonflower's night-blooming habit makes it an excellent choice for planting around a deck or patio where you sit on summer evenings. For daytime interest, interplant with 'Pearly Gates' morning glory (*Ipomoea tricolor*) to continue the white theme, or with another flowering vine for more color.

Problems and Solutions

Moonflower seldom has any problems in the garden.

Top Performer

Ipomoea alba (moonflower): Also called *Calonyction aculeatum*. Moonflower offers soft white (rarely palest pink) trumpets that are sometimes banded green. Each intensely fragrant bloom measures from 4 to 6 inches (10 to 15 cm) in diameter. The dark green leaves are attractive in their own right: huge, heart-shaped or sometimes three-lobed, and very tropical in appearance.

Smart Substitutes

For beautiful white flowers that you can enjoy during the day, try potato vine (*Solanum jasminoides*, sometimes called *S. laxum*). It is evergreen and ever blooming in frost-free climates, semi-evergreen and spring to fall flowering in Zones 8 and 9, and a summer-flowering annual elsewhere. Only 'Album', the white-flowered form, seems to be cultivated so far, and it has given rise to several variegated cultivars. Train this bushy scrambler up a support or let it cascade out of a container. Height: 3 to 20 feet (1 to 6 m). Spacing: 8 to 12 inches (20 to 30 cm).

Ipomoea

Quamoclit, cardinal climber, red morning glory, cypress vine

Cardinal climber, red morning glory, and cypress vine form a small but distinct subgroup—the quamoclits—within the vast morning glory (*Ipomoea*) genus. True, most morning glories share short-lived flowers, opening early in the morning and closing in the afternoon. But the quamoclits have finer stems, more deeply cut foliage, and most notably, smaller, more distinctly tubular flowers suddenly flaring out at the tip into a flat face that is either pentagonal or starlike, depending on the species. And did I mention their color range? Red, red, and red!

Plant Profile

IPOMOEA
ih-poe-MEE-uh

- **Bloom Color:** Red
- **Bloom Time:** Summer through early fall
- **Height:** Varies by species; see individual listings
- **Spacing:** 8 to 12 inches (20 to 30 cm)
- **Garden Uses:** Container planting, hanging baskets, groundcover, screening; on trellises, fences, and pergolas
- **Attracts:** Hummingbirds
- **Light Preference:** Full sun
- **Soil Preference:** Average, evenly moist but well-drained moist soil
- **Best Way to Propagate:** Sow seed indoors or outdoors in spring
- **Hardiness:** Half-hardy annual

Growing Tips

Quamoclits don't like to have their roots disturbed, so you're not likely to see plants for sale at your local nursery. Instead, you'll have to learn to grow them from seed—and that is easy enough to do.

In warm climates, you have a choice: Either start the seed indoors a few weeks before the last frost date or sow directly outside about 2 weeks after all danger of frost has passed, when the soil has warmed up. In short-season areas, though, starting the plant indoors 6 to 8 weeks before the last frost date is a better way to go. First, either nick the hard black seed or soak it in tepid water for 24 to 48 hours. Plant two or three seeds per peat pot, about ⅛ inch (3 mm) deep, and keep them at room temperature. Germination can be surprisingly fast: sometimes less than 1 week. After germination, thin to the strongest plant in each pot.

Wait until there is absolutely no danger of frost and the soil has warmed up thoroughly before planting quamoclits outdoors. Place them near a support so they can start climbing, or let them trail out of containers. Individual plants tend to be a bit thin, so grow them quite closely together, 8 to 12 inches (20 to 30 cm) apart, so their foliage can mingle. They prefer full sun but bloom better in partial shade than most other morning glories. Good garden soil that's well drained but not overly rich is ideal. Water thoroughly during drought.

FUN FACTS

The botanical name *quamoclit* certainly stands out from the crowd. Most botanical names have Latin or Greek origins, or have at least been "Latinized" but not *quamoclit*: It was taken directly from a native Mexican name for the cypress vine.

Warning: The seeds of quamoclits are poisonous, so keep them out of reach of children and pets.

Good Neighbors

Quamoclits have lacy leaves that don't so much block a view as soften it. Use them to dress up an already-beautiful trellis or arbor, or allow the fine-leaved cypress vine (*Ipomoea quamoclit*) to drape itself over an evergreen hedge or an upright juniper.

Problems and Solutions

Spider mites can be a problem during hot, dry weather; spray with water or insecticidal soap to control them.

Top Performer

Ipomoea × multifida (cardinal climber): Also called *Quamoclit × sloteri* and *I. × sloteri*. This is a hybrid between the two plants described below, with a more controlled habit and larger flowers. Also, although it will self-sow quite readily, it has less of a tendency to become a nuisance than *I. coccinea*. It produces crimson, somewhat star-shaped flowers about 1 inch (2.5 cm) wide, with a white throat. The leaves are dark green and more or less triangular in shape with three to seven deeply cut, narrow lobes. Height: 3 to 20 feet (90 cm to 6 m). **Self-sowing** 🌱

More Recommended Quamoclits

🌷 **Think Twice:** *Ipomoea coccinea* (red morning glory, star morning glory): Also called *Quamoclit coccinea*. The leaves of this species are heart shaped (although often deeply toothed), and the flower face is round, rather than star-shaped. The ¾-inch (2-cm) flowers are borne in clusters and are bright scarlet with a yellow throat. This is a fast-growing, more aggressive plant than the others and tends to self-sow to the point of weediness; keep it deadheaded for control. Height: 6 to 20 feet (1.8 to 6 m). **Self-sowing** 🌱

    I. quamoclit (cypress vine, star glory): Also called *Quamoclit pennata*. This distinctive species bears clusters of ¾-inch (2-cm), star-shaped flowers that are usually scarlet but sometimes pure white, dotted among the deeply cut, fernlike leaves. It does self-sow somewhat but is rarely weedy. Height: 6 to 25 feet (1.8 to 7.5 m). **Self-sowing** 🌱

'Cardinal' red morning glory (*Ipomoea coccinea* 'Cardinal')

Larry's Garden Notes

My garden could never be without quamoclits, not only because I just love their lacy foliage and tiny scarlet trumpets, but also because they are absolute hummingbird magnets. It's not only the color and shape that draw them so faithfully (although it is a well-known fact that hummingbirds prefer tubular red flowers to all others), but the constancy of their bloom. Once they begin to flower in earnest in midsummer, you can be sure there will be abundant bloom on them every single day until frost.

Ipomoea lobata

Flag-of-Spain, Spanish flag, firecracker vine, exotic love

You'd never guess that this species is closely related to the traditional trumpet-shaped morning glories (*Ipomoea* spp.). In fact, its blooms couldn't be more different! First, they're produced on thin, red-stemmed, arching sprays, with flowers arranged all along their lengths, pointing in the same direction. Then the tip of each flower barely opens—not into a "morning glory trumpet" but into a tiny, barely noticeable five-pointed star, with long, thin anthers and a pistil that sticks out briefly. It is, therefore, essentially the colored bud that is of interest rather than the flower itself.

Plant Profile

IPOMOEA LOBATA
ih-poe-MEE-uh low-BAH-tuh

- **Bloom Color:** Red, orange, yellow, white
- **Bloom Time:** Early or mid-summer to fall; year-round in frost-free climates
- **Height:** 6 to 20 feet (1.8 to 6 m)
- **Spacing:** 8 to 12 inches (20 to 30 cm)
- **Garden Uses:** Container planting, hanging baskets, groundcover, screening; on trellises, fences, and pergolas
- **Attracts:** Hummingbirds
- **Light Preference:** Full sun
- **Soil Preference:** Average, evenly moist but well-drained soil
- **Best Way to Propagate:** Sow seed indoors or outdoors in spring
- **Hardiness:** Frost-sensitive perennial grown as a tender annual

Growing Tips

You'll rarely see a flag-of-Spain plant offered in a pot, mainly due to its dislike of being transplanted, but it's usually fairly easy to find the seed for it.

Start this climber indoors in all but the very mildest climates; otherwise, you'll get bloom only at the very end of summer. Sow indoors 8 to 10 weeks before the last frost, first soaking the seed for 24 to 48 hours in warm water. I like to put the seed in an old thermos full of fairly hot water, then change it after 24 hours. Sowing in peat pots is important so you won't disturb the roots at transplanting time. Plant two or three seeds per pot, cover them with ⅛ inch (3 mm) of growing mix, and keep at 65° to 70°F (18° to 21°C). Look for seedlings in 1 to 3 weeks. Don't hesitate to repot them into larger peat pots if poor weather forces you to delay their planting outdoors because restricted root growth can delay their flowering by several weeks.

Wait until both the air and the soil outside have thoroughly warmed, perhaps 2 or 3 weeks after the last frost date, to move the seedlings outdoors. Then acclimate them gradually, from deep shade to light shade to full sun, over the period of a week or so before planting them out in their permanent spot.

For fullest coverage, set plants 8 to 12 inches (20 to 30 cm) apart. Full sun and a not-too-rich, well-drained soil are best; rich soil tends to stimulate lots of foliage but few flowers. Since flag-of-Spain prefers steady moisture, apply a mulch and water at least occasionally. This vine hates being cold, so it really isn't worth trying where night temperatures regularly dip below 50°F (10°C). Gardeners in the Deep South, however, will be thrilled at how well flag-of-Spain thrives in hot, humid summers!

Flag-of-Spain is short-lived perennial in mild climates and will even bloom throughout the year in truly tropical areas. In Zones 8 and 9, however, it will often lose its leaves in fall and sprout again in spring. Elsewhere, treat it as an annual or bring container-grown plants indoors for winter. Cut them back severely and grow them in a warm, sunny spot.

Warning: The seeds of flag-of-Spain are poisonous, so keep them out of the reach of children and pets.

Good Neighbors

Flag-of-Spain's warm colors look great with purples, either in a foreground planting—perhaps *Salvia verticillata* 'Purple Rain'— or in a companion vine, such as a purple clematis. Or let it climb up and over a forsythia to provide summer interest.

Problems and Solutions

Spider mite infestations sometimes occur during dry weather. Spider mites damage plants by piercing tiny holes in the leaves and drinking the sap that leaks out. Control them by spraying with water or insecticidal soap.

Top Performer

Ipomoea lobata (flag-of-Spain, Spanish flag, firecracker vine, exotic love): Also called *I. versicolor* and *Mina lobata*. Curved, somewhat inflated, tubular buds start out small and scarlet red, then mature through orange to lemon yellow to creamy white, with all colors present on the same stalk. The colored buds last for weeks, but they drop off only a few hours after they actually open. Borne on reddish, twisting stems, the heart-shaped leaves are beautifully cut into three or more lobes. If you're looking for a more subdued color effect, try 'Citronella', with buds that start off lemon yellow, then fade to white at opening. Flag-of-Spain will occasionally self-sow, especially in mild winter areas. **Self-sowing** 🖉

Flag-of-Spain
(*Ipomoea lobata*)

Smart Substitutes

If you enjoy climbers with hot-colored flowers, you should definitely try Chilean glory vine (*Eccremocarpus scaber*). This fast-growing tropical vine bears light green, deeply cut leaves, ending in branching tendrils and scores of bright orange, 1-inch (2.5-cm), tubular flowers that look like pot-bellied goldfish with pouting lips. Selections with red, pink, or yellow flowers are also available. Grow as per flag-of-Spain, but you don't need to soak the seed. Height: 10 to 15 feet (3 to 4.5 m). Spacing: 1 foot (30 cm).

Ipomoea

Morning glory

Morning glories are by far the most popular of climbing annuals. Generations of gardeners have found them prolific, productive, and easy to grow, so they make a great choice for beginners. They are instantly recognizable, either by their twisted, pointed buds or by the broad, trumpet-shaped flowers they unfurl into. The common name is quite appropriate: The flowers open with the first rays of the sun and close by noon (or late afternoon on cloudy days). Closed blooms never open again, but lots of new flowers open each day.

Plant Profile

IPOMOEA
ih-poe-MEE-uh

- **Bloom Color:** Varies by species; see individual listings
- **Bloom Time:** Early summer through fall; much of the year in mild climates
- **Height:** Varies by species; see individual listings
- **Spacing:** 8 to 12 inches (20 to 30 cm)
- **Garden Uses:** Container planting, hanging baskets, groundcover, screening; on trellises, fences, and pergolas
- **Attracts:** Hummingbirds
- **Light Preference:** Full sun
- **Soil Preference:** Average, evenly moist but well-drained soil
- **Best Way to Propagate:** Sow seed indoors or outdoors in spring
- **Hardiness:** Frost-sensitive perennial grown as a tender annual

Growing Tips

If morning glories have a flaw, it is that they don't transplant well, a fact that keeps them out of the usual nursery production facilities.

To grow your own plants, start the seed indoors or out. Outdoor sowing, a week or so after the last frost date, gives great results. Nick or soak the seed overnight and sow it ¼ inch (6 mm) deep and 2 inches (5 cm) apart. When the plants come up, thin them from 8 to 12 inches (20 to 30 cm) apart.

If you want flowers early, start the seed indoors 3 to 4 weeks before your last frost date. As above, either nick the seeds with a sharp knife or soak them overnight in warm water. Use peat pots to minimize transplanting shock later, sowing two or three seeds in each pot. Germination is rapid, often taking less than 1 week to sprout up. Thin to one plant per pot—the sturdiest—and plant outside when all danger of frost is past.

In very mild climates, many morning glories are perennials and may even bloom much of the year. Elsewhere, consider them annuals and start new plants each year.

Warning: The seeds of all morning glories are poisonous, so keep them out of reach of children and pets.

Good Neighbors

Morning glories provide such dense coverage that they're hard

FUN FACTS

Northern gardeners often find that their morning glories don't bloom until late in the season, when the summer is already half over. For faster results, try one of the *Ipomoea nil* cultivars recognized for their extra-early flowering habit, such as 'Early Call' (a blend of colors) or 'Scarlett O'Hara' (pinkish red).

to beat for hiding eyesores. They're also great for filling space temporarily while slower-growing perennial vines, such as clematis, are getting established.

Problems and Solutions

Spider mites can be an annoyance during dry weather. Spray them off with water or insecticidal soap.

Top Performer

Ipomoea nil (morning glory): Also called *I. imperialis.* Twisting, somewhat hairy stems produce medium green, heart-shaped leaves that are usually entire but sometimes three-lobed. The flowers are usually 2 to 4 inches (5 to 10 cm) in diameter, although some Japanese hybrids are up to 8 inches (20 cm)! The color range includes various shades of blue, purple, red, pink, and white, usually with a white throat; many cultivars are irregularly striped or edged. There are also types with variegated leaves. This species produces a tuberous root you can overwinter indoors, keeping it dormant in a cool but frost-free place. Height: 3 to 15 feet (90 cm to 4.5 m). **Self-sowing**

More Recommended Morning Glories

 Think Twice: *Ipomoea purpurea* (common morning glory): In spite of its common name, this species is not the most widely grown morning glory, although it *is* common as an escaped weed in warmer climates. This fast-growing annual vine produces heart-shaped to lobed leaves and innumerable flowers. The blooms are purple with a white throat in the species and range from white through pink, red, magenta, and maroon in cultivated varieties. Height: 6 to 10 feet (1.8 to 3 m). **Self-sowing**

I. tricolor (morning glory): Almost as popular as *I. nil,* this smooth-stemmed species has larger, heart-shaped leaves. It is best known for two cultivars: 'Heavenly Blue', with huge, sky blue flowers surrounding a yellow throat, and 'Pearly Gates', with pure white flowers. Other cultivars come in other shades, from crimson to purple, as well as bicolors. Height: 10 to 12 feet (3 to 3.6 m). **Self-sowing**

Morning glory
(*Ipomoea nil*)

Up and Coming

There's been an astounding array of new morning glories introduced over the last few years, many of them from Japan, where morning glories practically have cult status among serious gardeners. Where we Westerners simply choose easy-to-grow cultivars that are stable from seed, the Japanese adore strange mutations and delicate plants that can often be multiplied only by cuttings. As these strange plants are stabilized through careful plant breeding to come true from seed, look for more truly odd morning glories at a garden center near you!

Lablab

Hyacinth bean, lablab, Egyptian bean

Only a few years ago, hyacinth bean was relatively unknown; now many people regard it as a must-have vine for their garden. It's easy to understand the attraction! Ornamental strains usually have purple stems and purplish new leaves, followed by scented, pea-shaped, rose-purple flowers that turn into glossy maroon-purple pods. The leaves consist of three large triangular leaflets carried on twining stems. This is an easy-to-grow vine with only one major requirement: It needs warmth to thrive.

Plant Profile

LABLAB
LAB-lab

- **Bloom Color:** Pink, purple, white

- **Bloom Time:** Summer through fall; year-round in mild climates

- **Height:** 6 to 30 feet (1.8 to 9 m)

- **Spacing:** 2 to 3 feet (60 to 90 cm)

- **Garden Uses:** Container planting, cut-flower garden, hanging baskets, groundcover, vegetable garden, specimen plant, screening; on trellises, fences, and pergolas

- **Light Preference:** Full sun

- **Soil Preference:** Any well-drained soil

- **Best Way to Propagate:** Sow seed indoors or outdoors in spring

- **Hardiness:** Frost-sensitive perennial grown as a tender annual

Growing Tips

Although you may occasionally find hyacinth beans being sold in individual pots, in most cases you'll have to grow your own plants from seed.

Where summers are long, there isn't much advantage to starting seed indoors; just sow it outside when all danger of frost is past and the ground is warm—at least 65°F (18°C). In cooler climates, though, hyacinth bean will appreciate a 6- to 8-week head start. Indoors or out, soak the seed in warm water overnight to stimulate faster germination, then plant it just thinly covered. Indoors, sow into peat pots. Seedlings will be up and growing in about 2 weeks. Give indoor seedlings individual short stakes to climb on until it's time to plant them outside (when both the ground and the air have thoroughly warmed up).

Being legumes, hyacinth beans get much of their nitrogen from a symbiotic relationship with soil bacteria, so they do perfectly well in ordinary soil. If you've never grown beans in that spot before, dust a little soil inoculant for beans (sold in the vegetable-seed section of garden centers and catalogs) into the planting hole to provide the bacteria the beans will need. Good drainage is important, so raised beds are ideal; this is especially true in cooler climates, where they offer the added benefit of warming up rapidly in spring.

You can use hyacinth bean as a groundcover or let it climb up just about any kind of structure its twining stems can wrap themselves around. Don't expect 30-foot (9-m) plants in most gardens, though: hyacinth beans take about 2 years to reach that height. In most climates, 10 to 15 feet (3 to 4.5 m) is a reasonable height to expect for one summer's growth.

Summer care consists mainly of watering as needed. Although quite drought tolerant, the plants produce more flowers and more pods if you water regularly. In dry climates, use a mulch to keep the soil naturally moister while saving water.

Hyacinth beans are likely to overwinter only in Zones 9 to 11; elsewhere, treat them as annuals.

Good Neighbors

This is one vine that works great either with or without a structure. Whether adorning a fence or scrambling over and through established shrubs, hyacinth bean is always attractive. For a quick privacy shield, simply string up supporting twine or wire and allow it to fill in the gaps. Its rich colors also make a handsome backdrop trained on a fence behind low-growing shrubs or perennials.

Hyacinth bean
(*Lablab purpureus*)

Problems and Solutions

I've never seen any problem on hyacinth bean, but apparently leaf spot can occur near areas where the bean is grown as a food crop. Mulching and keeping the soil evenly moist without moistening the leaves could help prevent the problem.

Top Performer

Lablab purpureus (hyacinth bean, lablab, Egyptian bean, Indian bean, bonavist, sarawak bean): Also called *Dolichos lablab*. The species is actually quite variable, with flowers ranging from white to pink to bicolored, not just purple. The species has plain green leaves and blooms poorly in the North, so always ask for the ornamental types when you're shopping for seeds. The large seeds themselves also vary in color, from white to buff, reddish brown, brown, and black. This can actually help you pick your flower colors if you have mixed seed: White seeds will give white-flowered plants, buff seeds, pink ones, and so on. The darker the seed, the darker the flower! Flowering is nonstop all summer and can continue through much of the year in frost-free climates since hyacinth bean is a perennial—albeit a short-lived one. **Self-sowing**

Larry's Garden Note

Although North Americans and Europeans grow this plant strictly as an ornamental, hyacinth bean is a staple vegetable and forage crop throughout much of Asia and Africa. All of its parts are edible; you can even eat the young leaves, lightly steamed. Use the seed as you would garden beans. While the seed is still small and soft, eat the pods raw or cooked; once the beans are mature, cook and eat them fresh, sprout them, or dry them for future use. Throw away the cooking/sprouting water, though, since some people are allergic to it.

Lathyrus

Sweet pea

Sweet peas are pretty much what their name suggests: sweet-scented relatives of the garden pea. Well, at least they *used* to have a lovely perfume! Until recently, sweet pea hybridizers seemed to look primarily for plants with larger, more colorful flowers, while perfume was put on the back burner. That is now changing. Along with the sweetly perfumed, old-fashioned cultivars that are coming back in style, recent "show varieties" are featuring scent again. One final note: Sweet peas differ from garden peas in that their seeds are not only inedible but also *toxic*!

Plant Profile

LATHYRUS
LATH-uh-rus

- **Bloom Color:** Blue, lavender, pink, purple, salmon, maroon, red, rose, white

- **Bloom Time:** Late spring through early fall; fall through winter in mild climates

- **Height:** 6 to 72 inches (15 to 180 cm)

- **Spacing:** 6 inches (15 cm) for climbers; 1 foot (30 cm) for bush types

- **Garden Uses:** Container planting, cut-flower garden, hanging baskets, groundcover, mixed border, screening; on trellises, fences, and pergolas

- **Light Preference:** Full sun to partial shade

- **Soil Preference:** Humus-rich, evenly moist but well-drained, closer to neutral than acid soil

- **Best Way to Propagate:** Sow seed outdoors in late winter to spring or fall; indoors in late winter in hot summer areas

- **Hardiness:** Hardy annual

Growing Tips

Nurseries and garden centers seldom carry sweet pea plants, but they may sell seeds of more common cultivars. For seeds of the old-fashioned types, you'll probably need to mail-order them.

How you grow sweet peas very much depends on your climate. In mild winter regions with hot summers, enjoy them as winter and spring bloomers by sowing them outdoors in late fall. In areas with reasonably cool summers—nights generally below 75°F (24°C)—sow in the late fall or in very early spring, as soon as the soil can be worked, about 1 inch (5 cm) deep. They'll sprout when conditions are right. If you sow the seed later in the spring, close to your last frost date, nick the hard seeds first and soak them in water for 24 hours before planting; otherwise, they can take more than 1 month to sprout.

Sweet peas are most challenging to grow in regions with frosty winters and hot summers. Try starting them in a cold greenhouse or coldframe, or a cool but sunny spot in the home. Sow 6 to 8 weeks before the last frost date. The seeds need cool temperatures—55° to 65°F (13° to 18°C)—to germinate, and even cooler temperatures—40° to 50°F (4° to 10°C)—after that. Set seedlings outdoors in early to midspring.

Plant sweet peas in heavy, rich soil generously amended with compost or well-decomposed manure. If you've not grown peas in

FUN FACTS

For extra-long bloom in areas where summers aren't too hot, try mixing early-flowering cultivars (any one labeled "old-fashioned," for example) with the heat-resistant or summer flowering types. The early ones will ensure spring bloom, then the heat-resistant types will take over for the rest of summer.

that spot before, add a dusting of soil inoculant for peas (sold in garden centers and seed catalogs) to each planting hole. When plants are about 6 inches (15 cm) tall, pinch once to stimulate branching. During summer, mulch well and water as needed, preferably without moistening the leaves. Foliar applications of fertilizer can be *very* helpful in maintaining bloom on this greedy plant. And deadheading is essential because sweet peas stop growing if they go to seed. For climbing types, provide something quite narrow that the rather weak tendrils can grab onto, such as trellis net, chicken wire, chain-link fencing, or narrow bamboo stakes.

Sweet pea
(*Lathyrus odoratus*)

Good Neighbors

Sweet peas trained on a bamboo teepee provide an interesting garden accent and are easily accessible for cutting. They look particularly pretty used this way in a cottage garden, along with delphiniums, hollyhocks (*Alcea rosea*), baby's breaths (*Gypsophila* spp.), and bellflowers (*Campanula* spp.).

Problems and Solutions

Seedlings are susceptible to slug and snail damage, so surround the young plants with slug barriers. To help prevent diseases, use a mulch and avoid getting the leaves wet. Also, rotate your plantings to avoid growing any kind of peas in the same spot more than once every 4 years.

Top Performer

Lathyrus odoratus (sweet pea): Like garden peas, sweet peas have winged stems, leaves that end in branching tendrils, and typical "pea" flowers. They need about the same care, too. The main difference is that sweet peas offer a vastly wider range of flower colors—just about everything but yellow—and, of course, a sweet, almost honeylike perfume. The climbing types are still the most common, but more modern dwarf or "bush" cultivars are also available. Dwarf sweet peas tend to be weak-stemmed, though, so insert twiggy branches among the plants early in the season, or let them spill out of containers.

Larry's Garden Notes

To hear the British wax poetic over sweet peas, one would think they are simply the most marvelous garden plants in existence, but then the Brits usually have the cool, damp summers sweet peas need to thrive. North American gardeners, who generally have to deal with hot, dry summers, are rarely so enchanted: We find sweet peas pretty enough but a bit of a challenge to grow well. For most of us, cultivars labeled as "long blooming" or "heat resistant" are a better choice than ones with larger flowers in showier colors.

Phaseolus

Scarlet runner bean, Dutch runner bean

Is runner bean a vegetable or an ornamental? Actually, it's both! One of the most beautiful annual climbers, it deserves a prominent spot in the flower garden, but you can also harvest the abundant crops of delicious beans it produces. This fast-growing, easy-care vine provides excellent cover due to its abundant twining stems and large three-part leaves. And the pea-shaped scarlet flowers (more rarely, pink, white, or bicolor) are stunning, to say the least. Add the fact that butterflies and hummingbirds adore it, and you have one of the very best annuals in any category!

Plant Profile

PHASEOLUS
fay-see-OH-lus

- **Bloom Color:** Pink, red, white

- **Bloom Time:** Summer through early fall; throughout the year in mild climates

- **Height:** 1 to 30 feet (30 cm to 9 m)

- **Spacing:** 6 to 8 inches (15 to 20 cm)

- **Garden Uses:** Container planting, cut-flower garden, hanging baskets, ground-cover, vegetable garden, screening; on trellises, fences, and pergolas

- **Attracts:** Butterflies, hummingbirds

- **Light Preference:** Full sun

- **Soil Preference:** Humus-rich, evenly moist but well-drained soil

- **Best Way to Propagate:** Sow seed indoors or outdoors in spring

- **Hardiness:** Frost-sensitive perennial grown as a half-hardy annual

Growing Tips

You'll rarely find scarlet runner bean plants for sale; and even if you did, it wouldn't be worth buying them. Even if you need only one plant, it's cheaper to buy a packet of seed.

The value of starting plants indoors ahead of time is also questionable, except perhaps in the coldest climates. If you do decide to start from scratch, plant the seed in large peat pots 4 to 6 weeks before the last frost date, and germinate it at 60° to 70°F (15° to 21°C). Plant them out when all danger of frost has passed, and the ground has thoroughly warmed up.

For most of us, though, it's simplest to sow the seed outdoors about 1 week before the last expected frost. You *could* soak the seed overnight, but its germination is so fast (4 to 5 days) that soaking doesn't really give you any further head start. If you haven't grown any kind of beans in that spot before, dust a little soil inoculant for beans (sold in the vegetable-seed section of garden centers and catalogs) into the planting hole: It contains useful bacteria that will help the plants absorb nitrogen.

For both indoor and outdoor sowing, plant the kidney-shaped seed 1 inch (2.5 cm) deep with the eye of the bean (white mark) facing down. If you have mixed seed, you can partly work out your color scheme: White seeds will give white-flowered plants; dark or mottled seeds produce scarlet ones. Runner beans need a strong support. They may not reach their potential 30 feet (9 m) of growth in short-season areas but should attain at least 10 to 15 feet (3 to 4.5 cm) if the support is large enough.

Runner beans bloom just 4 to 5 weeks after sprouting and will already be producing harvestable beans within 60 to 75 days. The more beans you pick, the more the plants will bloom. For fresh eating, harvest the beans when they're 4 inches (10 cm) long. For shell beans, let them mature on the vine, although that may well put an end to blooming for the season. Unlike other beans, all of which love the heat, scarlet runner beans yield best in cool summer climates. Flowering is abundant even in hot climates, though: It's the bean production that can be weak.

Scarlet runner beans will keep on blooming and producing until frost brings them to a halt. In Zones 9 to 11, the plants can overwinter. Elsewhere, you *could* take cuttings in late summer and grow them indoors for the winter, but it's *much* easier to grow new plants from seed each year.

Scarlet runner bean
(*Phaseolus coccineus*)

Good Neighbors

Scarlet runner bean needs the support of a sturdy fence, trellis, or tripod. Its dramatic combination of scarlet flowers against dark green foliage nicely sets off salvias or summer phlox (*Phlox paniculata* and *P. maculata*). Add silvery artemisias or perhaps green-flowering tobacco (*Nicotiana* 'Lime Green') as a blending element.

Problems and Solutions

Watch out for slugs early in the season; hand-pick if needed. Prevent leaf diseases with crop rotation and mulching.

Top Performer

Phaseolus coccineus (scarlet runner bean, Dutch runner bean, dwarf runner bean): Also called *P. multiflorus*. Besides the traditional climbing runner beans, there are dwarf runner beans in the same range of flower colors. They make great choices both for the vegetable garden and the front or middle of the flower border. Oddly, white-flowered plants are called Dutch runner beans, even though they originated in Mexico. Scarlet runner beans may self-sow in warmer climates but rarely to the point of weediness.
Self-sowing 🖊

Kissing Cousins

Vigna caracalla (corkscrew flower, snail bean, snail flower): Also called *Phaseolus caracalla*. The leaves of this perennial, tropical, climbing bean are quite similar to scarlet runner bean, but white, pink, or yellow blooms are curiously twisted, like the corkscrew or snail suggested by the common names. Start it indoors 10 to 12 weeks before the last frost date, nicking and soaking the seed before sowing to speed up germination. Height: 4 to 25 feet (1.2 to 7.5 m). Spacing: 6 to 8 inches (15 to 20 cm).

Thunbergia

Thunbergia, black-eyed Susan vine, clock vine

From a distance, you might mistake the bright orange-yellow, brown-centered flowers of this annual vine for those of the popular black-eyed Susan (*Rudbeckia hirta*). Close up, though, it is clear that they are totally different plants. For one, black-eyed Susan vine is a climber with thin green stems that wrap themselves around stakes, trellises, or plant stems. Plus, the flowers are not at all daisylike but are instead trumpets, opening broadly at the tip to form five flat lobes. And the dark center is not a mass of florets, but a dark tube leading insects into the heart of the flower.

Plant Profile

THUNBERGIA
thun-BER-gee-uh

- **Bloom Color:** Varies by species; see individual listings

- **Bloom Time:** Late spring through early fall; year-round in mild climates

- **Height:** Varies by species; see individual listings

- **Spacing:** 12 to 18 inches (30 to 45 cm)

- **Garden Uses:** Container planting, hanging baskets, groundcover, specimen plant, screening; on trellises, fences, and pergolas

- **Light Preference:** Full sun to partial shade

- **Soil Preference:** Humus-rich, evenly moist but well-drained soil

- **Best Way to Propagate:** Sow seed indoors in late winter or take stem cuttings at any season

- **Hardiness:** Frost-sensitive perennial grown as a half-hardy annual

Growing Tips

Black-eyed Susan vine (*Thunbergia alata*) is available in six packs or cell packs, in individual pots, and as seed. If you're into container gardening and need only a plant or two, it might be worthwhile buying individual pots of them. Buying plants is also the best way to get blue trumpet vine (*T. grandiflora*), although you'll likely have to search for it at specialty nurseries.

If you want lots of plants of black-eyed Susan vine cheaply—or if you want orange clock vine (*T. gregorii*)—growing from seed is the way to go. For a head start on the season, sow the large seed indoors 6 to 8 weeks before the last frost, soaking them in an old thermos of warm water for 48 hours before sowing. Although they will tolerate root disturbance, they grow faster when their roots remain intact, so starting the seeds in peat pots is wise. Barely cover the seed. It'll germinate in 10 to 21 days at 65° to 75°F (18° to 24°C). Plant them out when there is no longer any danger of frost and the soil is thoroughly warm. Outdoor sowing is also a possibility, especially in Zones 7 to 11; follow the same instructions.

Choose a sunny spot protected from wind in cool summer areas. In hot climates, on the other hand, a regular breeze and partial shade, or at least protection from afternoon sun, will give better results. Thunbergias prefer rich soil that is moist but well-drained. Water as necessary to keep the soil evenly moist. Mulching is helpful to keep the roots cool and the soil moist.

Since all thunbergias are actually perennials, you can carefully dig them up and bring them indoors in fall, if you have the room to grow them in a spot with full sun. Alternatively, take cuttings in late summer, or start new plants each year.

Good Neighbors

Lush in foliage and bright in color, thunbergias will quickly outcompete most neighbors, making them more of a stand-alone plant than an easy companion. Try them in a good-size planting box on a porch or deck rail, where they can hang down and adorn the view from below. Or give them a planter with one or more stakes to climb to create a vertical accent.

Problems and Solutions

Spider mites and whiteflies are major annoyances during hot, dry weather and indoors. Spray repeatedly with insecticidal soap to control them.

Top Performer

Thunbergia alata (black-eyed Susan vine, clock vine): This old-fashioned climber is back in style again, in a wider range of colors: orange, buff, yellow, tan, or white, with or without a dark eye. The flowers measure 1¼ to 1½ inches (3 to 4 cm) in diameter. The mid-green, arrow-shaped leaves are carried on winged stalks. Height: 4 to 10 feet (1.2 to 3 m).

More Recommended Thunbergia

Thunbergia grandiflora (blue trumpet vine, skyflower, Bengal clock vine): This woody tropical climber is a much larger vine usually grown as a summer container plant in the North. The lavender-blue to violet-blue, trumpet-shaped flowers with yellow throats measure 3 inches (8 cm) across, and the elliptic to heart-shaped leaves are 4 to 8 inches (10 to 20 cm) long. Prune as needed to keep it in check. This species just loves the hot, humid summers that send the other two into the doldrums. Height: 30 feet (9 m).

   T. gregorii (orange clock vine): Also called *T. gibsonii*. This plant is very similar to the black-eyed Susan vine, both in appearance and culture. The most obvious differences are the hairy stems and ovate to triangular leaves, plus somewhat larger, clear orange flowers with each lobe indented at the tip. Height: 4 to 12 feet (1.2 to 3.6 m).

Black-eyed Susan vine
(*Thunbergia alata*)

Smart Substitutes

For another climber with bright blooms, try orange glow vine (*Senecio confusus*, also called *Pseudogynoxys chenopodioides*). Also known as Mexican flame vine, it is a bushy, dense climber with lance-shaped, fleshy, dark green leaves. The main attraction, however, is the dense clusters of orange-red, daisylike flowers, borne all summer (or through the entire year in Zones 10 and 11). It may die to the ground in Zone 9 in winter and then grow back when warm weather returns. Elsewhere, bring it indoors for winter.

ANNUALS FOR
Cut & Dried ARRANGEMENTS

Annuals can be so spectacular in bloom that you may hesitate to bring them indoors as cut flowers—but don't! Jump right in and harvest them. They are prolific bloomers, so you're not likely to miss a few flowers taken here and there. But even better, harvesting blooms inevitably stimulates the plant to produce more flowers than ever. Think of it as "pre-deadheading," if you wish. The plant (figuratively) thinks "I've lost my first attempt to produce seed, so this time I'll try twice as hard!" Soon it is blooming more heavily than ever. So harvest away to your heart's content: There's more where that came from!

◄Most cut-flower annuals, like these sweet scabious, have long stems that seem designed by Mother Nature for cutting—and the more you cut, the more they bloom!

A Long Tradition

Back in the Victorian era, practically every middle-class North American home had its cutting garden. It was inevitably located to the side or the back of the house, along with the vegetable garden, the clothesline, and other "utility" areas. The ornamental value of the cutting garden was rarely a consideration, and little effort was made to arrange colors in a decorative fashion, although the view from the house was often spectacular just because of the masses of color. The purpose of the cutting garden was practical: to supply masses of cut flowers for the big, blowsy flower arrangements that were so popular at the time. Decorum demanded fresh flowers in season and dried flowers in winter, yet florists were few and far between, so people rarely thought twice about it: There *had* to be a cut-flower garden!

The lower classes may not always have had the space for a cutting garden, but they still loved cut-flower arrangements. Given their lack of space, there was rarely room for a specific cut-flower garden, so their gardens mingled a bit of everything: vegetables, annuals, herbs, perennials, and bulbs. Plantings in these "cottage gardens" were generally informal; and self-sowing was not just encouraged but expected. Wherever the plant decided to grow was just fine, so these gardens took on a quite casual appearance. But at least there were flowers available to bring indoors to add a bit of color and beauty to an existence that was otherwise often quite drab.

The best time to collect cut flowers is in the morning before it gets too hot. Remove the leaves from the bottom part of the stems before adding the flowers to your arrangement.

so they'll produce the most flowers for harvest. You'll thus want to place your cut-flower garden in full sun (you can always shade plants preferring less sun between rows of taller plants). And you'll want to grow taller plants with long flower stems, as opposed to the dwarf border annuals currently so popular.

Fun for All
Even young children will get a kick out of a cut-flower garden. Just buy a pack or two of "cut-flower annuals" (most seed suppliers offer such blends), help them rake over a bare patch of ground, and then let them sprinkle seeds over the spot and rake lightly. Sprinkle a little water—and your kid's garden is well under way.

Sneaking Cut Flowers from Ornamental Beds
Even if you have no space for a cutting garden and cottage gardens are too disorganized for your tastes, you can still harvest plentiful quantities of flowers for cutting and drying from a mixed border. The secret is simple: Set out more plants than you normally would in each planting spot. A spot containing 15 annuals instead of the 10 you'd normally plant will give you half again as many flowers as you needed to create the impact you wanted. And if you harvest what is essentially one third of the flowers, this will stimulate the plants to produce even more of them, so you'll have a ton of flowers to cut as the summer goes on.

Reviving the Cut-Flower Garden
If you have the space, why not add a cutting garden to your landscape? Rather than raiding your flower borders out front, you'd be able to pick away with abandon. Narrow rows, incongruous color combinations, bare spots in midsummer, it really doesn't matter: You get to ignore any pretense of style here. Instead, think how to give plants the best conditions possible

Harvesting the Bounty

Whether you are hauling in armfuls of flowers from your cut-flower garden or just carefully picking a handful of blooms from a mixed border, there are a few secrets to getting the most out of your cut flowers.

First, although it may look incredibly bucolic to wander about a garden with an open basket over one arm, laying flower after flower on its side, be realistic: Cut flowers wilt quickly, and when they do, they rarely recover fully. You're going to have to learn to haul water and plunge each of the cut stems directly into it as you go, so a pail or a jug is a much more appropriate container than a basket for flower collecting!

Most flowers last longest if cut when their stems and tissues are fully charged with moisture, so avoid harvesting in the afternoon or early evening when they are naturally somewhat dehydrated. Midmorning, while the flowers are still fully rigid but the dew has evaporated, is perfect. Fill a pail with lukewarm or even hot water nearly to its brim, grab your pruning shears or sharp scissors, and off you go. If you're picking single-stemmed flowers, it's generally best to take them when they're recently but fully opened; plants with multiple flowers per stem should show a few open flowers and lots of buds showing color. As you harvest, cut the longest stem possible (you can always shorten it later), remove the lower leaves, and plunge the flower immediately into warm water up to its neck. Then harvest more blooms.

Don't arrange blossoms right after cutting because they will tend to fade quickly unless they are "conditioned." This simply means putting the container full of blooms in a cool, shaded spot for 2 to 8 hours and letting them soak in a solution of cut-flower preservative. You can use either a commercial product or 3 teaspoons (15 ml) sugar plus 1 drop of bleach to 1 pint (½ l) of warm water.

Before arranging flowers, get all your materials ready, including properly soaked floral foam if you're using an open container rather than a "form-fitting" vase. Now recut each stem under flowing water, at a 45 degree angle, place it immediately into the foam or vase, and add cut-flower preservative when you're done placing all the flowers. Every few days, change the water and recut the stems. Most cut flowers will last 7 to 10 days.

Flowers for Drying

Annuals not only make great cut flowers but many are wonderful dried flowers as well. Some of these are "everlastings," which dry pretty much on their own; they often have a papery texture even when fresh. You can sometimes simply harvest them as is and put them directly into your dried-flower arrangements, although a short period of air-drying will give you straighter stems.

There are also ordinary ornamental flowers that make good dried flowers if you know how to treat them. Some flowers dry best when harvested in the "open-bud" stage, others at full maturity: Read the entries in this chapter to know which applies to which plant. In both cases, simply harvest the flowers in the afternoon (when the plants are dry), strip the lower leaves, and tie them loosely together, hanging them upside down in an open, airy, dark space. Avoid dank conditions and full sun. You can dry flowers with their stems or without: In the latter case, you'll gain flexibility but will have to arrange the blossoms using flexible wire and floral tape.

15 More Cut and Dried Flowers

Annuals are such prolific bloomers that most of them can be used as cut flowers; many can be dried as well. Here are just a few plants that are especially well adapted to being used in indoor arrangements. Those that dry well (or have seedheads that dry well) are indicated by an asterisk (*).

Ammi

Lace flower, false Queen-Anne's-lace

It's easy to see why many people confuse white lace flower (*Ammi majus*) and Queen-Anne's-lace (*Daucus carota*). Both have deeply cut, fernlike leaves and the same dome-shaped, lacy inflorescences. The latter, though, is a biennial, so it takes 2 years to bloom, and it's very weedy thanks to the thousands of seeds it produces. Annual lace flower is faster growing and is less likely to get out of control. It also lacks the long white taproot that makes Queen-Anne's-lace impossible to transplant. Both plants, though, are highly attractive to beneficial insects that help prevent pest outbreaks in the garden.

Plant Profile

AMMI
AM-ee

- **Bloom Color:** Varies by species; see individual listings

- **Bloom Time:** Mid- to late summer through early fall; fall through winter in mild climates

- **Height:** 2 to 3 feet (60 to 90 cm)

- **Spread:** 1 foot (30 cm)

- **Garden Uses:** Container planting, cut-flower garden, herb garden, meadow garden, mixed border

- **Attracts:** Beneficial insects

- **Light Preference:** Full sun to partial shade

- **Soil Preference:** Humus-rich, evenly moist but well-drained soil

- **Best Way to Propagate:** Sow seed outdoors in spring or fall

- **Hardiness:** Hardy annual

Growing Tips

A few nurseries are experimenting with growing lace flower in six packs or cell packs, so maybe you'll be lucky and find them for sale. If you can't find plants, seed is readily available in catalogs and is very easy to grow.

It's easiest to start this hardy annual outdoors. Sow it in fall for bloom the following summer, or early in spring, a few weeks before the last frost, when the ground is still cool. Simply scatter the seed over the soil and rake in very lightly. Don't worry about frosts: The seed isn't bothered by cold, and by the time the young plants emerge, there'll be little danger of their freezing.

Lace flower takes from 12 to 14 weeks to reach blooming size, so direct-sowing outdoors will give flowers rather late in the season. For earlier bloom, or if you live in a short-summer area, start the plants indoors 6 to 8 weeks before the last frost. Just cover the seed and expose it to relatively cool temperatures: 55° to 65°F (13° to 18°C). Germination is sometimes irregular and can take from 1 to 3 weeks. The plants are frost hardy and enjoy cool spring temperatures, so you can risk slipping them into your garden a week or so before the last frost date (but wait 1 or 2 weeks if your spring has been unusually cool).

Lace flower definitely appreciates rich soil and regular moisture. Once established, though, it becomes quite drought tolerant. Full sun is best except in hot, humid summer climates, where this cool-climate annual will prefer partial shade or at least protection from the hot afternoon rays. Mulching heavily and keeping the soil slightly moist at all times can also help plants to beat the heat. Avoid planting lace flower in windy spots if possible, or supply a few twiggy branches as unobtrusive stakes to support the plant's slender stems.

You can't save lace flower from the fall frosts. In very mild winter climates, though, you can sow in early fall for winter bloom.

For long life as a cut flower, harvest lace flower when several flowers in the cluster are fully open and most others are in the advanced bud stage. It will last 7 to 10 days. For drying, harvest the flowers closer to full maturity and hang upside down in loose bunches. It also makes a lovely pressed flower.

Good Neighbors
Sow lace flower in drifts among grasses or perennials, or spot it here and there in the garden to look as though it had self-sown. For a charming fresh arrangement, combine lace flower with perennial balloon flower (*Platycodon grandiflorus*), brightly colored poppies (*Papaver* spp.), and several sprigs of bells-of-Ireland (*Moluccella laevis*).

Problems and Solutions
Lace flower is rarely bothered by pests or diseases in the garden. In fact, it attracts beneficial insects to feed on the nectar of its flowers.

Top Performer
Ammi majus (white lace flower, false Queen-Anne's-lace, white dill): This is the most commonly grown species, remarkable because of the pure white of its flowers. In continental Europe, you can't pass a florist shop without seeing pails of this flower out front; it is widely used there as filler material for bouquets, much as we use baby's breath (*Gypsophila paniculata*). It can self-sow, but rarely to the point of being an annoyance. Height: 2 to 3 feet (60 to 90 cm). Spread: 1 foot (30 cm). **Self-sowing** 🌱

More Recommended Ammi
Ammi visnaga (green lace flower): This is very similar to *A. majus,* but with charming chartreuse flowers instead of white. Its leaves are more deeply cut and are borne right up to the base of the umbel, giving the impression the flowers are floating in a haze of green. It sometimes self-sows. Height: 2 to 3 feet (60 to 90 cm). Spread: 1 foot (30 cm). **Self-sowing** 🌱

White lace flower
(*Ammi majus*)

Kissing Cousins

❗ **Think Twice:** Dill (*Anethum graveolens*), the popular herb, is a close relative of lace flower. It has the same lacy green foliage—this time deliciously aromatic—and bright yellow flowers that are lovely in the garden, freshly cut, or dried. Dill is a much faster-growing plant, coming into bloom in only 6 to 8 weeks. Make several sowings for continuous bloom, and harvest the flowers often for arrangements. Dill can be weedy if you let it go to seed. Height: 18 to 24 inches (45 to 60 cm). Spread: 10 to 12 inches (25 to 30 cm). **Self-sowing** 🌱

Ammobium

Winged everlasting

Here's a plant you could never mistake for any other! Young plants start off with a ground-hugging rosette of ragged, lance-shaped leaves, making them look very much like a woolly dandelion. Then come curious, branching, nearly leafless stems with four lengthwise broad, undulating, green wings. The blooms, made up of innumerable, pointed, papery white bracts surrounding a dome-shaped yellow center, do look somewhat like those of its close cousin, the strawflower (*Helichrysum bracteatum*); with those odd stems, though, there is no way you could mistake the two.

Plant Profile

AMMOBIUM
uh-MOE-bee-um

- **Bloom Color:** White

- **Bloom Time:** Late spring through early fall

- **Height:** 1 to 3 feet (30 to 90 cm)

- **Spread:** 8 to 15 inches (20 to 38 cm)

- **Garden Uses:** Container planting, cut-flower garden, mass planting, meadow garden, mixed border

- **Light Preference:** Full sun

- **Soil Preference:** Average to poor, light, well-drained soil

- **Best Way to Propagate:** Sow seed indoors in spring

- **Hardiness:** Frost-sensitive perennial grown as a tender annual

Growing Tips

Plants are occasionally offered and they will transplant well, but you may have to make a lot of phone calls to find a nursery that sells them. Thankfully, you'll often see the seed for sale in catalogs, and it's easy to grow.

In areas with a long summer season (roughly Zone 7 and south), it is a simple matter to sow winged everlasting outdoors, either in fall or in early spring, just pressing the seed into the soil. Elsewhere, they'll come into bloom too late from outdoor sowings to be of much use, so start the seed inside 6 to 8 weeks before the last frost. Right from the start, make sure winged everlastings have perfect drainage. Try sowing them in an equal mixture of sterile growing mix and horticultural sand. Seed germinates readily, in 10 to 15 days, at 50° to 60°F (13° to 15°C). Plant out seedlings when the soil has warmed and night temperatures remain above 50°F (13°C).

Winged everlasting needs very well-drained, even sandy, soil. If your soil tends to be moist, a raised bed will give the best results. This plant actually does best in poor soil; richer soil conditions produce soft, weak stems. Typically, the plant is upright at first, then the taller stems bend over and new ones rise, only to fall in their turn; the end result is a tangled mess. If you keep harvesting the stems as cut flowers before they start to flop, though, you can avoid the problem. Or you

FUN FACTS

This is the first of the "paper daisies" described in this chapter, so called for the papery texture of their flowers. The curious texture of these Australian natives is a protection from the drying winds of the arid landscapes where they grow wild.

can grow winged everlasting surrounded by low shrubs or sturdy perennials that it can lean on. True to its Australian outback origins, winged everlasting is highly drought resistant when it is well established; it will probably need watering only during the worst droughts.

Left on the plant, the blooms eventually turn brown in the center, but the bracts around them remain white. If you feel the brown centers detract, simply deadhead.

Although winged everlasting is in fact a perennial, it is hardly ever wintered over, even in Zones 10 and 11 where it is theoretically hardy. Most people simply sow it again each year as an annual. It will self-sow in Zones 7 to 11 but rarely enough to cause a problem. **Self-sowing**

To dry the flowers to perfection, harvest them when they are just starting to open and hang them upside down in open bunches. Flowers that have already fully opened can also be dried, but their centers tend to turn brown. And while you're at it, dry a few fully closed buds as well: They look great!

Good Neighbors

Try winged everlasting around yuccas or bear's breeches (*Acanthus* spp.), which thrive in the same well-drained, sunny conditions. In winter arrangements, winged everlasting's small, long-stemmed blossoms are good companions to dried flower heads of hydrangeas, stems of annual statice (*Limonium sinuatum*), and other dried pods and flowers.

Problems and Solutions

Planting in poor, perfectly drained soil will help avoid stem rot.

Top Performer

Ammobium alatum (winged everlasting): This species averages 18 to 36 inches (45 to 90 cm) tall with flowers about 1 inch (2.5 cm) in diameter. There is a larger-flowered subspecies, *A. alatum grandiflorum,* which produces a plant the same size but with flowers twice as big. For a smaller, sturdier plant, try 'Bikini', only 12 to 16 inches (30 to 40 cm) tall.

Winged everlasting
(*Ammobium alatum*)

Smart Substitute

If you're looking for a dried flower requiring much the same conditions as winged everlasting, but that you can direct sow in cooler climates, try safflower (*Carthamus tinctorius*). This prickly plant looks much like a gray-green thistle and even has fuzzy thistlelike blooms in shades of yellow and orange, or sometimes red, pink, cream, or violet. Direct sowing is best; but if you do want to start it indoors, sow it in peat pots because it dislikes root disturbance. Height: 1 to 2 feet (30 to 60 cm). Spread: 1 foot (30 cm).

Bracteantha

Strawflower, everlasting, helichrysum, immortelle

Strawflower is truly the queen of the paper daisies, those Australian daisy relatives with the papery-textured bracts: You can scarcely find a dried flower arrangement that doesn't feature it! But don't write it off as a dried flower only because it puts on a wonderful show in the garden as well. The single or double flowers, measuring from 1 to 3 inches (2.5 to 8 cm) across, come in a wide range of colors but always have a yellow center. Curiously, the blooms close not only during humid weather, but even if you spray them with water!

Plant Profile

BRACTEANTHA
brack-tee-ANN-thuh

- **Bloom Color:** Pink, purple, red, yellow, white

- **Bloom Time:** Summer through early fall

- **Height:** 1 to 5 feet (30 to 150 cm)

- **Spread:** 8 to 18 inches (20 to 45 cm)

- **Garden Uses:** Container planting, cut-flower garden, hanging baskets, edging, mass planting, meadow garden, mixed border

- **Light Preference:** Full sun

- **Soil Preference:** Average, evenly moist but well-drained soil; tolerates dry soil

- **Best Way to Propagate:** Sow seed indoors or outdoors in spring

- **Hardiness:** Half-hardy annual or perennial

Growing Tips

Strawflower plants are widely available in six packs or cell packs in the spring, but they are mostly dwarf cultivars—the least useful for drying. For taller plants with a stem truly worth mentioning, you'll probably have to grow your own plants from seed.

In areas with long, frost-free summers, sowing seed outdoors around the last frost date is certainly worthwhile. Elsewhere, start indoors 6 to 8 weeks before the last frost. Either way, press the cigar-shaped seed into the soil without covering it; it needs light for germination. Place in a brightly lit spot at 65° to 75°F (18° to 24°C). They should sprout in 5 to 21 days. Wait until there is no further risk of frost and the ground has warmed up thoroughly before you plant them out. Just about any soil will do, although they grow best in moderately rich conditions. Space dwarf types 8 to 10 inches (20 to 25 cm) apart; taller growers at 15 to 18 inches (38 to 45 cm) apart.

Although very drought tolerant, strawflowers stay healthier and bloom better if you keep their soil slightly moist at all times. The blooms hang on for much of summer, so deadheading isn't necessary if you're only growing strawflowers for garden color. If your goal is to produce cut or dried flowers, though, harvest them early and often to keep the plants productive.

Strawflowers last about 2 weeks in fresh arrangements. For drying, harvest when the flowers

FUN FACTS

Dried strawflowers readily absorb moisture, so they tend to droop in very humid conditions. Rather than wire the flowers into position, as many gardeners do, dry the flowers thoroughly in an upside-down position, and afterward they'll stay nicely stable.

are just about to open and hang them up-side down in loose bunches for a few weeks. You can also dry the flowers without their stems and then wire into arrangements. (To wire stemless flowers, run florist wire up through the flower, form a hook at the top, then pull the hook back down into the flower to secure it). Stemless flowers also look great displayed in clear decorative containers or mixed into pot-pourri to add color.

Good Neighbors
Combined with dried seedpods and flowers of contrasting shapes, such as poppy pods (*Papaver* spp.), lavender spikes, and baby's breaths (*Gypsophila* spp.), strawflowers add color and substance to a winter floral arrangement. In the garden, they combine well with other daisy-type flowers.

Problems and Solutions
Water carefully (without wetting the leaves) to prevent powdery mildew from discoloring the foliage.

Top Performer
Bracteantha bracteata (strawflower, everlasting, helichrysum, im-mortelle): This is a new name for a very well-known plant; you'll probably still see it listed as *Helichrysum bracteatum* on seed packets and in catalogs for years to come. This highly popular everlasting produces gray-green, lance-shaped leaves on generally upright stems topped with papery blooms in a wide range of colors, forms, and sizes. The original species reached a whopping 5 feet (1.5 m) tall, but most cut-flower types are more in the 2- to 3-foot (60- to 90-cm) range—long enough for cutting but not so long as to need staking. There are also dwarf cultivars, which grow about 1 foot (30 cm) tall. These are best used as border plants but can also work well in shorter dried arrangements. Both the dwarf and cut-flower types are true annuals and always grown from seed. There are also "container" cultivars with trailing stems, which are derived from the perennial form of the species; these are multiplied by taking stem cuttings.

Strawflower
(*Bracteantha bracteata*)

Kissing Cousins

Looking for more paper daisies? Rose everlasting (*Acroclinium roseum*, also called *Helipterum roseum* and *Rhodanthe chloro-cephala rosea*) is an upright an-nual with thin stems and pink to white flowers with yellow centers. Immortelle (*Xeranthemum an-nuum*) is an altogether more delicate-looking plant, with wiry stems and single or double flowers in purple, pink, crimson, or white. Both grow well from out-door sowing. Height: 1 to 2 feet (30 to 60 cm). Spread: 6 to 10 inches (15 to 25 cm).

Briza

Quaking grass

Many plants bring color to the garden, others perfume, but not many bring movement! However, that's the case of quaking grass, which, as the name suggests, trembles in the slightest breeze. It's a true grass, with the long, narrow, green leaves you'd expect. What you *won't* expect, however, are the beautiful and delicate blooms. The thin flowerstalks arch first up, then out, dividing toward the tips into hairlike segments, each supporting one puffy spikelet, its life hanging, as it were, from a thread! Of course, it is all perfectly solid, and in fact, you can harvest and dry the flower stems to maintain the show indoors for several years.

Plant Profile

BRIZA
BREE-zuh

- **Bloom Color:** Green

- **Bloom Time:** Late spring through early fall; fall through winter in mild climates

- **Height:** Varies by species; see individual listings

- **Spread:** Varies by species; see individual listings

- **Garden Uses:** Container planting, cut-flower garden, mass planting, meadow garden, mixed border

- **Light Preference:** Full sun to partial shade

- **Soil Preference:** Average to humus-rich, well-drained soil

- **Best Way to Propagate:** Sow seed outdoors in late spring or fall

- **Hardiness:** Hardy annual

Growing Tips

This is one annual you really do have to sow yourself: It simply isn't sold in nurseries. But then, you could scarcely ask for an easier plant to grow from seed.

Sow the seed where you want the plants to grow, either in spring, around the last frost date, or the previous fall. Just rake the seed in lightly and water, then thin the plants to 4 to 6 inches apart when they germinate. In truly mild climates, you can sow quaking grasses just about any time of the year.

If you're in a big rush, you can instead sow indoors, no more than 4 to 6 weeks before the last frost. Cover the seed with ⅛ inch (3 mm) of mix. Germination takes only 1 week or so at 55°F (13°C). Plant out when all danger of frost has passed.

Quaking grass will start to bloom as early as midspring in mild climates, early summer elsewhere. Creamy green at first, the spikelets mature to medium green, then reddish, then the whole plant turns a straw color in late summer. If you have a patch of them, it can be like looking at a field of wheat in miniature!

Not sure when to harvest the flowerstalks? You can do so any time after they form or wait until they dry on their own in late summer. You *could* hang them upside down to dry, but I find they will dry perfectly well when inserted directly into a dried

FUN FACTS

If there's a big quaking grass (*Briza major*) and a little quaking grass (*B. minor*), wouldn't it make sense that there be an intermediate quaking grass (*B. media*)? Well, there is—but its common name is simply "common quaking grass." It is actually a perennial and very similar to big quaking grass.

arrangement. Or harvest the stalks green for use in fresh arrangements; they stay green and in perfect shape for 2 weeks or more!

The two species described here are annuals and won't overwinter, even in mild climates. You can, however, collect the spikelets when they turn brown and save them for seed. To extract the seed, just break up the spikelets by rubbing them between the palms of your hand. There is no need to carefully pick through the chaff to remove the seeds—just sow the whole lot!

Actually, you may not need to sow anything: Quaking grass self-sows quite readily, possibly even a bit too much sometimes. Don't mistake it for quackgrass (*Agropyron repens*), though; it doesn't spread underground to make a real nuisance of itself, but only by seed. And it's easy to pull out young plants of quaking grass, or to transplant them elsewhere. **Self-sowing**

Big quaking grass
(*Briza maxima*)

Good Neighbors

A large clump of dried quaking grass in a container, accented with bunches of strawflowers (*Bracteantha bracteata*) and dried goldenrods (*Solidago* spp.), will keep its charm all winter. In the garden, quaking grass can add an interesting textural quality as its seed pods dangle among the foliage of peonies (*Paeonia lactiflora*) after their blooms have passed.

Problems and Solutions

Quaking grasses are easy-to-grow plants with few apparent problems.

Top Performer

Briza maxima (big quaking grass): This is the most popular of the quaking grasses and the one most often found in ornamental annual grass mixes. The ovate, scaly spikelets are produced in open clusters of 7 to 20 that measure about ½ inch (1.25 cm) long. Height: 18 to 24 inches (45 to 60 cm). Spread: 12 to 16 inches (30 to 40 cm).

More Recommended Briza

Briza minor (little quaking grass). This is the little brother of the big guy above. It produces clusters of 4 to 8 rounder spikelets about ¼ inch (6 mm) long. Height: 6 to 18 inches (15 to 45 cm). Spread: 4 to 6 inches (10 to 15 cm).

Kissing Cousins

There are lots of other annual grasses to try; here are two. Hare's tail (*Lagurus ovatus*) forms a dense clump of leaves topped in late summer by fuzzy white flower heads that look just like a rabbit's tail. The species reaches about 20 inches (50 cm) in height; 'Bunny Tails' is only 8 inches (20 cm) tall. Job's tears (*Coix lacryma-jobi*), from 18 to 36 inches (45 to 90 cm), produces separate clusters of male and female flowers, the latter maturing into hard, teardrop-shaped, ½-inch (1.25-cm) "beads" in creamy white, gray, or purple. **Self-sowing**

Craspedia

Drumsticks, drumstick flower, bachelor's buttons

This recent arrival from Australia is a relatively new kid on the block, but it's catching on quite nicely. And no wonder—it has a truly unique form that makes it stand out from the crowd. The foliage is interesting enough: a low-growing, dense rosette of woolly white, strap-shaped leaves. The flowers, however, are positively startling. On a tall, thin, leafless, wiry, unbranched stalk appears a perfectly round ball, about 1¼ inches (3 cm) wide, in bright mustard yellow. Each plant produces a whole forest of these drumsticks, certainly enough to start a decent percussion section.

Plant Profile

CRASPEDIA
crass-PEE-dee-uh

- **Bloom Color:** Yellow
- **Bloom Time:** Summer through early fall
- **Height:** 2 to 3 feet (60 to 90 cm)
- **Spread:** 10 inches (25 cm)
- **Garden Uses:** Container planting, cut-flower garden, edging, mass planting, meadow garden, mixed border, rock garden
- **Light Preference:** Full sun
- **Soil Preference:** Average to poor, very well-drained soil
- **Best Way to Propagate:** Sow seed indoors in late winter
- **Hardiness:** Frost-sensitive perennial grown as a tender annual

Growing Tips

Some of the better nurseries carry six packs or cell packs of this plant, and that's a good thing because it can be a bit delicate to start from seed.

Very slow to get going, it really does need to be started indoors just about everywhere, except perhaps in Zones 9 through 11. Figure at least 4 months—and sometimes even 5—from sowing until bloom. You'd have to have a *very* long season to accommodate this plant from an outdoor sowing!

The timing of indoor sowing depends on what you want from the plant. Is your goal to use drumsticks for summer-long bloom in the garden, harvesting the flowers only at the end of the season? You'll have to start your plants very early, a whopping 14 to 16 weeks before the last frost. This will give you well-established plants that will start to bloom shortly after you plant them out.

If you just want to have flowers for drying some time during the season, start the seeds indoors 6 to 8 weeks before your last frost date. This will give you flowers from mid- to late summer, depending on the length of your growing season.

Good drainage is critical, so you might want to prepare an especially well-drained mix by adding one-half horticultural sand to your usual germinating blend. Barely cover the seed. It germinates readily in about 14 days at 68°F (20°C) and isn't that difficult to maintain—just very slow to mature. Keep them a bit drier

FUN FACTS

Although it may not look the part, drumsticks is one of the paper daisies—in other words, a close relative of the strawflower (*Bracteantha bracteata*). Think of it as a strawflower that somehow lost its ray flowers and you might begin to see the resemblance.

than you would most other seedlings. Plant out when all danger of frost has passed.

Summer care is minimal. Although originally from a very dry environment, drumsticks will give better results if you water it occasionally. When you do water, try to avoid wetting the leaves.

The plants actually "bloom" for only a few weeks, then the flowers start to dry on the spot and look great right where they are through the summer. Why not wait, therefore, and harvest the bloom only at the very end, just before the first frosts? Of course, you could cut the flowers earlier for use as fresh flowers throughout the summer. The plant doesn't readily rebloom, though, so if you cut off all the flowers, it will just sit there as a little rosette of narrow leaves until frost. To dry the flowers, simply hang them upside down in open bunches for a few weeks.

Since drumsticks is actually a tender perennial, it may overwinter in Zones 9 to 11. However, that usually only happens under very dry conditions or in perfectly drained, gritty soil; it is very sensitive to winter wet.

Drumsticks
(*Craspedia globosa*)

Good Neighbors

Golden yellow drumsticks provide the perfect complement to shades of purple and blue. Once dried, combine it with purple and lavender statice (*Limonium sinuatum*) or larkspur (*Consolida ajacis*). In the garden, try it with mealy-cup sage (*Salvia farinacea*) or tall ageratum (*Ageratum houstonianum*).

Problems and Solutions

Spider mites can cause stippled foliage on young plants grown indoors; spray with insecticidal soap to control them. Slugs and snails can be a problem early in the season; hand-pick them.

Top Performer

Craspedia globosa (drumsticks, drumstick flower, bachelor's buttons): There are several species of *Craspedia*, but this is the most commonly grown. (Those offered as *C. uniflora* and *C. chrysantha* seem to belong here.) It is fully described above.

Smart Substitutes

! Think Twice: There is one "annual" (actually a short-lived perennial grown as an annual) that can imitate the ball-shaped flowers of drumsticks: feverfew (*Tanacetum parthenium*, also sold as *Chrysanthemum parthenium*). Two selections—'Golden Ball' (yellow) and 'Snowball' (creamy white)—have perfectly round, double flowers that resemble miniature versions of drumsticks. (There are also selections with single, daisylike flowers.) This old-fashioned herb self-sows and can often become invasive. Height: 9 to 24 inches (23 to 60 cm). Spread: 9 to 12 inches (23 to 30 cm). Self-sowing

Dianthus

Carnation

The carnation is one of the top commercially produced cut flowers, and no wonder! It produces beautiful, fully double, ruffled, 2- to 3-inch (5- to 8-cm) flowers that last up to 2 weeks when cut and are often sweetly scented. The plants are tufts of narrow, almost grasslike leaves in a range of colors from mid-green to grayish to chalky blue. They have a somewhat open, irregular habit and are not especially interesting when they are not in bloom. On the other hand, they almost always *are* in bloom, so that's not likely to be much of a problem.

Plant Profile

DIANTHUS
dye-ANN-thus

■ **Bloom Color:** Pink, purple, red, orange, yellow, white

■ **Bloom Time:** Late spring through midfall; may bloom through the winter in mild climates

■ **Height:** 10 to 30 inches (25 to 75 cm)

■ **Spread:** 8 to 10 inches (20 to 25 cm)

■ **Garden Uses:** Container planting, cut-flower garden, edging, hanging baskets, mass planting, mixed border, rock garden

■ **Attracts:** Butterflies

■ **Light Preference:** Full sun to partial shade to deep shade

■ **Soil Preference:** Humus-rich, well-drained soil; prefers neutral or slightly alkaline soil

■ **Best Way to Propagate:** Sow seed indoors in late winter

■ **Hardiness:** Hardy perennial grown as a hardy annual

Growing Tips

Annual carnations are usually sold in six packs or cell packs in the spring. If you can't find them, start seed indoors very early in the season for abundant bloom all summer. Seed sown outdoors will probably not even bloom until the following summer.

Before sowing, place the seed in the freezer for about 1 week. Then sow about ⅛ inch (3 mm) deep, 10 to 14 weeks before the last frost date. Seed germinates best with warm days—about 70°F (21°C)—and cool nights, closer to 60°F (15°C). Expect germination in 2 to 3 weeks. Repot or thin the young plants whenever they begin to touch, to maintain good air circulation.

Plant out at the last frost date or even 2 or 3 weeks beforehand. Space dwarf cultivars 8 inches (20 cm) apart, taller cultivars about 10 inches (25 cm) apart. The latter will probably need staking. For large-size, florist-quality cut flowers, pinch off buds from the sides, leaving only the flower bud at the end of each stem. This isn't as necessary if you intend to grow carnations mostly as garden plants or if you prefer the look of multiflowered carnations, called "sprays."

Summer care consists of mulching in hot summer areas and watering occasionally everywhere. Keep them deadheaded for summer-long bloom. To help "annual" carnations live over winter, cover them with a light mulch in fall, such as pine

FUN FACTS

Those striking blue-veined carnations seen in florist shops are actually produced by dyeing. To create blue carnations of your own, plunge the stem of a freshly cut white carnation in a glass of water containing a few drops of the blue food coloring. Within 12 hours, it will have a whole new look!

needles. Or bring plants or cuttings indoors to set on a sunny, cool windowsill.

For cut-flower use, choose flowers that have just opened or stems with one or two open flowers and lots of buds showing color. They'll last a good 2 weeks in bloom. Or hang them upside down, loosely bunched, for drying.

Good Neighbors

Carnations are the backbone of many flower arrangements due to their long-lasting good looks. Enjoy them in a traditional arrangement with ferns and baby's breath (*Gypsophila paniculata*), or go for a more dramatic contrast with the spikes of snapdragons (*Antirrhinum majus*) or delphiniums (*Delphinium* × *belladonna*).

Problems and Solutions

Watch out for slugs and snails early in the season; protect plants with barriers or hand-pick pests. Good drainage helps prevent crown rot and leaf diseases.

Top Performer

Dianthus caryophyllus (carnation, annual carnation): The original species had single, purplish pink flowers, but you'll almost never see it grown. The garden and cut-flower carnations we know and love are actually complex hybrids involving several species, but they're listed under the name *D. caryophyllus* for the sake of convenience. Dwarf types, some no taller than 10 inches (25 cm), are quite sturdy and won't require staking. They're often grown as border annuals or potted plants but also make nice bouquets of short-stemmed flowers. The taller types, up to 30 inches (75 cm), are often called cut-flower carnations. They have the long stems flower arrangers prefer but usually need staking to prevent floppy growth. I've found that the 'Floristan' series, however, produces strong stems that need staking only in the very windiest conditions. Some carnations are highly perfumed, with a sweet to clovelike scent, while others have no scent at all. So if you're looking for perfume, either sniff the flowers before you buy plants or carefully read the description in the catalog or on the seed packet.

'Chabaud's Giant Mixed' carnation (*Dianthus caryophyllus* 'Chabaud's Giant Mixed')

Larry's Garden Notes

Carnations are actually perennials, often surviving winter in Zones 6 through 11, and sometimes even Zones 4 or 5. But in their search for cultivars that would come into bloom relatively quickly, twentieth-century hybridizers developed "annual" strains: plants that would bloom the first year from seed sown indoors. But these were not as trustworthy in the garden. That's why many seed catalogs list carnations in two places: some strains in the annual section, others in the perennial section.

Emilia

Tasselflower, Flora's paintbrush, devil's paintbrush

Photographs of this plant really don't do it justice; for years, I thought it just looked like a weed. Once I saw it in person, though, I was hooked! It looks great in the garden and makes a wonderful cut flower, fresh or dried. It starts out quite inconspicuously, as a low-growing rosette of somewhat fuzzy, toothed lower leaves rather like the dreaded dandelion. Then up come the straight, wiry flowerstalks, bearing smaller leaves to about midheight and tipped with single blossoms or small open clusters of tassel-shaped flowers. Bloom is nonstop and the show is stupendous!

Plant Profile

EMILIA
eh-MIL-ee-uh

- **Bloom Color:** Red, orange, yellow
- **Bloom Time:** Late spring through early fall; fall through winter in mild climates
- **Height:** 18 to 24 inches (45 to 60 cm)
- **Spread:** 6 to 8 inches (15 to 20 cm)
- **Garden Uses:** Container planting, cut-flower garden, mass planting, meadow garden, mixed border
- **Light Preference:** Full sun
- **Soil Preference:** Average to poor, well-drained or even dry soil
- **Best Way to Propagate:** Sow seed outdoors in late spring
- **Hardiness:** Half-hardy annual

Growing Tips

I've never seen this plant offered in six packs or cell packs and don't expect I ever will unless it becomes much more popular, because it looks just like a weed until it starts to bloom.

Sow the seed directly outdoors where you want the plants to grow. In cool summer areas, sow it 2 to 3 weeks before the last frost date. In mild climates, you can also sow in early fall for winter bloom. Lightly cover the seed; it needs darkness to germinate. When the plants come up, thin them from 6 to 8 inches (15 to 20 cm) apart. Growth is incredibly rapid: Mine are often in bloom only 6 weeks after sowing!

That isn't fast enough for you? Start the seed indoors, about 6 weeks before the last frost date, covering lightly. Place in darkness at 60° to 70°F (15° to 21°C) until germination, about 1 week or so later, then expose to bright artificial light or full sun. Plant out when all danger of frost has passed. Young plants transplant well, but mature plants dislike disturbance.

Native to arid regions of Africa and Asia, tasselflower grows best in poor, but perfectly drained soil. It will still do well in cool, rainy climates as long as the soil is well drained; raised beds or containers are easy ways of ensuring good drainage even in a damp spot. On the other hand, tasselflower will not do well in hot, humid summers. In such climates, start it indoors as described above so you can enjoy it as a spring-flowering annual, or in Zones 9 to 11, grow it as a winter bloomer.

The best care for tasselflower is benign neglect. Don't mulch, don't fertilize, and don't water except in the worst droughts. Just hand-weed if needed and deadhead to stimulate prolonged bloom.

Think Twice: Although not invasive in cooler climates (where it doesn't self-sow), tasselflower can become a problem in mild winter areas: All the more reason to dead-head regularly! **Self-sowing**

For cut-flower use, harvest just as the flowers open. The fuzzy blooms will last for up to 2 weeks in a vase. Or dry the flowers instead, hanging them upside down in small bunches for a few weeks.

Good Neighbors

A drift of the jewel-like, red-orange flowers would sparkle among silver artemisias. In mixed bouquets, the bright tassels show up well against white roses and daisies, or offer a sparkling contrast to a generous clump of purple salvia (such as *Salvia verticillata* 'Purple Rain').

Problems and Solutions

Emilia is not subject to many problems.

Top Performer

Emilia coccinea (tasselflower, Flora's paintbrush, devil's paintbrush): Also called *Cacalia coccinea, C. sagittata, E. flammea,* and *E. javanica.* This species produces stalkless lower leaves to 5½ inches (14 cm) long and fluffy, brushlike flowers, usually in scarlet but also in various shades of red, orange, and yellow. They measure about ½ inch (1.25 cm) in diameter and arise from a bulging, cup-shaped green base. Each "flower" is in fact composed of dozens of individual tubular florets packed closely together. Height: 18 to 24 inches (45 to 60 cm). Spread: 6 to 8 inches (15 to 20 cm).

More Recommended Emilia

Emilia sonchifolia (Flora's paintbrush, yieh-hsia-hung): This plant is practically identical to *E. coccinea,* except that its flower color is closer to purple-red than scarlet and its leaves are somewhat shorter—to about 4 inches (10 cm)—and borne on a winged stalk. Under its Javanese name, yieh-hsia-hung, you'll sometimes find its young, tender rosettes in oriental markets, where they are sold as vegetables. Height: 18 to 24 inches (45 to 60 cm). Spread: 6 to 8 inches (15 to 20 cm).

Tasselflower
(*Emilia coccinea*)

Kissing Cousins

Pink hawk's beard (*Crepis rubra*) looks just like a pink dandelion! This close relative of tasselflower produces a ground-hugging rosette of toothed leaves, then upright stalks of showy, 1- to 1½-inch (2.5- to 3-cm) flowers that range in color from rose-red to pink to white. Grow this plant much as you would tasselflower, the main exception being it doesn't need darkness to germinate. A great cut flower, fresh or dried! Height: 12 to 16 inches (30 to 40 cm). Spread: 6 inches (15 cm). **Self-sowing**

Eustoma

Prairie gentian, Texas bluebell, lisianthus

With its waxy blue leaves and large cup-shaped flowers, prairie gentian truly stands out from the crowd. Its single blooms look similar to tulips, while the double ones more closely resemble roses. Some of the most charming varieties are bicolors, usually white flowers with purple or pink picotee edges. It makes an absolutely striking cut flower, and most people grow it more for cutting than for its rather dominant appearance in the garden.

Plant Profile

EUSTOMA
you-STO-muh

- **Bloom Color:** Lavender-blue, pink, purple, red, yellow, white

- **Bloom Time:** Late spring through early fall

- **Height:** 8 to 36 inches (20 to 90 cm)

- **Spread:** 1 foot (30 cm)

- **Garden Uses:** Container planting, cut-flower garden, mixed border, specimen plant

- **Light Preference:** Full sun

- **Soil Preference:** Humus-rich, well-drained, neutral to alkaline soil

- **Best Way to Propagate:** Sow seed indoors in early winter; outdoors in late summer for use as a biennial

- **Hardiness:** Half-hardy biennial grown as a half-hardy annual

Growing Tips

This is one tough plant to grow from seed, so it's a good thing that potted plants are widely available in spring. Just pop them into the garden without disturbing their roots, and they'll bloom for you all summer.

If you enjoy a real challenge, you could try to grow your own transplants. Although some seed companies suggest starting the seed indoors 10 to 12 weeks before the last frost date, the young plants are incredibly slow growing and won't have enough time to bloom the first year in most climates with such a short head start. It's generally best to start them 18 to 22 weeks before the last frost date, in December or early January.

For best results, buy pelleted seed: The germination rate is better, and you won't have to deal with sowing the tiny, dustlike seed. Most commercial seed-starting mediums hold too much moisture for the delicate seedlings, so it's best to blend the one you normally use with an equal amount of clean horticultural sand. Sowing into peat pots will save you the risky procedure of pricking out the seedlings later. Surface-sow the seed and expose to good light at 65° to 75°F (18° to 24°C), maintaining high humidity under a plastic tent or dome. Germination takes 2 to 3 weeks.

After germination, remove the plastic covering to help increase air circulation and prevent damping-off. Grow under cool conditions, 55° to 60°F (13° to 15°C), for more compact plants. Water the tiny seedlings only from below, waiting until the mix seems nearly dry before watering again. When the seedlings are a few weeks old, with 4 to 6 leaves, prick out into individual 4-inch (10 cm) pots if you haven't used peat pots. Pinch the taller growing plants two or three times to stimulate better branching.

When there is no longer any danger of frost, plant seedlings outside in full sun and rich, well-drained soil. While the young seedlings hate excess moisture, more mature plants prefer to be kept on the moist side. Mulch generously and water as needed. Stake taller-growing cultivars as needed. Harvesting the flowers regularly, or deadheading, will keep prairie gentian blooming through the summer.

In Zones 8 and 9 or the cool winter parts of Zones 10 and 11 (the only areas where the plant is reliably hardy), you can also sow prairie gentian directly in the garden in late summer for bloom the following spring. It is actually fairly easy to grow this way since it is a true biennial and this allows it to follow its natural habit.

Prairie gentian makes a spectacular cut flower, with individual blooms lasting up to 4 weeks!

Prairie gentian
(*Eustoma grandiflorum*)

Good Neighbors
In the garden, try prairie gentian in clusters of two or three, backed up by a foliage plant, such as a mass of ferns. In an arrangement, these substantial flowers will hold their own among the green bells-of-Ireland (*Moluccella laevis*), or in the midst of a mass of sea lavender (*Limonium latifolium*).

Problems and Solutions
Stem and leaf diseases are common in areas with high humidity; space plants generously apart to encourage air circulation, and avoid watering them from above.

Top Performer
Eustoma grandiflorum (prairie gentian, Texas bluebell, lisianthus): Also called *E. russellianum* and *Lisianthus russellianus*. The plant forms a rosette of oblong, 3-inch (8-cm) leaves, then produces more-or-less upright, somewhat leafy stalks ending in single flowers or small clusters of bloom. The flowers, each 2 to 2½ inches (5 to 6.5 cm) in diameter, open only during daylight hours. Many selections are available, from tall cultivars for cut-flower use to dwarf ones designed for growing in pots.

Larry's Garden Notes

True confessions time: This is one "annual" I simply cannot grow from seed. And it's not that I haven't tried! After 5 years of failures, I finally ended up with spindly little plants that failed to bloom in their first summer. Since it is not hardy in my area, I painstakingly overwintered the few remaining plants indoors. This time they were spectacular—but 18 months for one summer of bloom? I now buy my prairie gentians already started. Let the professionals break *their* backs at growing this persnickety plant from seed!

Gomphrena

Globe amaranth, gomphrena

This charming old-fashioned garden flower has undergone a major revival over the last few years, largely due to new hybrids in a much wider color range and to more compact cultivars better suited to the average border. It is a bushy plant with numerous stems and oval to lance-shaped green leaves. Its claim to fame, though, is its flower heads: globular inflorescences looking more than a bit like clover blooms. The difference is very obvious if you touch them, though; they are not soft like clover, but dry and papery—almost prickly.

Plant Profile

GOMPHRENA
gom-FREE-nuh

- **Bloom Color:** Varies by species; see individual listings

- **Bloom Time:** Early summer through early fall; nearly year-round in mild climates

- **Height:** Varies by species; see individual listings

- **Spread:** Varies by species; see individual listings

- **Garden Uses:** Container planting, cut-flower garden, edging, mass planting, meadow garden, mixed border, rock garden

- **Attracts:** Butterflies

- **Light Preference:** Full sun

- **Soil Preference:** Average, well-drained soil; tolerates dry soil

- **Best Way to Propagate:** Sow seed indoors in spring

- **Hardiness:** Tender annual

Growing Tips

You can buy ready-to-plant gomphrenas in six packs or cell packs just about anywhere. It's also easy to grow them yourself from seed.

You can sow gomphrena seed indoors or out. Sow outdoors if you're strictly interested in harvesting the plant as a dried flower, since it won't matter that the plants will be later to bloom. Indoor sowing is wise for season-long color, especially in short-season areas.

Wherever you sow, soak the seed in warm water for 24 hours before sowing to help speed up germination. Also, sow a bit more thickly than you would for many other flowers; gomphrena seeds have a notoriously low germination rate (often below 50 percent).

Outdoors, broadcast the seed when all danger of frost has passed and rake in lightly. Indoors, start the seed 8 to 10 weeks early. To minimize the chance of damping-off, blend your usual germination medium with an equal amount of clean horticultural sand to create a very well-drained mix. Press the seed into the mix, then cover with a black plastic bag or place the tray in darkness. Germination takes 6 to 15 days at 70° to 75°F (21° to 24°C). Place the seedlings in bright light once they have sprouted.

Seedlings prefer a mix closer to dry than wet, so water only when you see the leaves soften ever so slightly. Pinch the plants when they have 6 to 8 true leaves to stimulate better branching. Plant out when there is no further danger of frost and the ground has thoroughly warmed up; gomphrenas love warm conditions and can be set back by cool weather.

Plant dwarf types about 6 inches (15 cm) apart. The taller types normally need more space—about 1 foot (30 cm). For longer-stemmed cut flowers, though, trying spacing *G. globosa* plants more closely together—about 8 inches (20 cm) apart. This forces the plants to grow upward and produce longer flowerstalks. Although gomphrenas tolerate dry soil, it is still best to water during periods of prolonged drought. Deadheading is never required.

Gomphrenas can be harvested for cut flowers at just about any stage. They'll last for a good 2 weeks in a vase. For drying, strip off the leaves, then bunch the stems together loosely and hang them upside down for a few weeks.

Gomphrena
(*Gomphrena globosa*)

Good Neighbors

Brilliant magenta *Gomphrena globosa* combines well with orange and yellow lantana (*Lantana camara*). All gomphrenas work great as a filler around larger flowers, such as dahlias. They are equally useful in the vase, either fresh or dried. Combine with dried sprigs of goldenrods (*Solidago* spp.), lavender, and grasses for a winter bouquet.

Problems and Solutions

Prevent leaf spots and gray mold by providing a well-drained site with good air circulation. Water during dry spells to minimize the chance of powdery mildew affecting the foliage.

Top Performer

Gomphrena globosa (gomphrena, globe amaranth): The more common of the two species, this one produces distinctly rounded flower heads. The actual flowers are tiny white or yellow trumpets that are scarcely noticeable. It is the colorful bracts, arranged much like a pinecone, that draw the eye. It now comes in a much wider range of colors than the original magenta: lilac, pink, purple, red, and white. Height: 6 to 24 inches (15 to 60 cm). Spread: 6 to 12 inches (15 to 30 cm).

More Recommended Gomphrena

Gomphrena haageana (gomphrena, globe amaranth): This is a taller plant than *G. globosa* of a more open habit, with flower heads that are more elongated. Flowers are normally orange-red but can be lavender or pink. Plants may need staking. Height: 2 to 3 feet (60 to 90 cm). Spread: 1 foot (30 cm).

Larry's Garden Notes

Sometimes too much tinkering by hybridizers can spoil what is already a good thing. The dwarf gomphrenas, like the 6-inch (15-cm) 'Buddy' and 'Gnome' series, are a case in point. While I concede that these dwarf types can form an attractive mass for bedding, half the fun of growing gomphrena is harvesting the flower heads as dried flowers. Just try to put together an arrangement with the tiny stems the dwarf gomphrenas offer! I've always found the original species, already compact and mounded, just about perfect for garden use.

Limonium

Statice, sea lavender

Statice is well known to just about everyone who has ever arranged a flower. There are many hardy perennial species, but those grown as annuals are all frost-sensitive biennials or perennials that flower the first year from seed. They are unmistakable plants forming a ground-hugging rosette of dark green, wavy, deeply lobed leaves followed by stiff, winged, nearly leafless bright green stems. The stems rise straight upward, then branch at the tips into an intricate candelabra of one-sided flower clusters. It is the colorful, long-lasting calyces that give the flowers their charm.

Plant Profile

LIMONIUM
lih-MOAN-ee-um

- **Bloom Color:** Varies by species; see individual listings

- **Bloom Time:** Mid- or late summer through early fall

- **Height:** 12 to 30 inches (30 to 75 cm)

- **Spread:** 8 to 12 inches (20 to 30 cm)

- **Garden Uses:** Container planting, cut-flower garden, mass planting, meadow garden, mixed border, rock garden

- **Light Preference:** Full sun

- **Soil Preference:** Average, well-drained, even sandy soil; tolerates dry soil

- **Best Way to Propagate:** Sow seed indoors in spring

- **Hardiness:** Frost-sensitive perennial or biennial grown as a half-hardy annual

Growing Tips

Annual statice forms a long taproot that is not easy to transplant, a fact that has long limited its availability as a bedding plant in commercial nurseries. Fortunately, it's fairly easy to grow from seed.

Annual statice plants need up to 3 months from when the seed is sown to the start of flowering, so indoor sowing is preferable in all but the mildest areas. Start it 8 to 10 weeks before the last frost, covering the seed lightly. Sow the seed either directly into peat pots (to avoid transplant shock later) or into standard trays, transplanting them to individual pots when they have their second set of leaves (before the taproot forms). Most seed companies sell cleaned seed, with the chaff removed, which germinates within a week or so at 65° to 75°F (18° to 24°C). Uncleaned seed can take 3 weeks or more, and germination can often be irregular.

Plant out when all danger of frost is past and night temperatures remain about 45°F (7°C). Plant quite closely, 8 to 9 inches (20 to 23 cm) apart, for a full look in the garden. For cut-flower use, though, you'll find the stems mingle less (so harvesting is easier) if you set plants 1 foot (30 cm) apart. Well-drained soil is critical. Statice grows well in sandy soil and is actually native to seashores, so it takes salt air and strong winds in stride. It loves hot, dry summers (although occasional watering will help), but it hates hot, humid areas; it grows poorly in rainy climates as well.

As a garden plant, statice is at its prime for about 6 weeks after it starts to bloom. Afterward, the calyces fade and become less attractive. There's no use, though, in deadheading the plant to stimulate repeat bloom; it blooms only once. Instead, harvest the blooms for indoor use, and grow spreading plants nearby to fill in.

Pick the flowerstalks when about two-thirds of the flowers are fully open; most of the others will continue to open after harvesting. Statice makes a wonderful cut flower for fresh arrangements, lasting over 2 weeks. Its greatest value, though, is as a dried flower. Just hang the cut stems upside down in open bunches, until they are thoroughly dry: usually within a few weeks.

In Zones 8 to 11, plants *may* bloom again the following year but often act as annuals, dying out after their first flowering.

Good Neighbors

Combine the bright colors of statices with the natural hues of grasses and seed pods and dried goldenrods (*Solidago* spp.) in winter arrangements. In the garden, interplant statice with baby's breaths (*Gypsophila* spp.) to add some fullness to the stiff flower stems.

Problems and Solutions

Leaf diseases are frequent in hot, humid summer areas as well as in rainy climates. Perfect drainage and good air circulation can help alleviate these problems.

Top Performer

Limonium sinuatum (annual statice, sea lavender): The ½-inch (1.25-cm) funnel-shaped flowers are made up of a tiny, five-lobed, short-lived corolla (usually white) surrounded by a papery-textured calyx in a wide range of colors (including blue, purple, pink, and white). There are dozens of seed strains in various heights and colors. Height: 12 to 30 inches (30 to 75 cm). Spread: 8 to 12 inches (20 to 30 cm).

More Recommended Limonium

Limonium bonduellii (golden annual statice): Botanists often classify the yellow-flowered forms of annual statice under this name, although seed packs and catalogs inevitably simply lump them together with *L. sinuatum,* as do some botanists. And it *is* essentially identical, differing only in its coloration: yellow calyces and flowers. Plants with apricot calyces would be crosses between the two. Height: 12 to 30 inches (30 to 75 cm). Spread: 8 to 12 inches (20 to 30 cm).

Annual statice
(*Limonium sinuatum*)

Kissing Cousins

Pink pokers (*Psylliostachys suworowii*, also called *Limonium suworowii* and *Statice suworowii*) also travel under the common names rat-tail statice and Russian statice. Its wiry stems are rounded in cross section, without the wings characteristic of annual statice. Its rosy pink flowers are also different, produced in upright, branching, cylindrical, 8-inch (20-cm) spikes that look much like fingers. They are great as fresh or dried cut flowers. Height: 12 to 18 inches (30 to 45 cm). Spread: 8 to 12 inches (20 to 30 cm).

Moluccella

Bells-of-Ireland, lady-in-the-bathtub, shell flower

This old-fashioned annual is making a major comeback, notably as a cut flower, fresh or dried. It really looks like no other garden plant. To start with, it is mostly all "flower," with each flowerstalk blooming nearly from its very base to the tiptop. It is densely packed with whorled, cup-shaped green calyces that harbor the tiny, pink to white, delightfully perfumed but otherwise insignificant flowers, with a few scalloped leaves poking out here and there. The flowers drop off quickly, but the calyces remain for the rest of the summer—or year-round when dried.

Plant Profile

MOLUCCELLA
mol-you-CHEL-uh

- **Bloom Color:** Green

- **Bloom Time:** Midsummer through early fall

- **Height:** 2 to 3 feet (60 to 90 cm)

- **Spread:** 1 foot (30 cm)

- **Garden Uses:** Cut-flower garden, meadow garden, mixed border

- **Light Preference:** Full sun to partial shade

- **Soil Preference:** Humus-rich, well-drained, evenly moist soil

- **Best Way to Propagate:** Sow seed indoors or out in spring, or outdoors in fall

- **Hardiness:** Half-hardy annual

Growing Tips

This plant is too unusual to ever be a major hit, so you're unlikely to find it in a nursery in any form but seed packets.

After trying to sow it indoors and out, I've come to the conclusion that outdoor sowing is the best way to go with bells-of-Ireland, even in short-summer areas where it does take some time to reach flowering size. It just seems to give sturdier, taller, fuller plants. Sow early in spring, when the ground is still cool and there is still danger of frost. Or sow in the fall for bloom the following spring. Just press the seed into the soil, without covering because it needs light to germinate. It'll start to sprout as the soil warms up.

If you really want to start them indoors, sow into trays or peat pots 8 to 10 weeks before the last frost, without covering. For best germination, seal the seed containers inside a plastic bag and place in the refrigerator for 2 weeks; then place in bright light at cool temperatures—50° to 60°F (10° to 15°C). Higher temperatures are acceptable but tend to produce weak-stemmed plants. Plant outside when all risk of frost has passed but while nights are still cool.

If space is limited or you want to have perfectly straight stems, stake the plants. Unstaked, the tall stems will bend outward and then upward, creating an interesting and attractive look in the garden and in arrangements.

FUN FACTS

Bells-of-Ireland does not actually come from the Emerald Isle; it gets its common name from its bright green color. It is native to the arid Middle East, about as un-Irish a climate as you could imagine. It does grow beautifully in Ireland, though, and anywhere else where summers are cool.

In the garden, bells-of-Ireland remains green and attractive throughout much of summer, fading to beige only as fall approaches. For use as a fresh-cut flower, remove the leaves and singe the cut end of each stem with a match to burn off the sticky sap that can block the stem's circulation. Then place the stems in water and let them sit for a few hours in a cool, dark spot before placing them in an arrangement. Bells-of-Ireland will remain in top shape for 2 weeks or more.

Drying bells-of-Ireland is easy enough, but there are a few secrets. Florists often plunge it in glycerine to preserve its color, but that gives it a greasy appearance and changes the bright spring green to a darker shade. You can, however, dry bells-of-Ireland to a nice pale green if you're very careful. Just place it upright in a tall glass containing only about 1 inch (2.5 cm) of water. This allows it to dry slowly and helps it retain its color. It's not a perfect method—some stems do discolor—but it's worth trying.

Bells-of-Ireland
(*Moluccella laevis*)

❗ Think Twice: You scarcely need to think of how to sow bells-of-Ireland after the first year: It self-sows abundantly, sometimes a bit too much. To prevent this, harvest it when it is relatively young and no seeds have formed. **Self-sowing** 🖊

Good Neighbors

Try bells-of-Ireland with purple heliotrope (*Heliotropium arborescens*), annual verbenas, and other softly mounded annuals and perennials. In fresh or dried arrangements, it gives character and structure to otherwise standard arrangements of carnations (*Dianthus caryophyllus*) and baby's breaths (*Gypsophila* spp.).

Problems and Solutions

Bells-of-Ireland seems quite immune to insects and disease.

Top Performer

Moluccella laevis (bells-of-Ireland, lady-in-the-bathtub, shell flower): There are four species in this genus, but only the species described above is commonly grown.

Smart Substitutes

❗ Think Twice: Green flowers are so unusual that they always merit special attention. Besides bells-of-Ireland, thorow wax or thorough wax (*Bupleurum rotundifolia*) is another worth trying. This shrubby-looking annual or short-lived perennial produces numerous umbels of yellowish green flowers throughout much of the summer. It's an easy-to-grow annual for poor soil. *B. griffithii*, offered by some seed sources, appears to be an identical plant. **Self-sowing** 🖊

Nigella

Love-in-a-mist, love-in-a-puff, devil-in-the-bush, fennel flower

They just don't make common names like these any more! Modern plants have more practical names: They're short and to the point, as if we didn't have time any more to have fun naming things. Then you get the truly old-fashioned plants like this one, in culture for over four centuries, with its long list of ear-pleasers. Love-in-a-mist is a bushy annual with deeply cut leaves and curious and complex flowers in a wide range of colors. It's great as a fresh cut flower and even better dried—in the latter case, not for its flowers, but for its curious live-forever seed capsules.

Plant Profile

NIGELLA
ny-JEL-uh

- **Bloom Color:** Varies by species; see individual listings

- **Bloom Time:** Late spring through early fall; year-round in mild climates

- **Height:** Varies by species; see individual listings

- **Spread:** Varies by species; see individual listings

- **Garden Uses:** Container planting, cut-flower garden, edging, meadow garden, mixed border, rock garden

- **Light Preference:** Full sun

- **Soil Preference:** Average, well-drained soil

- **Best Way to Propagate:** Sow seed in fall or early spring outdoors; repeat sowings until July

- **Hardiness:** Hardy annual

Growing Tips

Love-in-a-mist plants quickly produce a taproot and don't take kindly to transplanting, so you'll seldomly find them for sale. But they are so easy to grow from seed, it wouldn't be worth buying them anyway!

Generations of gardeners have grown this old-fashioned favorite by simply dropping the seed in the garden and raking it in. Sow it in fall or early spring, as soon as the soil can be worked, to have the earliest flowers. To extend the bloom season, sow more seed once a month up until July for continuous bloom. (In frost-free climates, you can actually continue to sow monthly right throughout the year.) Early sowings sprout rapidly whenever the soil has warmed up enough; summer sowings sprout in about 10 to 15 days.

If you insist, you can start the seed indoors in peat pots, 6 to 8 weeks before the last frost date. Just barely cover; then provide 65° to 70°F (18° to 21°C) for germination.

Love-in-a-mist adapts to just about any type of soil, as long as it is well drained. It's not quite so adaptable when it comes to temperature, though, positively thriving in cool summer areas but burning out in hot ones. Where heat is a problem, sow it early outdoors for early bloom, then replace it with a more heat-resistant annual at the end of spring.

Love-in-a-mist adds a lovely lacy look to cut-flower arrangements, lasting 7 to 10 days. Pick stems when most of the flowers are fully open. It can also be dried at this stage: The flowers fade but retain their color. Generally, though, it's the swollen seed capsules that work best for drying.

Good Neighbors

Love-in-a-mist is a wonderful filler in the flower border and makes a nice complement to the stronger forms of euphorbias, irises, and roses. The interesting seedpods are good for winter arrangements, combined with irises and poppies (*Papaver* spp.) pods, dried grasses, and other everlastings.

Problems and Solutions

Generations of gardeners have grown this plant with nary a complaint. I don't think you'll have any problem either.

Top Performer

Nigella damascena (love-in-a-mist, love-in-a-puff, devil-in-the-bush, lady-in-the-bower): The flowers of this species are blue, purple, rose-red, pink, or white and either single or double. The common names all refer to the extremely fine foliage that grows on the stems and right up to the base of the flower, so that each bloom is sitting in a bed of lace. Devil-in-the-bush also refers to the vaguely sinister seed capsules, swollen into a globe and with devil-like horns. Harvest them when they take on a purplish tinge. Height: 1 to 2 feet (30 to 60 cm). Spread: 9 inches (23 cm). **Self-sowing**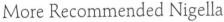

More Recommended Nigella

Nigella hispanica (fennel flower): Somewhat similar to *N. damascena,* but with larger blossoms in blue that are lightly fragrant and surround a curious mass of maroon-red stamens. Indeed, the plant is sometimes sold under the cultivar name 'Curiosity'. The leaves are deeply cut but not as threadlike as those of love-in-a-mist; the puffy seed capsules are also similar. Height: 24 to 30 inches (60 to 75 cm). Spread: 18 inches (45 cm). **Self-sowing**

N. orientalis (transformer): Otherwise similar to the others in foliage, the yellow flowers of this species make it very different in appearance. You won't grow this one for its blooms, though, but rather for its seed capsules: When dry, simply turn them inside out and they become perfect, little, parasol-shaped "flowers!" Height: 18 inches (45 cm). Spread: 9 to 12 inches (23 to 30 cm). **Self-sowing**

Love-in-a-mist
(*Nigella damascena*)

Smart Substitutes

If you enjoy unusual seed pods, try unicorn plant, also called devil's claw (*Proboscidea louisianica*, also called *P. jussieui*, *P. proboscidea*, and *Martynia fragrans*). Its pods are huge, monstrous things, each with a long beak: impressive! The plant itself is enormous, with huge, somewhat fuzzy, sticky leaves that catch aphids and whiteflies; it has large, trumpet-shaped, white, pink, or purple flowers with a yellow throat and a strong, musky perfume. Start indoors 6 to 8 weeks before the last frost date. Height: 2 to 3 feet (60 to 90 cm). Spread: 3 to 6 feet (90 to 180 cm).

Salvia

Clary sage, clary, annual clary sage

Somehow the name clary, originally referring to the medicinal biennial sage *Salvia sclarea,* became transposed onto a totally different sage, *S. viridis,* a scentless, strictly ornamental annual. Since then, these two plants have shared the same common name, causing no end of confusion. So different are these two plants that I can't even describe them together. Consider all the following information to apply strictly to *S. viridis,* the "annual" clary sage, shown in the photo. For true clary sage (*S. sclarea*), see "More Recommended Salvia" on the opposite page.

Plant Profile

SALVIA
SAL-vee-uh

- **Bloom Color:** Pink, purple, white

- **Bloom Time:** Late spring through early fall; fall through winter in mild climates

- **Height:** 16 to 24 inches (40 to 60 cm)

- **Spread:** 9 to 12 inches (23 to 30 cm)

- **Garden Uses:** Container planting, cut-flower garden, meadow garden, mixed border

- **Light Preference:** Full sun to partial shade

- **Soil Preference:** Poor to rich, well-drained soil

- **Best Way to Propagate:** Sow seed indoors or outdoors in spring or outdoors in fall

- **Hardiness:** Hardy annual

Growing Tips

I've yet to see annual clary sage (*Salvia viridis*) sold in six packs or cell packs. It transplants readily enough, but nurseries like to sell plants in full flower rather than in foliage; and by the time it has started to color up, it is already at full maturity and will no longer fill out when planted in the garden.

Most people sow annual clary sage directly outdoors, simply watering the seed in, either about 2 weeks before the last frost or in the fall. A fall sowing will give you plants that bloom the following spring in most regions. In mild winter areas, try two sowings—one in spring, one in fall—for bloom much of the year. Thin from 9 to 12 inches (23 to 30 cm) apart.

If you prefer to start seed indoors, sow it 6 to 8 weeks before the last frost, simply pressing it into the mix. It will germinate in 1 to 2 weeks at 60° to 75°F (15° to 24°C). Transplant outdoors after all risk of frost has passed.

Annual clary sage tolerates just about any soil, as long as it is not soggy. It will grow more thickly and possibly a bit taller in rich soil, but it blooms well even in poor soil. Annual clary sage grows best when kept evenly moist as a young plant. Adult plants are very drought tolerant but do appreciate occasional watering during dry spells.

Annual clary sage needs no deadheading because its true

FUN FACTS

Clary sage gets its name from the Latin *clarus* ("clear") because its leaves and seeds were used in making eye lotions. It also gives its name to claret, a red wine to which elderberries and clary are added to give it a muscatel flavor.

flowers are insignificant and there is no reason to want to stimulate rebloom. All the color comes from the bracts, which stay in perfect shape until fall, long after the flowers have faded. Of course, you may well be deadheading it indirectly by picking the stems for indoor use. It looks great in fresh arrangements and dries to perfection.

Annual clary sage self-sows in just about all climates but isn't invasive because the seedlings inevitably come up right around the base of the mother plant. Simply pull out any excess seedlings or move them to other parts of the garden.

Good Neighbors

Annual clary sage looks great spiking outward from daisy-shaped mums and soft sprays of baby's breaths (*Gypsophila* spp.) or white lace flower (*Ammi majus*). Pairing annual clary sage with green hydrangea blossoms in fresh or dried arrangements will emphasize the intricate green veins.

Problems and Solutions

Poor drainage can lead to rot.

Top Performer

Salvia viridis, often sold as *S. horminum* (clary sage, clary, annual clary sage): You'll grow this colorful annual not for its insignificant pink to pale purple flowers, but for the pink, purple, or white, green-veined bracts that develop at the top of each flower spike. The plant is bushy, with numerous hairy stalks and 2-inch (5-cm), mid-green, hairy leaves. Height: 16 to 24 inches (40 to 60 cm). Spread: 9 to 12 inches (23 to 30 cm). **Self-sowing** 🌱

More Recommended Salvia

Salvia sclarea (clary sage, clary, cleareye): Political correctness obliges a mention of this plant, the true clary sage. The large, felted, gray leaves are highly aromatic, and the huge, branching flower spikes last from spring throughout much of the summer. They are composed of hook-like, lilac-and-cream flowers with white to mauve bracts. Sow this biennial outdoors in summer for bloom the following year or indoors 8 to 10 weeks before the last frost for bloom the first year. Zones 5 to 9. Height: 3 feet (1 m). Spread: 2 feet (60 cm). **Self-sowing** 🌱

'Claryssa Blue' clary sage
(*Salvia viridis* 'Claryssa Blue')

Kissing Cousins

True clary sage (*S. sclarea*) has two very close relatives that, though biennials, are grown as annuals in most climates: Silver sage (*S. argentea*) and African sage (*S. aethiopis*). Both produce wide rosettes of spectacularly woolly leaves and are grown mainly for their foliage. I prefer to let them bloom the following year, though, for their white flowers. Hardy in Zones 5 to 8, silver sage forms a mound 1 foot (30 cm) tall and 2 feet (60 cm) across. African sage (*S. aethiopis*) is very similar but slightly hardier (to Zone 4).

Scabiosa

Sweet scabious, pincushion flower, mourning bride

Scabious is riding high on two waves: the increased interest in flower arranging and the discovery of a few exceptional perennial species have caused gardeners to take a second look at the whole scabious clan. The annual species are particularly attractive and easy to grow. They form a low-growing dome of hairy, mid-green foliage topped off by tall, wiry stems bearing large flower heads. Each is made up of broad outer florets and smaller, denser inner florets. The central florets form a dome with gray stamens that rise above the rest; it's easy to see where the name pincushion flower comes from!

Plant Profile

SCABIOSA
scay-bee-OH-suh

- **Bloom Color:** Varies by species; see individual listings

- **Bloom Time:** Early summer through early fall; fall through winter in mild climates

- **Height:** Varies by species; see individual listings

- **Spread:** 9 inches (23 cm)

- **Garden Uses:** Container planting, cut-flower garden, mass planting, meadow garden, mixed border

- **Attracts:** Butterflies, hummingbirds

- **Light Preference:** Full sun

- **Soil Preference:** Poor to humus-rich, evenly moist but well-drained soil

- **Best Way to Propagate:** Sow seed outdoors in mid spring

- **Hardiness:** Hardy annual

Growing Tips

You may be able to find sweet scabious (*S. atropurpurea*) hybrids for sale in spring. If possible, buy them when they're young, without any bloom because they form a taproot that does not tolerate being disturbed. (Peat pots are a better choice than six packs or cell packs for the same reason.)

Like many old-fashioned annuals, sweet scabious grows quickly enough from seed to make sowing it outdoors worthwhile. Sow the seed outside as soon as the ground is workable, or even the previous fall, barely covering it. The seed will germinate when the soil begins to warm up. Thin them to 9 inches apart or transplant the seedlings when they are still young, before their taproot makes moving them impossible.

For earlier bloom, start the seed indoors 4 to 6 weeks before the last frost date. Sow in cell packs or peat pots, at a rate of two or three seeds per pot. Germination takes about 2 weeks at 70° to 75°F (21° to 24°C). Thin to one plant per pot. Plant out when all risk of frost is over and the soil is beginning to warm up.

Just about any sunny spot will do, but the soil should be no more than slightly acid, and preferably neutral to alkaline. Soil fertility can pose a bit of a puzzle: The plants bloom the best in rich soil but then tend to flop over. In poor soil, bloom is sparser but the flowers remain more upright.

Scabious is attractive when it's in seed, so there is no need to deadhead to hide "fading flowers," nor does deadheading seem to stimulate future bloom. On the other hand, both species described here make interesting cut flowers, so you may find yourself pre-deadheading by harvesting the blooms anyway.

In very mild areas, scabious will some-times survive the winter for a second year, even though it is usually considered an annual plant by botanists.

Good Neighbors

These plants tend to have a weak form, so they look best when planted among stout neighbors in a cottage-garden set-ting, or in the cutting garden. The char-treuse flowers of euphorbias, blue or purple larkspur (*Consolida ajacis*), and pink dianthus or dahlias make attractive com-panions in a flower vase.

Problems and Solutions

Spider mites can produce stippled foliage in dry weather; spray with insecticidal soap.

Sweet scabious
(*Scabiosa atropurpurea*)

Top Performer

Scabiosa atropurpurea (sweet scabious, pincushion flower, mourning bride): This is the most common species and also the most beautiful in bloom. The dome-shaped, sweet-smelling flowers measure 3 inches (8 cm) in diameter and come in a wide range of shades of purple, blue, pink, rose-red, and white. There is also a beautiful dark burgundy shade, close to black, that is actually the original color of the wildflower. Most modern hybrids are doubles, with a fuller dome than the single cultivars. This is an excellent cut flower, lasting 10 days or more if you harvest it just as it starts to open and if you recut the stems regularly. Height: 18 to 36 inches (45 to 90 cm). Spread: 9 inches (23 cm). **Self-sowing**

More Recommended Scabious

Scabiosa stellata (starflower, Ping-Pong ball, paper moon): The flowers are of an unusual color that is very hard to describe. Some references refer to pale blue, pale lavender, or pale pink, but to my eyes, they are actually a light beige. The most interesting feature, though, is its dried seedheads: perfectly round and made up of cuplike bracts with a dark star in the center. They dry to a beautiful bronze shade. Har-vest them while they are still partly green because they tend to shatter if allowed to dry to full maturity on the plant. Height: 2 to 3 feet (60 to 90 cm). Spread: 9 inches (23 cm). **Self-sowing**

Larry's Garden Notes

Pincushion flower has a major flaw: It flops! Poorer, more alkaline soil will help, but after spending years improving your soil, would you honestly consider buying poor soil and pouring it into your garden? And making the soil more alkaline would be worthwhile only if you had several other alkaline-loving plants you wanted to grow with it. That leaves either staking (which can't be done pleasingly on a plant that's almost all stem and no leaf) or surrounding it with stur-dier plants that can hold it up (the best solution).

Trachelium

Throatwort

Flower arrangers just love blue throatwort (*Trachelium caeruleum*), and as a result, it's slowly creeping its way up the popularity charts with gardeners and nursery centers. The flower heads of this unusual annual are simply huge! They are made up of hundreds of tiny, trumpet-shaped, purple, pink, or white, lightly perfumed flowers that mingle with their neighbors to create an airy mass more than 1 foot (30 cm) in diameter. The plant is shrublike, with sharply toothed, dark green leaves and reddish branching stems.

Plant Profile

TRACHELIUM
tray-KEL-ee-um

- **Bloom Color:** Purple, white
- **Bloom Time:** Early summer through early fall
- **Height:** Varies by species; see individual listings
- **Spread:** Varies by species; see individual listings
- **Garden Uses:** Container planting, cut-flower garden, annual hedge, mass planting, meadow garden, mixed border
- **Attracts:** Beneficial insects, butterflies
- **Light Preference:** Full sun to partial shade
- **Soil Preference:** Average, evenly moist but very well drained soil
- **Best Way to Propagate:** Sow seed indoors in spring
- **Hardiness:** Frost-sensitive perennial grown as a tender annual

Growing Tips

You'll probably be able to find throatwort in some of the larger nurseries, especially those offering container plants. I've seen it sold only in individual pots so far, but then, you need just a few plants to create considerable impact.

If you can't find it locally as a plant, you can grow it from seed. Since it is actually a biennial or short-lived perennial, it is in no hurry to bloom the first year; sowing outdoors is worthwhile only in Zones 9 to 11, where it is hardy enough to come through the winter. There, you can sow it either in summer or very early in the new year for bloom the upcoming summer.

Elsewhere, start throatwort indoors 10 to 12 weeks before the last frost date. Don't cover the seed; it needs light to germinate. It'll sprout in 2 to 3 weeks at 55° to 60°F (13° to 15°C). Water carefully at first because the young seedlings are fragile (they quickly toughen up). Either thin out the trays or transplant the seedlings into more spacious quarters as they grow in size.

When there is no longer any danger of frost, harden off the young throatworts and plant them out. Full sun is best, although some shade from the afternoon sun is wise in hot climates. Ordinary garden soil will do just fine, although they will grow a bit better if the soil is neutral to just slightly alkaline. Be sure to pot up a few as moveable decorative accents; this plant is a true charmer in containers of all sorts.

Summer care is minimal: Simply water as needed and mulch to keep the soil reasonably moist. Remove fading flower heads to make room for their replacements.

Throatwort does not dry well but makes a truly superior cut flower. Pick it when most of the flowers in the head are fully open, and they'll last for 10 days or more in the vase.

Good Neighbors

An airy addition to the cut-flower vase, throatwort makes a nice complement to the warm colors of summer. Whether in the garden or in arrangements, zinnias, yarrows (*Achillea* spp.), and annual statice (*Limonium sinuatum*) look superb against throatwort's fluffy violet clouds.

Problems and Solutions

There are few problems outdoors, but spider mites and aphids may appear on indoor plants; spray with insecticidal soap.

Top Performer

Trachelium caeruleum (blue throatwort, common throatwort): You'll occasionally find pink- or white-flowered selections of this species, but shades of purple and violet are much more common. The common types, usually growing 30 to 48 inches (75 to 120 cm) tall, provide the longest flowerstalks. However, the dwarf cultivars, like 14- to 16-inch (35- to 40-cm) tall 'Passion in Violet', still offer good cut-flower material and are more compact plants. Blue throatwort may self-sow in very mild climates, although not to the point of weediness. Height: 14 to 48 inches (35 to 120 cm). Spread: 1 foot (30 cm). **Self-sowing** 🖊

More Recommended Trachelium

Trachelium rumelianum (creeping throatwort): Creeping throatwort is a dense, compact plant forming a carpet of pointed, oblong leaves. In summer, it produces upright, open umbels of starry blue flowers that have a fuzzy appearance due to the numerous extended stamens and stigma. Height: 8 to 12 inches (20 to 30 cm). Spread: 9 to 12 inches (23 to 30 cm).

Blue throatwort
(*Trachelium caeruleum*)

Larry's Garden Notes

I've been experimenting with blue throatwort as a houseplant and am very pleased with the results. I start a few stem cuttings in early summer and grow them outside until fall, then bring them indoors to bright light for winter. I found the regular types needed frequent pinching in fall to stay bushy, but the newer dwarf types do all the work! By February they're full of buds, then they bloom right through until about midsummer when they start to lose steam. Start new plants each year from cuttings or seeds.

Trachymene

Blue lace flower, didiscus

No, this is not a new plant, just an old-fashioned favorite with a newfangled name. When I was a kid, I grew it under the name *Didiscus,* and many gardeners still use that name. The 2- to 3-inch (5- to 8-cm) domes are open and lacy, composed of tiny little stars, each with bright yellow stamens in the center. The deeply cut leaves look like those of white lace flower (*Ammi majus*), a close relative. The flower heads appear on somewhat branching, curving, wiry stems with smaller stem leaves.

Plant Profile

TRACHYMENE
tray-KEH-men-ee

- **Bloom Color:** Blue, lavender, pink, white

- **Bloom Time:** Summer through early fall; winter and spring in mild climates

- **Height:** 18 to 36 inches (45 to 90 cm)

- **Spread:** 1 foot (30 cm)

- **Garden Uses:** Container planting, cut-flower garden, mass planting, meadow garden, mixed border

- **Attracts:** Beneficial insects, butterflies

- **Light Preference:** Full sun to partial shade

- **Soil Preference:** Poor to humus-rich, light, well-drained soil

- **Best Way to Propagate:** Sow seed indoors or outdoors in spring; fall in mild climates

- **Hardiness:** Frost-sensitive biennial grown as a half-hardy annual

Growing Tips

You'll almost never see blue lace flower sold as a started plant, mainly due to its dislike of transplanting. You can, however, sow it yourself indoors or out and get spectacular results.

To start blue lace flower outdoors, sow after the last frost, just covering the seed. Since it needs darkness to germinate, you might want to shield the planting areas with an inverted pot or other covering until germination. Outdoor sowing will give all-summer bloom only in very long season climates. In such places, sow it either in early spring for summer bloom or in early fall for winter flowers. Elsewhere, expect bloom in late summer or fall.

For much earlier results, start your seed indoors, 8 to 10 weeks before the last frost. Use peat pots or plan to prick out the seedlings into individual pots while they are still quite small, before they develop their long taproot. Barely cover the seed, then keep it dark and at 70°F (21°C) until germination, 2 to 3 weeks later. Plant the seedlings outdoors after the last frost, spacing them 8 to 9 inches apart. Pinch the plants when they're about 3 inches (8 cm) tall to encourage better branching.

Blue lace flower will do well in full sun or light shade. It also tolerates just about any soil that is well drained, even poor or sandy soil, but it blooms better in richer soil. It is not very heat tolerant, though, so give it a site with afternoon shade and mulch it generously in hot summer areas.

Blue lace flower stems are never perfectly straight: They arch and curve or even flop entirely. That's not a problem in flower arrangements; in fact, the curving stems and lacy blooms help compensate for the stiffness of so many other flowers. In the garden, though, it can be annoying. Try surrounding the plants with solid perennials or small shrubs they can lean on, or insert twiggy branches at planting time to support the stems as they grow upward. Or simply plant them densely so they can hold each other up (more or less)!

Pick this top-notch cut flower when most of the flowers are open. The blooms last up to 10 days.

Blue lace flower is actually a tender perennial, but it almost never overwinters outdoors, even in the milder climates. (It is not very drought tolerant, but it also hates winter wet.) It does make an attractive and easy-to-grow potted plant for a cool, bright spot indoors, although it tends to be short lived, lasting no more than 9 to 10 months.

Blue lace flower
(*Trachymene coerulea*)

Good Neighbors
In an arrangement, blue lace flower provides a gentle contrast with various shades of yellow and cream: for example, yellow statice and 'Italian White' sunflowers. In the garden, make sure to plant them where they will get some support from stronger neighbors, such as silvery artemisia.

Problems and Solutions
Blue lace flower is not really subject to any major problems, although rot and leaf diseases are possible in poorly drained soil.

Top Performer
Trachymene coerulea (blue lace flower, didiscus): Also called *Didiscus coeruleus.* There are some 12 species of *Trachymene,* but this is the only one that seems to be grown outside of its native Australia. A few years ago, there was only one choice for blue lace flower—the species in light blue. Now there are several strains available in paler shades of lavender, pink, and white, although you may have to search for them because they're not yet in every catalog.

Larry's Garden Notes

If your blue lace flower has very weak stems, part of the problem may be that it doesn't like the fertilizer you've been applying. In its native Australia, phosphorus is often in short supply, so many plants have learned to live with only very tiny quantities of it. When grown in areas where soil phosphorus is relatively abundant (including North America and Europe), they may have trouble adapting. Using a fertilizer low in phosphorus but rich in potassium, or not fertilizing at all, may help them produce straighter stems.

ANNUALS WITH DECORATIVE
Fruits or Foliage

The word "annual" is so closely associated with the word "flower" that, not so very long ago, you almost never heard the word annual used alone: The term was "annual flower." That being the case, it may seem a bit strange to devote a chapter to annuals that you don't grow for their blooms but instead for their foliage or their fruits. It won't seem strange once you get to know these plants, though! All the annuals described here are as colorful and attractive as any flower; and anything flowering plants can do, they can do at least as well—sometimes even better. In fact, several of these plants are so spectacular that you'll want to use them with discretion.

◄With foliage like this, who needs flowers! Coleus (*Solenostemon scutellarioides*) is just one example of an increasing range of annuals with outstanding foliage color.

Foliage Is Forever!

Plants with colorful leaves have a major advantage over flowering annuals: You can really count on their colors. Most annual flowers, you see, take time getting started in spring, then have their ups and downs, with long periods of light flowering interspersed with moments of heavy bloom. Where there is an absolute necessity for color right through summer, why then take a risk with flowering plants when foliage plants guarantee results?

And that is the main attraction of plants with decorative foliage: They're always at their peak. Annuals produce leaves from the time they germinate to the time they die. Their actual flowering period is much, much shorter: a few weeks, perhaps a few months at the most. All you need, therefore, is to find plants with foliage so attractive they match the finest flowers. From the brightest gold to the iciest silver to the deepest purple to the wildest variegation, foliage annuals offer a bit of everything.

The Secrets of Leaf Color

Logically speaking, all plants should have green leaves. After all, chlorophyll—that marvelous component that allows plants to absorb sunlight and convert it into storable, usable energy—is green. Why bother with any other color? This is so true that nearly all plants follow the plan and produce green leaves. Given the overwhelming mass of green in just about every environment, however, anything that *isn't* green immediately attracts our attention.

True confessions time: Coppertone hibiscus is simply my favorite foliage plant, bar none.

of extreme sun and heat (arid climates and sand dunes, for example). Transpose silvery plants into a less burning environment, though, and they still thrive, and they really stand out, as well.

Blue foliage (often called "glaucous" foliage), as seen in ornamental cabbage leaves, results from a similar situation and also exists as a protective device. Instead of fuzzy hairs, though, a waxy, white powder called "bloom" covers green leaves, making them look icy blue.

Purple Plus

Purple foliage, which we gardeners tend to call bronze or red, is *not* common in nature, at least not visibly so. Most plants, though, have hidden pigments deep down in their leaves, some of which come into the foreground in fall when for a brief period the chlorophyll in many leaves dies, revealing colors hitherto invisible. Red pigments serve a role of protection: They act as a sunscreen, warding off overly harsh solar rays. New leaves, for instance, are often reddish because red pigments dominate to protect them until they have developed a sun-resistant outer cuticle that does the same job; then the leaf goes back to being green again.

Purple foliage results when a mutation causes a plant to produce more than its share of red pigmentation while still producing plenty of the green stuff. Bright red cells mixed with green give a dark, purplish green color we call bronze, seen in such plants as bloodleaf (*Iresine herbstii*). It's a common enough mutation and one that hybridizers specifically work to highlight, to our delight. They cross purple-leaved plants together and pick out the darkest of all in the next generation.

Going for Silver

Silver is the most common nongreen foliage color in nature. In some climates, in fact, *most* plants have a silvery sheen. That's because silver really isn't silver, but rather a coating of white over green. A prime example is dusty miller (*Senecio cineraria*); if you scrape off its fuzzy white outer coating, you'll discover it is not the silvery gray it appears but dark green.

It so happens that a coating of white over green leaves reflects light, protecting plants from overly strong sunlight that could actually damage them. This coating of hairs also keeps drying air away from the leaf's tender cells. That's why silver foliage dominates in areas

All That Glitters . . .

"Golden" leaves are a bit of wishful thinking on the part of gardeners. "Gold" is usually a pale lime green much closer to chartreuse than gold. It's a particularly pleasing color to the eye, though, especially in contrast to the common dark greens in surrounding vegetation. Golden leaves, though, are actually a genetic flaw. They result when green pigments are present but very diffuse, allowing underlying yellow pigments to show through. Many coleus (*Solenostemon scutellarioides*) cultivars offer this kind of golden coloration. "Gold" foliage really stands out in a dark corner or when contrasted with dark foliage.

Spots and Dots

"Variegation" is the term gardeners use to describe irregular coloration, generally a green leaf with spots, splotches, or stripes of a contrasting shade. Parts of a variegated leaf are albino, totally lacking in green pigmentation; this allows the underlying white, pink, yellow, or red colors to show through. Generally, variegation is a genetic flaw, a mutation that would be fatal to the plant in the wild since it has less energy-absorbing chlorophyll than its neighbors do. But gardeners love this type of bright contrast and go out of their way to "save" these brilliant plants. A few types of variegation are even due to viruses.

Variegation is not always a genetic flaw or a disease, though. A few wild plants have learned to use it to their advantage. Snow-on-the-mountain (*Euphorbia marginata*), for example, uses the icy white bands along its leaf edges to attract pollinators to its insignificant flowers. Several other plants have developed similar tricks, but even so, most variegated annuals are manmade cultivars.

Many colorful foliage annuals do not come true from seed: You have to multiply them by taking cuttings or by division. Some do come true from seed, however, and are featured prominently in this chapter!

Colorful Fruit: A Totally Different Picture

As with foliage annuals, annuals with colorful fruit really stand out from the crowd that only produces a few showy blooms as their "talent." Unlike trees and shrubs, which can afford to expend time and energy producing juicy berries, annuals tend to concentrate on producing smaller, less colorful, faster-to-mature seed. Those annuals that do bear fruit often look rather plain while they're growing and flowering, saving up their display until their colorful fruits ripen near the end of the season, which somewhat reduces our interest in them. That's why the rare fruit-producing annuals that produce fruit fairly early in the season, such as ornamental peppers (*Capsicum annuum*), are highly prized and well worth growing. Of course, most of us are so impatient that we inevitably cheat by starting them indoors, thus giving them a head start!

13 More Annuals with Decorative Fruit and Foliage

It takes only a simple mutation to turn a green-foliaged annual into one with golden, purple, or variegated leaves. That's why so many flowering annuals offer at least one selection with colorful foliage. The following annuals, though, have fruit or foliage colorful enough that you might well grow them for that purpose alone.

Beta

Swiss chard, ornamental beet

Who says vegetables can't be beautiful? Swiss chard has long been a staple in home vegetable gardens (it is simply, in my opinion, *the* easiest leaf vegetable of all!), but it's only relatively recently gained acceptance as an ornamental as well. The plant is absolutely stunning: a broad fountain of large, shiny, dark green to deep purple leaves with thick petioles in bright red, pure white, yellow, orange, and lavender.

Plant Profile

BETA
BAY-tuh

- **Foliage Color:** Green, lavender, pink, red, yellow, white

- **Foliage Time:** Summer through late fall; fall through winter in mild climates

- **Height:** 9 to 18 inches (23 to 45 cm)

- **Spread:** 12 to 18 inches (30 to 45 cm)

- **Garden Uses:** Container planting, edging, groundcover, mass planting, mixed border, vegetable garden

- **Light Preference:** Full sun to partial shade

- **Soil Preference:** Light, humus-rich, evenly moist but well-drained soil

- **Best Way to Propagate:** Sow seed outdoors in spring or early fall in mild climates

- **Hardiness:** Half-hardy biennial grown as a hardy annual

Growing Tips

Nurseries are starting to offer cell packs of both Swiss chard and ornamental beet, which are a good option if you need only a few plants. Both are also easy to grow from seed, however, if you prefer to raise your own plants.

Sow seed outdoors in early spring, a month before the last frost date, or in the fall in Zones 9 to 11. Alternately, start them indoors in peat pots 6 to 8 weeks before the last frost, and set the plants out around the last frost date. Either way, sow the seed about 1 inch (2.5 cm) deep. If you sow the seed outdoors while the soil is still cold, it'll simply germinate when temperatures reach an appropriate level. Indoors, or if you get a late start on the season, soak the seed overnight before sowing to speed up germination. It'll sprout in 5 to 20 days at 50° to 85°F (10° to 30°C).

Each "seed" is actually a cluster of five or six seeds that produces several plants, so thinning is required. Simply eat what you pull out, though; the whole plant is perfectly edible. Try to space Swiss chard at least 14 inches (35 cm) apart for best ornamental appearance. Thinning ornamental beets to about 4 inches (10 cm) apart will give a denser, carpetlike appearance while still allowing room for their roots to fill out nicely.

The nice thing about it is you really *can* have your Swiss chard and eat it, too! If you harvest only the outer leaves, breaking them

FUN FACTS

Swiss chard and beets are actually the same plant. Back when the wild beet, a beachfront weed, was being domesticated, the Greeks set about to create a plant with thicker leaf stalks (petioles) that became Swiss chard, while the Romans developed its root and turned it into the beet we now know.

off at the base, it keeps producing throughout the summer until the ground freezes solid. You can likewise harvest beet greens for the table.

Both Swiss chard and beets are biennials and normally produce only foliage the first year. Where they overwinter (usually Zones 8 to 11), you can leave them in the ground for some spring color, but the show is over when the first flower heads appear.

Good Neighbors

The decorative chards are at their most beautiful with sunlight glowing through their large, crinkled leaves. Plants of a more delicate habit, such as annual phlox (*Phlox drummondii*), love-in-a-mist (*Nigella damascena*), and nasturtium (*Tropaeolum majus*), are effective companions.

Problems and Solutions

Leaf diseases are possible, especially in soggy soil or when the soil is dry but the air is humid late in the season. To prevent these diseases, grow in well-drained soil but water regularly during dry periods. Hand-pick caterpillars. Remove and destroy foliage infested with leafminers, which produce winding tunnels under the leaf surface. (See "Annual Pests" on page 34.)

Top Performer

Beta vulgaris cicla (Swiss chard): Prized for its large, usually crinkled leaves and its thick, colorful petioles (leafstalks). Until recently, red and white forms dominated the market, but there's now a whole range of Easter-egg colors. Height: 9 to 18 inches (23 to 45 cm). Spread: 12 to 18 inches (30 to 45 cm).

More Recommended Beta

Beta vulgaris crassa (ornamental beet, ornamental beetroot): Some spectacular, very dark red-leaved cultivars of garden beet are now available: 'Bloody Mary' and 'Bull's Blood' are two. They make exceptional border plants, yet are just as edible as any other beet. Of course, digging up the roots entirely destroys the show, so don't plan on harvesting early beets if you want season-long color! Height: 9 inches (23 cm). Spread: 1 foot (30 cm).

Swiss chard
(*Beta vulgaris cicla*)

Smart Substitutes

Ornamental beets aren't the only edible plants that can add a touch of purple to the flower garden. Basil (*Ocimum basilicum*), the popular aromatic herb, also offers a wide range of purple-leaved cultivars. There are well over a dozen cultivars; just take your pick! Sow indoors and don't place the plants outdoors until the air has warmed up. Or sow seed in pots in fall for winter color indoors—and for a supply of fresh basil for cooking. Height: 6 to 24 inches (15 to 60 cm). Spread: 1 foot (30 cm).

Brassica

Ornamental cabbage, ornamental kale

Common as cabbage may be as a vegetable, it has also produced some very attractive selections that make excellent ornamentals. Although they are sometimes called "flowering" cabbage, it's not the second-year flowers you'll grow them for but rather their foliage. After a summer of growing as a rather typical cabbage or kale with green to blue-green leaves, the center of the plant begins a radical color change to white, pink, or red as soon as the nights become cool in the fall. The color lasts until the plants disappear under the snow, or even right through winter.

Plant Profile

BRASSICA
BRASS-ih-kuh

- **Foliage Color:** Pink, red, white

- **Foliage Time:** Early to late fall; right through winter in some climates

- **Height:** 10 to 14 inches (25 to 35 cm)

- **Spread:** 12 to 18 inches (30 to 45 cm)

- **Garden Uses:** Container planting, cut-flower garden, edging, mixed border, specimen plant

- **Light Preference:** Full sun to partial shade

- **Soil Preference:** Humus-rich, well-drained soil; prefers neutral to alkaline soil

- **Best Way to Propagate:** Varies by climate; see "Growing Tips"

- **Hardiness:** Hardy biennial grown as a half-hardy annual

Growing Tips

The important thing to realize is that ornamental cabbages and kales *aren't* ornamental, not until fall. You, therefore, have to consider how to grow them so they won't detract from the appearance of your garden during their ugly-duckling phase, yet still instantly become stars when frost kills off everything else.

The easiest way to do this is to buy plants in full "bloom" (coloration) in the fall and simply plug them into empty spaces left by frosted annuals. Alternatively, start your own plants in spring but grow them in pots in an out-of-the-way spot. Keep moving them into larger pots, until they are in 8-inch (20-cm) pots by August; then plug them into the garden when you need them. Another possibility is simply growing them outdoors where you want them but hiding them behind frost-sensitive plants. They need to be checked regularly for caterpillar damage (or you won't have much of a show).

In short-season areas, start ornamental cabbage and kale indoors in spring, 4 to 6 weeks before the last frost date. Plant it out when all danger of frost has passed, or outdoors a week or so before the last frost. Elsewhere, sow indoors or out in mid-summer. (In mild climates where summers are too hot for cabbage seedlings, it's best to wait until September to sow, although this

FUN FACTS

Ornamental cabbage and kale are both edible, although sometimes a bit tougher than the cabbage you may be used to. The colored leaves work great as decorative elements for edging salads or even as small serving plates. Or cut the head off the top of a flowering cabbage and use it as an unusual indoor Thanksgiving decoration.

will result in plants that won't color up until the winter.) A sowing depth of ¼ inch (6 mm) is fine. Germination takes only 4 or 5 days at warm temperatures but will also occur, slowly but surely, at temperatures down to 45°F (7°C). Keep the sprouts cool if possible—they hate the heat. Thin regularly or plant when the leaves begin to touch each other.

Ornamental cabbages and kales grow best in full sun, although they appreciate some afternoon shade in hot summer areas. Mulching can help keep them cool in hot weather.

Where winters are mild, ornamental cabbages and kales overwinter and produce tall, branching stems of yellow flowers mixed with the colored leaves: definitely more odd than beautiful.

Ornamental kale
(*Brassica oleracea acephala*)

Good Neighbors

Spot ornamental cabbages and kales within beds of evergreen groundcovers for seasonal interest. They also combine well with ornamental grasses, which will soften their stiff form and brilliant foliage. In containers, replace tired summer annuals with ornamental cabbages and kales for a colorful display that will last into winter.

Problems and Solutions

Any insect or disease that attacks regular cabbage will also love the ornamental type: That means all kinds of leaf spots and rots, plus caterpillars, root maggots, and aphids. You can avoid most problems, though, by planting in a different spot each year and by spreading them throughout the garden rather than massing them.

Top Performer

Brassica oleracea capitata (ornamental cabbage, flowering cabbage) and *B. oleracea acephala* (ornamental kale, flowering kale): Both of these plants come from the same wild species and need exactly the same care. If you really want to tell them apart, ornamental cabbage has wavy but entire leaves and forms a dense head; when in flower, it looks a lot like a giant rose. Ornamental kale has loose, deeply cut or fringed leaves and forms no head.

Smart Substitutes

If you're into bold foliage plants, another good choice is cardoon (*Cynara cardunculus*). It has spectacular silvery, deeply cut foliage that really wakes up a dull border or container. In Zone 7 and warmer, it produces fuzzy, purple artichoke-like flowers on tall stems the second summer, then usually dies; elsewhere, it generally doesn't overwinter. Height: 2 to 6 feet (60 to 180 cm). Spread: 4 feet (1.2 m). Or try green-and-silver Our Lady's thistle (*Silybum marianum*), of a similar size but much spinier.

Capsicum

Ornamental pepper, chili pepper, Christmas pepper

One of the rare annuals with truly attractive fruits, ornamental pepper is a startlingly beautiful plant, yet all too often relegated to the vegetable garden. It's a shrubby plant with simple, mid-green leaves (deep purple or variegated purple-and-white on some cultivars) and small, pendant, star-shaped flowers that are usually white, but sometimes purple. The flowers are followed by fruits, which start out green and pass through several colors before maturing to their final shade of red, orange, yellow, purple, or chocolate brown.

Plant Profile

CAPSICUM
KAP-sih-kum

■ **Bloom Color:** Purple or white

■ **Fruit Color:** Chocolate brown, purple, red, orange, yellow

■ **Foliage Color:** Green, purple, variegated

■ **Fruiting Time:** Summer

■ **Height:** 8 to 30 inches (20 to 75 cm)

■ **Spread:** 8 to 15 inches (20 to 38 cm)

■ **Garden Uses:** Container planting, edging, mass planting, herb garden, mixed border, rock garden

■ **Light Preference:** Full sun

■ **Soil Preference:** Humus-rich, evenly moist but well-drained soil

■ **Best Way to Propagate:** Sow seed indoors in spring

■ **Hardiness:** Tender annual or short-lived perennial grown as a tender annual

Growing Tips

You can buy nursery transplants of ornamental peppers, although they're usually sold in individual pots, making them expensive. One solution is to buy flats of any small-fruited hot pepper and grow them as ornamentals. On the other hand, it's not difficult to grow your own transplants.

Start the seed indoors 6 to 8 weeks before the last frost date (10 to 12 weeks in areas with a short growing season). Plant the seed about ¼ inch (6 mm) deep and expose it to temperatures between 65° and 95°F (18° and 35°C). Germination takes 10 to 15 days. Pinch once or twice for fuller plants.

Plant out not only when all danger of frost is over but also when the soil and air have thoroughly warmed up. Unpinched plants may need to be staked. Maintenance simply involves watering them during periods of drought.

You can bring plants indoors in the fall to enjoy in pots, but fruiting plants of many varieties tend to be already near the end of their useful life and probably won't make it through the winter, although you may have luck if you provide really strong light. Instead, for "Christmas peppers" (any ornamental pepper grown for holiday color), sow seed in pots in early August. With no bees, getting fruits to form indoors will take an extra effort: Either shake the plants when they are in bloom or spray the flowers with water to encourage pollination.

FUN FACTS

Ornamental peppers are so hot that you should wear gloves when you harvest them so you don't burn your fingers. The heat comes from capsaicin, found in the fruits and seeds. It is especially concentrated in peppers grown in hot summer areas.

Good Neighbors

Bright pepper fruits make a handsome contrast to dark foliage, such as the deep purple leaves of 'Blackie' sweet potato pine (*Ipomoea batatas* 'Blackie'). And don't forget them when collecting cut flowers; they can make an exciting addition to any hot-hued arrangement.

Problems and Solutions

Leaf diseases and wilts are possible, especially in overly wet or excessively dry soils. Try rotating planting sites and using mulch, plus regular watering during times of drought, to prevent them. And use disease-resistant varieties. Control spider mites and aphids, both mostly problems indoors, with regular sprays of insecticidal soap.

Top Performer

Capsicum annuum (ornamental pepper, chili pepper, hot pepper, Christmas pepper): Botanically, there is no difference between a sweet pepper and a hot one—although your tongue can instantly tell the difference! Both are derived from *C. annuum*. Ornamental peppers are simply decorative cultivars of the edible pepper, almost always from the hot side of the family. The decorative cultivars tend to have many small fruits that are held upright, while most "strictly edible" peppers have larger, downward-hanging fruits. Ornamental peppers are still edible, though; just leave enough fruits on the plant for them to remain attractive! Some of the most decorative varieties include 'Black Prince', 'Fiesta', 'Poinsettia', and 'Varengata'. Height: 8 to 30 inches (20 to 75 cm). Spread: 8 to 15 inches (20 to 38 cm).

More Recommended Capsicum

Capsicum frutescens (tabasco, hot pepper, chili pepper, goat pepper): This species is essentially identical to *C. annuum*, but all its cultivars are hot. The most obvious difference is that its greenish white, drooping flowers are held on upright stalks, while with former species, both the flowers and their stalks droop. *C. frutescens* is also somewhat woodier and more likely to be perennial than an annual in frost-free climates! 'Tabasco' and 'Thai Hot' peppers belong here. Height: 8 to 30 inches (20 to 75 cm). Spread: 8 to 15 inches (20 to 38 cm).

'Rio Grande Chili' ornamental pepper (*Capsicum annuum* 'Rio Grande Chili')

Kissing Cousins

Peppers have lots of relatives with potential as ornamentals, but only one other edible is commonly grown that way: eggplant or aubergine (*Solanum melongena*). The ornamental eggplant cultivar you're most likely to find is 'Easter Egg', with egg-shape and egg-size white fruits that turn yellow-orange when fully mature; another is the self-descriptive 'Red Egg'. Eggplant needs the same care as ornamental peppers but will grow outdoors *only* in areas with long, hot summers. Height: 18 to 36 inches (45 to 90 cm). Spread: 12 to 18 inches (30 to 45 cm).

Cordyline

Grass palm, dracaena, spike, cabbage tree

For well over 100 years, grass palm has been *the* centerpiece plant for containers and annual beds of all sorts. Look at any mixed container, and there it is, stretching its spiky green leaves skyward. The name "grass palm" is both way off and totally appropriate. Botanists will argue it is neither a grass nor a palm, but it *looks* like a combination of both. Young plants consist solely of long, narrow, sword-shaped leaves pointing up at first, then arching out and downward at the tips, creating a grassy, fountainlike effect. And, if you keep it for a few years, it will develop a trunk, like a palm.

Plant Profile

CORDYLINE
kor-dih-LINE-nee

■ **Foliage Color:** Green, purple, variegated

■ **Foliage Time:** Late spring through late fall; all year in mild climates

■ **Height:** 1 to 4 feet (30 to 120 cm)

■ **Spread:** 10 to 24 inches (25 to 60 cm)

■ **Garden Uses:** Container planting, specimen plant

■ **Light Preference:** Full sun to deep shade

■ **Soil Preference:** Average, well-drained soil

■ **Best Way to Propagate:** Root cuttings at any season

■ **Hardiness:** Frost-sensitive tree grown as a half-hardy annual

Growing Tips

By all means, buy nursery-grown plants! Grass palm is very slow growing from seed: You literally have to start 1 year in advance to have one of a worthwhile size by summer. Commercial growers produce so many plants that the price is reasonably low, and you rarely need more than a few anyway.

You insist on knowing how to grow it from seed? Sow it in July for use the *following* summer. Soak the hard seed for 24 to 48 hours in warm water, and then sow on the surface of the soil, as it needs light to germinate. It germinates best at warm temperatures—80° to 85°F (27° to 30°C)—and takes about 1 month to sprout. After germination, keep the seedlings slightly moist and brightly lit, planting into individual pots as needed.

Few plants are as indifferent to growing conditions as an established grass palm. Plant it out around last frost date in any well-drained soil—rich or poor, acid or alkaline. It is quite drought tolerant but will only *really* grow if watered regularly. Although grass palm prefers full sun or partial shade, it will look fine in dark, dense shade as well. Of course, the secret is that it won't *grow* much at all in dense shade; it will just sit there. But we don't expect much growth from this plant anyway.

Of the millions of grass palms sold yearly, nearly all are left outside to freeze to death in winter; but if you have the space, why not pot yours up and bring it inside for winter? Either grow it as a houseplant for winter, in bright light with typical houseplant care, or store it in a cold room, protected garage, or cool basement, without any water or light, and then haul it outside the following spring.

With time, grass palm will grow and lose its lower leaves (pull them off when they dry), revealing a thick, beige, ringed trunk, making it look very much like a palm. If your plant gets too big, you can cut off the top and root it or air layer it. The "stump" will produce new shoots. Or to produce new plants in larger quantities, cut off some of the thick roots, slice them into 2-inch (5-cm) sections, and use them as root cuttings. They're slow off the mark, but at least as fast as growing the plant from seed!

Outdoors, in Zones 10 and 11, mature specimens may flower, producing huge panicles of creamy white flowers followed by white or blue berries. Don't expect anything of the sort from container-grown plants, though.

'Variegatus' grass palm
(*Cordyline australis* 'Variegatus')

Good Neighbors

Positioned in the center of the container, grass palm will lend height and drama to any combination. Try it with several colors of 'Wave' petunias, a mixed planting of lantana (*Lantana camara*) and edging lobelia (*Lobelia erinus*), or any other potted partnership.

Problems and Solutions

Spider mites, mealy bugs, and scale can attack indoor plants, causing weak growth and discolored foliage. Treat with insecticidal soap.

Top Performer

Cordyline australis (grass palm, dracaena, spike, spike grass, cabbage tree, cabbage palm): Also called *Dracaena australis*. This is the only species commonly grown as an "annual." *C. australis purpurea*, with reddish purple leaves, is an interesting variety that comes true from seed. Height: 1 to 4 feet (30 to 120 cm). Spread: 10 to 24 inches (25 to 60 cm).

More Recommended Cordyline

Cordyline indivisa (blue dracaena): Also called *Dracaena indivisa*. Unlike the medium to dark green leaves of *C. australis*, this one has blue-green foliage. Although many seed companies list seed of *C. indivisa*, seeds and plants sold under this name are almost always *C. australis*. Height: 1 to 4 feet (30 to 120 cm). Spread: 10 to 24 inches (25 to 60 cm).

Kissing Cousins

A "new" plant rapidly catching on for containers and gardens is New Zealand flax, which can be either *Phormium tenax* or *Phormium colensoi* or a hybrid between the two. It's a striking, grasslike plant with broad, sword-shaped leaves. The species, which can attain 8 to 15 feet (2.4 to 4.5 m) high, are rarely grown; but dwarf types, 1 to 3 feet (30 to 90 cm) tall, are popular. Some have green leaves, but most are purple-leaved or are striped in red, gold, white, or pink. North of Zones 9 to 11, bring them indoors for the winter.

Euphorbia

Snow-on-the-mountain, annual euphorbia, annual poinsettia

The only two annual euphorbias you're likely to find in seed catalogs were once widely grown, but they seem to be having a hard time making themselves known in modern times. They are particularly easy-to-grow plants, sprouting readily from seed and forming large, shrubby plants. The two plants described here look little alike, but they share one characteristic that's common to euphorbias in general: colorful leaves or bracts that change color at flowering time and serve to attract insects to the insignificant flowers.

Plant Profile

EUPHORBIA
you-FOR-bee-uh

- **Foliage Color:** Varies by species; see individual listings
- **Foliage Time:** Late spring to frost; fall through winter in mild climates
- **Height:** 1 to 3 feet (30 to 90 cm)
- **Spread:** 1 foot (30 cm)
- **Garden Uses:** Container planting, cut-flower garden, annual hedge, mass planting, meadow garden, mixed border, specimen plant
- **Light Preference:** Full sun to partial shade
- **Soil Preference:** Average to poor, well-drained soil
- **Best Way to Propagate:** Sow seed indoors or outdoors in spring
- **Hardiness:** Hardy annual

Growing Tips

You'll almost never find plants of annual euphorbias for sale. Fortunately, they're a snap to grow from seed.

Since annual euphorbias tend to color up late in the season, starting them indoors can be useful because it will give you a few weeks' head start. Sowing them 6 to 8 weeks before the last frost gives plants young enough to still transplant well (adults don't like being moved), yet not far from starting to color up. Sow the seed ¼ inch (6 mm) deep and place the tray in a warm spot: 70° to 75°F (21° to 24°C). Germination takes 1 to 3 weeks. Set the plants out at about the last frost date; they're quite cold tolerant.

Follow the same instructions for outdoor sowing, starting 2 to 3 weeks before the last frost. Then thin or move surplus plants to about 1 foot (30 cm) apart.

Annual euphorbias perform as well in hot, humid summers as in cool ones, though the stems are often more solid in the latter case. They are drought tolerant but still prefer even moisture. They'll grow in any kind of soil, even sandy or gravelly ones. In very rich soil, though, they grow larger than usual, with weaker stems that inevitably require staking.

Think Twice: Both euphorbias described here self-sow readily and can even become a bit invasive. They are fortunately easy to recognize even as young plants; pull out or transplant wayward ones promptly. **Self-sowing**

Don't neglect annual euphorbias when you gather material for arrangements: They're long-lasting and attractive. To help keep their milky sap from clouding up the water, sear the stems ends over a match flame or plunge them into boiling water until they stop "bleeding."

Warning: Euphorbias produce sticky, white latex that is bitter tasting and often caustic. Always wear gloves when you work with them because the sap can cause severe irritation if it gets into your eyes or in an open wound.

Good Neighbors

The showy foliage of annual euphorbias adds interest among drifts of colorful annuals or perennials such as black-eyed Susan (*Rudbeckia hirta*) and dark-leaved Joseph's coat (*Alternanthera ficoidea*). They make great fillers for gaps left by bleeding hearts (*Dicentra spectabilis*) or Virginia bluebells (*Mertensia pulmonarioides*) when these early bloomers go dormant.

Problems and Solutions

Euphorbias are generally problem free.

Top Performer

Euphorbia marginata (snow-on-the-mountain, ghost weed): This shrubby plant is upright at first, then becomes branching as it starts to color up. At first, the oval, smooth-edged leaves are entirely green, but they become more variegated toward the top of the plant. By mid- to late summer, clusters of white "flowers" appear. In fact, the true flowers are the tiny greenish growths in the center; the four rounded, white to greenish white "petals" that surround them are actually bracts. Height: 1 to 3 feet (30 to 90 cm). Spread: 1 foot (30 cm).

More Recommended Euphorbia

Euphorbia heterophylla (annual poinsettia, fire-on-the-mountain, painted leaf): May also be sold as *E. cyathophora*. This annual euphorbia (sometimes perennial in Zones 9 to 11) looks much like the popular Christmas poinsettia (*E. pulcherrima*), although less massive. The deeply lobed, dark green leaves resemble oak leaves. At flowering time, the base of the center leaves turns scarlet-red, forming a circle around the yellow-green true flowers. A cutting-grown selection with broad cream borders on green leaves and peach bracts is available under the name 'Yokoi's White' or 'Summer Sunset'. Height: 1 to 3 feet (30 to 90 cm). Spread: 1 foot (30 cm).

Snow-on-the-mountain
(*Euphorbia marginata*)

Larry's Garden Notes

Think Twice: Mole plant or caper spurge (*Euphorbia lathyrus*) is actually a biennial (Zones 6 to 11) grown as an annual where it is not hardy. Unscrupulous salespeople claim it drives moles from the garden, but don't believe that. It is, in fact, a pernicious weed of little ornamental value. The long, narrow leaves growing in a strictly symmetrical pattern are, at best, intriguing, while the olive-green bracts and tiny flowers are not terribly exciting. The sap is not just caustic, but violently purgative, as are the seeds. I suggest skipping this one! Self-sowing

Hibiscus

Coppertone mallow

The word "hibiscus" brings to mind huge, saucer-shaped blooms, so it's strange to think of a hibiscus you'll grow just for its foliage. That is certainly the case here, however! Coppertone mallow (*Hibiscus acetosella* 'Coppertone') is a tender perennial but looks more like a shrub, with semiwoody branches that arch out from a woody base. The shiny, deep maroon-purple leaves are deeply cut into three to five lobes, much like maple leaves. The plant *does* produce flowers, but very late in the season, so much so it doesn't have time to bloom in short-season climates.

Plant Profile

HIBISCUS
hy-BISS-kus

■ **Foliage Color:** Maroon-purple

■ **Foliage Time:** Late spring through early fall; year long in mild climates

■ **Height:** 2 to 5 feet (60 to 150 cm)

■ **Spread:** 3 feet (90 cm)

■ **Garden Uses:** Container planting, annual hedge, mass planting, mixed border, specimen plant, screening

■ **Light Preference:** Full sun to shade

■ **Soil Preference:** Humus-rich, evenly moist but well-drained soil

■ **Best Way to Propagate:** Sow seed indoors in spring; take stem cuttings at any season

■ **Hardiness:** Frost-sensitive perennial grown as a half-hardy annual

Growing Tips

For some reason, few retail nurseries offer coppertone mallow. Some mail-order sources sell individual plants, which is an option if you want only one or two but an expensive way to go if you need more than that. Likewise, only a few mail-order sources offer seed, which is unfortunate because they are certainly easy enough to grow.

A fairly long head start—sown indoors 8 to 10 weeks before the last frost date—is best, especially in short-season areas. Chip the hard seed before sowing or soak it overnight in tepid water. Press it into the surface of the soil (do not cover); then place in warm temperatures: 70° to 80°F (21° to 27°C). Germination can be a bit irregular, taking from 10 to 30 days. Wait until both the air and soil have thoroughly warmed up, usually 2 to 3 weeks after the last frost date, before setting out the seedlings.

If you live where coppertone mallow is perennial (Zones 10 and 11, plus the warmer parts of Zone 9), you could instead try sowing the seed outside. Start it in midsummer with the idea of using the plants as perennials the following year. Keep the seedlings moist at all times.

Full-sun sites produce the best leaf color. Mulching will help keep the soil evenly moist, but you'll probably still need to water occasionally during periods of hot weather or drought to keep the soil slightly moist at all times. Pinch transplants once to stimulate better branching. It's possible to clip the plants into hedges or geometric shapes, but they will naturally develop a pleasing bushy form if they get light from all sides.

Coppertone mallow makes an interesting indoor plant for winter because the foliage keeps its rich color (though it's somewhat less intense than when it's outdoors). Plus, even gardeners in short-season areas will get to see the flowers this way. (It takes about 10 months for the blooms to form after being sown the first year, and even plants grown from cuttings rarely bloom before November.)

Where coppertone mallow is hardy, it will often die back to the ground in winter. If it doesn't die down, prune it back harshly, nearly to the base of the plant, in early spring. Do the same thing with potted plants grown indoors for the winter.

Besides growing from seed, this plant is also easy to multiply by stem cuttings.

Good Neighbors

The tall form and purple foliage of this hibiscus plant make it a striking vertical accent and provide a dark background that makes brighter colors glow. For a handsome contrast, pair coppertone mallow with a variegated grass or silvery cardoon (*Cynara cardunculus*). Gardeners in subtropical and tropical climates can grow these plants as a low hedge.

Problems and Solutions

Caterpillars and Japanese beetles can chew holes in foliage: Handpicking is one solution. Watch out for discolored foliage, caused by aphids and thrips outdoors and whiteflies and mealy bugs on indoor plants; control them with insecticidal soap.

Top Performer

Hibiscus acetosella 'Coppertone' (coppertone mallow): Also called *H. acetosella* 'Red Shield' and *H. eetveldeanus*. This is the most common cultivar and generally comes true from seed, at least as far as foliage color is concerned. (The leaves can be rounded on some plants and more deeply cut on others.) The 2½-inch (6.5-cm) flowers are a deep purple-red, a color so close to the color of the foliage that they really don't stand out. The original species has green leaves that are only lightly flushed with red, and more-visible flowers that are either yellow with a red eye or red; it's rarely cultivated.

'Coppertone' mallow
(*Hibiscus acetosella* 'Coppertone')

Larry's Garden Notes

Think Twice: Want a red-leaved plant that you can sow directly outdoors? Red orach (*Atriplex hortensis* var. *rubra*) has medium red, arrow-shaped leaves that are very attractive. Pinch regularly to keep this plant nice and bushy. Sow seed directly outdoors in early spring, or in fall for a winter crop in mild climates. It often self-sows a bit too enthusiastically, though. Height: 1 to 4 feet (30 to 120 cm). Spread: 1 foot (30 cm). Self-sowing

Hypoestes

Polka-dot plant, freckle face

This charming little plant has only recently made the transition from being strictly grown as a houseplant to gaining popularity as a bedding plant—and it's about time! Of course, it isn't for the thin spikes of lavender to pink flowers that gardeners grow the polka-dot plant. Instead, the attraction comes from the numerous ovate, dark green leaves that are dotted with tiny translucent spots of white, pink, or red, as if a painter had flicked a brush over them. It's a very unusual form of variegation and, therefore, highly prized. This is certainly a plant to discover if you have shade!

Plant Profile

HYPOESTES
hy-poe-ES-tees

■ **Foliage Color:** Green to purple with white, pink, or red spots

■ **Foliage Time:** Late spring until frost; all year in mild climates

■ **Height:** 10 to 22 inches (25 to 56 cm)

■ **Spread:** 8 to 14 inches (20 to 35 cm)

■ **Garden Uses:** Container planting, edging, hanging baskets, groundcover, mass planting, mixed border, rock garden

■ **Light Preference:** Partial shade to deep shade

■ **Soil Preference:** Humus-rich, evenly moist but well-drained soil

■ **Best Way to Propagate:** Sow seed indoors in spring; take stem cuttings at any season

■ **Hardiness:** Frost-sensitive perennial grown as a tender annual

Growing Tips

Once a rarity in outdoor gardens, polka-dot plant has become so popular that most nurseries now offer it in trays and cell packs at planting-out season. And if your nursery doesn't sell them with the other annuals yet, you can still raid its houseplant department! On the other hand, if you want to have enough for a mass planting, it's probably cheapest to grow your own from seed. Fortunately, that's not a hard thing to do.

Outdoor sowing is an option only in the very mildest climates. In most areas, sow seed indoors 10 to 12 weeks before the last frost date, lightly covering it. It germinates in 10 to 14 days at 70° to 75°F (21° to 24°C). Pinch the young plants to stimulate branching, and thin or plant them as needed.

Wait until all danger of frost has passed and the ground has thoroughly warmed up before setting out your polka-dot plants. They prefer steady soil moisture and protection from strong sun and drying winds. Summer maintenance simply consists of watering them as needed and possibly trimming off the flowerstalks, which tend to appear in greater and greater numbers as the summer advances. On the other hand, you only have to remove them if you really dislike their appearance because blooming and setting seed seems in no way to harm the plant or lessen its impact.

Some of the taller-growing, old-fashioned cultivars benefit from an occasional pinching to encourage them to fill in. Most modern types are already nicely compact and have little need for pruning except to eliminate the occasional wayward stem. If you're using polka-dot plant as a shady-site groundcover in a frost-free climate and the plants get taller than you want, prune them back to about

2 inches (5 cm) from the ground, and they'll resprout from the base.

The first fall frost spells the end of the polka-dot plant, although it will grow on for years in areas free of frost. Before it freezes, though, you could either dig up a plant or two or take some cuttings for indoor growing. Or grow some all summer in containers so they'll be easy to bring inside. Although the plants need some shade outdoors, bright light is essential in keeping them happy in the home. And even the dwarf types tend to grow lankier indoors, so be prepared to pinch them back a bit. Overwintered plants can provide innumerable cuttings for the following summer's garden.

Good Neighbors

Best when planted in large groups, polka-dot plant offers a nice alternative or partner to impatiens in the shade or semi-shade. It also combines well with other foliage plants such as ferns and beefsteak plant (*Iresine herbstii*). Sweet woodruff (*Galium odoratum*) can also make a companionable neighbor, producing white flowers in late spring but turning a pleasant green by the time polka-dot plants are reaching a good size.

Problems and Solutions

Powdery mildew can cause grayish patches on the leaves when the soil is dry and the nights are humid. Keeping the soil slightly moist at all times will help prevent this problem. Aphids can produce shoots that are distorted and sticky; knock them off with a blast of water if they appear.

Top Performer

Hypoestes phyllostachya (polka-dot plant, freckle face): Also called *H. sanguinolenta*. There are several hybrid strains of the polka-dot plant; all are short, compact plants 8 to 12 inches (20 to 30 cm) tall. The old-fashioned, tall-growing species is still available, too; it can reach up to 22 inches (56 cm) or more in height if you don't pinch it back regularly.

'Rose Splash' polka-dot plant (*Hypoestes phyllostachya* 'Rose Splash')

Larry's Garden Notes

What a change polka-dot plants have undergone in just the last few years! The originals were lanky plants that bore small leaves very lightly speckled with pink. Then came cultivar strains—such as 'Splash' and 'Confetti'—with much more compact plants, a wider color range, and much larger spots. The most recent compact strain, 'Splash Select', is so heavily splotched that almost the entire leaf is colored, with only a bit of green along the nerves. Any less green and the plant will have no chlorophyll left to carry out photosynthesis!

Iresine

Bloodleaf, beefsteak plant

Once a star of the Victorian garden, this old-fashioned favorite has been passed from gardener to gardener through the generations, primarily as a houseplant. Fortunately, times and tastes have changed, and it is currently receiving renewed attention as a summer foliage annual! Few plants are as colorful or as easy to grow. The stems are bloodred, and the leaves are either deep purplish red with cerise veins or mid-green with yellow veins. Talk about stunning!

Plant Profile

IRESINE
eye-ruh-SEYE-nee

- **Foliage Color:** Green, red, yellow

- **Foliage Time:** Late spring until frost; year-round in mild climates

- **Height:** 1 to 3 feet (30 to 90 cm)

- **Spread:** 1 to 3 feet (30 to 90 cm)

- **Garden Uses:** Container planting, hanging baskets, mass planting, mixed border, specimen plant

- **Light Preference:** Full sun to partial shade

- **Soil Preference:** Humus-rich, evenly moist but well-drained soil

- **Best Way to Propagate:** Take stem cuttings at any season

- **Hardiness:** Frost-sensitive perennial grown as a tender annual

Growing Tips

Nurseries are starting to sell bloodleaf as a container plant for the outdoor garden or as a houseplant, and that's a good thing; I've never seen seed for sale. You just have to go about multiplying bloodleaf the way generations have: by taking cuttings.

Bloodleaf is singularly easy to grow from cuttings. You can even root them in water, a technique I normally wouldn't recommend for other plants because of the high failure rate. You can root bloodleaf cuttings at any time of the year, although the two most popular seasons are late summer (when you'll be bringing plants back in for the winter) and late winter (when you'll be creating new plants for your summer garden). Take 6-inch (15-cm) cuttings and remove the lower leaves, then insert them in a growing mixture. No rooting hormone is necessary. Keep them moist and cover the container with a clear plastic bag or inverted wide-mouth jar if the air is dry. When new growth appears, a sign the cuttings are well rooted, remove the covering and grow them as adult plants.

Don't move the tender plants outdoors until spring temperatures have thoroughly warmed up and there is no longer any risk of frost. When temperatures no longer dip below 50°F (10°C) at night, it is probably safe to move them to the garden.

Plant out in rich, moist, well-drained soil, in full sun or partial shade. Deeper shade is fine too, but the brilliant leaf coloration will be diminished. Pinch or prune the plants regularly to keep them bushy. Water as needed to prevent the soil from drying out.

Of course, bloodleaf makes a superb houseplant for a brightly lit spot. Make sure you keep pinching and pruning it, though! It will become quite scrawny looking—barren at the base and with unequal branches—if allowed to grow totally on its own.

Good Neighbors

Bloodleaf makes an outstanding color accent among ferns and other foliage plants, particularly the silvery gray leaves of licorice plant (*Helichrysum petiolare*). *Iresine herbstii,* a soft-pink flowering maple (*Abutilon* hybrid), and twinspur (*Diascia* hybrid) make a great trio for a container.

Problems and Solutions

Powdery mildew can occur when bloodleaf is stressed by drought, especially toward the end of the summer. Keep the soil at least slightly moist and there should be no problem. Watch out, too, for spider mites and aphids, especially when bloodleaf is grown indoors. Control pests with insecticidal soap.

Bloodleaf
(*Iresine lindenii*)

Top Performer

Iresine herbstii (bloodleaf, beefsteak plant, chicken gizzard plant): You can instantly recognize this species by its curiously deformed leaves, which are puckered and deeply notched at the tip as if someone had taken a pinch out of them. This odd shape has given rise to the no-less-odd name "chicken gizzard plant," referring to the similarity between the leaf's shape and organ in question. The species itself is unknown in culture, but two cultivars are widely available: 'Brilliantissima', with purple-red leaves and shocking red-pink veins, and 'Aureoreticulata', with green leaves and yellow veins, plus red stems and petioles. Height: 1 to 3 feet (30 to 90 cm). Spread: 1 to 3 feet (30 to 90 cm).

More Recommended Iresine

Iresine lindenii (bloodleaf): Just like *I. herbstii,* but with leaves that end in a point rather than a notch. The species bears bloodred leaves with cerise-red veins, while 'Formosa' has green leaves with yellow veins and red petioles. Height: 1 to 3 feet (30 to 90 cm). Spread: 1 to 3 feet (30 to 90 cm).

Smart Substitute

Persian shield (*Strobilanthes dyerianus*) is another member of the houseplant world that has decided to make a new life for itself as an outdoor annual. And it's a knockout! The upright, branching stems bear elliptic, dark green leaves, up to 6 inches (15 cm) long, that are flushed purple with a beautiful silver overlay. No description can do them justice; they have to be seen to be believed! Care is as for bloodleaf. This plant positively *thrives* in hot, humid summers! Height: 4 feet (1.2 m). Spread: 3 feet (90 cm).

Senecio

Dusty miller

Generations of gardeners have grown and loved this handsome foliage plant. It's so easy and so trustworthy that it's hard not to succumb to its charm. The silvery leaves range from broad and spoonlike, only lightly cut toward the base, to deeply cut lobes, like a thick-fronded fern. The stems are silvery, too. The flowers, usually only seen the second year (if the plant overwinters, of course) are dirty yellow daisies; they're of little interest, and most gardeners remove them on sight. But for beautiful foliage that looks great with any companion, dusty miller truly is a must for every garden!

Plant Profile

SENECIO
seh-NEE-cee-oh

- **Foliage Color:** Silvery gray
- **Foliage Time:** Late spring until the first snows; year-round in mild climates
- **Height:** 8 to 24 inches (20 to 60 cm)
- **Spread:** 6 to 10 inches (15 to 25 cm)
- **Garden Uses:** Container planting, edging, mass planting, mixed border, rock garden
- **Light Preference:** Full sun to partial shade to deep shade
- **Soil Preference:** Rich to poor, very well-drained soil
- **Best Way to Propagate:** Sow seed indoors in late winter
- **Hardiness:** Half-hardy subshrub grown as a half-hardy annual

Growing Tips

Good news for those who prefer their annuals ready-to-plant: nursery transplants of dusty miller are widely available.

That said, you really don't know a plant unless you've grown it from seed at least once, so here's what you'll need to do. There is little point in starting this slow-grower outdoors, except in truly frost-free environments. Instead, sow it indoors 10 to 15 weeks before the last frost date. Do not cover the seed because it needs light to germinate. Place at temperatures of 65° to 75°F (18° to 24°C). Germination takes 10 to 15 days.

Dusty miller is one annual you can plant out early, 2 to 3 weeks *before* the last frost. Or you could wait and plant it out when you're putting in your other annuals.

Just about any type of soil will do, from rich and humusy to poor and stony, but good drainage is vital. Its silvery color is best in full sun or only partial shade, but if you only have shade, grow it anyway; it may not grow much, but it will look good all summer! Dusty miller is a perfect seashore plant (in fact, in the wild, it is native to Mediterranean seacoasts) and tolerates salt and strong winds with equal aplomb.

Summer care is minimal. In shady spots or if you have second-year plants, you might want to shear the plant back a bit for a fuller look. And even though dusty miller is highly drought tolerant, it will do best if watered regularly.

Don't be in a rush to pull this plant out in fall. For one thing, it breezes right through the first frosts and adds color to the garden and to containers right up until snowfall, even all winter where snow is rare. Plus, just maybe it will still be alive the following spring. It's only truly hardy in Zones 8 to 11, but sometimes it manages to pull through winter even into Zone 4, especially in very well-drained soil. If it does survive, prune it back harshly, and be prepared to remove its not-so-lovely flowers!

You could also pot up a few plants in early fall to enjoy indoors during the winter. Then use these to supply cuttings in February for the summer garden ahead.

Good Neighbors

Dusty miller shines as a neat edging plant for flowerbeds, but it is also very useful as a neutral transition between flowers of different colors. Combined with plants that have a touch of white in their flowers—such as 'Strata' mealy-cup sage (*Salvia farinacea* 'Strata') or 'KLM' nemesia (*Nemesia strumosa* 'KLM')—the transition becomes ultra-smooth.

Problems and Solutions

Nearly problem-free, although rot is a problem in wet soil (where you shouldn't be planting dusty miller anyway!).

Top Performer

Senecio cineraria (dusty miller): Also called *S. maritima*. This "silver-leaved" annual is the closest to true silver. The leaves, especially when grown in full sun, are so heavily covered in fuzzy white felt that they look icy gray! 'Silver Dust' is the most popular cultivar and is typical of the deeply lobed cultivars. 'Cirrus' is the most popular broad-leaved type, with leaves only slightly indented. Height: 8 to 24 inches (20 to 60 cm). Spread: 6 to 10 inches (15 to 25 cm).

More Recommended Dusty Millers

Senecio viravira (dusty miller): A much rarer species, with a open, lacy look, rather like an intensely silver-gray California poppy (*Eschscholzia californica*). You may have to order plants by mail, as seed is rarely offered. Height: 8 to 24 inches (20 to 60 cm). Spread: 6 to 10 inches (15 to 25 cm).

'Cirrus' dusty miller
(*Senecio cineraria* 'Cirrus')

Smart Substitutes

Gardeners tend to call any deeply lobed, low-growing, silvery plant "dusty miller," including a few hardy perennials. There are, however, two other "annual" dusty millers. Silver lace (*Tanacetum ptarmiciflorum*, also called *Pyrethrum ptarmiciflorum*) has finely cut, silvery-blue leaves and, if it blooms, little white daisies. The rarer *Centaurea seridis maritima* and its look-alike cousin *C. cineraria* are often confused with *Senecio cineraria*, but if your dusty millers produce *purple* flowers, they belong here. Height: 8 to 24 inches (20 to 60 cm). Spread: 6 to 10 inches (15 to 25 cm).

Solenostemon

Coleus, painted nettle

After a long absence from our gardens, this old-fashioned favorite is now very much back in style, and all I can say is "what took so long?" No other plant offers such a wide array of leaf colors: just about everything, in fact, but blue. Some leaves are all one color, while others have contrasting edges or veins, or V-shaped markings, and still others are simply splotched with various colors. Leaf sizes and shapes vary, too, from broadly oval to fringed, long and narrow, deeply cut, and even duckfoot! Two things all coleus share, though, are square stems and narrow spikes of lavender to white flowers.

Plant Profile

SOLENOSTEMON
so-leh-NOH-ste-mon

- **Foliage Color:** Beige, near black, brown, green, purple, salmon, red, orange, yellow, white

- **Foliage Time:** Late spring until frost; year-round in mild climates

- **Height:** 8 to 36 inches (20 to 90 cm)

- **Spread:** 8 to 36 inches (20 to 90 cm)

- **Garden Uses:** Container planting, edging, hanging baskets, groundcover, annual hedge, mass planting, mixed border, rock garden, specimen plant, screening

- **Light Preference:** Full sun to deep shade

- **Soil Preference:** Humus-rich, evenly moist but well-drained soil

- **Best Way to Propagate:** Sow seed indoors in spring; take stem cuttings in at any season

- **Hardiness:** Frost-sensitive perennial grown as a tender annual

Growing Tips

Seed-grown coleus were considered the coleus wave of the future from the 1970s until the late 1990s. Seed strains featured self-branching plants far more compact than the original, upright, often ungainly coleus known before that, and the colors were much clearer and more distinct. There was a whole new range of leaf shapes, as well, from lightly fringed to deeply cut. And the range of colors had been improved beyond belief. Could there be anything better?

The last few years have shown there could be indeed! The problem is that seed-grown strains inevitably flower abundantly (to produce lots of seed). But flowering is not a desirable trait: The spikes of tiny blooms aren't particularly attractive, and stems often deteriorate after blooming, leaving a gaping hole. That means you have to pinch out the flowers—an extra step busy gardeners can do without.

Recently, named cutting-grown cultivars that do not flower readily have become available, and they appear to be the new coleus wave of the future. They will bloom eventually, of course, but usually not until very late in the season when a decline would no longer be so noticeable. They are, of course, considerably more costly, but once you own them, you can take cuttings to your heart's content.

All of this means you have a variety of options for starting with coleus in spring, depending on your budget and your time:

- If you want fast results at only moderate expense with little effort at planting time, but with quite a bit of pinching off unwanted blooms later on, buy trays of plants in the spring.

- If you have a meager budget, some time on your hands, and don't mind pinching, start your own coleus from seed. It's best to sow the seeds indoors, 8 to 12 weeks before the last frost date. (Sow outdoors only in Zones 9 to 11). Don't cover the seed because it needs light to germinate. It sprouts in 10 to 20 days at 65° to 75°F (18° to 24°C).

- If you have lots of cash and want the latest hybrids, none of which need much pinching, buy cutting-grown plants in whatever quantity you need.

- Finally, if you love the spectacular appearance and low care of the latest hybrids but are on a limited budget, buy one or two cutting-grown plants and multiply them like crazy. Cuttings root in just 3 to 5 days and are ready for the garden in 2 weeks.

Coleus
(*Solenostemon scutellarioides*)

Plant coleus outdoors only when the soil and air have warmed up. Water as needed to keep the soil evenly moist; coleus are *not* drought tolerant. They still have a reputation for needing partial to deep shade, but there are now sun-resistant cultivars, often sold as "sun coleus." In general, dark-leaved plants tolerate full sun, whereas paler shades—and especially the yellow-leaved selections—burn if they're not shaded.

Coleus are tropical plants and will overwinter only in Zones 10 and 11. Elsewhere, you must bring the plants in for winter or take cuttings in early fall.

Good Neighbors

Invaluable for container plantings, the foliage colors of coleus provide a strong middle ground against which a wide range of companions can shine. Dark red and chartreuse cultivars are particularly useful as foliage accents in the garden, allowing the eye to take a rest from vibrant flower colors.

Problems and Solutions

Coleus is generally problem-free outdoors but can be subject to mealy bugs, scale insects, and whiteflies indoors. Treat with insecticidal soap.

Top Performer

Solenostemon scutellarioides (coleus, painted nettle, flame nettle): See description above. There are hundreds of cultivars: Take your pick!

Kissing Cousins

Think Twice: Beefsteak plant (*Perilla frutescens*), also called Chinese basil or shiso, looks much like coleus but comes in a much more limited range of colors. 'Atropurpurea' has deep purple leaves only lightly toothed along the edges; *P. frutescens* var. *crispa* is the same color but has frilled leaf edges. Grow beefsteak plant as you would coleus. Deadheading is critical, though, because it self-sows to the point of weediness if you let it go to seed. Height: 8 to 36 inches (20 to 90 cm). Spread: 8 to 36 inches (20 to 90 cm). Self-sowing

Talinum

Jewels of Opar, fame flower

This annual is very hot among "gardeners in the know," yet is almost unknown otherwise. It starts off the season by producing shiny, mid-green, succulent leaves on spreading stems: a really stunning foliage effect. Then it develops hordes of upright flowerstalks branching into thin, hairlike segments each ending in a tiny flower bud. The actual flowers, cup-shaped and reddish pink, aren't all that impressive and each only lasts a day. However they are followed by perfectly round, pinkish red seed capsules that have the generosity to hang on for the rest of the summer, creating a frothy reddish haze over the crisp green leaves. What a show!

Plant Profile

TALINUM
ta-LINE-um

- **Bloom Color:** Pink, red, or yellow
- **Fruit Color:** Pinkish red
- **Foliage Time:** Summer through early fall
- **Height:** 1 to 2 feet (30 to 60 cm)
- **Spread:** 1 to 2 feet (30 to 60 cm)
- **Garden Uses:** Container planting, cut-flower garden, edging, groundcover, mass planting, mixed border
- **Light Preference:** Full sun
- **Soil Preference:** Average to poor, well-drained soil
- **Best Way to Propagate:** Sow seed indoors or outdoors in spring
- **Hardiness:** Frost-sensitive perennial grown as a half-hardy annual

Growing Tips

You're unlikely to find jewels of Opar for sale at your local nursery, so you'll probably need to get seeds or starter plants from a friend or buy them through a mail-order source.

In short-season climates, starting seed indoors is wise. Sow 6 to 8 weeks before the last frost date, barely covering the tiny black seed. It germinates at room temperatures in 2 to 3 weeks; give it as much light as possible. Wait until all risk of frost is over and both the soil and the air have thoroughly warmed up before setting out transplants.

Where summers are longer, roughly Zones 8 to 11, you can also sow jewels of Opar directly outside in early spring or a few weeks before the last frost date. It will germinate as soon as the temperature permits, usually late spring.

Plant jewels of Opar in full sun. It is totally indifferent to heat and, therefore, does perfectly well in the Deep South. It grows best in soil with poor to average fertility. Perfect drainage, however, is a must—it will not stand wet feet!

Summer care is almost non-existent. Jewels of Opar is extremely drought resistant, thanks to a thick, succulent, underground root that stores water in spring to release it as needed during summer. You won't need to worry about fertilizing or staking. And in most cases, you won't even have to bother with

FUN FACTS

Ever wonder where the name "jewels of Opar" came from? It is the title of an Edgar Rice Burroughs book featuring no-less prestigious a character than Tarzan. Whoever named this plant obviously chose to associate the jewel-like seed capsules of *Talinum* with the legendary jewels of the novel.

deadheading, since you'll want to enjoy the decorative seed capsules.

Of course, you might want to harvest some of the seed-producing stems for use in cut or dried arrangements. Fresh stems last up to 2 weeks in a vase. The seed capsules dry to a medium brown while keeping their shine, creating a charming effect.

 **Think Twice:** Jewels of Opar self-sows readily—in fact, sometimes a bit too much so. In areas with hot summers and mild winters, particularly, it can become out-and-out invasive. If you live in such a climate, you might prefer to remove the flowerstalks early and grow it strictly as a foliage plant. **Self-sowing**

To overwinter the plants indoors, either bring in potted specimens or take stem cuttings. It will behave as a perennial in Zones 10 and 11.

'Kingwood Gold' jewels of Opar (*Talinum paniculatum* 'Kingwood Gold')

Good Neighbors

Companions with lacy or narrow leaves, such as verbenas or moss roses (*Portulaca grandiflora*), make a handsome contrast to the broad, glossy foliage of jewels of Opar.

Problems and Solutions

Although usually trouble free, aphids sometimes can cause sticky, distorted growth. Control pests with a spray of water or insecticidal soap.

Top Performer

Talinum paniculatum (jewels of Opar, panicled fame flower): This is the most common species and usually has green leaves, but 'Variegatum', with cream-margined leaves, and 'Kingwood Gold', with golden leaves, are worth looking for. The former does not come true from seed, so you need to buy a plant and multiply it by cuttings; 'Kingwood Gold', on the contrary, is easy to grow from seed. Height: 1 to 2 feet (30 to 60 cm). Spread: 1 to 2 feet (30 to 60 cm).

More Recommended Talinum

Talinum calycinum (fame flower): Some seed catalogs offer this species, which is almost identical to *T. paniculatum,* although said to be smaller in size. Some seed sources seem to confuse the two. Height: 4 to 8 inches (10 to 20 cm). Spread: 1 to 2 feet (30 to 60 cm).

Larry's Garden Notes

Don't underestimate the value of jewels of Opar as a houseplant. It is very attractive both in foliage and in seed, and it's a snap to grow as well; just go easy on the watering, especially in winter. Cactus enthusiasts often grow this plant as a "caudiciform": They like to leave its thickened root partly exposed, then prune the plant and grow it very dry so its foliage is not too abundant, resulting in a twisted specimen very similar to a bonsai.

Flowering Annuals

FOR CONTAINERS & HANGING BASKETS

Container gardening is hot! From simple window boxes to sophisticated urns, from old-fashioned stone troughs to trendy wall pouches, there are containers everywhere, and I predict that this is only the beginning. After all, in this world of constant mobility, where you never know where that next career move will take you, it isn't always desirable to invest time and effort in a garden you may have to leave behind. And yards seem to be getting smaller and smaller, too. But containers solve both problems: If you move, just take the container with you! And who needs space when there are containers that will fit on the smallest windowsill?

◄ Ivy geranium is only one of the numerous annuals that, while they could easily grow in any garden, are decidedly at their best in containers!

When You're Hot . . .

The current container craze is great news for annuals. They had been languishing in the slow lane for many years while perennials shone on as the stars of our gardens. But perennials just don't have what it takes to be ideal container plants; they tend to be slow to fill in, and their bloom is too unreliable. When a perennial isn't looking its best in a mixed border, it can count on having a neighbor to cover for it. In a pot, though, any little bit of downtime will look like a glaring error. So you need plants that grow quickly, fill in gaps almost overnight, and bloom nonstop. And there's only one group of plants that can fill that role: annuals.

Annuals seem made for container culture. They're widely available, they're a snap to plant, they're fast off the mark, and they bloom through the entire summer and usually well into fall with only basic care. You can throw together a container garden of annuals a week before the garden club comes visiting and make it look like you'd been growing it for years—they're that fast!

The Best Container Annuals

Most annuals make great container plants, but some are greater than others. The 11 plants in this chapter are so superb in containers that most are grown almost exclusively that way. And you'll find even more "unbeatable" container plants in the list on page 307. There's a little secret to their success: Most of the very best container "annuals" aren't true annuals at all but rather tender perennials or shrubs. Used to a long growing season, they just

The containers you use can make as much of a statement as the plants you choose. Learn to be daring, and don't be afraid to splurge on a fabulous pot or tub every once in a while.

breeze right through summer as if expecting that it will never end. Most will be stopped only by frost in fall: Now *that's* blooming power!

There are a few things to look out for in a container annual, of course. Nonstop bloom is an obvious trait, or failing that, attractive foliage. Since containers look best when on the crowded side, you'll also want to pick plants that can take competition. And fast growth is ideal: Who wants to wait months for results? Some drought resistance is appreciated because it can get mighty dry in pots. The final factor is tolerance of average growing conditions. Container residents need to share their root space with each other, so you really don't want to include picky plants with needs that you'll have a hard time meeting.

Mix and Match

Most containers include a combination of different plants—just like a regular garden, but in miniature. And just as you would in a regular garden, you'll get the best effect if you put some thought into combining plants with different heights and habits. Start with a taller,

more upright plant for use as an accent, usually placing it right in the middle of the pot. That way the container will look equally good from all sides. Around it, in larger containers especially, you'll probably use filler plants (bushy plants of medium height). These are often regular garden annuals, such as begonias, impatiens, and geraniums. Surround these fillers with edging plants: extra-dwarf, dense plants that spread enough to cover pot edges. Then, to add a bit of zing, tuck in a few trailing plants: annuals that grow outward and downward rather than strictly upward. If your pot is not particularly interesting, use lots of trailers. If the pot is a decorative one, use trailers in moderation so you can still enjoy its appearance.

In medium-size containers—1 foot (30 cm) or less in diameter—you may not have enough space for all four types of plants. In this case, go straight from the central accent plant to edging plants and then trailers; skip the filler plants.

Long, narrow containers, such as a window box or deck-railing planter, take a slightly different approach. You'll rarely be able to turn them, so give them a distinct front and back. The accent plant can still go in the middle, but toward the back, with filler plants on either side, or you can skip the accent plant and use medium-height filler plants as accent material. Complete the effect with edging plants toward the front and the extremities of the pot, adding a few trailers here and there. It'll look great!

Swinging Singles

Mixed container gardens are only one possibility. If you have smaller containers that can hold only one plant each, or if you're using large plants that don't leave much room for companions, you can combine individual potted plants to compose great-looking container gardens. The same design guidelines apply here: pots of tall plants to the back, lower ones to the front, and filler pots tucked in here and there.

Another possibility is to underplant large container specimens with a few edging or trailing plants—just enough to cover the soil and soften the edge of the pot.

Happy Trails

You'll notice that many of the plants in this chapter have trailing habits. In other chapters, you'll find plenty of annuals that make great accent, filler, and edging plants. The trailing plants, however, really have nowhere else to go but containers. In gardens, they tend to sprawl beyond their limits, and who wants to spend summer pruning back invading annuals? On the other hand, few other annuals will not only spread outward, covering pot edges, but also downward, partly hiding pot sides. Underappreciated in flowerbeds, the weak, floppy stems of trailers suddenly make them stars in containers. And that is doubly true for hanging baskets: The only kind of plant that truly does look good in a basket is a trailer.

Container Care

For the best effect in a mixed container, really jam it full of plants. You'll want them to mingle, so they don't leave any bare spots. The crowded conditions and increased exposure to drying sun and wind that naturally come from raising a plant above ground level, however, mean that container plants will need care beyond what you would give other plants. In cool weather, they'll dry out quickly enough to need water every few days. In hot, dry, or windy weather, where plants lose more water to evaporation than they need to grow, you'll probably need to water daily, or even twice a day if your containers are exposed to full, blazing sun or are placed on hot spots, such as a driveway, concrete patio, or brick sidewalk. And all that watering plus the crowded conditions means that container plants need more fertilizing than the same annuals in the garden. Slow release organic fertilizer should do the trick.

15 More Flowering Container Plants

Of course, you can grow just about every annual in containers, so your choices are nearly unlimited. However, if you're looking for long-blooming, weather-resistant annuals, the following have a particularly good reputation as being great container annuals.

Abutilon

Flowering maple

A popular houseplant during the Victorian era (they called it "parlor maple"), this ever-bloomer is back in style again, offering its beautiful leaves and even more striking flowers to a whole new generation. This tropical shrub is easy enough to recognize: It has maplelike leaves and big, bell-shaped, nodding flowers. It is not related to true maples (*Acer* spp.), but as the flowers reveal, it's a close relative of hibiscus, even down to the column combining the anthers and stigma right in the flower's center. It blooms indoors, it blooms outdoors—you just can't stop this incredible plant!

Plant Profile

ABUTILON
uh-BEW-tih-lon

- **Bloom Color:** Varies by species; see individual listings

- **Bloom Time:** Summer through fall; all year in mild climates

- **Height:** Varies by species; see individual listings

- **Spread:** Varies by species; see individual listings

- **Garden Uses:** Container planting, hanging baskets, groundcover, annual hedge, mass planting, mixed border, rock garden, specimen plant, screening; on a standard

- **Attracts:** Hummingbirds

- **Light Preference:** Full sun to partial shade

- **Soil Preference:** Average, well-drained soil

- **Best Way to Propagate:** Take stem cuttings at any season

- **Hardiness:** Frost-sensitive shrub grown as a tender annual

Growing Tips

Many nurseries sell at least one type of flowering maple, usually in individual pots. Mail-order nurseries specializing in tender plants offer a wider selection. If you want variegated flowering maples, you'll need to buy plants; they don't come true from seed. Seed *is* an option if you need a lot of plants and don't mind having all-green leaves. Seed catalogs mostly offer the dwarf "bedding" types.

Sow the seed 10 to 14 weeks before the last frost date. Soak it overnight in tepid water; then cover lightly. Seed germinates in 10 to 14 days at average room temperature.

Wait until there is no danger of frost before moving flowering maples outdoors. They like full sun in cooler climates but appreciate partial shade, or at least some protection from strong afternoon sun in hot ones. Any of the planting mixes used for container growing is fine with them; in the garden, just make sure the soil is well drained and moderately fertile.

Abutilon flowers drop off on their own after they fade, so dead-heading is rarely necessary. Summer care mostly consists of fertilizing regularly and watering as needed when rainfall is in short supply. Pinch or prune overly rampant growth. You can also create a very nice standard by pruning out the lower branches of the shrubby types or training the trailers up a solid stake.

If you have the space, bring your flowering maples indoors in fall. They'll bloom all winter long if you give them bright light and temperatures above freezing. Prune harshly in spring to rejuvenate specimens that are aging. It's easy to multiply all types by stem cuttings.

Good Neighbors

Flowering maples stand alone very nicely, but if you'd like to pair them with something, the delicate spires of angelonia (*Angelonia angustifolia*) or twinspur (*Diascia* hybrids) would offer a pleasing contrast.

Problems and Solutions

Indoors, whiteflies, spider mites, mealy bugs, and scale insects can weaken growth and cause distorted, discolored leaves. (Whiteflies can be a problem outdoors as well.) Spray with insecticidal soap to control these pests.

Top Performer

Abutilon hybrids (flowering maple, parlor maple): Most flowering maples are complex hybrids, with a wide range of flower colors (white, yellow, orange, pink, or red) and leaf shapes that can range from broad and rounded to deeply lobed and maplelike. The bedding types and most of the shrubby cultivars belong here; many of the hybrids are trailers as well. While the older types have drooping flowers, the blooms of many modern hybrids are partially upright. Height: 18 to 96 inches (45 to 240 cm). Spread: 18 to 72 inches (45 to 180 cm).

More Recommended Abutilon

Abutilon megapotamicum (trailing abutilon): This is a popular species with smaller, more heart-shaped leaves than the others and a naturally spreading to trailing habit. This species is grown as much for the lantern-shaped calyces, which are a rich red in the best clones, as for the tubular, totally pendant, yellow flowers. 'Variegatum' is like the species, but with yellow-mottled leaves. 'Victoria' is a related hybrid with larger yellow flowers that makes a wonderful hanging-basket plant. Height: 3 to 6 feet (90 to 120 cm). Spread: 3 to 6 feet (90 to 120 cm).

  A. pictum (flowering maple): Also called *A. striatum*. One of the parents of most hybrids, this common species has deeply cut, distinctly maplelike leaves and pendant orange flowers with darker veins. 'Thompsonii' is a popular cultivar with yellow-mottled foliage. Height: 3 to 8 feet (90 to 240 cm). Spread: 4 to 6 feet (1.2 to 1.8 m).

Flowering maple
(*Abutilon* hybrid)

Larry's Garden Notes

There are three different types of flowering maple: the shrubby, upright growers; the trailers; and the dwarf bedders. The upright types make great accent plants. They can, theoretically, reach 12 feet (3.6 m) tall, although 3 to 5 feet (90 to 150 cm) is more usual. The trailers, with long, dangling branches, are ideal for hanging baskets and raised containers of all kinds. You can also train them to climb up a trellis. The bedding types are good for beds and borders, and they make great filler plants in containers.

Acalypha

Strawberry firetails, chenille plant, red-hot cat's tail

The genus *Acalypha* stands out from the crowd mainly because it is so singularly unremarkable. Most of the some 400 species are tropical trees and shrubs with boring leaves and insignificant flowers. Three species, however, save the genus from horticultural oblivion, and in truly spectacular ways, at that. Strawberry firetails (*A. reptans*) and chenille plant (*A. hispida*) produce striking tassels of red flowers that trail gracefully downward like crimson chenille. Copperleaf (*A. wilkesiana*), on the contrary, has totally lackluster flowers, but wildly colorful foliage, every bit the equal of coleus leaves.

Plant Profile

ACALYPHA
ak-uh-LIF-uh

- **Bloom Color:** Varies by species; see individual listings
- **Bloom Time:** Late spring through early fall; fall through winter in mild climates
- **Height:** Varies by species; see individual listings
- **Spread:** Varies by species; see individual listings
- **Garden Uses:** Container planting, hanging baskets; on a standard
- **Light Preference:** Full sun to partial shade
- **Soil Preference:** Humus-rich, evenly moist but well-drained soil
- **Best Way to Propagate:** Take stem cuttings at any season
- **Hardiness:** Frost-sensitive shrub grown as a tender annual

Growing Tips

You'll need to buy a plant to start with. Look for acalyphas in the houseplant section of your garden center or among the starter plants for containers.

Don't put these tropical plants outdoors until all danger of frost has passed and the air has thoroughly warmed up. Even then, keep them out of cool winds, especially in the North. They love heat and humidity and will positively glow in the Deep South where so many annuals fail. Full sun or partial shade is fine, as are all-purpose container growing mixes. If you plant acalyphas in the garden, make sure to supply humus-rich soil and good drainage.

Summer care consists mostly of watering as needed to keep the soil evenly moist and fertilizing container plants regularly. The tassels usually fall off on their own, so deadheading isn't necessary. A pinch every now and again will help plants fill in evenly.

In Zones 10 and 11, you can grow acalyphas outdoors year-round. Elsewhere, bring it indoors in fall as a houseplant or start new plants from cuttings. Indoors, give it bright light and temperatures no lower than 55°F (13°C) at night. A harsh pruning in early spring will give fuller-looking plants in summer.

Warning: *Acalypha* is closely related to the genus *Euphorbia* and like it, its sap is toxic. Keep these plants out of reach of children and pets.

Good Neighbors

Accentuate the color of the long catkins of flowering species by pairing them with a red foliage plant, such as bloodleaf (*Iresine herbstii*) or a dark red coleus. The showy foliage of copperleaf looks great with a wide array of companions.

Problems and Solutions

Acalyphas have few problems while outdoors, especially if you give them a site with good air circulation and keep the soil evenly moist. Indoors, spider mites, whiteflies, mealy bugs, and scale insects can attack; control with insecticidal soap.

Top Performer

Acalypha reptans (strawberry firetails, trailing chenille plant): Also called *A. repens* and *A. pendula*. This is a relatively new plant on the market and still something of a horticultural mystery. No one seems to know if it's a true species of its own or just a trailing variety of the chenille plant (*A. hispida*); either way, it's a winner! This creeping plant has small, oval, mid-green leaves and thin, trailing stems that quickly arch downward over the edge of a pot. Strawberry red hanging tassels, looking much like pipecleaners, dangle downward, giving the plant its main point of interest. It is used almost exclusively in containers since the flowers would simply lie on the dirt below if the plant were grown in the ground. Height: 4 to 8 inches (10 to 20 cm). Spread: 18 to 36 inches (45 to 90 cm).

More Recommended Acalypha

Acalypha hispida (chenille plant, red-hot cat's tail): An upright, shrubby version of *A. reptans* with much larger, shinier leaves and bright red tassels that reach up to 20 inches (50 cm) long. Height: 3 to 6 feet (90 to 180 cm). Spread: 2 to 6 feet (60 to 180 cm).

   A. wilkesiana (copperleaf, Jacob's coat): *A. godseffiana* is similar and sometimes considered to be a variety of *A. wilkesiana*. Very different from either of its brethren, copperleaf produces tiny, insignificant flowers that are half hidden among its leaves. Its main claim to fame is its large, toothed, oval, delightfully colored foliage. There are dozens of cultivars available with a variety of leaf colors, including deep copper, copper-splashed pink and cream, green with ivory margins, and maroon with bright red borders. Some are curiously twisted or narrow and willowlike. Height: 3 to 6 feet (90 to 180 cm). Spread: 3 to 6 feet (90 to 180 cm).

Strawberry firetails
(*Acalypha reptans*)

Larry's Garden Notes

Don't bother even looking for acalypha seed: it simply isn't available. Instead, multiply your plants by cuttings; they root readily if you give them warmth and high humidity. Apply a dusting of rooting hormone and insert the 6-inch (15-cm) sections into sterile growing mix or vermiculite, then cover with a plastic dome or a clear plastic bag and place in bright light but with no direct sun. Take cuttings in fall through late winter to get well-established plants for the upcoming summer.

Anagallis

Pimpernel

Not so long ago, few North American gardeners had ever heard of pimpernel. Recently, however, blue pimpernel (*Anagallis monellii*) has come to the forefront as a superb container plant in a rare shade—a startlingly brilliant, deep gentian blue—and it's presently giving the old-fashioned but far less heat-resistant edging lobelia (*Lobelia erinus*) a run for its money. There's *lots* more to discover in this small but very floriferous genus, although only one other species is currently available: scarlet pimpernel (*A. arvensis*).

Plant Profile

ANAGALLIS
an-uh-GAL-iss

- **Bloom Color:** Varies by species; see individual listings
- **Bloom Time:** Early summer through midfall; much of the year in mild climates
- **Height:** Varies by species; see individual listings
- **Spread:** Varies by species; see individual listings
- **Garden Uses:** Container planting, edging, hanging baskets, groundcover, mass planting, meadow garden, mixed border, rock garden
- **Light Preference:** Full sun to partial shade
- **Soil Preference:** Varies by species; see individual listings
- **Best Way to Propagate:** Sow seed indoors or out in spring; take stem cuttings in fall
- **Hardiness:** Frost-sensitive perennial or annual grown as a half-hardy annual

Growing Tips

Blue pimpernel is a tender perennial, hardy in Zones 9 to 11, but gardeners just about everywhere grow it as an annual. You can either buy starter plants or start your own. To grow it from seed, start it indoors 10 to 12 weeks before the last frost. Germination takes 2 to 3 weeks. Use a well-drained seed mix with added sterilized sand because the young seedlings are susceptible to damping-off in ordinary peat-based mixes. Sow the seed ⅛ inch (3 mm) deep and place the tray at room temperature. Plant out when all danger of frost has passed. Standard container mix is fine for growing in flower boxes and hanging baskets, but give it humus-rich, well-drained, evenly moist soil if you plant it in the garden. And keep it relatively moist all summer for best results.

Scarlet pimpernel is a fast-growing annual that doesn't really need a head start indoors. Either sow it directly in the garden or start it indoors, 6 to 8 weeks before the last frost date, but in peat pots to reduce the risk of root disturbance at transplanting time. It sprouts in about 30 days. It prefers 60° to 65°F (15° to 18°C) for germination. Outdoors, scarlet pimpernel does best in poor to average, well-drained soil. Don't give it any special treatment, other than watering during periods of extreme drought.

Both species bloom up a storm whether you deadhead or not, so you can simply let them grow,

FUN FACTS

Ever wonder where the Scarlet Pimpernel, that swashbuckling masked hero of the novel by Baroness Orczy and later star of television, stage, radio, and screen, got his name? From the flower, scarlet pimpernel (*Anagallis arvensis*). And you can grow it in your garden without having to buckle a swash!

only pinching out wayward branches. Of course, deadheading scarlet pimpernel could help moderate its invasive tendencies, but there are so many of the tiny flowers that only the most fastidious gardener would ever make very much headway.

Where blue pimpernel isn't hardy, bring a plant or two indoors for the winter or take cuttings before frost; grow them in bright light. Let scarlet pimpernel, a true annual, finish its life cycle outdoors and start new plants from seed the following spring—if it hasn't already self-sown throughout your garden!

Good Neighbors

Blue pimpernel can be a good alternative to the ever-present blue edging lobelia in the garden or in pots and window boxes. As a companion to red zonal geranium (*Pelargonium* × *hortorum*), it adds a touch of the unusual to the ordinary.

Problems and Solutions

Knock aphids off with a strong spray of water if they appear.

Top Performer

Anagallis monellii (blue pimpernel, flaxleaf pimpernel): Also called *A. collina*. The deep blue, ½-inch (1.25-cm) flowers are perfectly set off by a bright red center. The plant is bushy, with dark green oval to lance-shaped leaves in twos or threes. Flaxleaf pimpernel (*A. monellii linifolia,* also called *A. linifolia*) has narrower leaves and is the form you're most likely to find for sale. Red- and pink-flowered types also exist. Height: 4 to 8 inches (10 to 20 cm). Spread: 12 to 18 inches (30 to 45 cm).

More Recommended Anagallis

Think Twice: *Anagallis arvensis* (scarlet pimpernel, poor man's weatherglass): The tiny ¼-inch (6-mm), cup-shaped flowers are a beautiful brick red with a delicious honeylike scent. There are also pink and white cultivars, plus a subspecies, *A. arvensis caerulea,* with blue flowers. This short, spreading plant is a common weed in poor soil, which should give you an idea that it does tend to be invasive! Mulching well will help control it. Height: 6 to 12 inches (15 to 30 cm). Spread: 1 foot (30 cm). **Self-sowing** 🌱

Flaxleaf pimpernel
(*Anagallis monellii linifolia*)

Larry's Garden Notes

In the United Kingdom, scarlet pimpernel (*Anagallis arvensis*) is often called "poor man's weatherglass." That's because the flower has a fascinating habit: Its brilliant red flowers are fully open during sunny weather but close up entirely on cloudy days. They are even said to predict upcoming weather conditions, starting to unfurl even during gray weather if the sun is on its way and refusing to open on a sunny day if the air pressure is dropping.

Bidens

Golden goddess

Talk about back from the dead! Golden goddess had a few years in the sun back in the mid-1800s, when people commented on how pretty and easy to grow it was; then it seemed to disappear from gardens. Recently, it resurfaced in a big way. I first saw it in France and Great Britain in the mid-1990s when it was simply *the* star of hanging baskets and containers; now it is just as hot in North America. Golden goddess is a pretty daisylike flower, rather similar to a coreopsis, with deeply cut, lacy leaves. And boy does it bloom! You can count on hundreds of blooms per plant by midsummer.

Plant Profile

BIDENS
BYE-denz

- **Bloom Color:** Golden yellow

- **Bloom Time:** Summer through midfall; much of the year in mild climates

- **Height:** 12 to 30 inches (30 to 75 cm)

- **Spread:** 12 to 18 inches (30 to 45 cm)

- **Garden Uses:** Container planting, cut-flower garden, hanging baskets, mass planting, meadow garden, mixed border

- **Light Preference:** Full sun

- **Soil Preference:** Average to humus-rich, evenly moist but well-drained soil

- **Best Way to Propagate:** Sow seed indoors or outdoors in spring; take stem cuttings at any season

- **Hardiness:** Frost-sensitive perennial grown as a half-hardy annual

Growing Tips

How you start golden goddess depends on how you'll use it. Most cultivars grow readily from seed and are, of course, much cheaper to grow that way. The newer, weak-stemmed, container cultivars do not come true from seed, though, and have to be multiplied by cuttings.

You're most likely to find the trailing types sold as plants in spring. Just pot them up in containers and put them outdoors after all danger of frost has passed.

Growing the more upright cultivars from seed is scarcely more complicated. Golden goddess grows rapidly, so sowing outside at the last frost date will give you flowers in short order. For even faster bloom, sow indoors 6 to 8 weeks before planting time. Just barely cover the seed and place the growing tray at 55° to 60°F (13° to 15°C). Germination is fast: just 7 to 14 days. Plant out when all risk of frost is over.

Give golden goddess full sun and just about any kind of well-drained soil. During the summer, keep the soil evenly moist if possible; the plants tolerate drought but then will flower less. When I first tried this plant, I was told deadheading was vital in stimulating continuous bloom, but I found it hard to keep up with this fast-blooming plant. The following year I experimented with side-by-side plants, one deadheaded and the other allowed to grow as it wished, and to be honest, I could see *no* difference in bloom.

You can bring plants indoors in fall, pruning them back harshly, and they'll quickly come into

FUN FACTS

The name *Bidens* means "two teeth" and refers to the two often-hooked projections at the end of the seeds of most species.

bloom again on a bright windowsill. I find they'll bloom only weakly until midwinter, then really take off as the days become longer. You can likewise take cuttings in fall if you want smaller plants to maintain over winter. Obviously, the vegetatively propagated trailing cultivars are the worthiest contenders for a chance to overwinter indoors. The others grow so quickly from seed it doesn't seem worthwhile bothering to save them.

 **Think Twice:** In very mild climates, Zones 8 to 11, plants often overwinter on their own. Elsewhere, they'll self-sow quite readily and can even become weedy. That's not likely to be a problem on a balcony, but it could be if you grow them in a garden. Covering the soil each spring with a fresh layer of mulch will prevent them from getting out of control. Fortunately, the young plants, with their ferny green leaves, are easy to recognize and easy to pull out. **Self-sowing** 🖊

'Compact' golden goddess (*Bidens ferulifolia* 'Compact')

Good Neighbors

Golden goddess makes a wonderful companion to more upright daisies such as marguerites (*Argyranthemum* spp.). It also looks great with geraniums (*Pelargonium* spp.), purple edging lobelia (*Lobelia erinus*), and other traditional container favorites.

Problems and Solutions

Golden goddess is not generally subject to diseases, unless you grow it in the same place year after year. Aphids can be an annoyance; knock them off with a strong spray of water.

Top Performer

Bidens ferulifolia (golden goddess): Also called *B. aurea.* 'Golden Goddess' is actually the name of one of the earlier cultivars of *B. ferulifolia,* but it has caught on as a common name in many areas. Golden goddess produces 1¼- to 2-inch (3- to 5-cm) golden yellow, daisylike flowers with five broad "petals" (ray flowers) surrounding a yellow center. There are short, medium, and tall strains that come from seed, plus several cutting-grown, trailing types.

Larry's Garden Notes

Golden goddess itself is a beautiful and inoffensive plant, but you can't say the same for its nearest relatives. You see, it is a member of the dreaded beggar's-tick (*Bidens*) clan, also known as stick-tights, pitchforks, Spanish-needles, and tickseed. This group of noxious weeds is renowned for having annoying prickly seeds, which grab onto clothes and animal fur with their two curved hooks. There are dozens of species of the nasty ones, and you probably have one or two in your neighborhood right now.

Calibrachoa

Million-Bells

I just hate calling a plant by its commercial name, but with *Calibrachoa*, what's a guy to do but follow the crowd? Even introductions from competing companies are commonly called Million-Bells: 'Liricashower' Million-Bells, 'Colorburst' Million-Bells, and so on. The plant causing all the stir resembles a bushy, trailing, miniature, weather-resistant petunia, but its 1-inch (2.5-cm) flowers are more bell shaped than trumpet shaped like true petunias. And gardeners all over will be pleased to know they are *not* sticky to the touch, unlike the annoyingly gluey petunias.

Plant Profile

CALIBRACHOA
ka-lee-bra-KOE-uh

- **Bloom Color:** Pink, violet, blue, magenta, salmon, red
- **Bloom Time:** Late spring through late fall; early spring in mild climates
- **Height:** 6 to 10 inches (15 to 25 cm)
- **Spread:** 18 to 36 inches (45 to 90 cm)
- **Garden Uses:** Container planting, edging, ground-cover, hanging baskets, mass planting, mixed border, rock garden, wall planting
- **Attracts:** Hummingbirds
- **Light Preference:** Full sun to partial shade
- **Soil Preference:** Average to humus-rich, well-drained, slightly acid soil
- **Best Way to Propagate:** Take stem cuttings at any season
- **Hardiness:** Frost-sensitive perennial grown as a half-hardy annual

Growing Tips

The day will probably come when Million-Bells are available by seed, but at the time I wrote this, they were sold only as vegetatively propagated plants. They are widely available in nurseries and garden centers at spring planting time. When all danger of frost is out of the air, move them outside. Work them into container plantings, or plant them in the garden. A pinch at planting time will often result in much fuller-looking plants.

Ordinary container growing mix is just fine for Million-Bells, and it adapts to most garden soil as well, as long as the site is well drained. It prefers soil that's a bit on the acid side, so mix a bit of peat moss with the soil at planting if your soil is either neutral or alkaline. Most potting soils already are at the right level of acidity for Million-Bells.

Summer care is minimal, especially since Million-Bells is quite drought tolerant. It makes an excellent choice for containers that are out of reach or simply too hard to water regularly. It does still need watering during periods of extreme heat, but at least you won't have to water twice a day as you do with so many other container annuals. Fertilize container-grown Million-Bells regularly. Deadheading is an entirely optional activity: Plants bloom heavily straight through the summer whether you deadhead them or not.

Unlike its cousin, the petunia, Million-Bells usually doesn't go into decline in midsummer, especially in cool or short-season areas. Where summers are very long or very hot (it does bloom less in hot weather), you can always prune back by half any plants that seem to go downhill; they'll soon be as good as new.

Million-Bells is quite frost hardy and will probably bloom right through the first fall frosts. In protected spots of Zone 7, plus in Zones 8 through 11, there is a good chance plants grown in the garden will come back the following year as a perennial. In containers, where cold penetrates more deeply, that is less likely: Consider it hardy only in Zones 9 through 11. Where it isn't hardy, think about bringing in either a potted specimen or a few cuttings for the winter.

Good Neighbors

Million-Bells are excellent choices for both window boxes and hanging baskets. Pair them with deep purple heliotrope (*Heliotropium arborescens*) for a colorful planting combination or let a hot pink cultivar liven up the deep purple foliage of the 'Blackie' sweet potato vine (*Ipomoea batatas* 'Blackie'). When planted in the garden, Million-Bells can develop into a truly superior groundcover.

Problems and Solutions

Aphids and whiteflies can be a problem. Control them with sprays of insecticidal soap. Powdery mildew may show up when the air is cool and the plants a bit drought stressed. Try to keep the soil a bit moister in the late summer to prevent it. Poor growth and yellowed foliage may be due to a lack of micronutrients. Try spraying with liquid seaweed fertilizer for a fast green-up.

Top Performer

Calibrachoa hybrids (Million-Bells): There are now lots of cultivars of this plant, varying in habit and color. One particularly interesting selection is 'Terra Cotta', with flowers that range from brick red to orange to yellow to bicolored all on one plant. Expect more colors and larger flowers as this new plant gains in popularity and as hybridizers experiment with it more fully. And I wouldn't be surprised to see truly hardy perennial types appear as well, since some of the wild species are very cold resistant.

Million-Bells
(*Calibrachoa* hybrid)

Larry's Gardening Notes

Calibrachoa sounds like something really new, and it is, sort of. The first species were introduced back in the early nineteenth century, but under the name *Petunia*. One species, *C. parviflora* (*Petunia parviflora*), called beach petunia, was grown for a while, and this South American native is now well established as a garden escapee in California and from Florida to Maine. The hybrids we now know came about when the Japanese firm Suntory started working with wild species from South America in 1988, releasing the first hybrids nearly a decade later.

Melampodium

Melampodium

Melampodium has the curious habit of doubling its stems each time it flowers. The first bloom appears when the plant is still very small—basically an upright stick with just a few leaves. As the first flower opens, two new stems appear at the leaf node just below the flower. When these stems bloom in their turn, they each produce two stems, and so on. By midsummer, it is simply magnificent; by summer's end, the word "stupendous" is more appropriate. Melampodium is a showstopper, both in containers and in the garden.

Plant Profile

MELAMPODIUM
mel-am-POD-ee-um

- **Bloom Color:** Golden yellow

- **Bloom Time:** Summer through early fall

- **Height:** 8 to 24 inches (20 to 60 cm)

- **Spread:** 8 to 18 inches (20 to 45 cm)

- **Garden Uses:** Container planting, cut-flower garden, mass planting, meadow garden, mixed border

- **Attracts:** Butterflies

- **Light Preference:** Full sun

- **Soil Preference:** Average, relatively humus-rich, well-drained soil

- **Best Way to Propagate:** Sow seed indoors or outdoors in spring

- **Hardiness:** Frost-sensitive perennial grown as a tender annual

Growing Tips

Many nurseries sell this easy-to-grow annual in individual pots and in seed packs, and some are starting to offer it in cell packs, so you have a choice in how to grow it.

If you want to save money, start it from seed. In areas with very long growing seasons, you can sow the seed outdoors around the last frost date. Elsewhere, start it indoors 6 to 8 weeks before the last frost date, just barely covering the seed. It'll germinate in 7 to 14 days at room temperature. Thin or transplant them as they grow; they don't like to be overcrowded. When the soil has warmed up and all danger of frost is past, plant them outside. Set purchased plants out at the same period.

A spot in full sun with moderately fertile, well-drained soil is best. Avoid damp soils: This is one plant that prefers its roots on the dry side. Also avoid soils that are excessively rich, and don't fertilize too heavily; excess nutrients result in luxuriant foliage but scarcely a bloom.

Melampodium grows well in the garden, but it's particularly wonderful in a pot, thanks to its heat and drought resistance. When other container annuals have withered away, it will still be blooming as if nothing had happened. That's not to say you shouldn't water it, of course (just

FUN FACTS

***Paludosum* means "marsh loving,"** which could lead you to believe melampodium needs moist or even wet conditions, but nothing could be further from the truth. It's simply a case of mistaken identity. When Carolus Linnaeus was first classifying plants, he thought it came from a marshy area, and so gave it the name it still bears today.

about every drought-tolerant plant prefers even soil moisture), but at least it won't die just because you went away for the weekend! Gardeners in the Deep South will also appreciate this one: It seems totally immune to the combination of extreme heat and unbearable humidity that does in so many other plants.

Deadheading is unnecessary because the ray flowers simply fall off when their show is over, and the constantly dividing new growth quickly hides what's left of the flower head. Although melampodium has lots of good traits, frost tolerance isn't one of them. Where the frost-free season is long, though, it will just keep on blooming and blooming.

Rather than trying to bring a fully-grown plant indoors for the winter, just take a few cuttings in late summer. In a bright, sunny window, the show can be very attractive.

Melampodium
(*Melampodium paludosum*)

Good Neighbors
The small yellow flowers amid the healthy green foliage of melampodium gives the appearance, from a distance, of a fresh yellow-green, which mixes equally well with warm yellows and oranges and cool blues and pinks. And there's no better marigold substitute for those that are inclined to break from the crowd!

Problems and Solutions
Damping-off can be a problem with young seedlings. Make sure they get good ventilation and don't let them get crowded. Watch out for slugs on young plants, especially those growing in moist soil; hand-picking is one control.

Top Performer
Melampodium paludosum (melampodium, star daisy): Upright, bushy plants have large, apple green leaves, often undulating along the edges and quite rough to the touch, and ¾-inch (2-cm) golden yellow inflorescences like tiny sunflowers. There are several cultivars, all very much alike except for size. I don't find the dwarf types are always true to type; you'll always have to rogue out a few taller plants from a patch of dwarf ones.

Larry's Garden Notes

Be prepared for a bit of confusion when it comes to melapodium's botanical name. Some authors list this plant as *Leucanthemum paludosum*, a name also shared by the considerably different baby marguerite (variously called *Hymenostemma paludosum*, *Leucanthemum paludosum*, and *Chrysanthemum paludosum*), which has white ray flowers and a yellow center. However, all plant descriptions of *Leucanthemum paludosum* mention its toothed to pinnate leaves, which is true of baby marguerite, but is *not* true of melampodium.

Nolana

Nolana

A staple in hanging baskets back in Victorian times, nolana has been cruising along at a snail's pace ever since. With the increased popularity of container gardening, though, it should be due for a major surge in interest. It is, after all, particularly well adapted to container culture, with thick stems and fleshy leaves that store water, making it quite drought tolerant. And its naturally spreading, creeping nature turns it into an attractive trailing plant when you lift it off the ground. The bell-shaped flowers look very much like petunias, but they open only in sunny weather.

Plant Profile

NOLANA
no-LAH-nuh

- **Bloom Color:** Varies by species; see individual listings

- **Bloom Time:** Late spring through early fall; fall through winter in mild climates

- **Height:** Varies by species; see individual listings

- **Spread:** Varies by species; see individual listings

- **Garden Uses:** Container planting, edging, hanging baskets, groundcover, mass planting, mixed border, rock garden, wall planting

- **Light Preference:** Full sun to partial shade

- **Soil Preference:** Average to poor, well-drained soil

- **Best Way to Propagate:** Sow seed indoors in spring

- **Hardiness:** Frost-sensitive perennial grown as a half-hardy annual

Growing Tips

Not many nurseries sell started plants, so you'll most likely have to grow your nolanas from seed, starting outdoors or indoors.

Outdoors, sow seed 2 to 3 weeks before the last frost date. That will give you young plants that germinate just after the last frost date, but while the soil is still cool: perfect for nolana. (It prefers cool conditions but is only slightly frost tolerant.)

Indoors, a 6- to 8-week head start is sufficient. Nolana produces a long taproot and quickly becomes difficult to transplant, so you'll want to get it planted outdoors while it is still quite small. It is easiest, therefore, to sow directly into a peat pot, about three seeds per pot. If you do choose to sow in trays, be prepared to pot up individual seedlings when they have no more than six to eight leaves. Sow the hard, beige-colored seed about ⅛ inch (3 mm) deep in regular seed-starting mix. Germination takes about 10 days at 60°F (15°C). Thin to only one seedling per peat pot.

Plant outside around the last frost date in soil that is well drained. Average or even poor soil is fine because nolana is not a heavy feeder. In fact, very rich soil or heavy fertilizing encourages abundant leafy growth but poor flowering. Full sun is the best option for most climates, but in areas with very hot summers, some protection from the afternoon sun is wise.

Summer care is minimal. You can go easier on watering than you normally would for container plants because nolana is very drought resistant. Even so, plants in containers dry out more quickly than those in the garden, so some watering will be necessary. Pinch straggly plants occasionally to stimulate better branching and therefore a fuller look. Deadheading is not really necessary because fading

flowers drop off on their own, and removing the seed capsules doesn't seem to
stimulate better bloom.

In Zones 10 and 11, you can grow
nolana as a short-lived perennial. Elsewhere, you should plan to start new plants
from seed each year, or to bring in cuttings.
Nolana makes an attractive houseplant for a
sunny window location.

Good Neighbors

Combine this gentle trailer with other
succulent plants, such as hens and chicks
(*Sempervivum* spp.), to make an attractive
and drought-tolerant window box or
planter. Silver or white neighbors can be
particularly flattering; try nolana with
dusty miller (*Senecio cineraria*) or sweet
alyssum (*Lobularia maritima*).

Problems and Solutions

If aphids cause distorted, sticky growth, knock them off with a
strong spray of water. Leafminers may trace winding tunnels
in the leaves; remove and destroy infested foliage.

Top Performer

Nolana paradoxa (nolana, Chilean bellflower): Also called *N. napi-
formis*. This is a low-growing, sprawling plant with sticky leaves. It
forms a basal rosette of rather narrow leaves, with broader leaves on
the creeping stems. The flowers, about 2 inches (5 cm) in diameter,
are usually blue to purple with a white to pale blue throat and a
yellow to greenish center. There are a handful of cultivars that differ
mainly in the degree of purple of the flower, as well as a few white-
flowered, yellow-throated cultivars. Height: 6 to 10 inches (15 to
25 cm). Spread: 18 to 24 inches (45 to 60 cm).

More Recommended Nolana

Nolana humifusa (nolana): A lesser-known but no less valuable
species with a similar but more compact habit. It produces smaller,
1-inch (2.5-cm) flowers in lavender-blue with beautifully streaked
throats and smooth, purplish stems. Height: 4 to 6 inches (10 to
15 cm). Spread: 18 to 24 inches (45 to 60 cm).

'Blue Bird' nolana
(*Nolana paradoxa* 'Blue Bird')

Larry's Gardening Notes

Nolana's drought resistance
stands it in good stead in its native environment: dry, semidesert
areas of coastal Chile and Peru,
where it often grows on sand
dunes within reach of salt spray.
Seaside gardeners should take
special note of this plant's tolerance of dry conditions and air-
borne salt. It will be especially
useful in areas where off-shore
breezes blow cool more often
than hot; it doesn't appreciate the
burning sand of tropical regions.

Pelargonium peltatum

Ivy geranium

Anyone who has seen the incredible, flower-filled balcony plantings of a Swiss chalet will definitely want to try ivy geraniums. Growing them to such perfection isn't always quite as easy as in the Swiss mountains, where the sunny days and cool nights are very much to this plant's liking, but you can get very good results just about everywhere. Ivy geraniums get their name both from their growth habit—they creep and trail much like an ivy (*Hedera* spp.) does—and also from their ivylike leaves. They produce rounded clusters of individual flowers with generally well-spaced, often narrow petals.

Plant Profile

**PELARGONIUM
PELTATUM**
**pel-ar-GO-nee-um
pel-tah-TUM**

- **Bloom Color:** Lilac, mauve, pink, purple, red, white

- **Bloom Time:** Late spring through early fall

- **Height:** 12 to 30 inches (30 to 75 cm)

- **Spread:** 6 to 48 inches (15 to 120 cm)

- **Garden Uses:** Container planting, edging, hanging baskets, groundcover, rock garden, wall planting

- **Light Preference:** Full sun to partial shade

- **Soil Preference:** Humus-rich, well-drained soil; tolerates alkaline soil

- **Best Way to Propagate:** Sow seed indoors in winter; take stem cuttings at any season

- **Hardiness:** Frost-sensitive sub-shrub grown as a tender annual

Growing Tips

Traditionally, ivy geraniums have been offered as rooted plants. It's only recently that seed has become available, and even today, the choice of seed-grown cultivars is limited. I suggest you stick with cutting-grown plants unless you need a lot of plants at a good price, in which case seeds are a viable option.

Ivy geraniums grown from cuttings are widely available. Purchase small starter plants and pot up three or four per hanging basket, or buy an already-planted basket. Set out the plants any time after the danger of frost has passed. In fact, if you grow them in containers (and ivy geraniums usually *are* best suited to be container plants), you can always take the risk of putting them out early, as long as you bring them indoors if frost is a threat.

If you wish to grow ivy geraniums from seed, sow indoors 14 to 16 weeks before the last frost, barely covering it with mix. Seeds germinate in 1 to 14 days at 70° to 85°F (21° to 30°C). Move them to a cooler spot, 60° to 70°F (15° to 21°C), after germination. You'll probably need to pinch the young seedlings once or twice to get them to fill out well.

Ivy geraniums are less heat re-sistant than zonal geraniums (*Pelargonium* × *hortorum*) and usually do best with some protection from the sun's hottest rays. In areas where blazingly hot

FUN FACTS

One intriguing way of growing ivy geraniums is in "plant pillars." Insert a solid, column-shaped tomato cage in a large pot of cuttings and train them upward, letting them peek out along the edges. I've seen columns 6 feet (1.8 m) high so heavily covered with flowers that the foliage was scarcely visible!

summers are the norm, grow them on the eastern side of the house. Although quite drought tolerant, ivy geraniums grow and bloom much better if you water regularly.

Throughout summer, water ivy geraniums well and fertilize regularly. Most are self-cleaning, so deadheading isn't necessary.

In fall, except in Zones 10 and 11, bring your ivy geraniums back indoors or take cuttings for overwintering. Dip the cuttings in rooting hormone and insert into perlite or sterile growing mix. *Don't* cover them with plastic; they tend to rot in very humid conditions. Grow your ivy geraniums under cool conditions indoors, then take more cuttings in the spring for a large number of summer baskets.

'Cornell' ivy geranium (*Pelargonium peltatum* 'Cornell')

Good Neighbors

Ivy geraniums combine beautifully with edging lobelia (*Lobelia erinus*), golden goddess (*Bidens ferulifolia*), and petunias. The variegated types make interesting foliage accents around a bold, upright partner, such as a canna or an ornamental grass.

Problems and Solutions

Stem rot (black leg) is a common problem in cuttings. Increased air circulation can reduce the chance of infection. Edema, seen as raised brown patches under the leaves, results from excess watering. Control aphids and whiteflies with insecticidal soap.

Top Performer

Pelargonium peltatum hybrids (ivy geranium): It's unlikely you'll ever grow the true species; almost all ivy geraniums in culture are complex hybrids with various other *Pelargonium* species. The leaves of all are generally shield shaped with pointed lobes and can be green, deep purple, or variegated. There are many cultivars with intriguing leaves and curious flowers, but for truly spectacular results in a basket or flower box, try one of the European balcony types. The 'Balcon' and 'Cascade' series offer better-than-average heat and sun tolerance and are good choices if your local temperatures don't resemble those of the Swiss Alps.

Kissing Cousins

Looking totally different from ivy geraniums, but still very popular in containers, are the various scented geraniums (*Pelargonium* spp.). This complex group of plants includes both upright growers and trailers, with green, grayish, or variegated leaves in a wide range of sizes and shapes. The white or pink flowers generally aren't very showy. Their claim to fame is their highly aromatic leaves that come in a variety of fragrances: lemon, rose, apple, orange, coconut, and more! Grow them as you would ivy geraniums.

Sanvitalia

Creeping zinnia

Is creeping zinnia an edging plant that looks great in a container or a container plant that looks great as an edging? Well, you'll have to decide that one for yourself because this plant works equally well in the garden and in containers. The common name is certainly appropriate enough: It does creep and the leaves do bear an astonishing resemblance to tiny zinnia leaves. Of course, the flower *does* look more like a sunflower (*Helianthus annuus*), but who's quibbling when the plant is as terrific as this one is?

Plant Profile

SANVITALIA
san-vih-TAL-ee-uh

- **Bloom Color:** Orange, yellow
- **Bloom Time:** Early summer through early fall
- **Height:** 5 to 8 inches (13 to 20 cm)
- **Spread:** 12 to 16 inches (30 to 40 cm)
- **Garden Uses:** Container planting, edging, hanging baskets, groundcover, mixed border, rock garden, wall planting
- **Attracts:** Butterflies
- **Light Preference:** Full sun or partial shade
- **Soil Preference:** Average, humus-rich, well-drained soil
- **Best Way to Propagate:** Sow seed outdoors or indoors in spring
- **Hardiness:** Half-hardy annual or short-lived tender perennial

Growing Tips

This great annual has rarely received the attention it deserves in the past because of a "fatal flaw" (from the point of view of a commercial nursery, that is!): It dislikes being transplanted. That means it's generally been offered only in seed packs, a major drawback in a modern world where many gardeners want instant results. That may be changing, though! It turns out that while seed-grown plants quickly produce a taproot, making transplanting difficult, cutting-grown plants produce only fibrous roots; that means they're as easy to transplant as any other annual. As a result, vegetatively propagated creeping zinnias have started to appear on the market as starter plants and even in hanging baskets.

While waiting for your local nursery to sell transplants, you can still grow creeping zinnia the traditional way: from seed. For garden display, sow the seed outdoors 2 to 3 weeks before the last frost date, or even the previous fall if you live in a mild climate, for bloom from midsummer through fall. For container culture, though, there's no need to wait so late in the season. Start it indoors 6 to 8 weeks before the last frost, directly in a hanging pot; that way, you won't have to worry about transplanting it. Or sow it into peat pots, only 4 to 6 weeks before planting out, so that you'll be transplanting seedlings whose taproots haven't yet fully formed. In all cases, simply press the seed into the soil,

FUN FACTS

One can hardly imagine tiny little creeping zinnia as a good candidate for flower arrangements; however, the flowers dry wonderfully. To compensate for a lack of stem, you just have to wire them and wrap the wire in floral tape.

without covering it because it needs light to germinate. Germination is quite rapid: 10 to 14 days at room temperature.

Creeping zinnia prefers a relatively fertile, humus-rich soil but will settle for much less; even poor, rocky, or sandy soil will do. In a container, use a good basic potting mix. Don't go overboard fertilizing during summer, though, or you'll see lush foliage but few flowers.

Creeping zinnia seems to thrive in hot, humid weather, but it does well in cool summer climates, too. Full sun gives bushy, free-flowering plants, but creeping zinnia will still grow reasonably well in partial shade; just plant them a bit more densely so their more sprawling stems will mingle together. Quite drought tolerant, creeping zinnia will do fine in spots out of reach of your hose. For full, green foliage and lots of flowers, though, do make sure you water it regularly during periods of drought, especially if it is growing in a container. Deadheading is unnecessary.

Most creeping zinnias are true annuals and can't be saved except by collecting seed. However, some recent introductions seem to have a longer life span and will grow from cuttings, allowing you to overwinter them indoors.

Creeping zinnia
(*Sanvitalia procumbens*)

Kissing Cousins

A distantly related plant, sea daisy or sea aster (*Asteriscus maritimus*, also called *Odontospermum maritimum*) makes an interesting substitute for creeping zinnia. It produces golden yellow, daisylike blooms and small, spoon-shaped leaves lightly covered with silky hairs on semi-woody stems. This cutting-grown plant is perennial in Zones 8 to 11 but sold as an annual for container use. It tolerates salt spray and sandy or rocky soils but is not very heat tolerant. Height: 1 foot (30 cm). Spread: 2 feet (60 cm).

Good Neighbors

Creeping zinnia looks wonderful mass planted in a sunny spot, or in a large container. Planted alone in a hanging basket, it will bloom cheerfully for months.

Problems and Solutions

Creeping zinnia is generally pest free, but rot can be a problem in poorly drained soil; provide a well-drained planting site.

Top Performer

Sanvitalia procumbens (creeping zinnia): Creeping zinnia is a low-mounding plant forming a dense carpet of smooth, oval, mid-green leaves, with each of the numerous stems ending in a long-lasting dark-centered "daisy" with yellow to orange ray flowers. Most forms sold today are single to semidouble.

Scaevola

Fan flower, Australian fan flower

There are nearly 100 species of *Scaevola* found around the world, mostly in the South Pacific and Australia, but only this one has made any headway as an ornamental—so far. After languishing for several generations in the "Australian Flora" collections of botanical gardens, fan flower suddenly became a smash hit in the mid-1990s. This handsome plant forms a dense carpet of small, lightly toothed, spoon-shaped leaves. The innumerable ¾- to 1-inch (2- to 2.5-cm), tubular flowers each open into a broad, five-lobed fan, something like a broad-flowered edging lobelia (*Lobelia erinus*).

Plant Profile

SCAEVOLA
skuh-VOH-luh

- **Bloom Color:** Blue, mauve, pink, purple, white

- **Bloom Time:** Late spring through mid- to late fall; much of the year in mild climates

- **Height:** 4 to 8 inches (10 to 20 cm)

- **Spread:** 20 to 60 inches (50 to 150 cm)

- **Garden Uses:** Container planting, edging, hanging baskets, groundcover, mass planting, rock garden, wall planting

- **Light Preference:** Full sun to partial shade

- **Soil Preference:** Average, humus-rich, evenly moist but well-drained soil

- **Best Way to Propagate:** Take stem cuttings at any season

- **Hardiness:** Frost-sensitive perennial grown as a tender annual

Growing Tips

Don't bother looking for the seed of this plant: It simply isn't available. Instead, you'll find individually potted transplants and fully grown baskets of fan flowers in just about every nursery. Just remember to wait until all danger of frost is past before setting out your purchased plants.

As long as you give fan flower full sun to partial shade and don't let it soak constantly in water, it will probably do just fine. Although native to arid regions of its native land, it seems equally at home in the dry heat of the American Southwest, the heat and humidity of the Deep South, and the cool summers of the North. Evenly moist soil is best, although fan flower is somewhat succulent and can take occasional droughts. If possible, avoid using hard (alkaline) water (rain water is ideal).

Fan flower is remarkably adaptable, but it really thrives in a naturally fertile, humus-rich soil that's a bit on the acid side and low in mineral salts. For the best bloom display, fertilize with a low-phosphorus fertilizer, or preferably, one with lots of potassium, a fair amount of nitrogen, and no phosphorus at all. (Like many Australian plants, it evolved in a nearly phosphorus-free environment and has a hard time dealing with added phosphorus in the garden.) Once fan flower begins blooming, it will continue to bloom nonstop until frost. Deadheading is unnecessary.

Where it is hardy (Zones 10 and 11), fan flower often blooms

FUN FACTS

The botanical name for this plant is quite appropriate: It comes from the Latin *scaeva* ("left-handed") and refers to the one-sided, hand-shaped flowers.

right through winter. For most of us, though, it is a summer annual that we can bring inside for winter. Prune back all the stems to within 8 inches (20 cm) of the soil, and place in a sunny spot indoors. It tends to bloom modestly through winter and more abundantly as the days get longer.

In February, take cuttings for your summer displays. Cuttings root readily at warm temperatures. Use a rooting hormone and cover the tray or pot with clear plastic to maintain high humidity. Pinch rooted cuttings once or twice to stimulate branching.

'New Wonder' fan flower
(*Scaevola aemula* 'New Wonder')

Good Neighbors

Fan flower makes a good showing all on its own but it is also nice combined with a neighbor or two, such as the 'Limelight' licorice plant (*Helichrysum petiolare* 'Limelight'). As a bedding plant, fan flower is equally worthy, with each plant able to cover an incredible amount of ground. Try it with green-flowering tobacco (such as *Nicotiana* 'Lime Green') for a pleasing color harmony.

Problems and Solutions

Whiteflies can be a problem, especially indoors; spray with insecticidal soap or light horticultural oil to keep them under control. Remove and destroy any leaves with winding tunnels under the leaf surface (a sign of leafminers).

Top Performer

Scaevola aemula (fan flower, fairy fan flower, Australian fan flower, blue fan flower): The species itself, although attractive, is rarely grown; longer-blooming cultivars have taken its place, some possibly hybrids with other *Scaevola* species. The cultivars are mostly in the blue to purple range, plus some whites, mauves, and pinks, usually with a pale spot at the base of each fan. Standard types can spread to 5 feet (1.5 m) across or trail downward to a similar length. The stems of dwarf types are less than half that length, so they're better suited to smaller containers and gardens.

Smart Substitute

For a very different effect in practically the same blue to violet color range as many fan flowers, try streptocarpella (*Streptocarpella* hybrids, which are also called *Streptocarpus*). This shrubby perennial has succulent, arching stems and fleshy, rounded, somewhat fuzzy leaves. Slender, branching pedicels bear tubular flowers with flaring, fan-shaped lobes. Grow in full sun to partial shade and water regularly, although it does tolerate some drought. Bring indoors in fall. Height: 8 to 12 inches (20 to 30 cm). Spread: 18 to 30 inches (45 to 75 cm).

Sutera

Bacopa, sutera

This incredible plant appeared, seemingly out of nowhere, in the mid-1990s and really took the container world by storm. It wasn't so much the small, white flowers with five broad lobes that caused such a sensation, or the small, rounded, toothed leaves, but rather the long, trailing stems that cascade nearly 2 feet by summer's end. With the plant's dense growth habit, you'd only need a sprinkling of flowers for it to be attractive, yet it blooms so heavily that the small flowers pack quite a punch, even from a distance.

Plant Profile

SUTERA
soo-TAIR-uh

■ **Bloom Color:** Mauve, pink, violet, red, white

■ **Bloom Time:** Late spring through early fall

■ **Height:** 3 inches (8 cm)

■ **Spread:** 12 to 20 inches (30 to 50 cm)

■ **Garden Uses:** Container planting, edging, hanging baskets, groundcover, mixed border, rock garden, wall planting

■ **Light Preference:** Full sun to partial shade

■ **Soil Preference:** Average to humus-rich, evenly moist well-drained soil

■ **Best Way to Propagate:** Take stem cuttings at any season

■ **Hardiness:** Frost-sensitive perennial grown as a tender annual

Growing Tips

If you want to try bacopa, you'll have to buy plants. Seed simply isn't available, at least not yet. You'll usually find it in the form of already established hanging baskets, but better nurseries now often have a "starter plant" section where you can buy rooted cuttings so you can prepare your own containers.

If possible, get a head start on the season by planting up your containers indoors a month or so before the last frost date. Besides giving the plants time to settle in, it will give you a chance to pinch it a few times to encourage denser growth; otherwise, the center of the clump tends to be a bit thin. Bacopa is not hardy, so don't be in a hurry to set it outside. Wait until there is no further risk of frost.

A water-retentive potting mix is a good choice for container use. This plant does need good drainage, true enough, but it grows best if its soil never dries out completely. Bacopa prefers cooler conditions than some other container annuals, so a bit of afternoon shade and regular waterings, plus the cooling evaporation that results from the latter, will help make it a happy camper. In cool or rainy climates, though, you'll find you get more bloom if you grow bacopa in full sun.

This is really a dual-purpose plant. It's marketed as a container plant and, of course, looks great when used that way. However, it also makes an extraordinary garden plant as an edging for a bed, as an annual groundcover, or as a filler for an empty space in a rock garden. One of the best ways I've seen it used was dripping down over the edge of a stone retaining wall.

In fall, either bring container plants inside and cut them back hard, or bring in a few cuttings; they root readily under good light and warm temperatures. Indoors, they'll do best in full sun with only moderate watering. In Zones 9 to 11, you can grow bacopa outdoors year-round as a perennial groundcover.

Good Neighbors

Bacopa is an outstanding addition to all kinds of containers, and it looks great with any sun-loving companion. A planting of white zonal geranium (*Pelargonium* × *hortorum*), white marguerites (*Argyranthemum* spp.), silvery dusty miller (*Senecio cineraria*), and white-flowering bacopa makes an attractive grouping for the night garden.

Problems and Solutions

The most common problem is whiteflies; a light horticultural oil spray is the best control for them. (Avoid using insecticidal soap on this plant because it can cause leaf and petal burn). Root or stem rots are possible if you keep the soil too moist. Some greenhouse growers report gray mold is a problem, but that is less likely outdoors, especially if you can give the plants a site with good air circulation.

Top Performer

Sutera cordata (bacopa, sutera): Also sold as *Bacopa* 'Snowflake'. This incredibly varied genus includes more than 130 species of annuals, perennials, shrubs, and small trees. If it's possible to cross even some of those species to create new plants suitable for garden use, there's going to be a revolution in plant breeding! And it has already started. After the original introduction of the white-flowered plants of *S. cordata*, which were very close to the wild species, recent years have seen totally new shades appear on the market—pinks, purples, lavenders, and even a cerise red—all new characteristics brought into the species by hybridizing with other species. Given the number of wild *Sutera* species with yellow flowers, I suspect that will be the next color to appear. And there are large-flowered bacopas, bicolored bacopas, and much, much more. This plant's future looks *very* bright!

Bacopa
(*Sutera cordata*)

Larry's Gardening Notes

When I first saw *Sutera cordata* in the mid-1990s, it was being sold under the name of *Bacopa monnieri*. Now, I know *B. monnieri* quite well because I used to raise aquarium plants, so I couldn't believe this hanging basket annual could possibly be a *Bacopa*. After all, *B. monnieri*—better known as water hyssop—is a semi-aquatic plant, whereas the new plant was anything but. I later learned it was all a mistake and since then the plant has been sold under its real name, but that hasn't stopped "bacopa" from becoming popular as its common name!

LARRY'S LAST LOOK: FLOWERING ANNUALS FOR CONTAINERS & HANGING BASKETS

Here are a few more flowering "annuals" that, like most of the plants in this chapter, are really tropical or subtropical shrubs or perennials. Enjoy them year after year by overwintering them indoors as houseplants.

COMMON AND BOTANICAL NAMES	LIGHT AND SOIL PREFERENCES	DESCRIPTION
Lilies-of-the-Nile *Agapanthus* cultivars	Full sun to partial shade Average, well-drained soil	They don't readily share space with other plants but are great choices in tubs on their own. They have grasslike leaves and rounded umbels of tubular, blue, purple, or white flowers. Height: 1–4 feet (30–120 cm) Spread: 1–3 feet (30–90 cm)
Lion's ear *Leonotis leonurus*	Full sun to partial shade Average, well-drained soil	Upright, bushy plants with dense whorls of tubular, orange or scarlet flowers at each node. Although you can grow it as an annual from early-sown seed, it's usually treated as a subtropical container plant and multiplied by cuttings. Height: 3–6 feet (90–180 cm) Spread: 3 feet (90 cm)
Mandevillas *Mandevilla* cultivars (also called *Dipladenia* spp.)	Full sun to partial shade Average to rich, evenly moist but well-drained soil	This exotic climber has caught on in a big way as a patio plant. Let its thick stems and leathery leaves dangle down around its container or provide a trellis of some sort. Spectacular, funnel-shaped, red, pink, or white flowers appear all summer. Allamandas (*Allamanda* spp.) are similar but yellow. Height: 3–22 feet (90 cm–6.6 m) Spread: 2–10 feet (60 cm–3 m)
Passion flowers *Passiflora* spp. and cultivars	Full sun to partial shade Rich, evenly moist but well-drained soil	There are hundreds of different passion flowers, most of them vigorous climbers with tendrils. The flowers consist of a saucerlike base overlaid with a feathery crown and a central stalk. Some types bear edible fruit. *P. caerulea,* greenish white with blue filaments, is most popular. Height: 3–30 feet (90 cm–9 m) Spread: 3–30 feet (90 cm–9 m)
Cape fuchsias *Phygelius* cultivars	Full sun Rich, evenly moist but well-drained soil	This suckering shrub is fairly hardy (to Zone 7 with protection), but it's generally grown as a container plant and brought indoors for the winter. It bears oval to lance-shaped leaves and somewhat arching stems with numerous pendant, tubular, five-lobed flowers that are red, orange, pink, cream, or yellow. Hummingbird heaven! Height: 30–60 inches (75–150 cm) Spread: 3–5 feet (90–150 cm)

COMMON AND BOTANICAL NAMES	LIGHT AND SOIL PREFERENCES	DESCRIPTION
Cape leadwort *Plumbago auriculata* (also called *P. capensis*)	Full sun Rich, well-drained soil	This plant looks marvelous dripping over the edge of a container or climbing up a support. It bears dense, phloxlike clusters of pale blue or white flowers from spring through fall. Tolerates salt spray. Height: 3–20 feet (90 cm–6 m) Spread: 3–10 feet (90 cm–3 m)
Butterfly flower *Schizanthus pinnatus*	Full sun to partial shade Rich, evenly moist, well-drained soil	Also called poor man's orchid for its small but numerous orchidlike flowers in a wide range of colors, all with a golden throat overlaid with purple splotches. Bushy plants with deeply cut, ferny leaves are almost hidden in blossoms. Prefers cool nights. Some varieties popular as greenhouse plants. Height: 1 to 4 feet (30 to 120 cm) Spread: 9 to 18 (23 cm to 45 cm)
Blue potato bush *Solanum rantonnetii* (also called *Lycianthes rantonnetii*)	Full sun Average to rich, evenly moist but well-drained soil	This large, leafy shrub is often trained as a standard. It produces numerous 1-inch (2.5-cm) shallowly trumpet-shaped flowers in shades of blue-violet with a bright yellow center. Close relatives *S. wendlandii* and *S. crispum,* both called potato vine, are similar but are climbers or ramblers. Height: 3–8 feet (90–240 cm) Spread: 9 to 18 inches (23 to 45 cm)

Lion's ear
(*Leonotis leonurus*)

Lily-of-the-Nile
(*Agapanthus* cv.)

Foliage Annuals
FOR CONTAINERS & HANGING BASKETS

Looking for fabulous, no-fail containers? Just mix plenty of the plants covered in this chapter, and you're practically guaranteed to succeed! These plants are prized for their attractive foliage, and unless true disaster occurs, leaves *always* look good. Foliage plants tend to act as fillers and trailers, rather than accents, but they still can add lots of color and texture to complement and contrast with the showy flowers of their companions. These "mixers" are very adaptable plants, likely to survive in sun or shade, in damp soil or dry: whatever the blooming plants they live with is fine by them. Not that you can't use them on their own, of course, but they really do make the plants around them look just great!

◄English ivy (*Hedera helix*) is a traditional choice for containers and hanging baskets: Its dark green foliage looks good at all times, spring through fall.

Come On Down!

The majority of plants described in this chapter are trailers—and that's no accident. What could be more attractive than a fountain of foliage cascading toward the ground to set off a more upright flowering annual? Typically, these foliage trailers are planted near the brim of mixed containers. As the blooming plants fill in and begin arching over the edge of the pot, the trailers dangle even farther downward, always keeping ahead of the crowd.

You can also grow foliage trailers in their own pots. Enjoy them as individuals, as a foliage collection, or as part of a mixed grouping of foliage and flowering containers. For even more interest, combine trailing foliage with trailing flowering annuals, such as ivy geraniums (*Pelargonium peltatum* hybrids), in the same container.

Of course, there are also many good foliage plants for containers that aren't trailers. Think of the dramatic cardoon (*Cynara cardunculus*), with its upright habit and deeply cut, silver leaves, or the fountainlike appearance of grass palm (*Cordyline australis*); both are perfectly suited as accents for center stage. The bushy stars of silvery dusty miller (*Senecio cineraria*) and multicolored Joseph's coat (*Alternanthera ficoidea*) are just two great choices for filler foliage.

Indoors and Out

You'll note that many of the top foliage plants for containers and hanging baskets are not true annuals. Most are hardy or tropical perennials or shrubs, renewed annually from cuttings or divisions. Actually, you'll probably think of many of the plants described here as houseplants, a

This mixed planting gets much of its pizzazz from the bright chartreuse of the sweet potato vine: nary a flower, but what color!

role some have played for generations. But when you see how great they look in a basket or container outdoors, I'm sure you'll agree that sticking them in a corner of your living room barely scratches the surface of their potential. In the brighter light and fresher air of outdoors, they'll grow much faster than indoors and fill in more densely as well. You'll hardly recognize some of them after they've spent a few months outdoors. Obviously, the "house-plant contingent" will overwinter marvelously indoors. You can either bring in the mother plant (already conveniently planted in a pot) or take cuttings and root them on a bright windowsill.

There are also a few hardy perennials that make super foliage plants for containers. In moderately mild climates, up to about Zone 7, they'll probably overwinter outdoors in pots with no particular care. In colder areas, place their containers on the ground in a protected spot in late fall, water them well, and cover them up with leaves or landscape fabric. With a little luck, they'll come through winter just fine. Or, since all the hardy perennial types are easy to multiply by cuttings, simply keep a mother plant in the ground somewhere and take fresh cuttings every spring.

Keeping Them Happy

Foliage plants need less fussy care than flowering ones. There's no deadheading to worry about, and most foliage plants just fill in on their own with a minimum of pinching. But container plants of all sorts need more care than the same plants growing in the ground, and it's worthwhile considering how you can best meet their needs.

The first thing you'll notice about container annuals is that they dry out very quickly. The reason is simple: For the best effect in containers, you have to grow plants more densely than in the garden, so you have more plants competing for the same water. The average pot is also quite small, so it doesn't hold a lot of soil that can act as a water reservoir. Plus, container plants are generally more exposed to moving air, so they lose more water to evaporation than in-ground plants. All told, the result can be a need for very frequent watering. It's not unusual for plants in a small container in full sun to need a thorough watering twice a day during periods of extreme heat.

Fortunately, there are ways of preventing plants from drying out too quickly. One basic technique is to use bigger containers; the larger the soil mass, the more water is absorbed. Container plantings will also dry out less quickly if you place them in partial shade. And use a more moisture-retentive mix in outdoor containers than you would for seedlings (less sand and more peat or compost).

There are even biodegradable water-retention crystals that you can add to your container mix. These tiny white crystals expand to many times their original size as they absorb water, then slowly release moisture as the mix gets drier. Some manufacturers claim they can reduce watering needs by 50 percent. Do test these before you use them on a large scale, though. They work best in soil-based mixes and in hot, dry climates. And they work better in large containers than in small ones. I find they make no difference in my cool summer area, but I know people in other climates who can't get by without them.

Another solution is to use drip irrigation. Carefully placed behind pots or along the base of a wall or veranda, the larger feeder hose will be scarcely noticeable. Just run the thinner "spaghetti tubes" from the feeder hose to each pot and add an emitter. Each system is somewhat different, but usually you can either adjust the rate of flow of each emitter according to your plant's needs or switch to an emitter with a faster or slower rate as needed. With a programmable timer, you can control watering when you're not at home. You can even add a rain gauge that turns it off when Mother Nature steps in to lend a helping hand!

Feed Me!

Plants in containers need extra feeding. Crowded conditions are partly to blame but so is leaching. Raindrops and hand watering both rinse container soil of its natural nutrients faster than they would with plants in the ground. I always add a generous dose of slow-release organic fertilizer as I pot up plants, then use a liquid or soluble fertilizer each time I water, at about one-quarter of the recommended rate.

Playing Musical Plants

One of the nice things about foliage plants compared to flowering ones is that they usually need less light to grow well. But if foliage isn't enough for your needs and you haven't found enough choice among the shade-tolerant flowering annuals, here's a way to create a beautiful display in even the deepest shade: Start with plenty of containers of shade-tolerant foliage plants for a lovely green background. Now grow just a few pots of your favorite sun-loving flowering annuals, placing them in their favorite sunny spot for most of the summer, but move each of them in turn to the shady corner for 2 weeks. You'll find that 2 weeks in the shade isn't enough to harm even the most sun-loving of flowering plants; yet, if you already have a background of greenery, it will only take a pot or two of flowers to create a magical effect. A schedule of 2 weeks of shade and 4 weeks of sun will keep them in perfect shape all summer long.

11 Other Foliage Plants for Containers

There is no lack of foliage plants for containers, certainly not when you consider that 9 out of every 10 foliage houseplants could fit the bill! If that's not enough, here are a few more plants with attractive foliage that are covered in other chapters.

Asparagus

Asparagus fern

Is it a fern or an asparagus? Well, an asparagus, actually! Just take a glance at the new stems: They look exactly like very thin stalks of edible asparagus as they emerge from the ground. Asparagus fern is a particularly charming plant in containers because the arching to trailing stems are covered with bright green, ferny foliage, giving the plant a lively, bushy appearance. The tiny white flowers are not particularly showy, but the black to red berries, while usually few in number, do add a bit of interest.

Plant Profile

ASPARAGUS
as-PAIR-uh-gus

- **Foliage Color:** Green

- **Foliage Time:** Late spring through early fall; year-round outdoors in mild climates and indoors

- **Height:** 16 to 36 inches (40 to 90 cm)

- **Spread:** 18 to 36 inches (45 to 90 cm)

- **Garden Uses:** Container planting, hanging baskets, groundcover, mixed border, rock garden, screening, wall planting; on trellises, fences, and pergolas

- **Light Preference:** Full sun to deep shade

- **Soil Preference:** Humus-rich, evenly moist but well-drained soil

- **Best Way to Propagate:** Sow seed indoors in late winter; divide at any season

- **Hardiness:** Frost-sensitive perennial grown as a tender annual

Growing Tips

Young plants are readily available as starter plants for container use, and they are a good option because growing the plant from seed is a very long process.

If you do wish to try raising them yourself, you'll find that most seed catalogs carry seed packs. Look for fresh seed, though, as older seed germinates poorly if at all. Soak seed in tepid water overnight, then sow just below the soil surface and keep at room temperature. Germination is *very* slow: a month or more! Sowing 14 to 18 weeks before the last frost date will give small plants just the right size to use as filler material. If you want larger plants, already starting to trail, sow indoors 24 weeks before the last frost date.

Asparagus fern grows nearly equally well in full sun or deep shade, although it may become a bit yellowed in extremely bright locations. Keep evenly moist both indoors and out. The roots of mature plants quickly fill their containers and make watering a challenge. Rather than try to water from above, dunk the roots in a bucket of water and let them soak for 1 hour.

To keep plants healthy and control their size, it's a good idea to divide and repot them every year or two. First, cut all the stems about 6 inches (15 cm) from their base; otherwise, their intermingling stems will be impossible to separate. With a saw or an ax, cut through the center of the plant, leaving a few eyes

FUN FACTS

Ferny appearance to the contrary, asparagus fern is almost leafless. The true leaves are reduced to the tiny prickles it bears on its stems. What look like leaves or needles are actually flattened stems called "cladodes."

(buds or new shoots) with each new section. It sounds radical, but the plants respond rapidly with fresh new growth.

Think Twice: In Zones 10 and 11, make sure to remove all of the berries, otherwise asparagus fern can self-sow and become extremely invasive. **Self-sowing**

Good Neighbors

Trailing from a large container, light, airy emerald feather (*Asparagus densiflorus* 'Sprengeri') would nicely set off more massive flowering annuals, such as zonal geraniums (*Pelargonium* × *hortorum*). The more upright, light green, ferny fingers of foxtail fern (*A. densiflorus* 'Myersii') would be interesting alternating with tuberous begonias in a window box.

Problems and Solutions

Watch out for rot in poorly drained soil. Excessive leaf yellowing is usually a sign of drought stress; keep the soil moderately moist to avoid problems. Spider mites and aphids are sometimes a problem, usually indoors; treat with insecticidal soap.

Top Performer

Asparagus densiflorus (asparagus fern): Two very different clones of this plant are commonly available, and both come true from seed. Emerald feather or emerald fern (*A. densiflorus* 'Sprengeri') has arching, then pendant, stems and a very soft, open appearance. It is most popular in mixed plantings. Foxtail fern (*A. densiflorus* 'Myersii', also called *A. meyeri* and *A.* 'Myers') produces more upright, arching stems densely cloaked in needles and is best in individual pots or as an accent plant in larger containers. Both produce red berries. Height: 16 to 36 inches (40 to 90 cm). Spread: 18 to 36 inches (45 to 90 cm).

More Recommended Asparagus Ferns

Asparagus setaceus (asparagus fern): Also called *A. plumosus*. The most fernlike of these plants, this species has upright stems that bend in the middle, then form a flattened triangle of tiny needles. Young plants are quite bushy, while adults are distinctly climbing or trailing. The berries are black. Height: 16 to 36 inches (40 to 90 cm). Spread: 18 to 36 inches (45 to 90 cm).

'Myersii' asparagus fern (*Asparagus densiflorus* 'Myersii')

Larry's Garden Notes

In the wild, asparagus fern is a climber, and its long stems can reach well up into nearby trees and shrubs. I've seen the twisting stems of *Asparagus setaceus* reaching up at least 12 feet (3.6 m) into a mango tree in a Cuban public garden. In containers, plants at least 2 years old tend to send up longer and longer stems. Either divide the plant, which will send it back to a more juvenile state, or cut off growing stems about 1 foot (30 cm) from their base to encourage branching and shorter new stems.

Chlorophytum

Spider plant

Everybody knows spider plant as a houseplant, but few realize that it makes a great outdoor plant as well: notably in hanging baskets and containers, but also in the garden. It has a rather grasslike appearance, with a dense central tuft of arching, sword-shaped leaves. The tufts produce long, arching stems (called stolons) that are actually modified flowerstalks; these first form small white flowers, then plantlets. The plantlets produce stolons of their own plus plantlets, which produce more in their turn. Well-tended plants can trail a good 6 feet (2 m), creating quite an impact in a hanging basket.

Plant Profile

CHLOROPHYTUM
klor-o-FYE-tum

- **Foliage Color:** Green, green and white

- **Foliage Time:** Late spring through early fall; year-round outdoors in mild climates and indoors

- **Height:** 6 to 8 inches (15 to 20 cm)

- **Spread:** 1 to 3 feet (30 to 90 cm)

- **Garden Uses:** Container planting, edging, hanging baskets, groundcover, rock garden, wall planting

- **Light Preference:** Full sun to deep shade

- **Soil Preference:** Humus-rich to poor, evenly moist but well-drained soil

- **Best Way to Propagate:** Root plantlets or divide at any season

- **Hardiness:** Frost-sensitive perennial grown as a tender annual

Growing Tips

Spider plants are sold everywhere, but why buy one? You certainly have a friend with plants to spare! Simply remove a plantlet from the mother plant by cutting its "umbilical cord" (stolon) and press its base, which will already have begun to sprout roots, into moist growing mix. Or place a pot of growing mix under or beside the mother plant and nestle the plantlet into its surface. When the "baby" has rooted, you can cut the cord. Or you can divide the plant at any season.

Spider plants growing outdoors will produce capsules of black seeds that you can sow when fresh. (They grow quite readily, but seed from variegated plants will produce only green seedlings.) Otherwise, seed is not commercially available.

Spider plants are as easy to grow outdoors as indoors. Just remember to place them in a shady spot outdoors at first, gradually moving them to more light over a week or so; setting them in full sun right away will cause leaf burn. Outdoor-acclimated plants can take full sun to deep shade and practically any kind of soil. For best results, keep them evenly moist. The roots of mature plants soon fill up the pot, however, making effective watering difficult. The best way to water adult plants is through drip irrigation or by soaking the entire rootball in a bucket of water.

Occasionally spider plants fail to produce stolons and plantlets, leading to the curious belief that

FUN FACTS

With the realization that the air in our homes is generally far more polluted than the air outdoors, spider plant merits extra attention as a houseplant. NASA studies have shown it to be one of the best plants for cleaning the air of toxins. Make sure to bring yours inside for the winter; your lungs will thank you!

they are male plants. That's nonsense, of course: All spider plants have "perfect" flowers (containing both male and female reproductive organs). And even if they didn't, male plants could still produce plantlets; it's only seeds they wouldn't be able to produce. Very low light and constant drought are the usual culprits, although plants constantly exposed to long days may also fail to offset.

Use adult spider plants on their own, in baskets or other containers where their cascades of trailing stolons and plantlets can show off: Their roots are far too domineering to allow them to share a pot with other plants! Young plantlets root readily, making an inexhaustible source of plants for decorating containers or even planting in the garden. (Spider plants make a very choice edging plant, for example.)

Think Twice: In Zones 10 and 11, where it is hardy, spider plant works great as a groundcover. Be forewarned, though, that it's very invasive: Those stolons that hang so prettily from baskets will quickly run through the garden, rooting as they go.

Spider plant
(*Chlorophytum comosum*)

Good Neighbors

A large spider plant adorned with plantlets makes a satisfying display by itself for a hanging basket. Or start with a young plant and add 'Imagination' verbena or bacopa (*Sutera cordata*) to the basket for summer color.

Problems and Solutions

Spider plant is basically trouble free. Drought stress causes brown leaf tips, especially if the container soil contains excess mineral salts. Keep the soil evenly moist, and occasionally water extra heavily so water runs out the bottom of the pot, carrying with it the excess salts.

Top Performer

Chlorophytum comosum (spider plant, ribbon plant): Entirely green plants with green stolons are occasionally found and correspond to the wild species (*C. comosum*). Much more popular, however, is 'Vittatum', with a broad cream to white stripe up the center of each leaf. The inverse variegation, with a green center and white margins ('Variegatum') is not as common, but just as lovely.

Smart Substitute

Another narrow-leaved plant that looks great both in a pot and in the garden is ornamental corn (*Zea mays* cultivars). Currently, there are essentially two selections with ornamental foliage, one with white stripes on green leaves (*Z. mays* 'Variegata') and either one or several similar selections called *Z. mays japonica*, 'Quadricolor', or 'Harlequin' with multicolor foliage. Sow indoors in peat pots 3 to 4 weeks before the last frost date or directly outdoors when the soil warms up. Height: 3 to 5 feet (90 to 150 cm). Spread: 2 feet (60 cm).

Glechoma

Ground ivy, creeping Charlie

"Onward and downward" seems to be this plant's motto: It has no desire to grow upward at all. Grown in the ground, it spreads out evenly in all directions, creating a solid mat of greenery. In a container, it reaches the rim and heads straight down, creating a perfect curtain of greenery in no time. Ground ivy appears in this chapter because its pairs of rounded leaves with prettily scalloped edges are its main attraction; it does, however, also produce tiny, tubular, light purple flowers in late spring and early summer. They are quite charming but create an impact only from up close.

Plant Profile

GLECHOMA
glay-KOE-muh

- **Foliage Color:** Green, green and white

- **Foliage Time:** Late spring through midfall; year-round outdoors in mild climates and indoors

- **Height:** 4 inches (10 cm)

- **Spread:** Indefinite

- **Garden Uses:** Container planting, edging, hanging baskets, groundcover, herb garden, rock garden, woodland garden, wall planting

- **Light Preference:** Full sun to deep shade

- **Soil Preference:** Average to humus-rich, evenly moist to damp but well-drained soil

- **Best Way to Propagate:** Divide or root plantlets at any season

- **Hardiness:** Hardy perennial

Growing Tips

Variegated ground ivy does not come true from seed (and in fact, rarely produces any). For your first time, buy one starter plant in early spring, then start dividing; you'll quickly have as much as you need. You *could* grow the all-green species from seed, available from herb seed catalogs, but why bother? It's an inferior plant that you can probably already find for free as a lawn weed!

The good news here is that variegated ground ivy is incredibly easy to grow. All you need to do is keep it evenly moist and it will thrive. Drought is its only enemy: It will recover from some drying out, but repeated exposure to dry conditions will do it in. Variegated ground ivy will tolerate any kind of soil, even sandy or rocky. Anything from full sun to deep shade is fine, although it's hard to keep this plant at its optimum moisture level in full sun, so it's better to place the container in at least afternoon shade in hot climates.

Besides working well in containers, variegated ground ivy also makes an interesting, soil-hugging groundcover, especially for semishady, moist spots. Just plant it somewhere its invasive habit won't be a problem, even though the variegated foliage makes it easy enough to spot and pull out if it does escape.

FUN FACTS

Is ground ivy invading your lawn? It has mine, and I think it's just great because I enjoy a mixed lawn where all sorts of grasses and flowers live together. I do realize, though, that not everyone agrees. If you want to get rid of it, get down on your hands and knees and pull it out! You *can* get rid of it, but only if you yank out each and every piece. If you don't have ground ivy, be very careful of ever letting this plant loose near your lawn.

Ground ivy is a snap to grow either from divisions or by rooting the numerous plantlets that form wherever the plant touches moist soil. In many climates, it will survive winter outdoors in pots, especially if you place them on the ground, although you'd better not count on that in Zones 1 through 6. It makes a truly superior houseplant if you grow it in bright light indoors.

Good Neighbors

Variegated ground ivy (*Glechoma hederacea* 'Variegata') is a good alternative to that other window-box staple, large periwinkle (*Vinca major*). It's a natural choice for combining with a wide variety of traditional container favorites, such as zonal geraniums (*Pelargonium × hortorum*) and verbenas. For a harmonious mix, combine it with the large, fuzzy foliage of peppermint geranium (*P. tomentosum*) and the delicate pink flowers of twinspur (*Diascia* hybrid). Or use it as an addition to a pairing of cascading petunias and licorice plant (*Helichrysum petiolare*).

Problems and Solutions

Not subject to insects or diseases.

Top Performer

Think Twice: *Glechoma hederacea* 'Variegata' (ground ivy, creeping Charlie, gill-over-the-ground, alehoof, cat's foot, field balm, dollar plant): I don't recommend growing the straight species, even in a pot, unless you're sure it can't escape. It is pretty enough, with deep green leaves that take on a purplish tinge in fall, but it is simply too invasive to be trustworthy. Instead, grow 'Variegata', with leaves that are irregularly bordered in white, sometimes with a pinkish tinge in cool weather. It is only slightly invasive. It isn't nearly as hardy as the species, though; consider it as fully hardy only in Zones 6 to 11. Elsewhere, bring it indoors and enjoy it as a spectacular houseplant for winter. If you already have variegated ground ivy in your garden, of course, you don't even need to bother overwintering it in containers; just dig up a few sprigs each spring for container use. **Self-sowing** 🖊

Varigated ground ivy
(*Glechoma hederacea* 'Variegata')

Smart Substitutes

Think Twice: Here's a plant with the same growth habit as ground ivy, hanging straight down from pots as much as 3 feet (90 cm), and a similar leaf shape: Australian violet, also called Tasmanian violet, ivy-leaved violet, or trailing violet (*Viola hederacea*, also called *V. reniforme*, *Erpetion hederaceum*, and *E. reniforme*). This outstanding basket plant blooms much of summer, with small, violetlike (not surprising, since it is a true violet) flowers in pale violet, purple, white or bicolors. In Zones 8 to 11, it also makes a superior groundcover, although it can be invasive.

Hedera

English ivy

If ever a plant could be called "all-purpose," English ivy is it! Long grown as a climbing plant for outdoor use, it was enjoyed as a houseplant during the Victorian era (and still remains popular for that purpose). It became popular as an evergreen groundcover at the end of the twentieth century and is now gaining ground as a trailer for containers. And all that from a plant that never even flowers, at least not in containers! Grow it indoors, grow it outdoors—ivy always satisfies.

Plant Profile

HEDERA
HEAD-ur-uh

- **Foliage Color:** Chartreuse, green, green and white, green and yellow

- **Foliage Time:** Late spring through early fall; year-round outdoors in mild climates and indoors

- **Height:** 6 inches (15 cm) when used as a hanging plant; 20 feet (6 m) or more as a climber

- **Spread:** 1 to 3 feet (30 to 90 cm); indefinite as a groundcover

- **Garden Uses:** Container planting, edging, hanging baskets, groundcover, rock garden, woodland garden, screening, wall planting; on a standard; on trellises, fences, walls, and pergolas

- **Light Preference:** Full sun to deep shade

- **Soil Preference:** Humus-rich, evenly moist but well-drained soil

- **Best Way to Propagate:** Take stem cuttings at any season

- **Hardiness:** Hardy climbing shrub grown as a half-hardy annual

Growing Tips

You'll find a wide range of ivies in any nursery, both as starter plants and in baskets and mixed containers, ready for display. There is, therefore, little need to grow them from seed, which can be, at any rate, a long process.

Ivy will grow just about anywhere, from rich, humusy soils to poor, stony ones. Green-leaved ivies tolerate the widest range of light conditions. Yellow- or white-variegated ivies tend to grow weakly or to lose their coloration in deep shade, and they may burn in full sun; but partial shade is perfect! All ivies need regular moisture and thrive in spots sheltered from strong sun and drying winds.

Ivies make exceptionally beautiful, easy-to-grow houseplants, so when winter is on the way, simply move them indoors. They'll tolerate extremely low light indoors, more than almost any other houseplant, as long as you summer them outside.

Multiply ivies by stem cuttings, or cut out the plantlets that form where a stem touches the soil and starts to root.

Warning: All parts of ivy are toxic and some people even react to ivy sap. Keep these plants out of reach of children and wear gloves while working with them if you are subject to skin problems.

Good Neighbors

A collection of ivies with different leaf shapes and colors makes an attractive container planting with year-round interest. In a mixed planting, allow ivy to cascade below colorful zonal geraniums (*Pelargonium* × *hortorum*) and petunias, or train it around a wire frame to create an interesting vertical accent.

Problems and Solutions

Rot and leaf diseases are possible in overly humid conditions; ensure good drainage and aeration to prevent them. Spider mites, scale insects, and mealy bugs are common indoors, causing weak growth and discolored, distorted foliage; treat these pests with insecticidal soap.

Top Performer

Think Twice: *Hedera helix* (English ivy): This plant is so variable it's hard to know where to begin! In general, though, look for self-branching, trailing types for outdoor use in containers. There are a nearly unlimited number of cultivars, with all sorts of variegation and leaves ranging from heart-shaped to maple-shaped to fan-shaped! I recommend finding a local or mail-order ivy specialist and picking out whatever strikes your fancy. English ivy can escape from culture and become a serious weed where it is hardy (Zones 5 to 10). It is harmless in containers, but if you plant it in the ground, make sure you don't let it wander! Height: 6 inches (15 cm) in a pot; 20 feet (6 m) or more as a climber. Spread: 1 to 3 feet (30 to 90 cm) in a pot; indefinite as a groundcover. **Self-sowing**

English ivy
(*Hedera helix*)

More Recommended Hedera

Think Twice: *Hedera canariensis* (Canary Island ivy, North African ivy, Algerian ivy): Also called *H. algeriensis*. This is a faster-growing ivy with huge, glossy, emerald green leaves from 4 to 8 inches (10 to 20 cm) long and almost as broad. The leaves, borne on purplish stalks, are usually heart shaped or three lobed. 'Gloire de Marengo', with irregular white to cream margins and gray splashes toward the center of the leaf, is the most popular of several variegated clones. Canary Island ivy is considerably less hardy than English ivy (Zones 7 to 11), so it could be a better choice where you're worried about ivy escaping into the environment. Height: 8 inches (20 cm) in a pot; 20 feet (6 m) or more as a climber. Spread: 1 to 3 feet (30 to 90 cm); indefinite as a groundcover.

Larry's Gardening Notes

To grow your own weeping "ivy tree," graft a trailing ivy onto an upright plant in the same family, such as *Schefflera* or × *Fatshedera*. Grafting sounds complicated but is easier than you think. Just cut slits at a sharp angle into the "trunk" of the future tree and insert ivy cuttings (with the cut end trimmed at an angle) into the slits. Use several cuttings per slit. Wrap the wounds in Teflon pipe tape until the cuttings show signs of life; then cut off the top of the original plant and remove all of its leaves. Pinch your ivy so it fills in nicely. You can then either let it trail (it will remain in its juvenile form) or keep pruning it for a more upright appearance. Do bring your ivy tree indoors for the winter, as it won't be hardy beyond Zone 10.

Helichrysum

Licorice plant

I first saw this plant in the United Kingdom in the early 1990s and was blown away by its incredible soft, rich texture and silvery gray color. I just love the felty texture of stems and the rounded, silvery leaves, as well as the undisciplined way the silvery stems creep in and out in every direction. Licorice plant is neither upright nor pendant, but somewhere in between. You might think of it as "semi-trailing": growing outward more than up, with the stems arching downward under their own weight as they leave the confines of the pot.

Plant Profile

HELICHRYSUM
hel-ih-CRY-sum

- **Foliage Color:** Chartreuse, silver, silver and chartreuse
- **Foliage Time:** Late spring through early fall; year-round in mild climates and indoors
- **Height:** Varies by species; see individual listings
- **Spread:** Varies by species; see individual listings
- **Garden Uses:** Container planting, edging, hanging baskets, ground cover, annual hedge, rock garden, specimen plant, wall planting
- **Light Preference:** Full sun to partial shade
- **Soil Preference:** Average to poor, very well-drained soil; tolerates neutral to alkaline soil
- **Best Way to Propagate:** Divide or take stem cuttings in late spring or summer
- **Hardiness:** Frost-sensitive shrub grown as a tender annual

Growing Tips

Licorice plant isn't a true annual but a relatively slow-growing shrub always grown from cuttings. You can begin with a starter plant, available in nurseries that have a container-plant section, or by buying a mixed planting or basket that contains it.

Full sun is best, but partial shade is sufficient. Licorice plant adapts to moderate moisture but prefers somewhat dry conditions, so it can accompany annuals that prefer better drainage or drier conditions than most, like marguerites (*Argyranthemum* spp.) and Madagascar periwinkle (*Catharanthus roseus*).

Allowed to grow entirely on its own, licorice plant is inclined to be a bit straggly. Pinch it at planting time, and snip off wayward stems as needed, and it will fill in nicely. Overwintered plants will probably bloom the second year, usually toward fall. The flowers are not unattractive but tend to detract from the exceptionally beautiful foliage, so many people simply pinch them out.

In frost-free climates, you can grow licorice plant outdoors year-round. Elsewhere, you can keep it going year after year by bringing the original plant indoors for the winter or by starting new plants from cuttings at the end of summer. Indoors, it will need to have full sun and does best if it is not overwatered.

Good Neighbors

I'm not sure how we ever got along without this mixer, which has become a staple in container

FUN FACTS

Ever wonder where the name "licorice plant" came from? On a really hot, dry, windless day, when the plants are a bit drought-stressed, the leaves give off a faint odor rather like licorice.

plantings. Licorice plant has the somewhat unique ability to weave among all types of flowering and foliage plants, enhancing their good looks. Winding along a garden path, purple-leaved sweet potato vine (*Ipomoea batatas* 'Blackie') and licorice plant make a charming couple.

Problems and Solutions

Licorice plant is usually insect free, but it can be subject to rot or leaf spots in poorly drained conditions; give it well-drained soil or potting medium, and avoid overwatering it.

Top Performer

Helichrysum petiolare (licorice plant, licorice vine, silver licorice): Also called *H. petiolatum*. Described above, this is the plant that has caused such a sensation. Besides the usual silver-leaved form, often sold as 'Silver' although it's simply the normal species, there are a few very interesting cultivars. 'Petite Licorice' is a smaller-leaved variety while 'Limelight' (also called 'Aurea') is a beautiful chartreuse shade, a color rarely seen in foliage plants. Also charming are 'Variegatum' and its smaller cousin 'Roundabout', which are irregularly mottled with chartreuse and silver. Most other plants sold as *H. petiolare* cultivars really belong to one or another of the other silver-leaved plants described in "Kissing Cousins" (at right). Height: 20 inches (50 cm). Spread: 1 to 5 feet (30 to 150 cm).

More Recommended Helichrysum

Helichrysum italicum subsp. *serotinum* (curry plant): Formerly called *H. angustifolium*. A hardier plant (to Zone 7) with beautiful silvery white, very narrow leaves. Furthermore, the foliage gives off an intense aroma of curry when bruised or pinched. In spite of its common name, it is not the plant curry is derived from (curry is, in fact, a mixture of spices based on turmeric), although you can use it to add a slight curry taste to salads. Curry plant is an upright, shrubby plant that works well as a filler in a container or in the garden. It produces clusters of bottlebrush-like yellow flowers in fall. Height: 2 feet (60 cm). Spread: 3 feet (90 cm).

Licorice plant
(*Helichrysum petiolare*)

Kissing Cousins

Recent years have seen a veritable "silver rush" among container enthusiasts! *Plecostachys serpyllifolia*, also called *Helichrysum microphyllum* and *H. nanum*, is a trailing plant with much smaller leaves, reaching about 8 inches (20 cm) high and 18 inches (45 cm) wide in containers. Cushion bush (*Leucophyta brownii*, also called *Calocephalus brownii*) is also silvery white, but very different, forming an intricate mass of silvery stems. Height: 16 to 30 inches (40 to 75 cm). Spread: 16 to 36 inches (40 to 90 cm).

Ipomoea batatas

Sweet potato vine, sweet potato

Originally tall climbing plants, domesticated sweet potatoes have been selected for shorter, nonclimbing stems and much larger, edible tubers. Since they are multiplied by vegetative means, flowering was considered a waste of energy and has been largely bred out of the edible types, although they still do occasionally produce lavender to pale purple, trumpet-shaped flowers. The ornamental cultivars so popular for containers are a new development, with large heart-shaped leaves that are entire or three- to five-lobed in various colors: deep purple, chartreuse, or variegated.

Plant Profile

IPOMOEA BATATAS
ih-poe-MEE-uh ba-TA-tus

- **Foliage Color:** Chartreuse, deep purple, variegated
- **Foliage Time:** Early summer through early fall; year-round in mild climates and indoors
- **Height:** 8 inches (20 cm)
- **Spread:** 18 inches to 8 feet (45 to 240 cm)
- **Garden Uses:** Container planting, edging, hanging baskets, groundcover, rock garden, specimen plant; on trellises
- **Light Preference:** Full sun to partial shade
- **Soil Preference:** Humus-rich, evenly moist but well-drained soil
- **Best Way to Propagate:** Divide roots at any season
- **Hardiness:** Frost-sensitive perennial grown as a tender annual

Growing Tips

Most nurseries now carry ornamental sweet potatoes as starter plants, as well as baskets and containers already planted with them. Seed is not available nor will it be because sweet potatoes don't come true from seed.

Wait until average nighttime temperatures remain above 60°F (15°C) before putting sweet potatoes outdoors; they really can't stand cool weather. In the garden, they love a warm spot protected from strong wind, which can tear their tender leaves. Just being in a container helps them grow better because the soil will be warmer than in the garden, but gardeners in hot summer areas can plant sweet potatoes in the ground as well. For rapid leafy growth, feed them generously with nitrogen-rich fertilizer. Sweet potatoes prefer soil that remains at least somewhat moist; they will wilt badly when conditions are dry.

Sweet potatoes look just wonderful cascading downward from a pot, but you can also train them up onto a trellis or other support for a different effect.

At summer's end, you have a choice of ways of overwintering your sweet potatoes. You could just let them freeze, but that's a waste considering how easy they are to keep for the winter. You can bring in a container-grown plant or early fall stem cuttings before the first frost, keeping them well watered and in bright light over winter. Or you can bring in the tubers. Cure them first by exposing them to full sun and hot temperatures for 1 week; then store in peat moss or vermiculite at 50° to 60°F (10° to 13°C). When new sprouts appear in early spring, cut the tuber into sections, each with at least one eye (bud). Let the sections dry overnight, then pot them up, just covering the tuber slice with soil.

In Zones 10 and 11, you can leave sweet potatoes outdoors in containers year-round. They often overwinter in the ground (although they will lose their leaves during cold weather) even in Zone 9.

Good Neighbors

The large leaves of the sweet potato vine work beautifully with other foliage plants, especially those with strong personalities, such as caladiums and cannas. A combination of 'Pretoria' canna with the chartreuse-leaved 'Margarita' and almost black 'Blackie' sweet potato vine is beautiful with or without flowers.

Problems and Solutions

Leaf and stem diseases are most common in the garden in spots where sweet potatoes have grown year after year: Rotate plantings over a 3- to 4-year period and you should be able to control them. Indoors, watch out for foliar thrips, which cause silvery streaking on leaves; spray with insecticidal soap to control them.

Top Performer

Ipomoea batatas (sweet potato vine, sweet potato): This tuberous-rooted plant has recently started to make a splash in ornamental gardens, and it is already very popular. There are several cultivars of very confused nomenclature, but all fall into three distinct color categories: purple, chartreuse, and variegated. 'Blackie', with its five-lobed, almost star-shaped leaves, is a dark purple that is nearly black. 'Ace of Spades' is the same shade, but it has heart-shaped leaves. Among those with vivid chartreuse, heart-shaped leaves (a color that looks particularly nice against a dark background) are 'Margarita', 'Terrace Lime', and 'Sulfur'. I think they are one and the same plant, but others insist that 'Terrace Lime' is more compact than the other plants. Then there is the more variable 'Pink Frost,' which may or may not be the same as 'Variegata'. It has irregularly shaped green leaves that are heavily splashed with pink and white.

'Ace of Spades' sweet potato vine (*Ipomoea batatas* 'Ace of Spades')

Larry's Garden Notes

Ornamental sweet potatoes produce the same edible tubers that have made the sweet potato a valuable food source. But if you're interested in getting the largest tubers for harvest, try growing regular sweet potatoes in containers. It's the ideal solution for Northern growers whose summers are too short to mature sweet potatoes in the ground. Use a fast-maturing type, like 'Georgia Jet' or 'Carver', starting them indoors in early spring. Plant them out in large containers and in full sun when the weather warms up.

Lamium

Lamium, yellow archangel, dead nettle

Now, you might wonder, what is such a hardy perennial doing in a book about annuals? The answer is simple: It's probably best grown *as* an annual, in containers. This plant is a low-growing, spreading groundcover with terribly invasive habits—which don't matter a fig if you grow it in containers! Each textured leaf looks like it has been gilded with silver, and to heighten its effect, it usually takes on a reddish tinge in cold weather. The hooded, late-spring or early-summer flowers are not unattractive, but it's the plant's cascading habit and gorgeous leaves that always steal the show.

Plant Profile

LAMIUM
LAY-mee-um

- **Foliage Color:** Green and silver

- **Foliage Time:** Late spring through early fall; year-round in mild climates and indoors

- **Height/drop:** 6 to 12 inches (15 to 30 cm)

- **Spread:** Varies by species; see individual listings

- **Garden Uses:** Container planting, edging, hanging baskets, groundcover, mass planting, woodland garden, wall planting

- **Light Preference:** Full sun to deep shade

- **Soil Preference:** Average, well drained, evenly moist soil

- **Best Way to Propagate:** Divide or take stem cuttings at any season

- **Hardiness:** Hardy perennial

Growing Tips

Grow lamiums from purchased plants, which are readily available in just about every nursery. Young rooted cuttings ("starter plants") are fine, but the real bargain may well be an established plant that already has plenty of shoots; these plants are incredibly easy to multiply through cuttings or division.

Lamiums are very tolerant plants, taking full sun and deep shade with equal aplomb. In containers, however, full sun often equals regular droughts, and lamiums *hate* drying out. You'll find they grow most readily in fairly deep shade, where the air remains cool and the soil is more likely to remain moist.

Plant lamiums in containers in early spring; then pinch the young plants a few times to stimulate branching. Water as needed to keep the soil at least moderately moist. Fertilizing is essentially unnecessary, and there is no need to deadhead.

In Zones 7 to 11, lamiums will probably overwinter in their container, even if they remain exposed all winter. In colder climates, try placing the container on the ground near an east or north wall and covering it with dead leaves or a piece of landscape fabric. Or bring a plant or a cutting indoors for the winter; lamiums make great houseplants.

Good Neighbors

Lamiums cascade attractively from containers of sturdy growers such as cardoon (*Cynara*

FUN FACTS

Don't feel threatened by the common name "dead nettle"; this plant will not sting you like true nettles do. In fact, the word "dead" means, in this case, "unarmed." In other words, it's a nettle without the bite!

cardunculus), hibiscus, or even small shrubs. The silver-white variegation of many selections will accent the white flowers of woodland tobacco (_Nicotiana sylvestris_) beautifully in a good-size container, creating an excellent display for an evening garden.

Problems and Solutions

Leaf diseases can be a problem in sheltered parts of the garden but rarely show up in containers, where air circulation is usually excellent. Slugs and snails may attack plants grown in the ground, but are likewise generally absent from container plants.

Top Performer

Think Twice: _Lamium galeobdolon_ (yellow archangel): Also called _Galeobdolon luteum_ and _Lamiastrum galeobdolon_. First a warning: This plant is terribly weedy and really shouldn't be set loose in a garden setting. On the other hand, it's an absolutely wonderful container plant; just be careful to place it somewhere where it can't root its way into the soil. Yellow archangel's small hooded flowers are yellow with brown spots and are produced on short spikes. 'Florentinum' (also called 'Variegatum') is the usual cultivar for containers, although there are others. It has large leaves beautifully marked in silver on either side of a green center vein. This plant has no upward growth at all but hangs straight down for several feet if it is in a pot or basket. Height/drop: 6 to 12 inches (15 to 30 cm). Spread: Indefinite. 'Hermann's Pride' is an upright-growing, noninvasive variety you might want to try in the garden.

More Recommended Lamium

Think Twice: _Lamium maculatum_ (dead nettle): This species is also invasive, although much less so than _L. galeobdolon_; you can grow it in your garden without having to worry that it will take over. In pots, it hangs downward only about 18 inches (45 cm) or so, so it isn't as impressive as yellow archangel. However, the leaves are highly attractive (often nearly entirely silver), and the pink, purple, or white flowers are longer lasting and more beautiful, so it still makes an excellent container plant. Height/drop: 6 to 12 inches (15 to 30 cm). Spread: 1 to 3 feet (30 to 90 cm).

'Florentinum' yellow archangel (_Lamium galeobdolon_ 'Florentinum')

Larry's Garden Notes

If you already have lamiums growing in your yard, why bother buying new plants each spring or even trying to overwinter container plants? You already have all the propagation material you'll ever need! Just dig up a few clumps in early spring and pot them up; they'll soon be at full size. And, back in the garden, the plants grow fast enough that they'll soon fill in any gaps. Or start new plants from stem cuttings inserted directly into the container. Just water regularly at first; they root quickly and will soon be in full growth!

Lotus

Lotus vine, parrot's beak

Decisions, decisions! Do you want to make the special effort necessary to get this plant to bloom, or are you willing to take the easy way out and grow it primarily for its foliage? I suggest treating it as a foliage plant while coming as close as you can to its rather particular needs as is reasonably possible. That way if it doesn't bloom, you'll still get to enjoy its long, trailing stems and soft, silvery, needlelike foliage. And if it does bloom, you can invite friends over to admire the startling, beaklike flowers in brilliant shades of yellow, orange, or red.

Plant Profile

LOTUS
LOW-tus

- **Foliage Color:** Silvery green

- **Foliage Time:** Late spring through early fall; year-round in mild climates and indoors

- **Height:** 8 inches (20 cm)

- **Spread:** Indefinite

- **Garden Uses:** Container planting, edging, hanging baskets, groundcover, rock garden, wall planting

- **Light Preference:** Full sun to partial shade

- **Soil Preference:** Average, light, very well-drained soil

- **Best Way to Propagate:** Take stem cuttings at any season

- **Hardiness:** Frost-sensitive subshrub grown as a tender annual

Growing Tips

The most common way of obtaining lotus vine is as a rooted cutting (a "starter plant"), sold in the container-plant section of better nurseries in spring. You may also find it already planted into a mixed container or hanging basket. If your local nursery doesn't carry it, you can obtain it by mail order.

With a little luck, you may also be able to find seed. If so, start it indoors 8 to 10 weeks before the last frost date at 60° to 65°F (15° to 18°C). It germinates in 10 to 14 days. Sow into a starting mix with added sterilized sand. (The tiny seedlings are quite fragile and may suffer from damping-off in an overly moisture-retentive mix.) In frost-free climates, you might instead choose to sow the seeds outdoors. If so, start them very early, while the soil is still cool (perhaps in February or March).

Put the plants outdoors after all risk of frost has passed. Full sun or very light shade is a must in most climates, although partial shade is preferable in very hot summer areas; lotus vine doesn't appreciate extreme heat. Let the soil get nearly dry, then water well. This will be easier if you use a mix that drains more rapidly than usual; try mixing one part sand to two parts of your regular mix. Lotus vine loves seaside conditions and readily tolerates cool breezes and salt spray.

Seed-grown plants will not bloom the first year. Cutting-grown plants *may* bloom, but they're more likely to simply put out numerous new stems. If a few flowers do occur, enjoy!

Lotus vine is hardy in Zones 9 to 11. Elsewhere, overwinter it indoors; bring in the original plants or start some cuttings. If you hope to see your lotus vine bloom, you'll need to expose it to cool winter temperatures: 45° to 50°F (7° to 10°C) at night and not much more than 60°F (15°C) during the day. Supply the brightest light possible, even full sun, and don't overwater. With this kind of treatment, there's a good chance your lotus vine will start to bloom indoors toward the end of winter and will continue to bloom until early summer when it goes outside.

Good Neighbors

The soft gray, needlelike foliage of lotus vine looks particularly nice with the richly textured foliage of purple heliotrope (*Heliotropium arborescens*) or purple sage (*Salvia officinalis* 'Purpurascens'). Persian shield (*Strobilanthes dyerianus*), 'Purple Wave' petunias, and lotus vine make a lovely potted trio.

Problems and Solutions

Lotus vine is subject to leaf diseases under high humidity and stagnant air; prevent them by increasing air circulation around the plant. Indoors, spider mites, aphids, and mealy bugs can cause distorted, discolored foliage; control these pests with insecticidal soap.

Top Performer

Lotus berthelotii (lotus vine, parrot's beak, coral gem): Probably the more common of the two species usually grown, this one has narrower, more silvery leaves. The flowers, when they occur, are upward pointing and bright orange-red to scarlet. They look somewhat like pea flowers, but with two arching points that meet at the tip, rather like a partly open parrot's beak or a lobster's claw. Height: 8 inches (20 cm). Spread: Indefinite.

More Recommended Lotus Vines

Lotus maculatus (lotus vine, parrot's beak, coral gem): Almost identical to the previous species, but with yellow flowers tipped orange or red. 'Gold Flash' has flowers with more orange than yellow. Height: 8 inches (20 cm). Spread: Indefinite.

Lotus vine
(*Lotus berthelotii*)

Kissing Cousins

For experts only, another silvery-leaved member of the pea family is *Clianthus formosus,* an Australian native known as Sturt's desert pea, glory pea, or desert pea. Each pinnate (featherlike) leaf is 5 to 7 inches (13 to 18 cm) long, with many oval leaflets cloaked in soft, silky, gray hairs. The spectacular flowers are shaped like elongated lobster claws and are fiery red with a brilliant black projection in the middle. Grow as per lotus vine, but even greater care is needed with growing conditions—be especially careful to avoid overwatering. Height: 8 inches (20 cm). Spread: 4 feet (1.2 m).

Plectranthus

Mintleaf, Swedish ivy

The old-fashioned houseplant known as Swedish ivy (*Plectranthus australis*) has almost been lost among the wave of new species coming to the forefront as top-of-the line foliage plants for containers. Although you might have a problem finding *all* the plants described here, you'll find at least some in every nursery. Most of those offered as container plants are spreading to prostrate, shrubby perennials that either trail slightly or dangle straight down. They share square, often somewhat succulent stems and fleshy, often fuzzy leaves with scalloped edges.

Plant Profile

PLECTRANTHUS
plek-TRAN-thus

- **Foliage Color:** Varies by species; see individual listings

- **Foliage Time:** Late spring through early fall; year-round in mild climates and indoors

- **Height:** Varies by species; see individual listings

- **Spread:** Varies by species; see individual listings

- **Garden Uses:** Container planting, edging, hanging baskets, groundcover, herb garden, rock garden, woodland garden, specimen plant, wall planting

- **Light Preference:** Partial shade; some prefer full sun

- **Soil Preference:** Average to humus-rich, well-drained soil

- **Best Way to Propagate:** Take stem cuttings at any season

- **Hardiness:** Frost-sensitive perennial grown as a tender annual

Growing Tips

Seed of Swedish ivies is almost never available, so buy starter plants or ready-to-hang baskets at your local nursery. Put Swedish ivies outdoors after the air has warmed up in spring. They'll grow in just about any kind of soil but prefer average to rather rich conditions. Most will grow in full sun to fairly deep shade, but they prefer partial shade, especially in hot summer climates; they can burn in truly intense sunlight. In mixed containers, though, you can grow all of them in full sun because they're mostly trailing plants that will be shaded by their neighbors.

As companion plants to more spectacular flowering annuals, Swedish ivies usually adapt to whatever regime you give their roommates: They do equally well in evenly moist soil and in drier conditions, although they dislike both constantly soggy soil and extreme drought. Most of them flower rather readily, with terminal spikes of tiny, two-lipped, tubular flowers in white, pink, or purple. The branches that bloom tend to degenerate afterward, though, so it's best to clip off the spikes while they are still in the bud stage.

Think Twice: Bring in plants or cuttings for winter, or dig up any prostrate stems that have rooted on their own. They make incredibly easy houseplants to care for in bright or even, in some cases, low-light conditions. Swedish ivies are hardy only in Zones 10 to 11, but be careful if you plant them in the soil in those zones; they can become invasive.

Good Neighbors

For a soft color scheme, try variegated mintleaf (*Plectranthus madagascariensis* 'Variegated Mintleaf') with a pink verbena and silvery licorice plant (*Helichrysum petiolare*). Enhance the beauty of soft gray silverleaf plectranthus (*P. argentatus*) with a more delicate mixer, such as 'Imagination' verbena or fan flower (*Scaevola aemula*).

Problems and Solutions

Swedish ivy is rarely bothered by insect or disease problems.

Top Performer

Plectranthus madagascariensis 'Variegated Mintleaf' (variegated mintleaf, miller's wife): Also called *P. madagascariensis* 'Marginatus', *P. coleoides* 'Marginatus Minimus', and *P. coleoides* 'Variegatus'. This selection has become immensely popular for containers, and understandably so: It's a totally prostrate plant with stems that hang straight down, reaching as much as 30 inches (75 cm) or longer. It has the smallest leaves of any common Swedish ivy: Only 1¼ to 1½ inches (3 to 4 cm) long, they are dark green with a white margin, and they smell strongly of mint when crushed. This plant rarely blooms, but its all-green parent, *P. madagascariensis*, produces pale lavender to white flowers. Height: 4 inches (10 cm). Spread: Indefinite.

More Recommended Plectranthus

Plectranthus argentatus (silverleaf plectranthus): This massive, shrubby, upright plant is very different from the others as it has no tendency to trail. It bears very large leaves for a Swedish ivy: to 4½ inches (11 cm) long. They are fully covered in silvery fuzz, giving the plant an attractive gray-green appearance with a silvery sheen. Its massive terminal spikes of lilac or pink flowers don't need to be removed and are quite stunning. Give this species full sun. Height: 2 to 3 feet (60 to 90 cm). Spread: 2 to 3 feet (60 to 90 cm).

P. forsteri (Forster's mintleaf): Also called *P. coleoides*. This plant looks very much like a somewhat larger version of *P. madagascariensis* with a much more upright habit. 'Marginatus' (also called 'Albomarginatus'), with white-edged leaves, is the most commonly grown form. Height: 10 inches (25 cm). Spread: 3 feet (90 cm).

Variegated mintleaf (*Plectranthus madagascariensis* 'Variegated Mintle[...]

Larry's Garden Notes

Ask for "thyme" in a public market in Mexico or the West Indies, and people will probably point you to *Plectranthus amboinicus* (also called *Coleus amboinicus*). Commonly called Spanish thyme, Cuban oregano, Mexican mint, or Indian borage, this strongly scented, spreading to trailing herb is widely used in cooking in tropical areas of the New World. The species has gray-green foliage, but there is a popular cultivar, 'Variegata', with leaves edged in white and sometimes flushed pink.

Senecio

German ivy

Among the thousand-plus species of *Senecio,* one group of great interest for the container gardener is the "daisy ivies," including German ivy (*S. mikanioides,* now more correctly *Delairea odorata*) and wax ivy (*S. macroglossus*). Climbing plants in their native southern Africa, these species are handsome, easy-to-grow trailers for container gardens. Both produce nearly prostrate growth if they have nothing to wrap themselves around, then cascade straight downward when they reach the edge of the pot, creating a dense waterfall of greenery that can drop 10 feet (3 m) or more. Try them from a second-floor window box: Breathtaking!

Plant Profile

SENECIO
seh-NEE-cee-oh

- **Foliage Color:** Green or variegated
- **Foliage Time:** Late spring through early fall; year-round in mild climates and indoors
- **Height:** 4 to 6 inches (10 to 15 cm) when grown as a trailer; to 10 feet (3 m) or more when allowed to climb
- **Spread:** Indefinite
- **Garden Uses:** Container planting, edging, hanging baskets, groundcover, rock garden; on trellises, fences, and pergolas
- **Light Preference:** Full sun to deep shade
- **Soil Preference:** Average, well-drained soil
- **Best Way to Propagate:** Take stem cuttings at any season
- **Hardiness:** Frost-sensitive perennial grown as a tender annual

Growing Tips

Seed of German and wax ivies is rarely, if ever, available, so start with a purchased plant. Look for starter plants or ready-to-use baskets, or buy a mixed container that has used them as trailing material.

Plant German and wax ivy outdoors when all danger of frost is past. Pinch young plants a few times early in the season to stimulate branching. These tough plants will take just about anything (except frost)—even deep shade, although partial shade will give it thicker growth. A bit of protection from full afternoon sun is also wise for wax ivy. Both plants adapt well to evenly moist soil but also have some drought resistance.

Except in the mildest climates, you'll need to bring German and wax ivies indoors over winter, either as the original plants or as cuttings (which are easy to root).

Good Neighbors

German and wax ivies will work equally well in a window box or outdoor container. Let them trail below a showier companion, such as zonal geranium (*Pelargonium* × *hortorum*), or train them on a framework for a vertical accent.

Problems and Solutions

Whiteflies, spider mites, and aphids are occasional problems indoors; control these pests with repeated sprayings of insecticidal soap.

FUN FACTS

I just love the scent given off by a crushed leaf of German ivy. I'm sure some people don't appreciate it, but to me, its fresh "green" scent, somewhat like wintergreen, is very springlike. Try it and see what you think!

Top Performer

Think Twice: *Delairea odorata,* formerly known as *Senecio mikanioides* (German ivy, parlor ivy, Cape ivy). This evergreen South African plant became known as German ivy because it first became popular in that country. A rather weak climber usually grown as a trailer or groundcover, it produces fleshy, bright green leaves with five to seven lobes, much like a maple leaf. Don't count on it for flowers, though. Its small, yellow flowers usually bloom only in fall, just after most of us have either cut back the plant to bring it indoors (thus removing the flower buds) or have started new plants from cuttings, which are too young to bloom. German ivy will often survive winter by dying to its roots and resprouting in Zone 9. In fact, use precaution when planting it in mild climates, as it has been known to escape from culture and become a noxious weed. Height: 4 to 6 inches (10 to 15 cm) when grown as a trailer; to 10 feet (3 m) or more when allowed to climb. Spread: Indefinite.

German ivy
(*Delairea odorata,* formerly known as *Senecio mikanioides*)

More Recommended Senecio

Senecio macroglossus (wax ivy, Cape ivy, Natal ivy): This plant is similar to *Delairea odorata* in its general appearance and growing habits. A closer look, though, reveals that it has more distinctly triangular leaves that are even fleshier than those of German ivy. Furthermore, the leaves are brilliantly shiny, looking as though they have been dipped in wax. It is also a more vigorous climber, so while it dangles quite nicely from a pot, you'll also find stems that wrap around their companions and start to climb back up. The white to cream-colored daisy flowers are beautiful, but unfortunately quite rare when the plant is grown in a container. This plant is hardy only in Zones 10 and 11. 'Variegata' is a popular cultivar with irregular cream to yellow margins. It tends to occasionally sport all-green stems (which you should remove so they don't take over) and totally albino growth with creamy yellow leaves and pretty pink stems. Height: 4 to 6 inches (10 to 15 cm) when grown as a trailer; to 10 feet (3 m) or more when allowed to climb. Spread: Indefinite.

Larry's Garden Notes

During the mid- to late-twentieth century, when mixed container plantings were considered totally passé, most of the trailing container plants of the Victorian era went the way of the dinosaur. There were two exceptions though: German ivy and vinca vine (*Vinca major*). Generations of gardeners kept up the tradition of planting German ivy outdoors in containers each summer and bringing in cuttings each fall. Even though more colorful trailers are now widely available, this dependable and handsome plant is definitely still worth growing!

Tradescantia

Purple heart, wandering Jew

This genus has provided a number of great candidates for container culture. Many have long been grown as houseplants, but they also make wonderful plants for outdoor containers, either during the summer months or in mild climates. For outdoor use, though, one stands out from the crowd: purple heart (*T. pallida* 'Purpurea'). The whole plant is an extraordinarily rich violet-purple. A closer inspection shows this striking color is composed of deep purple leaves overlaid with bluish bloom: What an exceptional combination!

Plant Profile

TRADESCANTIA
trad-es-KANT-ee-uh

- **Foliage Color:** Varies by species; see individual listings

- **Foliage Time:** Late spring through early fall; year-round in mild climates and indoors

- **Height:** Varies by species; see individual listings

- **Spread:** Varies by species; see individual listings

- **Garden Uses:** Container planting, edging, hanging baskets, groundcover, mixed border, rock garden, specimen plant, wall planting

- **Light Preference:** Varies by species; see individual listings

- **Soil Preference:** Average to humus-rich, well-drained soil

- **Best Way to Propagate:** Take stem cuttings at any season

- **Hardiness:** Frost-sensitive perennial grown as a tender annual

Growing Tips

Look for starter plants or already-planted baskets in the container plant or houseplant sections of your local nursery. Seed is rarely, if ever, available.

Don't put these tropical or subtropical plants outdoors until nighttime temperatures remain above 50°F (10°C). Give them a sheltered spot because strong winds can easily break their fragile stems. Pinch them regularly to keep them compact and full; otherwise, they tend to become straggly. And prune off flowering stems after they bloom because they become unattractive.

By the end of the season, the whole plant will probably look very tired and often barren at the base. It's rarely worthwhile saving the whole mother plant because this plant is exceedingly simple to grow from cuttings. If you insist, though, you could prune it severely, forcing it to sprout anew.

Think Twice: In frost-free areas, you can grow purple heart and its kin outdoors year-round. They are popular groundcovers, although with an annoying habit of escaping and becoming weeds. This is, of course, not a problem in areas with frosty winters. In most climates, you'll need to overwinter purple heart and its kin indoors as houseplants, a role they play to perfection.

Good Neighbors

The dark foliage of purple heart makes a dramatic foil to yellow-green and gray foliage. Let it mingle with the fuzzy, yellow-green leaves of *Helichrysum petiolare* 'Limelight' or cascade from the base of a potted cardoon (*Cynara cardunculus*). It's useful also in a window box, combined with a flowering companion, such as a pink verbena.

Problems and Solutions

Purple heart rarely suffers from problems with insects or diseases.

Top Performer

Tradescantia pallida 'Purpurea' (purple heart): Also called *Setcreasea purpurea*, *S. pallida* 'Purple Heart', and *T. pallida* 'Purple Heart'. This is a denser growing plant than most of the tradescantia clan, with larger leaves. Its 4- to 6-inch (10- to 15-cm), strap-shaped leaves fold into a 'V' at the base and wrap themselves around thick but weak stems. In summer, three-petaled pink flowers appear at the tips of the stems. Each lasts only a day, but they are replaced regularly over several weeks. This species prefers full sunlight or only light shade outdoors and is quite drought tolerant. Indoors, give it the brightest light possible. Height: 8 inches (20 cm). Spread: 12 to 16 inches (30 to 40 cm).

Purple heart
(*Tradescantia pallida* 'Purpurea')

More Recommended Tradescantia

Tradescantia fluminensis (wandering Jew): Also called *T. albiflora*. Several species of wandering Jews make good outdoor plants, but this is the most common one. It's a totally prostrate plant and simply pours over the pot edge, making no pretense of wanting to grow in any direction but down. The leaves are thin, pointed and ovate, with no petiole (leaf stem). In the original species, they are medium green, but there are many cultivars with leaves variously striped with white, yellow, pink, or purple. They range in size from ¾ inch (2 cm) long to more than 4 inches (10 cm). Some cultivars produce tiny white to pink flowers while others rarely bloom. Cultivars with tiny leaves are more compact plants, while those with large leaves are long, trailing plants that can easily hang downward 4 feet (1.2 m) or more in one season. Some variegated types produce all-green stems; remove these. Give wandering Jews semishade to shade or at least some protection from full sun, and make sure their potting mix remains moist. Height/drop: 4 to 6 inches (10 to 15 cm). Spread: Indefinite.

Kissing Cousins

The other long-popular wandering Jew is best known under the name *Zebrina pendula*, but it's now considered part of the *Tradescantia* clan under its new name: *T. zebrina*. As the botanical name suggests (*zebrina*, obviously, derives from zebra!), this species has striped leaves, with two broad, bright silver bands on either side of the central nerve. Since the rich purple of the leaf's underside shows through, the result is an attractive purplish leaf with silver highlights. Height: 4 to 6 inches (10 to 15 cm). Spread: Indefinite.

Vinca

Periwinkle, vinca vine

You can never have too many truly easy foliage plants for containers. And this one is a snap, adapting to just about any set of conditions. The trumpet-shaped flowers, though lovely, aren't around for long. Instead, enjoy the gracefully hanging stems and shiny foliage. The stems, upright at first, soon began to arch outward; then they bend downward and continue growing until they reach the soil. You'll sometimes see them trailing 4 feet (1.2 m) or more. In mild climates where the stem tips don't freeze, variegated greater periwinkle (*Vinca major* 'Variegata') has been known to cascade downward a full 10 feet (3 m)!

Plant Profile

VINCA
VING-kuh

- **Foliage Color:** Green, variegated

- **Foliage Time:** Late spring through early fall; year-round in mild climates and indoors

- **Height:** Varies by species; see individual listings

- **Spread:** Indefinite

- **Garden Uses:** Container planting, edging, hanging baskets, groundcover, rock garden, woodland garden, wall planting

- **Light Preference:** Full sun to deep shade

- **Soil Preference:** Poor to humus-rich, well-drained soil

- **Best Way to Propagate:** Divide or take stem cuttings at any season

- **Hardiness:** Frost-sensitive perennial grown as a tender annual

Growing Tips

You can find periwinkle for sale just about everywhere, either as a starter plant in the container sections of local nurseries or in already-potted baskets or mixed plantings. Don't even bother looking for the seed; it isn't available and, besides, the variegated types don't come true from seed.

If bloom really is of no interest to you, you can plant periwinkle even in very deep shade, where it will grow beautifully, but without flowering. If you want the most flowers, give it full sun. Periwinkles adapt to just about any kind of soil: rich or poor, humusy or rocky. They do prefer constantly moist soil, and although they will grow in soils that regularly approach dryness, they do not tolerate drought.

Winter care depends on your climate. Grown in the ground, greater periwinkle is hardy to Zone 7, but if you're growing it in a container that's fully exposed to winter cold, don't count on it surviving winter north of Zone 9. In Zones 7 and 8, place the container on the ground, up against a north or east wall, and cover it with dead leaves or landscape fabric. It will usually come through winter in fine shape. Where greater periwinkle *isn't* hardy (north of Zone 7), bring plants or cuttings indoors for winter, or place established plants in a barely heated garage or in a cold room. Don't let them dry out entirely, and they'll do just fine.

FUN FACTS

Although periwinkles are considered poisonous (not life-threatening, but capable of causing a very painful stomachache), greater periwinkle (*V. major*) has also been widely used in producing medications for dilating blood vessels and controlling high blood pressure.

Although periwinkles are evergreen, unpruned plants tend to become straggly in containers. Cut them back harshly in spring to encourage them to grow back from the base.

The easiest way of multiplying periwinkle is to dig up sections that have rooted all on their own. You can also take cuttings of the semiwoody stems; they will root quite readily when you apply a light dusting of rooting hormone.

Good Neighbors

Just about any colorful bloomer that suits you will suit periwinkles. Petunias and verbenas, for example, will add some height. A contrasting trailer, such as edging lobelia (*Lobelia erinus*) or golden goddess (*Bidens ferulifolia*), will add a spark of interest.

Problems and Solutions

Insects or diseases rarely bother periwinkles.

Top Performer

Vinca major 'Variegata' (variegated greater periwinkle, vinca vine): Its appearance is unmistakable, with dark green, ovate leaves irregularly bordered in creamy white. If you find it too common, try the all-green form (*V. major*)—it's also a heavier bloomer—or 'Maculata', which has centers irregularly splashed in gold. Height: 18 inches (45 cm). Spread: Indefinite.

More Recommended Vinca

Vinca minor (lesser periwinkle, creeping myrtle): This low-growing, hardier, less-aggressive species is widely used as a groundcover as far north as Zone 4 (even Zone 3 under snow cover). While it's rarely used in containers, it looks marvelous grown that way, trailing down a good 2 to 3 feet (60 to 90 cm) in a single summer. It has smaller leaves but is usually a much heavier bloomer than greater periwinkle, even in shade. It comes in a huge array of cultivars, with flowers ranging from the usual blue-purple to white, lilac, and deep plum-purple, plus all types and shades of leaf variegation. My current favorite is 'Illumination', which is entirely yellow with only thin, green leaf margins. Height: 4 to 8 inches (10 to 20 cm). Spread: Indefinite.

'Variegata' variegated greater periwinkle (*Vinca major* 'Variegata')

Larry's Garden Notes

Think Twice: Greater periwinkle makes a lovely groundcover, but watch out! Where it is hardy, it spreads like crazy. When planted in the ground, the long stems take root wherever they touch the soil. Since they can grow up to 6 feet (1.8 m) in a single season, this plant can easily take over your yard. And that's the advantage of growing it in containers. It has nowhere to root. Of course, if yours cascades down over a garden or a lawn, it could easily break free, so trim it back any time it comes within 1 foot (30 cm) of the ground.

LARRY'S LAST LOOK: FOLIAGE ANNUALS FOR CONTAINERS & HANGING BASKETS

Here is a quick overview of some other great foliage plants for containers. Some are trailers designed to make the flowering plants in your tubs and baskets look better; others are so dramatic in form or color that they look great in pots of their own. None are true annuals, so multiply them by division or cuttings and overwinter them indoors.

COMMON AND BOTANICAL NAMES	LIGHT AND SOIL PREFERENCES	DESCRIPTION
Aeoniums *Aeonium* spp.	Full sun to partial shade Average, well-drained to dry soil	These succulents produce dense, saucerlike rosettes of spoon-shaped leaves, usually on trunklike stalks. *A. arboreum*, with green leaves, and its cultivar 'Zwartkop', with black-purple foliage, are especially popular. Height: 8–36 inches (20–90 cm) Spread: 8–72 inches (20–90 cm)
Baby sun rose *Aptenia cordifolia* (also called *Mesem-bryanthemum cordi-folium*)	Full sun to partial shade Average to poor, extremely well-drained to dry soil	This plant produces starlike pink, red, or orange flowers, but it's mainly grown for its long trailing stems of succulent, heart-shaped leaves. 'Variegata', with green leaves edged in white, is especially popular. Height: 2–8 inches (5–20 cm) Spread: Indefinite
'Powis Castle' artemisia *Artemisia* 'Powis Castle'	Full sun Rich, well-drained soil	This plant's finely cut, silvery foliage sets off other plants perfectly. Although it's fairly hardy (to Zone 6) in the ground, you'll probably want to bring this plant indoors for the winter if you grow it in containers. Other species, like beach wormwood (*A. stelleriana*, Zone 3), are just as good but hardier. Height: 2 feet (60 cm) Spread: 3 feet (90 cm)
Japanese aucuba *Aucuba japonica*	Full sun to deep shade Average to rich, evenly moist but well-drained soil	A beautiful evergreen shrub with shiny green leaves that are often speckled with yellow. Semihardy (to Zone 7 in the ground) but best grown in containers and overwintered indoors in most climates. Height: 3–10 feet (1–3 m) Spread: 3–10 feet (1–3 m)
Elephant ears *Colocasia esculenta*	Full sun to partial shade Rich, moist to wet soil	A spectacular semi-aquatic plant with huge, arrow-shaped leaves, often with purple markings; some cultivars are entirely purple-black. Although it tolerates drier soils, it grows best in a tub *without* drainage holes so the roots are constantly wet. Store dry tubers indoors over winter. Height: 2–5 feet (60–150 cm) Spread: 2 feet (60 cm)

COMMON AND BOTANICAL NAMES	LIGHT AND SOIL PREFERENCES	DESCRIPTION
Purple toatoa *Haloragis erecta* 'Melton Bronze'	Full sun to partial shade Average, well-drained soil	This plant has branching stems clothed in shiny, saw-toothed, bronze-green leaves. Can grow from seed sown indoors in early spring. Excellent in the garden as well! Height: 1–2 feet (30–60 cm) Spread: 1–2 feet (30–60 cm)
Creeping Jenny, moneywort *Lysimachia nummularia*	Full sun to deep shade Rich, evenly moist soil	A popular hardy groundcover (Zone 4) whose normally prostrate stems drip down beautifully from a pot. The bright yellow flowers are a plus. 'Aurea', with golden yellow spring leaves turning lime green, is most striking. *L. congestiflora* is similar, with more bloom. Height: 2 inches (5 cm) Spread: Indefinite
Basket grass *Oplismenus africanus* 'Variegatus' (also called *O. hirtellus* 'Variegatus')	Full sun to partial shade Average, evenly moist but well-drained soil	A pretty little ornamental grass with thin, lance-shaped leaves striped white and green and heavily overlaid in purple-pink. It quickly covers its pot, rooting at every node, then rains downward: a perfect foil for flowering annuals. Height: 6–8 inches (15–20 cm) Spread: Indefinite
Variegated St. Augustine grass *Stenotaphrum secundatum* 'Variegatum'	Full sun to partial shade Rich, evenly moist but well-drained soil	A charming variegated version of a common mild-climate lawn grass. Light green leaves with rounded tips and ivory stripes on trailing to hanging stems, rooting where they touch the soil. Don't put outside until the air has thoroughly warmed up. Will not tolerate drought. Height: 6 inches (15 cm) Spread: Indefinite

'Powis Castle' artemisia
(*Artemisia* 'Powis Castle')

'Variegata' Japanese aucuba
(*Aucuba japonica* 'Variegata')

ANNUALS FOR
Bees, Birds & Butterflies

I think every garden should be a mini wildlife sanctuary. We didn't ask our native birds, mammals, and insects if we could move in with our bulldozers and work crews, flattening forests, digging up prairies, and filling in marshes and ponds to build yet another subdivision. We just went ahead and did it; and in the process, we chased some of these creatures away. While few of us have the room to invite the larger wildlife back, the least we can do is to re-create an environment that will support some life. Insects and many birds, especially, readily return to backyards that have what it takes—and it really takes so little.

◄ Tubular flowers attract hummingbirds while clustered ones attract butterflies: With many annuals like star cluster (*Pentas lanceolata*), you'll attract both!

Variety Is the Spice of Life

Just by planting annuals, you're off to a flying start in your effort to create a mini wildlife sanctuary in your yard. Their nonstop bloom beats out almost any other plant group when it comes to attracting hummingbirds, bees, and butterflies. Annuals will attract meadow birds and insects, but there are other interesting wildlife species that need a bit of height. Most birds, for example, will nest only in shrubs or trees. That's why a yard that mixes low grass and wide flowerbeds, plus shrubs and trees of varying heights will attract the widest range of visitors. Adding a bit of open space—perhaps a few flat stones or a rock garden that is more rock than flowers—will attract birds and animals that like to sun themselves. Here are some more tips for planning your garden for wildlife:

- Most birds are seed- or insect-eaters. Letting plants like sunflowers go to seed is one good way to provide food for seed-eaters; not being too picky about controlling *all* the harmful insects in your yard will give the others plenty of insects and grubs to eat. (Spraying will kill not only their food supply but also often the birds themselves.)

- Hummingbirds like tubular or trumpet-shaped flowers, notably in reds, oranges, and bright pinks.

- For the most part, butterflies are nectar feeders and prefer small flowers grouped together (as they are in daisy-type flowers, for example).

- Bees like bright colors and are attracted to perfumes. They visit a wide range of flowers.

- Sphinx moths are drawn to plants with white flowers that have strong perfumes, especially at night.

The long, skinny beak of a hummingbird is just right for reaching the nectaries at the bases of many garden flowers.

Water, Water . . . Somewhere

One element that is essential to many types of wildlife is water. Birds have to drink daily and will often choose to nest and live near a supply of moisture. Many insects need water, as well.

A simple wash basin set into the ground and filled mostly with stones, with just enough water to barely cover them, will do as much to attract wildlife as many ponds, since most small insects and birds don't like deep water anyway. If you *do* have a water garden, pile up some stones here and there so there'll be some shallow water as well. A mud puddle (just let water dribble onto clayey soil in an open part of the garden) is very popular with many butterflies. Be sure to empty, clean, and add fresh water to your birdbath at least once a week.

Oddly, most commercial birdbaths attract few birds. Many prefer to bathe near ground level and won't appreciate baths put on a pedestal; putting the same container on the ground will often be more effective. Commercial birdbaths also tend to be too deep for short-legged birds; add stones so the water is never more than 1 inch (2.5 cm) deep.

Feed Me!

Besides providing a nonstop display of flowers that supply pollen and nectar to bees, butterflies, and hummingbirds, you can also set up feeding stations for other wildlife. Seed-eating birds will visit a bird feeder year-round, not just in winter. In fact, a variety of feeders with a variety of foods will attract the widest possible range of birds. Hummingbirds readily visit feeders specially designed for them and filled with a supply of sugar solution, changed regularly (up to every 3 days in hot weather). Put your hummingbird feeders out early in the growing season to catch hummingbirds' attention as they migrate through your area; you may well encourage them to adopt your yard as their principal larder.

Don't Forget Shelter

Shrubs and trees offer shelter to many birds and insects when it rains and snows. To attract even more critters, pile up a few rocks here and there, or leave a few hollow logs out; toads, lizards, and many butterflies will thank you. If possible, leave a small corner, perhaps out of sight, for a "wild garden." Being overly tidy—always picking up dead branches, fallen leaves, faded flowers, and so on—eliminates many vital hiding places, so pick a spot and just let things grow; many weeds, including nettles (*Urtica dioica*) and milkweeds (*Asclepias* spp.), are prime food sources for butterflies!

Learn to Attract Beneficials

Of all the "bugs" you see in your garden, most are actually helpful, and only a very few are harmful to your plants. So if you see an unknown insect, don't automatically squash it; unless you actually see it eating a plant, it's probably a friend. These beneficial insects actually help maintain an equal balance in the garden by eating harmful insects. The group includes a lot of insects you do see, including lady beetles, ground beetles, lacewings, and mantises, plus many you won't. (For instance, most predatory wasps—those whose larvae penetrate and devour pests from the inside—are so tiny that you'll never even see them.)

Although you can now buy many kinds of beneficial insects, that's often a waste of money: Most are already present in your garden or will visit all on their own if you give them a chance. There are two main keys to maintaining a healthy population of beneficial insects: Avoid indiscriminate spraying with pesticides, and supply a wide range of conditions and plants. Many beneficial insects feed on pollen and nectar when pest populations are low, so providing a variety of flowers will help support them. Plants that bear many tiny flowers combined into dense heads are particularly good; think of daisylike blooms, such as cosmos and sunflowers (*Helianthus* spp.), and lacy blooms, such as blue lace flower (*Trachymene coerulea*).

You may be able to find a seed packet collection that includes many of the plants that attract beneficial insects. Johnny's Selected Seeds, in conjunction with *Organic Gardening* magazine, offers a special Beneficial Borders Flower Seed Collection that includes seven ornamental plants (alyssum, anise hyssop, bachelor's buttons, blue lace flower, borage, California poppy, and cosmos) proven to attract and shelter beneficials.

Say No to Pesticides

Of course, it makes little sense to attract wildlife to your garden only to poison it with pesticides. Keep your use of insecticides, especially, to a minimum; even organic pesticides, such as rotenone, can be harmful. If I must spray, I choose nontoxic contact pesticides, like oil sprays and insecticidal soap, applying them only when absolutely necessary and only on those plants that obviously need them. Unlike pesticides that function as insect poisons and can remain effective for days, weeks, or even months, oil and soap are effective only when you first apply them. If you spray them only on damaging pests and not over the whole garden, they won't destroy the mini-ecosystem you are building up.

17 Other Annuals for Birds, Bees, and Butterflies

Don't think that the plants in this chapter are the only annuals good for attracting wildlife to your garden! In fact, just the fact that a plant has pretty flowers means it is designed to attract pollinators of some sort, so *most* of the plants in this book will do a good job. But the following annuals are particularly valuable for attracting birds, bees, butterflies, and beneficial insects to your yard.

Asclepias

Blood flower

This brightly colored, free-flowering tropical milkweed is related to the various milkweed species found throughout North America. It's a tufted, upright plant producing narrow, lance-shaped, mid-green leaves and sturdy stalks topped off by rounded clusters of flowers. Unlike hardy milkweeds, most of which bloom all at once from the stem tips, blood flower also blooms from secondary branches, thus prolonging the flowering season through the entire summer. In tropical climates, it will bloom sporadically all year!

Plant Profile

ASCLEPIAS
as-KLEE-pea-us

- **Bloom Color:** Orange, yellow
- **Bloom Time:** Summer to early fall; late winter to early summer and sporadic bloom year-round in mild climates
- **Height:** 2 to 3 feet (60 to 90 cm)
- **Spread:** 2 feet (60 cm)
- **Garden Uses:** Container planting, cut-flower garden, mass planting, meadow garden, mixed border
- **Attracts:** Bees, butterflies
- **Light Preference:** Full sun to partial shade
- **Soil Preference:** Average to humus-rich, evenly moist but well-drained soil
- **Best Way to Propagate:** Sow seed indoors in spring
- **Hardiness:** Frost-sensitive perennial grown as a tender annual

Growing Tips

Blood flower is definitely catching on as a garden annual, but it's still not widely available from nurseries. It's likely you'll have to send for seed from a mail-order source and grow your own. Fortunately, that's easy to do.

In very mild climates, you can sow blood flower directly in the garden. Elsewhere, it's best to start the seed indoors in individual peat pots, 8 to 10 weeks before the last frost date. Keep it warm—at least 60°F (15°C)—and look for seedlings in 30 days. Grow the young plants in full sun. Transplant them with care to the garden or to outside containers when the outdoor air has thoroughly warmed up.

This plant is *very* generous with its nectar and attracts lots of visitors; bees, syrphid flies (striped beelike flies), and butterflies are a constant presence in summer.

Before using blood flower in arrangements, though, sear the cut end with a flame or plunge it into boiling water for a few seconds. This will stop the flow of thick white sap, which can be toxic to other flowers in the arrangement.

In fall, you can bring in potted plants or dig up plants from the garden, taking care to minimize damage to the thickened roots. Cut them back harshly and grow them in the brightest light available. They'll make nice foliage plants in the dead of winter and will usually start blooming again as soon as the days start to grow longer.

Warning: The thick white sap of blood flower is very bitter and even somewhat toxic. Some people break out in a rash if it touches their skin, so always wear gloves when working with this plant.

Good Neighbors

The hot colors of blood flower (*Asclepias curassavica*) add a vibrant spark to blues and purples. Try them near tall blue salvias, such as *Salvia farinacea* 'Blue Bedder', or alongside anise hyssop (*Agastache foeniculum* 'Blue Spike'). Echo the red-orange with a low plant such as 'Profusion Orange' zinnia.

Problems and Solutions

Watch out for the orange-red aphids that flock to this plant (and, in fact, all milkweeds) at flowering time. Knock them off with a strong spray of water. Indoors over the winter, you may find this plant infested with spider mites, mealy bugs, or whiteflies; control with insecticidal soap.

Blood flower
(*Asclepias curassavica*)

Top Performer

Think Twice: *Asclepias curassavica* (blood flower): Each curious flower is made up of five reddish orange to yellow calyces arched backward around a yellow crown of hooded appendages, often glistening with nectar. The narrow, pointed, 3-inch (8-cm) seed capsules burst open in the fall to reveal flattened seeds, each equipped with a tuft of silky hair. This plant is considered a pernicious weed in many tropical countries because its parachute-like seed routinely carries it into the wild. If you live in Zones 10 and 11, grow it only if you're willing to snap off the seedpods before they open. Elsewhere, frost ensures it is totally harmless. Height: 2 to 3 feet (60 to 90 cm). Spread: 2 feet (60 cm). **Self-sowing**

More Recommended Milkweeds

Think Twice: *Gomphocarpus physocarpus* (swan plant, balloon plant): Although now officially a *Gomphocarpus,* this plant is commonly sold as *Asclepias physocarpa*. It's taller than blood flower, with narrow, gray-green leaves. Somewhat pendant, open clusters of white to greenish flowers appear all along the upright stems. The real interest, though, comes from the round, inflated, lightly spiny, pale green seed capsules, which are up to 2½ inches (6.5 cm) in diameter. Watch it: This plant is just as invasive in tropical climates as blood flower. Height: 4 to 6 feet (1.2 to 1.8 m). Spread: 2 feet (60 cm). **Self-sowing**

Larry's Garden Notes

Who doesn't know the orange and black monarch butterfly that migrates from Central America to North America and back each year? Monarchs feed only on milkweeds, whose bitter sap renders the butterflies repulsive to birds. Planting blood flower will make them feel right at home in your garden; it's one of the species they feed on in Central America. If you find their brightly striped caterpillars chomping on the leaves, let them eat their fill. These baby monarchs will need the energy for their long trip home at the end of summer!

Cerinthe

Honeywort

Honeywort burst onto the ornamental annual scene in a big way in the late 1990s, and now all the "in" gardeners are growing it! Although quite eucalyptus-like in leaf, its odd flowers put it in a class all by itself. It is an upright plant, with blue-green, white-mottled, heart-shaped leaves that wrap around the stem at the base. The stems branch at the tips, then arch downward, with the upper "leaves" (actually bracts) becoming tinged with purple. Pendant, bell-shaped flowers, either purple or yellow and maroon, appear among the bracts. Weird? Definitely! Wonderful? Most assuredly!

Plant Profile

CERINTHE
ceh-RIN-thee

■ **Bloom Color:** Purple, bicolor (yellow and maroon)

■ **Bloom Time:** Summer through early fall; fall through winter in mild climates

■ **Height:** 1 to 2 feet (30 to 60 cm)

■ **Spread:** 9 to 12 inches (23 to 30 cm)

■ **Garden Uses:** Container planting, cut-flower garden, mass planting, meadow garden, mixed border

■ **Attracts:** Bees

■ **Light Preference:** Full sun to partial shade

■ **Soil Preference:** Average, well-drained soil

■ **Best Way to Propagate:** Sow seed indoors or outdoors in spring or fall

■ **Hardiness:** Frost-sensitive perennial grown as a hardy annual

Growing Tips

Some of the more progressive nurseries now sell honeywort in spring. If you locate starter plants, you'll find they transplant readily. In most cases, though, you'll have to grow them yourself from seed, available from speciality catalogs.

In long-season climates, it's easiest to direct-sow; just toss the seed on the ground and rake them in lightly. Sow them either in early spring, while the soil is still cool, or in fall. Don't worry if, in Zones 8 and warmer, fall-sown seed starts to sprout soon after planting; honeywort is actually an evergreen biennial or short-lived perennial in its native Europe and is quite frost resistant. The young plants will simply stop growing when truly cold weather hits, then start up again where they left off when spring arrives. In Zones 10 and 11, where there is no cold to tell them to go dormant, you can even sow them in early fall for winter to early spring bloom.

You can sow honeywort outdoors in short-season climates as well, but for color all season long, I suggest starting the seed indoors 6 to 8 weeks before the last frost. Soak the seed overnight; then sow, just barely covering them. It germinates in 5 to 21 days at 65° to 85°F (18° to 30°C). Plant out around the last frost date, or even a bit sooner if the spring seems to be milder than usual.

Where summers are cool, plant honeywort in full sun or only light shade. In hot summer areas, though, give it at least afternoon shade; also make sure you mulch its soil and keep it evenly moist. It is quite happy in ordinary or even poor soil and indeed can be a bit floppy in soils that are too rich.

Summer care couldn't be easier: Just water enough to keep the soil from drying out entirely. Deadheading is simply a waste of time, as faded petals drop off on their own and producing seed does not seem to in any way reduce the number of blooms nor shorten their duration.

Honeywort produces copious quantities of nectar, a fact that your local bees will almost certainly discover and welcome!

Honeywort generally self-sows, but only moderately, rarely causing any problems. With their unusual leaf shape and color, seedlings are easy to spot; simply pull out any plants you don't want or move them to other parts of your garden.

Self-sowing

Although theoretically a short-lived perennial, honeywort acts like an annual in most climates. It grows so readily from seed that it's not worth trying to protect it for the winter or bringing it indoors out of the cold. Just save a few seeds for the next year's garden!

'Purpurascens' honeywort (*Cerinthe major* 'Purpurascens')

Good Neighbors

Honeyworts make a unique accent around sturdier plants, such as irises or agapanthus. They're also a good choice for covering up yellowing bulb foliage. A sprinkling of wall baby's breath (*Gypsophila muralis*) among honeywort's sprawling stems will add sparkle to the garden picture.

Problems and Solutions

Honeywort seems largely insect and disease resistant, although root rot can be a problem in poorly drained soil; make sure you plant it in a well-drained site.

Top Performer

Cerinthe major (honeywort): This species produces blue-green bracts usually only lightly tinted purple, and flowers that are deep maroon-purple at the base and bright yellow at the tip. Even more popular is *C. major* 'Purpurascens' (also called *C. major purpurescens*): The entire tip of the plant turns bluish purple at flowering time, and the blooms are purple outside and cream inside.

Smart Substitute

❗ **Think Twice:** If you appreciate the look of honeywort's eucalyptus-like leaves, why not grow the real thing? Also called gum trees, eucalyptuses are mostly tall trees in their native Australia, but several can work as annuals in cold-season climates. Silver dollar plant (*Eucalyptus cinerea*) is one of the most popular; its young growth bears aromatic leaves that are round and silvery, with the stem passing through their center. Start indoors. Be warned that in Zones 9 to 11, eucalyptuses often reach massive sizes and may even become invasive through self-sowing. Height (when used as an annual): 1 to 3 feet (30 to 90 cm). Spread: 1 to 2 feet (30 to 60 cm). Self-sowing 🌱

Cleome

Spider flower

Looking for an annual that not only will bloom for a long season but will actually improve with age? Spider flower may be just the choice for you. It starts blooming when it is only 1 foot (30 cm) or so high, then just keeps growing taller, with fading blooms toward the base being replaced by newer ones at the top. By summer's end, when so many other plants are in decline, it is absolutely at its peak. Best of all, bees, butterflies, and hummingbirds just love the flowers!

Plant Profile

CLEOME
klee-OH-me

- **Bloom Color:** Pink, purple, white

- **Bloom Time:** Summer through mid- to late fall

- **Height:** 4 to 5 feet (1.2 to 1.5 m)

- **Spread:** 1 to 2 feet (30 to 60 cm)

- **Garden Uses:** Container planting, cut-flower garden, annual hedge, mass planting, meadow garden, mixed border, screening

- **Attracts:** Bees, butterflies, hummingbirds

- **Light Preference:** Full sun to partial shade

- **Soil Preference:** Humus-rich, well-drained, even sandy soil

- **Best Way to Propagate:** Sow seed indoors or outdoors in spring or fall

- **Hardiness:** Half-hardy annual

Growing Tips

Spider flower is a snap to grow, whether you buy plants or grow them yourself from seed. Packs and flats of these plants are widely available, and they transplant readily. About the only reason to grow spider flower from seed is to save some money—which is, of course, reason enough!

You can sow spider flower outdoors in fall or in early to mid-spring, when the ground is still cool to the touch, but the resulting plants won't begin to bloom until midsummer. For earlier flowers, start the seed indoors 8 to 10 weeks before the last frost date. Scatter the seed evenly over a tray of seed-starting medium (do not cover) and moisten lightly. Insert the tray into a clear plastic bag and place it in the refrigerator for about 2 weeks; then remove the tray and place it in a warm spot. Germination will take place in 10 to 14 days at room temperature.

Set out seedlings or transplants when all danger of frost has passed and night temperatures remain above 40°F (4°C). Space plants 1 to 2 feet (30 to 60 cm) apart in a sunny to lightly shaded and well-drained location. Keep the soil evenly moist for a few weeks after planting; established plants are generally very drought resistant.

In spite of its height, spider flower rarely needs staking, especially if you set out plants while they're still relatively young. Summer care is nil: Deadheading is practically impossible (there's just too much to trim off), and besides, the long, thin seed capsules add to the plant's attractive spidery appearance. In fall, let spider flower freeze; start fresh plants in spring or just wait for self-sown seedlings to pop up.

Good Neighbors

Try growing spider flower (*Cleome hassleriana*) around castor bean (*Ricinus communis*) for a handsome textural contrast. In the foreground, plant something bushy and sturdy to conceal spider flower's late-summer legginess, such as red fountain grass (*Pennisetum setaceum* 'Purpureum') or 'Powis Castle' artemisia.

Problems and Solutions

Leaf spots are possible during rainy growing seasons; remove the damaged leaves. Aphids, spider mites, and whiteflies are occasional problems, causing distorted, discolored foliage; control with insecticidal soap.

Spider flower
(*Cleome hassleriana*)

Top Performer

Think Twice: *Cleome hassleriana* (spider flower): Also called *C. spinosa* or *C. pungens*. This species produces upright, branching, sticky, thorny stems and leaves that are divided in a palmate (handlike) fashion. Long, thin stamens and almost as narrow seed capsules enhance the open clusters of white, pink, rose, and violet flowers, giving the plant the "spidery" appearance suggested by its common name. Spider flower self-sows quite readily but tends to be truly invasive only in mild winter climates. (Mulch abundantly in such climates to keep it under control.) Height: 4 to 5 feet (1.2 to 1.5 m). Spread: 12 to 18 inches (30 to 45 cm). **Self-sowing**

More Recommended Cleome

Cleome serrulata (Rocky Mountain bee plant, stinking clover): You'll sometimes see this species offered as a "florist friendly" spider flower because it lacks the thorny stems of its cousin. There's no denying that it looks good in flower arrangements, but as the common name "stinking clover" suggests, it shares the same musky odor as its relative. It's a more compact plant than spider flower, with smaller, three-leaflet leaves and a denser flower head in white or very light pink with crimson stamens. 'Solo' is a dwarf cultivar, only 16 inches (40 cm) tall; it makes a good bedding plant. Height: 2 to 5 feet (60 to 150 cm). Spread: 1 foot (30 cm). **Self-sowing**

Larry's Garden Notes

I can't really talk about spider flowers without some mention of their odor. You see, the leaves and stem give off a distinctly musky aroma. I've heard that some people find this odor pleasant, but to me, spider flower smells of skunk! It's not intense enough to strike casual visitors, but you'll definitely notice it if you linger in the garden, especially near a grouping of these plants. And I would definitely suggest *not* planting spider flower near windows or doors.

Fuchsia

Fuchsia, lady's eardrops

Fuchsia's pendant, distinctly two-part flowers always reminds me of a ballerina in a tutu! The flowers even move like ballerinas, as each blossom dangles from a thin, threadlike pedicel that dances in the slightest breeze. To finish the portrait, the ballerina stands on extended "legs," actually the stigma and anthers. There are thousands of hybrids of this hummingbird favorite; just choose according to your color preferences and your needs. Trailers and hanging types are, of course, the top choices for hanging baskets, while bushy cultivars look best in the garden and in containers seen from above.

Plant Profile

FUCHSIA
FEW-shuh

- **Bloom Color:** Blue-violet, pink, purple, salmon, red, white

- **Bloom Time:** Late spring through early fall; much of the year indoors and in mild climates

- **Height:** 6 to 60 inches (15 to 150 cm)

- **Spread:** 12 to 42 inches (30 to 105 cm)

- **Garden Uses:** Container planting, edging, hanging baskets, annual hedge, mass planting, meadow garden, mixed border, rock garden, woodland garden, specimen plant; on a standard

- **Attracts:** Hummingbirds

- **Light Preference:** Full sun to partial shade

- **Soil Preference:** Humus-rich, evenly moist but well-drained soil

- **Best Way to Propagate:** Take stem cuttings at any season

- **Hardiness:** Frost-sensitive shrub grown as a tender annual

Growing Tips

Chances are you'll be buying fuchsias either in fully grown baskets or as rooted cuttings. Just about every nursery offers a few; for more variety, check out specialist mail-order nurseries.

Seed for hybrid fuchsias is sometimes available. These plants need a long head start (14 to 24 weeks) for early bloom; check the seed packet for recommended sowing times. Sow the seed on the surface of the mix and expose to 13 hours of light per day. Germination takes 3 to 4 weeks at 75°F (24°C).

Wait until there is no danger of frost before putting fuchsias out for summer. While they are popular in containers, you'll probably find they do better in the garden, where the soil is cooler.

In cool climates, full sun is ideal; elsewhere, try for full morning sun with afternoon shade. Although often promoted as a shade plant, fuchsia does not bloom all that well in full shade. Summer care consists mostly of watering and fertilizing. Fuchsia will not tolerate drought conditions, so keep it at least slightly moist at all times.

To overwinter fuchsias, bring in plants or cuttings before frost. Grow them as houseplants in bright light and at cool temperatures, or cut them back hard and keep them nearly dry in a cold room or barely heated garage until March.

Good Neighbors

Fuchsia flowers are so outstanding that companions may seem superfluous! But should you choose to embellish them, you might try matching the flower color with different flower forms—for example, white fuchsia with white bacopa (*Sutera cordata*).

Problems and Solutions

Fuchsias are subject to a wide variety of insects and diseases. Perhaps the worst pests are whiteflies that tend to follow fuchsias when you bring them indoors for winter and then spread to other plants. Never bring a fuchsia into your house until you have thoroughly washed all of its leaves with a solution of insecticidal soap.

Top Performer

Fuchsia hybrids (fuchsia, common fuchsia, hybrid fuchsia, lady's eardrops): Also called *F.* × *hybrida*. These widely variable plants range from tiny to gigantic and from upright to bushy, trailing, or hanging. The green, reddish, gold, or variegated leaves can be large or small, and the flowers range from smaller than a pinkie nail to over 2½ inches (6.5 cm) in diameter. One thing they do share is the distinct two-part flower form. The top part of each blossom is made up of a tube spreading out into four relatively thick, white, pink, or red sepals. The bell-shaped "tutu" of softer petals hanging below can be single, semidouble, or double. It comes in a wide range of shades and is rarely the same color as the sepals, so the blooms are usually bicolored. Height: 6 to 60 inches (15 to 150 cm). Spread: 12 to 42 inches (30 to 105 cm).

More Recommended Fuchsias

Fuchsia magellanica (hardy fuchsia): This small-flowered fuchsia with red sepals and purple petals is often hardy to Zone 7, and even beyond with winter protection. It is a spreading shrub to 10 feet (3 m) tall and wide in mild climates, but cold usually kills it to the ground north of Zone 8, forming a much smaller plant. Height and spread: 2 to 3 feet (60 to 90 cm).

F. 'Triphylla' group (honeysuckle fuchsia): This rather distinct group of hybrids produces upright plants with leaves usually tinged purple underneath and long, narrow flowers that are mostly all sepal. Orange-red is the principal color. 'Gartenmeister Bonstedt', almost never out of flower, is typical of this group. Height: 24 to 30 inches (60 to 75 cm). Spread: 18 to 24 inches (45 to 60 cm).

'Blue Eyes' fuchsia
(*Fuchsia* 'Blue Eyes')

Smart Substitutes

Think Twice: Coral fountain (*Russelia equisetiformis*, also called *R. juncea*) is ideal for replacing fuchsias in hot, humid climates where the latter don't thrive. Also known as coral plant or firecracker plant, it produces narrow green stems (upright at first, then trailing) and short-lived, scalelike leaves. The narrow, pendulous, scarlet flowers appear in abundance from early spring to fall. It can self-sow, and even become invasive, in Zones 10 to 11; elsewhere, overwinter it indoors. Height and spread: 2 to 5 feet (60 to 150 cm). Self-sowing

Gaillardia

Blanket flower, Indian blanket

Once considered a staple in annual borders, blanket flower seems to have fallen out of favor with gardeners, other than for use in wildflower gardens. The only explanation I can think of is that it is too easy to grow. There is, after all, a certain class of gardeners (and a very influential class at that) who generally look down on easy-to-grow plants, considering them beneath their skills. I say, though, the easier the better! This plant is definitely near the top of the sure-bet list, right up there with cosmos and marigolds.

Plant Profile

GAILLARDIA
guh-LAR-dee-uh

- **Bloom Color:** Red, yellow, cream

- **Bloom Time:** Late spring through early fall; fall through winter in mild climates

- **Height:** 12 to 18 inches (30 to 45 cm)

- **Spread:** 6 to 12 inches (15 to 30 cm)

- **Garden Uses:** Container planting, cut-flower garden, mass planting, meadow garden, mixed border, rock garden

- **Attracts:** Beneficial insects, butterflies, seed-eating birds

- **Light Preference:** Full sun

- **Soil Preference:** Average to poor, well-drained soil; tolerates sandy, even stony soil

- **Best Way to Propagate:** Sow seed outdoors or indoors in spring or fall

- **Hardiness:** Hardy annual

Growing Tips

Only a very few knowledgeable nurseries offer started plants of annual blanket flower, so you'll probably have to grow your own plants from seed.

In long-season climates, sow the seed in late fall or early spring, when the ground is still cool. Just rake the ground very lightly and sprinkle the seed where you want the plants to grow; then water them in. Later, simply thin out the resulting seedlings to give each one at least 6 inches (15 cm) of growing space. From this point on, blanket flowers will grow pretty much on their own.

Elsewhere, sow blanket flower seed indoors in spring. A 4- to 6-week head start is sufficient. Just press the seed into the growing mix without covering (it needs light to germinate), and moisten lightly. Place the tray in bright light at about 70°F (21°C). The seed will sprout in a week or so.

Full sun and average garden soil are perfect. In very fertile, rich soil, blanket flower tends to produce weak stems that need some support; plants are perfectly sturdy in poorer soil, though. Gardeners in coastal areas will appreciate blanket flower's drought and salt tolerance, while those in the Deep South and arid climates will just love the way this plant puts up with unbearable heat. In all

FUN FACTS

Double blanket flowers are the result of a curious mutation. Instead of a domed center of tiny, fertile florets surrounded by a ring of much larger, flattened, sterile ray flowers (which is typical of daisies), double blanket flowers produce greatly lengthened, fertile center florets and no ray flowers at all.

climates, it is a magnet for butterflies; it seems like these beautiful creatures just can't get enough of its numerous nectar-filled florets.

During the summer, water only when the soil is becoming very dry, and don't bother with supplementary feeding. I used to deadhead this plant but found that it seems to bloom perfectly well whether I deadheaded or not. Now I let my resident goldfinches do the deadheading for me; they love blanket flower seedheads!

 **Think Twice:** Leave open space in your garden, especially in a dry spot, and you'll find blanket flower will happily self-sow into it. It's rarely invasive enough to cause any real problems, though. **Self-sowing**

Blanket flower
(*Gaillardia pulchella*)

Good Neighbors

Blanket flower lends itself to the informal garden. The single-flowered types combine particularly well with other self-sowers, such as calliopsis (*Coreopsis tinctoria*) and bachelor's button (*Centaurea cyanus*), to create a relaxed and colorful look.

Problems and Solutions

Watch out for mildew in late summer, especially when the soil is dry but the morning air is very heavy with dew. Watering a bit more generously at that time can help prevent the problem of mildew. Control thrips and aphids, which can cause distorted and sticky or silver-streaked foliage, with repeated sprays of a light horticultural oil or insecticidal soap.

Top Performer

Gaillardia pulchella (blanket flower, Indian blanket): Gray-green leaves, which are lance or spoon shaped and somewhat hairy, appear mainly toward the base of the plant; the upper part of each stem is mostly leafless. Single-flowered types are usually sold as mixes and include red, yellow, golden, cream, and reddish purple flowers, plus bicolors. Much more popular are the doubles and semidoubles in the same color range. 'Red Plume', an All-America Selection winner, and its light yellow cousin, 'Yellow Plume', are both dwarfs only 12 to 14 inches (30 to 35 cm) tall. They remain sturdy and upright even in rich soil.

Smart Substitutes

Gaillardia pulchella is one parent of the well-known perennial blanket flower *G.* × *grandiflora*. (The other parent is a yellow-flowered perennial species native to the prairies: *G. aristata*.) This hybrid inherited the red-and-yellow color combination of *G. pulchella*, as well as its fast growth rate and all-summer bloom. It got its perennial habit from the other parent, but even that is modified by the annual parent: *G.* × *grandiflora* tends to last only 2 to 3 years. Height: 1 to 3 feet (30 to 90 cm). Spread: 1 to 2 feet (30 to 60 cm). **Self-sowing**

Heliotropium

Heliotrope, cherry pie

The first time I smelled heliotrope, a wave of memories flooded over me: It was exactly the same fragrance as my grandmother's talcum powder! Heliotropes can also have other scents including baby powder, vanilla, cherry pie (another common name), and even cloves. These shrubby plants bear beautifully textured, dark green leaves and masses of tiny, trumpet-shaped flowers in violet, lavender, white, or even (I have been told, although I have yet to see this color) rose. This old-fashioned annual seems to be making a definite comeback, as each year sees yet more new cultivars.

Plant Profile

HELIOTROPIUM
he-lee-oh-TROH-pea-um

- **Bloom Color:** Lavender, violet, rose, white

- **Bloom Time:** Late spring through early fall; sporadically throughout the year indoors and in frost-free climates

- **Height:** 1 to 5 feet (30 to 150 cm)

- **Spread:** 1 to 2 feet (30 to 60 cm)

- **Garden Uses:** Container planting, cut-flower garden, edging, hanging baskets, mass planting, mixed border, rock garden, wall planting; on a standard

- **Attracts:** Bees, butterflies, hummingbirds

- **Light Preference:** Full sun to partial shade

- **Soil Preference:** Humus-rich, well-drained soil

- **Best Way to Propagate:** Take stem cuttings at any season; sow seed indoors in late winter

- **Hardiness:** Frost-sensitive shrub grown as a tender annual

Growing Tips

Most larger nurseries sell heliotrope plants, either cutting grown or seed grown. The former are usually sold individually as rooted cuttings; the latter in packs or trays at a much lower cost.

You can also grow heliotrope from seed, started indoors. A 10- to 12-week head start is a minimum (I prefer 18 weeks) because heliotrope is slow to germinate and even slower to come into bloom. Barely cover the seed, then give it high humidity and room temperatures. Germination can take 1 month or even longer.

If you want bushy plants for containers or the garden, it's a good idea to pinch the young plants to stimulate branching. You may need to pinch again whenever the plant begins to look scraggly. (While many modern cultivars are disappointing in the fragrance department, they do have the advantage of staying bushy and compact without pruning.) Deadhead to removing fading flower clusters: The plants will look better with the brown flowers removed, and you'll encourage better bloom in the future. Just watch out for bees, which enjoy the flowers as much as you do! (Hummingbirds and butterflies appreciate the nectar-rich blooms, too.)

Heliotrope is very sensitive to cold, so wait until the air and soil have thoroughly warmed up before planting it out—at least 2 to 3 weeks after the last frost date. Plant it in full sun or only very

FUN FACTS

Not only is heliotrope a delight to the nose, but it was long a major element in colognes, soaps, powders, and perfumes. Today the real thing has been largely supplanted by artificial scents, but for my money, there is no nicer perfume than that given off by a living heliotrope—especially one growing in your own yard!

light shade in cool summer areas. Where summers are hot, though, partial shade, or at least some protection from hot afternoon sun, is best. Rich, evenly moist soil is ideal; heliotrope dislikes both dry and soggy conditions. Container-grown plants will need regular watering, up to twice a day if they are in nearly full sun; dry soil can be fatal.

Since heliotrope is not a true annual but actually a tropical shrub, it makes sense to overwinter it indoors. This is necessary even in Zone 10; only in Zone 11 is it really hardy enough to remain outdoors year-round. Either bring in mature plants (it's really easy if they're already growing in pots) or take cuttings. Don't wait too long, though, or you run the risk of plants being stunted or killed by an early cold snap. I like to bring my heliotropes in before nights even begin to cool, which can mean in late August or September in many climates. They often bloom all winter long in bright light. By late winter or early spring, a good pruning is usually necessary; you can cut straggly plants down to only 2 or 3 inches (5 or 8 cm) from their base.

Heliotrope
(*Heliotropium arborescens*)

Good Neighbors

Heliotrope's textured foliage and deep purple flowers make an elegant contrast to softer textures and lighter colors, such as soft pink verbena or light purple Swan River daisy (*Brachyscome iberidifolia*).

Problems and Solutions

Whiteflies are a major problem, especially indoors over the winter. Never bring a heliotrope in from the garden without having carefully washed both sides of its leaves with a soft rag dipped in insecticidal soap. Leaf spots are an occasional problem; pick off any infected leaves. If the problem reappears, get rid of the infected plant and grow a disease-free one from seed.

Top Performer

Heliotropium arborescens (heliotrope, cherry pie): Also called *H. peruvianum.* There are some 250 species of heliotrope, many of them deliciously scented; but this species, described above, is the only one that is currently being cultivated.

Larry's Gardening Notes

Recent years have seen a whole range of "new, improved" heliotropes: usually much more compact plants with larger flower heads and deeper purple shades. Despite the descriptions promising a delicious scent, however, lines such as 'Marine' and 'Mini Marine' are, to my nose, almost scentless—and a heliotrope without a perfume has no reason to exist. I suggest going plant hunting in a local nursery and buying the most perfumed plant you can find. Once you have it, you can multiply it *ad infinitum* by cuttings.

Iberis

Candytuft

The more experience I gain in gardening, the more I appreciate a truly easy plant. That's why annual candytufts are among my favorites. There are two common species, both with narrow leaves and rather sprawling stems that rise at the tips to form dome-shaped clusters of flowers. The charming blooms have a distinctive form, with two large lower petals and two tiny upper ones. Both species of annual candytuft deserve much wider recognition than they now get!

Plant Profile

IBERIS
EYE-ber-iss

- **Bloom Color:** Varies by species; see individual listings
- **Bloom Time:** Midspring through early fall; fall through winter in mild climates
- **Height:** Varies by species; see individual listings
- **Spread:** Varies by species; see individual listings
- **Garden Uses:** Container planting, cut-flower garden, edging, groundcover, hanging baskets, mass planting, mixed border, rock garden, wall planting
- **Attracts:** Bees, other beneficial insects, butterflies
- **Light Preference:** Full sun to partial shade
- **Soil Preference:** Average to poor, evenly moist but well-drained, with neutral to alkaline soil
- **Best Way to Propagate:** Sow seed indoors or out in spring or outdoors in fall
- **Hardiness:** Hardy annual

Growing Tips

Candytufts really are cool-season annuals. Where summer temperatures remain over 80°F (27°C) for weeks on end, plant or sow very early in the season, while the air is still cool, then replace them with more heat-resistant plants when summer arrives. In fact, in Zones 9 and 10, you can sow in early fall for bloom through much of the winter. Where summers are cool, the story is quite different: Candytufts are among the first annuals to come into bloom and, if you keep deadheading them, the last to stop blooming in fall.

You may find candytufts in better nurseries in spring. Whenever possible, buy young plants; flowering-size plants don't handle transplanting very well. If you can only find them in bloom, cut the plants back harshly to force them to sprout from the base. In most cases, you'll get better results growing candytufts yourself from seed.

It's generally best to sow seed directly outdoors, either in fall or in early spring, as soon as you can work the soil. Lightly rake the seed in and water; it'll germinate when the time is right. Thin to 5 to 8 inches (13 to 20 cm) apart.

For truly early bloom, you can also sow seed indoors from 4 to 6 weeks before the last frost. Sowing into peat pots helps because candytufts dislike having their roots disturbed. Since the plants are somewhat frost resistant, you can begin planting out a week or so before the average last frost date, especially if the spring seems especially warm.

FUN FACTS

Candytuft didn't get its "sugary" name because the flowers are so sweet. Instead, it comes from *I. umbellata*, which was introduced from Crete. The old English word for Crete was "Candie," and the plant grew in tufts: hence, candytuft. Curiously, the genus name, *Iberis*, comes from Iberia, or Spain, home to a different species.

Sow or plant candytufts into average to poor soil that has very good drainage. Full sun will give the best results in cool summer areas, but some protection from the afternoon sun is needed elsewhere. Mulch in hot climates to help keep the soil cooler.

In summer, water to keep the soil evenly moist. And deadhead regularly, by cutting off entire flower heads when their bloom starts to decrease. Other than that, just stand back and enjoy the procession of bees, butterflies, and beneficial insects drawn to the fragrant flowers.

Good Neighbors

Candytufts make great fillers for both the garden and for the flower vase. They offer a pleasant contrast of form and color to Swan River daisy (*Brachyscome iberidifolia*) or browallia (*Browallia speciosa*). The compact habit of annual candytuft (*Iberis umbellata*) makes it ideal for a formal edging.

Problems and Solutions

Not generally subject to diseases. Slugs and snails, however, may attack young plants, but they usually recover on their own and quickly outgrow any pest damage.

Top Performer

Iberis amara (rocket candytuft, hyacinth-flowered candytuft): This species forms upright, elongated domes of highly perfumed flowers. White is the most common color; pink, lavender, and red types exist but are rarely offered. It usually self-sows, but not invasively. Height: 6 to 18 inches (15 to 45 cm). Spread: 6 inches (15 cm). **Self-sowing** 🌰

More Recommended Iberis

🌱 **Think Twice:** *Iberis umbellata* (annual candytuft, globe candytuft, fairy candytuft): This is a smaller plant with a more spreading habit than *I. amara,* producing smaller, rounder, but more numerous domes of lightly scented, smaller flowers. The color range is also wider: white, pink, rose, lavender, lilac, carmine, and red. This one self-sows with abandon and has been known to escape from culture, especially along seashores. Height: 6 to 12 inches (15 to 30 cm). Spread: 9 inches (23 cm). **Self-sowing** 🌰

'Giant Hyacinth' rocket candytuft (*Iberis amara* 'Giant Hyacinth')

Larry's Garden Notes

There *is* a way of getting your annual candytufts to bloom all summer, even in hot summer areas. You see, young plants don't seem to mind the heat and will bloom abundantly. The problem is that, after their first flush of bloom, they don't seem to have the capacity to regenerate from the base unless nights are cool. So instead of deadheading, simply sprinkle seeds over the same area every 2 weeks and then rake them in. When older plants begin to dry up, simply cut them out; well-established replacements will be ready to take their place.

Lantana

Lantana

Visitors to tropical and subtropical climates can't help but notice this plant: It's everywhere! A lot of gardeners don't realize, though, that it makes an interesting bedding plant in cooler climates as well. Tiny, trumpet-shaped flowers appear at stem tips, grouped into dense, rounded clusters. These butterfly magnets produce different flower colors in the same cluster, giving a rainbow effect that is highly attractive. Some types also produce attractive black berries, which are relished by some birds.

Plant Profile

LANTANA
lan-TAN-uh

- **Bloom Color:** Varies by species; see individual listings
- **Bloom Time:** Late spring through early fall; all year indoors and in mild climates
- **Height:** Varies by species; see individual listings
- **Spread:** Varies by species; see individual listings
- **Garden Uses:** Container planting, edging, hanging baskets, groundcover, annual hedge, mass planting, mixed border, rock garden, specimen plant, wall planting; on a standard
- **Attracts:** Berry-eating birds, butterflies, hummingbirds
- **Light Preference:** Full sun to partial shade
- **Soil Preference:** Average to poor, evenly moist but well-drained soil; tolerates sandy or stony sites
- **Best Way to Propagate:** Take stem cuttings at any season
- **Hardiness:** Frost-sensitive shrub grown as a tender annual

Growing Tips

Most nurseries carry at least one lantana, either as small plants or full grown in baskets. If you can't find plants locally, you may decide to grow your own from seed.

Lantana seed can take over 1 month to germinate, so you'll need to give it a long head start; sow indoors 14 to 16 weeks before the last frost date. Soak the seed overnight in tepid water before sowing it about ⅛ inch (3 mm) deep. Germination and growth are best at 70° to 75°F (21° to 24°C).

Wait until night temperatures remain above 60°F (15°C) before putting plants outdoors for the summer. Full sun is best in most climates, but partial shade is fine where temperatures get very hot. Any well-drained soil will do. Lantana is highly resistant to salt spray and salty soil, so it makes a good seaside plant.

Benign neglect is the main key to success with lantana. It blooms most generously in rather poor, dry soil, so don't fertilize or water heavily. In containers, though, soil can go from slightly dry (acceptable) to bone dry (not acceptable) in only a few hours, so there you'll need to water quite frequently. Pinch and prune plants regularly to keep them within bounds.

Think Twice: Lantana easily escapes from gardens in tropical and subtropical regions and is a widespread noxious weed in Florida, California, and Hawaii. It spreads only by self-sowing, though; so if you remove the berries before they ripen, there's no problem. **Self-sowing**

In mild climates (Zones 9 to 11), winter care is minimal: Just prune out any parts that get frosted. In Zone 9, lantana often acts as a perennial, dying to the ground each winter. Elsewhere, bring cuttings or plants in for winter and grow them in as much sun as possible.

Warning: Lantana leaves and flowers are toxic, and some people may even break out in a rash just from handling the foliage. It's best to wear gloves when working with this plant and to keep it out of the reach of children and pets.

Good Neighbors

Lantanas' mounding, rambling habit complements more upright forms, such as yuccas, and their warm colors contrast nicely with annual and perennial blue salvias (*Salvia* spp.). They are also striking in a container with Brazilian vervain (*Verbena bonariensis*) and California bluebells (*Phacelia campanularia*).

Problems and Solutions

Spider mites, aphids, and whiteflies are possible. The latter are often a serious problem, especially when you bring plants indoors for winter. Carefully wash both sides of lantana leaves with a soft cloth dipped in insecticidal soap before bringing any lantana, even just a cutting, indoors; outdoors, spray with insecticidal soap.

Top Performer

Lantana camara (common lantana, yellow sage, red sage): The species is a large upright or spreading shrub often with spiny branches and flowers that open yellow, then turn pink and finally orange-red. It has scented, toothed, often wrinkled leaves that are usually very rough to the touch. Few gardeners still grow the species, though; most choose from among the hundreds of dwarf, upright, spreading, or trailing cultivars. Colors include white, pink, yellow, cream, red, lilac, and purple, plus plenty of combinations. Height: 6 to 72 inches (15 to 180 cm). Spread: 1 to 6 feet (30 to 180 cm).

More Recommended Lantana

Lantana montevidensis (weeping lantana): Also called *L. sellowiana.* This species has a spreading or trailing habit and rose-lilac flower clusters. It's a parent of many hybrid lantanas, especially the trailing types. Height: 6 to 40 inches (15 to 100 cm). Spread: 2 to 4 feet (60 to 120 cm).

Common lantana
(*Lantana camara*)

Larry's Garden Notes

Having always been told that lantana was toxic, I was shocked when a friend calmly harvested some berries from his plant and popped them into his mouth, claiming they were delicious. When I returned home, I made a few phone calls and discovered that the plant actually *is* toxic—*except* for the fully ripe berries. The green berries are particularly dangerous. That being the case, it's probably best *not* to eat even the ripe fruits, so that you don't take the risk of accidentally swallowing any immature ones.

Matthiola

Stock

If you're a fan of fragrance, these two heirloom annuals belong in your garden. Hard to find only a few years ago, common stock (*Matthiola incana*) is again back in style, with its upright stalks of colorful flowers and intense clovelike scent. Evening-scented stock (*M. longipetala bicornis*) remains little known outside of serious gardening circles, but it has many fans there due to its delightful perfume, which is noticeable only at night. Both species are easy-to-grow annuals best adapted to cool summer areas or to growing during the cooler months of the year in hot climates.

Plant Profile

MATTHIOLA
math-ee-OH-luh

- **Bloom Color:** Varies by species; see individual listings

- **Bloom Time:** Late spring through early fall; fall through winter in mild climates

- **Height:** Varies by species; see individual listings

- **Spread:** Varies by species; see individual listings

- **Garden Uses:** Container planting, cut-flower garden, edging, mass planting, meadow garden, mixed border, rock garden, wall planting

- **Attracts:** Bees, moths

- **Light Preference:** Full sun to partial shade

- **Soil Preference:** Average to humus-rich, evenly moist but well-drained soil; prefers neutral to alkaline soil

- **Best Way to Propagate:** Sow seed indoors or outdoors in spring

- **Hardiness:** Hardy annual or biennial grown as a hardy annual

Growing Tips

Common stock is widely sold as plants in spring, and that's a good thing. You see, the most desirable form of common stock has double flowers because they offer more visual impact and a more intense perfume than the singles, but even the best seed strains rarely give more than 60 percent doubles. Nurseries select only the doubles when potting up the seedlings.

If you grow your own plants, you'll have to know how to tell the two apart. In the case of the popular 'Ten Week' stocks, so-called because they bloom about 10 weeks after sprouting, seedlings of single-flowered plants have dark green leaves whereas those of doubles are yellow-green. This color difference is most evident at cooler temperatures—about 45°F (7°C). In 'Trisomic' types (7-week stocks), the doubles produce sturdier, faster-growing seedlings than the singles. And in other strains, like the 'Stockpot' series, the seedling leaves of the doubles have a notch in them, but those of singles don't. These curious but useful traits were bred into hybrid stocks as genetic markers so growers could easily distinguish the doubles from the singles at an early stage and thus be able to offer trays of identical plants. Refer to the seed packet to learn which trait to watch for in your chosen seeds.

Start the seed indoors 6 to 8 weeks before the last frost. Simply press it into the mix without covering; it needs light for germination. A very well drained mix is vital because stocks are subject to damping-off. They germinate best at 55° to 65°F (13° to 18°C). After a week or so, thin by removing the single-flowered plants. Plant out the remaining seedlings when all risk of frost is over.

Alternatively, you can sow common stock seed directly outdoors in early spring or late fall. (It won't be as easy to distinguish between the singles and doubles outdoors, but they will bloom abundantly—and is having a mix of singles and doubles really all that unfortunate?) In frost-free areas, sow in September for winter bloom.

Stocks are a snap to grow in cool summer areas, and they will bloom right through summer into fall, often surviving the first frosts. Deadhead only to clean up and leave room for new flowerstalks: The popular double forms produce no seed. In hot summer climates, their bloom is much briefer; try repeat sowings every 2 weeks for continuous bloom.

Good Neighbors

These cool-weather flowers are not the easiest plants to place in the hot summer garden, but it's worth growing them just for their fragrance. In the flower border, you could dot a few among seedlings of love-in-a-mist (*Nigella damascena*), which will fill in as the stocks fade.

Problems and Solutions

Watch out for damping-off (keep seedlings on the dry side) and aphids (spray with insecticidal soap).

Top Performer

Matthiola incana (common stock): This species comes in a wide range of colors, including white, pink, red, mauve, purple, and violet as well as creamy yellow. There are dozens of dwarf, half-high, and tall annual strains and mixes to choose from. There are even some biennials, hardy in Zones 8 to 11. Height: 8 to 30 inches (20 to 45 cm). Spread: 10 to 12 inches (25 to 30 cm). **Self-sowing**

More Recommended Matthiola

Think Twice: *Matthiola longipetala bicornis* (evening-scented stock, night-scented stock): Also sold as *M. bicornis*. This rather open plant has unimpressive pink, mauve, or purple, narrow-petaled flowers that open only at night—but what a perfume! Mix them with day-scented Virginia stock (*M. maritima*) for more impact without losing the punch of their perfume. No special care needed here; just sow where they are to grow. This species self-sows to the point of weediness; mulch heavily to minimize unwanted seedlings. Height: 12 to 14 inches (30 to 35 cm). Spread: 9 inches (23 cm). **Self-sowing**

'Nordic Lilac Rose' common stock (*Matthiola incana* 'Nordic Lilac Rose')

Kissing Cousins

Virginia stock (*Malcolmia maritima*) is practically identical to the evening-scented stock (*M. longipetala bicornis*), but it offers more colorful, broader flowers that open in daytime. Its flowers are deliciously scented, although not as intense as those of evening-flowered stock. Just toss the seed on the ground in spring and rake it in; the plants are in bloom within 6 weeks. Sow again about every 4 weeks until late summer. Height: 6 to 18 inches (15 to 45 cm). Spread: 4 to 6 inches (10 to 15 cm). **Self-sowing**

Mirabilis

Four-o'clock, marvel of Peru

An old-fashioned favorite, four-o'clock has a lot to offer contemporary gardeners, too. The narrowly tubular flowers, which open into five broad lobes, come in some particularly powerful colors, and they are wonderfully fragrant, especially early in the evening. They open only in late afternoon (around 4 o'clock, as the common name suggests), then stay open all night, closing only with the heat of the day. On gray days, though, they will stay open all morning; in truly rainy weather, they're open all day.

Plant Profile

MIRABILIS
meer-AB-ill-iss

- **Bloom Color:** Pink, magenta, salmon, red, rose, yellow, white

- **Bloom Time:** Midsummer through early fall; much of the year in frost-free climates

- **Height:** 20 to 48 inches (50 to 120 cm)

- **Spread:** 1 to 2 feet (30 to 60 cm)

- **Garden Uses:** Container planting, cut-flower garden, annual hedge, mass planting, meadow garden, mixed border, specimen plant

- **Attracts:** Hummingbirds, moths

- **Light Preference:** Full sun to partial shade

- **Soil Preference:** Average to humus-rich, evenly moist but well-drained soil

- **Best Way to Propagate:** Sow seed indoors or outdoors in spring

- **Hardiness:** Frost-sensitive perennial grown as a tender annual

Growing Tips

There are several different possibilities when it comes to buying four-o'clocks. You'll occasionally find seedlings for sale in spring, which gives you a number of plants at a quite reasonable price. Sometimes you'll see the tuberous roots sold in the bulb section, along with dahlias and gladiolus; this is the most expensive way to go, but it gives you second-year plants that bloom much earlier and more heavily than those grown from seed. Growing your own plants from seed is obviously the least expensive method and gives you the widest choice of heights and colors, especially if you order seed from catalogs; and it's easy to do.

In long-season climates, start the seed outdoors, either in fall (where winters are mild) or about 1 week after the last frost date. Elsewhere, sow them indoors 6 to 8 weeks before the last frost date. Use peat pots because young plants don't like root disturbance. The large, hard seed germinates best if you soak it for 48 hours in tepid water. Press the seed into the surface of the mix, without covering it; it needs light to germinate. Sow 2 to 3 seeds per pot. Germination takes 5 to 10 days at 70° to 85°F (21° to 30°C). When all the seeds are up, pinch out the weaker seedlings, leaving only one plant per pot.

Whether you have purchased plants, grown your own seedlings, or started your four-o'clocks from tuberous roots, plant them out when all danger of frost has passed. Despite tropical origins, four-o'clocks seem pretty much indifferent to cold (other than frost) and likewise thrive in hot and dry or hot and humid air. They will also adapt to just about any type of soil, even sand, although they will grow more lushly and quickly in rich, well-drained, evenly moist soil. They are moderately drought tolerant as well but will do much better if you never let them dry out severely.

Summer care consists mostly of watering and fertilizing. Deadheading isn't necessary since faded blooms will fall off on their own.

In frost-free climates, four-o'clocks are perennials and often keep blooming throughout the year. Where frost is light, as in Zone 9, they will likely die to the ground and resprout in spring. In Zone 8, a thick mulch might get them through the winter. Elsewhere, you can dig up the dark-skinned tuberous roots and store them in barely moist peat moss or vermiculite for winter, then plant them out again in spring.

Warning: All parts of four-o'clock are poisonous. Keep plants out of the reach of children and pets.

Four-o'clock
(*Mirabilis jalapa*)

Good Neighbors

With their shrublike habit, these Victorian favorites can create a fragrant hedge that looks great along a walk, or around a patio where you might sit in the evening. Use young transplants to fill in space left by early-blooming bulbs and perennials. The yellow-flowering types make an excellent backdrop for purple basil.

Problems and Solutions

Leaf diseases are most likely in humid climates; spraying the foliage regularly with seaweed-based liquid fertilizer seems to help it resist these diseases. Insects are rarely a major problem.

Top Performer

❗ **Think Twice:** *Mirabilis jalapa* (four-o'clock, marvel of Peru, beauty-of-the-night): Upright, bushy plants have dark green, nearly heart-shaped leaves. Both regular and "dwarf" types—dwarf, for this species, meaning under 2 feet (60 cm) tall—are available. Four-o'clocks self-sow in milder climates; it has been known to escape from gardens and become a weed in Zones 9 to 11. **Self-sowing** 🌱

Larry's Garden Notes

Mirabilis means "marvelous"—and this plant most certainly is. In fact, it attracted immediate attention from the time it was first discovered in Peru in the sixteenth century. The flowers astounded botanists not only by their time-keeping abilities but also by their habit of "breaking" (displaying several colors on the same flower). What excited early botanists even more was that one plant can bear flowers that are two entirely different colors!

Pentas

Star cluster, star flower

Just a few years ago, the only people who grew star cluster were Floridian and Hawaiian gardeners, for whom it was a fairly large shrub, and houseplant maniacs, like me, for whom it was an ungainly indoor specimen. Then the hybridizers "discovered" it—and no one will ever look at this plant the same way again. Formerly up to 6 feet (1.8 m) tall, many newer selections grow no more than 8 to 14 inches (20 to 35 cm) tall, meaning they can even work as edging plants. The dome-shaped flower clusters are much larger, too, with many more of the narrowly tubular blooms that open into five-lobed stars.

Plant Profile

PENTAS
PEN-tus

■ **Bloom Color:** Lilac, pink, magenta, red, white

■ **Bloom Time:** Late spring through early fall; almost all year indoors and in mild climates

■ **Height:** 8 to 72 inches (20 to 180 cm)

■ **Spread:** 1 to 3 feet (30 to 90 cm)

■ **Garden Uses:** Container planting, cut-flower garden, edging, hanging baskets, groundcover, mass planting, mixed border, rock garden, woodland garden, specimen plant

■ **Attracts:** Butterflies, hummingbirds

■ **Light Preference:** Full sun to partial shade

■ **Soil Preference:** Humus-rich, evenly moist but well-drained soil

■ **Best Way to Propagate:** Sow seed indoors in spring; take stem cuttings at any season

■ **Hardiness:** Frost-sensitive perennial grown as a tender annual

Growing Tips

Many nurseries now offer star cluster plants for sale: in packs and flats with other annuals, in individual pots in the container-plant section, or as established plants in the houseplant department. If you can't find plants locally, check seed racks and catalogs.

The only problem with growing star cluster from seed is that it needs a long head start in most climates: 14 to 16 weeks before the last frost. (I tried the 6- to 8-week head start suggested on seed packets and ended up waiting until almost the end of summer for flowers.) Sprinkle the seed over the surface of the mix and press lightly, without covering; it needs light to germinate. Germination can take up to 1 month at 60° to 65°F (15° to 18°C). Pinch young plants once or twice to stimulate branching. In mild winter climates, you can sow star flower directly outdoors in early spring and still get it to bloom early enough in summer to be worthwhile.

Don't plant purchased or home-grown star clusters outside until all risk of frost has passed and the soil temperature has reached at least 50°F (10°C). Full sun is best in most climates, although providing some shade from the midday heat is wise in those areas where hot summers are the norm. During summer, water the plants as needed and fertilize regularly with a foliar spray. Star flower prefers evenly moist soil, so mulching is a good idea. Pinch

FUN FACTS

Some botanical names are truly obscure, but *Pentas lanceolata* is an easy one. Think Pentagon or pentagram and you'll quickly guess *Pentas* derives from the word "five," referring to the plant's five-pointed flowers. And *lanceolata* is pretty obviously a reference to the lance-shaped leaves.

out faded flower clusters and prune any ungainly or wayward stems.

In frost-free climates (Zones 10 and 11), star cluster won't need any winter protection. You may be able to get it through winter in Zone 9 by mulching heavily in fall, then pruning off any frost damage in spring. North of Zone 9, you'll need to overwinter it indoors to keep it from year to year. Bring in cuttings or pot up plants from the garden in late summer, before the first frosts. Grown indoors in very bright light, star flower will bloom much of the winter.

Good Neighbors

This summer-long bloomer is a good choice for a large patio pot. Because it thrives in moist soil, give it companions that will not suffer from too much water: cannas and elephant's ear (*Colocasia esculenta*) are two good candidates. It also looks striking underplanted with the chartreuse foliage of yellow-leaved creeping Jenny (*Lysimachia nummularia* 'Aurea').

Problems and Solutions

Watch out for spider mites, aphids, and whiteflies, especially on plants growing indoors. Control them with insecticidal soap.

Top Performer

Pentas lanceolata (star cluster, star flower, Egyptian star flower): Also called *P. carnea*. This is the most common species and a parent of the increasing numerous hybrid forms described below. The original form, which is still sold occasionally, is a tall, shrublike perennial that tends to become woody at the base. It has fuzzy, medium green, elliptical leaves. Modern cultivars are generally similar but more compact. Height: 8 to 72 inches (20 to 180 cm). Spread: 1 to 3 feet (30 to 90 cm).

More Recommended Pentas

Pentas hybrids (hybrid star cluster): Most plants sold today probably belong here, but you won't be able to tell them apart from the compact forms of *P. lanceolata*. Height: 8 to 36 inches (20 to 90 cm). Spread: 1 to 3 feet (30 to 90 cm).

Star cluster
(*Pentas lanceolata*)

Kissing Cousins

While Brazilian firecracker (*Manettia luteorubra*, also called *M. bicolor* or *M. inflata*) and star cluster are members of the same family, the two plants couldn't look more different. Brazilian firecracker is a fast-growing, twining climber that can reach 13 feet (3.9 m) tall in only a few months. It has shiny, broad, ovate leaves and tubular flowers that are bright red at the base and brilliant yellow at the tip. Other than its need for a trellis, care for Brazilian firecracker is the same as for star cluster.

Reseda

Mignonette

If ever a plant was an ugly duckling, this is it. The leaves can only be described as "ordinary"; and as for its flowers, well, the closest thing I can think of to compare them to would be wispy broccoli. This is truly a flower only its mother could love. But here comes the "swan" part: Mignonette is simply the most sweetly perfumed of all annuals—even, some would say, of all flowers. The odor is indescribable: I suggest you grow it and smell for yourself!

Plant Profile

RESEDA
reh-SEE-duh

- **Bloom Color:** Reddish green, yellowish green, white

- **Bloom Time:** Summer through early fall; fall through winter in mild climates

- **Height:** 8 to 24 inches (30 to 60 cm)

- **Spread:** 6 to 12 inches (15 to 30 cm)

- **Garden Uses:** Container planting, cut-flower garden, meadow garden, mixed border, rock garden; topiary

- **Attracts:** Beneficial insects, butterflies, hummingbirds

- **Light Preference:** Full sun to partial shade

- **Soil Preference:** Average to humus-rich, evenly moist but well-drained, alkaline soil; tolerates most soil types

- **Best Way to Propagate:** Sow seed outdoors in spring or fall

- **Hardiness:** Hardy annual

Growing Tips

Don't look for mignonette plants in your local nursery: in a pot, mignonette looks more like a weed than a garden flower, and its chances of selling would be about zero. Fortunately, it's a snap to grow from seed, especially in cool summer areas.

The traditional way to start mignonette is to sow the seed outdoors, where you want the plants to bloom. In Zones 9 to 11, sow in the fall for winter to spring bloom; elsewhere, sow early in the spring for summer flowers. Simply rake the soil lightly among other plants that can cover it up a little, then scatter the seed over the soil and water it in. When seedlings appear, thin to about 6 inches (15 cm) apart; pinch to stimulate better branching and more flowerstalks. In cool climates, mignonette will bloom right through the summer; elsewhere, sow every 3 weeks until midsummer to ensure continuous bloom.

For extra-early bloom, start the seed indoors 6 to 8 weeks before the last frost date. Use in peat pots because mignonette does not tolerate root disturbance. Don't cover the seed; it needs light to germinate. It will sprout in a week or so at 70°F (21°C). Plant out after the last frost date.

Except in cool climates, where full sun is ideal, mignonette does best in light shade. Just about any well-drained soil will do, but richer soil encourages plants to produce more flowerstalks and, therefore,

FUN FACTS

One curious Edwardian hobby involved creating potted tree mignonettes by attaching the plant to a stake and pinching out all side stems. The result looks something akin to sickly broccoli on stilts. Personally, I prefer the modern concept: Growing mignonette so it can be smelled but not seen!

more fragrance. Try to keep the soil evenly moist; mulch will help.

Mignonette can be a short-lived perennial in frost-free climates, but even there, it tends to dry up and die after several months of growth. For that reason, it's best to grow mignonette as an annual and allow it to die in the fall.

Mignonette makes a wonderful cut flower and keeps its scent for months when dried. To dry it, harvest when most of the flowers have opened, but before the lower flowers have faded.

This plant's intoxicating perfume attracts pollinating insects to its insignificant flowers, where those visitors are rewarded with a copious supply of nectar. You'll find your mignonette constantly buzzing with bees, butterflies, and other pollinators, as well as a horde of beneficial insects.

Common mignonette
(*Reseda odorata*)

Good Neighbors

Mignonette has little appeal as an ornamental, but in fragrance it's among the best, so it deserves a spot among colorful neighbors. In a large pot, sow it around a showy, upright plant such as flowering maple (*Abutilon* spp.).

Problems and Solutions

Mignonette rarely suffers from insects or diseases.

Top Performer

Reseda odorata (common mignonette): Mignonette is a small, upright to slightly spreading, branching plant with medium green leaves that range from spoon shaped to distinctly lobed. It produces open spikes of tiny, star-shaped flowers, usually yellowish green but sometimes white or reddish green, surrounding a tuft of orange stamens. Recent years have seen the introduction of more ornamental types, such as 'Red Monarch', with distinctly red flowers; sadly, though, increased color seems to also mean reduced perfume—and who wants an odorless mignonette? This annual self-sows abundantly; but since it readily shares space with other plants, that's a "flaw" most gardeners are more than willing to forgive. **Self-sowing**

Larry's Garden Notes

Legend has it that Napoleon sent Empress Josephine seeds of this plant from his Egyptian campaign. Whether that is true or not is unknown, but what *is* clear is that Josephine first popularized this plant, calling it *mignonnette d'Égypte* ("little darling of Egypt") and recommending it to all her friends. Not to be undone, the British soon adopted it as well, dropping one "n" in the process. Until World War I, this plant figured prominently in just about every ornamental garden.

Acknowledgments

Many readers probably don't realize that writing a book is a collaborative effort: The author may get most of the credit, but there is always an entire team behind him or her. After having written a first book with Rodale Organic Gardening Books entirely from afar (isn't e-mail wonderful?), I was especially thrilled to finally meet much of the team during a trip I took to Emmaus while I was writing this book. I'd like to thank the entire Rodale team for all their efforts, with extra-special thanks to Karen Bolesta for her tactful but insistent way of getting me to produce text, to Fern Bradley for keeping watch over a tight deadline, and to Nancy Biltcliff for a solid, usable book design. Thanks, too, to Nancy Ondra for the terrific editing

and photo selection and to Pam Ruch for her assistance with the "good neighbors" and nomenclature research. Another thanks to both Nancy and Pam for their help in choosing the best annuals to cover. I'd also like to thank the designers of the beautiful garden plans: Stephanie Cohen, Sarah Wolfgang Heffner, Nancy Ondra, and Pam Ruch.

On the home front, my assistant Susanne Roy was helpful, as always, in keeping things running while I was busy writing. And my wife, Marie, the "writing widow," deserves a thorough round of applause for putting up with all those months when I simply showed up for meals and then crawled back to my basement office for more writing.

Photo Credits

Jim Block 91, 115, 119, 165, 235, 295, 373, back cover

David Cavagnaro 353

Linny Morris Cunningham 331 (left)

Grace Davies 6, 332, 343, 345

Alan & Linda Detrick 16, 77, 157, 249, 287

Ken Druse ii, 10, 40, 72, 98, 152, 174, 216

Garden Image/Dency Kane 37

Garden Picture Library/Chris Burrows 311

Garden Picture Library/Brian Carter 145, 213, 229

Garden Picture Library/Densey Clyne 359

Garden Picture Library/John Glover 289, 379

Garden Picture Library/A. I. Lord 339

Garden Picture Library/Howard Rice 257

Garden Picture Library/J. S. Sira 192, 209

Garden Picture Library/Friedrich Strauss 341

Garden Picture Library/Didier Willery 357

Garden Picture Library/Aaron Woods 355

Anne Gordan Images 239

Larry Hodgson 18 (blue), 141, 223, 389

Saxon Holt 30, 35 (left), 69 (left), 95 (left), 113

Bill Johnson 53, 163, 171, 271, 293, 297, 367

Dency Kane 87, 125 (right), 219, 331 (right), 361 (right & left), 383

Lynn Karlin v, vii, ix, 1, 18 (red, orange & violet), 43, 45, 51, 59, 68 (right), 69 (right), 79, 81, 85, 95 (right), 105, 121, 126, 131, 137, 147, 149, 155, 159, 185, 191, 197, 201, 205, 207, 211, 214, 221, 233, 241, 244, 247, 251, 253, 255, 259, 261, 265, 275, 277, 280, 283, 285, 291, 309, 317, 319, 325, 351, 369, 375, 381, 385, back cover

Richard Lavertue 89, 103, 139, 161, 167, 199

Andrew Lawson 93, 111

Janet Loughrey 125 (left), 181, 203, 334

Alison Miksch 306

Ralph Paonessa 364

Jerry Pavia 12, 18 (yellow & green), 65, 109, 128, 133, 150, 169, 179, 183, 187, 231, 269, 315, 337, 349, back cover

Richard Pomerantz 35 (right), 327

Richard Sheill 63, 123, 194, 227, 237, back cover

Connie Toops 55, 304, 323, back cover

Mark Turner 2, 15, 28, 70, 75, 135, 143, 189, 299, 313, 321, 329, back cover

Scott Vlaun 49, back cover

Kurt Wilson vi, 8, 31, 38, 47, 57, 61, 67, 68 (left), 83, 96, 101, 107, 117, 172, 177, 225, 242, 263, 267, 273, 278, 301, 303, 347, 362, 371, 377, 387, back cover

Sources

Common annuals are, of course, widely available in nurseries everywhere. If you're looking for rarer plants or the latest colors, though, turn to catalogs and mail-order sources. The choice they offer is simply mind-boggling! The following companies sell seed packets for annuals or offer plants by mail.

W. Atlee Burpee & Co.
300 Park Avenue
Warminster, PA 18974
Phone: (800) 888-1447
Fax: (215) 674-4170
Web site: www.burpee.com

Chiltern Seeds
Bortree Stile
Ulverston, Cumbria
England LA12 7PB
Phone: 01229 581137
Fax: 01229 584549
Web site:
   www.chilternseeds.co.uk

The Cook's Garden
P.O. Box 535
Londonderry, VT 05148
Phone: (800) 457-9703
Fax: (800) 457-9705
Web site:
   www.cooksgarden.com

Fedco Seeds
P.O. Box 520
Waterville, ME 04903
Phone: (207) 873-7333
Fax: (207) 872-8317

The Fragrant Path
P.O. Box 328
Fort Calhoun, NE 68023
Catalog, $2.00

J.L. Hudson, Seedsman
Star Route 2, Box 337
La Honda, CA 94020
Catalog, $1.00

Thomas Jefferson Center for Historic Plants
Monticello
P.O. Box 316
Charlottesville, VA 2290
Phone: (804) 984-9821
Web site:
   www.monticello.org/shop/

Johnny's Selected Seeds
R.R. 1, Box 2580
Albion, ME 04910
Phone: (207) 437-4301
Web site:
   www.johnnyseeds.com

Mason Hogue Gardens
3520 Durham Road 1, R.R. #4
Uxbridge, ON
Canada L9P 1R4
Phone: (905) 649-3532
Fax: (905) 649-3532

Park Seed Company
1 Parkton Avenue
Greenwood, SC 29647-0001
Phone: (800) 845-3369
Fax: (864) 941-4206
Web site: www.parkseed.com

Pinetree Garden Seeds
P.O. Box 300
New Gloucester, ME 04260
Phone: (207) 926-3400
Fax: (888) 527- 3337
Web site: www.superseeds.com

Scents of Time Gardens Company, Ltd.
204-11948 207th Street
Maple Ridge, BC
Canada V2X 1X7
Web site:
   members.tripod.com/~
   scents_of_time_gardn/

Seed Savers Exchange
3076 North Winn Road
Decorah, IA 52101
Phone: (319) 382-5990
Fax: (319) 382-5872
Web site: www.seedsavers.org

Seeds of Change
P.O. Box 15700
Santa Fe, NM 87506
Phone: (800) 957-3337
Web site:
   www.seedsofchange.com

Select Seeds
180 Stickney Hill Road
Union, CT 06076
Phone: (860) 684-9310
Fax: (800) 653-3304
Web site:
   www.selectseeds.com

Stokes Seeds Inc.
P.O. Box 548
Buffalo, NY 14240
Phone: (716) 695-6980
Fax: (888) 834-3334
Web site:
   www.stokeseeds.com

Territorial Seed Company
P.O. Box 158
Cottage Grove, OR 97424
Phone: (541) 942-9547
Fax: (541) 942-9881
Web site:
   www.territorialseed.com

Thompson & Morgan Inc.
P.O. Box 1308
Jackson, NJ 08527-0308
Phone: (800) 274-7333
Fax: (888) 466-4769
Web site:
   www.thompsonmorgan.com

Recommended Reading

When it comes to growing plants, you can never have enough information at your fingertips. I have literally hundreds of gardening books in my library, and I keep buying more. It is especially important to locate good books on annuals—they are quite rare, and the cultural details and plant descriptions they include are invaluable. I suggest checking them out in your local library, then purchasing those you'll really want to have on hand at all times. The following are just a few of my favorites.

ANNUAL GARDENING

Bennett, Jennifer, and Turid Forsyth. *The Harrowsmith Annual Garden.* Willowdale, ON, Canada: Firefly Press, 1988.

Brickell, Christopher, and Judith D. Zuk, eds. *The American Horticultural A–Z Encyclopedia of Garden Plants.* New York: DK Publishing, 1996.

Brown, Deni. *Encyclopedia of Herbs & Their Uses.* New York: DK Publishing, 1995.

Christopher, Thomas, and Michael A. Ruggiero. *Annuals with Style: Design Ideas from Classic to Cutting Edge.* Newtown, CT: Taunton Press, 2000.

Ellis, Barbara W. *Taylor's Guide to Annuals: How to Select and Grow More Than 400 Annuals, Biennials, and Tender Perennials.* New York: Houghton Mifflin Co., 2000.

Hole, Lois. *Lois Hole's Northern Flower Gardening Bedding Plants: A Guide for Cooler Climates.* Renton, WA: Lone Pine Publishing, 1994.

Hodgson, Larry. *Perennials for Every Purpose.* Emmaus, PA: Rodale Inc., 2000.

Hougue, Marjorie Mason. *Amazing Annuals.* Willowdale, ON, Canada: Firefly Books, 1999.

Lane, Clive. *Cottage Garden Annuals: Grown from Seed for Summer-Long Colour.* London: David & Charles, 1997.

Loewer, Peter. *Step-by-Step Annuals.* Des Moines, IA: Better Homes & Garden Books, 1997.

Marken, Bill. *Annuals for Dummies.* Foster City, CA: IDG Books Worldwide, 1998.

Phillips, Roger, and Martyn E. Rix. *The Random House Book of Summer Annuals.* New York: Random House, 2000.

Powell, Eileen. *From Seed to Bloom: How to Grow Over 500 Annuals, Perennials & Herbs.* Pownal, VT: Storey Communications, 1995.

Proctor, Rob, and Nancy J. Ondra. *Rodale's Successful Organic Gardening: Annuals and Bulbs.* Emmaus, PA: Rodale Inc., 1995.

Winterrowd, Wayne. *Annuals for Connoisseurs.* New York: Prentice-Hall, 1992.

CONTAINER GARDENING

Cole, Rebecca. *Potted Gardens: A Fresh Approach to Container Gardening.* New York: Clarkson Potter, 1997.

Heitz, Halina. *Container Plants: For Patios, Balconies, and Window Boxes.* London: Barrons Educational Series, 1992.

Holmes, Roger. *Taylor's Guide to Container Gardening.* New York: Houghton Mifflin Co., 1995.

FLOWER GARDENING

Benjamin, Joan, and Barbara Ellis. *Rodale's No-Fail Flower Garden.* Emmaus, PA: Rodale Inc., 1997.

Creasy, Rosalind. *The Edible Flower Garden.* Boston: Periplus Editions LTD, 1999.

Halpin, Anne, and Betty Mackey. *Cutting Gardens.* New York: Simon & Schuster, 1993.

Hillier, Malcolm. *Malcolm Hillier's Color Garden.* New York: DK Publishing, 1995.

Sombke, Laurence. *Beautiful Easy Flower Gardens.* Emmaus, PA: Rodale Inc., 1995.

Van Der Horst, Jan. *Art of the Formal Garden.* London: Seven Dials, 2000.

Index

Note: Page references in **boldface** indicate photographs.

USDA Plant Hardiness Zone Map

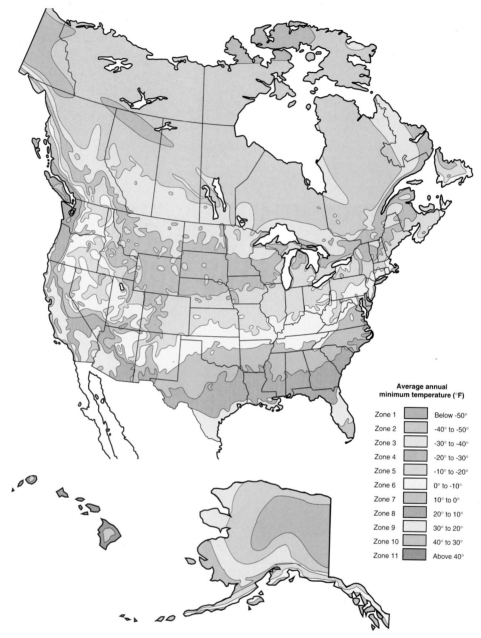

**Average annual
minimum temperature (°F)**

Zone 1	Below -50°
Zone 2	-40° to -50°
Zone 3	-30° to -40°
Zone 4	-20° to -30°
Zone 5	-10° to -20°
Zone 6	0° to -10°
Zone 7	10° to 0°
Zone 8	20° to 10°
Zone 9	30° to 20°
Zone 10	40° to 30°
Zone 11	Above 40°

Revised in 1990, this map is recognized as the best indicator of minimum temperatures available. Look at the map to find your area, then match its color to the key at the right. When you've found your color, the key will tell you what hardiness zone you live in. Remember that the map is a general guide; your particular conditions may vary.